The Joan Palevsky Imprint in Classical Literature

In honor of beloved Virgil—

"O degli altri poeti onore e lume . . ."

—Dante, *Inferno*

The publisher gratefully acknowledges the generous contribution to this book provided by the Classical Literature Endowment Fund of the University of California Press Associates, which is supported by a major gift from Joan Palevsky.

A Critical History of Early Rome

A Critical History
of Early Rome

From Prehistory to the First Punic War

Gary Forsythe

UNIVERSITY OF CALIFORNIA PRESS

Berkeley   Los Angeles   London

University of California Press
Berkeley and Los Angeles, California

University of California Press, Ltd.
London, England

First paperback printing 2006
© 2005 by the Regents of the University of California

Library of Congress Cataloging-in-Publication Data
Forsythe, Gary.
    A critical history of early Rome: from prehistory to the first
    Punic War / Gary Forsythe
        p.   cm.
    Includes bibliographical references and index.
    ISBN-13: 978–0–520-24991–2 (pbk. : alk. paper)
    ISBN-10: 0–520–24991–7 (pbk. : alk. paper)
        1. Rome—History— To 510 B.C.   2. Rome—History—
    Republic, 510–265 B.C.   I. Title.
    DG209.F735   2005
    937—dc22   2004008505

Manufactured in the United States of America

13   12   11   10   09   08   07   06
10   9   8   7   6   5   4   3   2   1

Printed on Ecobook 50 containing a minimum 50% post-consumer
waste, processed chlorine free. The balance contains virgin pulp,
including 25% Forest Stewardship Council Certified for no old
growth tree cutting, processed either TCF or ECF. The sheet is
acid-free and meets the minimum requirements of ANSI/NISO
Z39.48–1992 (R 1997) (*Permanence of Paper*).

CONTENTS

TABLES AND ILLUSTRATIONS

ix

ACKNOWLEDGMENTS

The many debts of gratitude incurred in the course of researching and writing this book are too numerous to be easily enumerated, but common decency requires that the author at least make an attempt to acknowledge the most obvious and important ones. Thanks are due to Kurt A. Raaflaub, A. John Graham, Martin Ostwald, Michael Alexander, Brent Vine, Mark Toher, Richard Mitchell, and Ernst Badian for their comments, criticisms, and suggestions. Thanks are due also to Kate Toll, the copy editrix, whose intelligent and well-informed editing of the text has made it more readable. A great debt is owed to Scott Pathel for his computer expertise employed in the preparation of the maps and other illustrations used in this book. Thanks are due to the people at the reference desk in the Westchester Public Library in Chesterton, Indiana for their assistance in obtaining many books and articles through inter-library loan.

Although the author was occupied with the research and writing of this book from the summer of 1997 to the spring of 1999, in a certain sense this book has been in the making for very many years; and as a direct consequence of the author's blindness, he is greatly indebted to many friends and fellow college students, who over the years have given him many hours of their time in order to read books and articles to him. Out of this very long list of devoted volunteer readers the author wishes to mention by name the following persons whose voices recorded on tape have been the author's constant companions as he wrote the present volume: Lloyd Daly, Peter Denault, Becky Harrison, Sarah Kimball, Scott Rusch, Nell Wright, Sina Dubovoj, and especially Terry Trotter (who now teaches mathematics in San Salvador), Peg Decker (who died at about the time the work on this book was begun), Kitty Reip and her sister Kandi Kaliher (the latter of whom died of cancer in November of 1994). Special thanks are also due to the author's dear college friend of many years ago, Bryan McMurray, and his gracious wife, Joanna, for allowing the author to enjoy the hospitality of their home in Champaign, Illinois, while he made use of the University of Illinois's vast library resources. Unfortunately, due to her death the author's wife, Dorothy Alice Forsythe, was not able to assist in the final proofreading of the copyedited text. This task was carried out by a very dear friend, Marnie Veghte. Yet the greatest debt of gratitude by far is owed to the author's wife, Dorothy, for her countless hours of assistance in every conceivable capacity. Attempting to record the innumerable ways in which this book is indebted to this extraordinary woman would involve an entire chapter of its own.

Toward the end of the five-year period during which this work has gone from manuscript to published book, my most lovely, loving, and beloved wife Dorothy Alice died of cancer (March 8, 2003). Over the past thirty-one years she has assisted me in countless ways, has been the light of my life, and has been the best love-mate, life-mate, and help-mate a person could ever hope to have.

To thee, my dearest love, the most perfect person whom I have known, I dedicate this book. You were my first love, my one and only love, and the great passion of my life. Words cannot express how much I love and miss you, and how grateful I am to you for having blessed and graced my life with your supreme goodness, incomparable sweetness, and infinite love.
As your name suggests, you have been and continue to be a truly divine gift to all of us who knew and loved you.

Dedicated to Dorothy Alice Forsythe on July 29, 2003, my darling's seventy-fifth birthday.

ABBREVIATIONS

ad Att.	Cicero, *Letters to Atticus*
ad Q. Fr.	Cicero, *Letters to His Brother Quintus*
Akten 1981.	*Akten des Kolloquiums zum Thema die Göttin von Pyrgi: Archäologische, Linguistische und Religionsgeschichtliche Aspekte (Tübingen, 16–7 Januar 1979)*. 1981. Instituto di Studi Etruschi ed Italici, Florence. Appian *Bell. Civ.* Appian, *Bella Civilia*
Aug. *Civ. Dei*	Augustine, *City of God*
Caes. *Bell. Gall.*	Caesar, *Bellum Gallicum*
CAH	*Cambridge Ancient History*
Cat.	Cicero, *Against Catiline*
CIL.	*Corpus Inscriptionum Latinarum*
Cic. *Amic.*	Cicero, *De Amicitia*
Cic. *De Re Pub.*	Cicero, *De Re Publica*
Cic. *Phil.*	Cicero, *Philippics*
Cic. *Tusc. Disp.*	Cicero, *Tusculan Disputations*
CLP	*Civiltà del Lazio Primitivo*, Exhibition Catalogue
CSE	*Corpus Speculorum Etruscorum*
Diod.	Diodorus Siculus, *The Library*
Dion. Hal.	Dionysius of Halicarnassus, *Roman Antiquities*
Frontinus *Strat.*	Frontinus, *Stratagems*
Gell.	Aulus Gellius, *Attic Nights*
Hdt.	Herodotus, *The Histories*
ILLRP	*Inscriptiones Latinae LiberaeRei Publicae*
ILS	*Inscriptiones Latinae Selectae*. H. Dessau, ed. 1892–1916.

Pliny *NH*	Pliny the Elder, *Natural History*
Plutarch *QR*	Plutarch, *Roman Questions*
Plutarch *Rom.*	Plutarch, *Life of Romulus*
Polyb.	Polybius, *Histories*
Sallust *Bell. Iug.*	Sallust, *Bellum Iugurthinum*
Seneca *Controv.*	Seneca the Elder, *Controversiae*
Serv. *ad Aen.*	Servius, *Commentary* on the *Aeneid* of Vergil
Serv. *ad Ecl.*	Servius, *Commentary* on Vergil's *Eclogues*
SIG	*Sylloge Inscriptionum Graecarum*
Suet. *Tib.*	Suetonius, *Life of Tiberius*
Suet. *Vitellius*	Suetonius, *Life of Vitellius*
Tacitus *Ann.* and *Hist.*	Tacitus, *Annales* and *Histories*
Theophrastus *Hist. Plant.*	Theophrastus, *Historia Plantarum*
Thuc.	Thucydides, *The Peloponnesian War*
Ulpian *Tit.*	Ulpian, *Tituli*
Val. Max.	Valerius Maximus, *Memorable Deeds and Sayings*
Varro *Ling. Lat.*	Varro, *De Lingua Latina*
Vell. Pat.	Velleius Paterculus, *History*
Vir. Ill.	*De Viris Illustribus*

FOREWORD

This book narrates the early history of Rome, one of the most successful imperial powers of world history. Although the story told here ends with the subjugation of Italy and thus does not treat the great wars of overseas conquest, during Rome's advancement from a small town on the Tiber River to the ruling power of the Italian peninsula the Romans in large measure developed the social, political, and military institutions that formed the foundations of their later imperial greatness.

Throughout human history there have been many nations or peoples who have greatly extended their power or territory by conquest, but only a small number of such states have been able to retain their conquests beyond three or four generations. Conquest requires little more than the successful application of military might, whereas the lasting success of an imperial power depends upon its ability to adapt military, political, social, economic, cultural, and religious institutions to accommodate change over time and to serve more than the narrow self-interest of a ruling oligarchy. Unlike many ancient Greek city-states, such as Athens and Sparta, which excluded foreigners and subjects from political participation, Rome from its beginning did not hesitate to incorporate conquered peoples into its social and political system. Allies and subjects who adopted Roman ways were eventually granted Roman citizenship and became fully participating members in Roman society.

Rome's early development occurred in a multi-cultural environment, and its institutions and practices were significantly affected by such diversity. Since the site of Rome, situated twelve miles inland from the sea on the Tiber River that separated Latium from Etruria, commanded a convenient river crossing and lay on a land route from the Apennines to the sea, geography brought together three distinct peoples at the site of early Rome:

Latins, Etruscans, and Sabines. Though Latin in speech and culture, the Roman population must have been somewhat diverse from earliest times, a circumstance which doubtless goes far in explaining the openness of Roman society in historical times. Given present-day interests in issues of ethnicity, multi-culturalism, and cultural diversity, Rome's successful unification of the diverse peoples of early Italy is a subject worthy of careful and serious study.

This volume is aimed at three rather different constituencies: the general educated reader interested in having a general but sophisticated account of early Roman history, the college undergraduate enrolled in survey or more advanced courses on ancient Rome, and the more specialized graduate student and professional scholar of classical studies and ancient history. Attempting to satisfy three such divergent groups is likely to be overly ambitious; and although the author has tried to keep them constantly in mind, some portions of the narrative will inevitably serve one group better than the other two. On the one hand, in order to produce a coherent narrative, much of the book necessarily sets forth many issues on which there is substantial agreement among modern scholars. This will best serve the needs of the general educated reader and college undergraduate. On the other hand, however, the study is much more than a mere general survey or statement of current orthodoxy. It contains many original interpretations by the author and bears clear signs of his particular interests, which are intended to engage the more specialized reader and instructor. The book will be best understood and appreciated when read concurrently with Livy's first ten books, the *Roman Antiquities* of Dionysius of Halicarnassus, or Plutarch's biographies of Romulus, Numa, Publicola, Coriolanus, Camillus, and Pyrrhus. In fact, the book's organization is patterned to some degree after the arrangement of Livy's first ten books, which are our single most important source on early Rome. The first three chapters serve as an introduction to the subject as a whole by treating the prehistoric, cultural-historical, and historiographical background. Chapter 4 corresponds to Livy's first book in treating the period of the early kings; and following the excursus on early Roman religion in chapter 5, chapters 6 and 7 correspond to Livy's second and third books. Chapter 8 covers the same material found in Livy Books IV–VI, and chapter 9 is parallel to Livy Books VII–IX.

Modern scholarship on early Roman history in some ways resembles that of the Homeric poems and their historicity. Differences of opinion and interpretation largely hinge on individual scholars' divergent assessments of the relative historical value or worthlessness of the data. These problems of evaluating ancient source material are complicated by the fact that both Homer and Livy were highly skilled story tellers. They constructed such vivid and compelling narratives of personalities and events that the modern scholar, interested in basic questions of historicity, may often find it difficult to suspend belief and thereby be seduced by their verisimilitude. As a result, both modern Homeric scholarship and the study of early Roman history have been characterized by wide divergences of opinion, which have tended to run in cycles from one generation to the next (see Heurgon 1973, 244–50). Indeed, early Roman history can be regarded as a classic illustration of the old adage, "there are as many opinions as there are people (*quot homines tot sententiae*)." It is inevitable, therefore, that many other scholars will disagree sharply either with the basic approach taken or with various individual interpretations set out in this book.

As indicated by the title, the overall approach adopted throughout this volume is rather critical toward the general reliability of the surviving ancient sources on early Roman history. Agreeing with M.I. Finley's famous dictum that "the ancients' ability to invent and their capacity to believe are persistently underestimated," the author regards a critical approach as entirely justified and necessary. Archaeological finds have been useful in tracing Rome's overall development during the pre-republican period, but Roman history for the fifth and first half of the fourth centuries B.C. remains extremely problematic due to the nature of the surviving ancient historical tradition. Then from the middle of the fourth century onwards this tradition gradually becomes more reliable as the events described approach the period of Rome's earliest historians.

It must always be kept in mind that the ancient Romans did not begin to write their own history until c. 200 B.C. By that time a well formulated tradition about the early kings and the early republic was already firmly established, and this historical tradition continued to be reshaped during the next 170 years until it was given final literary expression in the works of Livy and Dionysius of Halicarnassus. Herodotus's description of the Persian Wars may offer us an instructive historiographical parallel. Although the Greek historian conducted his research and composed his historical account only one or two generations after Xerxes' invasion of Greece, his narrative offers clear testimony to the fact that already by his day these historical events were becoming mythologized.

Recent work by T.P. Wiseman in reference to Rome's foundation legend (Wiseman 1995, 117 ff.) and by J. von Ungern-Sternberg concerning the formation of the historical tradition surrounding the early kings and early republic (Ungern-Sternberg and Reinau 1988, 237–65; Eder 1990, 91–102) has shown that when the first Roman historians composed their accounts, much of what they recorded was simply the historical tradition currently accepted by Roman society, but this tradition, as those of other peoples, had little relation to or interest in historical truth, but rather reflected contemporaneous concerns and ideology. Indeed, tradition is itself the product of the historical process, is capable of being manufactured, and can readily gain currency within a society as representing the historical truth (see Hobsbawm and Ranger 1983). The more we learn about the workings of oral tradition, the more it becomes evident that it has the capacity to transform historical truth both swiftly and massively. Thus, modern historical scholarship on early Rome cannot simply base its conclusions upon the supposed unanimity of later Roman historians, but instead, critical analysis must be employed. Abandoning the safe shelter of the hallowed ancient tradition may be psychologically difficult; it is certainly quite inconvenient; and it forces us to engage in the hard work of historical reconstruction of an imperfectly documented period of the past, but the endeavor is both intellectually challenging and rewarding.

In November of 1994 the University of California Press approached the author to inquire whether he would be interested in writing a book narrating the history of early Rome. The author gladly agreed to undertake this task, but in the very next year there was published T. J. Cornell's *The Beginnings of Rome*, which covers the same period as the present volume. Thus, it might be reasonably asked why we need another narrative history of early Rome. The answer is that despite Cornell's masterful synthesis of the ancient evidence and modern scholarly research, as well as his achievement in having written a very detailed but quite readable work on this subject, reputable Roman historians (e.g., Wiseman 1996; McDonnell 1997) regard his general approach to the ancient source material as too trusting and overly optimistic. Indeed, even before the publication of his book in 1995 Cornell's general working hypothesis concerning the ancient sources, which argues against large-scale invention by distinguishing between structural facts and narrative superstructure, had come under criticism (see Wiseman 1983; Raaflaub in Raaflaub 1986, 47–51; Ungern-Sternberg in Ungern-Sternberg and Reinau 1988, 242). Consequently, since the serious study of history involves the juxtaposition and evaluation of different interpretations of the same data, another narrative history of early Rome, which adopts a more critical approach to the ancient sources, may prove to be helpful in stimulating and advancing modern research on this subject. The present book is certainly not intended as a deliberate criticism of Cornell's fine work, but its own working hypothesis concerning the ancient sources is rather different.

Finally, with the exceptions of Raaflaub 1986 and *CAH* VII.2 1989 (which contains three excellent chapters by Cornell) the subject of early Rome was generally ignored in the English-speaking book trade for nearly twenty years following the publication in 1973 of Jacques Heurgon's *The Rise of Rome to 264 B.C.*, but the decade of the 1990s has witnessed a major reawakening of interest (see Mitchell 1990, Pallottino 1991, Bietti Sestieri 1992, Ridgway 1992, Holloway 1994, Forsythe 1994, Wiseman 1995, Smith 1996, Grandazzi 1997, Oakley 1997, Oakley 1998, Stewart 1998, and Forsythe 1999). In addition to these books in English, Raaflaub's collection of scholarly essays in 1986 was soon followed by similar volumes in Italian, German, and French (Campanile 1988, Eder 1990, *Crise et Transformation* 1990, and *Bilancio Critico* 1993); and *CAH* VII.2 1989 even has its Italian counterpart in Momigliano and Schiavone 1988. As a result, teachers and students should now be able to juxtapose the present volume profitably with a considerable body of other recent work. It is therefore hoped that the ensuing clash of ideas, like that of flint and iron, will have the salutary effect of producing illuminating sparks and perhaps even a strong steady flame of critical historical enlightenment in the minds of readers.

June 1, 1999

Chapter 1

Italy in Prehistory

The past two hundred years of human history have witnessed continuous and rapid technological change and progress on an unparalleled scale. Yet despite the highly advanced nature of present-day technology, geographical and climatic factors still exercise a profound influence upon the regional economies and cultures of human populations worldwide. The presence or absence of mountains, desert, rich farmland, water, forests, petroleum, coal, and other mineral resources continue to shape modern societies and nations in many fundamental ways. It therefore should come as no surprise that an inverse relationship has long existed between human technology and geographical determinism: the less control people have over their physical surroundings, the greater is the impact that their physical environment has upon their existence and way of life. Consequently, much of human prehistory and history has been a struggle to develop a material culture that mitigates the effects of climate, environment, and geography. The prehistory of Italy was no exception to this general rule.

The Italian peninsula, measuring 116,372 square miles (roughly the size of Nevada), exhibits great diversity of mountains, plain, and hill country, which frequently exist together in the same locale (see map 1). Situated in the middle of the Mediterranean, Italy consists of two distinct areas determined by the Alpine and Apennine mountain ranges. One of these two regions, the Po Valley of northern Italy, is roughly triangular in shape. It is bounded on the north by the Alps, on the south by the Apennines, and by the Adriatic Sea to the east. Since during the fifth and fourth centuries B.C. Celtic tribes (termed Gauls by the Romans) from continental Europe crossed the Alps and took up residence throughout the Po Valley, the ancient Romans called this region Cisalpine Gaul, meaning "Gaul on this

Map 1. Physical map of Italy.

side of the Alps." This plain is good for agriculture and is bisected by the Po River, the largest river of Italy, which flows west to east for 418 miles, receives the runoff from both mountain ranges in numerous streams, and empties into the Adriatic. Since the land nearest the Po was often marshy, the earliest human inhabitants of northern Italy tended to settle in areas away from the river. Settlement of the mountain slopes and plain promoted the exchange of commodities peculiar to each environment. The arc of the Alps separates northern Italy from continental Europe. Yet despite their height, they never constituted an insuperable barrier to early man, but several passes were routinely used for travel to and from southern France to the west and the central Danube to the east. Although the Po Valley was the last area of Italy to succumb to Roman arms, its geographical ties to continental Europe played an important role in the prehistory and early history of Italy by its reception of new cultural influences and peoples beyond the Alps and transmission of new ideas across the Apennines.

The other major area of Italy is the peninsula south of the Po Valley. This region is geographically very complex and diverse. The Apennine Mountains form a compact range along the southern side of the Po Valley, but after they turn southeastward to run the length of the peninsula, they diverge into parallel ranges separated from one another by deep gorges. This terrain was well suited for pastoralism. Herders kept their cattle, sheep, pigs, and goats down in the valleys to avoid the rigors of winter, but drove them into the uplands to enjoy the cooler pastures of summer. This pattern of seasonal pastoralism is termed *transhumance*. It originated at some time during Italy's prehistoric period and continued to be practiced until modern times. In addition, mountain ridges and valleys formed important paths which facilitated the movement of people, goods, and ideas.

For much of their southeasterly course the Apennines are much closer to the eastern coast of Italy and often run right down to the Adriatic. As a result, the northern and central areas of western Italy open up into a complex tangle of plain and hill country, which form the three major areas of Etruria, Latium, and Campania, all possessing a rich volcanic soil, enjoying a moderate annual rainfall, and destined to play the most important roles in the history of ancient Italy. Etruria, enclosed by the Arno and Tiber Rivers, the Tyrrhenian Sea, and the Apennine Mountains, was blessed with rich metal deposits, primarily iron and copper; and because Phoenicians and Greeks from the more highly civilized eastern Mediterranean came in search of these ores, Etruria became the homeland of the first high civilization of Italy. Campania possessed the richest agricultural land of Italy and was later famous for its bountiful crops and wine. In early historical times, the northern Campanian coast was settled by Greek colonists, who thus constituted the first Greek neighbors to the Romans. Latium, bordering Etruria along the lower Tiber and separated from Campania by mountains, although initially lagging behind Etruria in economic and cultural development, was the homeland of the Latins and of Rome itself, which eventually emerged as the ruling power of all Italy. Since the Apennines swing away from the Adriatic coast in southern Italy, turn toward the Tyrrhenian Sea, and terminate in the foot and toe of Bruttium, the southeastern coast of the peninsula comprises the large plain of Apulia, which was receptive to influences from across the Adriatic.

Although Italy has a coastline of approximately two thousand miles, and no place south of the Po Valley is more than seventy miles from the sea, it has very few large navigable rivers, and the native peoples did not take to the sea to a significant degree until early historical times when they adopted the superior maritime technology and seafaring skills of the Greeks and Phoenicians. Many of the rivulets that flowed down from the mountains or hill country into the sea were little more than winter torrents that usually dried up during the summer, when their beds could be used as roads for pedestrian travel, wheeled transport, or the driving of livestock. Nevertheless, the country was by no means isolated. In particular, the people along the eastern coast from the Neolithic period onwards were in communication with the inhabitants of the opposite shore of the Adriatic. Thus, although surrounded by the Mediterranean on three sides and bounded on the north by the Alps, prehistoric Italy at different times and in varying degrees received new ideas and peoples from all quarters.

Since language has always been a principal factor in defining a people's cultural and ethnic identity, a region's linguistic history can be useful in understanding major cultural patterns. Even more than in Greece, Italy's complex geography fostered the growth of cultural and linguistic diversity, which is perhaps best illustrated by a map showing the distribution of languages in pre-Roman times (see map 2). Before Rome embarked upon its conquest of the peninsula, the land was inhabited by peoples speaking several different languages that were unintelligible to one another. It is therefore a great testimony to the political skills of the ancient Romans that they succeeded in forging unity out of such diversity. The modern study of the pre-Roman languages of ancient Italy is a very complex and difficult subject, involving many unanswered questions due to the fact that many local languages are now known only from a relatively small body of inscribed texts. Nevertheless, scholars of historical linguistics have been able to arrive at many firm conclusions about the overall character of these languages and their historical links to one another.[1]

Before Latin began to drive the other languages of ancient Italy into extinction during the first century B.C., a substantial portion of the country's inhabitants spoke one of four languages: Venetic, Latin, Umbrian, and Oscan, which because of shared similarities of vocabulary and grammar have been grouped together by modern scholars into the Italic family of Indo-European. Venetic was spoken by the people of the eastern Po Valley.

---

1. For general surveys see Whatmough 1937; L. Palmer 1954, 3–49; Devoto 1978, 1–72; Salmon 1982, 1–39; Penney in *CAH* IV. 1988, 720–38; Wallace 1998; and Baldi 1999, 118–95. See n.1 of chapter 5 for references to major collections of texts.

Map 2. Linguistic map of Italy c. 350 B.C.

As the result of the migration of Celtic tribes into northern Italy during the fifth and fourth centuries B.C., the inhabitants of the western and central districts of the Po Valley were Celtic in speech, although Ligurian, Lepontic, and Raetic, which are not well understood due to the paucity of surviving evidence, continued to be spoken by peoples dwelling in and along the Alps. The inhabitants of Latium, including the Romans, spoke Latin. The various peoples dwelling in the Apennine Mountains of peninsular Italy spoke one of several languages belonging to the Sabellian subgroup within Italic. These dialects included the speech of the Umbrians, Sabines, Marsi, Marrucini, Vestini, Paeligni, Frentani, Aequi, Volsci, and Samnites. Umbrian, known almost entirely from seven inscribed bronze tablets from Iguvium outlining public religious rites of the community, was the language of the people dwelling in the Apennines in an area south of the Po and bordering on Etruria. The other major Sabellian dialect was Oscan, which was the speech of the Samnites, the non-Greek inhabitants of Campania, and the people of Lucania and Bruttium. The people living in the southeastern portion of the peninsula spoke an Indo-European language called Messapic, which was not Italic but might have been related to the speech of the Illyrians, who dwelled on the Balkan coast of the Adriatic. Most enigmatic of all is the language of the Etruscans. Not only is it non-Indo-European, but there is no other known language to which it can be clearly related. Exactly how this linguistic diversity arose in Italy in prehistoric and protohistorical times is still largely shrouded in mystery, but the phenomenon alone is solid proof of the complexities of cultural evolution and formation during Italy's prehistory.[2]

MODERN ARCHAEOLOGY AND PREHISTORY

History and prehistory differ in that the former involves studying a past society with the benefit of written accounts, whereas in the latter no written records exist to aid the investigator. A prehistoric people of the past can be studied only by analyzing the surviving material remains of their culture, and these physical remains are recovered by archaeological excavations of inhabited sites or graves. Although modern archaeology has become extremely sophisticated and can call upon many scientific analytical methods, this has not always been the case. Consequently, since the beginning of the modern study of Italian prehistory during the mid-nineteenth century, manifold valuable archaeological data have been lost as the result of unscientific methods of excavation. In addition, two very important ideas should always be kept in mind when archaeological data are being discussed. The first one is that archaeological finds are quite often totally fortuitous, resulting from bulldozing for a new highway or digging the foundations of a new

2. For the overall problem of correlating archaeological finds and the emergence of various languages see Renfrew 1987 and Mallory in Blench and Spriggs 1997, 93–121, which treat this matter in reference to the Indo-European family of languages. See Drews 1988b for this question in reference to the prehistory of Greek. See Dench 1995, 186 ff. for this issue in reference to the early inhabitants of the central Apennines.

office building, and they therefore may not be representative of an entire society. Sometimes graves of a past people are discovered but not their place of residence. In other instances the foundations of their huts and hearths are unearthed but not their cemetery. Thus an excavated site may offer information about only certain aspects of the people's lives. Indeed, archaeological data for much of Italian prehistory are quite often confined to items that were buried with the dead, and the range of such items is usually of limited variety, being the product of prevailing funerary customs and religious beliefs.[3]

Secondly, archaeology can only recover physical manifestations of a culture that have happened to survive in the particular soil or water conditions of a site, and what has perished may be as important in understanding a culture as what has survived. In addition, the surviving physical remains of a culture can often tell us about a people's diet, the floor plan of their dwellings, their funerary practices, and what kind of stone, ceramic, or metal utensils were in daily use, but many other aspects of their culture, such as their language, social organization, political structure, or religious beliefs, are more often than not archaeologically invisible. It should therefore be realized that while modern archaeology can often succeed in reconstructing many aspects of a past society's material culture, there are many other important questions that excavations cannot answer. In order to assess prehistoric data judiciously, we must be well aware of what archaeology can and cannot do. These observations apply not only to the study of the earliest inhabitants of Italy treated in this chapter but also to the beginnings of Etruscan and Latin culture and Roman history described in chapters 2 and 4.

Archaeologists have traditionally divided European prehistory into periods of time that take their names from the technology used in making tools. Thus, Italy's prehistory consists of the Paleolithic (Old Stone) Age, Neolithic (New Stone) Age, Copper Age, Bronze Age, and Iron Age. These periods are often subdivided into early, middle, and late or numbered phases, as has seemed best to prehistorians for the purpose of charting the changes in material culture. Moreover, since the material remains of prehistoric peoples within the same time period exhibit major differences from region to region, archaeologists employ other terms, often taken from the names of excavated sites such as Remedello or Villanova, in order to distinguish one prehistoric culture from another. These differences can include such things as how people disposed of the dead (inhumation or cremation), or how they shaped and decorated their pottery or jewelry. In addition, changes in burial customs or pottery styles can provide important

---

3. For the problem of correlating funerary remains with society as a whole during historical times of classical antiquity see Morris 1992, 1–30.

evidence for the exchange of ideas from one region to another. Unfortunately, archaeology cannot usually determine whether such exchanges were brought about through trade networks or by people migrating from one area to another and bringing their characteristic material culture with them. It should also be realized that two population groups who lived next to one another could have shared the same material culture while they spoke different languages and regarded one another as ethnically distinct. Consequently, the material remains of prehistoric peoples uncovered by archaeology can usually provide only a partial picture of past cultures.

PREHISTORIC ITALY

During the past two million years, the world's climate has undergone major warming and cooling trends as reflected in the advance and retreat of glaciers. Prolonged cold climatic conditions have fostered the growth of enormous ice sheets, whose movements have left their marks on the earth's surface. For example, the lake beds of Maggiore, Como, and Garda below the Alps in northern Italy were carved out by glacial action. Furthermore, glaciers are composed of such massive amounts of water that their expansion and contraction have drastically affected sea levels worldwide. Thus, at the height of the Wurm glaciation periods (i.e. four intervals occurring during the past 125,000 years) the level in the Adriatic dropped so far that dry land at times extended as far south as Ancona. Conversely, in interglaciation periods the sea level rose as glaciers melted, and parts of what are now the Tyrrhenian coast and the eastern Po Valley were submerged beneath the sea. Plant and animal life throughout Europe and Asia fluctuated in accordance with these geological and climatic changes, and Paleolithic hominids (*Homo erectus, Homo sapiens neanderthalensis,* and *Homo sapiens sapiens*) adjusted to regional conditions by hunting animals and gathering edible plants, by using fire, caves, and animal skins to shelter themselves from the rigors of cold weather, and by fashioning various utensils and tools out of wood, animal bone or horn, and stone.[4] Under such conditions human existence was extremely hard and precarious and differed little from that of the animals upon whom early people depended for food, clothing, and tools. The landscape was very thinly populated by small bands of our hominid ancestors, who were often obliged to change their abode frequently in their pursuit of deer, bison, mammoth, and other animal populations. Those dwelling near major bodies of water also supplemented their diet with aquatic and marine life. Human survival depended upon

---

4. For general but detailed treatments of the prehistoric peoples and cultures of Italy, see Trump 1966; Barfield 1971; Potter 1979, 30–51; Holloway 1981; and MacKendrick 1983, 1–27. For the prehistory of the Mediterranean as a whole, see Trump 1980.

close cooperation within the group. As in hunting and gathering societies in different parts of the world studied by modern anthropologists, the adult males were probably responsible for hunting big game and making tools, while the women stayed close to the home site, watching the children, gathering edible plants, berries, and nuts, and performing other tasks.

This general pattern of life prevailed across Europe and Asia during much of the Paleolithic Age (c. 400,000–10,000 B.C.); and although the remains of hominid culture during the Old Stone Age are rather scanty in Italy, the same must also have applied to its prehistoric hominid inhabitants. The country's mountains furnished numerous caves suitable for human habitation, and the Lessini Mountains north of Verona in the Po Valley contained large flint deposits which were constantly worked by prehistoric miners for making tools.

The glaciers of the last ice age gradually melted around 12,000–5,000 B.C., and ushered in higher sea levels and milder climatic conditions throughout the Mediterranean. In the Near East, in the area often termed the Fertile Crescent, the end of this period also witnessed one of the most important developments of human history: the so-called agricultural revolution, perhaps more accurately termed the agricultural transformation (Redman 1978, 2 and 88 ff.), during which people began to support themselves by systematic agriculture. Since despite this major transition from hunting and gathering to agriculture the earliest farming peoples continued to fashion their tools from stone, the term Neolithic or New Stone Age is used to distinguish this period of human culture from that which had gone before. Moreover, since people could quite often grow more crops than they consumed, the existence of an agricultural surplus led to significant population growth, the division and specialization of labor, and incipient trade between communities and regions as surplus commodities of one sort were exchanged for others. The concatenation of these factors brought into being the first towns of the Near East; and in the course of time human settlement along the great river valleys of the Nile and Tigris-Euphrates resulted in the rise of the two early civilizations of Egypt and Mesopotamia, as complex political and social structures developed out of the need for people to cooperate in constructing and maintaining irrigation works that exploited the agricultural potential of these river basins.

The idea and practice of agriculture gradually spread westward from the Fertile Crescent and Anatolia in the eastern Mediterranean through the Balkan peninsula and thence to Italy, perhaps arriving around 5000 B.C. Exactly how this process of diffusion occurred is still unknown, but one route by which agriculture was introduced into Italy is suggested by archaeological finds in Apulia. In 1943, aerial reconnaissance of northern Apulia by the British Royal Air Force, designed to collect information about military air fields and railway traffic, disclosed peculiar dark crop circles.

Following the conclusion of World War II, these were investigated and found to be associated with ditches surrounding Neolithic sites (Stevenson 1947; Bradford 1950; and Bradford 1957, 85–110). Agriculture therefore could have been introduced into Apulia by enterprising farmers from the opposite Balkan coast in search of new land to cultivate. From this region, agriculture may have gradually spread into other areas of Italy as the farming population grew and brought more land under cultivation, or as indigenous hunters and gatherers learned the art of agriculture from farming settlements. From aerial photography, traces of over two thousand Neolithic sites have been detected in an area of 1,650 square miles in the Tavoliere plain around Foggia. This indicates that Apulia during the fifth and fourth millennia B.C. supported a substantial farming population organized into many small villages. The latest of three successive settlements at Passo di Corvo is the largest Neolithic site discovered thus far not only in Italy but in all of Europe, measuring 500 by 800 yards.

These same early farming settlements of Apulia have yielded tools made from obsidian (a black volcanic glass) originating from the Lipari Islands north of Sicily, thus demonstrating the existence of a trade network during Neolithic times. Their bones show that the raising of domesticated animals such as cattle, sheep, pigs, and goats also accompanied the cultivation of crops in Neolithic Italy; and unlike Paleolithic hunters and gatherers, Neolithic peoples augmented their material culture with handmade pottery, whose varying shapes and decorative styles are used by archaeologists to date sites and to trace the spread of new ideas. Vessels for making cheese have been found at many sites; and stone arrowheads of various shapes, perhaps used for both hunting and warfare, are first found in strata databable to the later fourth millennium B.C. Spindle whorls and loom weights, testifying to the widespread custom of spinning thread and weaving it into cloth, first appear at sites in the Po Valley also dating to the late fourth millennium. This technology probably entered northern Italy across the Alps from central Europe, and it spread southward down the peninsula. Consequently, by the close of the fourth millennium B.C. the human population in Italy had increased substantially from what it had been before the advent of agriculture, and human culture had been enriched by several major innovations.

Since over time the prehistoric cultures of Europe and the Mediterranean area exhibited increasing sophistication in metallurgy, archaeologists have traditionally divided the period between the Neolithic Age and the dawn of history into three large intervals whose names reflect the most advanced metallurgical knowledge of the period: Copper Age, Bronze Age, and Iron Age. Of these three metals, copper is the simplest to smelt from ore and to fashion into objects, and it was therefore the first metal to be mined and worked by prehistoric cultures, but it is also the softest of the three metals, even softer than flint. Consequently, even after prehistoric

Map 3. Prehistoric sites.

peoples learned how to refine copper from its ore, stone continued to be used as well. In Italy, the knowledge of mining and working copper first appeared in the Po Valley. Archaeologists have excavated several Copper Age sites dating to the third millennium B.C. located north and south of the Po River in the central region of the plain, and the human remains of their cemeteries display an admixture of both long-headed and round-headed people. Since the latter physiological trait has rarely been encountered at Neolithic sites, the presence of this genetically determined attribute strongly suggests that a new round-headed people entered northern Italy at the beginning of the Copper Age. It can be further surmised that these immigrants crossed the Alps from central Europe, whence they brought with them the copper-working technology that had gradually spread up the Danube River during the fourth millennium B.C. Copper was used primarily for making axes and knives, which were often buried with the dead. The stylistic motifs present in the material artifacts of the Italian Copper Age have been interpreted by modern archaeologists as evidence that during the third millennium B.C. Italy was affected by the contemporary cultures of southern France, central Europe, and even the Aegean. These influences doubtless reflect complex interactions associated with copper prospecting, mining, and refining, and with the distribution of manufactured objects.

THE ICE MAN

In September of 1991 a German couple, while hiking through the Alps bordering western Austria and northern Italy southwest of Innsbruck, inadvertently came upon what might be considered the single most remarkable archaeological find of European prehistory: the frozen body of a man who had died some 5000 years ago. Summer melting of the Similaun Glacier had exposed the man's head and shoulders. At first he was thought to be another hiker who had met with a fatal accident, but the artifacts accompanying the corpse soon dispelled this presupposition. Before scientists arrived on the scene to extricate the dead man, some damage was inflicted upon the body's left hip by a jackhammer, and certain objects were removed by curiosity seekers. Nevertheless, a nearly intact corpse of a prehistoric man with all his gear was recovered, and has become the focus of intense scientific analysis.[5]

Carbon 14 dating indicates that this man lived around 3500–3000 B.C., which makes him approximately as old as the earliest civilizations of Mesopotamia and Egypt. Moreover, unlike the mummies from ancient Egypt who had their internal organs removed when embalmed, the body of the Ice Man is almost fully preserved, and scientists have begun to study his internal anatomy in detail. He stood about five feet two inches tall and weighed about 110 pounds. Although his age at time of death was initially

---

5. On this topic see Roberts 1993 and Spindler 1994. As this book was written and revised, new findings concerning the Ice Man have continued to be announced. For the current state of knowledge consult the Ice Man's official website: www.iceman.it.

estimated at twenty-five to forty years, subsequent analysis of bone and blood vessels has shown him to have been forty to fifty years old and beginning to suffer from degenerative arthritis. He had brownish black hair, wore a beard, and would easily blend into the local Alpine population today if put in contemporary dress. The hair on his head is only three and a half inches long, demonstrating that the people of his culture regularly cut their hair. His body also bears several marks: a cross behind the left knee, stripes on the right ankle, and three sets of short vertical parallel lines to the left of his spine on his lower back. At first these marks were thought to be tattoos, but further examination revealed them to be cauterized cuts, possibly intended to counter the pain of arthritis.

But perhaps the most informative aspects of this discovery pertain to his clothing and other artifacts. Unlike the grave goods uncovered from prehistoric burials, which were placed with the dead according to the prevailing funerary customs and religious beliefs, the Ice Man was not formally buried but died with all his regular gear about him, and its remarkable state of preservation offers unique insights into the living conditions and technology of his culture. He wore leather boots bound around his legs with thongs and stuffed with straw for insulation against the cold. He was clad in a fur-lined coat composed of deer, chamois, and ibex skin stitched together, and over this he wore a cape of woven grass similar to those worn by local Tyrolean shepherds as late as the early twentieth century. A disk-shaped stone may have been worn around his neck as an amulet. He had with him a bow, fourteen arrow shafts, and what is now the world's oldest known quiver, made of deerskin. The arrows are fitted with feathers at an angle so as to impart spin for greater stability and accuracy. His bow measures six feet in length and is made of yew, the best wood available in Europe for bow making, the same as that used to make the famous English long bow. His bow, however, had not yet been notched and fitted with a string, suggesting that the Ice Man had only recently obtained the wood from a tree. He also had a bone needle, a small flint knife fitted with a handle of ash wood, a copper axe, and a small tool of deer antler that was probably used for sharpening flint blades and arrowheads. The flint knife was carried in a delicately woven grass sheath. Pieces of charcoal contained in a grass packet were used for making a fire. Two mushrooms (*Piptoporus betulinus*) bound on a cord are conjectured to have constituted the Ice Man's medicine for fighting off stomachache and pain resulting from arthritis. The discovery of parasitic worms in the lower part of the large intestine suggests that the Ice Man suffered from the former ailment. His equipment was carried in a backpack made of wood and bark.

A sloe berry found at the site has been interpreted as a remnant of the Ice Man's food; and since sloe berries are in season at the end of summer and the beginning of autumn, its presence seems to fix the time of year when the Ice Man died. The body and all the artifacts were located in a natural depression, which accounts for the fact that they were not destroyed by glacial action but were covered in ice and snow until the present day. The site is at an altitude of 10,530 feet, about 3000 feet above the tree line of that time. It has therefore been conjectured that the Ice Man was engaged in traveling across the mountains when the onset of a sudden snow storm forced him to seek refuge in the hollow where he froze to death and his corpse and equipment were preserved. He could have belonged to one of several local Copper Age cultures that flourished then on both sides of the Alps, and the discovery offers striking testimony to the existence of human traffic across these mountains in prehistoric times. The shape and style of his copper axe closely resemble those of the so-called Remedello Culture of northern Italy, known from a series of 124 graves and dating to the third millennium. The Ice Man also had with him a collection of unshaped pieces of flint of high quality, which might have come from flint deposits in northern Italy.

THE BRONZE AND IRON AGES

The Bronze Age of Italy, roughly coinciding with the second millennium B.C., exhibits not only more advanced metallurgical technology but also more widespread use of metal and continuous contacts with the Bronze-Age peoples of central Europe and the eastern Mediterranean.[6] Bronze is a metal alloy formed by adding a small amount of tin to copper. The result is a harder metal, which melts at a somewhat lower temperature, is more fluid than molten copper, and is therefore superior for casting into molds. The major problem, however, is the relative scarcity of tin deposits (Maddin, Wheeler, and Muhly 1977). Although small tin deposits might have been located and mined out in various areas in ancient times, one major source of tin that was probably exploited during the Bronze Age was Cornwall in southwestern England. After being mined and cast into ingots, the tin could have been transported along the major rivers and land portages from northern to central Europe and the Mediterranean. This would have brought into being a complex interlocking network of commercial contacts; and given the considerable demand for tin among the Bronze-Age civilizations of the Aegean and Near East, the growth and prosperity of Mycenaean civilization c. 1600–1200 B.C. may have been in part the result of Mycenaean involvement in the central Mediterranean segment of this tin trade. This surmise can be further supported by the parallel trade in amber, which has

6. In addition to the works cited above in n.4, good treatments of the Bronze and Iron Ages of Italian prehistory are to be found in Hencken 1968, 27–96 and the essay by Peroni (containing further bibliography) in Ridgway and Ridgway 1979, 7–30.

been found in the Mycenaean shaft graves and probably reached Greece from the Baltic by a sequence of overland and Adriatic travel (Harding and Hughes-Brock 1974).

The distribution of Mycenaean pottery of the fourteenth and thirteenth centuries B.C. revealed thus far can serve as a rough indicator of the degree to which the more highly developed civilizations of the eastern Mediterranean during the late Bronze Age interacted with the prehistoric cultures of the central Mediterranean (Taylour 1958, Vagnetti 1970 and 1982, and Harding 1984, 244–61). The most plentiful finds of late Mycenaean pottery have been made at a number of sites on the Ionian and Adriatic coasts of Italy and in eastern Sicily (especially at Thapsus, a trading post situated on a promontory not far to the north of the Great Harbor of Syracuse), whereas the Tyrrhenian coast of Italy has so far yielded only small amounts of Mycenaean potsherds (e.g., the small island of Vivera in the Bay of Naples). This situation, however, is likely to change as more Bronze-Age sites in the latter area are carefully excavated. Some remains of Mycenaean pottery have been found at Luni sul Mignone, a site located about twenty miles upstream from the coast along the Mignone, which flows south of Tarquinii into the Tyrrhenian Sea. At this site Swedish archaeologists uncovered three building-like structures dating to the late Bronze Age, one of which measured 13 feet wide and 138 feet long. All three structures were dug down into the tufa rock surface to a varying depth of four to six feet, and the walls above ground consisted of irregularly shaped stones piled one on top of the other and not bound together by any kind of mortar (Potter 1979, 37–41 and Drews 1981, 146–47). Since Luni sul Mignone is situated on the northern edge of the Tolfa-Allumiere Mountains of southern coastal Etruria, a region rich in copper, it is possible that these curious structures and the presence of Mycenaean pottery testify to the exploitation of mineral deposits and commercial interaction with the eastern Mediterranean during the late Bronze Age.

Scoglio del Tonno, a headland in the harbor of Tarentum, the finest anchorage in Italy, seems to have served as a convenient port of call for eastern merchants and prospectors on their voyages in western waters. Similarly, the presence of Mycenaean pottery in the Lipari Islands may indicate that ships put in there before sailing on to Sardinia, whose southwestern coast has also yielded the remains of Mycenaean pottery. This island's rich deposits of copper are thought to have been exploited to supplement the metal resources of the eastern Mediterranean. In fact, the so-called Nuragic Culture of Sardinia, characterized by large stone defensive towers and chamber tombs of stone masonry whose architecture was far in advance of the contemporary cultures of Bronze-Age Italy, probably arose in response to these eastern contacts and commercial interaction. Indeed, during the late Bronze Age native Sardinians were apparently hired as mercenaries in the armies of Libya, Egypt, and other states of Syria and Palestine (Trump 1980, 202).

As had been the case during the preceding Copper Age, the Bronze-Age sites of the Po Valley, especially during the second half of the second millennium, were heavily influenced by the Transalpine culture of central Europe. Throughout much of the Po Valley, cremation replaced inhumation as the standard way of disposing of the dead, and this practice clearly entered northern Italy from the Urnfield Culture of the Danube. This innovation has been the subject of much speculation. Was this major transition brought about by the exchange of ideas mediated through trade, or by the influx of new people, or by both these means? Besides funerary customs, the pottery and metalwork in the Po Valley of the late bronze age also exhibit new features similar to the those in the cultures of central Europe. Sites along the Apennine edge of the Po Valley, which were first investigated by L. Pigorini at the end of the nineteenth century, have been collectively termed the Terramara Culture, taking its name from a local Italian word meaning "black earth," which refers to the fertile mounds of dark soil produced by prolonged human habitation. Like the lakeside settlements farther north, Terramara structures were erected upon wooden platforms in order to avoid the hazards of flooding in the river plain.

Perhaps the single most intriguing site of the late and final Bronze Age in Italy (c. thirteenth to eleventh centuries B.C.) is that of Frattesina located in the eastern part of the Po Valley. By prehistoric standards it was quite large, 700 by 190 yards, an area of 27.5 acres, and its remains show that it was an industrial community that refined metal, fashioned deer antler into tools, and produced colored glass beads, making it the earliest known site in Italy to manufacture glass. Ivory, amber, and fragments of ostrich eggs have been uncovered there as well, testifying to external commercial contacts. Frattesina can therefore be viewed as a prehistoric forerunner of Spina and Hatria, two important commercial sites located near the mouth of the Po, to be discussed in the next chapter. The progressive and innovative character of Bronze-Age northern Italy is further demonstrated by the fact that during the thirteenth century B.C. the spring safety pin was invented, probably in the area between Lake Garda and the Austrian Alps. Termed a "fibula" by modern archaeologists from its Latin name, the pin was henceforth used throughout antiquity to fasten at the shoulder or chest a garment wrapped about the body. Fibulae are therefore often found in graves, and the changing decorative style of their catch-plates provides archaeologists with valuable information for dating and concerning possible artistic influence.

During the second millennium B.C., bronze gradually drove out flint as the primary material used for making tools, utensils, and weapons. Metalworking and the exchange of manufactured metal objects are clearly evident from numerous bronze hoards found at various sites throughout the peninsula, sometimes revealing unworked ingots and at other times stashes of knives or axes, the latter possibly the unclaimed buried caches of traveling merchants. Buried assemblages of bronze objects discovered near or in lakes or rivers, however, are generally interpreted as representing collections of religious votive offerings to a local deity. Excavations of sites located at the edges of the lakes of the Po Valley have also yielded many wooden artifacts preserved for more than 3000 years under water, including dugout canoes and Europe's earliest known plow and spoked wheel. The earliest Italian finds of horse bones come from these same prehistoric lakeside villages of the third millennium.

While the material culture of the Po Valley developed in response to influences from central Europe and the Aegean, peninsular Italy during the late Bronze Age lagged somewhat behind for the most part. Inhumation continued to be the funerary practice of this region. Although agriculture doubtless remained the mainstay of human subsistence, other evidence (the occupation of mountainous sites not conducive to farming, the remains of cattle, sheep, pigs, and goats, and ceramic vessels used for boiling milk and making cheese) indicates that pastoralism was also very widespread. This suggests that transhumance was already a well-established pattern of human existence. In fact, since the material culture of central and southern Italy was relatively uniform at this time, it has been conjectured that this so-called Apennine Culture of c. 1600–1100 B.C. owed its uniformity in part to the migratory pattern characteristic of ancient Italian stockbreeding.

During the first quarter of the twelfth century B.C. the Bronze-Age civilizations of the eastern Mediterranean came to an abrupt end. The royal palaces of Pylos, Tiryns, and Mycenae in mainland Greece were destroyed by violence, and the Hittite kingdom that had ruled over Asia Minor was likewise swept away. The causes and reasons for this major catastrophe have long been debated without much scholarly consensus (see Drews 1993, 33–96). Apart from the archaeological evidence indicating the violent destruction of many sites, the only ancient accounts relating to this phenomenon come from Egypt. The most important one is a text inscribed on the temple of Medinet Habu at Thebes, which accompanies carved scenes portraying the pharaoh's military victory over a coalition of peoples who had attempted to enter the Nile Delta by land and sea. The text reads in part:

Year 8 under the majesty of Ramses III (1179 B.C.). The foreign countries made a conspiracy in their islands. All at once the lands were removed and scattered in the fray. No land could stand before their arms, from Hatti, Kode, Carchemish, Arzawa, and Alashiya on being cut off at one time. A camp was set up in one place in Amor (Syria). They desolated its people, and its land was like that which has never come into being. They were coming forward toward Egypt while the flame was prepared before them. Their confederation was the Philistines, Tjeker, Shekelesh, Denyen, and Weshesh, lands united. They laid their hands upon the lands as far as the circuit of the earth, their hearts confident and trusting: "Our plans will succeed!" . . . Those who reached my frontier, their seed is not; their heart and their soul are finished forever and ever. Those who came forward together on the sea, the full flame was in front of them at the river mouths, while a stockade of lances surrounded them on the shore. They were dragged in, enclosed, and prostrated on the beach, killed and made into heaps from tail to head. Their ships and their goods were as if fallen into the water. I have made the lands turn back from even mentioning Egypt; for when they pronounce my name in their land, then they are burned up. . . . (Pritchard 1969, 262–3)

The carved Egyptian scenes of these so-called peoples of the sea show them not only in boats but also on land with wagons, women, and children, suggesting that this abortive invasion of Egypt involved some kind of migration. Much scholarly effort has been vainly expended in trying to identify the groups mentioned in this text. Suffice it to say that whatever was responsible for the collapse of the Mycenaean and Hittite civilizations, the end of the second and the beginning of the first millennia B.C. witnessed major changes in the cultural, linguistic, and political geography of the eastern Mediterranean. Archaeology reveals that in mainland Greece the destruction of the Mycenaean palace-centered states and economies was followed by a drastic decline in the material culture and the abandonment of many sites. In fact, historians have traditionally labeled the period c. 1100–800 B.C. the Greek dark age, characterized by village societies headed by local chieftains, from which the city-state eventually arose. The unsettled conditions of the late second millennium B.C. might have extended as far west as eastern Sicily. Coastal sites exposed to sea raids were abandoned, and the inhabitants occupied defensible positions of the interior, such as Pantalica near Syracuse (Holloway 1981, 107–14). It is also noteworthy that at the close of the Bronze Age the major site in the Lipari Islands met with violent destruction and was reoccupied by people from the Apennine Culture of Italy.

The most important technological advance which came in the wake of the collapse of the Bronze-Age civilizations of the eastern Mediterranean was ironworking. Iron ore is much more plentiful than copper and tin and even has a lower melting point, but the methods necessary to extract iron from ore and to work it into a much stronger metal are far more complex than bronzeworking. Simple smelting produces only an unusable iron bloom, which has to be further refined by repeated hammering and controlled heating. The Hittites had already mastered this technology during the late Bronze Age, and with the collapse of the Hittite kingdom in the twelfth century this knowledge was dispersed among other people, thus spawning the beginning of the Iron Age. Iron metallurgy did not reach Italy until the ninth century B.C., and even then it was two or more centuries before iron displaced bronze as the most commonly used metal. Thus, archaeologists date the beginning of the Iron Age in Italy to c. 900 B.C.; and although the Italian Bronze Age is generally assigned to the period c. 1800–1100 B.C. and is subdivided into early, middle, and late phases, the 200-year interval between the late Bronze Age and early Iron Age has been labeled the Final Bronze Age.

During this period the practice of cremation spread south of the Po Valley and is attested at numerous sites throughout the peninsula. Since this cultural tradition developed into the Villanovan Culture which prevailed in Etruria and much of the Po Valley c. 900–700 B.C., modern archaeologists have devised the term "Proto-Villanovan" to describe the cremating cultures of the Italian Final Bronze Age. As might be expected, the spread of cremation throughout the peninsula has been the subject of much speculation and has been variously explained:[7] (a) cultural interaction between the Terramara Culture of the north and the Apennine Culture of the south to produce a composite culture of the Final Bronze Age; (b) the extension of Terramara cremating people and their culture to the south beyond the Po Valley; or (c) the migration or invasion of new people from the Danubian Urnfield Culture. The fact that some of the earliest urnfield sites of peninsular Italy are located on the coast (e.g. Pianello in Romagna and Timmari in Apulia) is interpreted by some archaeologists as an indication that cremating people had come into Italy by sea, and that their migration was part of the larger upheaval which affected the eastern Mediterranean at the end of the Bronze Age (so Hencken 1968, 78–90). On the other hand, the same data can be explained in terms of indigenous coastal settlements adopting new cultural traits as the result of commercial interaction with foreigners. In any case, by the end of the Final Bronze Age inhumation had reemerged as the dominant funerary custom of southern Italy, but cremation continued to be an integral aspect of the Villanovan Culture of northern and much of central Italy. Was the widespread practice of cremation during the Final Bronze Age a passing fad, so to speak, adopted and then abandoned by the indigenous peoples of the peninsula, or was it introduced by new peoples who were eventually absorbed into the inhuming tradition of the south? This puzzle may serve as an instructive illustration of the limitations of modern archaeology in examining prehistoric peoples solely from the surviving remains of their material culture.

7. For a general survey of this question, with further modern bibliography, see Fugazzola Delpino in Ridgway and Ridgway 1979, 31–48.

Figure 1. Biconical Villanovan
ash-urn covered with a helmet.

ANCIENT LANGUAGES AND MODERN ARCHAEOLOGY

With the advent of the early Iron Age in Italy in the ninth century B.C.,
regional differences begin to manifest themselves in the archaeological
record, probably reflecting in some degree the linguistic and ethnic diversity which later characterized pre-Roman Italy in historical times. For example, to take funerary customs, for which archaeological data are the most
plentiful, inhumation predominated in the region east and south of an
imaginary line drawn between Rimini and Rome, whereas cremation was
the most prevalent burial custom west and north of this line. The inhabitants of the latter area placed the ashes in a biconical urn, covered it with
an inverted bowl or helmet, and deposited the vessel in a pit grave (see fig. 1).
This culture, which was common throughout Etruria and much of the Po
Valley, takes its name from Villanova, a hamlet near Bologna in southeastern Cisalpine Gaul, which was the first site of this type excavated by Count
Gozzadini during the 1850s. By the middle of the eighth century B.C. the
Villanovan Culture of Etruria was evolving into what soon became the Etruscan civilization, while the Villanovan Culture of the eastern Po Valley
developed into what archaeologists call the Este Culture. Linguistically, the
former was characterized by a non-Indo-European language whose origin
and connection with other known languages are still enigmatic. The tongue
of the Este Culture, Venetic, belongs to the Italic family of Indo-European
languages. This development may illustrate once again the limitations of

archaeological data, for if, as seems likely, the Etruscan and Venetic languages were already established in their respective areas at the beginning of the Iron Age, these two populations, though linguistically distinct, for a time shared a common material culture.

Similarly, of the four major Italic languages (Venetic, Latin, Umbrian, and Oscan) the first two, though separated by considerable geographical distance, are linguistically more closely related to one another than they are to Umbrian, while Oscan and Umbrian are themselves clearly kindred and are even grouped together by historical linguists into a larger Sabellian class of Italic. A likely explanation for this circumstance is suggested by the geographical distribution of these dialects during historical times: namely, that at some time during prehistory people speaking what later became the Venetic-Latin branch of Italic split into two separate groups; and furthermore, this separation might have been caused by the interposition of a population speaking what later evolved into the Sabellian dialects. If so, we would have another instance in which major linguistic and possibly ethnic differences were brought about by movements of people in prehistoric Italy, and these movements have thus far not been clearly detectable in the archaeological record. A third such case is provided by some of the inhabitants along the eastern coast of Italy, for although the preservation in historical times of tribal names such as Iapyges in Apulia and Iapusci in Umbria, related to Illyrian Iapudes, strongly suggests migration across the Adriatic, archaeology cannot offer clear proof concerning when Illyrians might have established themselves in Italy. In conclusion, the current state of our archaeological knowledge of prehistoric Italy and of the country's pre-Roman linguistic history testifies to the extraordinarily complex cultural processes operating before the dawn of history and to our inability to fathom them except in the broadest of terms.

Chapter 2

Archaic Italy c. 800–500 B.C.

Cultural and technological advancement in Italy from the Neolithic Age onwards was largely bound up with influences received directly or indirectly from central Europe, the Balkan peninsula, and the Near East. This pattern continued during the period covered in the present chapter, but with far more important consequences. Phoenician and Greek permanent settlement and commercial activity throughout the western Mediterranean brought about major economic, social, and political changes on a hitherto unparalleled scale that led to the rise of true civilization in Italy. Ancient historians continue to debate the nature of the ancient Mediterranean economy during Greek and Roman times, the two antithetical models being primitive and modern. There can be no doubt that agriculture occupied 80 to 90 percent of the inhabitants of classical antiquity, which suggests that the overall economy was primitive. Nevertheless, there also existed a significant amount of both long-distance and short-distance trade for various essential raw materials and manufactured goods as well as luxury commodities, which suggests a modern economic system. Both elements were integral to the ancient Mediterranean in Greek and Roman times. If the economy had been entirely agricultural, Greek and Roman town life and urban culture never would have come into being. They were made possible by the modern-looking aspects of the ancient economy, no matter that their scale appears modest in comparison to contemporary industrialized societies. These new economic conditions arose throughout much of the Mediterranean during the period treated in this chapter and were responsible for drawing Italy into this larger Mediterranean world.

PHOENICIANS IN THE WEST

Ancient Phoenicia, located at the eastern end of the Mediterranean, between Syria and Palestine, was a narrow strip of land about two hundred miles in length, enclosed by the Mediterranean Sea and the mountains of Lebanon.[1] Its principal towns were Beirut, Byblos, Marathos, Sidon, Tripoli, and Tyre, and the inhabitants spoke a Semitic language closely related to ancient Hebrew. The land's limited agricultural potential, its easy access to the sea, and the timber of its cedar forests, desired for building by the Egyptians and Mesopotamians from early times, encouraged the Phoenicians to take to the sea and to become famous maritime traders of the ancient world. This seafaring tradition began as early as the Bronze Age, and their voyages do not seem to have been confined to the eastern Mediterranean. In 1956, off the southwestern coast of Sicily near the ancient site of Selinus, a fisherman's net brought up from the sea a bronze figurine of the Semitic god Resheth, whose style resembles the art of Ugarit during the fourteenth and thirteenth centuries B.C. This find may indicate that Syrian and Phoenician traders were already active in Sicilian waters during the late Bronze Age, and they may have been in part responsible for the distribution of Mycenaean pottery found in eastern Sicily, southern Italy, and the Lipari Islands, mentioned in the preceding chapter. Passages from the Old Testament (1 Kings 10:22 and 2 Chronicles 9:21) record that during the tenth century B.C. the Phoenicians of Tyre were regularly sending out ships on trading missions lasting three years. The vessels returned with cargos of gold, silver, ivory, apes, and baboons. These voyages were probably along the coast of North Africa and perhaps reached as far west as southern Spain, which possessed rich mineral deposits, and where the Phoenicians at some relatively early date founded permanent settlements at Gades (modern Cadiz) and Sexi.

Phoenician activity in the western Mediterranean during the ninth century is suggested by six cinerary urns from a cemetery near the ancient site of Sexi, for these funerary containers are adorned with cartouches of Egyptian pharaohs of the ninth century. Also dated to this same period is a stone plaque inscribed with eight lines of Phoenician writing. The stele was discovered in 1773 built into the wall of a church at Nora in southern Sardinia, hence its name, "the Nora Stone." The text's date is established by the style of the Phoenician letters, but its interpretation is problematic, because what now survives may not be the complete text of the inscription. Nevertheless, F.M. Cross (1972) has offered the following translation:

> He fought with
> the Sardinians at Tarshish, and he drove them out. Among the Sardinians he is
> now at peace, and his army is at peace: Milkaton son of Subna, general of
> King Pummay.

1. For modern treatments of the Phoenicians see Harden 1963; Moscati 1968; Heurgon 1973, 54–75; Herm 1975; Trump 1980, 240–50; Moscati 1988; and Aubet 1993.

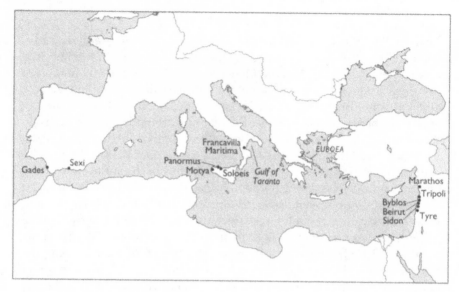

Map 4. The ancient Mediterranean.

According to Cross's interpretation, Tarshish, a Semitic word meaning "foundry," refers neither to Tarsus in southeastern Cilicia in Asia Minor, nor to southern Spain, known as Tartessos among the Greeks, but to the mining area of Sardinia where the Nora Stone was found. The inscription was set up by a Phoenician leader to commemorate a military defeat of the local inhabitants, and the Pummay mentioned at the end of the text is none other than the famous king of Tyre known to the Greeks as Pygmalion, who ruled from 831 to 785 B.C. If this interpretation is accepted, it would demonstrate early Phoenician presence in Sardinia and exploitation of its mineral deposits. Moreover, on the basis of similarities between various Cyprio-Levantine and Sardinian artifacts, some scholars have recently argued that mining interests in Sardinia were maintained by traders from the eastern Mediterranean during the Greek dark age despite the collapse of the Mycenaean commercial network during the twelfth century (see Ridgway 1992, 26–29 and 147–48).[2] Ancient historical sources indicate that from at least the sixth to the third centuries B.C. Sardinia lay within the Phoenician and Carthaginian sphere of influence, and Semitic culture continued to be prominent in the more civilized coastal areas of the island long after it had been annexed as a Roman province.

2. For detailed treatments of numerous aspects of Sardinian prehistory, see the collection of essays in Tykot and Andrews 1992. This volume (pp. 355–63) also includes an essay by D. and F.R.S. Ridgway, who carefully set forth arguments in favor of ongoing relations between Sardinia and Cyprus during the Greek dark age.

Although these data for Phoenician commercial involvement in the western Mediterranean are scanty and not without problems of interpretation, the physical signs of such Phoenician activity may continue to elude modern archaeology, given the transient nature of their trading practices. According to the *Odyssey* (14.287–313 and 15.415 ff.) and Herodotus (4.196 with 1.1) Phoenician merchants were in the habit of beaching their ships among foreign peoples and then sailing off again for another promising port of call when their business was concluded. According to the Greek historian Timaeus (Dion. Hal. 1.74.1), Carthage was founded by Tyre in 814 B.C., but the earliest archaeological finds from the site date to the middle of the eighth century, making the birth of this Phoenician colony coincide roughly with the beginning of Greek colonization in southern Italy and eastern Sicily. The Phoenicians also established settlements in northwestern Sicily at Motya, Soloeis, and Panormus (modern Palermo). Even though the location of these colonies suggests that the Phoenicians were primarily concerned with controlling the African coastal route to southern Spain as well as access to Sardinia, other data (discussed below) show that during the sixth and fifth centuries B.C. the Phoenicians and Carthaginians also enjoyed close relations with the Etruscans. Thus, given their early activity in the western Mediterranean, it may be plausibly conjectured that the Phoenicians would not have entirely bypassed Italy in earlier times. Indeed, the site of Francavilla Maritima, located near an obvious portage route across the foot of Italy between the Ionian and Tyrrhenian Seas, displays Phoenician influence in the bronze work contained in three tombs of high-ranking individuals dating to the first half of the eighth century B.C. (Zancani Montuoro 1977 and Ridgway 1992, 110–11).

GREEK COLONIZATION IN THE WEST

In the modern study of Greek history, the three centuries c. 800–500 B.C., roughly corresponding to the regal period of Rome (i.e., the period of the early kings), are generally termed the archaic period. It was during this age that the rather simple society of the Greek dark age reflected in the Homeric poems evolved into the politically, economically, and culturally advanced society of classical Greece. This extraordinary transformation was intimately bound up with the rise of the city-state as the basic political unit in the Greek world. A Greek city-state (*polis*) was a politically sovereign entity with discrete territorial boundaries and having an urban center that served as the major political and social focal point of the state. The local kings of the Greek dark age gave way to aristocratic oligarchies, which in the course of time evolved into constitutional governments consisting of elected magistrates, advisory councils, and citizen assemblies. From the late seventh century B.C. onwards, the Greek city-states developed law codes that

clarified the rights and duties of their citizens. This process of "state formation" also involved the introduction of hoplite military service and the levy-
ing of taxes, facilitated by the invention of coinage. During the eighth and
seventh centuries B.C., increased economic activity led the Greeks to
reestablish contacts with the more advanced civilizations of the Near East.
This resulted in the creation of the Greek alphabet, the flowering of Greek
epic and lyric poetry, and the transformation of Greek arts and crafts as
Levantine and Egyptian artistic techniques and methods of representation
were adopted and developed into a distinctively new Greek style. Indeed,
because Greek art of the seventh century was so heavily indebted to that of
the Near East, archaeologists and art historians often call it the orientalizing period. The expansion of the Assyrian Empire in the Near East during
the eighth century B.C., involving the violent conquest of cities and the
forcible resettling of entire communities in new areas, may have encouraged many Phoenician and Syrian artisans to leave their homelands and to
seek their fortunes abroad in the Aegean and even in the western Mediterranean; and such a transfer of talent might have been a key ingredient in
contributing to the orientalizing character of Greek and Etruscan arts and
crafts in archaic times.

One of the most important phenomena of the Greek archaic period was
colonization.[3] From the second half of the eighth century B.C. onwards,
many Greek city-states sent out organized expeditions and established new
communities along the coasts of the Black Sea, the northern Aegean, North
Africa, the Adriatic, southern Italy, Sicily, and even southern France and
northeastern Spain. In fact, some of the more prominent cities of modern
Europe, such as Marseilles, Naples, and Istanbul, can trace their origins
back to a Greek colonial foundation. Once firmly established, these new
communities became fully functioning, independent city-states in their own
right, although they were bound to their mother-cities by their shared culture and heritage. The social, economic, and cultural impact of Greek colonization on the history of the ancient Mediterranean can hardly be
exaggerated. It greatly expanded the geographical limits of the Greek
world, spread Greek institutions and culture into less civilized areas, and
substantially broadened the economic basis of the ancient Mediterranean
world as a whole by creating a complex network of long-distance trade in
essential raw materials, basic manufactured products, and luxury goods.

3. For more detailed treatments of this subject, see Dunbabin 1948; Woodhead 1962;
Heurgon 1973, 75–105; Boardman 1980, 161–229; Holloway 1981, 133–54; and Graham in
CAH III.3 1982, 94–113 and 163–95. For a detailed analysis of the important archaeological
data from the Greek colonial site of Pithecusa see Ridgway 1992. For the Greeks in Campania
see Frederiksen 1984, 54–116.

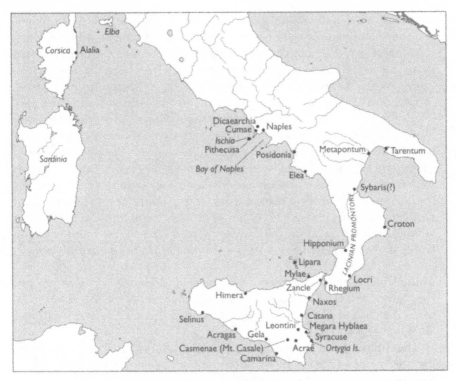

Map 5. Greek colonization in Sicily and Southern Italy.

This Greek colonizing movement seems to have first concentrated on Sicily and southern Italy, and it was these "western Greeks" with whom the Romans of the regal period and early republic first came into close contact, and by whom they were influenced. Many Greek colonial ventures probably began with the sending out of a relatively small body of settlers in a few ships, whose duty was to scout out a site, secure it from the native inhabitants, and begin the task of constructing a new community. Once this was done, additional colonists arrived in much larger numbers from the homeland. Colonies were generally established on easily defended sites such as small offshore islands or promontories of the mainland, and usually in areas where the native population did not pose a major threat to Greek settlement. The area around the Gulf of Taranto inside the heel of Italy received several Greek colonies, perhaps because native pastoralism made it less densely populated than other regions. The geographical designation "Italy" was originally applied only to the foot of the peninsula and implied such pastoralism, for it had the meaning, "Calf-land."

The primary purpose behind Greek colonization was to provide new economic opportunities for people of the Greek homeland; and since colonists received an allotment of land, and most of them probably settled down to become farmers, agriculture must often have been the leading economic motive behind a colonial enterprise. Thus Metapontum, Croton, Sybaris, and Leontini occupied fine farmland and became flourishing agricultural communities. Yet from the very beginning of the colonizing movement, the Greeks did not overlook the commercial potential of various sites. Pithecusa on the island of Ischia and Cumae on the opposite coast of Italy just north of the Bay of Naples were among the earliest Greek colonies founded in Italy, if not actually the first, and they were the northernmost foundations and the most distant from Greece. Moreover, the Chalcidians and Eretrians of Euboea who established these colonies were at the time among the most economically advanced and commercially enterprising Greek states (Ridgway 1992, 11 ff.). It has therefore been plausibly conjectured that these colonies were founded with a view to trade with the flourishing Villanovan settlements of Campania and Etruria. In addition, not long after the foundation of these two communities, the Chalcidians colonized Zancle and Rhegium which commanded the strait between Italy and Sicily.

The following is a chronological listing of western Greek colonial foundations.[4] As can be seen, it was not at all uncommon for a colony such as Cumae or Syracuse to found its own colonies.

750–725: Pithecusa and Cumae (Chalcis and Eretria)
750–725: Zancle and probably Rhegium (Chalcis)
734: Naxos (Chalcis)
733: Syracuse (Corinth)
729: Leontini (Sicilian Naxos)
728: Catana (Sicilian Naxos)
728: Megara Hyblaea (Megara)
725–700: Mylae (Zancle)
720: Sybaris (Achaea)
709: Croton (Achaea)
706: Tarentum (Sparta)
688: Gela (Crete and Rhodes)

4. In this list parentheses are used to enclose the name of the state or states by which the colony was founded. The dates in regular print refer to those colonies whose dates of foundation have been recorded in ancient historical accounts such as Thucydides 6.3–5, Diodorus, *The Chronograph* of Eusebius (which survives in Jerome's Latin translation), etc. Those in italics refer to colonies whose foundation dates have not been recorded in surviving ancient historical accounts but can only be roughly determined from archaeological finds; and since these dates derive from pottery styles that are estimated to have lasted for about a generation, they can usually be determined only approximately within a twenty-five-year period.

679–673: Locri (Locris)
663: Acrae (Syracuse)
650: Hipponium (Locri)
650: Naples (Cumae)
650–600: Metapontum (Achaea)
648: Himera (Zancle and Syracuse)
643: Casmenae (Syracuse)
628: Selinus (Megara Hyblaea)
600: Massilia (Phocaea)
598: Camarina (Syracuse)
580: Acragas (Gela)
580–576: Lipara (Cnidus and Rhodes)
540: Elea (Phocaea)
531: Dicaearchia (Cumae and Samian exiles)

Colonies were often founded to extend and consolidate the mother-city's political control and economic interests; and because the subsidiary colonies were often not distant from their mother-cities, they tended to be somewhat dependent or even subservient entities. This policy was pursued most successfully and aggressively in Sicily by Syracuse. By founding Acrae, Casmenae, and Camarina, the Syracusans extended their political control over the surrounding native Sicel population and made themselves the leading state in the island. Locri, Croton, and especially Sybaris, all situated on the Ionian coast of Italy, established colonies opposite themselves on the Tyrrhenian coast to serve as *termini* for land routes across the foot of Italy (but see Holloway 1981, 142). Sybaris in fact founded several such colonies, including Posidonia; and as can be judged from the text of a treaty concluded between Sybaris and an otherwise unknown people called the Serdaioi, inscribed on a bronze tablet discovered at Olympia, Sybaris also extended its influence into the Italian hinterland by making alliances with native peoples (Meiggs and Lewis 1975, #10). Indeed, by the sixth century B.C., Sybaris's commercial activity and agricultural prosperity made it proverbial in the Greek world for wealth and luxury. Similarly, even though the Greek colonies began as rude settlements of single-room houses, as shown by excavations at Megara Hyblaea and the initial Syracusan settlement on the island of Ortygia, by the sixth century many of these communities had blossomed and had become quite populous and flourishing; their economic prosperity is clearly reflected in their construction of magnificent temples.

Perhaps the single most interesting example of commercially oriented colonization is offered by Phocaean settlement in the western Mediterranean (see Hdt. 1.163–67). In 600 B.C. the Phocaeans, who inhabited a peninsula on the western coast of Asia Minor, and who were probably already engaged in overseas trade on a significant scale, founded the colony of Massilia (modern Marseilles) just east of the mouth of the Rhone River on the southern coast of France. This site controlled the flow of raw materials and manufactured goods between the Mediterranean and the less civilized Celtic tribes of the interior. It is generally supposed that the most valuable commodity the Celts had to offer Mediterranean merchants was tin from Cornwall in Britain, transported along the major rivers of France and across adjoining portage routes. In return, the ruling elite of Celtic tribes purchased manufactured luxuries such as fine pottery, metalwork, and wine, as physical manifestations of their status. A striking illustration of this commercial traffic has been discovered at Mt. Lassois on the Seine, one hundred miles southeast of Paris. The site has produced a large quantity of Greek pottery, and the nearby burial mound of a Celtic princess, replete with a gold diadem and other fine objects dating to the late sixth century B.C., has yielded a bronze krater used for mixing wine. The vessel is of Greek workmanship, beautifully crafted, and stands five and a half feet tall.

The Phocaeans of Massilia further expanded their sphere of activity by establishing a settlement on the coast of northeastern Spain. Its very name, Emporiae (modern Ampurias), meaning "trading center," clearly demonstrates its commercial character. Following the conquest of Asia Minor by Persia during the 540s B.C., a body of Phocaeans abandoned their Aegean homeland and sailed west, where they established a new community at Alalia (later known as Aleria) on the eastern coast of Corsica, but their piratical activities soon resulted in a major naval battle with the combined forces of the Carthaginians and the Etruscans of Caere. The Phocaeans were technically victorious but were themselves so badly mauled that they abandoned Alalia and allowed the Carthaginians and Etruscans to absorb Sardinia and Corsica respectively into their spheres of influence. These refugee Phocaeans then proceeded to found Elea on the southern Tyrrhenian coast of Italy.

THE FORMATION OF ETRUSCAN CIVILIZATION

The Etruscan civilization[5] offers the single best testimony to the extraordinary impact that Phoenician and Greek settlement and commercial activity in the western Mediterranean had upon the people of Italy, but as a consequence of the non-Indo-European nature of the Etruscan language and of

5. Modern bibliography on the Etruscans is enormous. The interested reader can begin with the following works: Bloch 1961; Heurgon 1964; Scullard 1967; Hencken 1968; Banti 1973; Pallottino 1975; De Grummond 1982; MacKendrick 1983, 29–70; Bonfante and Bonfante 1983; Bonfante 1986; Ridgway in *CAH* IV. 1988, 623–75; Spivey and Stoddart 1990; De Puma and Small 1994; and Brendel 1995. In addition to the long-running Italian scholarly journal *Studi Etruschi*, there is now the English *Etruscan Studies*, whose first volume was published in 1994.

a quaint tale told by Herodotus (1.94), modern scholars have long debated whether the Etruscan people were indigenous or immigrants.[6] At the end of his narrative concerning the Lydian kingdom and its conquest by Cyrus the Great, Herodotus wraps up the Lydian portion of his history by briefly noting the customs and traditions of Lydia, in which he includes the claim that they invented many of the games common among ancient peoples. Herodotus then proceeds to explain how this came about. During the reign of King Atys, which from an earlier section of Herodotus (1.7) can be regarded as corresponding roughly to the time of the Trojan War (c. 1200 B.C.), the Lydians suffered from a dreadful famine and, in order to cope with the crisis, they first decided to eat every other day and to divert themselves on days of fasting by playing various games they devised for the occasion; but when even this stratagem failed, they divided the population into two groups. One, placed under the leadership of Tyrrhenus, was sent out of the country and eventually came to northern Italy where they became the Tyrrhenians (i.e., the Etruscans). The other half of the population remained in Lydia and lived under the rule of Lydus, from whom they took their name.

In later historical times the Etruscans generally accepted and promoted the notion of their kinship with the Lydians of Asia Minor, but Dionysius of Halicarnassus denied the historicity of Herodotus's tale when, writing during the reign of Augustus, he composed his description of the myths and traditions surrounding the earliest peoples of Italy (1.25–30). In addition to observing that the languages and customs of these two peoples had nothing in common, and that the Etruscans called themselves Rasenna and not Tyrrhenians, he cited other Greek historians of the fifth century B.C. whose accounts differed from Herodotus's. According to the Lydian historian Xanthus, Lydus and Torebus (not Tyrrhenus) were the eponymous rulers of two related peoples of Asia Minor; and according to Hellanicus of Lesbos, the Etruscans were an offshoot of the Pelasgians who had inhabited Thessaly before the coming of the Greeks, because some of them had migrated across the Adriatic to Spina and had come thence into Etruria. In fact, Herodotus himself seems to record a variant of this Pelasgian origin of the Etruscans in 1.57, when describing the Dorian invasion of Greece. Moreover, in narrating the military campaign of the Spartan general Brasidas in the northern Aegean during the year 424 B.C., Thucydides (4.109.4) characterizes a Pelasgian people of the Chalcidic Peninsula as being of the Tyrrhenian race who once inhabited Lemnos and Athens. On the basis of

6. For a detailed survey of different modern views on this subject, see Pallottino 1975, 61–84. For a detailed treatment of Herodotus 1.94 and associated modern scholarship see Drews 1992. For treatment of recent relevant archaeological finds see Moser in Hall 1997, 29–43.

these last three data from Hellanicus, Herodotus, and Thucydides, we may surmise that the Greeks of the fifth century B.C. generally equated the terms "Pelasgian" and "Tyrrhenian," and that they were applied to non-Greek indigenous peoples.

The notion that the homeland of the Etruscans lay somewhere in the Aegean or Asia Minor has received support from an inscription found on the island of Lemnos in the northern Aegean, dating to about 600 B.C. The text is an epitaph written in a Greek script but it is clearly not Greek in language. It is in fact the only substantial surviving example of the island's pre-Greek language, which began to be driven out of existence during the second half of the sixth century B.C., when the island was conquered and settled by the Athenians. Even though the Lemnian text cannot be understood, the language's morphology resembles Etruscan, suggesting that the two tongues were somehow related.[7] The "oriental thesis" of Etruscan origins has been further buttressed in modern scholarship by the archaeological record, because beginning in the late eighth century B.C. the material culture of many Etruscan sites, particularly those of southern Etruria, gradually loses the characteristics of the Villanovan Culture of the early Iron Age and takes on features typical of the eastern Mediterranean. Not only are curvilinear and animal motifs of Near Eastern origin used in place of Villanovan simple geometric designs on pottery and metalwork, but inhumation begins to replace cremation for disposing of the dead.

Although this interpretation of Etruscan origins was dominant throughout much of the twentieth century, it has increasingly come under attack during the past three decades, so much so that it can now be regarded as a minority view. It has largely been replaced by the idea that Etruscan civilization resulted when the native inhabitants of Etruria came under and responded to the cultural influence of the higher civilizations of the eastern Mediterranean. In this interpretation, the oriental aspects of Etruscan material culture have the same explanation as those exhibited in Greek society at roughly the same time. Dramatic changes in artistic styles and even in burial customs need not be taken to signal the arrival of a new people. Indeed, despite the Near Eastern attributes of seventh-century Greek arts and crafts, no one today would seriously argue that this indicates a Levantine invasion of the Greek mainland during the archaic period. Furthermore, the Etruscan language could have been the only pre-Indo-European language that happened to survive in Italy into historical times,

---

7. The Lemnian inscription consists of only fifteen words written in six short lines on either side and above the carving of a human head in profile. The text can be transliterated as follows: "evistho zeronaith zivai I sialchueiz aviz I maraz mav I vanalasial zeronai morinail I aker tavarzio I holaiez naphoth ziazi." See Pallottino 1975, 72–73; MacKendrick 1983, 30–32; and especially Best and Woudhuizen 1989, 139–51.

and its similarity to Lemnian could stem from the fact that both languages were related parts of the same Mediterranean linguistic substratum, which was submerged by the infiltration and diffusion of the various Indo-European languages of Anatolia, the Balkan Peninsula, and Italy. Thus Etruscan and Lemnian, which the ancient Greeks classified as pre-Greek Pelasgian, might represent linguistic islands in an Indo-European sea, resembling the survival of Basque in the Pyrenees. Consequently, no credence should be attached to Herodotus's tale of a Lydian migration to Etruria seven hundred years or so before the Greek historian lived and wrote. It should be accorded the same trust as the story that assigned a Trojan origin to the Latins, and which is also first attested in a Greek writer of the fifth century B.C., Hellanicus of Lesbos. Both tales should be consigned to the realm of Greek mythography and not be given serious historical consideration.[8]

Important as language is in defining a people's ethnic identity, it is only one aspect of cultural formation. Thus, even if the Etruscan language was a successful holdout against the spread and evolution of the Italic languages, this fact alone tells us very little about Etruscan ethnogenesis, except perhaps in liberating us from simplistic explanations involving the migration of an Anatolian people and in compelling us to seek answers in Etruria itself during the early Iron Age. Though we are wont to speak of Etruscan civilization as if it were a monolithic entity, we should always keep in mind, as Luisa Banti demonstrated so clearly in her detailed survey of the Etruscan cities, that cultural development and change did not progress throughout Etruria at the same pace and according to the same timeline; there were major differences, the general pattern being that Near Eastern and Greek cultural influences and their concomitant social and economic changes occurred first and more rapidly in southern Etruria near the coast, but later and more slowly at northern and inland sites. In addition, the archaeological record demonstrates that despite the relative uniformity of Etruscan civilization there was, nevertheless, a degree of cultural diversity between regions and even from one locale to the next.

One principal factor contributing to the rise of the Etruscan civilization was the land's wealth in copper, iron, and, to a smaller degree, silver. The largest deposits were situated in northwestern Etruria in the so-called *Colline Metallifere,* "the Metal-bearing Hills," an area roughly defined by Populonia, Vetulonia, and Volaterrae. Populonia was the only Etruscan city situated on the coast. It commanded major iron deposits, including those on the offshore island of Elba, and it was famous throughout classical antiquity

8. Despite the current scholarly trend to view Etruscan civilization as indigenous to Italy, F. C. Woudhuizen has recently been analyzing the Etruscan language with the working hypothesis that it is related to the languages current in western Anatolia during the early Iron Age. See Best and Woudhuizen 1989, 139–79 and Woudhuizen 1992.

Map 6. Etruria.

for iron smelting. Vetulonia was the only northern Etruscan city that came into being and flourished during the first two centuries of the Etruscan civilization (c. 750–550 B.C.). Its graves have yielded substantial amounts of amber jewelry, suggesting its involvement in a trade network that included central and northern Europe; and its artisans became expert in intricate gold work. The other two major concentrations of mineral deposits lay in southern Etruria, and were responsible for the growth and prosperity of the area's three principal coastal sites: Caere, Tarquinii, and Vulci. The Tolfa-Allumiere Mountains lay in the hinterland of Caere and Tarquinii, and Monte Argentario lay on the Tyrrhenian coast a short distance west of Vulci. All three of these Etruscan cities lay a few miles inland from the sea, but were located on rivulets that gave them ready access to the coast. Caere and Tarquinii, like Veii farther inland, were also built on plateaus that were rendered easily defensible by surrounding deep ravines.

Yet, though of great importance, mineral resources alone did not account for the formation of Etruscan civilization. The land's thin but rich volcanic soil was good for agriculture; and by the beginning of the eighth century Etruria must have been inhabited by a population sufficiently numerous, technologically advanced, and well organized to deter Phoenicians and Greeks from establishing permanent settlements as they were doing in southern Italy, Sicily, North Africa, and southern Spain. Etruscan metal ores were responsible, however, for bringing eastern prospectors and traders into contact with the natives; and the latter were both eager consumers of the traders' manufactured goods and, even more importantly, willing pupils of their arts and crafts. It was this complex coincidence of factors that produced the first great civilization of Italy.

PHOENICIANS, GREEKS, AND ETRUSCANS

Because of their early foundation dates and proximity to Etruria, the Euboean settlements at Pithecusa and Cumae are likely to have played a leading role in introducing the Etruscans to the products, arts, and crafts of the eastern Mediterranean.[9] The Greeks first established the settlement of Pithecusa on the island of Ischia. With an area of about eighteen square miles, it is the biggest offshore island in the region of the Bay of Naples, and is only seven miles from the coast at its nearest point. The Greek colony flourished on the island during the second half of the eighth century; and during its early existence, when the colonists had become sufficiently strong and sure of their surroundings, they established a second colony at Cumae on the opposite Italian coast, just north of the Bay of Naples. Once Cumae was securely established, the initial settlement on the island went into decline. Abandonment of the site was apparently encouraged in part by volcanic activity on Ischia. Judging from the number of early graves in the

9. For more detailed treatments of the relations between Phoenicians, Greeks, and Etruscans, consult the contributions of Torelli and MacIntosh Turfa in Bonfante 1986, 47–91; Asheri in *CAH* IV. 1988, 739–80; and Pallottino 1991, 59–93.

cemetery, the settlement on Ischia must have been substantial very early on. David Ridgway (1992, 101–3) has estimated its population to have been between 4,800 and 9,600 people. The graves display a mixture of burial rites: cremation for adults, and inhumation for infants and children. The finds also confirm a high infant mortality rate: of the 493 early graves thus far excavated and analyzed, 27 percent are infant burials. Moreover, since many of the adult females were interred with fibulae that were not Greek in style but characteristic of the native Italians, it has been suggested that many of these women were native to the area and were taken as wives by Greek male colonists. One large storage vessel recycled to serve as an infant's coffin in a family burial plot was inscribed with a triangular Semitic character that was a religious symbol commonly used by the Phoenicians. This has been interpreted to mean that at least one of the dead infant's parents was Phoenician (Ridgway 1992, 114). Excavations have also shown that pottery production and ironworking occurred at Pithecusa. The site has yielded the earliest instance of a Greek potter's signature, and the clear remains of a shop where iron was forged (Klein 1972).

Among other things that Greeks and Phoenicians introduced into central Italy were new forms of house construction and the concept of the city (Drews 1981). Since Neolithic times the inhabitants of Italy had been living in single-room huts, circular or oval in floor plan, with walls of wattle and daub, covered with a thatched roof (Brown 1976), but they now adopted the building techniques and principles of urban planning used by Greeks and Phoenicians in their western Mediterranean settlements. From the early seventh century B.C. onwards, villages of simple huts in Etruria and Latium began to be replaced by communities of houses built on stone foundations, constructed of durable mud brick, and covered with terracotta roof tiles. Excavations at sites such as San Giovenale near Tarquinii have revealed clear signs of town planning: blocks of houses and alleys arranged in a regular pattern. The construction of such a site presupposes political and social organization of a considerable degree, because it would have involved decision making by a ruling authority as well as the coordination of communal labor.

In examining the impact that the Greeks and their culture had upon southern Etruria during the period 750–480 B.C., Mario Torelli (1976, 136–37) has suggested the four following phases:

1. 750–670: Villages coalescing into towns; introduction of wheel-made pottery and limited Etruscan imitation of Greek colonial styles; greater specialization of labor and crafts.

2. 670–630: The rise of urban society and social classes, including aristocratic families and the earliest attestation of the *praenomen-nomen* system of nomenclature (explained below, p. 160); adoption of writing; artistic reception of Greek myths and pottery shapes.

3. 630–580: Arrival of Greeks in Etruscan communities; beginning of sculpture, wall painting, and monumental architecture; horizontal mobility of foreigners into Etruscan society; increased Etruscan pottery production for local consumption and foreign export; aristocratic consumption of foreign imported goods.

4. 580–480: Increased self-consciousness of aristocratic status and power; decrease in social fluidity; confining of Greek artisans and merchants to controlled sites such as Graviscae and Pyrgi; rise of the Etruscan urban *demos* (i.e., people below the aristocratic class).

A few graffiti and artisans' signatures on pottery offer tantalizing clues concerning the presence of highly skilled foreign workers in Etruria during the seventh century B.C. Aristonothos was a Greek potter and vase painter who flourished around the second quarter of the century and seems to have worked at Caere. He is well known to art historians for a ceramic wine-mixing bowl (krater) signed with his name, decorated on one side with a scene of two Etruscan ships engaged in a sea battle, and on the other with a depiction of Odysseus blinding the cyclops. His name in Greek literally means "Best Bastard." He therefore might have been a native of Greece, the son of a noble father, whose illegitimate status obliged him to seek his fortunes abroad; alternatively, he could have been the offspring of a mixed marriage between a Greek immigrant and a native Italian. A chamber tomb near Tarquinii dating to the same period contained a wine pitcher (oinochoe) which bore the name Rutile Hipukrates (Pallottino 1968, #155). It is uncertain whether the name was that of the owner or of the vessel's maker. In any case, the first element of this compound name is the Latin name Rutilus (meaning "red") with the Etruscan nominative singular ending *-e,* and the second element is clearly Greek. It is tempting to surmise that this name belonged to a Greek who had become a member of Etruscan society. A compound Etruscan and Greek name of the same type, Larth Telicles, is found on a perfume bottle (aryballos) of the mid-seventh century (Pallottino 1968, #761–62).

Excavations at Graviscae, located at the mouth of the rivulet that connected Tarquinii to the sea, have revealed the remains of a Greek trading settlement which flourished during the sixth and early fifth centuries B.C. (Torelli 1971, 1976, 1977, and Ridgway *CAH* IV. 1988, 669–70). Traces of post holes indicate that the earliest occupation of c. 600 B.C. consisted of simple huts around a small shrine to Aphrodite, which had received dedications from Ionian Greeks. The shrine was replaced around 580 by a more permanent rectangular structure that remained in use until about 530–520, when it was itself replaced by an even larger building. Four of the dedications to Aphrodite were inscribed, three in Ionic Greek and one in Etruscan. Later in the sixth century there were dedications to Apollo, Hera, and Demeter, including more than three thousand votive lamps to the last-named goddess of grain, which is likely to have been a common commodity of exchange at the site. Perhaps the most remarkable find is a stone anchor dedicated to Apollo of Aegina and bearing the Greek inscription, "I belong to Aeginetan Apollo; Sostratus, the son of —, made me (or had me made)." This man is likely to have been the same Sostratus of Aegina whom Herodotus mentions (4.152) as having been the richest Greek merchant before his own day. Other inscribed names of devotees include the Greek Alexandros, Deliades, Eudemos, Themistagoras; the Lydian Paktyes; and Ombrikos, perhaps a Hellenized native of Umbria. Thirty of the fifty or so inscribed dedications were to Hera. Like the goddess Uni-Astarte of Pyrgi discussed immediately below, Hera of Graviscae was probably viewed as a divinity who protected seafarers; and given the myth of Aphrodite's birth from the foam of the sea, the same tutelary nature may have been associated with her as well, and may therefore account for the prominence of her worship at this site. The settlement appears to have received newcomers from the Greek cities of Asia Minor in the wake of the Persian conquest of Anatolia during the 540s B.C., and some modern scholars have connected their arrival with the tradition of wall painting in the chamber tombs of Tarquinii, which began during the second half of the sixth century. Nevertheless, the Greek character of the site abruptly ended around 475, coinciding with major military conflicts between the western Greeks and both Carthaginians and Etruscans. From that point onwards down to the founding of a Roman colony on the site in 181 B.C., Graviscae was patronized by local Etruscans. A few inscribed votive offerings dating to this later period bear the Etruscan divine names Uni and Turan, corresponding to Greek Hera and Aphrodite.

A similar settlement has been uncovered at Pyrgi, located about thirty miles west-northwest of Rome (Colonna 1966 and in *Akten* 1981, 13–37). It lay on the coast at the mouth of the rivulet that joined the Etruscan city of Caere to the Tyrrhenian Sea. Caere lay seven miles inland, and the rivulet that flowed past the city divided into two branches before entering the sea. Pyrgi and Punicum were the ancient names of Caere's two harbor communities. Pyrgi is a Greek name meaning "tower" or "fort," and Punicum is simply the Latin for "Phoenician" or "Carthaginian." Thus the two toponyms would seem to reflect both Greek and Phoenician trade with Caere. Like Graviscae, Pyrgi began as a settlement around 600 B.C. It was laid out in an orthogonal plan and had a road connecting it to Caere. Thus far archaeological excavations have not turned up clear signs of Greek occupation. Considerable remains of two temples have, however, been found. The two structures stood side by side facing the sea. Temple B measured 67 by 100 feet, and surviving terracotta decorations date it to the end of the sixth century. It was built according to Greek style: a peripteral or tetrastyle temple with columns along all four sides, four along the width and seven along the length. It had a single inner chamber or *cella* for the statue of a divinity. Temple A was somewhat larger, 80 by 114 feet, and was built around 480–460 B.C. It was Etruscan in style, with columns only along the front and walls of unfired brick covered in stucco on the other three sides. It contained three *cellae*, the central one larger than the two side ones. In the area between the two temples, there was a rectangular altar with a cylindrical shaft through the center, which descended into a pit six feet deep. This was probably designed to receive libations. In addition, one corner of the altar was pierced by a circular well. Both shrines were richly decorated with terracottas depicting several enigmatic figures, such as a winged male with a rooster's head, as well as scenes from Greek mythology, including an Amazonomachia and Hercules' battle with the Hydra. One terracotta relief from Temple A portrayed the Seven against Thebes: Zeus striking Capaneus with lightning, and Tydeus gnawing on the head of the dying Melanippus while Athena recoils in disgust.

The two temples remained in use until their destruction by violence, indicated by arrowheads and sling bullets, during the first half of the third century B.C. Their destruction presumably was at the hands of the Romans, who shortly thereafter founded a small maritime colony on the site, but the rubble from the two temples was carefully laid down and paved over, and amid these remains were discovered the most remarkable finds from the site: three inscribed gold plaques measuring about three and a half by seven inches. One contained a Phoenician text (Fitzmyer 1966), and the other two had Etruscan texts of thirty-six and fifteen words each (Pallottino 1964; Heurgon 1966; and Best and Woudhuizen 1989, 155–77). Each gold plaque was pierced with holes along the edges and had been buried with gold-headed bronze nails that had apparently been used to attach the plaques to one of the temple's wooden columns or doors. The style of letters employed in the texts date them to the first part of the fifth century. J.A. Fitzmyer has offered the following translation of the Phoenician text:

> To Lady Astarte is dedicated this shrine which Thefarie Velianas, king over Kaisrie [= Caere], constructed, and which he donated in the month of Sacrifices to the Sun as a gift in the temple. And I built it because Astarte requested it from me in the third year of my reign in the month of Krr on the day of the burial of the deity (= Adonis?). And may the years of the statue of the deity in her temple be years like the stars of El (= Phoenician god of heaven)!

The two Etruscan texts have largely eluded modern interpretation, but since the longer text seems to be a paraphrase of the Phoenician, some of it can be understood. It records the name of the goddess honored by the dedication as Uni-Astre, clearly combining Etruscan Uni with Phoenician Astarte and indicating close relations between Phoenicians and Caere.

Moreover, it gives Thefarie Velianas's official title as *zilac,* not *lauchume* (= "king," cf. Latin *lucumo*), and refers to "three years."

Etruscan *zilac* or *zilath* is generally thought to correspond to Latin *praetor* and can therefore either have the generic meaning of "magistrate" or specify a particular official of high rank. Since the texts indicate that Thefarie Velianas held this office at least into a third year, much modern scholarly speculation has arisen concerning the nature of Caere's political structure at this time. Was it still a monarchy, or had the kingship given way to a republican form of government, and could Thefarie Velianas have enjoyed a position akin to a Greek tyrant's?

The Phoenician goddess Astarte, equivalent to Mesopotamian Ishtar, was usually equated with Greek Aphrodite, and was the divinity of female beauty and love. Etruscan Uni, however, is equivalent to the Roman goddess Juno, who was a divinity of youthfulness, marriage, and child bearing, and was equated with Greek Hera. On the other hand, Greek writers identified the tutelary deity of Pyrgi as either Leucothea or Eileithyia. The latter was a minor Greek goddess of childbirth, whereas in Greek myth the former was the deified Ino, one of the daughters of Cadmus and the aunt of Dionysus, whom she was thought to have tended when the god was an infant. Ino was supposed to have committed suicide by jumping into the sea with her son Melicertes, whereupon they became the deified Leucothea and Palaimon. Consequently, Ino was associated with the protection of seafarers and children (Krauskopf in *Akten* 1981, 137–49). Thus it seems likely that the chief goddess of Pyrgi was worshipped by seafaring merchants for safe navigation, and this religious ideology may also have been associated with the cult of Aphrodite at Graviscae. Furthermore, in both instances we should not exclude the possibility that the worship of Uni-Astarte at Pyrgi and of Aphrodite at Graviscae likewise stemmed from the sexual needs of sailors. In the course of time, the sacred precinct at Pyrgi became quite wealthy from religious offerings made by grateful merchants and sailors; according to the Greek historian Diodorus (15.14), in 384 B.C. Dionysius I of Syracuse, in search for funds to finance a war with Carthage, sent sixty triremes against Pyrgi to rob it of its riches. The sea raid upon the sacred site produced one thousand talents, and the sale into slavery of prisoners of war taken from Caere realized another five hundred talents.

GROWTH AND DECLINE OF ETRUSCAN CIVILIZATION

Southern Etruria enjoyed its greatest prosperity during the seventh and sixth centuries B.C., while areas of central and northern Etruria lagged behind in their social, economic, and cultural development, and reached their zenith somewhat later. Our best source of information about Etruscan society comes not from ancient literary accounts or the remains of Etruscan

cities, but from its cemeteries. Members of the upper class were usually buried in chamber tombs, which in southern Etruria were subterranean, cut out of the soft tufa rock of the land, whereas in other areas of a different geology the tombs were constructed of stone above ground; but in both instances they were often covered with a mound of earth. In addition to containing the bodies of the deceased, the tombs of the orientalizing period (c. 720–580 B.C.) were usually furnished with fine pottery and metalwork, whereas those dating from the mid-sixth century onwards frequently had walls painted with scenes from Etruscan daily life, religion, and myth. Taken together, this abundant funerary material provides us with an amazingly detailed look into Etruscan culture. Grave goods demonstrate that the Etruscans were consumers of imported luxuries. In fact, a very large proportion of the fine Greek pottery of the archaic and classical periods on display in museums throughout the world has come from the cemeteries and chamber tombs of Etruria. Carved ivory and silver objects of Near Eastern provenance are also well represented in the early "princely tombs" (*tombe principesche*) as they have come to be called. For example, silver bowls found in the famous Regolini-Galassi tomb at Caere, one of the earliest and most magnificent of Etruscan chamber tombs, were of Levantine workmanship. Since the Etruscan upper class adopted the Near Eastern and Greek institution of the symposium or formal drinking party, vessels characteristic of ancient sympotic culture such as pitchers, mixing bowls, and drinking cups abound among Etruscan funerary goods (Rathje 1990).

By the sixth century B.C., however, the Etruscans had assimilated Greek and Levantine ceramic and metallurgical skills and techniques, and were producing their own distinctive pottery and metalwork. Indeed, Etruscan bronze casting and granulated gold work were unsurpassed in their skill and beauty. Art historians to this day still marvel at the latter; and the large corpus of decorated and inscribed bronze mirrors that were buried with the dead forms another important source of information on Etruscan society, religion, and mythology (see De Grummond 1982 and *CSE*). Furthermore, since, unlike Greece, the land of Etruria did not possess marble for architecture or sculpture, the Etruscans instead made extensive use of clay, and became expert in producing terracotta busts, statues, and reliefs for decorating buildings, and even artistically pleasing clay items of daily use. Enterprising Etruscans imitated the Greeks and Phoenicians in taking to the sea to enrich themselves through trade and piracy. As early as the Homeric Hymn to Dionysus, the Etruscans had a reputation as pirates among the Greeks. By the beginning of the sixth century B.C., the Etruscans were also exporting their own Bucchero pottery, fragments of which have been found at numerous sites throughout the entire Mediterranean. The most striking illustration of the Etruscan export trade comes from an ancient shipwreck off the coast of southern France near Antibes, dating to the second quarter of the sixth century. Among the ship's cargo were 170 Etruscan transport amphorae filled with wine.

Etruscan tomb paintings vividly portray many aspects of daily life, such as hunting and fishing, juggling and dancing to music, feats of horsemanship and chariot racing, and athletic contests (Steingräber 1985). In the tomb of the leopards at Tarquinii, women are shown reclining on couches together with their husbands at a banquet. Such social equality between the genders was alien to Greek and Near Eastern societies, where respectable women were not allowed to participate in drinking parties. Moreover, since Etruscan women are depicted as wearing more outer clothing, hats, and sturdier footwear than their eastern Mediterranean counterparts, it has been surmised that the well-to-do ladies of Etruria led much more public lives (Bonfante 1981). The dress and insignia of Etruscan magistrates resemble those known for the Roman republic. The tomb of the lictor at Vetulonia, dating to the seventh century B.C., takes its name from the fact that found in it was a double-headed iron axe surrounded by eight other iron rods similar to the *fasces* carried by lictors before Roman consuls and praetors. The curule chair employed by the same Roman officials is also encountered in several Etruscan tomb paintings. In the famous François Tomb at Vulci dating to c. 300 B.C., Vel Saties is depicted wearing what the Romans called a *toga picta,* which was worn by a Roman commander celebrating a triumph. The same tomb contains bloody scenes from Greek mythology, revealing a darker side of Etruscan culture: sanguinary fighting from the Seven against Thebes, and Achilles' sacrifice of Trojan captives at the pyre of Patroclus. The tomb of the augurs at Tarquinii depicts a bloody combat between a man and dog. The man, naked except for a loin cloth and wearing a sack over his head as a kind of blindfold, wields a club, while another person arouses against him a fierce dog, which has already inflicted bloody wounds upon the man. This has been taken to suggest that the Etruscans regarded the shedding of human blood as fitting, if not actually religiously necessary, for the funerals of prominent people. Herodotus (1.167) says that, following the naval battle fought by the Phocaeans against the Carthaginians and Etruscans c. 540 B.C., the people of Caere stoned their Greek captives to death. Barbarous though this act may have been, it is probably to be connected with funerary rites intended to appease the spirits of the Etruscans who had lost their lives in the same sea fight. From such funerary rites there evolved the Roman tradition of public gladiatorial contests, which were first performed in Rome in 264 B.C. in conjunction with the funeral of a senator (Van Der Meer 1982).

Like the Greeks, the Etruscans were bound together by a common language and culture but were not politically united into a single state or empire; rather, they inhabited independent city-states. Also like the Greeks,

the Etruscans extended the influence of their culture beyond the borders of their homeland by establishing new towns in Campania and the Po Valley. Archaeology suggests that already by the eighth century B.C. Etruscans had settled at Capua on the Volturnus and at other sites throughout Campania. In the course of time, Capua became one of the most important and powerful cities of central Italy, and the Etruscan language and civilization continued to be a significant element in Campanian culture long after the area had been overrun in the late fifth century B.C. by Oscan-speaking Samnites from the Apennines (Frederiksen in Ridgway and Ridgway 1979, 277–311; and Frederiksen 1984, 117–33). By the close of the sixth century B.C., the Etruscans were expanding northward into the Po Valley. They took over the flourishing Villanovan site at Bologna, a collection of villages that measured more than a mile in diameter, and they organized it into the Etruscan city of Felsina. Both before and after the Etruscan phase of its history, the site enjoyed great prosperity from its considerable production of high-quality iron and bronze objects. A discovered hoard of bronze, apparently collected to be recycled, contained 14,838 objects and weighed more than 3,100 pounds.

Twenty-five miles south of Bologna, where the Reno River flows down from the Apennines and meets the plain of the Po Valley, the Etruscans founded another city, whose ancient name is unknown, but which goes by the modern name of Marzabotto. This site was carefully excavated during the 1880s and has revealed much about Etruscan town planning (Mansuelli in Ridgway and Ridgway 1979, 353–60). The town was laid out according to an orthogonal plan precisely in alignment with the four points of the compass. There were four main avenues measuring fifteen meters in width, and eight other streets that were five meters wide. Three of the former ran east-west and were intersected by the fourth major avenue and the other eight streets. Thus the town was divided into orthogonal blocks. At the intersection of two of the avenues, there was a boundary stone on whose top was cut a cross marking out north-south and east-west. An elevated area in the northwestern sector served as the arx or citadel, complete with a sacred precinct.

By the end of the first quarter of the fifth century B.C., the economic prosperity enjoyed by the coastal cities of Etruria sharply declined, as the profitable long-distance trade between the Mediterranean and northern Europe shifted away from the Tyrrhenian Sea and moved eastward to the Adriatic and westward to Spain. During the second half of the sixth century, two new trading communities had arisen at Spina and Hatria near the mouth of the Po, and they became flourishing commercial centers during the fifth and fourth centuries, with mixed populations of Etruscans, Greeks, and native Umbrians and Veneti. Both may have been Etruscan foundations, but uncertainty still surrounds the circumstances and nature of their origin. Hatria's prominence is reflected in the fact that it gave its name to the Adriatic Sea. Spina, situated on the coast at the southernmost part of the Po delta, resembled modern-day Venice in having canals to serve as thoroughfares, which were laid out in an orthogonal pattern with a "Grand Canal" intersected by five other waterways. More than 3,500 graves in two different cemeteries at Spina have been excavated and have yielded enormous quantities of fine Attic pottery of the classical period, many pieces of which are on display in museums throughout the world. Grave goods also indicate that a flourishing trade existed between Spina on the Adriatic coast and the inland Etruscan city of Felsina.

By the end of the sixth century B.C., economic interests and commercial rivalries brought the western Greeks into violent conflict with the Phoenicians and Etruscans. The Carthaginians successfully opposed the Greek attempt to colonize northwestern Sicily, which was led by the Spartan royal prince Dorieus (Hdt. 5.43–48). Conflict between the two peoples finally culminated in the battle of Himera in 480 B.C., when the Carthaginians landed a large army on the northern coast of the island and were beaten by a coalition of Greek states (Hdt. 7.165–67). Following this battle, there were no other major engagements in Sicily between the Phoenicians and Greeks until the last decade of the fifth century, when Carthage renewed hostilities and embarked upon the conquest of the island. After that, Sicily was the scene of war between Syracuse and Carthage until the seesaw struggle was ended by Rome's military intervention in the First Punic War.

Conflict between the Greeks and Etruscans during the late sixth and early fifth centuries B.C. largely centered upon Cumae, the northernmost Greek foothold on the western coast of Italy. In 524 the Cumaeans succeeded in defeating a military offensive aimed against them by the Etruscans of Capua. Twenty years later in 504, an ambitious Cumaean aristocrat named Aristodemus led a force of two thousand Cumaeans to Aricia in Latium to lend aid to the Latins against an Etruscan army led by Arruns, the son of King Porsenna of Clusium, who at the time held Rome within his power. After defeating the Etruscans at Aricia, Aristodemus returned to Cumae and succeeded in making himself tyrant. He abolished the oligarchic constitution and introduced populist reforms, but after twenty years the new generation of aristocrats, some of whom had been living in exile at Capua, banded together and began waging a guerilla war against Cumae. Aristodemus was killed, and aristocratic rule was reinstated (Dion. Hal. 7.3–11). Finally, in 474 the Etruscans mounted another major attack upon Cumae, this time from the sea. Cumae appealed to Hieron I of Syracuse for assistance, and the result was a decisive Greek defeat of the Etruscans (Diod. 11.51). The victory was celebrated by the Greek poet Pindar in his first Pythian Ode, and Hieron commemorated his success by dedicating captured Etruscan helmets at Olympia (Meiggs and Lewis 1975, #29).

The victories at Himera and Cumae secured prosperity for the western Greeks for the remainder of the century, while coastal Etruria experienced a drastic decline in maritime commerce, which was not reversed until the fourth century. At the same time, the Etruscan communities in the Po Valley and Campania were threatened by and eventually succumbed to the migrations of Celts and Samnites respectively; and during the fourth and third centuries the Etruscan homeland itself came under Roman rule.

THE ALPHABET

Perhaps the single best indication and illustration of the impact that the Phoenicians, Greeks, and Etruscans had upon the peoples and culture of early Italy can be seen from the history of the alphabet.[10] Cuneiform and hieroglyphics, the two earliest systems of writing developed in the ancient Near East by the Sumerian and Egyptian civilizations, employed hundreds of pictographic symbols or ideograms and were therefore not easily mastered but required years of diligent study. Consequently, the number of people who could read and write in ancient Egypt and Mesopotamia was extremely small, and literacy was confined to a professional group of learned priests and scribes, who enjoyed considerable status and power within their societies as the result of their control of written knowledge. As the idea of civilization spread throughout the Fertile Crescent, so did the practice of writing. During the second millennium B.C. the Semitic-speaking peoples of Syria, Phoenicia, and Palestine developed their own systems of writing and created the first consonantal alphabets of twenty-two to thirty letters in which only consonants (not vowels) were represented. During the late Bronze Age, the Mycenaean palaces of Greece developed a system of writing which modern scholars call Linear B. This script consisted of eighty-seven characters, each of which stood for a consonant plus a vowel (hence the term "Linear B syllabary"). Because of the relatively large number of characters involved and the requirement to spell everything syllabically in segments consisting of a consonant followed by a vowel, this form of writing and reading Mycenaean Greek was rather difficult to learn and was only used to keep palace records, the purpose for which the script was devised. The Linear B syllabary and the knowledge of writing in general died out among the Greeks with the destruction of Mycenaean civilization during

10. For the early history of the alphabet, see Healey 1990 and Powell 1991, 5–118. For a general survey of the complex relationship between memory, orality, and literacy in archaic and classical Greece, see Thomas 1992. For the origin, diffusion, and other issues of the Etruscan alphabet, see Cristofani 1972 and the same author's essay in Ridgway and Ridgway 1979, 373–412. For the question of literacy during the early and middle Roman republic, see Harris 1989, 149–74, and for a treatment of literacy in early central Italy with particular attention to the question of the nature of the surviving evidence, see Cornell 1991.

the early twelfth century B.C. The Phoenician consonantal alphabet of twenty-two letters, on the other hand, survived the collapse of the Bronze Age civilizations and, during the early Iron Age, formed the basis of the Hebrew and Aramaic consonantal alphabets. Similarly, when the Greeks reestablished contacts with the Near East around 800 B.C., one of the first cultural borrowings and adaptations they effected was this same Phoenician script, which they modified into the world's first true alphabet with characters used to represent both consonants and vowels, thereby producing a simple, precise, and unambiguous script that made the skills of reading and writing easier to acquire.

The concept of writing spread very quickly throughout the Greek world, and slight changes were made from region to region, thus spawning so-called local Greek scripts. This process of diffusion and differentiation seems to have been completed by the third quarter of the eighth century B.C., when the Greeks began founding colonies in Sicily and southern Italy. As might be expected, colonies employed the local script of their mother-cities; and it was the alphabet of the Euboeans, probably of Pithecusa and Cumae, that the Etruscans borrowed and adapted to express their own language in writing. The earliest Etruscan writing, consisting of simple signatures and labels on ceramic and metal objects, dates to about 700 B.C. Not only were the Etruscans the first people of Italy to use a writing system, but the Etruscan alphabet was in turn adopted and adapted by the other indigenous peoples of Italy, including the Latins and Romans. In fact, the numeric symbols we now term roman numerals were devised by the Etruscans, and taken over by the Romans. Thus it is fair to say that the Phoenicians, Greeks, and Etruscans formed the successive links of a complex chain of creative cultural borrowing and adaptation that planted the seeds of literacy in the soil of ancient Italy.

Although the number of surviving Oscan, Umbrian, Venetic, Latin, Picene, and Messapic inscriptions earlier than the third century B.C. is quite small, the present corpus of Etruscan inscriptions numbers about ten thousand, of which a large proportion antedates 300 B.C.[11] Nevertheless, fewer than ten of these inscribed texts are of any substantial length. Virtually all are very short funerary epitaphs or labels on votive offerings, wall paintings, pottery, mirrors, and other objects of daily use. Yet the sheer ubiquity of such brief *tituli* conveys the impression that reading and writing were not arcane skills in Etruria. This suggests that the Etruscans were by far the most literate native people of Italy before the fourth or third centuries B.C. During the past few decades some modern scholars have argued that the Greek cultural revolution of the archaic and classical periods was in part due to the invention of the Greek alphabet, whose simplicity significantly

11. For a selection of these texts, see Pallottino 1969.

broadened literate culture and encouraged the development of rational institutions (e.g., Havelock 1982 and Goody 1986). Even though these claims are difficult to prove conclusively due to the scanty nature of the surviving evidence, and have therefore been challenged or played down by other scholars (e.g., Harris 1989, 45–64 and Thomas in Bowman and Woolf 1994, 33–50), it seems likely that the alphabet had a significant impact upon the cultural history of ancient Greece. The same may be cautiously concluded with respect to the alphabet's importance to the early inhabitants of Etruria, Latium, and Campania.

THE ARCHAEOLOGY OF EARLY LATIUM

Before ending this overview of major social, economic, and political developments in early central Italy, it is necessary to survey the archaeological data concerning early Latium.[12] Along with Greek colonization of southern Italy and the rise of Etruscan civilization, this subject forms the general background to the origin and growth of the early Roman state and society. In addition, although the data are far from complete, thanks to excavations at several sites during the past twenty-five years, our knowledge and understanding of what archaeologists now term Latial Culture have been greatly expanded. The following are the chronological phases and subdivisions of Latial Culture that have been devised in recent years by archaeologists and are now in general use (all dates, of course, being approximate and before the common era):[13]

1000–900: LC I
900–830: LC II.A
830–770: LC II.B
770–740: LC III.A
740–720: LC III.B
720–620: LC IV.A
620–580: LC IV.B

The first and second phases of the Latial Culture correspond respectively to the Proto-Villanovan and Villanovan archaeological cultures of Italy as a whole, whereas the fourth phase is contemporary with the orientalizing

12. For more detailed treatments of this subject, see Ridgway 1973–74; *Civiltà del Lazio Primitivo* 1976; Cornell 1980; Ampolo 1980; *Enea nel Lazio* 1981; Anzidei 1985; Cornell 1986; Bietti Sestieri 1992; Holloway 1994, 103–64; and Smith 1996. Gierow 1964–66 is a comprehensive synthesis of the early archaeological data from the area of the Alban Hills.

13. For an overview of the scholarly history behind this chronological system in the larger context of modern archaeology of early Italy, see J.C. Meyer 1983, 9–29, and for a detailed analytical demonstration of the relative chronology of the different phases of the Latial Culture, see the same work, 30–60.

period of Etruscan civilization, and the third phase is transitional between the second and fourth phases. LC I is characterized by simple undecorated pottery and cremation as the dominant funerary rite, whereas in LC II cremation is replaced by inhumation, and pottery is decorated with simple patterns. Foreign influences are detectable in the pottery of LC III, and in the fourth and final phase both foreign pottery and its local imitation are represented. Different styles of female fibulae also play an important role in this chronological scheme. Broadly speaking, developments in the material culture of Latium in many ways resembled those in Etruria. Since the land of Latium, however, did not possess the mineral resources which attracted Phoenician and Greek prospectors and traders and formed the basis of the economic growth and prosperity of the coastal cities of southern Etruria, Latium was significantly poorer and in some ways resembled inland Etruria in its agricultural orientation and slower pace of cultural change.

During the first two phases of the Latial Culture people lived in very small villages whose populations probably numbered no more than a few hundred at the very most. Before the advent of the masonry house to central Italy in the seventh century B.C., the typical dwelling was the simple hut, consisting of a single room, oval in floor plan with the major axis rarely exceeding twenty feet, and constructed of wattle and daub walls and a thatched roof pierced by a smoke-hole above the hut's hearth. All pottery was handmade with each household probably producing what they needed. Since the potter's wheel was not introduced until the eighth century, the round shape of vessels was produced by coiling; and since pottery was heated in the open fire and not in a kiln with a diaphragm used to shield the vessel from the fire, its appearance was black. The only specialized skill in this simple society of subsistence agriculture was metalworking. In LC I the dead were cremated, and their ashes were buried in urns, accompanied by miniature replicas of everyday utensils. Ash urns of this period discovered in the Roman Forum and in the Alban Hills are miniature models of the people's huts and were apparently designed to serve as the deceased's dwelling for eternity (see fig. 2), but during LC II inhumation gradually replaced cremation as the usual means of disposing of the dead.

Our most detailed view of Latial Culture during the second and third phases comes from the site of Osteria dell'Osa located near ancient Gabii, thanks to the careful excavation and thorough analysis of six hundred graves by Anna Maria Bietti Sestieri. The population of this settlement is estimated to have ranged between one hundred and three hundred people, and the graves of its cemetery are arranged in fourteen clusters which seem to represent family lineages over more than one generation. Grave goods accompanying the dead present the picture of a simple and poor society in which one's age and gender largely determined one's role and status. Moreover, although a rise in the quality of the grave goods over time reflects a

Figure 2. Hut-shaped cremation urns.

tend to be relatively uniform at any particular time and reveal only small differences in wealth. Given the high mortality rate for infants and children, it is not surprising to discover that their graves received worn and used pottery, whereas adults of vigorous years were buried with more and better-quality items. Inhumation was the general rule; but cremation, requiring a greater expenditure of energy, was used as a more honorific funerary rite and was reserved almost exclusively for adult males seventeen to forty-five years of age. These cremation graves were accompanied by full-size or miniature weapons, clearly indicating the males' role as warriors. Young females, on the other hand, were almost always buried with a spindle whorl used in making thread for weaving, which exemplified one of their more important roles in the society. Drinking sets were most often buried with the elderly, perhaps as a mark of honor or because their age had allowed them to accumulate a larger number of valuable objects. Women were buried with more personal ornaments than men. Adult males were usually buried with only a fibula, whereas women were often interred with beads and rings. In three inhumation graves (two female and one male), beads and rings. In three inhumation graves (two female and one male), the body was covered or wrapped with a sheet whose edges were bordered with small bronze rings.

Eventually, the community's gradual increase in wealth and reception of outside influences are reflected in the grave goods. For example, miniature weapons alone accompanied male cremation graves of the earliest period, but full-size bronze ones were occasionally buried in later graves. The presence of amber jewelry and several vessels resembling Villanovan styles current in Etruria and Campania demonstrate the infiltration of outside influences. Similarly, the grave goods of LC III do not exhibit the same degree of consistency in terms of gender and age as those in the burials of LC II. This may reflect changes in a simple traditional society resulting from economic growth and increasing social differentiation. Most striking of all is a globular flask associated with one of the few female cremation graves. On it, scratched with a metal point, are the five Greek letters, *EULIN*. The graffito probably represents a personal name that may not even be Greek. The grave is dated to LC II.B and is probably no later than the first quarter of the eighth century. Consequently, the incised letters constitute the earliest example of Greek alphabetic writing thus far discovered.

The bronze hoard discovered at Ardea, consisting of both unworked and worked metal, had probably been accumulated for recycling and suggests a growing demand for metal objects and the concomitant expansion of the metallurgical craft. With the introduction of the potter's wheel in the eighth century, pottery production joined metallurgy as a skilled industry, and wheel-made ceramic ware drove out domestically produced handmade pottery. Archaeological surface survey work in the vicinity of Antemnae, Fidenae, and Crustumerium along the Tiber north of Rome indicates that the countryside began to be occupied by farmsteads during the seventh century. This points to population growth and the intensification of farming. The grape and olive must have been cultivated in Latium during the archaic period, but it cannot be known on what scale. The increased exploitation of the land resulted in an agricultural surplus that brought into being a new affluent lifestyle of local elites. Their conspicuous consumption is best illustrated by the graves of Castel di Decima and the princely tombs of Praeneste.

Just as the site of Osteria dell'Osa has revolutionized modern understanding of LC II and III, the graves of Castel di Decima, located ten miles south of Rome on the Via Ostiensis and thought to be the ancient site of the early Latin community of Politorium, have done the same for LC IV. The site's cemetery has yielded three hundred graves dating to LC III and IV. The majority are simple inhumations accompanied by no or only modest grave goods, but the richer ones clearly show a gradual increase in wealth, culminating in the richest graves of the seventh century. Several women were buried dressed in garments ornamented with amber and glass beads and wearing silver or gold fibulae, with their hair bound with silver wire. Bowls for mixing wine were also buried with women. This suggests that, as in contemporary Etruria, the well-to-do women of Latium participated in symposia and were even responsible for dispensing the drinks. Punic wine amphorae testify to the importation of foreign wine, which was probably served at banquets to display the host's wealth. Weapons were commonly buried with males. The richest grave contained a lance, sword, breastplate, three shields, and a small two-wheeled chariot. Indeed, two-wheeled chariots were included in six graves, one of them that of a woman whose body was adorned with an amber and gold pectoral, gold hair rings, and a robe decorated with amber and glass beads.

In 1855 and 1876, there were discovered at Praeneste the Barberini and Bernardini tombs, the two richest sepulchers of early Latium. Both in their date (second quarter of the seventh century) and in the extraordinary quantity and splendor of their precious objects, they correspond to the Regolini-Galassi tomb of Caere, and their contents are on display in Rome in the Museo Nazionale di Villa Giulia (Densmore Curtis 1919 and 1925). The Bernardini tomb was an underground chamber constructed from a pit five and a half feet deep, approximately seventeen feet long, and twelve and a half feet wide; its walls were lined with tufa blocks. The vast amount of bronze, silver, gold, amber, and ivory objects (plaques, tripods, cauldrons, bowls, cups, shields, knives, etc.) present in these two tombs testifies to the incredible wealth accumulated by the deceased. The occupant of the Bernardini tomb might have been a woman who bore the Latin name Vetusia, because one of the tomb's silver bowls is engraved with this name. The artistic style of this material, depicting human figures, animals, and mythical creatures, derives from the Near East, but many of the objects are believed to have been manufactured in western colonial workshops by artisans operating within this artistic tradition. Nevertheless, some of the objects are likely to have been imported from the Near East itself. One such object is a silver bowl whose central decorative scene shows an Egyptian pharaoh killing his enemy. The accompanying hieroglyphic inscription is gibberish and was apparently included to add color to the Egyptian content of the artwork, but a Phoenician inscription gives the name of the artist: "Eshmunazar son of Asto."

Until recently, modern scholars had generally regarded the Barberini and Bernardini tombs as indicating that, like Rome during much of the sixth century B.C., Praeneste came under the rule of Etruscan overlords for part of the seventh century. But the rich tombs discovered at Castel di Decima have now rendered this conjecture unnecessary. Moreover, similar "princely tombs" dating to the seventh century B.C. have been found at Cumae, Pontecagnano in southern Campania (D'Agostino 1977), and even as far afield as Novilara on the Adriatic coast in Picenum (Trump 1966, 164–65).

Thus, these rich Praenestine sepulchers can be viewed as the Latin manifestation of a larger aristocratic cultural koine that pervaded central Italy during the orientalizing period and cut across ethnic and linguistic boundaries.

From the middle of the seventh century B.C. onwards, houses built on stone foundations and covered with roof tiles began to replace simple wattle and daub thatched huts. Conversely, the prodigal display of personal wealth in tombs ended with the close of the orientalizing period c. 580 B.C. This major change in funerary practice was not confined to Latium but was characteristic of central Italy as a whole, which once again suggests the existence of a larger cultural koine. This shift is likely to have stemmed from a major change in social attitude, according to which it seemed more fitting to expend resources on the living than on the dead. Indeed, the sixth century was a period characterized by considerable public building of temples, such as that of Minerva at Lavinium and the one to Mater Matuta on the acropolis of Satricum, to name just two. Thus, by the end of the sixth century, Latium had experienced many of the same social and economic changes that were responsible for transforming Greece and Etruria from societies of simple villages into ones organized into city-states: the development of skilled metallurgical and ceramic manufacturing, population growth and increased agricultural production, the replacement of villages by towns, and the rise of local elites whose wealth was converted into social status, religious authority, and political power. Nevertheless, Latium's lack of mineral resources relative to Etruria meant that in general its communities were not as fully integrated into the commercial activities of the western Mediterranean. For example, although Lavinium and Ardea resembled Caere and Tarquinii in being settlements located a few miles inland from the coast on rivulets that joined them to the sea, the former did not experience the growth and prosperity of the latter because of the absence of mineral deposits. Nor were trading settlements such as Pyrgi and Graviscae established on the Latin coast downstream from Lavinium and Ardea. Yet the discovery at Lavinium of a bronze plaque dating to the late sixth century and recording a dedication to Castor and Pollux, the twin Greek gods who watched over seafarers (see Gordon 1983, #2), indicates that by this date Latium was certainly not impervious to foreign cultural influences.

Chapter 3

The Ancient Sources for Early Roman History

The history of Rome's regal period and early republic is highly problematic due to the fact that ancient accounts were written during the second and first centuries B.C., long after the events that they described.[1] Consequently, modern historians often disagree substantially in their interpretations and reconstructions, depending upon their presuppositions concerning the reliability of the ancient sources and the criteria by which ancient traditions should be considered accurate. Thus a serious study of early Roman history cannot be undertaken without a clear understanding and continual examination of the nature and veracity of the ancient sources that purport to record the history of Rome's distant past. The two most important ancient accounts of early Rome that have survived from antiquity are the first ten books of Livy's *History of Rome* and the *Roman Antiquities* of Dionysius of Halicarnassus, both of which were composed during the closing decades of the first century B.C. But since these two narratives came at the end of nearly two hundred years of a long and varied historiographical tradition, and were the authors' own synthesized redactions of earlier histories which are now lost except in fragments,[2] a survey of the ancient sources for early

1. For other treatments of this subject, see Raaflaub and Cornell in Raaflaub 1986, 47–65; Ogilvie and Drummond in *CAH* VII.2 1989, 1–29; Cornell 1995, 1–30; and Oakley 1997, 3–108.

2. The term "fragment" is used by modern scholars of ancient history to refer to a portion of a lost ancient historical account that now survives in another surviving ancient literary text. A fragment can be either a verbatim quotation from a lost work or a paraphrase of a portion of its content. See Brunt 1980. In some instances (e.g., Cincius Alimentus, Postumius Albinus, and C. Acilius), we possess only a few fragments from a lost work and are therefore almost entirely ignorant of the work's nature and content, but in other cases (e.g., Cato, Calpurnius Piso, Claudius Quadrigarius, and Valerius Antias), the fragments are sufficiently numerous to

Roman history may properly begin with an overview of Livy's and Diony-sius's predecessors.[3]

THE ANNALISTIC TRADITION

As they did in many aspects of culture and literature, the Romans adopted the practice of historical writing from the Greeks, but the Greeks them-selves did not begin to pay serious attention to Rome in their historical accounts until the Pyrrhic War (280–275 B.C.), when Rome was completing its subjugation of Italy and was involved in a war with the Greek city of Tarentum. Timaeus, a native of the Sicilian Greek town of Tauromenium, in his detailed history of the western Greeks from earliest times down to the eve of the First Punic War between Rome and Carthage (i.e., 264 B.C.), not only narrated the events of the Pyrrhic War but also treated Rome's mythi-cal origin and early history in some detail. He visited Lavinium in Latium and made inquiries concerning the nature of the Penates worshipped by the Latins. He was somewhat familiar with the Roman yearly sacrifice of the October Horse, which he explained with reference to the Romans' descent from the Trojans. He dated the foundations of Rome and Carthage to the same year (814/3 B.C.); and he ascribed the invention of Roman bronze money to King Servius Tullius.[4] Another Sicilian Greek, Philinus of Acragas, wrote a contemporary historical account of the First Punic War (264–241 B.C.), but it was the momentous nature of the Second Punic or Hannibalic War (218–201 B.C.) that apparently prompted two Roman sen-ators, Q. Fabius Pictor and L. Cincius Alimentus, to write the first native

---

give us a fairly clear picture of the work's structure, overall reliability, and historical method-ology. The fragments of the lost histories of Roman republican authors are set out in their Greek and Latin texts in Peter 1914. It should be noted, however, that Peter ignored as ficti-tious the numerous citations of republican writers in the *Origo Gentis Romanae,* a short Latin treatise of late antiquity concerned with Roman mythology from primordial times down to the city's foundation by Romulus. For the rehabilitation of this work's citations see Momigliano 1958. The Latin text of this treatise is published in Pichlmayr 1970. In recent years, other edi-tions of the lost histories of republican Rome have been produced, usually accompanied with a detailed introduction, notes, commentary, and/or translation into a modern language: Chassignet 1996 for Q. Fabius Pictor, L. Cincius Alimentus, A. Postumius Albinus, C. Acilius, and the *Annales Maximi;* Chassignet 1986 for Cato; Santini 1995 for Cassius Hemina; Forsythe 1994 for Calpurnius Piso; and Walt 1997 for Licinius Macer.

3. For other surveys of some or all of these writers, see Badian 1966; Gabba in *Origines de la République Romaine* 1967, 135–69; Gentili 1975; Rawson 1976; Forsythe 1994, 25–73; and Forsythe 2000.

4. For Timaeus in general see T.S. Brown 1958, Momigliano 1977, and Pearson 1987. Concerning the Penates, October Horse, foundation date, and Servius Tullius, see Dion. Hal. 1.67.4; Polyb. 12.4 b 1; Dion. Hal. 1.74.1; and Pliny *NH* 34.43. All Timaeus's fragments are col-lected in Jacoby 1950, no. 566.

histories of Rome.[5] Their works were written in Greek, the literary language of the Hellenistic world, and they did not simply narrate the history of the Second Punic War but also recounted Roman affairs from mythical times down to their own day. Fabius Pictor's surviving fragments suggest that the traditions of the regal period were already well developed and in large measure resembled what we find in Livy's first book. Yet Dionysius (1.6.2) indicates that although the histories of Pictor and Alimentus were relatively detailed concerning Rome's foundation and the period of the Punic Wars, they passed over the intervening time span in a summary fashion.

Two other Roman senators, A. Postumius Albinus and C. Acilius, composed similarly all-encompassing histories of Rome, but since we possess very few fragments from these works, their scale and nature are unknown.[6] The first Latin narrative of Roman history was written by the poet Q. Ennius (239–169 B.C.), who composed his *Annals* in dactylic hexameter verse (see Skutsch 1985). This national epic—heroic, moralizing, and patriotic in nature—was a staple for educating Roman schoolboys and thus shaped the Romans' view of their past until its account of Rome's Trojan origin was supplanted by Vergil's *Aeneid* during the Augustan principate. The poem treated the Trojan connection and the regal period in the first three books, the early republic in the next two, and Roman affairs from the Pyrrhic War onwards in the remaining thirteen. The first Roman history composed in Latin prose was written by Cato the Elder (234–149 B.C.), and after that, with few exceptions, the Romans wrote their histories in Latin. Cornelius Nepos in his brief biography of Cato (3.3–4) describes the work as follows:

> He set about writing history in his old age. It consists of seven books. The first book contains the deeds of the kings of the Roman people, whereas the second and third books describe the origin of each Italian community, and for this reason it seems, all the books were called *Origines*. The First Punic War is in the fourth book, and the Second Punic War is in the fifth book. All these matters are described in a summary fashion. He narrated the remaining wars in the same manner down to the praetorship of Servius Galba [150 B.C.], who plundered the Lusitanians. He did not mention the commanders of these wars by name, but he recorded affairs without names. In these books he set forth the events of Italy and the two Spains as well as what seemed marvelous in these areas. He expended much energy and care upon these books but no learning.

5. In addition to the modern works cited above nn.2–3, see Timpe 1972 and Verbrugghe 1979 for two contrasting treatments of Fabius Pictor, and see Verbrugghe 1982 for Cincius Alimentus.

6. Since Fabius Pictor, Cincius Alimentus, Postumius Albinus, and C. Acilius wrote their Roman histories in Greek, their fragments were collected in Jacoby 1958 as historians nos. 809–10 and 812–13.

The numerous fragments from this work bear out Nepos' description. The second and third books seem to have resembled the kind of Greek ethnographic history found in Herodotus and the fragments of Timaeus. The fragments from the last four books are largely concerned with the military affairs of the middle republic, and the fragments from the first book treat the regal period. Thus there is a strong possibility that Cato ignored the traditions of the early republic altogether, or at least treated them in a very cursory fashion.[7]

Following Cato, L. Cassius Hemina wrote a history probably comprising no more than five books, the first of which seems to have resembled the second and third books of Cato's *Origines* in recounting the mythical origins of the towns and peoples of central Italy. The work's second book covered both the regal period and the early republic. The surviving fragments suggest that Hemina had relatively little interest in military affairs but was keenly interested in religion and cultural history.[8] L. Calpurnius Piso Frugi composed a historical account in seven or eight books, which he probably published after his censorship of 120 B.C. Like Livy and Cato, Piso treated the regal period in his first book, while the events of the early republic were narrated in his second and third books. The latter, probably the most detailed account of the early republic written thus far, described events by using an annalistic framework and may have been the very first Roman historical account to employ this kind of structured narrative to depict the early republic (Forsythe 1994).

All histories of Rome written thus far by Romans had been composed by senators and were relatively brief accounts of names, dates, and major events. By the close of the second century B.C., however, detailed Greek histories such as that of Polybius, comprising thirty-nine books to describe in great detail Rome's conquest of the Mediterranean during the period 264–146 B.C., inspired Romans to write much lengthier works and to experiment with writing historical monographs on individual wars. Moreover, the writing of history was no longer a preserve of the Roman senator experienced in public affairs. It now became the occupation of men who possessed great literary skills, but who often lacked a practical knowledge of politics, diplomacy, and warfare. Thus, for example, Coelius Antipater (c. 100 B.C.), using earlier detailed histories written by Greeks, wrote a history of the Hannibalic War in seven books; and Sempronius Asellio, patterning his work after Polybius, devoted fifteen books to the period c. 150–90 B.C. Conversely, from this point onward other authors wrote greatly expanded

---

7. On this matter see Forsythe 1994, 46–48; 2000, 4. For a general discussion of Cato's *Origines*, see Astin 1978, 211–39 with Kierdorf 1980.

8. For Hemina see Rawson 1976, 690–702; Scholz 1989; Forsythe 1990; and Santini 1995.

histories of Rome from its foundation down to their own day. The first such was Cn. Gellius, whose work comprised at least ninety-seven books. His first book seems to have been patterned after the second and third books of Cato's *Origines* and the first book of Cassius Hemina in describing the mythical origins of the various peoples and communities of Italy. Romulus's reign was treated at the end of his second book and the beginning of his third. The expansive scale of Gellius's history is apparent from the fact that he described events of the year 389 B.C. in his fifteenth book, whereas Livy treated the same matters in his sixth. This literary expansion was largely achieved through the inclusion of lengthy speeches and battle narratives, which—for early Rome—were entirely invented and were intended to enliven his work and make it more entertaining for his readers. Although Livy did not make direct use of Gellius's history, Gellius was a major source for Licinius Macer and for Dionysius, who was apparently attracted to his rhetorical incontinence and meticulous attention to fictitious details.[9]

During the 80s and 70s B.C., Q. Claudius Quadrigarius, probably in reaction against the fictional character of Gellius's treatment of early Rome, compiled a history whose starting point was not Rome's mythical origin but the Gallic capture of Rome in 390 B.C. Quadrigarius chose to begin his narrative at this point because he believed that during the Gauls' occupation of the city all written records had been destroyed, and all historical traditions concerning events prior to 390 could therefore be regarded as untrustworthy (see Plutarch's *Numa* 1.2). Livy paraphrased this sentiment at the beginning of his sixth book and used Quadrigarius as a source throughout his second pentad. The fragments suggest that Quadrigarius was almost exclusively interested in military affairs.

During the last generation of the Roman republic, major histories were written by C. Licinius Macer, Valerius Antias, and Q. Aelius Tubero, all of whom Livy and Dionysius used as sources for their own works (see Ogilvie 1965, 7–17). As tribune of the plebs in 73 B.C., Macer was a staunch proponent of the populist politics of the day, which sought to restore full, traditional powers to the plebeian tribunate by overturning the restrictions placed upon the office in the recent constitutional reforms of the dictator Sulla.[10] Macer's fragments clearly display his keen interest in the struggle of the orders during the early republic. In fact, three fragments (Livy 7.9.3, 9.46.3, and 10.9.7–13 with 10.11.9) demonstrate that Macer was not averse to outright fabrication in order to enliven his narrative with spurious

---

9. For Gellius see Rawson 1976, 713–17 and Forsythe 1994, 163–64 and 229–32. For the practice of literary embellishment in ancient historiography see Wiseman 1979a, 3–40.

10. For Sallust's rendition of Macer's fiery political oratory during his tribunate, see Sallust *Historiae* III.48.1–28 = pp. 420–31 of the Loeb Classical Library edition of Sallust. For a detailed analysis of this speech see Walt 1997, 11–28.

conflicts between patrician and plebeian officials. But perhaps the most sensational and shameless fabricator of the Roman annalists was Valerius Antias, who probably composed his history, consisting of at least seventy-five books, during the period c. 65–45 B.C. His work is frequently cited by Livy, who complains of his unreliability and indicates that he enjoyed inventing both major occurrences and minor details.[11] Thus by the time that Livy and Dionysius came to write history, Roman historiography had a complex development of nearly two hundred years behind it, and there were numerous sources at hand from which they could fashion their own works.

THE ANTIQUARIAN TRADITION

In addition to this rich and varied historiographical tradition, antiquarian scholarship, a similar but separate literary tradition, likewise arose and flourished during the last two centuries B.C., and the results of its research often provide modern scholars with valuable information about early Rome. Like the ancient historical accounts just surveyed, however, the antiquarian literature of the Roman republic survives almost entirely through its use by later extant authors. Roman antiquarians were not directly concerned with reconstructing and narrating the political and military history of the Roman state. They were interested in the history of the Latin language, including the original meaning and history of words. Nonetheless, since much of their research involved investigating the language, meaning, and terminology of religious and legal documents surviving from earlier times, their writings often devoted considerable attention to the history of Roman social, political, military, religious, and legal institutions and practices. The Roman antiquarian tradition can perhaps be said to begin with the publication of a treatise on the Roman religious calendar, written by M. Fulvius Nobilior, consul in 189 B.C. and a patron of the poet Ennius.

Several significant antiquarian writers flourished during the second half of the second century B.C. Besides writing histories of Rome, Fabius Maximus Servilianus (consul 142 B.C.) and Numerius Fabius Pictor (a descendant of Rome's first native historian) both wrote treatises on pontifical law. Junius Gracchanus, who received his surname from having been a close friend of the revolutionary politician C. Sempronius Gracchus (died 121 B.C.), wrote a work entitled *De Potestatibus*, which concerned the history of Roman customs and institutions and the powers of

---

11. For example, see Livy 3.5.12–13. For Antias and Livy in general, see Howard 1906, and for a discussion of Antias' influence upon the late annalistic tradition in his glorification of members of the Valerian family during the regal period and the early years of the republic, see Wiseman 1998, 75–89.

the various magistrates.[12] L. Aelius Stilo (c. 150–80 B.C.) published works on the archaic language of the hymn of the Salian priests and on the Law of the Twelve Tables. Atticus (110–32 B.C.), intimate friend of Rome's greatest orator, Cicero, not only shared his antiquarian learning with the latter (whose voluminous extant writings were thus enriched), but his Book of Chronology (*Liber Annalis*) outlined the whole of Roman history in a single volume and set forth its chronology in such a definitive and convincing manner that the scheme was adopted by Varro, and from the Augustan age onward this so-called "Varronian" chronology was the official chronology of the Roman state (see the Appendix).[13]

The greatest Roman antiquarian of all was M. Terentius Varro (116–27 B.C.), who throughout his long life wrote at least fifty-five treatises on a wide range of subjects.[14] According to one ancient source, Varro had completed the writing of 490 volumes by his seventy-eighth year. Unfortunately, the only one of his works that has survived to us intact is a treatise on agriculture (*De Re Rustica*), but substantial portions of his twenty-book examination of the Latin language (*De Lingua Latina*) have come down to us and contain much valuable information on early Roman institutions. In addition, a considerable amount of his scholarship, especially in the area of religion, has been preserved for us indirectly in the writings of later ancient authors such as Pliny the Elder, Aulus Gellius, Servius, Macrobius, and the Christian writers Tertullian, Lactantius, Arnobius, and Augustine.

The last major Roman antiquarian important for the study of early Rome is Verrius Flaccus, who flourished during the Augustan age and was therefore a contemporary of Livy and Dionysius. A significant portion of his scholarship, like Varro's, has been preserved indirectly in the writings of later surviving authors. One of his most important treatises, *De Significatu Verborum,* was a kind of antiquarian dictionary, in which archaic Latin words and phrases were arranged in alphabetical order, and their meanings were discussed and explained. Although this work has not survived, we possess a later abridgement of it by Sex. Pompeius Festus (c. 200 A.D.). A substantial portion of Festus's text (A-L) has been lost, but this loss is partially remedied by the survival of an eighth-century A.D. summary of the work by Paulus Diaconus. Despite the unfortunate state of its preservation, Festus's text contains much valuable information for the modern student of early Rome.[15]

12. For the fragments see Bremer 1896 I. 37–40.
13. For Atticus's life and scholarly activity, see Münzer 1905 and Perlwitz 1992.
14. For an evaluation of Varro see Baier 1997.
15. Modern scholars normally cite Festus according to the pagination of the Teubner text edited by W. M. Lindsay; and in order to signify the fact that this text, rather than some other earlier edition, is being used, *L* is placed after the relevant page number.

LIVY AND DIONYSIUS OF HALICARNASSUS

Livy (59 B.C.–A.D. 17) was born at Patavium (modern Padova or Padua) in northeastern Italy, not far from Venice. He does not appear to have held any public office or to have performed any military service, but allusions to him in the works of Seneca the Elder and Quintilian indicate that he was a rhetorician by training and profession.[16] In his later years, after he had gained a reputation as a writer of Roman history, he is said to have encouraged the literary endeavors of Augustus's grandnephew Claudius (later emperor 41–54 A.D.), who wrote two histories: one of Carthage, and another of the Etruscans. Livy seems to have begun writing his history of Rome around 30 B.C. and might have still been writing right up to his death. The history comprised 142 books, beginning with Rome's foundation and ending with the year 9 B.C. The books of the history were clearly organized into groups of five (pentads) or of ten (decades) and were probably published in installments of five or ten books (Stadter 1972). Of the 142 books, only 1–10 and 21–45 have survived. The first ten books cover Roman affairs down to 293 B.C. and constitute our single most important source on early Roman history. This first decade may have been published around 20 B.C. (Luce 1965). Books 21–45 narrate Roman history for the years 218–167 B.C. Livy's history was so successful that it was soon acknowledged as the standard account of the Roman republic and eventually supplanted all earlier histories. Nevertheless, the work's huge size proved a hindrance to its complete preservation. In later centuries abridged versions abounded. Consequently, although only about one-third of the entire work has survived intact, we possess brief summaries of all the books, as well as later ancient condensations and adaptations of the history.

Livy did not possess the keen analytical intellect of a Thucydides, nor was he a shameless fabricator like Valerius Antias. Livy's real talent lay in his ability to arrange his material skillfully and economically, to construct an artistically pleasing narrative, and to depict individual episodes with great dramatic effect. Since most events covered in his history long preceded his own time, Livy did not engage in any original research into official documents, but was content to compare and synthesize the different accounts of earlier historians. Generally speaking, he adopted an agnostic attitude toward the received traditions of early Rome, and he did little more than try to reconcile discrepancies in his sources by using arguments from probability, a mainstay of ancient rhetorical training. Thus Livy was not particularly concerned with ascertaining detailed points of historical fact. Rather, he was much more interested in larger moral and patriotic themes. Like many other ancients, he believed that the value of history lay in providing

---

16. Seneca *Controv.* 9.1.14; 9.2.26; 10. praef. 2; Quintilian 1.5.56; 1.7.24; 2.5.20; 8.1.3; 8.2.18; 10.1.39; and 10.1.101.

people with good and bad models of conduct to be emulated and to be avoided respectively. His history has a decidedly moral and patriotic tone.[17]

Dionysius of Halicarnassus was an exact contemporary of Livy.[18] He came to Rome in 30 B.C. and began teaching Greek rhetoric to members of the Roman upper class. In addition to having written critical treatises on famous Greek orators, Dionysius wrote a stylistic critique of the Greek historian Thucydides, which he dedicated to the Roman historian and jurist Q. Aelius Tubero (Pritchett 1975). A century earlier, Polybius had published his detailed history in Greek of Rome's conquest of the Mediterranean during the period 264–146 B.C., but since all other historical accounts written in Greek had failed to treat early Roman history in as much detail as the Latin annalists of the late republic, Dionysius undertook to write such an account for his fellow Greeks. The product was his *Roman Antiquities*, comprising twenty books and covering Roman affairs from earliest times down to 264 B.C. The work was completed by 7 B.C. and was Dionysius's own synthetic redaction of the histories of Cn. Gellius, Licinius Macer, Valerius Antias, Aelius Tubero, and other native Roman writers. Only the first eleven books of this work, treating events down to 449 B.C., have survived. Portions of the remaining nine books have come down to us in excerpts made by later Byzantine writers. The work is far more lavish and rhetorical than Livy's first decade. This often makes for tedious reading. Even the most casual comparison of Dionysius's history with Livy's first ten books reveals the latter's judiciousness and discriminating restraint and the former's unbridled verbosity. Nevertheless, since Dionysius was writing for a Greek audience whom he assumed to be not particularly well informed concerning Roman customs and institutions, his narrative is oftentimes more informative than Livy's, because the latter tends to omit many details with which his Roman readers were familiar. Furthermore, even though Livy and Dionysius generally drew upon the same earlier historical accounts

17. Walsh 1963 and 1974 are two excellent surveys of Livy and his work. Dorey 1971 and Schuller 1993 are collections of essays written by different authors on various aspects of Livian scholarship. Ogilvie 1965 is a detailed commentary on the first pentad. Oakley 1997 is a thorough introduction to the second pentad and exhaustive commentary on Book VI. Oakley 1998 is a similarly detailed commentary on Books VII-VIII. A third volume soon to be published by the same author will treat Books IX-X. Phillips 1982 is a detailed bibliographical essay concerning modern scholarship on Livy's first ten books. Luce 1977, 139–297 is an excellent treatment of Livy's methods in writing his history by synthesizing earlier historical accounts. Forsythe 1999 discusses Livy's historical methods and judgment throughout the first decade. Gutberlet 1985 attempts to detect the influence of the political violence of the late republic in Livy's first ten books. Ridley's study in Eder 1990, 103–38 is the single best essay on Livy's attitude toward the struggle of the orders.

18. For a relatively recent treatment of Dionysius and his *Roman Antiquities* in the broader context of Augustan Rome and Greek society, see Gabba 1991. For an examination of his ideas on historical writing, see Sacks 1983. For his ideology in portraying the regal period, see Fox 1996, 49–95.

for compiling their narratives, their treatments of individual events often diverge markedly, thus providing modern scholars with important glimpses into the heterogeneity of the Roman annalistic tradition.

CICERO AND DIODORUS SICULUS

Two other ancient writers important for early Roman history and therefore deserving comment are Cicero and Diodorus. M. Tullius Cicero (106–43 B.C.) was Rome's greatest orator, whose numerous speeches and nearly one thousand letters make the years 65–43 B.C. the best documented period of classical antiquity. Besides speeches and letters, Cicero wrote a large number of philosophical and rhetorical essays that contain valuable allusions to events in earlier Roman history. Two essays of particular interest to the modern scholar of early Rome are *De Re Publica* and *De Legibus,* which were roughly patterned after Plato's two famous works, *The Republic* and *The Laws.* Book 2 of *De Re Publica* traces the political and constitutional history of the Roman state as an ideal model for the evolution of the mixed constitution. Unfortunately, the text is not complete and contains many gaps, but it is still an important narrative for the tradition of the regal period and of the early republic down to 449 B.C. Books 2–3 of *De Legibus* discuss the laws that an ideal state should possess; and since these laws are largely those of the Roman state, the treatise is a valuable source of information concerning Roman institutions.

Diodorus Siculus was a Sicilian Greek, who wrote a universal history of the ancient world in forty books, beginning with the mythical past and coming down to the year 60 B.C. He seems to have written during the 50s, 40s, and 30s B.C. Only Books 1–5 and 11–20 have been fully preserved, and the latter narrate the events of the fifth and fourth centuries B.C.; but since Diodorus for this period is almost entirely interested in recording the events of mainland Greece, the Persian Empire, and the western Greeks, he describes Roman affairs very briefly and usually only when there is some truly momentous event to relate, such as the decemviral legislation, the Gallic capture of Rome, or major events of the Second Samnite War. Otherwise, he is content merely to record the names of Rome's eponymous magistrates for each year along with the name of the eponymous archon of Athens. Consequently, his narrative is an additional source for the early list of Roman magistrates, even though the lists, especially of the colleges of military tribunes with consular power, often contain omissions and errors due to his carelessness or that of later copyists (Drummond 1980). Nevertheless, Diodorus's list of Roman magistrates contains a few major differences from those of Livy, Dionysius, and the *Fasti Capitolini* which are of historiographical interest (Drachmann 1912). Since some of his detailed Roman material differs from Livy's account, there has been much modern scholarly speculation concerning the nature and identity of his Roman source or sources (Perl 1957 and Cassola 1982, 724–58). Since Mommsen (1879) advanced the view that Diodorus's source for Roman affairs was Fabius Pictor, modern scholars have sometimes given his account of events preference to others, but Mommsen's hypothesis has now been generally discredited (Beloch 1926, 107–32 and Klotz 1937), and the oddities of Diodorus's Roman material can usually be attributed to the author's own carelessness and general indifference to the details of the annalistic tradition.

ANCIENT DOCUMENTARY SOURCES

Now that Rome's annalistic and antiquarian traditions have been briefly sketched, it may be reasonably asked upon what kind and quality of information these ancient historical and antiquarian works were ultimately based. One possible source of information that has figured prominently in modern scholarly treatments of early Roman history is the Pontifical Chronicle or *Annales Maximi*, whose genesis Cicero (*De Oratore* 2.52–53) describes as follows:

> From the beginning of Roman affairs to the chief pontificate of P. Mucius [130–115 B.C.], the chief pontiff [= pontifex maximus] used to write down all matters year by year, publicized (or recorded) them on a whitened board (*album*), and placed the tablet (*tabulam*) in front of his house, so that the people could learn from it. Even now they are called the Chief Annals (*Annales Maximi*). This form of writing has been followed by many who have left behind unembellished records of mere dates, persons, places, and deeds.

Servius Auctus, commenting in late antiquity on Vergil's *Aeneid* 1.373, gives the following description of the chronicle's content:

> Every year the pontifex maximus had a whitened tablet (*tabulam dealbatam*), upon which he first wrote the names of the consuls and of other magistrates. He then used to jot down day by day the events at home and abroad, both on land and sea, worthy of record. The ancients filled eighty books with these yearly commentaries of the pontiff's diligence, and they called them the Chief Annals (*Annales Maximi*) from the chief pontiffs by whom they were composed.

The nature and history of Roman pontifical record keeping has been much discussed, and many different theories have been advanced.[19] The most

---

19. For an overview of modern scholarly opinions, see Frier 1979 10–20, 162–72, and 179–80. See also Crake 1940; Bauman 1983, 290–98; Drews 1988a; Forsythe 1994, 53–71; Bucher 1995; and Forsythe 2000, 6–8.

likely explanation, supported by ancient Babylonian astronomical diaries and medieval monastic Easter calendars, is that the whitened board of the chief pontiff was calendrical in nature.[20] Other ancient sources indicate that during republican times, at the beginning of each month the rex sacrorum announced to the assembled Roman people the festivals to be observed that month. This announcement probably included the month's legal calendar as well (Varro *Ling. Lat.* 6.27, Servius Auctus *ad Aen.* 8.654, and Macrobius *Saturnalia* 1.15.9–13). A whitened notice board must have been employed to supplement and reinforce these monthly oral proclamations, and in the course of time the chief pontiff, who was in charge of the custom, used the board to record events bearing upon his supervision of the public religion. The early Romans believed that the individual days of the year were either auspicious or inauspicious; and the pontiffs, who were responsible for regulating the calendar, were probably interested in recording the dates of major public events in order to determine empirically the favorable or unfavorable nature of each day of the year. Moreover, at the end of each year any pertinent data must have been copied from the whitened board into a more permanent and less bulky record, such as a linen scroll or wooden codex, and a new notice board was used for the next year. According to Cicero, the custom of this notice board went far back into the past and was not discontinued until P. Mucius Scaevola was chief pontiff.

Many modern scholars have concluded that while Scaevola was chief pontiff, all accumulated pontifical data were compiled into the eighty books of the *Annales Maximi,* but Frier (1979, 27–48 and 192–200) has argued that Scaevola simply discontinued the custom of posting a notice board, and that the eighty-book edition mentioned by Servius Auctus was not compiled until early imperial times. This view, however, has been refuted in detail (Forsythe 1994, 53–71 and 2000, 7–8). Among other things, the contemporaneous works on pontifical law by N. Fabius Pictor and Fabius Maximus Servilianus constitute very strong circumstantial evidence that interest in such matters was characteristic of the late second century B.C. In fact, Pictor's and Servilianus's works were probably reworkings of the recently consolidated *Annales Maximi,* whose content they helped to disseminate and to incorporate into the developing Roman annalistic tradition. More recently, Bucher (1995) has argued that the *Annales Maximi* took the form of a series of inscribed bronze tablets nailed up on the outer wall of the Regia, but his thesis rests upon a flawed interpretation of Cicero's *De Oratore* 2.52 quoted above (Forsythe 2000, 8–25). He regards *album* and *tabulam* as referring to two different objects, a whitened notice board and a bronze

---

20. For analogous ancient Babylonian record keeping, see Sachs 1948. For a discussion of the origin and nature of medieval monastic chronicles, see Thompson 1942, 158 ff.

tablet; but the variation is more plausibly taken as Cicero's use of two different words to describe the same thing so as to avoid verbal repetition in two adjacent phrases. Note that Servius Auctus combines *tabula* with an adjectival form of *album* to describe the pontiff's wooden notice board. Even if we were to factor in pontifical material relevant to the civil law, which in fact was most likely preserved in its own separate archive, there never could have been enough pontifical material to fill eighty papyrus scrolls of the average size used for books of literary prose. To judge from the nature of our surviving sources, by Scaevola's day the amount of authentic pontifical material preceding the middle of the fourth century B.C. must have been quite modest. Frier's down-dating of the eighty-book edition to the early empire only shifts this embarrassing problem from one chronological context to another. On the other hand, when supplemented with other religious material and traditions already recorded in published histories, the pontifical material accumulated during the early and middle republic might have easily filled eighty wooden codices: for a bulky codex, even one of numerous thin wooden leaves, could not hold as many columns of writing as a papyrus scroll. Thus, eighty wooden codices comprising the *Annales Maximi*, suspended by hooks from rafters in a public building like other Roman official records, might have contained the equivalent of only fifteen to twenty average-sized books written on papyrus.[21]

The historical accounts of Livy and Dionysius contain certain kinds of information that modern scholars have generally supposed to derive ultimately from the Pontifical Chronicle: the list of annually elected consuls (*fasti consulares*), major military defeats and the celebration of triumphs, the deaths of priests, the dedications of new temples and the institution of new religious celebrations, plagues, food shortages, and the occurrence of unusual phenomena that the Romans regarded as divine prodigies requiring expiation (e.g., eclipses, monstrous births, and damage or death caused by lightning).[22] Such material forms a very small portion of Livy's and Dionysius's narratives. At most the historical data preserved in the *Annales Maximi* would have provided their accounts with a skeletal chronological framework of major events, whose narrative had to be fleshed out by other means. The surviving fragments from the works on pontifical law written by N. Fabius Pictor and Fabius Maximus Servilianus, whose content probably resembled that of the *Annales Maximi,* largely contain detailed contemporary religious regulations and verbal formulae used in ceremonies (Peter 1914, 114–16 and 118). This suggests that the eighty books of the *Annales*

21. For the history of the ancient book form, see Kenyon 1951, and for a survey of Roman archival practices, see Posner 1972, 160–223.

22. For a skeptical view concerning the Pontifical Chronicle as the source of Roman prodigy lists, see Rawson 1971a, but for counterarguments see Ruoff-Väänänen 1972. On the names of priests preserved in Livy, see Rüpke 1993.

Maximi comprised a relatively small amount of truly historically relevant data. It seems likely that histories such as that of Calpurnius Piso, written about the time of the compilation of the *Annales Maximi,* were the first works to incorporate systematically the relevant historical data gleaned from the Pontifical Chronicle, including an annalistic framework, and that subsequent historians did not need to consult the work directly but simply took the material over indirectly from other accounts.

Another important source of documentary information for later ancient writers is thought to have been the texts of treaties and laws inscribed on durable materials such as stone or bronze, so that they still existed in historical times and were thus available to those interested in examining them. According to Dionysius (4.58.4), an ox-hide shield bearing the text of a treaty between Rome and Gabii, concluded during the reign of Tarquinius Superbus, was preserved in the temple of Dius Fidius on the Quirinal. Cicero (*Pro Balbo* 53) indicates that the Cassian Treaty with the Latins, dating to the year 493 B.C., was still to be seen during his own day engraved on a bronze column behind the Rostra in the Forum. Polybius (3.22–26) succeeded in locating the texts of three early treaties between Rome and Carthage, and used their contents to reconstruct the early diplomatic history between the two states. There can be no doubt that if such texts were properly dated and their main provisions accurately related, treaties could serve as important landmarks in charting Rome's growing sphere of interest and influence in international affairs over the course of time. But the surviving ancient evidence suggests that Polybius's translation and detailed explication of the early treaties between Rome and Carthage rarely, if ever, had parallels in other ancient accounts of early Rome.

Dionysius (4.26) states that the sacred law attributed to King Servius Tullius, prescribing sacrificial procedures for the cult of Aventine Diana, could still be seen in his day, carved in archaic letters on a bronze tablet; and inscriptions of the early principate indicate that this so-called Aventine Canon was still serving as a model for Roman religious ceremonies.[23] Dionysius (10.32.4) also says that a law passed in 456 B.C., which regulated private settlement on the Aventine Hill, was inscribed on a bronze tablet and placed in Diana's temple. According to Livy (3.55.13), the plebeian aediles from the middle of the fifth century B.C. onwards were responsible for preserving the texts of senatorial decrees in the temple of Ceres on the Aventine. Thus it appears that at least some original documents of the early republic still existed in later historical times. The chances of a document's survival must have been enhanced if it had been engraved on bronze or a

---

23. Inscriptions of the early empire from Narbo in Gaul, Salonae in Dalmatia, and Ariminum in northern Italy refer to this canon as forming the basis of cultic charters. See respectively *ILS* 112, 4907, and *CIL* XI: 361.

durable type of stone, if it happened to be deposited in a temple where it might be left undisturbed as a religious dedication, and if its provisions did not become obsolete but continued to be somehow relevant. Only documents of particular importance, however, were likely to be engraved on stone or bronze, and many of the inscribed bronze tablets from early times were probably eventually melted down so that the metal could be reused. The great majority of laws and other official documents must have been written on much more perishable materials such as wood, parchment, and linen.

Apart from the question of preservation, we may wonder how accurately ancient historians and antiquarians could read and interpret archaic Latin texts. Polybius (3.22.3) states that the language of the oldest treaty between Rome and Carthage was so archaic that even the most learned Romans of his day had difficulty in understanding it. As a general rule, legislative language tends to be convoluted and cryptic, and the actual content of laws is frequently complex, so that the brief summaries of supposed landmark statutes which we encounter in Livy and Dionysius, reported at second hand from earlier accounts at best, may not be very reliable. Furthermore, even if the text of a law survived into later times and was readily comprehensible, the document would have contained no information regarding the political and historical circumstances surrounding its passage. This could only be supplied by oral tradition or by the researcher's own imagination, both of which might be quite unreliable.

It just so happens that the chance discovery of an archaic Latin inscription furnishes us with one clear instance in which we can see how ancient historians and antiquarians dealt with such material. In 1899, the Italian archaeologist Giacomo Boni unearthed an inscribed stone from beneath a black marble pavement in the Forum near the Comitium and Rostra. The stone is oblong, measuring about two feet in length with four lateral faces; since one end is thicker than the other, it has the shape of an obelisk. It is therefore likely that before it was buried beneath the ancient pavement of the Forum in imperial times, it stood upright on its thicker end. Along the length of the four lateral faces have been inscribed sixteen lines of very early Latin, whose meaning is rendered even more problematic by the fact that a portion of the stone's upper end was broken off, so that the text is incomplete (see Gordon 1983, #4). On the basis of the shapes of the inscribed letters, modern scholars generally agree in dating the inscription to about 500 B.C., making it one of the oldest surviving Latin texts. Although the precise meaning of the document is uncertain,[24] four words are beyond

24. For two differing interpretations, see R.E.A. Palmer 1969 (a sacred law protecting a grove from pollution) and Dumézil 1979 259–93 (a sacred law regulating the procession of the rex sacrorum along the Sacra Via). Cf. Vine 1993, 31–64. Coarelli (1983, 161–99) has cogently argued that the stone belonged to the Volcanal, a precinct sacred to Vulcan, which contained an archaic altar and column.

dispute: (1) *sakros* = classical Latin *sacer*, masculine nominative singular, meaning "sacred" or more likely "accursed," thus alluding to the imposition of a religious sanction upon an offender of this law; (2) *recei* = classical Latin *regi*, indirect object in the dative case of *rex*, meaning "king," thus referring either to the Roman king or to the rex sacrorum of the fledgling republic; (3) *kalatorem* = classical Latin *calatorem*, direct object in the accusative case, meaning "herald" or "crier," referring to a minor official who was a kind of usher, possibly for the *rex*, whose duty was to clear a path for the king in public; (4) *iouxmenta* = classical Latin *iumenta*, nominative or accusative neuter plural, meaning "beasts of burden" and hence also "wagons," "carriages," "vehicles."

Since this so-called *cippus* of the *lapis niger* was not taken down and solemnly buried until imperial times, it must have stood near the Rostra throughout the republic and was therefore on permanent display for inspection by anyone interested in it. Ancient Roman historians and antiquarians, who probably had the benefit of examining the text in an undamaged state, thought that this inscribed stone was a tombstone, one thing which it certainly is not. At least three different views were offered concerning the identity of the alleged grave's occupant. One was that it was the tomb of Faustulus, the herdsman who had rescued and raised Romulus and Remus, and who had been killed at this site in the Forum when the followers of Rome's twin founders fell to quarreling over the auspices for naming the city. A second view was that it was the tombstone of Hostus Hostilius, the grandfather of King Tullus Hostilius, who had been killed during the fighting in the Forum Valley between the Romans under Romulus and the Sabines under T. Tatius, following the rape of the Sabine women. A third view was that it was the grave of Romulus himself.[25] All three of these conjectures associate the inscribed stone with the reign of Romulus, thereby dating it to the second half of the eighth century B.C.

ROMAN ORAL TRADITION AND GREEK MYTH

If we liken the use of the ancient literary tradition of early Roman history to modern paleontologists' hypothetical reconstruction of a long-extinct, large, magnificent creature, the documentary data of the Pontifical Chronicle and the texts of laws, treaties, and religious dedications correspond to bones retrieved from an incomplete fossil record, whereas native oral tradition, Greek literary models, and the creative imagination of Roman writers are like the reconstructed flesh, organs, and skin. In this model we may suppose that ancient Roman writers did not possess a complete skeletal framework of early Roman history, that the skeletal remains might even have derived from more than one creature, and that their assemblage of

25. See Dion. Hal. 1.87.2; 3.1.2; and Festus 184L s.v. *niger lapis*.

this basic structure might not have been free of errors. B.G. Niebuhr, a German scholar of the early nineteenth century, postulated that much of the content of the later literary tradition concerning the regal period ultimately derived from Roman bardic poems, sung at banquets during the early and middle republic. According to this "ballad theory," the historical deeds of the kings were preserved, albeit distorted, in mythicizing heroic songs, whose content was taken over by ancient historians. An important component of Niebuhr's thesis is Cicero's citation of Cato's *Origines* for the assertion that in earlier times banqueters were accustomed to sing the praises of famous men to the accompaniment of a flute.[26] Although Niebuhr's ballad theory has generally been dismissed by modern scholars,[27] Zorzetti (1990, 289–95) has plausibly explained Cicero's remarks as evidence that early Roman society adopted Greek sympotic culture, including the singing or recitation of lyric verse as a popular form of entertainment. Consequently, while Niebuhr's notion of a fully developed bardic tradition in early Rome is to be rejected, aristocratic banquets could have provided a setting in which the singing of songs contributed in some degree to the formation of a national historical tradition. Yet as modern critics of Niebuhr have pointed out, Cicero's words indicate that this tradition no longer existed in Cato's day.

From the middle of the third century onward, at major annual festivals, Roman playwrights produced for the public stage *fabulae praetextae* (tales in Roman formal dress) that dramatized both major contemporary events and episodes from the received historical tradition (Flower 1995 and Wiseman 1998, 1–16 and 153–64). In recent years, T. P. Wiseman has revived and further refined the notion that performances on the Roman stage were important in the development of Roman historical traditions. His basic working hypothesis is that, in a society in which literacy was not widespread, public spectacles at annual festivals or accompanying triumphs, temple dedications, and aristocratic funerals constituted an important medium for creating, adapting, and propagating popular traditions, which in many instances became part of the later literary historical tradition of the Roman state. Wiseman (1994, 1–22) argues that Roman society was open to Greek and

---

26. Cic. *Brutus* 75: "Would that there existed those poems which, as Cato has written in his *Origines,* used to be sung many generations before his age at banquets by individual diners concerning the praises of famous men!"

Cic. *Tusc. Disp.* 1.3: "It is written in the *Origines* that diners at banquets were accustomed to sing of the virtues of famous persons to the accompaniment of a flute player."

Cic. *Tusc. Disp.* 4.3: "Cato, a very weighty authority, has stated in his *Origines* that among our ancestors there had been a custom at banquets for those who reclined on couches to take turns singing the praises and virtues of famous men to the accompaniment of a flute."

27. For a detailed discussion of Niebuhr's thesis and its history in modern scholarship, see Bridenthal 1972. Cf. Momigliano 1957 and Fraccaro 1957.

Etruscan influences from very early times, and he uses archaeological finds
to suggest that Greek myths and related stories were in circulation in central Italy during the archaic period. He further surmises that despite the
silence of our all-too-faulty sources, public performances of some sort
existed at Rome much earlier than is generally supposed; and he conjectures that the stage was the place where the Roman community in large
measure created and shaped its collective identity. As will be discussed in
chapters 4 and 10 , Wiseman (1995, 126–43) has used this drama hypothesis to explain the evolution of Rome's foundation story. Even though many
of his ideas are unavoidably speculative due to the scanty nature of our
sources, Wiseman's drama hypothesis offers modern scholars of ancient
Rome a new paradigm with which to reexamine old and familiar issues from
a fresh perspective.

A less controversial source of early traditions was the well-established
practice of delivering a funeral eulogy for a deceased aristocrat, an oration
in which not only his own but his ancestors' deeds, virtues, and public
offices were enumerated. Polybius (6.53 with Flower 1996, 91–127) gives
us a detailed description of this custom for the middle of the second century B.C., but the tradition was obviously much older. Ancient writers even
indicate that written copies of such funeral orations were sometimes kept in
family archives. Thus aristocratic family traditions, either written or oral,
could have been incorporated into later historical accounts. For example,
Livy's narration in 8.30 of military operations in Samnium conducted by
Q. Fabius Maximus Rullianus in 324 B.C. may derive ultimately from Fabian
family tradition through Fabius Pictor. Nevertheless, both Cicero and Livy
regarded such family traditions as a principal means by which early Roman
history was contaminated with exaggerated or falsified claims. Cicero (*Brutus*
61–62) concluded that by his own day the early history of Roman oratory
could not be documented with written texts any earlier than Cato (234–149
B.C.); and he comments on family funeral orations in the following words:

> We regard Cato as quite ancient. He died in the consulship of L. Marcius and
> M'. Manilius, eighty-six years before my consulship. Nor in fact do I think that
> there is anyone more ancient whose writings I think should be adduced for
> sure, unless perchance someone likes this same speech of Ap. Caecus con-
> cerning Pyrrhus and some funeral eulogies. By Hercules, they do indeed exist.
> The families themselves preserved them as their own trophies and records, to
> be used when someone in the family died, for remembering the praises of
> their house and for demonstrating their noble lineage, despite the fact that
> our country's history has been made less accurate by these eulogies. Written
> in them are many things which did not occur: false triumphs, too many con-
> sulships, even forged genealogies, and transitions to the plebs in which people
> of lower station have been inserted into a clan of the same name, as if I should
> claim to be descended from the patrician M'. Tullius who was consul with Ser.
> Sulpicius in the tenth year after the expulsion of the kings.

Livy (8.40.3–5) writes in similar disparaging terms at the very end of his eighth book, assessing conflicting accounts of Roman military operations against the Samnites in 322 B.C.:

> It is not easy to prefer one thing over the other or one author over another. I think that the tradition has been contaminated by funeral eulogies and by false inscriptions on busts, since various families have fraudulently arrogated to themselves the repute of deeds and offices. As a result, both individuals' deeds and the public records of events have certainly been thrown into confusion. Nor is there any writer contemporary with those times who could serve as a reliable standard.[28]

As already noted, the surviving fragments of Fabius Pictor indicate that his account of the regal period was already well developed: Aeneas's arrival from Troy, the Alban king list, the birth and exposure of Romulus and Remus, the rape of the Sabine women, the treachery of Tarpeia, Servius Tullius's institution of the census and tribal organization, the construction of the Capitoline temple by the Tarquins, and the rape of Lucretia. This suffices to demonstrate that, from Fabius Pictor onwards, Roman historical accounts were a complex mixture of Roman traditions and adaptations of Greek tales and historical episodes.[29] For example, the story of how the infant twins Romulus and Remus were exposed to die but survived is a Roman version of a popular ancient legend told in reference to numerous figures of the Near East and Greece. The tale of Tarpeia is a Roman adaptation of a common Greek folktale in which a maiden of a besieged town falls in love with the commander of the enemy army, betrays her country to her beloved, but is punished with death for her treachery. The rape of Lucretia appears to be a Roman adaptation of the popular story of the homosexual love affair which contributed to the downfall of the Peisistratid tyranny and paved the way for the Cleisthenic democracy at Athens in 510 B.C. This having been said, however, whenever we identify a story in early Roman history as having been patterned after something from Greek literature or history, the question still must be asked whether the Roman account is a mere invention, or whether it is a genuine bit of tradition that has been fleshed out and given greater vividness by the use of a Greek model. In many instances modern scholars have arrived and will continue to arrive at different conclusions, and it is this kind of discretionary interpretive process that makes the modern study of early Roman history such a problematic but exciting endeavor.

---

28. For an excellent discussion of how aristocratic family traditions have muddied the historical waters of the fifth and fourth centuries B.C., see Ridley 1983.

29. For detailed treatment of this subject, see the excellent essays of Ungern-Sternberg and Timpe in Ungern-Sternberg and Reinau 1988, 237–86.

Chapter 4

Rome During the Regal Period

Our two primary sources of information for Rome during the regal period are the ancient literary tradition and archaeological data, both of which are highly problematic for different reasons. As the surviving fragments from Fabius Pictor's historical account show, the traditions surrounding Rome's early kings were already well established at the time of the Hannibalic War, but this relatively early date for the existence of these traditions by no means guarantees their reliability. Comparison of Livy's first book with the other nine books of his first decade clearly reveals that the Romans of later times knew far less about the alleged 244 years of the seven kings (753–509 B.C.) than they did about the 245 years of the early republic (509–264 B.C.). The ancient literary tradition concerning the early kings can perhaps be best likened to a contemporary Hollywood blockbuster concerning some major historical episode. Though the movie is beautifully produced and tells a story in a powerful and memorable fashion, the viewer is left wondering what parts of the film are historically accurate, and what parts are distortions or outright fabrications introduced into the plot to make the movie more appealing. In the case of Hollywood movies, the curious viewer can resolve this enigma by consulting books by reputable and well-informed scholars, but no such option is available to modern students of early Rome. The ancient tradition of the early kings, like the supposed Hollywood movie, tells the story of Rome's foundation and early growth with much vivid detail and considerable drama. The script is a combination of Roman oral traditions and adaptations of Greek myths, all artfully woven together by generations of skillful Roman storytellers.

One might suppose that modern archaeology could come to the rescue and deliver us from the same kind of epistemological enigma that confronts

a moviegoer in a Hollywood film devoted to a historical subject, but the archaeology of early Rome is such that it can be of only limited use in testing the accuracy of the ancient literary tradition. First of all, since archaeological data generally pertain only to a past society's material culture, there will always be many areas in which the literary and archaeological records do not overlap, and archaeology neither corroborates nor contradicts the written testimony. Secondly, even when there is overlap between the historical tradition and archaeology, the latter often has its own problems of interpretation; and although it is tempting to do so, we should resist the urge to use the problematic literary tradition to settle questions surrounding the archaeological data. Doing so perpetrates a grave injustice upon modern archaeology by reducing it to an obliging servant whom we ask to lie down on the Procrustean bed of the ancient literary tradition. Modern historians of early Rome should respect archaeology and grant it scholarly autonomy.

Thirdly and perhaps most importantly for early Rome, we must always keep in mind that the archaeological record is far from being complete. Modern Rome has long been one of the great cities of the world, and its continued habitation and continual rebuilding have placed severe restrictions on what areas can be investigated by archaeologists. The current archaeological record for early Rome is therefore extremely scanty, so that using it to correct the ancient literary tradition is akin to trying to explicate the historicity of a Hollywood film with only a handful of pages randomly torn out of an authoritative textbook. Our archaeological knowledge for matters pertaining to early Roman history is exceptional, whereas our archaeological ignorance is the general rule. In addition, archaeological excavations themselves can sometimes lead to the formation of circular arguments, in that sites are quite often deliberately chosen for excavation in accordance with what the ancient literary tradition has deemed important. In these cases, when archaeologists come upon what they think the written record has told them to look for, many are quick to hail the discovery as confirming the ancient historical tradition. Consequently, in trying to reconstruct Rome's early development, our analysis should operate along two parallel lines: the archaeological, and the historical-historiographical. The two should be allowed to interact only with deliberate care.

Lastly, one important area in which the ancient literary tradition and modern archaeology do overlap is Roman topography. Although many of the city's physical features have been altered since Roman times, careful modern-day study of the city's topographical history, informed by the ancient sources, can offer valuable clues about Rome's early growth and urban development. Much important information on Roman topography is preserved in the surviving antiquarian tradition, which is often independent of ancient historical accounts. Nevertheless, like the annalists in their tradition, later Roman antiquarians frequently associated archaic sites in the city with various kings and employed fanciful tales to account for their significance.

THE SITE OF ROME

Like Caere, Tarquinii, and Vulci of southern Etruria, Rome was located inland on a river that flowed into the Tyrrhenian Sea, but Rome lay somewhat farther inland (twelve miles) than its Etruscan counterparts, and was also different in that the river along which it arose was the largest river of central Italy and formed the boundary between Etruria and Latium.[1] The Romans were thus the northernmost inhabitants of Latium and close neighbors of southern Etruria.

The hills of Rome were on the left or eastern bank of the Tiber. Other geographical factors seem to have singled out this site early as desirable for human habitation. An island in the Tiber divided the river's current and made it easy to ford at Rome. Moreover, the salt fields at the mouth of the Tiber on the right bank are likely to have occasioned in very early times a frequently traveled route from the Apennines through Rome and down to the sea to obtain this much-used and highly prized commodity. In later times, one road leading northeast out of Rome into the Sabine interior was known as the Via Salaria, the Salt Road. The other portion of the ancient salt route lay along the other side of the Tiber and was called the Via Campana, taking its name from the fact that it terminated by the Tiber's mouth at the Campus Salinarum ("Field of Salt Pans").

Another thoroughfare with a suggestive name is the Vicus Tuscus, the Etruscan Street. It ran across the Forum Romanum and ended at the riverbank in the Forum Boarium ("Cattle Market"). Later ancient writers explained its name by affirming that many Etruscans from King Porsenna's army settled there at the beginning of the republic, but it is more likely that the street received its name because it ran down into the early riverside market area, which faced westward toward Etruria. In addition, since the Etruscan community of Veii lay upstream on the Cremera, which flows into the Tiber, and Caere was also not far distant along the Tyrrhenian coast, the site of Rome must have been routinely visited by Etruscan merchants and artisans, at least from the seventh century B.C. onwards. Thus the geography of Rome's site is likely to have encouraged the coming together of Latins, Sabines, and Etruscans from a relatively early date, thereby giving early Rome an ethnically and culturally diverse population; and this early diversity may have contributed

1. Since the late nineteenth century, the topography and monuments of ancient Rome have been the subject of extensive modern study, which has become a major scholarly discipline in its own right. Much of the early scholarship is consolidated in Platner and Ashby 1929 and Nash 1968. The results of more recent work are contained in Richardson 1992 and the ongoing multi-volume project coordinated by Margareta Steinby. For a brief but thoughtful assessment of recent work specifically in reference to the Roman Forum see Purcell 1989.

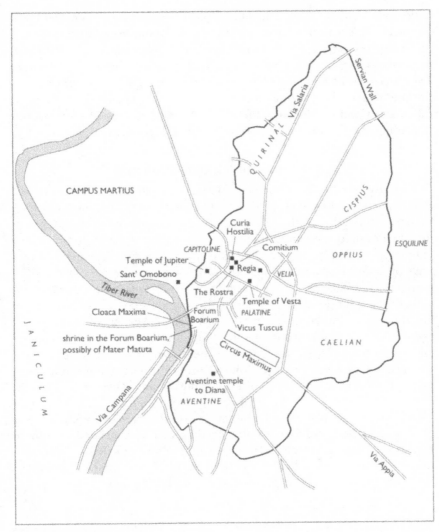

Map 7. Rome.

substantially to the relative openness of Roman social and political institutions so important to Rome's success as an imperial power in later times.

By the end of the republic Rome was known as the city of the seven hills, which probably stemmed from a popular reinterpretation of the Septimontium, an annual religious celebration of early origin that was observed on December 11 and involved seven areas of the city. Rome's famous seven hills consist of two groups (see map 7). Moving from north to south, the Capitoline, Palatine, and Aventine lay close to the river, stood up from the bottomland, and were separated from one another by valleys that in early times were prone to flooding from the Tiber. The other group of hills comprised westward projections of a plateau that lay to the east. Again moving from north to south, they were the Quirinal, Viminal, and Esquiline. The last named terminated on the west in two spurs: the Cispius to the north, and the Oppius to the south. The Caelian lay between the Esquiline and the Aventine. North of the Capitoline and west of the Quirinal, the bend of the Tiber enclosed a large plain called the Campus Martius, "the Field of Mars," which, like the Forum Romanum, later formed an important public and civic area of the city.

THE ARCHAEOLOGY OF EARLY ROME

The earliest significant archaeological remains from Rome consist of a relatively small number of cremation and inhumation graves, most of which were discovered during the 1870s and the first decade of the twentieth century. Following the political unification of Italy in 1871 and Rome's designation as the new nation's capital, the city of Rome experienced its first stage of modern urban development, as new streets were laid out and large numbers of public and private buildings were erected. In the course of leveling the land for development during the 1870s, workers removed massive amounts of accumulated ancient debris in which were included five early graves from the Quirinal and 164 from the Esquiline. But since this material was removed in great haste and was not properly stored, little of it was still available for study in 1905 when Giovanni Pinza published a major monograph on the prehistory of Rome and Latium.[2] Given the new light that cemeteries such as those of Osteria dell'Osa and Castel di Decima have shed upon the prehistory of Latium as the result of recent careful excavations and analysis, the loss of much of the material associated with these early Roman graves is truly unfortunate, and we can only hope that future urban development in Rome may turn up a hitherto unknown series of early tombs that can be properly excavated and examined.[3]

2. For more detailed accounts of this material, consult Bloch 1963, 63–84 the contributions of Ridgway, Pallottino, and Colonna in Ridgway and Ridgway 1979, 187–235; MacKendrick 1983, 71–112; J.C. Meyer 1983; Torelli in *CAH* VII.2 1989, 30–51; Momigliano ibid. 63–82; Holloway 1994, 1–90; and Smith 1996, 129–223. The first four volumes of Einar Gjerstad's *Early Rome* 1953–1966 represent a well-organized and comprehensive synthesis of archaeological data concerning early Rome: vol. I 1953, Stratigraphical Researches in the Forum Romanum and along the Sacra Via; vol. II 1956, The Tombs; vol. III 1960, Fortifications, Domestic Architecture, Sanctuaries, Stratigraphic Excavations; vol. IV 1966, Synthesis of Archaeological Evidence.

3. A striking illustration of the fortuitous nature of archaeological finds relating to early Rome is offered by the following example. As the author was making final revisions in the text of this book, the tomb of a small girl was discovered on the Capitoline near the present-day City Hall. According to newspaper reports, her teeth indicate that she was about four years old when she was buried along with pottery and small toys. The grave seems to date to the eighth century B.C. and was located beneath the floor of the family's dwelling.

In sharp contrast to these discoveries were the unimpeachable excavations of Giacomo Boni from 1902 to 1905, which uncovered forty-one early cremation and inhumation graves in the Forum near the Palatine and Velia. In the latter, the bodies were placed in hollowed-out oak logs, and in the former, the ashes of the dead were stored in hut urns, which were in turn placed inside larger clay vessels. Grave goods accompanying the dead consisted of handmade pottery, bronze fibulae, amber or glass beads, grain, fish, etc. One grave even contained a clay model of a sheepdog, whose curly fur was represented by impressed arcs. Since Boni's excavations, some additional graves have been uncovered on the Palatine and in the Forum.

Until quite recently, modern scholars generally interpreted the presence of both cremation and inhumation graves at the site of early Rome as indicating that two distinct ethnic groups, Latins and Sabines, inhabited the area together. With the establishment of the new chronology for the Latial Culture, however, it has become apparent that the two funerary rites reflect a difference in chronology: cremation was characteristic of LC I, and inhumation of LC II–IV. Moreover, the excavations at Osteria dell'Osa have also revealed the presence of both rites within one homogeneous community, each ceremony having its own symbolic significance. Thus, when compared with the new funerary data from other Latin sites, the earliest Roman graves show that the people who lived at the site of Rome during the tenth and ninth centuries B.C. partook of the same Latial Culture.

Excavations conducted on the Palatine during the first decade of the twentieth century and shortly after World War II revealed the remains of floors and post holes from early wattle and daub thatched huts (Gjerstad III. 48 ff.). When we combine this information with the hut-shaped cremation urns, we can visualize the structure of these dwellings in considerable detail. The one whose traces were least disturbed by later human occupation had a floor measuring thirteen feet five inches by eleven feet nine inches. The floor itself had been dug one foot eight inches below the surrounding ground level. The post holes were fifteen and three-fourths inches in diameter and went down about one and a half feet. A post in the center of the hut helped to support the ridgepole of a gabled roof. The doorway was built into one of the narrower sides and included a small covered porch.

During the 1950s, the Swedish archaeologist Einar Gjerstad excavated a grid measuring sixteen by eleven feet to a depth of nineteen feet, down to virgin soil, in the middle of the Forum near the large base of the equestrian statue of Domitian. The trench revealed a series of twenty-nine successive layers (Gjerstad I, 29 ff.). Layers twenty through twenty-two were three gravel pavings of the regal period, which Gjerstad dated to about 575 B.C., and which he interpreted as marking the beginning of the Forum as a public center. Below layer twenty-two there were found six layers (twenty-three through twenty-eight) containing traces of huts, which Gjerstad dated back to about the middle of the seventh century. Consequently, Gjerstad conjectured that the settlements on the Palatine and other hills eventually outgrew their hilltops and spread down into the Forum valley. Furthermore, careful study of the graves uncovered in the Forum suggests that they formed a cemetery which began near the Palatine and gradually spread outward away from the hill as the inhabitants of the Palatine buried their dead during LC I–III.

Between 1985 and 1988, the Italian archaeologist Andrea Carandini excavated an area on the northern slope of the Palatine. Carandini's excavations first uncovered the remains of houses of the middle republic, which had been built above four substantial atrium-style houses of the late sixth century B.C., which in turn had been erected upon an artificial platform about six feet deep. Further digging beneath this platform revealed the remains of four successive walls constructed of tufa blocks and clay. Associated pottery and other material allowed these four walls to be approximately dated 550–530, 600, 675, and 730–720 B.C. The earliest of these structures had been erected on virgin soil (Carandini 1990, Steinby 1996 III, 315–17, and Grandazzi 1997, 149–50).

The evidence of graves, huts, and walls could be taken to confirm the ancient literary tradition concerning Rome's foundation. After all, the ancients believed that the Palatine was the initial site of Romulus's settlement, and it was thought to sustain the most venerable cults of the Roman people. Even in the time of Augustus, the Romans were still faithfully preserving on the Palatine a thatched hut believed to have been the one in which Romulus and Remus had lived (Dion. Hal. 1.79.11). Romulus was also supposed to have built a wall around the Palatine, and in imperial times its course was still marked out with stones as representing the city's original sacred boundary, the pomerium (Tacitus *Ann.* 12.24). Indeed, the date for the earliest of the walls discovered by Carandini corresponds to the later years of Romulus's reign according to the standard Varronian chronology.[4] Alexandre Grandazzi (1991 = the English translation of 1997) has centered an entire book around this newest archaeological discovery, in which he dates Rome's foundation on the Palatine to the later part of the eighth century, just as the ancient tradition maintains. Carandini himself (1997) has produced a massive volume of nearly eight hundred pages, in which he develops a similar thesis. By synthesizing archaeological, topographical, and ancient historical, antiquarian, religious, and even mythological evidence (often quite uncritically), Carandini traces Rome's earliest growth through pre-urban, proto-urban, and urban phases. During the former two periods, separate villages arose at the site of Rome and gradually formed

---

4. It should be pointed out that the date of this early wall corresponds exactly to Rome's foundation as recorded by L. Cincius Alimentus, i.e., 729/8 B.C. (see Dion. Hal. 1.74.1).

themselves into a loose union; this development culminated c. 725 B.C. in the beginning of Rome as a unified city centered about the Palatine.

Indeed, topographical arguments can be adduced in favor of an early Palatine settlement. The hill's steep sides offered natural protection, and the area of the hilltop itself was certainly substantial enough to support a settlement typical of Latium in the early Iron Age. The nearby location and later commercial importance of the Forum Boarium may suggest that the site could also have been appealing due to its proximity to the river. Although modern archaeology, the ancient literary tradition, and considerations of topography seem to converge in indicating the Palatine's significance to early Rome, this is still a far cry from demonstrating that the hill played the central role in the city's genesis. The same topographical arguments can be applied in varying degrees to the other hills; and given the small size of Latin settlements during LC I and II, we should expect that some of the other hills were likewise inhabited, independently of one another. The early graves discovered fortuitously on the Quirinal suggest that this area was in fact inhabited in LC II. If modern excavations had not concentrated entirely upon the Palatine and Forum but had explored other parts of the city, such as the Aventine or Caelian, for evidence of the earliest signs of human occupation, we might have a very different view of settlement patterns for this early period. Furthermore, since excavations over the past few decades have revealed that ditches and walls were constructed during the eighth century B.C. at other Latin settlements, Ficana and Castel di Decima for instance, we may plausibly suppose that if other hills of Rome had been settled at this time, they might also have received encircling walls similar to those of the Palatine.

Two aspects of archaic Roman religion point to the existence of several early settlements on the hills of Rome. The Salii, the leaping priests, formed one of the minor priesthoods, whose duties primarily concerned the performance of ceremonies at the end of February and the beginning of March to mark the end of the old year and the beginning of the new one. They were organized into two bodies: the Salii Palatini and the Salii Collini, representing the Palatine and Quirinal Hills respectively. Secondly, the festival of the Septimontium has been interpreted by many modern scholars as representing a loose religious union of several settlements at some early time before Rome was organized into a city. According to Festus (458L and 474–76L), the Septimontium included the two eminences of the Palatine (the Palatium and Cermalus), the Velia, the Caelian, and three areas of the Esquiline: the Oppius, Fagutal, and Cispius. Since this festival was observed on December 11, it would have been at the close of the autumn planting, and could therefore have been a celebration marking the close of the year's agricultural work, before the winter months of relative inactivity. Festivals of a similar nature, such as the Saturnalia of December 17 and the Paganalia and Compitalia of January, were later celebrated by the entire Roman people, whereas the Septimontium was always observed only by the inhabitants of the seven areas mentioned above.

As touched upon in chapter 2, from the middle of the seventh century B.C. onwards central Tyrrhenian Italy experienced a major urban transformation, as villages of huts were gradually replaced by towns exhibiting rational planning and organization, monumental public architecture, and private houses built on stone foundations with roofs of timber and terracotta tiles. These physical features were the outward manifestations of state formation, and archaeological data from the Roman Forum and its immediate environs indicate that this process began at the site of Rome during the last quarter of the seventh century. As mentioned above, Gjerstad's excavations of one area of the Forum suggest that huts there were covered over by a gravel pavement around 575 B.C., but since Gjerstad's pottery chronology is generally regarded as erring on the late side, most archaeologists of early Rome have adjusted his dating of the Forum's first gravel pavement to about 625 B.C. Moreover, A. Ammerman (1990) has argued that the wattle and daub material beneath this gravel pavement, which has been interpreted as a sign of earlier human habitation in the Forum, actually represents landfill carried to the spot to raise the level of the Forum so as to reduce the danger of flooding from the Tiber. On the basis of a series of sample soundings down to virgin soil, Ammerman has attempted to reconstruct a relief map of the Forum Valley before it was altered by human activity. He maintains that at least the middle area of the Forum was originally too low and too susceptible to flooding to have made human habitation in simple huts practicable. Rather, he regards the debris revealed by the Forum excavations of Boni and Gjerstad as the product of a massive project, involving the coordination and expenditure of communal labor on a vast scale, to reclaim the marshy areas of the valley for the community's use. The thesis is bold and exciting, and could carry with it important implications regarding the scale and nature of cooperative activity in Rome toward the end of the seventh century B.C., though its revolutionary character can be modified by assuming that this reclamation project was carried out piecemeal over many years.

Excavations have revealed that the early paving of the Forum was accompanied by its organization into public space, with the erection of structures central to the community's political and religious activities. The earliest material, found deposited in a well at the temple of Vesta, dates to c. 600 B.C. (Gjerstad III, 359–74) and suggests cultic activity in this area from that time onwards. The temple of Vesta housed Vesta's perpetual fire, which was tended by the Vestal virgins. Their sacred precinct was close to the Regia, whose early history is well documented from archaeological excavations summarized in the next paragraph. Ongoing excavations in this part of the

Forum may soon provide additional data concerning the early history of the temple of Vesta itself. Likewise dating to c. 600 B.C. are a gravel paving and fragments of roof tiles from a building in the northwestern area of the Forum, which have been interpreted to be the earliest paving of the Comitium and the original senate house of Rome, the Curia Hostilia (Gjerstad III, 217–23 and Coarelli 1983, 119–30). In later times, the Comitium was one of the areas where assemblies of the Roman people congregated. In the later official religious calendar, it was closely associated with the rex sacrorum, who conducted rites there on February 24, March 24, and May 24. The first of these days was the Regifugium or King's Flight, in which the priest king performed ceremonies symbolic of the ending of the old Roman year. The early close association between the Roman king and the Comitium is further indicated by the discovery near the Rostra of the so-called *cippus* of the *lapis niger* discussed in the preceding chapter (see above p. 73–74). The *cippus* is inscribed with what was probably a sacred law, in which the word "king" is mentioned. Moreover, the black marble pavement (*lapis niger*), measuring ten by thirteen feet, which was laid down in imperial times to cover over the earlier hallowed site, had beneath it not only the famous inscribed stone but also the lower courses of an altar dating to the sixth century B.C. (Coarelli 1983, 161–99 and Holloway 1994, 81–87).

During the last quarter of the seventh century B.C., an area at the eastern end of the Forum, which might previously have been occupied by small huts, was cleared away and laid out to receive the earliest version of the Regia, a sacred edifice at which the rex sacrorum supervised many important public religious rites. This oblong building was rebuilt several times during the course of the sixth century, its design changing subtly with each reconstruction (Brown in *Origines de la République Romaine* 1967, 47–60 and Brown 1974–75). Around 540–530 B.C., a fire destroyed everything in this general area, and the sacred building was rebuilt once again, this time remaining unchanged as the Regia of the early and middle republic. A fragment of a ceramic vessel dating to the third quarter of the sixth century B.C. has been found at the site and is inscribed with the single word "rex." The length of the structure was oriented east to west and was divided into three areas of unequal size. The central chamber was an open-sided roofed area granting entry into the other two chambers to the east and west. A street, together with a paved sidewalk, ran along the building's length to the south, and attached to the north side of the Regia was an irregularly shaped courtyard, probably to be identified with the Atrium Regium mentioned in literary sources, where some public rites were performed in the open air. The eastern chamber was by far the smallest of the three and was probably the *sacrarium* ("sacred room") of Ops Consiva, a divinity concerned with agricultural abundance. This room was off-limits to all except certain priests. The western chamber of the building was the largest and was probably the *sacrarium* of Mars, which contained the god's sacred spear and the special shields (*ancilia*) carried by the Salii in their sacred dance. In the northwestern corner of this room was discovered a circular stone structure that probably formed the foundation of a hearth. This was apparently the hearth on which was collected the blood dripping from the tail of the sacrificed October Horse of October 15, blood that was carefully preserved to be used in rites of purification on April 21 at the festival of the Parilia supervised by the rex sacrorum and the Vestal virgins.

Rome's development into a city-state during the late seventh and sixth centuries B.C. is further suggested by additional evidence for organized religion. Fragments of terracotta decorations found in or near the Forum point to the use of monumental architecture in the construction of public religious sanctuaries, whereas votive deposits found on the Capitoline and Quirinal contain material as early as the late seventh century. One terracotta relief panel associated with the Regia portrays the Minotaur of Crete, indicating that depictions of Greek mythology were already common in Rome during the sixth century. But perhaps the most intriguing find, one that has attracted considerable scholarly attention since its discovery in 1880, is the so-called Duenos Vase, probably recovered from a votive deposit on the Quirinal and dating to the sixth century. The object is quite small, consisting of three brownish-black clay vases fused together with cylindrical arms to form a kind of equilateral triangle measuring about four inches per side. The vases are less than one and a half inches high, and around the perimeter of the three vases has been cut a Latin inscription of three lines whose meaning is still debated with little agreement.[5] The inscription reads as follows:

> Iovesat deivos qoi med mitat, nei ted endo cosmis virco sied. | As ted noisi opetoitesiaipacarivois. | Duenos med feced en mano meinom duenoi. Ne med malos tatod.[6]

This object takes its name from the phrase "duenos med feced en mano meinom duenoi" = "a good man [or the personal name Duenos = later Latin *bonus*] made me as a fine gift for a good man (*duenoi*)." Some kind of wordplay or antithesis seems to be involved at the end, where "good" (*duenos* and *duenoi*) is contrasted with "bad" (*malos*). The first part of the text seems clear enough except for the initial *iovesat deivos*. The first of these

---

5. For a detailed description and illustration of this curious object, see Gordon 1975 and 1983 #3 (= *ILLRP* 2). For recent discussion of the Latin inscription itself, see Vine 1999 and Baldi 1999, 197–200. For earlier modern linguistic scholarship, consult the bibliography contained in the works here cited.

6. Word divisions and punctuation have been indicated where the general sense seems to require.

two words appears to be a verb form from later Latin *iuro* ("swear"), whereas *deivos* could be either the nominative singular or the accusative plural of later Latin *deus* ("god") and thus could be either the subject or the object of the verb form. Consequently, these two words could be construed in two different ways: (1) "he swears by the gods;" (2) "the god swears." The next nine words may be rendered, "who sends/gives me —— that the fair maiden not be against thee." The central portion of the inscription (*as ted noisi opetoitesiaipacarivois*) poses the greatest difficulty and seems to be a conditional statement: "but if . . . not . . . thee. . . . " The final four words (*ne med malos tatod*) are probably a negative imperative: "let not a bad man touch (?) me."

A consideration of the unusual shape of the object suggests at least two very divergent interpretations. One is to regard the three small bowls as having been intended to hold a woman's cosmetics and perfume. The person being addressed in the inscription would then be a man who is giving this object as a gift to his fair maiden *(cosmis virco)*. Alternatively, the object might be a *kyrnos,* a cluster of small vessels joined together, used in the Eleusinian mysteries of Demeter and Persephone to hold assorted offerings made to the divinities. According to this interpretation, the "fair maiden" should be none other than Persephone herself, or some Latin or Italic divinity such as Feronia who was equated with the Greek goddess. Moreover, the euphemistic adjective *mano* is suggestive of the Di Manes ("gentle gods") of the Roman underworld and would thus strengthen the object's chthonic significance. In this regard it is noteworthy that the Latin is inscribed upside down; for the inscription to be read, the object must be held with the mouths of the three bowls turned downward toward the earth.

If the latter of these two interpretations be favored (which is by no means certain), this curious object with its accompanying Latin text could provide evidence for the presence of some degree of Orphic or Eleusinian religious ideology in early Rome. The two occurrences of *Duenos* (= "good") could have two rather different meanings: one referring to the skilled craftsman who fashioned the object, and the other referring to its recipient and alluding to his mystic belief. *Malos* would then refer to anyone not conversant with the rites associated with the object. This all-too-tentative interpretation can be given additional context by a graffito found on a Corinthian vessel dating to the middle of the seventh century, which was buried in a tomb on the Esquiline. The graffito consists of a single word, a person's name written in Greek, variously read as *Ktektou* or *Kleiklou* or the like (see Solin 1983). In any case, the genitive form of the name implies that it represents the identity of the vessel's owner. Unless it was exchanged through aristocratic gift-giving or by trade, it could have been buried with its Greek owner on the Esquiline.

The single best example of an archaic Roman sanctuary discovered thus far is a temple that was located in the Forum Boarium near the foot of the Capitoline. Its remains were found buried beneath two other shrines of the third century B.C., which were in turn covered by the Church of Sant' Omobono built in the sixteenth century. Consequently, this early Roman sanctuary generally goes by the designation, "the archaic temple under Sant' Omobono" or the like (see *Enea nel Lazio* 1981, 124–30; Coarelli 1988, 205–34; and Holloway 1994, 68–80). A deposit of remains from sacrifices found beneath the archaic altar indicates that the site was already sacred before the construction of the temple. Also discovered in the pre-temple strata was a pottery fragment bearing the graffito "uqnus." A similar pattern is seen at Ardea and Satricum, where huts at sacred precincts were replaced by masonry-built edifices. The archaic shrine under Sant' Omobono was built during the second decade of the sixth century and continued to be used until the last decade of the same century, at which time it was remodelled and continued in use for some time thereafter. The temple stood on a podium and measured thirty-five feet square. Among its fragments of terracotta decorations has been found a nearly full-size statue group of Hercules and Minerva, possibly representing the former's apotheosis upon his introduction to Olympus by the latter (Sommella Mura 1981). Floral and faunal remains indicate that the temple received offerings of assorted grains and hazelnuts and the sacrifice of young pigs, goats, sheep, cattle, dogs, and even some turtles, fish, geese, and doves. The wealth of dedications included loom weights, spindle whorls, perfume bottles, bronze fibulae, imported Greek pottery, figurines, amber, and carved bone plaques which decorated other objects. An ivory plaque carved into the shape of a crouching lion was inscribed on its smooth back with the Etruscan name, "Araz Silqetenas Spurianas," and a fragment of pottery was inscribed with the single word, "ouduios." These simple graffiti constitute some of the earliest samples of writing discovered at Rome.

When compared with other votive deposits found in Rome and dating to the archaic period, the remains of dedications made at this shrine are rather exceptional for their variety and high quality. Although it shares with other votive remains large numbers of miniature clay vessels, models of bread loaves, and human figures cut out of sheet bronze, its other remains are rarely encountered. Modern scholars therefore regard this sixth-century shrine as displaying a more diverse clientele, and its location in the Forum Boarium beside the Tiber has suggested parallels to the contemporary sites of Graviscae and Pyrgi. Furthermore, although the identity of the divinity worshipped at this shrine is unknown, many scholars have followed the conjecture of A.M. Colini that it was the temple of Mater Matuta, who did in fact have a shrine in the Forum Boarium; this Roman goddess of female maturation (and later of the dawn) is seen as corresponding to

Aphrodite, Hera, and Uni-Astarte attested at Graviscae and Pyrgi. Even though the temple's association with Mater Matuta must be considered unproven, the conjectured correspondence between it and the sanctuaries at the harbor communities of Caere and Tarquinii is attractive and plausible.

Rome's urban development also involved domestic architecture. It is likely that from the late seventh century B.C. onwards wattle and daub thatched huts were gradually replaced by masonry-built houses with roofs of timber beams and terracotta tiles. Above the earliest cremation and inhumation graves of the Forum, Giacomo Boni discovered portions of an early house, the lowest portion of whose walls was composed of square-cut tufa blocks. The house was not very large. It measured seventeen by thirty-three feet and was subdivided into three rooms arranged side by side along the building's length (see Gjerstad I, 139 and Holloway 1994, 55), but its construction was a great improvement over that of the earlier huts. By the end of the sixth century B.C., however, well-to-do Roman families were living in spacious town houses like those known from Pompeii at a much later date. The foundations of four such structures have been recently uncovered by Andrea Carandini on the northern slope of the Palatine. They were built upon an artificial platform about six feet in depth, which had been laid down c. 530–520 B.C. The houses faced north onto the Sacra Via and remained in existence for about three hundred years until they were destroyed by fire in 210 B.C. Even from this early date, they must have been part of a fashionable section of the city inhabited by Rome's elite families (*Grande Roma dei Tarquini* 1990, 97–99).

These physical signs of Rome's urban transformation have prompted scholars to ask whether this process resulted from the consolidation of several villages into one social, political, and religious community (synoecism, to use a convenient ancient Greek term) or was effected by a single village's expanding and incorporating other neighboring areas into itself (nuclear expansion). The festival of the Septimontium points to the former, whereas the preeminence assigned to the Palatine in the ancient literary tradition suggests the latter. Yet as shown by the political history of ancient Greece, these two models need not be mutually exclusive; the process of synoecism could be greatly facilitated by a larger settlement's taking the lead in unification. For example, J. C. Meyer (1983, 91–138) has combined both these concepts to explain the history of human habitation at Rome during the early Iron Age. He has interpreted the ancient literary evidence and the extant archaeological data to argue that the Palatine settlement first expanded to form the Latin community of the Septimontium, which later merged with a Sabine settlement on the Quirinal. In the present state of our knowledge this reconstruction is at least plausible, but we should bear in mind that the archaeological record for early Rome is so sketchy that our current conclusions are likely to be myopic, if not actually erroneous.

Furthermore, the Palatine's preeminence in the ancient literary tradition may simply be the product of a mythical civic tradition forged in later times.

Parallel to the modern discussion of Roman synoecism vs. nuclear expansion has been a debate about whether Rome's urban development was the product of evolution or of a punctual event of foundation, *Stadtwerdung* vs. *Stadtgrundung* to use their pithy German compound nouns (see Cornell 1995, 97–103). Historians by virtue of their training are generally inclined to view change in terms of continuous ongoing processes rather than as stemming from discontinuous quantum jumps. This inclination tends to predispose them against the ancient tradition of punctual city-foundation in favor of gradual evolution from village to city. Nevertheless, Drews (1981) has advanced compelling arguments in support of *Stadtgrundung*, urging that two of the most important cultural developments among the early peoples of central Tyrrhenian Italy, the masonry house and the concept of the organized city-state, were borrowings from the Phoenicians and Greeks. This thesis maintains that, contrary to the evolutionary model, there is no logical or inevitable development from a village of huts into a city-state with rational institutions and coherent physical layout. Rather, the planned city-state was a novel concept introduced into central Italy as the result of Phoenician and Greek colonization.

As Cornell (1995, 102–3) has argued , adducing the example of classical Sparta, which was still a collection of unwalled villages in Thucydides' day, state formation and urban development need not be parallel processes. Indeed, the purposeful planning required of rational urban development implies the pre-urban existence of political authority and social organization capable of carrying out such a physical transformation. Furthermore, once the ruling authority or authorities made the momentous decision to reorganize and to rebuild their community as a planned city, the transformation is likely to have been an ongoing process spanning years if not decades, as suggested by the excavations at Ficana south of Rome and at San Giovenale near Tarquinii. Yet these objections only qualify and do not undermine the case for *Stadtgrundung*. There is a clear qualitative difference between a collection of huts on the Palatine during the eighth century and the community of the last quarter of the seventh century represented by the Regia, the gravel paving of the Comitium, and the Curia Hostilia. The late seventh century layout (and the initial decision to build it) clearly presuppose the existence of a self-conscious ruling elite and a strong sense of community. These too, like the masonry house and concept of the city-state, can perhaps be largely attributed to the social and economic effects of Phoenician and Greek settlement and commercial activity in the western Mediterranean. Thus the impact that Greeks and Phoenicians had upon central Tyrrhenian Italy was extraordinary, comparable to critical mass in radioactive substances: before critical mass is achieved, radioactive material emits subatomic particles at a low-level, naturally occurring rate, but when a catalyst intervenes in the form of human scientific knowledge and engineering, the threshold of critical mass can be reached and the natural process of radioactive emission is quantitatively and qualitatively altered and immediately becomes something entirely new, a self-sustained nuclear reaction that releases tremendous amounts of energy. To be sure, Italy was a fertile field in which the cultural seeds from Greece and the Levant were unwittingly sown, but there might never have been any urban growth and city-state development in central Tyrrhenian Italy without those seeds from the eastern Mediterranean.

THE ANCIENT LITERARY TRADITION

The later canonical ancient literary tradition of Rome's foundation involving Aeneas, Lavinium, the Alban Kings, and Romulus and Remus was the product of an evolutionary process that began at least as early as the fifth century B.C. and was largely completed by the time Rome's first two native historians, Q. Fabius Pictor and L. Cincius Alimentus, wrote their histories at the close of the third century B.C.[7] The subject is a complex one, including as it does Greek mythography and foundation tales, indigenous Italian folklore, Roman oral tradition, and even Roman political and cultural ideology. It has therefore attracted much modern scholarly attention,[8] but since it was totally unhistorical and is more relevant to the formation of Rome's national identity from the middle of the fourth century B.C. onwards when Rome appropriated unto itself the religious symbols of Latin leadership, only certain aspects of the myth's development need be noted here.

Although Greek historians did not write seriously about Rome until the Pyrrhic War, they were aware of Rome's existence long before. In accordance with their custom of explaining the origins of foreign peoples by connecting them with the wanderings of one of their own mythical heroes such as Jason and the Argonauts, Hercules, or Odysseus, Greek writers from the fifth century B.C. onwards succeeded over time in generating no less than sixty different myths to account for Rome's foundation (see Wiseman 1995, 160–68 with Bickermann 1952). A representative cross section of

7. For other treatments of the regal period examined in the remainder of this chapter, see Ogilvie 1965, 30–232; Heurgon 1973, 106–55; Scullard 1980, 42–77; Momigliano in *CAH* VII.2 1989, 82–112; Forsythe 1994, 75–244; and Cornell 1995, 56–80 and 114–214. Ungern-Sternberg's essay in Ungern-Sternberg and Reinau 1988, 237–65 is extremely important for its assessment of the generally mythological quality of the later Roman tradition surrounding the early kings.

8. See, for example, Trieber 1888, 1894; Bickermann 1952; Classen 1963; Galinsky 1969; Cornell 1975; Horsfall 1979; Bremmer and Horsfall 1987, 12–48; Gruen 1992, 6–51; and Wiseman 1995.

these tales is found in Plutarch's *Romulus* 1–2 and in Festus 326–30L s.v. *Romam*. Many of these Greek tales involve an eponymous Rhomos or Rhome, whereas Romulus seems to have been the original founding hero in the native Roman tradition. Dionysius of Halicarnassus (1.45.4–48.1 and 1.72.2) indicates that a contemporary of Herodotus and Thucydides, Hellanicus of Lesbos, who wrote numerous mythological and historical treatises, in his *Troica* traced Aeneas's wanderings from Troy to Aeneia in the Thermaic Gulf, to Epirus, and thence to Latium where the burning of his ships by a travel-weary woman named Rhome led to the foundation of a town named after her. For reasons that are still unclear, out of the numerous mythical foundation tales told by Greek writers concerning Rome, the Romans chose to associate themselves with the Trojans and incorporated the story of Aeneas into their own folklore about the beginning of their city. Moreover, the combination of competing Greek and Roman accounts could have contributed to the creation of a foundation tale involving twins named Romulus and Rhomos.

Roman historians knew that the republic had begun c. 500 B.C. because their annual list of magistrates went back that far. Before that time, they thought, Rome had been ruled by seven kings in succession. By using Greek methods of genealogical reckoning, they estimated that seven kings would have ruled no more than 250 years, making Rome's regal period begin somewhere around the middle of the eighth century B.C. In fact, Fabius Pictor and Cincius Alimentus dated Rome's foundation to 748/7 and 729/8 B.C. respectively (Dion. Hal. 1.74.1). By the end of the republic, however, the chronological scheme worked out by Atticus and taken over by Varro became the officially accepted chronology of the Roman state (see the Appendix), according to which Rome had been founded in 753 B.C., and the republic had begun in 509 B.C. Since the Trojan War was supposed to have been fought four hundred or more years before Rome's foundation, Troy's unhistorical connection with Rome was maintained by inventing the Alban kings, whose reigns were made to span the chronological gap between Troy's destruction (1184/3 B.C. according to Eratosthenes) and Rome's foundation. The wording in Plutarch's *Romulus* 3.1–2 suggests that the list of kings was already present in the historical account of Fabius Pictor; and this conclusion has received additional support from the remains of an ancient library discovered at Tauromenium in Sicily, for on its walls were painted various descriptive labels to accompany books stored there, including the following one for Rome's first historian (Manganaro 1974, 394):

> Quintus Fabius, nicknamed Pictorinus, the Roman, son of Gaius, who recorded Hercules' arrival in Italy, as well as the "return" [*nostos*] of Lanoios, his ally Aeneas, and Ascanius. Romulus and Remus were much later, and Rome's foundation by Romulus, who was the first to rule as king.

Three of the most striking features of the story of Romulus and Remus (their twin birth, the newborns' survival despite having been exposed to die, and their suckling by a wild animal) are common in folklore and Greek mythology; and more than one hundred years ago Conrad Trieber (1888) pointed out striking similarities between the tale of Romulus and Remus and the plots of Greek tragedies involving similar stories. Indeed, from the time that stage performances were introduced to Rome from Etruria in 364 B.C. (Livy 7.2), this form of popular entertainment is likely to have played an important role in disseminating such tales (Wiseman 1998, 153–64). Stories of divinely begotten twins have been documented in many cultures worldwide, and they were a common feature of Greek mythology: Castor and Pollux, Hercules and Iphitus, Otys and Ephialtes, Amphion and Zethus, Calais and Zetes, Neleus and Pelias. It will be remembered that the first pair, Castor and Pollux, was worshipped at Lavinium as early as c. 500 B.C. The motif of the twins' survival after being exposed to die is the Roman version of a widespread ancient Mediterranean folktale told of several national leaders, such as the Akkadian king Sargon (c. 2300 B.C.), the biblical Moses, the Persian king Cyrus the Great, the Theban king Oedipus, the Greek hero Telephus, and the two sets of twins, Neleus and Pelias and Amphion and Zethus of Greek mythology. In these stories, the power of the future leaders' divine destiny is graphically demonstrated by the vulnerable infants' success in evading the deadly designs of mortals. The element of an infant exposed in the wild being suckled by an animal is associated with Cyrus the Great, Telephus, and the twins Neleus and Pelias.

Even if not actually present in native Italian folklore, these motifs are likely to have been known from Greek mythology in central Tyrrhenian Italy from relatively early times, as we can judge from numerous mythological scenes depicted on Etruscan mirrors, pottery, and tomb paintings. In fact, an Etruscan sandstone funerary monument from Felsina dating to c. 400 B.C. depicts a panther or lioness suckling a boy. A similar scene is found on a cista from Praeneste of about the same date, but most striking of all is a bronze mirror discovered at Volsinii in 1877, which was long thought to be a fake but in recent years has been vindicated as genuine. It dates to the third quarter of the fourth century B.C. and depicts a lioness suckling two infants (see Wiseman 1995, 65–71). Moreover, inclusion of the animal wet-nurse in the tale of Romulus and Remus might have been suggested, at least in part, by the Etruscan rendering of Rome's name and its meaning in Latin: since the Etruscan alphabet did not include the letter *o*, the Etruscans spelled Rome's name as Ruma, which in Latin means "teat" or "nipple." Given the importance of female lactation and nursing for the survival of infants in a pre-industrial society, we should not be surprised to discover that the Romans paid serious homage to a goddess of nursing,

Rumina. Her open-air precinct (*sacellum*) was located on the Palatine near the Lupercal, the cave of the Luperci; an aged fig tree nearby was known as the Ficus Ruminalis ("Rumina's Fig Tree"). Later historians and antiquarians associated all three monuments with the suckling of the twins by a she-wolf and even derived the tree's name from Romulus (Hadzsits 1936).

Yet, this having been said, the single most curious aspect of Rome's foundation story is the fratricide, described in different ways in the surviving accounts. In some versions Romulus is portrayed as having killed his brother with his own hand, but in other authors Remus is killed amid a general brawl between the supporters of the twins. Why have the city's beginning coincide with such a dreadful deed? During the last two centuries B.C., as Rome conquered and consolidated its control over the Hellenistic world, this element in Rome's foundation tale served as convenient propaganda for Rome's enemies, who portrayed Roman rule as sanguinary and ruthless. The enigma of the primordial fratricide has recently been scrutinized by T. P. Wiseman (1995). After examining the ancient traditions concerning Romulus and Remus and after criticizing modern scholarship, Wiseman has proposed a most interesting answer to this puzzle. He plausibly maintains that when the tradition was first created, the twins must have embodied some basic duality in Roman society. Wiseman dates the tale's formation to the later fourth century and associates the twin founders with the political ideology of the new patricio-plebeian nobility. At that time the Greek eponymous Rhomos had his name changed to Remus, was characterized as slow, and was connected with the *aves remores* ("delaying birds") of augury. He therefore represented the noble plebeians as political latecomers. His death, connected in one version with Romulus's fortification of the Palatine community, was originally a human sacrifice to insure Rome's invulnerability. In Wiseman's view (1995, 117–25), the inclusion of this element into Rome's foundation story came about as the result of the Romans' resorting to human sacrifice in 296 B.C. prior to the battle fought at Sentinum in the following year against a powerful coalition of Etruscans, Gauls, and Samnites. Since both consuls were placed in command of this campaign and its victory was achieved at the cost of one of their lives, Wiseman's thesis makes perfectly good sense.

Romulus, traditionally Rome's first king, was an unhistorical figure, created by early Greek and Roman tradition as the city's eponymous founder. His fictitious reign was filled with deeds expected of an ancient city founder and a son of the Roman war god Mars. He was thus described as waging war against neighboring states and as establishing Rome's early political, military, and social institutions: he was credited with creating the senate, the distinction between patricians and plebeians, the patron-client relationship, the institution of marriage and family obligations, and division of the populace into the three archaic tribes and thirty *curiae*. Romulus was also thought to have shared his royal power for a time with a Sabine named Titus Tatius. The latter name may be that of an authentic ruler of early Rome, and its priority in the list of kings might also be genuine, but given the working methods of Greek and Roman storytellers concerning the origins of peoples and cities, T. Tatius was necessarily reduced to a shadowy companion of the eponymous Romulus.

The names of the other six kings are likely to be authentic recollections of real people, but it also seems probable that few reliable details were known about their reigns. The later Romans wished to have explanations for their early customs and institutions, and consequently oral tradition and later historians ascribed various innovations to these kings, using stereotypical and simpleminded reasoning. The three kings who followed Romulus are hardly more than names, but the deeds of the last three kings have often been regarded as more historical, because they seem to be confirmed by archaeology.

According to ancient tradition the warlike founder, Romulus, was succeeded by the Sabine Numa Pompilius, whose reign was characterized by complete tranquility and peace. Numa was supposed to have created virtually all of Rome's religious institutions and practices: the religious calendar, the priesthoods of the pontiffs, augurs, Vestals, Salii, and flamens, as well as all their duties and privileges. His religiosity is probably unhistorical and simply derives from the ancients' connecting his name with the Latin word *numen*, meaning "divine power," which suggested to them that his reign must have been concerned with religion. Numa was succeeded by Tullus Hostilius, whose reign was filled with warlike exploits, most notably the fabled combat between the Horatii and Curiatii triplets, which concluded with Alba's destruction and the incorporation of its people into Rome. It is likely that Tullus's reign was depicted as warlike because the name Hostilius was later interpreted to suggest hostility and belligerence. Tullus was followed by Ancus Marcius, who was believed to have been the grandson of Numa. Although his reign was described as having combined the watchwords of his two predecessors, involving both religious innovations and warfare, later historians clearly had difficulty in finding things with which to fill up his reign, as the brevity of their accounts shows. Finally, according to the later established tradition, Rome's fifth and seventh kings, Tarquinius Priscus (Tarquin the Elder) and Tarquinius Superbus (Tarquin the Proud), were father and son of Etruscan origin, but since the standard chronology for the regal period placed between them the forty-four-year reign of Servius Tullius, the historian L. Calpurnius Piso Frugi pointed out the genealogical improbability of their father-son relationship and proposed instead that they must have been grandfather and grandson (see Dion. Hal. 4.6.1–7.5; 4.30.2–3; and 4.64.2–3; cf. Livy 1.46.4).

What is perhaps most striking about the list of early Roman kings is that their names (apart from the two Tarquins) indicate the absence of a hereditary principle. This peculiarity can be explained in at least two different ways. If we assume that Rome came into being as the result of synoecism of several villages already existing on various hills, the king list could be the product of forging the remembered names of prominent rulers from more than one community into a single unified tradition. Alternatively, the ancient literary tradition could be correct in depicting the kingship in nonhereditary terms. As was the case in Homeric society and in Greece during the early archaic period, hereditary royal succession was possible, but since an early Greek community required a king of vigorous adult years who could protect it and give it his personal leadership in war, kingship tended to devolve upon the most capable aristocratic leader in the community. If we take this to be our model for early Rome, the presence of two Tarquins in the later part of the list may point to a shift away from Homeric-style kingship and toward a hereditary monarchy, as Roman political structure evolved from a simple village to a more advanced city-state.

Another aspect of the early king list worth examining is its chronology. As seen from the list of dates here, the ancient literary tradition consistently assigned relatively long reigns to all seven kings.

753–716: Romulus (37 years)
716–715: One year interregnum
715–672: Numa Pompilius (43 years)
672–640: Tullus Hostilius (32 years)
640–616: Ancus Marcius (24 years)
616–578: Tarquinius Priscus (38 years)
578–534: Servius Tullius (44 years)
534–509: Tarquinius Superbus (25 years)

Given the vagaries of human mortality in early central Italy, it seems very unlikely that these regnal years for seven successive kings accurately reflect the history of the regal period. Rather, their numerical values and symmetry betray the obvious fact that they were the product of later historical reconstruction. The reigns form three consecutive pairs ending with the neat twenty-five-year rule of Tarquinius Superbus, a period of time commonly used as the length of a generation in ancient genealogical estimates. Romulus and Numa reigned for a total of 80 years: Romulus for 37 (= 40 – 3) and Numa for 43 (= 40 + 3). It might have been thought appropriate to give Numa the edge in span, since his reign was characterized by continual peace and tranquility, whereas Romulus had waged numerous wars. The reigns of the next two kings, Tullus Hostilius and Ancus Marcius, are consecutive multiples of 8: 32 = 4 × 8, and 24 = 3 × 8 respectively. The reigns ascribed to Tarquinius Priscus and Servius Tullius correspond to those of

Romulus and Numa and exceed them by exactly one year: 38 = 37 + 1 for the former, and 44 = 43 + 1 for the latter. Thus, no historical reliability should be attached to the lengths of the kings' reigns recorded in the ancient literary tradition. They were contrived by some early writer with a penchant for numerology.

One means of readjusting this fictitious ancient chronology of the kings is offered by archaeology, a procedure which many might regard as a classic case of analyzing one obscure matter by having recourse to an even more obscure one (*obscurum per obscurius*). Nevertheless, if nothing else, the exercise may at least serve to enhance our assessment of the ancient literary tradition. As mentioned above, there have been uncovered in the Comitium traces of a building tentatively dated to c. 600 B.C. If we associate these remains with the Curia Hostilia and accept its attribution to Rome's third king as the name and the literary tradition suggest, we could perhaps assign the reigns of T. Tatius, Numa Pompilius, and Tullus Hostilius to the second half of the seventh century and fit the reigns of the last four kings within the sixth century. This would scale down the regal period to about 140 years, c. 650–510 B.C., giving each of the seven kings an average reign of twenty years. By this reckoning, the rule of Tullus Hostilius would be c. 610–590 B.C. If correct, this would produce a regal period considerably shorter than that given by the ancient tradition, but it would have the advantage of chronologically associating the entire list of kings more closely with the period of Rome's formation as a city-state, from the late seventh century B.C. onwards.

Far more complex problems confront the modern investigator in examining and evaluating the ancient literary tradition concerning Rome's last three kings. Rome's fifth king, Tarquinius Priscus, was believed to have come to Rome from the Etruscan city of Tarquinii during the reign of Ancus Marcius and to have succeeded in getting himself declared king after the latter's death, even though Ancus left behind two sons of nearly adult years. Tarquinius's father was not a native of Tarquinii but an immigrant named Demaratus, a Greek aristocrat who had left his native Corinth because of political unrest. During his reign Tarquin the Elder was thought to have engaged in major public works in the city: he built the Circus Maximus in the valley between the Palatine and Aventine to entertain the public with horse and chariot racing, oversaw the erection of new shops and private houses in the Forum, and directed the laying of the massive foundation for the temple of Jupiter Optimus Maximus on the Capitoline. The ancient tradition assigned similar public works to his two successors. Servius Tullius enclosed the city with a defensive stone wall, divided and organized the city and surrounding countryside into districts called tribes, introduced the census of citizens together with evaluation of their property, formulated the timocratic comitia centuriata, and built the Aventine temple to Diana to rival the one at the Latin town of Aricia. Tarquinius Superbus built the Capitoline temple of Jupiter and constructed the sewer system of the Cloaca Maxima.

The last three kings were thus thought to have carried out what amounts to a comprehensive program of urban development; and since this portrait generally fits with the archaeological record for Rome during the sixth century B.C., many modern scholars have considered the latter as having corroborated the former. Moreover, because Rome's fifth and seventh kings were supposed to have been of Etruscan origin, modern scholars have often viewed Rome's transformation into a city as having been brought about by Etruscan overlords who had seized control of the site because of its location at the island crossing of the Tiber (Alföldi 1965, 176–235). Nevertheless, this opinion, like the one which attributed the splendor of the Barberini and Bernardini Tombs of Praeneste to Etruscan overlords, is based upon a notion of Etruscan cultural superiority and of Latium's relative social and economic backwardness during the archaic period, a view that has now been called into question by the discovery of rich tombs from the seventh century B.C. at Castel di Decima. Consequently, recent researchers such as J. C. Meyer (1983, 139–69) and T. J. Cornell (1995, 127–30 and 151–72) have challenged the modern conception of *la grande Roma dei Tarquinii* and have preferred to see Rome's development as occurring within a central Tyrrhenian cultural koine rather than as having been indebted to a higher Etruscan culture and overlords. These are indeed important and complex issues that require thoughtful and careful consideration and will be discussed below in the closing section of this chapter.

Given the transparently simplistic way in which ancient historians formulated the reigns of Numa Pompilius and Tullus Hostilius from their names, we should perhaps regard the ancient claim that Tarquinius Priscus came from Etruscan Tarquinii in the same light. We are fortunate to have the Etruscan form of his name recorded in the famous François Tomb of Vulci (discussed immediately below) dating to c. 300 B.C. It is written as *Cneve Tarchunies Rumach* (Cn. Tarquinius the Roman). The name *Tarchunies* is exactly analogous to Latin Tarquinius in being a clan name derived from the toponym: Etruscan Tarchuna = Latin Tarquinii. Nevertheless, since the François Tomb may precede Rome's first historians by less than a century, the Etruscan rendering of the king's name may not have as much independent value as we would like. It should be noted that the name in the François Tomb has the *praenomen* Cneve (= Gnaeus), whereas in the Roman tradition both Tarquinius Priscus and Tarquinius Superbus were given the *praenomen* Lucius, doubtless because of its resemblance to the Etruscan word for king (Etruscan *lauchume* = Latin *lucumo*). In any case, the obvious derivation of both the Etruscan and Latin forms of the name from a toponym conforms to a larger pattern of ancient Italian nomenclature, by which a clan name could be nothing more than an adjectival form of a city's name used to specify origin. Thus among the tombstones from the cemetery of Praeneste of republican times we encounter the clan name Fidenatius (*CIL* XIV. 3135), suggesting that someone from Fidenae who settled at Praeneste assumed a name reflecting his origin. Similarly, thanks to a newly discovered fragment from Livy's lost eleventh book, we now know that the family of A. Gabinius, the consul of 58 B.C., whose hometown was the Roman colony of Cales in Campania, owed the name Gabinius to the fact that an ancestor or ancestors had left the Latin town of Gabii to be part of the original colonial foundation (R.E.A. Palmer 1990a with *ILLRP* 1211–16).

The ancient literary tradition concerning Tarquin's Etruscan origin receives additional support from Ampolo's study (1976–77), which shows that horizontal social mobility between communities was characteristic of Etruscan society during the archaic period. Buried in a rich chamber tomb at the Etruscan city of Veii in the late seventh century B.C. was a man who bore the Etruscan name Tite Latine (= Titus Latinius, *CLP* 1976, 376 #131). The name seems to indicate the man's origin in Latium, but his tomb shows his integration into the Etruscan society of Veii. Thus, given the nature of social conditions and nomenclature in central Tyrrhenian Italy during the seventh and sixth centuries B.C., it is certainly possible that Tarquinius Priscus or his family came from Etruscan Tarquinii. His association with Demaratus of Corinth, on the other hand, is probably not historical but is likely to have been the result of later writers conflating two totally different tales into one: (1) the story of Demaratus of Corinth coming to Tarquinii with various artisans (Pliny *NH* 35.152), which was used to account for Tarquinii's "industrial" leadership in southern Etruria during the archaic period; and (2) the story of a Tarquinian noble who came to Rome and ruled as king.

According to the ancient literary tradition, Tarquinius Priscus's rule ended when he was violently assassinated. His murderers were two brothers hired by the two sons of Ancus Marcius, who resented their exclusion from royal power and hoped that one of them would gain the vacated throne. Instead, the elder Tarquin was succeeded by Servius Tullius, who was encouraged to take up the reins of government by the late king's wife, Tanaquil.[9] This man, we are told, had been given the name Servius because he had been born a slave (*servus*) in the Tarquin household. This item should no doubt be dismissed as a later ancient attempt to deduce biographical information from the king's name. Servius's name likewise

---

9. For more detailed treatments of the various questions surrounding the reign of Servius Tullius, consult Pais 1906, 128–51; Last 1945; Ridley 1975; and Thomsen 1980.

prompted later historians to attribute to him the customary rights and duties of freed slaves in early Roman law and society. In any case, in order to give this supposedly slave-born monarch a suitably royal pedigree, the ancient tradition also maintained that he was of noble lineage: when Tarquin had captured the town of Corniculum, its ruler had been slain, and his wife had been brought into Tarquin's palace, where she subsequently gave birth to Servius Tullius. According to one version, which is also told of Caeculus the founder of Praeneste (Bremmer and Horsfall 1987, 49–62), she was impregnated by a mysterious male member that had appeared in the fire of Tarquin's hearth. Thus Servius Tullius was alleged to have been divinely begotten by the fire god Vulcan or by the Lar Familiaris, guardian spirit of the household (Dion. Hal. 4.2). After a lengthy rule in which he did much to establish the foundations for the later republican form of government, Servius Tullius also fell victim to a political assassination, this one orchestrated by his own ambitious daughter and her husband, L. Tarquinius Superbus, who then became king.

Other ancient data derived from an independent Etruscan tradition seem to give a totally different picture of the death of Tarquinius Priscus and the accession of Servius Tullius, and have understandably stimulated considerable modern scholarly debate and attempted historical reconstructions.[10] One important text in this matter is a portion of a speech delivered by the Emperor Claudius in the Roman senate in 48 A.D. concerning his decision to enroll nobles from the provinces of the Three Gauls into the senate for the first time. Since the speech was greatly valued by the leading citizens of Gaul, it was inscribed on a bronze tablet which was discovered at Lyons in 1528 (*CIL* XIII. 1668 = *ILS* 212). Like the plebeian tribune Canuleius in Livy 4.3–5, the Emperor Claudius justified his policy of recruiting new senators by adducing various historical innovations in the Roman state, including the nonhereditary and foreign extraction of the early kings:

> Kings once ruled this city. Nevertheless, it happened that they did not pass it on to members of their own house. Unrelated persons and some foreigners succeeded them, as Romulus was followed by Numa who came from the Sabines, a neighbor to be sure but a foreigner at that time. Ancus Marcius was followed by Tarquinius Priscus. The latter was prevented from holding public office in his own hometown due to his tainted blood because he was the

10. The modern bibliography concerning Servius Tullius, Mastarna, and the painted figures in the François Tomb is very large. Discussions can be found in most books on Etruscan civilization. Important treatments in English are Alföldi 1965, 212–31; Cristofani 1967; Ridley 1975, 162–69; L. Bonfante 1978; Thomsen 1980, 57–104; Momigliano in *CAH* VII.2 1989, 94–96; and Cornell 1995, 133–41. For the wall paintings themselves, consult Messerschmidt and von Gerkan 1930, Tafeln 14–26 and the exhibition catalogue = Buranelli 1987. For the question of Etruscan historical writing and historical traditions independent of Rome, see Cornell 1976, 1978.

offspring of Demaratus the Corinthian and a woman of Tarquinii, well-born but poor, so that she had to accept such a husband by necessity; but after he migrated to Rome, he obtained the kingship. In addition, Servius Tullius came between this man and his son or grandson; for writers disagree even on the latter point. If we follow our own countrymen, he was born of a captive woman named Ocresia; but if we follow the Etruscans, he had once been the most faithful companion of Caelius Vibenna and shared in all his fortunes. After he had been driven out by changing fortune and had left Etruria with all the survivors of Caelius's army, he occupied the Caelian Hill and named it after his leader. Then after changing his own name (for his name was Mastarna in Etruscan), he was called by the name as I have said, and he obtained the kingship, to the greatest advantage of the state.

Other ancient passages (Varro *Ling. Lat.* 5.46 and Tacitus *Ann.* 4.65) also derive the name of the Caelian Hill from Caelius Vibenna. This man and his brother, Aulus Vibenna, were well-known figures in Etruria. They were displayed on funerary urns at Clusium, and they are found engraved on an Etruscan bronze mirror from Volsinii dating to the third century B.C. But the most extraordinary information concerning these brothers comes from the wall paintings of the François Tomb at Vulci, in which the following five pairs of men are depicted, with labels that give their names:

1. Marce Camitlnas, naked and bearded, is drawing his sword from a sheath about his neck and is rushing upon a bearded Cneve Tarchunies Rumach.
2. Avle Vipinas (= Aulus Vibenna), naked and bearded with an empty sheath about his neck, is using his left hand to pull back the head of Venthi Caules [. . .]plsachs and is stabbing him in the side of his chest with a sword held in the right hand.
3. Rasce, naked and bearded with an empty sheath about his neck, is using his left hand to grab the hair of Pesna Arcmsnas Svetimach and is stabbing him in the chest with a sword held in the right hand.
4. Larth Ulthes, bearded and wearing a belted tunic, is stabbing in the ribs a man named Laris Papathnas Velznach.
5. Macstrna (= Mastarna), naked and bearded, with a sword and sheath about his neck to give to his comrade, is using his own sword to cut through rope that binds together the wrists of an obviously captive Caile Vipinas (= Caelius Vibenna), who is also bearded and naked. (see fig. 3).

The partial clothing and postures of the four persons being attacked and killed have been interpreted to suggest a surprise attack upon sleeping men. Only these four figures have a third element in their name, which seems to specify their city of origin; Rumach = "of Rome," Velznach = "of Volsinii," but the cities of the other two men are in doubt. Since Macstrna,

Figure 3. Wall painting from the François Tomb at Vulci: Macstrna freeing Caile Vipinas from his bonds.

Caile Vipinas, and the four attacking figures have no such element in their names, they are all thought to belong to Vulci. If so, and if the tomb painting represents some historical episode, it could pertain to a struggle between Vulci and a coalition of other states including Rome and Volsinii, but in the absence of a written narrative we cannot be sure what this wall painting portrays. Yet it seems to involve Mastarna's liberation of his friend Caelius Vibenna from captivity, as well as the killing of Cneve Tarchunies Rumach. Since all but one of the men from Vulci are naked, Alföldi has plausibly suggested that the nude figures had been captured, stripped, and bound, but their ally Larth Ulthes, wearing a belted tunic, has come to their rescue with the swords they are using to kill their captors. The depicted scene appears to be entirely independent of the later Roman historical tradition, and it is still very much a mystery exactly how the two accounts are related and should be interpreted. Alföldi has combined this material with the traditions that Tarquinius Priscus came from Etruscan Tarquinii and that Porsenna seized Rome as clear evidence that during the sixth century B.C. Rome was involved in warfare with Etruscan states, which resulted in Rome's intermittent rule by Etruscan adventurers. In any case, the historical existence of Aulus Vibenna appears guaranteed by a Bucchero vase dating to the first half of the sixth century B.C., found at the Portonaccio temple of Veii and bearing the dedicatory inscription (Pallottino 1968, #35), "mini muluvanece Avile Vipiiennas" = "Aulus Vibenna dedicated me."

It has been observed that the name Macstrna appears to be nothing more than an Etruscan rendering of the Latin *magister,* a title associated under the republic with the dictator (magister populi) and his subordinate, the master of the horse (magister equitum): for -*na* is a common Etruscan termination, and *macstr* is simply the Latin *magister* minus the vowels, in accordance with Etruscan stress placed on the first syllable. Since the Etruscan alphabet did not have the letter *g,* all such sounds were represented by *c.* Consequently, if Servius Tullius bore the title magister, the latter might have evolved into a personal name in the Etruscan tradition (Mazzarino 1945, 177 and Ogilvie 1976, 63 and 88). This ancient evidence suggesting the equation between Servius Tullius and Macstrna-Mastarna has been interpreted by many scholars to mean that Servius Tullius usurped power in Rome and ruled in the fashion of a Greek tyrant.

In fact, Cornell (1995, 127, 132–33, and 145–50), following the highly speculative reconstruction of Coarelli (1988, 301–63), has adduced further considerations in support of this characterization. In his view, Servius Tullius's alleged divine sonship was used to confer legitimacy upon a charismatic usurper, and both his association with the goddess Fortuna and Tanaquil's public announcement from an upstairs window are seen as reflecting a common Near Eastern tradition concerning rulers and sacred marriages. Moreover, the currency of this latter notion in central Tyrrhenian Italy during the late archaic period may also be seen in the close association of Thefarie Velianas of Caere with Uni-Astarte in the Pyrgi texts, as well as in the statue group of Hercules and Minerva found at the archaic temple beneath the Church of Sant' Omobono, often identified as a shrine of either Mater Matuta or of Fortuna, built by Servius Tullius. Consequently, Cornell views Rome's last two monarchs as usurpers, whose policies and behavior are best understood in the larger context of Greek tyranny in the archaic period. Cornell (1995, 233–35) even further speculates that under these two rulers the monarchy itself was reduced to the religious office of the rex sacrorum, which both the ancient tradition and modern scholars have generally associated with the foundation of the republic and the consulship. Thus, according to Cornell's hypothetical reconstruction, Rome during the late regal period was under a kind of dual monarchy: a charismatic tyrant-like political usurper, and a religious figurehead. These ideas have the advantage of offering a unified explanation for several puzzling data. The interpretation is at least plausible, but like so many aspects of early Roman history (especially of the regal period), it remains largely speculative due to the problematic nature of each of its separate ingredients. Nevertheless, if the interpretation could be further corroborated and accepted as valid, it would provide important new information about Rome's political history during the sixth century B.C., showing that its development as a city-state was in large measure parallel to that of some contemporary Greek communities.

Finally, to complicate further our attempts to unravel the truth about Servius Tullius, let us be reminded of the sobering analysis of Etore Pais (1906, 142–48) concerning the monarch's resemblance to the slave-king at Aricia immortalized in Sir James Frazer's *Golden Bough*. Even in imperial times, the sacred grove of Diana at this Latin town was still vigilantly guarded by the rex nemorensis, the king of the wood, a runaway slave who received asylum from the sacred grove, but in order to benefit from this right of sanctuary, he first had to kill the currently reigning king of the wood, whose status he then assumed, only to be deposed and replaced at some future time by yet another runaway slave. According to the Roman tradition, Servius Tullius was a slave-born king who came to power as the result of the violent murder of his predecessor, and he was likewise removed from office by violence. Given the ancient tradition that connected the king with the Aventine temple of Diana, built to rival the cult at Aricia, we are justified in wondering whether, to what extent, and in what ways the tradition of the rex nemorensis has influenced the formation of the ancient historical accounts of Servius Tullius.

Archaeology can be enlisted to test in some degree the claims of the ancient literary tradition concerning two alleged public works carried out during the late regal period. Unlike Greece, central Italy did not possess good stone for building. Only various tufas, sediments formed from volcanic ash, were available for this purpose. In 1924, Tenney Frank published a monograph in which he employed the Romans' use of tufas at different times to reach important conclusions concerning Rome's urban development and architectural history during the republic. Before Rome's conquest of Veii in 396 B.C., the only tufa available to the Romans for building was the local Cappellaccio. Since this was the poorest in quality of the various tufas they used, the Romans largely, but not entirely, discontinued its use after they had access to the quarries of Grotta Oscura near Veii. By the time of the First Punic War, the Romans began using a third kind of tufa called Peperino, obtained from the Alban Hills, the earliest datable use of which is the base of a monument of M. Fulvius Flaccus to commemorate his capture of Volsinii in 264 B.C. Thus during the regal period and early republic, the Romans generally used only two varieties of tufa for their major building projects: local Cappellaccio before the beginning of the fourth century B.C., and Grotta Oscura from Veii together with Cappellaccio from the early fourth to the first part of the third century. This basic rule of thumb can therefore be applied to the remains of the so-called Servian Wall and the Capitoline temple, structures which the ancient literary tradition attributed to Rome's last three kings.

Two areas of Rome possess significant remains of the Servian Wall: the Esquiline next to the main railroad station, and the southern slope of the Aventine. The former consists of a stretch of stone masonry about three hundred feet in length, thirty-three feet high in seventeen courses of blocks, and thirteen feet wide. The Aventine has two sections of the wall, each about 140 feet long. These surviving portions of the ancient city wall are composed of blocks of Grotta Oscura tufa, which indicates that they were not constructed before the early fourth century B.C. A few other smaller sections of the ancient wall have survived, but none of them can be dated earlier than the fourth or third centuries B.C.[11] As a result, construction of the stone wall has been associated with two brief statements in Livy 6.32.1 and 7.20.9. The former records that in 378 B.C. the citizen body was taxed in the form of labor to build a wall with stone blocks provided under contract by the censors, whereas according to the latter the Roman legions in 353 finished out an uneventful campaigning season by repairing the wall and its towers. Given the scale of the project, it is likely to have taken several years to complete. Nevertheless, since archaeology has shown that other Latin communities, such as Ardea, Antemnae, and Gabii, were fortified with trenches and earthen mounds during the sixth century B.C., and since Rome's stone wall was backed up by an earthen mound and was fronted in places by a deep, wide trench, it is possible that the stone wall of the fourth century had been preceded by defensive earthworks in the more vulnerable areas of the city. Nonetheless, the ancient literary tradition that depicts Rome as encircled by a mighty stone wall from the sixth century B.C. is clearly incorrect.

11. For detailed treatment of the so-called Servian Wall, see Frank 1924, 111–24; Säflund 1930; *Roma Medio-Repubblicana* 1973, 7–31; and Holloway 1994, 91–101. See Cornell 1995, 201–2 concerning fortification walls of other states during Rome's late regal period and early republic.

Some achievements, such as the sewer system of the Cloaca Maxima and the construction of the Capitoline temple, were attributed to both the Tarquins by the ancient tradition. This is certainly unhistorical and results either from later confusion as to which Tarquin did what, or from simple duplication by later writers who had little information about the Tarquins and thus ascribed the same deeds to both. In the case of the Capitoline temple, this duplication could have been suggested by the appearance of the podium, the only portion of the ancient structure that now survives: for of the fifteen courses of blocks, the first twelve measure about one foot in height, whereas the upper three are about sixteen inches high, suggesting that the foundation was laid down in two stages (Gjerstad III, 175 and Holloway 1994, 3). In any case, since these blocks are of Cappellaccio tufa, we may conclude that this portion of the structure was built no later than the fifth century B.C. Although this dating does not actually confirm the ancient tradition, it does not contradict it. Furthermore, since the annalistic tradition does preserve information from pontifical records concerning the vows and dedications of several temples in the fifth century, the tradition's failure to record similar information with respect to the most magnificent temple in Rome, except for its dedication at the beginning of the republic, could be regarded as evidence that the temple was indeed constructed during the regal period.

ARCHAIC ROMAN INSTITUTIONS

By the end of the sixth century B.C., Rome had become a substantial, thriving city-state and had acquired important social and political institutions that continued to exist and function during republican times. Later Roman historians and antiquarians, wishing to give precise histories of these institutions, attached their creation and subsequent alteration to the various kings. Although we need not doubt the antiquity of these institutions, their association with specific kings cannot be accepted without good reasons.

We can be certain that by the end of the regal period the Roman state possessed a tripartite political organization: people, senate, and king. The earliest organization of the Roman populace (ascribed to Romulus) involved thirty units called curiae. These curiae were grouped into three sets of ten, which were termed tribes: Ramnenses, Titienses, and Luceres. The tribes were said to have taken their names from Romulus, T. Tatius, and a third person named Lucumo or Lucerus, who had given Romulus military aid in his war against the Sabines. The exact nature, origin, and history of these divisions have been the subject of considerable modern discussion and speculation with little agreement, but what does seem certain is that these tribal and curial units formed the basis of the earliest political and military structure of the Roman state. The earliest-organized Roman infantry and cavalry must have been recruited on the basis of these divisions. Even in later times, when the three archaic tribes and thirty curiae had long lost any meaningful significance for the functioning of the state, the cavalry units still retained a link to this structure by being organized into multiples of three: namely, the *sex suffragia* (six votes) and the other twelve centuries of *equites equo publico* (knights with a public horse) of the comitia centuriata. In fact, the *sex suffragia* were themselves grouped into two sets of three, and were named after the three archaic tribes.

Besides providing a basis for military recruitment, the thirty curiae also served as voting units in Rome's oldest popular assembly: the comitia curiata. Since it was almost entirely supplanted in later times by the tribal and centuriate assemblies, little is known about its original powers and functions. Even in republican times, however, it could be convoked in the Comitium to witness the making of wills and to give its assent to a special kind of adoption called *adrogatio*, in which the adoptee was legally independent and not under paternal authority. Indeed, the term *adrogatio* indicates that this form of adoption was a legislative act in which a question (*rogatio*) was put to the curiate assembly, which then gave or denied its approval. We are left to speculate as to whether the powers of this body during the regal period may have extended beyond such matters of private law and involved legislation in the public and constitutional spheres.

The abolition of the monarchy and the establishment of the consulship imply that by the close of the sixth century B.C. there existed in the Roman state a well-established and powerful aristocracy. The rich graves discovered at sites in Latium dating to the seventh century B.C. (especially those containing chariots), as well as the traces of substantial town houses built during the late sixth century on the Palatine, corroborate and amplify this picture. We may further surmise that, like those in contemporary Greek city-states, the early Roman aristocracy was organized into an advisory or deliberative body consulted by the king. Under the republic, this body was called the senate. Although it often met in temples, its own established meetinghouse was the Curia Hostilia in the Comitium. Once again, given the nature of our evidence, we cannot know how this body was organized under the kings, or what its powers and functions were. Its membership must have comprised the adult men of considerable wealth and social status. Like other relatively flexible communities of central Tyrrhenian Italy, Roman society during the late seventh, sixth, and early fifth centuries B.C. is likely to have been open to horizontal social mobility and even to some degree of vertical social mobility. Consequently, the membership of the early senate is likely to have been characterized by a certain social fluidity.

According to the ancient tradition, the Roman kings commanded the army in war, exercised judicial powers, and discharged religious duties; and when the monarchy was ended, these royal powers were divided between the two consuls and the rex sacrorum. This portrait has been widely accepted, but it must be stressed that even though the office of the rex sacrorum may render this view plausible, the later ancient tradition that paints the picture of complete and neat legal and constitutional continuity between the monarchy and the republic is not above suspicion. This major transition, especially in reference to the consulship, is unlikely to have been so tidy. Generally speaking, the historical process is a rather messy business and often works itself out in total defiance of neat legal or logical schemes. On the other hand, legal and constitutional theory usually follows in the wake of major historical change and then constructs *post eventum* systems that are unhistorical, but logically coherent, to justify the change and to demonstrate continuity.

This pattern is detectable in the ancient tradition of the legal mechanisms involved in the choosing of a new king. According to the tradition recorded in Livy's first book (1.17.5–11; 1.22.1; 1.32.1; 1.35.1–6; 1.41.6; 1.46.1; and 1.47.10), when a king died, the state reverted to the senate (*res ad patres rediit*), and the senate appointed a series of interim kings (*interreges*) until the people were summoned to a meeting of the comitia curiata, at which time a candidate proposed by the presiding interrex received the affirmative vote of the people (*lex curiata*) and the endorsement of the senate (*patrum auctoritas*). An identical procedure was employed during republican times whenever the chief curule magistrates of the state left office without successors. The only difference was that consuls and praetors were actually elected by the comitia centuriata, but they also had to have their election confirmed by a *lex curiata* (curiate law) of the comitia curiata.[12] Given the correspondence between the later republican procedure and the alleged method of appointing a king, we are fully justified in suspecting that the ancient tradition concerning the latter is anachronistic. Nevertheless, the later republican constitutional procedure could have been the legally elaborated outgrowth of customs surrounding the inauguration of a king. In the end, however, given the unsatisfactory nature of the ancient evidence, we can say nothing certain about the kingship except that the kings are likely to have been created through some process of nomination and ratification (no doubt involving aristocratic power politics) and exercised considerable power. It must also remain an open question whether, to what extent, and in what ways a king's authority was circumscribed by or exercised in conjunction with the will of the people and the approval of the senate.

12. For more detailed discussions of the ancient evidence concerning the *interrex, patrum auctoritas,* the *lex curiata,* and the auspices, see Lübtow 1952; Staveley 1954–55 and 1956, 84–90; Friezer 1959; Magdelain 1964a and 1964b; Nichols 1967; Develin 1977; Giovannini 1985; and Linderski in Eder 1990, 34–48 = Linderski 1995, 560–74.

According to the ancient tradition, Servius Tullius is supposed to have laid the foundations for the republic by his creation of the comitia centuriata, a popular assembly based upon the census and the military obligations of the citizens to the state. This assembly took its name from *centuria,* a military unit of the legion. Each legion was composed of sixty centuries, and in theory each century contained one hundred men. The obvious military character of this assembly is indicated by its powers and place of meeting. Under the republic, this body was responsible for electing all officials who exercised any form of *imperium,* which involved the raising and commanding of troops or the exercise of jurisdiction: consuls, praetors, censors, and curule aediles. These were the so-called curule magistrates. Besides having the power to legislate by voting in favor of proposals placed before it by a presiding curule magistrate, the centuriate assembly voted on declarations of war, ratified treaties, and even acted as a high court in capital cases. Since it was considered to be an army sitting as an assembly, it was not permitted to convene within the sacred boundary (pomerium) of the city but always met in the Campus Martius, the Field of Mars.

By the third century B.C., this organization had gone through a very long and complicated process of evolution, which we cannot reconstruct in any detail. We simply know of the final product of this evolutionary process. At that time, the assembly consisted of 193 centuries or voting units, which were organized into blocks according to property qualifications. The census assigned citizens to one of five economic classes based upon the assessed value of their property, and the members of each class were required to arm themselves for military service according to specified standards, the wealthier citizens more heavily armed and the Romans of lesser means more lightly armed. In the centuriate assembly, there were eighty units of the first class along with eighteen additional units of knights and two more of engineers for constructing siege machines. The second, third, and fourth classes were each allotted twenty units, and the fifth class was given thirty along with two additional ones for the horn blowers who issued military signals. Those whose property fell below the minimum qualification of the fifth class were lumped together into a single century of the proletariat and were exempt from military service.

The voting in this assembly was sequential in the order of the classes and centuries as outlined in table 1. Accordingly, since those citizens with a property qualification for the first class were distributed among eighty units of the first class, eighteen units of knights, and two units of engineers, this segment of the citizenry commanded a majority of the votes, although they constituted a numerical minority within the citizen body as a whole. Conversely, the single century assigned to those having a property qualification below the minimum of the fifth class must have been quite numerous. The Roman upper class of the republic took great pride in this timocratic

TABLE 1. Outline of the Later
Centuriate Organization

Class	Qualification[a]	Centuries
Knights	<100,000–	12
First Class	<100,000–	80
Sex Suffragia	<100,000–	6
Engineers	<100,000–	2
Second Class	75,000–100,000	20
Third Class	50,000–75,000	20
Fourth Class	25,000–50,000	20
Fifth Class	12,500–25,000	30
Horn Blowers	12,500–25,000	2
Proletarii	>12,500	1

SOURCES: Livy 1.43; Dion. Hal. 4.16–18; Polyb. 6.22–23; and Cic. *De Re Pub.* 2.39–40.

[a]These property figures are in terms of *asses,* and the amounts reflect the census requirements of the late third and/or second centuries B.C. Originally an *as* was one pound of bronze (one Roman pound = 324 grams), which was further subdivided into twelve *unciae* (whence the English word "ounce").

structure, which gave them secure control over the elections of the curule magistrates, and they regarded it as superior to the "arithmetic equality" encountered in Greek democratic states like classical Athens, for the reason that voting power in the centuriate assembly was distributed in proportion to the voters' wealth and military obligations to the state. As a result, they looked upon its alleged creator, King Servius Tullius, with much favor and viewed him as the founder of republican liberty.

A few data provide two possible clues concerning the earlier history of this complex organization. The five classes of centuries were equally divided between those of military age (*iuniores* = men seventeen through forty-five years old) and those over the age for military service (*seniores*): forty units for each group in the first class, ten units for each in the second, third, and fourth classes, and fifteen units each in the fifth class. Since the comitia centuriata had begun as an army acting in the capacity of an assembly, it must have originally been composed solely of men of military age, but at some point when the body became viewed more as a popular assembly than as an army, those over the age for military service must have been included and given equal representation throughout the five classes. In addition, information preserved by Gellius (6.13; cf. 10.15.4) and in Festus (100L s.v. *infra classem*) indicates that during the second century B.C. there existed a distinction between *classis* = "the class" and *infra classem* = "below the class," these categories referring to those of the first class vs. those of the other four classes. But a consideration of the weaponry employed by the five different classes suggests that in even earlier times this distinction pertained to those who were included in the army and the comitia centuriata vs. those who were not. Since the armor and weapons required of the first three classes differ little and correspond to those of a standard infantryman, whereas the members of the fourth and fifth classes were lightly armed, it seems likely that the first three classes originally comprised Rome's undifferentiated hoplite army, in which all soldiers (except for the aristocratic cavalrymen) were equipped with a helmet, cuirass, greaves, shield, and thrusting spear. The conjecture is reinforced by the observation that the uppermost three classes of *iuniores* amounted to sixty centuries (40 + 10 + 10), which is the number of centuries composing a Roman legion. Thus, the distinction between *classis* and *infra classem* is likely to have pertained originally to a stage of the centuriate organization in which only those capable of equipping themselves to fight as regular legionaries were entitled to a place in the assembly.

This interpretation of the meaning of *classis* vs. *infra classem* in early times receives support from an odd passage in Livy (4.34.6–7) concerning the year 426 B.C. After mentioning that Mam. Aemilius celebrated a triumph for capturing Fidenae during his third dictatorship, Livy adds, as if by way of a final footnote on the Fidenate War, that according to some writers the Roman fleet (*classis*) had been deployed on the Tiber and had taken part in the battle. In criticizing this variant, Livy first observes that the Tiber was too narrow for a naval action. He then conjectures that the use of a few ships in the river to block the enemy's escape was later magnified into a naval engagement. Ogilvie (1965, 583) correctly interprets *classis* as "army" and sees it as referring to the archaic Roman military levy of the undifferentiated comitia centuriata, in contrast to those who were *infra classem*. Interpreting *classis* as "fleet" seems to be a later annalistic misunderstanding of the word, which must have appeared in some documentary source, such as a dedication in the Capitoline temple to commemorate the victory (see Livy 4.20.4). If this is the correct interpretation of this oddity in Livy's text, as seems likely, we would then have an important datum showing that in 426 B.C. the primary distinctions in the centuriate organization were among cavalrymen, hoplite infantrymen, and those below the hoplite census, although some provision could have already been made for a small number of light-armed auxiliary forces.

The centuriate assembly was intimately bound up with two other important Roman institutions: the census, and the division of Roman territory into geographical districts called tribes. Although the latter had the same name as the three archaic tribes ascribed to Romulus mentioned above, they formed an entirely different system of organizing the citizen body into units, according to their residence within the confines of the Roman state.

Before 387 B.C., when the territory of recently conquered Veii was annexed and formed into four new tribes (Livy 6.5.8), Roman territory had been divided into twenty-one tribes. The city itself formed four urban tribes, and the surrounding countryside was organized into seventeen rustic tribes. Membership in these geographical tribes was assigned by censors. Although the office of censor was created in 443 B.C., it was not until the late fourth century B.C. that the Romans began to elect censors regularly about every five years. During the early history of the office (443–318 B.C.), censors were elected on average about every nine years (Astin 1982). The censors were always two in number and held office for eighteen months. Their primary duty was to conduct a census of the Roman people, which involved taking statements under oath from adult male heads of households as to the members of their family and their property holdings; on the basis of these formal declarations, the censors assigned every adult male to a tribe, to an economic class, and to a place within the comitia centuriata, and every household's taxes to the state were calculated according to the assessed value of its property. This entire nexus of the comitia centuriata, census, tribal organization, and state taxation was attributed to King Servius Tullius by the ancient tradition.

The historical accuracy of this claim is likely to resemble that concerning the Servian Wall. Although Servius Tullius was not responsible for the construction of the stone wall that encircled Rome, in the sixth century B.C. the city might have been defended in places by earthen mounds and ditches. Similarly, although Servius Tullius was certainly not the creator of the fully developed centuriate system, archaeological data and comparative studies make it likely that sixth-century Rome witnessed the introduction of hoplite warfare and organization. Hoplite panoplies have been discovered in the so-called Tomb of the Warrior at Vulci, dating to c. 530 B.C., as well as in a tomb at Lanuvium in Latium dating to the early fifth century (Torelli in *CAH* VII.2 1989, 35–36 and Drummond ibid., 170–71). The latter tomb also contained a bronze discus, strigils, and vessels for sand, oil, and perfume, indicative of athletic activity associated with the Greek gymnasium. The introduction of hoplite organization into Greek city-states during the seventh and sixth centuries B.C. is generally regarded as one of several important indications of state formation; and there is no reason why the same should not apply to the contemporary communities of central Tyrrhenian Italy. The uniformity of the typical hoplite phalanx and the universality with which hoplite organization was applied to a state's adult male population clearly reflect the rise of a state with rational institutions and with the ability and need to organize its citizenry into a systematic scheme for military activity.

Yet in its initial stages hoplite organization does not need to have been all that complicated, and two incidents from the Peloponnesian War clearly show how easy it was for a hoplite army to be an important element in a state's constitution. In the spring of 418 B.C., the armies of the Argives and the Spartans and their allies confronted one another at Nemea, but instead of fighting a battle, as the soldiers of both sides wished and expected, the young King Agis of Sparta conferred with two Argives, a general named Thrasylus and the Argive proxenos for Sparta. When these men agreed to a four-month truce and led the armies away, both armies were angry with the decision; and according to Thucydides (5.60.6), the Argives "on returning proceeded to stone Thrasylus in the Charadrus where they judge cases arising from a campaign before they enter the city. He took refuge at the altar and was spared, but they confiscated his property." This meting out of rough justice by an army outside the city reminds one of the comitia centuriata meeting in the Campus Martius outside the pomerium to elect its leaders, to decide on war and peace, and to try people on capital charges. The second incident involves the downfall of the oligarchy of the Four Hundred in Athens in 411 B.C. (Thuc. 8.97.1). After the Peloponnesian naval defeat of the Athenians off Euboea, the island revolted from Athens, which caused such a panic among the Athenians that they convened on the Pnyx and voted the Four Hundred out of power. In their place, "they handed the government over to the five thousand, and it was to be of those who provided themselves with hoplite armor."

In conclusion, the military organization of the thirty curiae and three archaic tribes can perhaps best be dated to the period of Rome's early unification, during the second half of the seventh century B.C.; but as a consequence of Rome's urban development during the sixth century, which involved increased economic activity, a rise in population from growth and incorporation of foreigners as new citizens, and the increase in the territorial extent of the Roman state, a new military organization was introduced to take advantage of these economic, demographic, and geographical changes, and the result was a hoplite phalanx recruited from new territorial districts called tribes.

ROME'S GROWTH AND EXPANDING HORIZONS

Despite the unsatisfactory nature of the surviving ancient evidence, some modern scholars have attempted to estimate Rome's size and strength at the end of the sixth century by making surmises, based upon ancient religious and historical data, concerning the supposed limits of Roman territory in early times. Although the results are little more than educated guesses, the endeavor is at least instructive when the estimates are compared with estimates concerning other Latin, Etruscan, and Greek states.[13]

13. See Ampolo in *Formazione della Città nel Lazio* 1980, 15–30 and 168–75 for detailed treatment (including earlier modern estimates) of the size of Rome's early population, territory, and urban area. Cf. *CAH* VII.2 1989, 164 and 248; and Cornell 1995, 204–7.

For example, K. J. Beloch (1926, 178) estimated that prior to Rome's annexation of Crustumerium, which the ancient tradition assigned to the early years of the republic, the Roman state encompassed an area of 822 square kilometers = 317 square miles. This area would have constituted 35 percent of all Latium, and the next five largest states at this time, according to Beloch's estimates, were Tibur at 351 square kilometers, Praeneste at 262.5, Ardea at 198.5, Lavinium at 164, and Lanuvium at 84. The other nine towns of Latium (Ficulea, Crustumerium, Pedum, Aricia, Tusculum, Fidenae, Gabii, Nomentum, and Labici) had territories estimated as ranging between 37 and 72 square kilometers. Conversely, Alföldi (1965, 288–318) argued that the Roman state at the end of the regal period was considerably smaller. Using his approximate boundaries, Ampolo (1980, 28) calculates that according to Alföldi's reconstruction Roman territory would have measured only 435 square kilometers. On the other hand, there seems to be little doubt that Rome's urban area at the end of the sixth century was comparatively quite large.[14] Rome's total population c. 500 B.C. has been variously estimated in the low tens of thousands. Ampolo (1980, 27) has demonstrated that Beloch's estimate of fifty thousand (1926, 217) is far too high. Ampolo's own estimate of twenty to thirty thousand can probably be taken as a reasonable guess (*Formazione* 1980, 29–30), as can his surmise that Rome might have been able to put into the field something on the order of 5700–8500 soldiers, corresponding roughly to a single legion of full strength or to two legions of three-quarters strength and each commanded by a consul. This would have been quite a substantial army in comparison with neighboring states. Ampolo's estimate for the size of Rome's population c. 500 B.C. compares well with Heurgon's estimate for the population of Etruscan Caere. Using demographic methods of analysis entirely different from those of Ampolo (i.e., working from the number of graves in Caere's famous ancient cemetery), Heurgon (1964, 145–48) concluded that from the seventh to the first century B.C. this state had a population of approximately twenty-five thousand. The growth in Rome's material resources can also be gauged from the size of the Capitoline temple of Jupiter Optimus Maximus, Juno Regina, and Minerva. The podium upon

---

14. Rome's urban area at this time is estimated to have been 285 hectares, and the area enclosed within the so-called Servian Wall of the mid-fourth century measured 426 hectares. Ampolo (*Formazione della Città nel Lazio* 1980, 168) lists the urban areas of the following ancient cities. All figures are in hectares (1 hectare = 2.471 acres). Latin communities: Ardea and Satricum each c. 40; Etruscan communities: Volsinii-Orvieto 80, Caere 120, Tarquinii 150, Vulci 180, Veii 242; western Greek colonies: Selinus 29, Caulonia 47.5, Cumae 72.5, Velia 72.5, Massilia 75, Naples 80.5, Heraclea 110, Posidonia 127, Metapontum 141, Gela 200, Hipponium 225, Locri 232.5, Croton 281, Tarentum 510, Sybaris 515, Acragas 517; Mainland Greek communities: Megara 40, Thasos 52, Mytilene 155, Rhodes 200, Halicarnassus 250, Sparta 450, and Athens with Peiraeus 585.

which it stood measured 175 by 200 feet, making it one of the largest sacred edifices in the Mediterranean world at the time (see Gjerstad III, 168–89 and IV, 388–98).

It is therefore evident that by the end of the regal period Rome had emerged to be the largest and most powerful state in Latium, approximating in size the largest city-states of Etruria. This growth was no doubt due to a significant extent to Rome's command of the Tiber at the important island crossing. As suggested at the beginning of this chapter, this location is likely to have brought together Latins, Etruscans, and Sabines, and perhaps even Greek and Phoenician traders. Onomastic data from early Rome bear out this conjecture. Although we may dismiss as fanciful the tradition that Numa Pompilius was summoned from Cures in the Sabine territory to rule Rome as king, his name is definitely Sabine, thus pointing to the presence of people of Sabine descent in early Rome. Likewise, Oppius, the name of one of the western spurs of the Esquiline, may be Sabine. At least four clan names occurring in the consular *fasti* of the early fifth century are of Etruscan origin: Aquillii, Herminii, Larcii, and Volumnii. The Voltinia, one of the names of the early rustic tribes probably created at the end of the sixth century, also seems to derive from an Etruscan clan name. Furthermore, although examples of writing at Rome are quite rare for this period, the ivory plaque carved into the shape of a crouching lion found in the remains of the archaic temple below the Church of Sant' Omobono in the Forum Boarium is inscribed with an Etruscan name: Araz Silqetenas Spurianas.

Rome's position on the Latin frontier with Etruria is likely to have resulted in a lively interchange between Latin and Etruscan cultures. In a lengthy treatment of this complex topic, T. J. Cornell (1995, 151–72) has properly rejected the more exaggerated modern claims for a Rome thoroughly dominated by an Etruscan presence during the sixth century B.C. Through careful analysis of the ancient evidence, he has shown how difficult it often is to attribute specific cultural traits to the Etruscans as opposed to ascribing them to the ethnically diverse inhabitants of central Tyrrhenian Italy as a whole. In addition, according to Cornell, the later Romans' belief in their indebtedness to Etruscan civilization resulted from the fact that many aspects of Etruscan culture remained relatively unchanged into historical times, and these archaic features were erroneously interpreted as the source of Rome's own bygone institutions and customs that resembled them. Rather, Cornell wishes to view Rome and Etruria as having developed their societies within a larger cultural koine and as having engaged in peer-polity interaction and cultural exchange, with the ultimate result that Etruscan cultural influence on Rome was superficial. In many respects this model is quite appropriate. For example, by the end of the archaic period itinerant artisans and artists working within the same traditions were responsible for the creation of a generally homogeneous monumental architecture in

Campania, Latium, and Etruria. Nevertheless, in correcting the more obviously exaggerated modern claims concerning Roman subservience to Etruscan culture, Cornell has perhaps gone too far in minimizing the significance of early Rome's borrowings from its Etruscan neighbors. Although the nature of our evidence may make it difficult for us to pinpoint cultural borrowings or to document them accurately, they certainly did take place among the peoples of central Tyrrhenian Italy. We should also acknowledge that the traffic was never in only one direction. The Etruscans, like the Romans, succeeded in building a vigorous and lasting civilization because they did not hesitate to borrow numerous things from others. Initially this involved imitating the more civilized Greeks and Phoenicians, but the Etruscans were not shy about borrowing things from their Latin neighbors as well, as we see in their worship of the deities Uni and Selvans, who were the Latin divinities Juno and Silvanus.

It is likely that the Etruscans were the first native people of Italy to adopt the art of writing from the Greeks. Like many other Italian peoples, the Romans and Latins learned to read and write from the Etruscans and even took over their numeral system, which we now know as roman numerals. By the second century B.C., the Romans regularly employed only seventeen different *praenomina* to name their male offspring. Two of these may have been of Etruscan origin: Aulus and Spurius. The latter might have been the Etruscan equivalent of Latin Publius, since both were derived from words meaning "people" or "state." As indicated by a double-headed axe surrounded by eight iron rods in the so-called Tomb of the Lictor at Vetulonia, dating to the seventh century B.C., the ancient tradition that ascribed Etruscan origin to the official insignia of Roman curule magistrates is probably correct (cf. L. Bonfante 1970b, 57–60). The Latin word *triumphus,* used in later historical times to describe a formal military parade led by a Roman commander to celebrate a great victory, ultimately derived from *Thriambos,* an epithet of the Greek god Dionysus, but the word reached the Romans indirectly through Etruscan mediation: Greek *thriambos* > Etruscan *triumpe* > Latin *triumphus* (L. Bonfante 1970a and Versnel 1970, 11–55). Unfortunately, despite the Roman borrowing of this Etruscan term, the murky nature of the extant evidence does not allow us to reconstruct the early history of the Roman ceremony with any degree of certainty. Consequently, we cannot as yet determine whether Etruscan influence accompanied the loanword. Volturnus, whose name appears to be Etruscan, was a deity worshipped by the early Romans, of sufficient importance to be served by one of the minor flamens and to have his own festival in the religious calendar, the Volturnalia of August 27; but like several other divinities, such as Falacer and Furina, who were also served by flamens, he had become so obscure by the late republic that the Romans no longer had any clear conception of him. Nevertheless, if he was in fact of Etruscan origin, as the formation of his name suggests, his flamen and festival would offer strong proof of Etruscan religious influence at a very early date.

One other possible example of Etruscan mediation of a Greek cultural artifact is the Greek god Herakles, whom the Etruscans called Hercle, and whom the Romans worshipped as Hercules. Like the word *triumphus,* the different spellings of the god's name suggest Etruscan mediation. When the Etruscans adopted the worship of the god from the Greeks, the second vowel in his name was deleted as the result of initial stress and syncope, which were common features of the Etruscan language. This produced the disyllabic Hercle with three consecutive consonants. If the Romans and Latins had adopted the worship of Hercules directly from the Greeks, we might expect them to have borrowed the Greek spelling of the divine name along with the god himself, as they did in the case of Apollo. The Latin omission of a vowel between the r and c follows the Etruscan spelling instead, and the insertion of the vowel u between the c and l is inconsistent with the Greek form of the name but has the appearance of a modification of the Etruscan spelling, designed to interrupt the cluster of three consonants. It is noteworthy that the Oscan-speaking people of Campania, who came into direct contact with the Greeks of Cumae and Naples, spelled the god's name *Herekleis,* with a vowel between the r and k as in the Greek form of the name.

Hercules was worshipped in early Rome in the Forum Boarium at the Ara Maxima (Greatest or Oldest Altar) and at a nearby small round temple. According to the ancient tradition (Livy 1.7 and Dion. Hal. 1.39–40), the cult was established by Hercules himself. Traveling homeward from Spain after killing the three-headed (or three-bodied) monster, Geryon, and taking his fine cattle, Hercules stopped to spend the night beside the Tiber, but a local shepherd named Cacus stole some of the cattle while Hercules slept. After awakening and detecting the theft, Hercules slew Cacus and was then received into friendship by Evander, the ruler of the Palatine, who had migrated to Rome from Arcadia in Greece. To commemorate their friendship, Hercules and Evander erected the Ara Maxima and offered on it the first sacrificial tithe from Hercules' herd of cattle. Moreover, the cult was placed under the supervision of two families, the Potitii and Pinarii; and the rites were conducted according to Greek fashion, with the head uncovered. Members of these two families continued to supervise the cult until 312 B.C., when the Roman censor Ap. Claudius Caecus placed it under the control of public slaves who were responsible to the urban praetor (Livy 9.29.9–11).

Although we tend to think of Hercules as a hero of great strength who in Greek myth performed mighty exploits and was deified after his death, he was widely worshipped by ancient traders and merchants, who are known to have honored the god in later Roman times with a tithe of their profits.

The ideology of such worship may have stemmed in part from Hercules' reputation for long-distance travel and in part from his early identification with the Phoenician Melqart, the chief deity of both Tyre in Phoenicia and Gades in southern Spain (Hdt. 2.43–44, cf. Bonnet 1983). In 1960 and 1967, D. Van Berchem published two articles in which he argued that the cult of Hercules at the Ara Maxima was of Phoenician origin. His thesis largely rested on two things: the offering of tithes and the significance of the Potitii. The offering of tithes is well attested in the Near East, and Van Berchem suggested that the Potitii did not constitute a Roman family but were slaves possessed by the god whom they served: for although the family of the Pinarii is well attested in the early consular *fasti,* the existence of the Potitii is not known apart from their alleged association with this cult. Van Berchem proposed that their name derives from the Latin verb *potior* meaning "take possession" and alludes to the widespread Near Eastern custom of temple slaves.

Van Berchem's bold thesis has stimulated responses from other scholars, who have offered their own ideas concerning trade in early Rome and the Phoenician or Greek origin of the cult at the Ara Maxima.[15] Despite the late date of the ancient sources concerning the Ara Maxima (mostly second to first centuries B.C.) and their clear debt to later Greek and Roman mythography, it seems clear that the story of Hercules, Cacus, and Evander served as a charter myth for the commercial protocol governing the interaction between Romans and foreigners in the Forum Boarium. The presence of Hercules' cattle beside the Tiber provides a convenient etiology for the Forum Boarium (= Cattle Market) itself, but more importantly the myth provides models of behavior to be avoided and to be followed. When Cacus (Greek *Kakos* = "Bad Man") misappropriates the property of a stranger, he is punished with death, whereupon the stranger is received into friendship by Evander (= "Good Man" in Greek). The message is clear: foreign merchants are to be afforded hospitality in the Forum Boarium and are to be secure against misappropriation of their goods or other forms of outrage; in return, they are to honor the protecting deity of the place with an offering of a tithe of their profits.

The great antiquity of the cult at the Ara Maxima seems guaranteed by the fact that, according to Tacitus (*Ann.* 12.24), the border around the Palatine, which the later Romans regarded as the pomerium of Romulus's settlement and whose outline they continued to preserve even in imperial

---

15. See Piganiol 1962; Rebuffat 1966; La Rocca 1977; and Bonnet 1988, 278–304. Cf. R. E. A. Palmer 1990b. For a detailed treatment of the numerous ancient versions of the story of Hercules and the Ara Maxima, see Winter 1910. For interesting observations concerning the importance of a church as a center for foreign trade in the Hanseatic League of the Middle Ages, see Holloway 1981, 48–49.

times, enclosed the part of the Forum Boarium in which the Ara Maxima stood. The offering of tithes and the non-Roman nature of the rites do in fact point to a foreign origin for the cult there, rendering Van Berchem's interpretation of the Potitii attractive. Unfortunately, in the absence of archaeological data, the matter can hardly be taken any further than that. We need not doubt that Greek and Phoenician traders regularly visited Rome during the archaic period. Yet given Rome's location, twelve miles inland from the sea on the border with Etruria and downstream from the Etruscan city of Veii, we may perhaps more plausibly conjecture that the most frequent foreign visitors to early Rome were Etruscans. Etruscan interaction with both Greeks and Phoenicians is well documented, and it could have been they who were responsible for introducing into the Forum Boarium a cult bearing Greek and/or Phoenician features which sanctioned and protected international trade.

Finally, three data indicate that Rome's horizons were expanding by the close of the regal period: the Sibylline Books, the Aventine temple of Diana, and Rome's first treaty with Carthage. According to the ancient tradition, one of the Tarquin kings purchased several books of cryptic prophecies written in Greek hexameter verse from a mysterious old woman, the Sibyl of Cumae. These were the famous Sibylline Books, carefully preserved by the Romans and consulted by order of the senate in times of crisis. A sixth or fifth century date for the Roman acquisition of this sacred Greek literature is plausible and would offer evidence of early Roman relations with the Greeks of Campania. H. W. Parke (1988, 85–89) has argued convincingly for a late sixth-century date for the origin of the Sibylline tradition at Cumae. It should be remembered that Tarquinius Superbus is supposed to have gone into exile and died at Cumae, which was then ruled by the tyrant Aristodemus (Livy 2.21.5). According to the later annalistic tradition, the two earliest occasions on which these books were consulted date to the years 496 and 433–431 B.C. According to the version of the battle of Lake Regillus followed by Dionysius (6.17.3, cf. Livy 2.21.3–4), a food shortage on the eve of the campaign prompted the Romans to consult the books and to vow to Ceres, Liber, and Libera a temple which was later dedicated in 493 B.C. On the other occasion (Livy 4.25.3 and 4.29.7), a plague resulted in the construction of a temple to Apollo Medicus.

Another sign of Rome's leading position in Latium and its involvement in the larger cultural world of the western Mediterranean is the Aventine temple of Diana attributed to King Servius Tullius. We need not doubt the tradition that the shrine was erected in order to rival the goddess's temple at Aricia, which was famous among the Latins and was patronized by them. During ancient times the founding of major religious festivals and the construction of temples were often used by states to promote their political and cultural ambitions and rivalry with one another. According to the Greek geographer Strabo (4.1.4–5 with Ampolo 1970), the wooden statue of the goddess in the Aventine temple was deliberately patterned after the cult statue of Artemis worshipped by the people of Massilia, which in turn was copied from the statue in Artemis's most famous temple, at Ephesus in Asia Minor. As described in chapter 2, the Phocaeans, who had founded Massilia at the mouth of the Rhone c. 600 B.C., were the most active maritime merchants of the western Greeks; and their fervent worship of Artemis is suggested by the fact that they founded a colony on the southern coast of France called Artemisium. Consequently, when the Romans decided to erect a temple to Diana to rival the one at the small Latin town of Aricia, the choice to model the cult statue after Artemis of Massilia must have been designed to enhance Rome's prestige by advertising its arrival in the larger cultural community of the western Mediterranean. Indeed, because the Aventine lay in the direction of the sea, the area between the Aventine and the Tiber was dominated by trade and activities connected with shipping in later times, so the temple could also have been intended to please foreign visitors and residents.

In the course of his analysis of what led the Romans and Carthaginians to embark upon the Second Punic War, Polybius (3.22–25) records the texts of three treaties concluded between Rome and Carthage, which he found inscribed upon bronze tablets in the Treasury of the Aediles beside the Capitoline temple. The third treaty dates to the time of the Pyrrhic War; the second one, for which Polybius fails to offer a date, is to be associated with brief statements in Livy (7.27.2) and Diodorus (16.69.1) concerning the Romans' making a treaty with Carthage during the 340s. Polybius dates the first of these treaties to the very first year of the republic, "the consulship of L. Junius Brutus and M. Horatius, the first consuls elected after the overthrow of the kings, under whom it also occurred that the temple of Capitoline Jupiter was dedicated."[16] Before the discovery of the Etruscan and Phoenician texts at Pyrgi dating to the early fifth century B.C., many modern scholars were reluctant to accept such an early date for Polybius's first treaty, but the Pyrgi texts have banished such concerns. Furthermore, even though Polybius's dating of the treaty to the very first year of the republic looks too good to be true, we can at least safely assume that the treaty was concluded some time toward the end of the archaic period, in either the late sixth or the early fifth century B.C., before the Volscians had overrun the Pomptine coast along which Circeii and Terracina were situated. The great age of the treaty is also shown by Polybius's characterization

---

16. This treaty has attracted enormous scholarly attention. For detailed discussions and further bibliography, consult Toynbee 1965, I. 519–55; Alföldi 1965, 350–55; Walbank 1970, 337–45; Heurgon 1973, 250–57; Cornell in *CAH* VII.2 1989, 254–57; and Scardigli 1991, 47–87.

of its language: it was so old that even the most learned Romans of Polybius's day had great difficulty in understanding it. The extremely archaic language of the *cippus* of the *lapis niger* from the Roman Forum, usually dated to c. 500 B.C., would fit Polybius's description.

In his *Politics,* written during the late fourth century B.C., Aristotle (*Pol.* 1280a36) cites the Carthaginians and Etruscans as examples of commercially oriented states that have agreements between one another to facilitate trade; the first treaty between Rome and Carthage has the appearance of a standard, boilerplate agreement of this kind. The first half of the text (Polyb. 3.22) spells out the conditions under which the Romans can conduct trade in North Africa, Sardinia, and Sicily; in the second half, the Carthaginians pledge themselves not to harm the Latins subject to Rome. It is this part of the treaty that has interested modern historians of Rome for what it suggests concerning the extent of Roman power in Latium at the end of the archaic period. According to Polybius's rendering of the text, this part of the treaty consisted of three principal clauses:

1. The Carthaginians will not harm the coastal cities of Lavinium, Ardea, Antium, Circeii, and Terracina, or any other Latins who are subject to Rome.
2. The Carthaginians will not harm the Latins who are not subject to Rome, but if they happen to capture any such city, they will hand it over to the Romans unharmed.
3. The Carthaginians will not construct a fort in Latin territory; and if they enter the land in arms, they will not spend the night there.

The first half of the treaty seems to address the commercial concerns of the Carthaginians, whereas the second part appears to relate to the Romans' political concerns for their sphere of influence. Describing Latin states as subject to Rome most likely distorts the political reality. This distortion could be due to Polybius's less than perfect translation of the archaic Latin text, and could also owe something to a habit among the leading Romans of his day of regarding all Latins as under Rome's dominion. In any case, it seems obvious that the Carthaginians were quite willing to acknowledge Rome as the leading power in Latium and as the one state in the area with which they needed to have an agreement. Lavinium at this time was doubtless an independent Latin community, important among the Latins for its religious cults. Ardea and Antium were certainly independent from Rome at this time as well. In fact, according to the ancient literary tradition, Tarquinius Superbus was engaged in a war with Ardea at the time of his downfall. According to the same tradition (Livy 1.56.3), Tarquin was supposed to have colonized Circeii. Terracina might have been included in the treaty not because of any Roman control of the site, but because it marked a convenient and easily recognizable geographical limit to Rome's hegemonic interests: for at this point along the coast the mountains come down almost to the sea, forming an obvious boundary separating the coast-line into Latin and Campanian segments. Rome certainly did not rule over the coastal towns listed by Polybius as having been contained in this treaty, but the Roman state was sufficiently strong to claim successfully that this area lay within its sphere of influence.

In conclusion, various indications, including modern demographic esti-mates and ancient historical data, seem to converge in showing that by the end of the sixth century B.C. Rome had emerged as the single most impor-tant state in Latium.

Chapter 5

Archaic Roman Religion

Given the important role religion played in early Roman affairs and in shaping Rome's institutions, an overview of the subject may be considered essential for a full understanding of early Roman society and its cultural and political development.[1] Since we possess a substantial amount of ancient evidence about religious ideas and practices among other peoples of Italy, Rome's religious history can also serve as a useful model in suggesting how Rome's cultural development occurred within a larger Italian context. Unlike much of our other ancient evidence, it can even offer interesting glimpses into early modes of Roman thought, behavior, and patterns of life. Furthermore, since Roman religion evolved over time as the Romans adapted themselves and their institutions to new circumstances, familiarity with archaic Roman religion can serve to illustrate the tremendous change and growth in Roman society from early to historical times. Such flexibility was central to Rome's success as an imperial power. Roman religion is fairly well documented: the names, powers, and shrines of deities, the religious calendar, the organization and duties of priestly colleges, and the nature of religious ceremonies and procedures are quite well known. Even though the surviving ancient evidence for archaic religion comes to us from sources written in later historical times and has been distorted by later modes of thought in many ways, a comparative study of other primitive religious

---

1. For the Iguvine Tablets from Umbria see Rosenzweig 1937, Coli 1958, Poultney 1959, Devoto 1974, and Ancillotti-Cerri 1996. Buck 1904, Vetter 1953, Prosdocimi 1978, and Poccetti 1979 are scholarly editions of non-Latin Italic texts important for comparative study of the early native peoples of Italy. Radke 1979 is an excellent encyclopedic source for the divinities of archaic Rome and early Italy.

systems (early Italian, ancient Mediterranean, and others) can often be used to clarify early Roman religious thought and practices.[2]

SOME IMPORTANT ROMAN DIVINITIES

To begin with, the Romans, like so many other ancient peoples, believed in the existence of numerous deities, each of whom possessed specific powers exercised over discrete aspects of the physical world. Unlike the Greeks, however, the Romans did not develop a complex and colorful mythology; they simply conceived of the gods in rather practical terms as being powerful entities, whom they diligently worshipped in order to receive benefactions and to avert evil. Supreme in the divine sphere was Jupiter (or Jove), who was the god of the sky and its weather. His name is etymologically related to Zeus, the Greek sky god, so that Jupiter's name is testimony to the Romans' primordial link to other Indo-European peoples. As the god of the sky and weather, Jupiter was believed to control lightning, which the Romans regarded as one of the most important ways in which divine favor and displeasure were made manifest to humankind. His supremacy in the Roman state religion was symbolized by the great temple on the Capitoline Hill, the single most important shrine in Rome, dedicated to the worship of the Capitoline triad: Jupiter, Juno, and Minerva.

Janus was the god of doors, passageways, and comings and goings. His name most likely derives from *ire,* the Latin verb "to go," and is probably cognate with Sanskrit *yana,* the path which led souls to their proper abode. Janus's two chief epithets, *Patulcius* ("opener") and *Clusivius* ("closer"), were illustrated iconographically by depicting the god's head as having two faces. Since he was thought to exercise power over accessibility, he was usually invoked first in official prayers, along with Jupiter, in order to gain access to the other gods. His most famous shrine in Rome was a small oblong structure with doors on each end which were kept closed in peacetime but opened in wartime (Müller 1943). According to one modern scholar (Holland 1961, 118 ff.), this shrine was originally an early Roman crossing over a brook in the Forum, which was later completely paved over.

---

2. Despite their age, perhaps the two best modern treatments of early Roman religion are still Fowler 1899, 1911. Although Scullard 1981 covers the same ground as Fowler 1899 and contains more recent bibliography, it is not informed by an insightful understanding of early Roman religion. Wissowa 1912 and Latte 1960 are detailed and well-documented accounts of Roman religious history, but Wissowa is sometimes gullible in accepting later Roman explanations of early practices. Dumézil 1966 treats Roman religion in terms of his overarching hypothesis of Indo-European trifunctionalism, on which see Renfrew 1987, 250–62. Harmon 1978a and 1978b present good treatments of some of the more important Roman festivals from the perspective of primitive religious thought. The most recent detailed survey of early Roman religion is Beard, North, and Price 1998, 1–72.

Before being converted into a temple, this bridge must have had a wooden door-like frame at each end and handrails along its sides. It was transformed into Janus's famous shrine by placing a door at each end, walling up the area beneath the handrails, and covering the remainder with an arched roof. Since this bridge stood on the edge of the early Roman settlement, it was always kept passable (the space from bank to bank closed with a walk-way) in peacetime, but in time of war it was always broken down (opened over the brook) in order to protect the community.

Mars was a very important god among the early Romans as well as for the other Italic peoples of early Italy. In later times he was regarded as the god of war, but his nature was much more complex in archaic times. He may originally have been the god of the wilderness lying just beyond the edge of the peasant's farmstead, who therefore was thought to exercise power over both farmland and wilderness. Consequently, he was invoked to protect crops and to assist Roman arms in waging war beyond the borders of the state. Ancient prayers and rituals clearly demonstrate his dual agricultural and warlike character. Cato, in section 141 of his treatise on agriculture, records the following prayer to be used in conjunction with sacrificial rites for purifying the land of a farm:

> Pray with wine to Janus and Jupiter, and speak thus. "Father Mars, I pray and beseech thee that thou be gracious and merciful to me, my house, and my household. To this intent I have ordered the *suovetaurilia*[3] to be led around my land, my ground, my farm; that thou keep away, ward off, and remove sickness, seen and unseen, barrenness and destruction, ruin and unseason-able influence; and that thou permit my harvests, my grain, my vineyards, and my plantations to flourish and to come to good issue, preserve in health my shepherds and my flocks, and give good health and strength to me, my house, and my household. For these reasons and for purifying my farm, my land, my ground, as I have said, be thou magnified (*macte esto*) by the sacrifice of these suckling victims of the *suovetaurilia*. Father Mars, to the same intent be thou magnified with these suckling victims of the *suovetaurilia*."

Mars's power over vegetation is further indicated by the fact that the early Romans began the year with the month of March, which took its name from the god and marked the return of spring and plant life. The Salii (leaping priests) performed their leaping dance through the streets of Rome during this month, beating spears upon shields and singing an archaic hymn. The growth of crops was supposed to be encouraged through the sympathetic magic of their leaping, and their hymn commemorated the passing of the old year's spirit of vegetation (Veturius Mamurius = Old Mars) and the return of the new year. Mars also had a role in divination, because a specific

---

3. The *suovetaurilia* was a ritual of purification involving the sacrifice of a pig, a sheep, and a bull, whose entrails were carried around the area to be purified.

breed of woodpecker (*picus Martius*) was greatly revered by many Italic peoples as a bird of great augural significance.

Juno was the goddess of youthful vigor and maturation (R. Palmer 1974, 3ff.). Thus the Romans applied her name to the month of June, the time when the crops were reaching full maturity for the summer harvest. During historical times, Juno was exclusively considered a goddess of women and childbirth, but her role in early Roman religion was not so restricted. Her domain over youthful vigor may have included the young men capable of bearing arms (*iuniores*) and hence the defense of the state. This may explain her inclusion in the Capitoline triad. She was likewise the tutelary deity of the Latin town of Lanuvium and the Etruscan city of Veii. The Etruscans adopted her worship from the Latins under the name Uni, testifying to the lively cultural interchange between these two peoples in archaic times.

Another important female deity in early Roman religion was Ceres. The genesis and history of her cult reveal much about early Roman religious thought and practice. Her name is related to the verb "to grow" (*crescere*) or "to create" (*creare*). She was therefore simply the goddess of agricultural increase. Comparative evidence from Oscan and Umbrian religious texts shows that the names of many Italic deities were often coupled with an adjective similar in form to Ceres's name because of their involvement in some kind of growth. It appears that although the Romans worshipped Ceres as a goddess from very early times, as witnessed by the fact that she was served by a flamen, she may not originally have been recognized as an actual divinity among other Italic peoples, who merely conceived of her as an abstract function associated with other divinities. She therefore represents a phenomenon not uncommon in the history of Roman religion: an attribute that becomes a divinity. Already by the beginning of the republic, Ceres was equated with Demeter, the Greek goddess of agriculture, for when the Romans built a shrine to Ceres on the Aventine (dedicated in 493 B.C.), her cult was patterned after the worship and rites of Demeter practiced among the western Greeks of southern Italy and Sicily. The Romans employed Greek artists to decorate the shrine (Pliny *NH* 35.154); and even though the cult was an integral part of the Roman state religion, the Romans always employed a Greek priestess from Magna Graecia or Sicily to conduct some of its rites (Cic. *Pro Balbo* 55). Thus, Ceres' cult exhibits one of the earliest instances of hellenization, one of the most important processes that affected Roman religion and culture in later centuries. Moreover, as the result of their responsibility for Rome's grain supply, the plebeian aediles quite naturally used Ceres' Aventine temple as their headquarters; and their practice of preserving official records there must have stemmed from one interpretation of Demeter's Greek epithet, Thesmophoros, as meaning "Lawgiver."

THE OFFICIAL RELIGIOUS CALENDAR

Rome's official religious calendar contains festivals of many other divinities, and a survey of the more important ones can further illustrate early Roman beliefs and concerns.[4] The earliest festivals of the religious calendar clearly indicate that archaic Roman religion was the religion of the Roman peasant farmer, whose survival depended upon his success in agriculture. In some instances, farmers performed religious rites on their own land to enlist divine assistance or to ward off harm. In other cases, the religious ceremonies were conducted by Roman priestly officials who were acting on behalf of the entire community. They insured that the rituals were performed correctly so as to obtain the desired favor of the gods. Our knowledge of Roman religious ceremonies is more detailed for the festivals celebrated during the months from January to June, thanks to Ovid's poem on these months of the calendar, the *Fasti;* in many instances we know relatively little about the actual rites of festivals observed during the other six months of the year.

Originally, each month of the Roman year began when the pontiffs observed the beginning of a new lunar cycle, but at some unknown early date this lunar calendar was replaced by a calendar of 355 days in which March, May, Quinctilis (later named July), and October all had thirty-one days, February twenty-eight, and all other months twenty-nine. The insertion of an additional intercalary period of twenty-two days every two years or so kept the calendar in agreement with the solar year (Michels 1967, 145–72). Besides having a length roughly equal to the lunar cycle, the months reflected their original lunar character in the Roman system of calendrical dating by counting backward from the three dividing days of the kalends, nones, and ides. The kalends was the first day of each month and corresponded to the appearance of the new moon. The ides was the thirteenth day of the shorter months of twenty-eight or twenty-nine days and the fifteenth day of months having thirty-one days, so that the ides corresponded to the full moon. The nones was the ninth day (counted inclusively) before the ides of each month and corresponded roughly to the moon's first quarter; it was therefore the fifth day of the shorter months and the seventh day of the longer ones. Since Jupiter was the god of the sky and daylight, all ides were sacred to him, because the full moon was the time when the night was most fully illuminated. Given Juno's and Janus's concern for birth and beginnings respectively, all kalends were sacred to them. Moreover, the lengths of the months and the assignment of festivals to

---

4. For scholarly treatment of the complexities and history of the official Roman calendar, see Michels 1967 and Rüpke 1995. For the texts of the various epigraphic calendars with exhaustive commentary, see Degrassi 1963. For the text and translation (with extensive commentary) of Ovid's *Fasti,* a poem describing the mythology and religious lore associated with six months of the Roman year (January–June), see Frazer 1929 and Bömer 1957–58.

specific days were largely determined by the early Romans' superstitious notions concerning the qualities of numbers. In general, odd numbers (especially prime numbers) were regarded as auspicious, whereas even numbers were inauspicious and inherently unstable because they all could be divided in half by two. Consequently, virtually all festivals were assigned to odd-numbered days in a month; and all the months except February contained either twenty-nine or thirty-one days, both being prime numbers, not divisible by any other number. February alone was allowed to have an inauspicious even number of days because its rites were largely concerned with the dead.

The first four months of the old Roman year had names associated with the growth and maturation of crops during the spring and early summer, and the major festivals were directly connected with this same agricultural process. As already mentioned, March took its name from Mars, who in early times was believed to have power over vegetation. April was the month of opening (*Aprilis* < *aperire*), referring to the blossoming of plants. May was the month of "bigness" (cf. Latin *magnus* = "big"), while June, associated with Juno, was the month of maturation leading up to the summer harvest. In contrast, the next six months simply took their names from the numbers five through ten: Quinctilis (later renamed July in honor of Julius Caesar), Sextilis (later renamed August in honor of the Emperor Augustus), September, October, November, and December; and their festivals were related to the heat and harvest of summer followed by the autumn planting. In addition, festivals associated with the human life cycle of birth, maturation, and death were coordinated with the yearly agricultural cycle.

The first day of the old Roman year, March 1, was sacred to Juno Lucina, the goddess of childbirth. In later times, the day was termed the Matronalia and was a kind of Mother's Day. The midpoint of the month, March 15, was sacred to a minor divinity, Anna Perenna, who symbolized the perennial annual cycle. The Liberalia of March 17 was sacred to a primitive god of fertility, Liber, whose worship was widespread among the other Italic peoples. In later times, however, he was equated with the Greek Bacchus/Dionysus and therefore became the Roman god of wine. The second half of April contained festivals pertaining to the protection of crops and herd animals. April 15 was the Fordicidia, in which pregnant cows were sacrificed to Tellus (Mother Earth) in order to guarantee the earth's fertility. April 19 was the Cerialia, the anniversary of the dedication of Ceres' Aventine temple in 493 B.C. It should be noted that throughout Roman history the day of a temple's dedication was carefully recorded and was henceforth regarded as the birthday (*dies natalis*) of the specific cult or divinity. It was therefore not unusual for Roman priests or officials to choose the day of dedication carefully so as to associate the deity and the temple with a pertinent time of the year. April 21 was the Parilia, a festival devoted to the worship of Pales, a divinity concerned with herdsmen and their livestock. In preparation for taking herd animals out to summer pastures, bonfires were set alight, and the animals were driven over them as a rite of purification. In later times, believing that Romulus and Remus had been shepherds before founding the city, the Romans regarded this day as the one on which Rome had been founded. It thus lost its original significance and was celebrated as Rome's birthday. April 25 was the Robigalia on which sacrifices were performed in order to avert red rust disease from the grain crops. The animal chosen for sacrifice was a dog (preferably red), perhaps because the vigilant nature of this animal was thought best suited to keep away the unwanted blight.

The period from the first of May to the middle of June was a critical time for the growth and maturation of crops, and the religious rites of this season suggest that the early Roman farmers, whose entire existence depended upon a good yield, anxiously awaited the outcome, in fear that seen or unseen forces of nature might cause harm. In keeping with that anxiety, marriages were not conducted during this period, for it was regarded as inauspicious. May 1 was sacred to the Protecting Lares (Lares Praestites), who were guardian spirits of the farmland. May 9, 11, and 13 were collectively known as the Lemuria. The Romans believed that during this time spirits or ghosts from the netherworld roamed about and had to be appeased (Rose 1944). These days were followed by the great purification of May 15, on which a group of priests solemnly proceeded through the city, collecting as they went a series of twenty-seven scarecrow-like figures called *argei*, which were finally thrown into the Tiber from Rome's oldest bridge, the Pons Sublicius (Nagy 1992). These figures were made of rushes and were stationed at specific sites throughout the city every year on March 16 and 17. After remaining on display for sixty days, they were rounded up and discarded as described. The anthropomorphic figures were probably designed to divert the attention of hostile spirits in springtime, and once the Lemuria had passed the community rid itself of the pollution by casting away the rush puppets. This great purification of the city was followed by a similar purification of the farmland at the end of the month. Farmers performed the Ambarvalia (Circuit of the Fields) by leading animals chosen for sacrifice about the borders of the land, thereby forming a sacred circle to enclose the good and exclude the evil.

June 1 was sacred to a minor divinity named Carna, who protected the vital organs of human beings. This day was thus a kind of religious physical-fitness day on which Carna received offerings of bean meal and lard. June 9 was the Vestalia, in honor of the goddess Vesta, whose sacred fire was kept burning perpetually by the Vestal virgins. Her temple was one of the oldest structures in the city. Its round floor plan was unlike later orthogonal sacred buildings. Its shape may have imitated that of the primitive thatched huts of the earliest Romans. The ceremonial cleaning of Vesta's temple on June 15 symbolized the community's readiness for taking in the summer harvest. June 11 was the Matralia in honor of Mater Matuta, whose name most likely means "Ripening Mother." Her worship was a safeguard for the ripening of crops, but she also received offerings for the ripening of pubescent girls (Rose 1934). Even in early times her simple character was further complicated by identification with the Greek goddess Leucothea, who protected seafarers and was thus patronized by merchants (Krauskopf in *Akten des Kolloquiums zum Thema die Göttin von Pyrgi* 1981, 137–51). She was also associated with the dawn (Dumézil 1980, 175–209).

July 5, the Poplifugia, was a primitive military ritual involving the assembly and purification of Rome's adult male population, followed by a ceremonial rout of Rome's foreign enemies. The ceremony was later replaced by the censorial lustrum at the end of a census and by the Transvectio Equitum (Procession of Cavalrymen) of July 15, instituted in 304 B.C. (Forsythe 1994, 322–30). July 7, the Caprotine Nones, celebrated the pollination of fig trees during midsummer. The Neptunalia of July 23 honored the early Roman god of springs and streams at a time when fresh water was at a premium. In later times, Neptune was equated with the Greek Poseidon and thereby was changed from the god of fresh water worshipped by the early Roman peasant into a mighty god of the sea. Vulcan, the Roman god of destructive fire, received worship on August 23 when the dry heat of summer must have posed a serious threat of combustion (Rose 1933). The end of the summer harvest was marked by the Consualia of August 21 and the Opiconsivia of August 25. Consus was the god of storage. On his holiday, his underground altar in the Circus Maximus was unearthed and received offerings, and horse races were held there in his honor. Opiconsivia was simply "the abundance of Consus" and probably originated as a mere attribute of the god before evolving into a minor divinity in her own right. She was, however, kept closely associated with Consus in the religious calendar by Roman priests.

During the autumn months, the Roman farmer was busy with plowing and planting next year's crops as well as with harvesting grapes to be processed into wine. The end of the autumn vintage was marked in the religious calendar by the festival of the Meditrinalia of October 11. Similarly, the autumn planting of wheat and barley was represented in the rites of October 5 and November 8, in which a ceremonial storage pit called the Mundus was opened, signaling the removal of seed grain to be planted. This religious ceremony, intended to confer ritual correctness and thus divine favor upon this important agricultural activity, was later reinterpreted to mean that on these days the doorway to the underworld was opened and ghosts were about (Fowler 1912). This infernal reinterpretation might have been encouraged or suggested by the belief that the term Mundus derived from the Etruscan word *mun, muni* = "underground chamber," "tomb." If so, it would constitute an important datum in the cultural interaction between the Romans and the Etruscans.

The end of the military campaigning season was marked by the Armilustrium of October 19, in which men assembled under arms and underwent ritual purification. October 15 was the Day of the October Horse, a curious ceremony whose precise significance has been much discussed by modern scholars with little consensus about its meaning (see Pascal 1981). Chariot races were held in the Campus Martius and a horse from the winning team was sacrificed, after which his head and tail were cut off, and two groups of people from different districts of the city fought for possession of these two objects. In the end the blood of the sacrificed horse was preserved to be used the following spring at the Parilia in rites for purifying livestock. Modern discussion of this peculiar festival has largely concentrated on the question of whether the ceremony was agricultural or military in nature. Given that the celebration was placed halfway between the Meditrinalia, marking the end of the harvest, and the Armilustrium, signaling the end of the campaigning season, the early Romans may have viewed the festival from both perspectives. In any case, the actual close of the planting season was marked in the religious calendar by the Saturnalia of December 17 and the Opalia of December 19. These two holidays were the autumnal counterparts to the Consualia and Opiconsivia of August 21 and 25. Saturn was originally the Roman god of sowing, and like Consus, the god of storing grain, he was given the attribute of abundance (*ops*), for the Roman farmer's prosperity depended upon his planting's producing an abundant yield. Ops, however, later evolved into an independent deity, whom the Romans regarded as Saturn's divine consort.

During the wintery months of January and February Roman farmers busied themselves with various odd jobs of maintenance and repair work. This season of relative inactivity allowed the Romans to spend time with their neighbors and relatives. In January the Compitalia was celebrated in the city, and the Paganalia was observed in rural districts (*pagi*). In both instances people came together with their neighbors at crossroads (*compita*) and enjoyed their company and hospitality while rendering homage at the shrines of the Lares Compitales.

February, the last month of the old Roman year, was dominated by the nine days of *Dies Parentales* (February 13–21), which were holidays in honor of deceased relatives. The Lupercalia of February 15 was originally a primitive ritual performed to protect livestock, especially sheep and goats, from the depredations of wolves; it might also have been intended to safeguard their fertility and lactation from unseen hostile forces. At some very early date, the Romans must have associated the warding off of wolves with superstitious ideas about werewolves (Michels 1953), and the pontiffs therefore assigned the festival to mid-February, reinterpreting the rite as a defense against unwelcome hostile spirits. This infernal interpretation of the Lupercalia might have been encouraged by a curious linguistic coincidence: Latin *lupus* (= "wolf") resembles Etruscan *lupuce* (= "he died"), a word frequently

Figure 4. Wall painting from the Tomb of Orcus at Tarquinii: Etruscan god of the underworld wearing a wolf's head.

encountered in Etruscan epitaphs. This linguistic and conceptual connection is further suggested by the fact that in the Tomb of Orcus at Tarquinii the Etruscan Lord of the Underworld is depicted wearing a wolf's head (see fig. 4). Thus the lore of the Lupercalia may testify to complex interplay between Etruscan and Roman religious thought. In addition, the Lupercalia's concern for the fertility of herd animals was extended to include the fecundity of humans: after sacrificing a goat and dog, the Luperci, the priests of this festival, clad only in loin cloths of goat skin, ran about the city, striking women with strips of the same goat skin. It was believed that the goat's potency was thereby transferred to the women, both increasing their fertility and insuring them safe and easy delivery.

The *Dies Parentales* ended on February 21 with the Feralia, on which people were supposed to bring offerings of various kinds to the graves of their deceased relatives. February 23 was the Terminalia in honor of Terminus, god of the boundary stones used to mark off the ownership of land. The Romans considered boundary stones to be sacred; according to an early law, if a man plowed one up, both he and his oxen were ruled accursed and could be killed with impunity (Festus 505L s.v. *Termino*). This was a clear instance in which religion was used to reinforce social order, because moving boundary stones undermined property rights. Originally, Terminus appears to have been an epithet of Jupiter who, as the sky god, was all-seeing and could therefore be counted on to witness and punish human misconduct. Accordingly, in the Capitoline temple of Jupiter Optimus Maximus, a boundary stone representing Jupiter Terminus was positioned below an opening in the roof so as always to have an unobstructed view of the sky. The Terminalia was also deliberately placed in this part of the calendar to symbolize the end of the old Roman year (Merrill 1924). This can be seen from the fact that even though there remained five more days in February, the Romans always inserted the intercalary month immediately after the Terminalia.

THE RELIGIOUS PRIESTHOODS

Rome's public religion was supervised and administered by various priests, each of whom had specific duties and expertise.[5] They were collectively responsible for Rome's success in war and for the general welfare of the people by maintaining the good will of the gods (*pax deorum*) towards the Roman state. Some offices, such as those of pontiffs and augurs, were held by a specified number of people simultaneously. These were organized into what the Romans called priestly colleges. In other instances, such as the rex sacrorum, only one person filled the position. Many priests were distinguished by their official dress or other insignia of office. All priesthoods were held for a lifetime term, and they were always filled by members of aristocratic families. Given their relatively small number and the influence that they could sometimes have on the conduct of public affairs, Roman priesthoods were highly coveted and regarded as marks of honor and

5. For more detailed treatment of this topic, see Beard and North 1990, 19–48.

political recognition. Furthermore, since priestly offices tended to be passed on from father to son or at least retained within the same aristocratic family, tenure of the priesthoods seems to have played an important role in the self-definition of the patriciate (see below p. 167ff). Contention over access to these offices was a significant element in the so-called struggle of the orders, as politically aspiring members of newly arrived families sought to validate their public careers by tenure of a religious office.

According to an entry in Festus (198L s.v. *ordo sacerdotum*), the five highest-ranking priests in the state religion were, in descending order of priestly prestige, the rex sacrorum, the flamens of Jupiter, Mars, and Quirinus, and the pontifex maximus. In historical times, however, the chief pontiff was the titular head of the state religion. As spokesman and head of the pontifical college, he was responsible for overseeing all aspects of Roman public religion, and he exercised jurisdiction over all other priests, including the rex sacrorum and the flamens of Jupiter, Mars, and Quirinus, even though they technically outranked him in the priestly hierarchy. Nevertheless, even in later times the offices of the rex sacrorum and of the three flamens were deemed to be of such importance for the state religion that the lives of these priests were governed by numerous religious restrictions, so much so that, unlike other Roman priests, they were often hampered in pursuing a political or military career, because they were not allowed to be absent from Italy. In fact, the ancient sources for the middle republic record several instances in which the chief pontiff prevented one of these flamens who had been elected to a political office from assuming the governorship of an overseas province.

The later Romans believed that the office of the rex sacrorum represented the religious duties and functions of the early kings of Rome. Although there is likely to have been a historical connection, we cannot know how much continuity or change there was from the regal period to the early republic, since we have no accurate knowledge concerning the religious duties and activities of the early kings. This priest's official cultic center was the Regia in the Forum (see above p. 87–88), and one of the earliest Latin inscriptions appears to be a sacred law in which the rex and his herald are mentioned (see above p. 73–74). Besides presiding over the rites of the Parilia on April 21, the rex sacrorum was responsible for performing sacrifices on other specified days throughout the year. On the nones of every month, he officially proclaimed that month's religious and legal calendar to the assembled Romans. Likewise, on February 24, March 24, and May 24 he performed ceremonies of some kind in the Comitium before the people. On the first of these three days, after performing the rites, he fled away. This ceremony, coming one day after the Terminalia, was called the Regifugium (the King's Flight), and later Roman antiquarians erroneously explained it as commemorating the anniversary of the overthrow of the monarchy. In fact, the rex sacrorum, representing the Roman people and their place within the divine order, was dramatizing in ritual the waning of the old Roman year.

A flamen was a Roman priest who was devoted to the service of a single divinity.[6] The word seems to be etymologically related to the Hindu priestly title Brahman, which suggests that the Roman term was of great antiquity. The flamens were of two types, major and minor, the former being those of Jupiter, Mars, and Quirinus. They were the most important ones. There were twelve minor flamens, but only the divinities served by ten of them are recorded in the ancient sources: Carmenta, Ceres, Falacer, Flora, Furrina, Palatua, Pomona, Portunus, Volturnus, and Vulcan. Carmenta was a minor deity of childbirth; Flora was the goddess of flowers and flowering plants; Pomona was a goddess of fruit; and Portunus was a minor deity of harbors and gateways. Despite the fact that Falacer, Furrina, Palatua, and Volturnus were important enough in early times to warrant their own flamens, they later became so obscure that Roman writers in historical times no longer had any clear idea of their natures. This fact alone hints at the great difference between the religious systems of archaic and historical times.

As suggested by the fact that he was served by one of the three major flamens, Quirinus was a very important god among the early Romans. His nature, too, was unknown in later times, and he continues to elude modern analysis as well. His priest was involved in the rites of the Robigalia of April 25, the Consualia of August 21, and the Larentalia of December 23. His connection to the first two festivals suggests that he was somehow concerned with agriculture. One possible etymology of his name links him with Quirites, an archaic term used to describe the Roman people. If the Latin etymon *quir-* is related to the Sanskrit adjective *cirá* meaning "resting," "abiding," the title Quirites could have originally designated the settlers or inhabitants of Rome. If so, Quirinus could have been the god of the settlement, so that the functions of Mars and Quirinus might have been initially complementary: while Mars ruled over the wilderness just beyond the Roman settlement, Quirinus held sway over the settlement itself. In any case, Roman antiquarians and historians, for whatever reason, regarded Quirinus as the deified Romulus, and by deriving his name from *quiris*, an alleged Sabine word meaning "spear," they considered him to be a war god similar to Mars. Moreover, because of Quirinus's association with Romulus and his flamen's involvement in the Consualia and Larentalia, these two festivals were explained with reference to Romulus's life: the former was associated with the rape of the Sabine women, and the latter was supposedly established by Romulus to honor his dead foster mother, Acca Larentia.

6. For a more detailed treatment of these priesthoods, see Vanggaard 1988.

Thanks to a chapter of Aulus Gellius's *Attic Nights* (10.15) and numerous sections of Plutarch's *Roman Questions* (see Rose 1924), we possess an extensive list of restrictions that surrounded the flamen of Jupiter (*flamen Dialis*). This elaborate religious code must have arisen in part because this flamen served the single most important deity of the Roman pantheon. Since he was not allowed to mount a horse or to gaze upon an army, he could not hold political offices that involved exercising military powers. The flamen's hair and finger nails had to be cut with bronze utensils, not iron ones. This restriction has usually been interpreted as indicating that the priesthood antedated the advent of the Iron Age in central Italy, but Rüpke (1995, 510–11) has instead postulated that the ban on iron was due to the metal's use in the ground and hence its association with the netherworld and death. In addition, the flamen's hair and finger nail clippings had to be buried beneath a fruitful tree. Their disposal must have been carried out in secret so as to prevent magic from being worked upon the priest; and their burial beneath a fruitful tree was doubtless intended to insure his well-being. Many of the other prohibitions are explicable as insuring that the priest not be constrained or confined in any way, because such constraints might impinge upon his priestly powers and efficacy. Thus, he was forbidden to bind himself by an oath. His clothing had to be free of knots, and he could not wear a ring that was a solid, unbroken band. He could neither touch ivy nor walk under grapevines.

The pontifical college was originally composed of four, five, or six members until it was increased to eight or nine by the Ogulnian Law of 300 B.C. (see note 29 in chapter 9). The title *pontifex* literally means "bridge builder." Modern scholars are generally in agreement that this priesthood took its name from the pontiffs' original responsibility for constructing and maintaining the Pons Sublicius, Rome's oldest bridge over the Tiber River (Hallett 1970). Since in early times the river was believed to be divine or inhabited by a water deity, the erection of a bridge was thought to require special care so as not to anger the river god, who could devastate the city by flooding. The religious character of this structure is demonstrated by the fact that it could not contain any metal. Despite the rather narrow scope of this primordial office, the priesthood's competence grew in time to become a general overseeing of the entire state religion. This supervision might have been the natural outgrowth of the pontiffs' responsibility for regulating the calendar and thus for keeping the community's religious records, which the pontifex maximus kept on a whitened board, as discussed in chapter 3. Another important duty of the pontiffs was the expiation of unusual natural phenomena believed to be signs of divine displeasure. As the result of their supervision of Roman families' private religious rites when these were either transmitted or interrupted by inheritance, adoption, or emancipation from paternal authority, throughout the early republic the pontiffs were Rome's legal experts and exercised enormous influence in determining the legal calendar and in shaping and interpreting Roman private law.

The augurs, originally six in number, then increased to nine by the Ogulnian Law of 300 B.C., were the experts in inaugurating sacred precincts as well as in taking and interpreting the auspices for the Roman state (Linderski 1986). Latin *auspicium* literally means "bird watching," and it did in fact involve the observation of birds, but it also included the interpretation of lightning and thunder as manifestations of divine will. The augurs divided the sky into four quarters and regarded the two sectors on the left as more auspicious than those on the right, and the front quarters as more favorable than the rear ones. Some species of birds were observed for their flight, and others gave signs by their cries. Roman auspices were of two types: deliberately sought by the augur (*impetrativa*), or unsought but offered by the gods (*oblativa*). No assembly of the people (electoral, legislative, or judicial) could be held unless favorable auspices had been received beforehand, and an assembly could be disbanded while in progress if an augur announced the observation of an unfavorable sign. Augurs employed a crooked staff called a lituus in making their observations, and their discipline was the Roman version of a religious tradition common throughout early Italy. The Umbrian tablets from Iguvium (VI.A1–21, with Poultney 1959, 231 ff.) describe the taking of auspices, and the procedure is similar to Roman practice. Etruscan auspices, however, formed a more complex system, because each of the four quarters of the sky was further subdivided into four parts, thus producing sixteen sectors in which signs were observed (Weinstock 1946).

To a considerable degree, the pontiffs and augurs expiated prodigies and took the auspices within a well-established tradition and according to accepted rules. On various occasions, however, unprecedented phenomena were observed for which Roman pontifical or augural law had no prescriptions or rulings. In such instances, the Roman senate usually sought the expert advice of Etruscan diviners called haruspices. By this means, aspects of Etruscan divination were incorporated into Roman religion. Besides interpreting divine will by observing birds, thunder, lightning, and other natural phenomena, haruspices performed divination by observing the shape and coloration of the livers of sacrificed animals. This form of divination is termed hepatoscopy. In 1877, a bronze model of a sheep's liver, measuring about five inches long and about three inches at its widest part, and weighing about one and a half pounds, was discovered five miles southwest of Piacenza (ancient Placentia) in northern Italy (see fig. 5). The object was obviously used by haruspices for divination and perhaps even for teaching the Etruscan discipline, because it is inscribed with forty-two

Figure 5. Bronze model of a sheep's liver, subdivided into sections and labeled with the abbreviated names of Etruscan gods.

Etruscan divine names.[7] Like the Etruscan augural sky, the outer margin of the liver is divided into sixteen areas, indicating that livers of sacrificed animals were thought to represent a microcosm of the universe. Similar liver models have been discovered at ancient sites in the Near East; and the Near Eastern origin of Etruscan hepatoscopy is evident from the fact that in Babylonian omen texts a Sumerian ideogram with the phonetic value 'har' is used to refer to the liver (Burkert 1992, 46–47). Thus, the *haru* element in Latin *haruspex* accurately reflects the Near Eastern derivation of this Etruscan religious science. The term *erus,* encountered in the Iguvine Tablets and referring to an organ of a sacrificed animal, may be the Umbrian rendering of this same linguistic element.

An even more important source of foreign influence upon Roman religion were the Sibylline Books.[8] According to Roman tradition, these texts, written in Greek dactylic hexameter verse, were acquired by one of the Tarquins from the Sibyl of Cumae. Down to 83 B.C., the books were kept beneath the throne of Jupiter Optimus Maximus on the Capitoline. At first, two men, termed *duoviri sacris faciundis* ("two men for performing rites"), were in charge of consulting and interpreting these books whenever the senate instructed them to do so (see Dion. Hal. 4.62). This religious

7. For a detailed discussion of this important artifact, see Van Der Meer 1987 with Linderski 1995, 595–99. A clay model of a sheep's liver has also been found at Falerii in southern Etruria, but it is not inscribed with divine names. See Nougayrol 1955.

8. For a detailed treatment of the Greek and Roman tradition of prophetic Sibyls and of Sibylline prophecy, see Parke 1988.

commission was increased from two to ten members in 368 B.C. and was henceforth known as the *decemviri sacris faciundis*. The books were consulted only in times of grave crisis, but since they had presumably been composed by Greeks, their religious content was likewise Greek. Thus, religious remedies divined from them invariably resulted in the Romans' adopting some aspect of Greek cultic practice. From the middle of the fourth century B.C. onwards, this priesthood and the pontifical and augural colleges were the most highly coveted religious offices for enhancing an aristocrat's political career.

The Vestal virgins were six in number; and like the pontifical college they were headed by a chief Vestal (*Vestalis maxima*). Although they participated in many of Rome's public rites, their primary responsibility was to tend the sacred fire of Vesta and to keep it burning perpetually as symbolic of the community's life and continuity. Not only were they emancipated from their father's paternal authority when they were inducted into office, but they were the only females in early Roman society who were not obliged to be under the legal guardianship of a male. This privilege was not, however, a matter of showing them honor, as ancient writers and modern scholars have generally supposed. Rather, it should be viewed in light of the various rules surrounding the flamen of Jupiter that prevented the priest from being physically, legally, or magically constrained. Freedom from legal guardianship must have been regarded as essential in order for the Vestals to perform their religious duties without any kind of impediments. They were, however, under the supervision of the chief pontiff, who was obligated, if Vesta's sacred fire were ever extinguished, to expiate the sin, by beating the delinquent Vestal. Moreover, if a Vestal allowed herself to be seduced and ceased to be a virgin, the chief pontiff atoned for this religious offense against the cult by clubbing the miscreant male to death in the Comitium. The priestess was not directly executed, but was subjected to an ordeal from which the goddess could extricate her servant if she so desired. The Vestal, furnished with food and water, was enclosed in an underground chamber in the Criminal Field (*Campus Sceleratus*) just inside the Colline Gate. Although ancient sources recount a number of marvelous tales of Vestals carrying water in a sieve or rekindling the sacred fire by uttering a prayer, they do not record any instances in which a Vestal was miraculously rescued from this subterranean chamber.

The Vestals' official dress and hair style resembled those of a bride, except that the Vestal wore a white veil instead of the bride's red one. Their sexual status was therefore both ambiguous and all-encompassing, embodying virginity and motherhood (Beard 1980); for them, every day was a kind of wedding day of great exaltation. Their official cult center was the temple of Vesta, a round sacred structure near the Regia in the Forum. Besides housing Vesta's sacred fire, the building was the repository of other sacred objects which were under the exclusive care of the Vestals, and it even had an area curtained off from the view of men. Just as Roman priests performed various rites on behalf of the entire community, so the Vestals embodied and represented the religious functions and duties of girls and women in Roman public ceremonies. They alone were responsible for baking the salted meal (*mola salsa*) used in public sacrifices of animals; and they were quite conspicuous in numerous festivals, among them the Fordicidia of April 15, the procession of the *argei* on May 15, the Vestalia of June 9, the cleaning and purification of Vesta's shrine on June 15, the Consualia of August 21, and February 13, the first day of the *Dies Parentales*.

Although many religious systems throughout human history have forbidden menstruating women to participate in certain rites or have allocated religious functions differently to premenopausal and postmenopausal women, the ancient sources say nothing explicit along these lines respecting the Vestals. This silence could mean that no such distinctions were present in Roman religion, or it could be the product of the all-too-successful secrecy in which the priestesses conducted so many of their rites. Dionysius (2.67.2) and Plutarch (*Numa* 10.1), however, record that it was customary for Vestals to serve for thirty years: ten years of learning their sacred duties, ten years of performing them, and ten years of teaching them to others. It is possible that these remarks have no basis in fact but are merely the neat, overly rationalistic scheme of some Roman antiquarian. Such skepticism is supported by the evidence of inscriptions from imperial times which show that some Vestals served well beyond thirty years. On the other hand, since this alleged thirty-year limit roughly corresponds to the interval between female puberty and menopause, it could hark back to some early requirement that Vesta must be served by ovulating women.

Two priesthoods of less prominence require mention for what they reveal concerning the nature and origin of early Roman religion. As already discussed, the Lupercalia of February 15 centered around the activities of the Luperci. These priests comprised two different bands: the *Fabiani* and the *Quinctiales*. These epithets derived from the names of two of the most distinguished patrician clans of early Rome: the Fabii and Quinctii. Thus, this public priesthood may have originated as the private religious office of two families whose prominence led to their incorporation into public cult; or alternatively, members of these two families could have so dominated this priesthood through hereditary succession that the office took on the names of the families. In either case, the priesthood's titulature testifies to the strong connection between aristocratic family lineages and priestly offices in archaic Rome. A similar phenomenon is seen in the Iguvine Tablets, for the Atiedian Brethren, the priests who were charged with performing the public religious rites of Iguvium outlined in these texts, also took their name from a prominent local clan. Moreover, the appellation "Brethren" of this Umbrian priesthood further illustrates how archaic Roman religion was in many ways just one particular version of a religious heritage common to many peoples of early Italy, because the title also occurs in the Roman Arval Brethren (*Fratres Arvales*).

ROMAN RELIGIOUS PRACTICES AND IDEOLOGY

Like those of the Atiedian Brethren of Iguvium, the religious activities of the Arval Brethren are well documented in a large corpus of inscriptions discovered in their sacred grove and dating to imperial times, when they were primarily concerned with performing sacrifices for the welfare of the emperor and his family.[9] Nevertheless, they still preserved and continued to perform a substantial portion of their archaic rites, so that their inscriptions offer our most detailed look into Roman religious cultic activities. The Arval Brethren were twelve in number; and as the epithet "Arval" indicates, they were concerned with the fertility of the farmland. They conducted their rites in a sacred grove located at the fifth milestone along the Via Campana, on the right bank of the Tiber. The site was dedicated to an otherwise unknown deity named Dea Dia. They performed their most important ceremonies every year toward the end of May, coinciding with the Roman farmers' observance of the Ambarvalia for purifying their fields. It was during the rites of this day that the priestly brotherhood sang its archaic Arval Hymn (see Gordon 1983 #75):

> Oh! Help us, ye Lares! Oh! help us, ye Lares! Oh! help us, ye Lares! Nor let bane and bale, O Marmar, assail more folk. Nor let bane and bale, O Marmar, assail more folk. Nor let bane and bale, O Marmar, assail more folk. Be full satisfied, fierce Mars. Leap the threshold! Halt! Beat the ground! Be full satisfied, fierce Mars. Leap the threshold! Halt! Beat the ground! Be full satisfied, fierce Mars. Leap the threshold! Halt! Beat the ground! By turns address ye all the Sowing-Gods. By turns address ye all the Sowing-Gods. By turns address ye all the Sowing-Gods. Oh! Help us, Marmor! Oh! Help us, Marmor! Oh! Help us, Marmor! Triumpe, triumpe, triumpe, triumpe, triumpe.

Note that with the exception of the last word "triumpe," which is repeated five times, every clause in this hymn is uttered thrice. Since the number three figures prominently in both religion and magic, the triple repetition was obviously intended to increase the prayer's efficacy. Marmar and Marmor are simply archaic forms of Mars's name. Although he is styled "fierce," he is nevertheless invoked along with agricultural deities: the Lares and the Sowing-Gods.

9. For these texts and their explication, see the progressively more complete editions of Henzen 1874, Pasoli 1950, and Scheid 1990. See also the discussions of Olshausen 1978, Beard 1985, and Linderski 1995, 600–2.

Like the Iguvine Tablets written in Umbrian, the official acts of the Arval Brethren document in lavish detail the strict formalism observed in Roman public cult. In order for rites to be efficacious, they had to be performed exactly in accord with a carefully prescribed procedure. Furthermore, just as the flamen of Jupiter was forbidden to use iron instruments to cut his hair or finger nails, a similar ban on iron applied to the sacred grove of Dea Dia. Thus, whenever workers needed to enter the grove, to do repair work on the buildings or to inscribe the priestly records on stone, a pig was first sacrificed in order to atone for the offense of bringing iron tools into the grove. It was not uncommon in other Roman religious ceremonies to begin by offering the sacrifice of a pig as expiation for any involuntary mistakes committed by the priest. The correct performance of all Roman public religious rituals was insured by requiring that several attendants oversee and assist the presiding priest or magistrate. In order to make sure that the prayer was spoken without mistakes, one person read the prayer aloud to the priest or magistrate, who then repeated it word for word, while a second attendant checked these proceedings against his own written text. Moreover, since the ceremony could be invalidated by the intrusion of an unwanted sight or sound, the presiding official kept his head partially covered with his toga so as to restrict his vision, and a flute player furnished the ceremony with a kind of sacred background noise. If any errors or interruptions were detected, the entire ceremony had to be repeated.

Another important feature of Roman religion, both public and private, was its votive character. It was customary for officials and private citizens to make a vow (*votum*) to some deity, according to which the divinity would receive some promised offering if the state, official, or private person obtained some desired end (e.g., victory in war, an excellent harvest, prosperity in commerce, recovery from illness, or health and success in childbearing). It was largely through commanders vowing temples for success in battle that the city of Rome was adorned with its numerous shrines. Likewise, modern archaeological excavations of ancient sacred sites have uncovered countless small objects of clay or metal that were deposited as offerings by private persons in return for some deity granting their prayers.[10] Many modern scholars have characterized Roman votive religion as little more than bargaining, a kind of *quid pro quo* or *do ut des* mentality. This view is valid, but it is also too simplistic in that it overlooks the reverence of the mortal petitioners and their gratitude for the divine favor. Roman worshippers did not perceive themselves as demanding or extorting benefits from the gods. Rather, they made their vows with humility, and consigned fulfillment or denial to the power of the divinity; but if fulfillment was

10. For discussions of votive offerings uncovered by archaeology, see Bonfante and MacIntosh Turfa in Swaddling 1986, 195–210; Ginge 1993; and MacIntosh Turfa in De Puma and Small 1994, 224–40.

granted, the vow was gladly discharged. Given the extraordinarily harsh living conditions of the ancient Romans, who did not have the benefits of modern medicine or technology, there should be little wonder why they sought the favor of the gods so earnestly, and why votive religion played such an important role in their lives.

The language of sacrifice and prayer provides interesting clues to the way the early Romans viewed the nature of the gods. The Latin word *magmentum* was an old term meaning "sacrificial victim." The suffix *-mentum* is a relatively common termination which simply indicates that the word refers to an object or concept, whereas the element *mag-* has the meaning of "big," "large," "great." The same etymon occurs in another archaic phrase, *macte esto*, found in prayers in which the ancient worshipper exhorted the divinity, "Be thou magnified!" Taken together, these two linguistic items suggest that the early Romans thought sacrifice was essential in order to provide the deities with or to compensate them for the energy necessary to accomplish a petitioner's request. Otherwise, the god or goddess might not have been inclined to expend vital energy simply to gratify the worshipper.

Additional evidence demonstrates that in public rites Roman priests were accustomed to invoke specific attributes of deities, indicating what particular quality or qualities were believed necessary for the deity to bring about the desired end. This practice testifies again to the extraordinary exactitude and formalism of Roman public rites, and it also shows the careful attention which early Roman priests paid to the powers of the various gods. Aulus Gellius, in 13.23 of his *Attic Nights,* has preserved some of these priestly *indigitamenta:* "maia Volcani, salacia Neptuni, hora Quirini, nerio Martis." *Maia Volcani* means "might of Vulcan," whereas *salacia Neptuni* means "effervescence of Neptune," referring to the ability of the primitive Roman god of fresh water to cause wells, springs, and brooks to flow forth from the earth. *Salacia* is etymologically related to Salii, the leaping priests. The other two phrases are more obscure and are understandable only with recourse to the other Italic languages. Thus, *hora Quirini* means "will of Quirinus," and *nerio Martis* means "strength of Mars." In later historical times, however, some of these divine attributes had evolved into minor divinities whom the Romans believed to be closely related or subservient to the major deity. In other instances, the Romans no longer remembered the original meaning of such attributes and reinterpreted them as representing the divine consorts of the gods with whom they were associated. Accordingly, the two phrases *hora Quirini* and *nerio Martis* were taken to mean that the wives of Quirinus and Mars were two obscure goddesses named Hora and Nerio.

Once again, the Umbrian religious texts furnish illuminating parallels to this Roman material. Tablets V–VII are primarily concerned with describing the ritual for purifying the Fisian Mount of Iguvium and the Iguvine people. After the auspices had been taken, a series of sacrifices and prayers were performed at three separate gates of the city, with three animals offered inside and three offered outside each gate to different divinities. The prayer uttered in connection with the purification of the assembled Iguvine people involved an execration of neighboring peoples and a blessing of the Iguvine folk. The god invoked in this prayer is Cerfus Martius, a compound deity, consisting of Mars (= Umbrian *Martius*) and Cerfus, an Umbrian masculine divine name cognate with Roman Ceres, the goddess of growth. Furthermore, two attributes of Cerfus Martius are specifically invoked in this prayer: *tursa Cerfia* and *prestota Cerfia*. In both instances the adjective *Cerfia* is used to underscore the fact that these qualities belong to Cerfus Martius. The first attribute means "terror" or "rout" and was employed to confound neighboring communities, whereas the second was used to place Iguvium under divine protection. Umbrian *prestota* is related etymologically to the Latin epithet of the Lares Praestites, the guardian spirits who watched over Roman fields. As in this example, many aspects of archaic Roman religion can be understood, when viewed in the larger context of early Italy, as expressions of a cultural koine. Despite their differences, many communities in early Italy were the heirs of a common storehouse of traditions. Practices we know to have been specifically Roman or Iguvine were merely variant local manifestations of a shared ancient heritage which had gradually developed during several centuries of prehistory in the Italian peninsula.

Chapter 6

The Beginning of the
Roman Republic

HOW DID THE MONARCHY END?

According to the ancient literary tradition, Rome's last king, Tarquinius Superbus (Tarquin the Proud), was a cruel tyrant. He murdered Servius Tullius, usurped royal power, oppressed the senate, and worked the Roman people to exhaustion by making them labor on the sewer system of the Cloaca Maxima which drained the runoff from the hills into the Tiber. He even used underhanded means to quell opposition throughout Latium in order to make himself the leader of the Latin League. His downfall, however, resulted from the outrageous conduct of his wicked son Sextus. His rape of the virtuous Lucretia and her consequent suicide so angered the Roman people that they rose up in revolt, banished the Tarquin royal family from Rome, and replaced the king with two annually elected consuls and a priest called the rex sacrorum, who held his office for life.[1]

Comparison with other ancient literature clearly shows that Tarquinius Superbus was portrayed by later writers in stereotypical terms of a tyrant (Dunkle 1967 and 1971). In addition, the tale also conforms to ancient Greek and Roman political theory concerning the evolution of a state's constitution from monarchy to tyranny to aristocracy; and the story of Lucretia appears to be little more than a Roman adaptation of the famous story of how the downfall of the Peisistratid tyranny in Athens c. 514–510 B.C. was set in motion by an assassination arising from a homosexual love affair gone bad (Thuc. 6.53–59). Indeed, ancient writers had a penchant

---

1. For other modern treatments of the period and topics covered in this chapter, consult Ogilvie 1965, 233–389; Momigliano 1969; Heurgon 1973, 156–69 and 176–80; Scullard 1980, 78–86 and 92–97; Drummond in *CAH* VII.2 1989, 172–226; Cornell ibid. 243–97; Forsythe 1994, 245–301; and Cornell 1995, 215–72 and 293–309.

for using such stories to explain major political transitions. For example, in the sixth chapter of his *Life of Cimon,* the Greek biographer Plutarch tells a story involving the attempted rape and murder of an innocent maiden of Byzantium by the Spartan Pausanias in order to explain why, in the aftermath of Xerxes' invasion of Greece, the Greeks of the Aegean abandoned Sparta's leadership in favor of Athens. In the debate of the Persian nobles over what form of government to establish following the deaths of Cambyses and Smerdis, Herodotus (3.80) has Otanes characterize the rule of a tyrant by three things: the setting aside of laws, the execution of people without trial, and the raping of women. The last element is even found at the beginning of the early Mesopotamian *Epic of Gilgamesh,* where Gilgamesh's highhanded behavior toward the people of Uruk is epitomized by his violation of young women. This prompts the people to pray to the gods to rid them of their insolent king.

The ancient tradition concerning Rome's last king could be regarded as basically correct in the sense that Tarquin's corrupt, abusive, or ineffectual exercise of power could have led to his deposition by an opportunistic and ambitious group of aristocrats. Kingship is the simplest form of government and also the most easily corrupted, since its proper functioning depends upon the character and abilities of a single individual; the end of a monarchy can ensue simply from its tenure by one person unfit to occupy the office. This is especially the case when kingship is based upon hereditary succession, and it is noteworthy that Rome's last king appears to have been the only monarch who owed his position at least in part to a hereditary connection. Unfortunately, as with so many matters pertaining to the regal period, the ancient tradition is so overlaid with later stereotypical features customary in the portrayal of a tyrant that we cannot be sure what details, if any, should be accepted as genuine.

Despite these difficulties, A. Alföldi (1965, 72–84) has offered a compelling picture of the events that might have brought about the end of the Roman monarchy. Following in the footsteps of earlier modern critics of the ancient tradition surrounding the beginning of the republic, Alföldi has argued that the monarchy ended as the result of the capture of Rome by King Porsenna of Clusium. Tarquinius Superbus either could actually have been deposed by Porsenna, or he could have fled from Rome after Porsenna's defeat of the Romans and advance upon the city. Tarquin then took refuge among the Latins, while Porsenna used Rome as a bridgehead in an attempt to expand his control in Latium. This situation resulted in the battle of Aricia in 504 B.C., in which the invading Etruscans, led by Porsenna's son Arruns and supported by the occupied city of Rome, fought against the other Latin states, which received important military assistance from Aristodemus of Cumae. When the latter were victorious, Porsenna withdrew from Rome, and the Romans were left to face alone a coalition of the other Latin states, who supported Tarquin's restoration as king. Eventually this standoff was resolved in the battle at Lake Regillus of either 499 (Livy 2.19–20) or 496 B.C. (Dion. Hal. 6.2 ff.), in which Rome defeated the Latins or at least fought them to a draw, and Tarquinius Superbus went into exile at the court of Aristodemus, who was now tyrant of Cumae.

According to the later standard tradition, Porsenna attacked Rome because he was trying to restore Tarquinius Superbus, but due to Horatius Cocles' brave defense of the bridge across the Tiber and to Mucius Scaevola's display of courage after his abortive attempt to assassinate Porsenna in his camp, the king of Clusium stopped before actually taking the city. He lifted the siege, and decided to make peace with Rome on condition of receiving hostages. At last, further impressed by the Romans' virtues, exemplified in the courage and honesty of the hostage Cloelia, he even became Rome's friend, withdrew his forces altogether, and refused to lend further support to Tarquin, who then sought aid from the Latins. Two ancient passages, however, suggest that Porsenna did in fact occupy Rome. In describing the burning of the Capitoline temple in December of 69 A.D. in the course of civil war in Rome between the supporters of Vitellius and Vespasian for the imperial throne, Tacitus (*Hist.* 3.72) characterizes this disaster as the worst catastrophe that ever befell Rome, even worse than those of the city's surrender to Porsenna or its capture by the Gauls. Pliny (*NH* 34.139) says that in the treaty which Porsenna granted to the Romans the latter were forbidden to use iron except in agriculture.

Tacitus could be guilty of using loose language, but other considerations make the literal meaning of his words plausible. The toppling of Tarquin from power and Porsenna's attack upon Rome form quite a striking coincidence. Signs of violent destruction dating to the end of the sixth century at the central Etruscan sites of Murlo and Acquarossa suggest that Etruria at this time was the scene of major inter-state conflict. The tales of Horatius Cocles, Mucius Scaevola, and Cloelia appear to be laudatory tales designed to redeem Roman pride and to disguise the embarrassing fact that Porsenna did in fact occupy the city. It is certain that Horatius Cocles and Mucius Scaevola are not historical figures; their stories are historicized folktales in which a one-eyed, one-handed, or one-legged man saves his people by killing an evil king, tyrant, or pretender (see Lincoln 1991, 244–58). The prohibition against using iron bespeaks someone who was firmly in charge and capable of dictating terms. This provision could have been meant to disarm the Romans by forbidding them to use weapons, or it could have been designed to divert all of Rome's iron production except for essential agricultural needs into making weapons for Porsenna's growing military forces, as he endeavored to push farther south into Latium.

THE NATURE AND ORIGIN OF THE CONSULSHIP

The two consuls were always regarded as the chief magistrates of the Roman republic,[2] so much so that they were the eponymous officials of the state: that is, the year in which they held office was officially dated by their names. They were the supreme military leaders in the Roman state. The term for their constitutional power was *imperium*, which gave them authority to raise troops, to issue orders, and to command in war. Given the military nature of their office, they were elected by the timocratic comitia centuriata, which originated as the Roman army serving as a popular assembly. Their insignia of office were quite distinctive and impressive. They wore a purple-bordered toga (*toga praetexta*) and sat on a special kind of folding chair adorned with ivory (curule chair = *sella curulis*). They were each attended by twelve subordinates called lictors, who took their name from the fact that they would arrest, bind (*ligare*), and punish with beating those whom the consuls ordered them to seize. As symbols of their power, the consuls shared the right, alternating from month to month during their year of office, of having the lictors carry bundles of rods (*fasces*) before them in public. The rods could be used for inflicting corporal punishment; and when the consul was outside the pomerium and exercising full military authority, the *fasces* were bound together with an axe, because when in the field the consul could have soldiers executed by beheading for insubordination or other serious military offenses. The consuls were equal partners in their office, and the action of one could be blocked by the opposition of the other. Thus the constitutional configuration of the office included an important check and balance of power. Agreement with or at least tacit acquiescence from one's colleague was necessary to carry things out; disagreement and opposition resulted in inaction.

Despite the advantages of consular collegiality, in times of extraordinary military crisis unity of command was desired and needed. The Roman state's solution to this problem was the office of the dictator, a thoroughly constitutional office, not to be confused with the modern term for a despotic ruler. The dictator was appointed by one of the consuls, probably in accordance with a decree of the senate urging him to take this course of action. The appointment may have required the assent of the comitia centuriata as well. The dictator exercised *imperium* greater than that of the two consuls, symbolized by the fact that he was attended by twenty-four lictors, but his term of office was not to exceed six months. He was also termed the master of the army (*magister populi*), and he appointed a subordinate called the master of the horse (*magister equitum*), who commanded the cavalry forces. According to

2. For other discussions of various modern views about the issues treated in this and the following sections—the origin and nature of the consulship and the reliability of the early consular *fasti*—see Staveley 1956, 90–112; Drummond 1978b; Ridley 1980a and 1983; Staveley 1983, 42–44; Drummond in *CAH* VII.2 1989, 172–77; and Cornell 1995, 226–41.

the ancient tradition, this office was created in 501 B.C.; down to the Hannibalic War it was periodically employed to deal with military crises.³ Moreover, as Roman territory expanded during the fourth and early third centuries B.C., and as the two consuls exercised their commands farther and farther from Rome, a dictator was often appointed for a short time, in the absence of the two consuls, in order to preside over the consular elections in the city.

As with virtually every aspect of early Roman history, modern scholars have posed important questions concerning the origin and nature of the consulship. Much of this discussion has hinged upon terminology. The title "consul," used to describe the two annually elected eponymous officials of the Roman state, simply meant "colleague" and probably did not gain currency until some time after the major reorganization of the government in 367 B.C., when it came into use to distinguish these two officials from the occupants of the newly created office of praetor, who resembled the consuls in many ways. It seems likely that in early times the consuls were themselves called praetors, a name meaning "leaders" (Latin *praeire* = "to go before") and referring to their role as the military leaders of the Roman state (see Stewart 1998, 113–15). Nevertheless, considerable modern discussion has arisen concerning this office, stemming in large measure from a particular passage in Livy (see Ogilvie 1965, 230–31 and Oakley 1998, 77–80). In describing Roman attempts to avert a persistent plague during the years 364–363 B.C., Livy (7.3) says that the Romans revived the practice of appointing a dictator to drive a nail into the wall of the Capitoline temple, because according to the recollection of the elders a plague had once been alleviated by this means.⁴ Livy then records a variant explanation of this odd custom of driving the nail:

> There was an ancient law, inscribed in antique letters and words, that whoever was the praetor maximus on September 13 should drive the nail. The chamber of Jupiter Optimus Maximus was nailed on the right side next to the shrine of Minerva. They say that this nail was a marker for the number of years because writing was scarce in those times, and that the law was devoted to the shrine of Minerva because counting was Minerva's invention. Cincius, a diligent authority of such records, asserts that at Volsinii there are also to be seen nails in the temple of the Etruscan goddess Nortia as indicators of the number of years. The consul M. Horatius in accordance with the law dedicated the temple of Jupiter Optimus Maximus in the year after the expulsion of the kings. The rite of driving the nail was subsequently transferred from the consuls to dictators, because their *imperium* was greater. Then after the custom had been discontinued, the matter seemed worthy even in its own right for appointing a dictator.

3. For a convenient summary of different modern views on the origin of the dictatorship, see Ridley 1979.
4. For the magical significance of this ceremony, see Foresti 1979 with Oakley 1998, 74–75.

The custom of driving a nail-like object into the side of a sacred building to mark the passage of a year is known from ancient Mesopotamia and is depicted on an Etruscan mirror dating to c. 320 B.C. (Bonfante 1983, 122). The Capitoline temple was dedicated to the worship of three divinities: Jupiter Optimus Maximus, Juno Regina, and Minerva; and the inner part of the temple contained three chambers, one for each of the deities with their cult statues, with Jupiter in the middle and the two goddesses on either side. September 13 was significant to the Romans as the anniversary of the dedication of the temple, and from early times a celebration called the *Ludi Romani* ("Roman Games"), extending over several days, was observed every year at this time in honor of the chief tutelary god of the Roman state. But this passage of Livy has attracted the attention of modern scholars largely because of its reference to an old law specifying the driving of a nail every year by the praetor maximus (= greatest praetor). Who was the praetor maximus? Was this another name for the dictator, whose office was supposed to have been created a few years after the consulship, and if so, does it suggest that the Roman republic was originally headed by a dictator and master of the horse rather than by two equal consuls? Alternatively, since the chronological context of this passage is the year 363 B.C., was the term praetor maximus the contemporaneous appellation of the holder of the newly created office of praetor, whose duties were primarily confined to the city of Rome and who therefore would have been an obvious candidate to perform this annual ritual? Or thirdly, does Livy's old law pertain to one of the two consuls, and did praetor maximus simply refer to the one who happened to be holding the *fasces* when the month of September rolled around?

Two points can be made about the title of praetor maximus. First of all, when Greek historians narrated Roman history and referred to a consul, they used a two-word phrase to translate the Roman title of consul: *strategos hypatos* (= highest general). It is quite evident from both Greek and Roman historians that Latin *praetor* was always translated as Greek *strategos,* and Greek *strategos* was always rendered into Latin as *praetor.* Moreover, since, like Latin *maximus,* the Greek word *hypatos* was a superlative adjective often used by itself without *strategos* to translate Latin *consul,* it is quite clear that the Greek phrase *strategos hypatos* was an exact translation of Latin *praetor maximus.* Since the first Greek historians to write seriously about Roman affairs probably date to the early third century B.C. (e.g., Timaeus of Tauromenium and Hieronymus of Cardia), we may date this Greek rendering of Latin *consul* to that time and take it as contemporary evidence for official Roman titulature. Secondly, it should be stressed that Livy cites the old law concerning the driving of an annual nail by the praetor maximus in connection with the year 363 B.C. As usual, Livy is himself very brief in discussing such a tangential matter and is eager to move on in his narrative to describe the important domestic and military affairs of the Roman state. The ultimate source of this information, however, must have been someone who actually saw and read this document in its entirety in the Capitoline temple, and it could have contained a consular date, which could have decided Livy to treat this matter under the year 363 B.C. If so, the term praetor maximus should be related to the historical context following the major reorganization of the Roman government in 367 B.C., which suggests that the superlative *maximus* was used to distinguish the consul who held the *fasces* from his consular colleague and the praetor. If so, the term praetor maximus may not have any relevance to the period before 367 B.C., or to the origin and nature of the consulship at the beginning of the republic.

Some modern scholars have even questioned whether the equal sharing of power between the two consuls was original to the office; if it was, they wonder where the Romans got the idea of organizing their affairs in this manner. These questions and doubts seem excessive. On the one hand, we should give the Romans considerable credit for practical political thinking and organization. After all, they did become the masters of the Mediterranean world, and we need not doubt that they were capable of political shrewdness in early times. On the other hand, the concept of collegiality was already part of the Roman experience in the form of priestly colleges of the augurs and pontiffs; and collegiality among public magistrates was also common among the Greek city-states of the archaic period (probably including the western colonies), suggesting that it was a widespread feature of contemporary political culture. Thus there do not seem to be adequate grounds to call into question the fact that the Romans replaced the king with two annually elected magistrates who shared equal power.

The late annalistic tradition, however, as seen in both Livy and Dionysius of Halicarnassus, assigned five consuls to the first year of the republic. L. Junius Brutus and the husband of Lucretia, L. Tarquinius Collatinus, were first elected, but Collatinus was forced to abdicate from office and to leave Rome simply because of his Tarquin name. He was replaced by Lucretius, the father of the raped Lucretia; when Lucretius died in office he was replaced by P. Valerius Publicola, who, like Brutus, had been present at Lucretia's suicide. Brutus, however, fell in battle against the Tarquins, and M. Horatius Pulvillus was elected in his place. The later tradition obviously wished to cram as many important people and events into this first year of the republic as possible. In fact, Livy (2.8.5) indicates that in some old writers Lucretius's consulship was not to be found. Let us recall that, in dating the first treaty between Rome and Carthage to the first year of the republic, Polybius (3.22.1) assigned it to the consulship of L. Junius Brutus and M. Horatius, although according to the later annalistic tradition these two had never held office at the same time in this year.

Since P. Valerius Publicola is listed as consul with another Lucretius for the second year of the republic, we may suppose that both names, Valerius and Lucretius, were duplicated to be consuls of the first year, and the clan name of the Lucretii was further used to concoct Lucretia as the wife of Tarquinius Collatinus. This supposition seems confirmed by the fact that in the accounts of Livy and Dionysius the two men are associated as friends: Lucretia's father asks Valerius to attend the meeting at which Lucretia kills herself. The same pattern of using names from the consular *fasti* for one year to formulate characters for action in another year is also seen in Livy 2.11.7–10 and Dion. Hal. 5.23 and 5.26.3–5, where the consuls of 506 B.C., Sp. Larcius and T. Herminius, are introduced as subordinate officers or ambassadors when Porsenna is besieging Rome. Valerius's involvement in the republic's first year was deemed necessary in order to have this new era of freedom marked by the passage of a Valerian Law concerning *provocatio,* a Roman's citizen's right to have a capital charge tried before an assembly of the people. This Valerian Law of 509, however, is fictitious; it is patterned after an actual Valerian Law on *provocatio* of 300 B.C. (Livy 10.9.3–6).

M. Horatius was firmly associated with the dedication of the Capitoline temple, probably because his name was preserved in later times in a dedicatory inscription. Yet both Tacitus (*Hist.* 3.72) and Dionysius (3.69.2 and 5.35.3) differ from Livy in assigning the temple's dedication to the third year of the republic, when Horatius was consul for a second time. It therefore seems likely that in order to have the temple's dedication take place in the momentous first year of the republic, later writers moved Horatius back two years and made him one of the first consuls. If so, we are then left with L. Junius Brutus and L. Tarquinius Collatinus. The latter hardly seems to be the product of later fabrication or manipulation: for it would have seemed quite incongruous to the later Romans for their forefathers to have elected a Tarquin to the consulship right after they had driven out the king's family. Thus, his name among the first consuls may be retained as authentic. Furthermore, since L. Junius Brutus was always associated in the later tradition with the founding of republican liberty (see the emphatic wording of Tacitus *Ann.* 1.1), we may suppose that this tradition derived from the simple fact that his was the very first name in the early list of consuls. Many moderns have challenged the historicity of his tenure, since the Junii are not attested again in the consular *fasti* until the late fourth century B.C., but other family names exhibit a similarly discontinuous pattern.

Consequently, Brutus and Collatinus should be retained, but Lucretius, Valerius, and Horatius should be removed from the first year of the republic. Brutus and Collatinus were really the first two consuls following the downfall of the monarchy; the other three names have been added from the next two consular years in order to assign the dedication of the Capitoline temple and a Valerian Law establishing *provocatio* to the very first year of the republic. Moreover, if we accept the notion that the monarchy was terminated as the result of Porsenna's capture of Rome, we may offer the additional suggestion that Brutus and Collatinus were appointed by Porsenna to govern affairs in the city. The king of Clusium deliberately chose a member of the Tarquin family because of his connection with the royal house, in order to lend legitimacy to his rule, but he also appointed L. Junius Brutus to serve as a watchdog over his colleague and vice versa. Then, when Porsenna's army was defeated at Aricia, his ambitions in Latium collapsed and he withdrew from Rome. The Roman aristocratic families readily filled the vacuum, and the division of power between two officials was maintained as a sensible arrangement.

THE EARLY CONSULAR *FASTI*

The foregoing analysis of the first year of consular government may serve as a convenient illustration of how the later Roman tradition and later historians could fabricate events, and it also serves to introduce the question, how reliable and accurate was the later Roman list of chief magistrates for the early republic? This list comes to us principally through four sources: Livy, Dionysius of Halicarnassus, Diodorus Siculus, and the inscribed list set up in the Forum by the Emperor Augustus and now known as the *Fasti Capitolini* (= Degrassi 1947, 1–142). This material, set out in chronological order along with the names of all other magistrates recorded for the Roman republic, has been systematically collected and published in two volumes by T. R. S. Broughton in *The Magistrates of the Roman Republic* (1951–52). But these two volumes are far more than a mere list of Roman magistrates. They contain all ancient references to these officials, brief summaries of events associated with them, critical remarks by Broughton himself, and citations of other pertinent modern scholarly work. Volume I covers the period 509–100 B.C., and volume II covers the years 99–31 B.C. In addition, the second volume (pp. 524–636) contains an Index of Careers, in which all the data concerning office holding are organized in alphabetical order according to clan names. This Index of Careers is extremely valuable for examining and reconstructing the history of specific noble families. In 1986 Broughton published a third, supplemental volume containing valuable additions and corrections, as well as a more up-to-date bibliography. These three volumes constitute an indispensable aid for the student and scholar of Roman republican history.

The overall reliability of the list of Roman chief magistrates (consuls, dictators and masters of the horse, and military tribunes with consular power) has been much discussed over the past 150 years, and many criticisms and interpretive approaches have been offered (see Ridley 1980a and 1983). It is apparent that the four different lists have come to us ultimately from a single official source, the records kept by the pontifex maximus, which were consolidated into the *Annales Maximi* during the 120s B.C. Since the pontifical records must have required copying and recopying periodically, as the material on which they were written deteriorated, we should not be surprised that for the earliest period (509–300 B.C.) the list contains errors, and that there are differences among our four major sources. For example, Livy's narrative does not include the consulships of 507 or of 490–489 B.C. Conversely, Diodorus has three extra consulships between the years 458–457, 457–456, and 428–427, which are found in no other source. There are three other major anomalies in the early list: (1) the second year of decemviral legislators for 450 B.C. is likely to be a later invention; (2) the years of anarchy (absence of eponymous curule magistrates) for one or more years preceding the reorganization of Roman government in 367 B.C. are also a later invention; and (3) the so-called four dictator years (333, 324, 309, and 301 B.C.) were probably devised by Atticus in the last years of the republic; they are found only in the *Fasti Capitolini*.[5] These are only the most obvious problems evident in the early consular list. Many others have been suspected, but they are usually hard to prove, since in most instances we have little more than the names to go on and are therefore at the mercy of an uncheckable tradition. Despite these difficulties, the overall chronology of the *fasti* seems to be correct. We have confirmation from the independent historical tradition of the Greeks that Rome was captured by the Gauls in 387 or 386 B.C., and that the battle of Aricia occurred in 504 B.C. (see Dion. Hal. 7.3–11 with Alföldi 1965, 56–72). These data demonstrate that the Roman chronology, although off by a few years, is basically accurate for the beginning of the republic and the Gallic occupation of Rome.

But the single most thorny problem of the early consular *fasti* is the presence, among consuls of the fifth century B.C., of names of clans which are known to have been of plebeian status in later republican times. These are anomalous according to the later annalistic tradition, which declares that the first plebeian to hold the consulship was L. Sextius in 366 B.C. Before that time, all consuls were supposed to have come from patrician families. Indeed, the clan names found in the early list of magistrates fall into three categories: (1) those which are known to have been patrician in later historical times; (2) those which in later historical times are only known as plebeian; and (3) those whose status cannot be determined, either because they became extinct before later historical times, or because the immense lapse of time between early officeholders bearing these clan names and later people with the same name makes the connection between the two uncertain. If we classify the names in the consular *fasti* for the sixty-five

5. See the Appendix for a fuller discussion of the chronological problems of the anarchy and dictator years.

years 509–445 B.C., before the creation of the office of military tribune with consular power (excluding suffect consuls, dictators, masters of the horse, and the second board of decemviral legislators of 450 B.C., whose historicity is in doubt), we come up with a total of forty-three different clan names, of which sixteen (37.2 percent) belong to the first category, ten (23.3 percent) belong to the second category, and seventeen (39.5 percent) belong to the third category.[6] Moreover, the offices held during this period consist of sixty-three pairs of consuls and one board of decemvirs, for a total of 136 offices, of which seventy-five (55.1 percent) were held by clans in the first category, twenty (14.7 percent) by clans of the second category, and forty-one (30.1 percent) by clans of the third category. These data seem to contradict the later annalistic tradition concerning patrician monopoly of the consulship in the early republic. Numerous theories have been put forth either to explain the discrepancy or to eliminate it. This is a very complex issue, but it is such a central and fundamental problem of early Roman history that it deserves and requires detailed explanation.

PATRICIANS AND PLEBEIANS

According to the late annalistic tradition as found in Livy and Dionysius, Rome's internal development during the early republic was characterized by a political struggle between two social orders, the patricians and the plebeians.[7] The patricians constituted a closed group of specific aristocratic clans, whereas all the other clans in Roman society were classified as plebeian. By the middle of the fourth century B.C. this social dichotomy had become well defined, but exactly how and when it arose is still imperfectly understood. According to tradition, the distinction between patricians and plebeians was as old as Rome itself. Romulus had created it by his appointment of the first one hundred senators, whose descendants became the patricians. Modern opinions put the origin of the social dichotomy anywhere from the regal period to the late fifth century B.C. In any case, by the

6. The patrician clans are the Aemilii, Claudii, Cloelii, Cornelii, Fabii, Furii, Julii, Manlii, Nautii, Postumii, Quinctilii, Quinctii, Servilii, Sulpicii, Valerii, and Veturii. The clan names of later plebeian status are the Aquillii, Cassii, Cominii, Genucii, Junii, Minucii, Sempronii, Sestii, Siccii, and Volumnii. The clan names of uncertain status are the Aebutii, Aternii, Curiatii, Curtii, Geganii, Herminii, Horatii, Larcii, Lucretii, Menenii, Numicii, Pinarii, Romilii, Tarpeii, Tarquinii, Tullii, and Verginii.

7. For other discussions and additional bibliography on this, the most complex and troublesome problem of the early Roman republic, consult R. Palmer 1970, 243 ff.; Heurgon 1973, 165–66; Ranouil 1975; Richard 1978; Staveley 1983; the essays by Richard, Mitchell, and Momigliano in Raaflaub 1986, 105–97; Drummond in *CAH* VII.2 1989, 178–86; Forsythe 1994, 266–72; and Cornell 1995, 242–56. Two important treatments of patricians and plebeians in the larger context of the struggle of the orders are Raaflaub in Raaflaub 1986, 198–243, and Raaflaub in *Bilancio Critico* 1993, 129–57, which contain valuable additional bibliography.

middle republic the patriciate comprised the following nineteen clans: Aemilii, certain Claudii, Cloelii, Cornelii, Fabii, Folii, Furii, Julii, Manlii, Nautii, certain Papirii, Postumii, Quinctii, Quinctilii, Sergii, Servilii, Sulpicii, Valerii, and Veturii. The plebeian order was quite heterogeneous and consisted of at least three major social subgroups: (1) a destitute rural proletariat; (2) independent and self-sufficient peasant farmers in the countryside and artisans in the city; and (3) rich and prominent families, whose members aspired to the same religious and political offices and high social status enjoyed by patricians. At the beginning of the republic the patricians were supposed to have monopolized positions of power (the consulship, the senate, and all religious offices), whereas the plebeians began with nothing except the right to vote. During the course of the struggle, through political agitation and confrontation, the plebeians gradually won concessions from the patricians and eventually attained legal equality, emancipation from harsh economic conditions, and access to high office.

There can be no doubt that the early Roman population was periodically plagued by indebtedness and food shortages; that before the take-off in Roman expansion during the later fourth century B.C. opportunities to acquire, own, and work land to support oneself might have been limited within Roman territory; and that by the middle of the fourth century B.C. the exclusive group of patrician families had been forced to share high office with aristocratic plebeians. At the same time, changing military, political, and administrative conditions resulted in the creation of new institutions and the adaptation of old ones. The late annalistic tradition, however, explained all early Roman internal problems, legislation, and institutional innovations in the same monotonous terms. Every development was described as a consequence of the plebeians' contending with the patricians. Though this late annalistic thesis has generally recognized problems—it is simplistic and stereotypical, and has anachronistic elements borrowed from the social, political, and economic conditions of the late republic—it has nonetheless been adopted with only minor modifications by most modern scholars. Three important points can be made and should always be kept in mind when analyzing aspects of this tradition. First of all, in many modern accounts of the early republic, the struggle between the two orders is described as a single sustained social movement, beginning with the first secession of the plebs in 494 and ending about two hundred years later in 287 B.C. with the passage of the Hortensian Law; the ancient tradition, however, depicts conflict between the two orders as beginning as early as the interregnum between the reigns of Romulus and Numa Pompilius and as lasting at least as late as the Hannibalic War.[8] Secondly, in view

8. On this important point see Forsythe 1994, 266–68 with Ungern-Sternberg in Raaflaub 1986, 353–78; Hölkeskamp 1988b, 299–306; and Ungern-Sternberg in Eder 1990, 91–102.

of the fact that this process is thought to have lasted about two hundred years, Raaflaub (1986, 198–201) is correct to protest against regarding Rome's internal social and political history during this period as having conformed to a single uniform pattern. We should indeed not assume that the nature of social conflict in 500 B.C. was more or less the same as it was in 400 or 300 B.C. Moreover, events which the later annalistic tradition related in terms of the struggle of the orders could have been unconnected to one another; and different segments of Roman society are likely to have had their own specific grievances and goals, which makes a unifying account suspect. Thirdly, apart from the consular *fasti,* the Law of the Twelve Tables, and a bare outline of key events, the fifth century B.C. in Roman history resembles a dark age whose void the later Roman tradition filled with stories and interpretations that must be critically evaluated.[9]

In 367 B.C., when the office of military tribune with consular power was finally abolished and replaced by the reinstatement of the consulship as the state's highest office, the elite families (both patrician and plebeian) seem to have agreed that henceforth the two consular positions would be filled every year by a member from each order, but as things turned out, this power-sharing arrangement was not consistently implemented until 342 B.C. For the succeeding 170 years, at the consular elections plebeian candidates competed for one position, and patrician candidates competed for the other. But as several patrician families gradually faded into obscurity or actually became extinct, and as there were always plebeian families endeavoring to establish themselves in Roman politics, by the beginning of the second century B.C. this power-sharing arrangement was quickly becoming outmoded. Consequently, in 172 B.C. for the first time two plebeians were chosen consuls, and henceforth the earlier sharing of the consulship was abandoned.

During the last three centuries B.C. the distinction between patricians and plebeians within the Roman ruling class primarily affected certain specific offices. The plebeian tribunate and aedileship could be held only by members of plebeian families, whereas the priesthoods of the rex sacrorum and the three major flamens (of Jupiter, Mars, and Quirinus) and the office of interrex had to be filled by members of patrician clans. The priestly colleges of the pontiffs, augurs, and the *decemviri sacris faciundis* were composed of roughly equal numbers of both groups, and there was equal power sharing with respect to the offices of curule aedile, consul, and censor. The modern reader should therefore not be misled by the pejorative connotation of "plebeian;" and it also must be understood that in later times patrician was not synonymous with noble. The latter term had a very specific meaning in Roman society. During the middle and late republic, a noble was

9. For amplification of all these points, see Raaflaub in *Bilancio Critico* 1993, 129–37.

anyone who was descended from someone who had held the consulship, and the Roman nobility comprised all such descendants (Shackleton Bailey 1986 with Burckhardt 1990). Thus, from the middle of the fourth century B.C. onwards, when the consulship was equally shared between members of the two orders, both patrician and plebeian families comprised the Roman nobility, and the patricians formed only a part of it, a part that gradually diminished in size with the passage of time, but which continued to enjoy great prestige and political prominence.

Finally, before addressing the apparent discrepancy between the early consular *fasti* and the late annalistic tradition, it seems best to explain first the peculiarities of Roman nomenclature. From at least the third century B.C. onwards, Roman men bore two and often three names: a *praenomen* or first name, a *nomen* or clan name, and (optionally) a *cognomen* or surname. The first of these was bestowed upon a newborn child by the parents, often repeating the *praenomen* of the father or grandfather. In later times only seventeen such names were commonly used. These were generally abbreviated by one or more letters: A. = Aulus, Ap. = Appius, C. = Gaius, Cn. = Gnaeus, D. = Decimus, K. = Kaeso, L. = Lucius, M. = Marcus, M'. = Manius, N. = Numerius, P. = Publius, Q. = Quintus, Ser. = Servius, Sex. = Sextus, Sp. = Spurius, T. = Titus, and Ti. = Tiberius. The clan name usually ended in *-ius* (e.g., Fabius, Cominius) and in theory it indicated that all bearers of the name could trace their descent back to a common ancestor, although (as argued above concerning the Etruscan origin or descent of Tarquinius Priscus, see p. 100–101) in some instances a clan name could be simply invented or borrowed. The Latin word for clan was *gens* (plural *gentes*); fellow clan members were termed *gentiles;* and in modern scholarship the clan name itself is often called the *nomen gentilicium* or gentile name. Since substantial numbers of people often shared a clan name, surnames (*cognomina*) were used to distinguish one branch or group within a clan from another. These surnames often endured generation after generation, especially among aristocratic families where name recognition with a voting public was important. For example, the Cornelii, the most prolific patrician clan of the Roman republic and the most successful in attaining high office, consisted of several collateral branches, each having its own distinctive *cognomen*: Cornelius Cethegus, Cornelius Dolabella, Cornelius Lentulus, Cornelius Scipio.

Before World War II modern scholars generally adopted one of two approaches to the problem posed by the early consular *fasti*. Some scholars, such as K. J. Beloch (1926, 12–22 and 43–52), accepted the view that the patricians had a monopoly of the consulship before 366 B.C., and they therefore regarded the names of plebeian clans in the early list as forgeries inserted into the *fasti* to glorify the history of plebeian noble families. The problem with this approach is that it places complete faith in the late annalistic tradition, which was developed long after the events described, and upon this basis it sweeps aside as forgeries a substantial number of names included in the early list of consuls. A second, less drastic, and more promising approach was to assume that the presumed plebeian clan names actually represent homonymous patrician clans that had died out before later historical times, leaving no other trace of their existence. This hypothesis would permit us to accept as accurate both the ancient tradition and the early consular *fasti;* and in fact, that patricians and plebeians could share the same clan name is shown by the cases of the Papirii and the Claudii.

Patrician Papirii are attested from the late fifth century B.C. to the early second century, and plebeian Papirii are known from the early second century B.C. onwards. The patrician Claudii were prominent throughout republican and imperial times; the family's first consulship belongs to the year 495 B.C. Likewise, from the time of their first consulship (332 B.C.), the plebeian Claudii Marcelli were an eminent Roman noble family of the republic and early empire. Although these two prominent families bore the same clan name, epigraphic evidence indicates that the name was quite common in various parts of Italy from early times, suggesting that the two Roman families were not actually connected by blood. The Etruscan form of the name (*Klautie*) was inscribed on a red-figure kylix dating to the late fifth century B.C. found in a grave at the Etruscan settlement of Aleria on Corsica (Heurgon in Jehasse 1973, 551); and the name also occurs in an Oscan inscription from the Mamertine community of Messana in Sicily (Buck 1904, 369 #63) dating to the early third century. An inscription on a tomb dating to the third century at Caere indicates that the tomb contained the remains of a family of Etruscan Claudii (Pallottino 1969, 79). The Claudii Marcelli can perhaps be regarded, then, as having descended from one or more non-Roman persons of that name who migrated to Rome from a Latin community during the fourth century B.C.

The same can be conjectured for T. Veturius Calvinus, the plebeian consul of 334 and 321 B.C. Although all other Veturii who held public office in Rome during the republic were patricians, he alone was a plebeian; but since a silver cup from the Bernardini Tomb at Praeneste dating to the middle of the seventh century B.C. is inscribed with the name Vetusia, we may likewise suppose that Veturius was not an uncommon clan name in early Latium, and the consul of 334 and 321 B.C. was not related to the patrician Veturii, although he shared their name. Yet despite the usefulness of this hypothesis of extinguished patrician clans in explaining some of the aberrant names in the early consular list, it hardly seems applicable in all cases. For example, Genucii, Minucii, and Sempronii appear in the consular *fasti* of the fifth century, and members of plebeian clans bearing these same names held the consulship from the fourth century B.C. onwards. Rather than concluding that these were fifth-century patrician clans which died out, it is more reasonable to suppose that these three families enjoyed prominence during the fifth century but failed to become part of the patriciate, and then reemerged again in the fourth century as important plebeian clans in the new nobility.[10]

Since World War II, one important trend in the study of this problem has been to take seriously the possibility that the late annalistic tradition was wrong about a patrician monopoly of the consulship from its inception to 366 B.C., and to regard the non-patrician names in the consular list as both reliable and genuinely non-patrician (see Bernardi 1945–46). This hypothesis has often been combined with an idea proposed by the Italian scholar Gaetano De Sanctis (1956, vol. 1 228–30) that, like so many other things, the patriciate was the product of historical evolution, and the group of families which composed it did not become a closed, exclusive body until some time during the early republic. E. J. Bickermann (1969, 402–7) reinforced the plausibility of this idea by pointing out its similarity to much-better-documented cases of self-defined closed ruling oligarchies in the free communes of late medieval Italy. Consequently, De Sanctis's concept of the closing of the patriciate (*la serrata del patriziato*) has been widely accepted and has been applied by various scholars to the surviving data in attempting to determine exactly when the patriciate came into being. Indeed, an evolutionary approach to the question of the patriciate's origin receives support from both the ancient literary tradition and archaeology.

Ancient writers connected the patriciate to membership in the senate during the regal period, portraying the patriciate as comprising the families who had enjoyed senatorial status under the kings. Moreover, since the size of the senate was supposed to have been expanded in stages by the kings' enrolling new members from additional families, the patriciate too was thought to have come into being through these same stages of augmentation. Romulus was depicted as having created the senate and patriciate at the same time, by appointing the senate's first one hundred members (Livy 1.8.7 and Dion. Hal. 2.8.1–3). Another one hundred or fifty new members were added when the Sabines under King T. Tatius were incorporated into the Roman state (Dion. Hal. 2.47.1 and Plutarch *Rom.* 20.1). King Tullus Hostilius

---

10. Despite Cic. *Brutus* 62 and Livy 4.16.3, I have deliberately left out of consideration *transitio ad plebem* as a possible means of explaining the anomalies in the early consular *fasti*. Such an explanation seems to be an obvious case of trying to solve one difficult problem by recourse to an even more problematic issue. Although occasionally invoked in modern scholarship, *transitio ad plebem*, a legal procedure by which a patrician could legally give up his patrician status and become a plebeian, is poorly understood and has not received much serious scholarly attention. The sole exception is an unpublished Bryn Mawr College dissertation of 1993 by Matthew Slagter entitled Transitio Ad Plebem: The Exchange of Patrician for Plebeian Status, in which the author argues that the earliest possible case of *transitio ad plebem* detectable in the surviving ancient sources involved C. Servilius, the praetor of 218 B.C.

included others when Alba Longa was destroyed and its elite families were absorbed into the Roman aristocracy (Livy 1.30.2 and Dion. Hal. 3.29.7). Tarquinius Priscus increased the size of the senate from two hundred to three hundred by enrolling another one hundred new members (Livy 1.35.6 and Dion. Hal. 3.67.1). After the downfall of Tarquinius Superbus, the senate again received new members, with the enrollment of people from well-to-do families which had previously not enjoyed senatorial status (Livy 2.1.10–11 and Dion. Hal. 5.13.1). It was believed that this last measure did not actually increase the size of the senate but simply brought it back up to three hundred members, as it had been before the murderous purges of Tarquin the Proud. Although this scheme was clearly the product of later antiquarian reconstruction, it may embody a basic truth: namely, that from very early times until *la serrata del patriziato*, the Roman aristocracy was socially fluid and receptive to outsiders, including Latins, Sabines, and Etruscans. The theory receives support from the ancient tradition that in 504 B.C. Appius Claudius migrated to Rome from the Sabine territory and not only was given land and citizenship (as were his large number of clients) but was accepted into the patriciate (Livy 2.16.3–5 and Dion. Hal. 5.40). It should, however, be stressed that if this were so, the patriciate as such must not have yet existed, because the one thing that distinguished the patriciate from other aristocracies was the fact that it was a closed group of specific families which did not admit newcomers. Thus, the tale of Appius Claudius the Sabine can be taken as evidence for the openness of the Roman aristocracy in the early years of the republic.

Archaeological excavations during the past few decades have revealed, through the discovery of numerous rich graves, that during the seventh century B.C. Latin communities underwent major social and economic changes resulting in the formation of elite groups, which can be assumed to have functioned as local ruling aristocracies. Moreover, the important study of C. Ampolo (1976–77) has shown that horizontal social mobility was a common feature of the cities of southern Etruria during the archaic period, as indicated by the ethnically diverse names of Larth Telicles, Rutile Hipukrates, and Tite Latine. We may surmise with justification that the same horizontal mobility was happening in Rome and Latium. Given the substantial economic growth and other concomitant changes accompanying state formation in central Tyrrhenian Italy during the archaic period, there also must have been considerable vertical social mobility. Consequently, social fluidity is likely to have been the general rule during the seventh and sixth centuries B.C. Evidence for this is offered by the names of the seventeen original rustic tribes of the Roman territory, dated by tradition to the mid-sixth century. All but the Clustumina have names that seem to derive from clans. In fact, seven of them (Aemilia, Claudia, Cornelia, Fabia, Papiria, Sergia, and Voturia) are the names of patrician clans prominent in

Roman affairs from the fifth century B.C. onwards. Three other names (Horatia, Menenia, and Romilia) are attested in the consular *fasti* only during the early republic and thus seem to represent clans that enjoyed considerable prestige during the fifth and fourth centuries but then died out. The remaining six names (Camilia, Galeria, Lemonia, Pollia, Pupinia, and Voltinia) are not otherwise attested and therefore may have been the names of clans that were sufficiently prominent to lend their names to divisions of the Roman territory during the sixth century but then faded into obscurity. Ampolo (1975) has provided further support with a case study of horizontal social mobility involving an Etruscan family's integration into early Roman society. By using three inscribed wine pitchers, one from the Portonaccio sanctuary at Veii and two in a tomb dating to the early sixth century B.C. near Vulci, all three bearing the Etruscan name *Avile Acvilnas* (= Latin Aulus Aquillius), Ampolo has argued persuasively that the C. Aquillius Tuscus recorded as consul for 487 B.C. was of Etruscan origin. A principal question to answer, then, is at what point an inner group of the Roman aristocracy set itself apart from other prominent families and succeeded in becoming the closed and exclusive patriciate.

The approximate date of this phenomenon is perhaps indicated by three characteristics of the consular *fasti* of the late fifth century B.C. The first of these relates to fluctuations in the number of new clans attaining high office (i.e., the consulship or consular tribunate) for the first time over the course of the fifth century B.C. The variation for the entire period of the early republic covered in this book is illustrated in figure 6. The x-axis is treated as a time-line from 509 to 260 B.C. with each unit representing a decade: 500s = 509–500, 490s = 499–490, 480s = 489–480, etc. to 260s = 269–260 B.C. The figures along the y-axis represent the number of new clan names appearing for the first time in the *fasti* for that particular decade. For the ten decades spanning the years 359–260, following the restoration of the consulship and its annual sharing by patricians and plebeians, there was a total of twenty new clans, thus averaging about two new clans per decade. This figure is about the same for the middle republic; and since there were twenty consuls elected within a ten-year period, this would work out to be 10 percent. On the other hand, since before 172 B.C. one consular position every year was reserved for a patrician, there were only ten available consular openings for new plebeian clans each decade. Consequently, the average figure for new clans reaching the consulship for the period 359–260 B.C. should be taken as 20 percent.[11]

11. Although the possibility exists that the consular *fasti* did not closely reflect major political trends (cf. Badian 1990, 411 for the period 179–49 B.C.), these data should not be ignored, for they may offer an important consideration in analyzing the political history of early Rome. For a detailed study of the phenomenon of social fluidity with respect to the Roman aristocracy for the middle republic, see Hopkins and Burton in Hopkins 1983, 31–119.

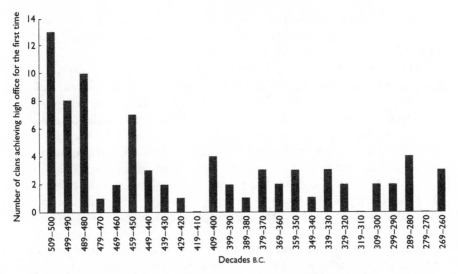

Figure 6. Chronological distribution of new clans attaining high office.

Now then, if we examine the chronological distribution of new clans reaching high office for the first time during the fifth and early fourth centuries, it is not surprising to see high figures for the first three decades (14, 8, and 10 respectively), since the consulship had never existed before, and thus there had never been any other consular families. Then there is only one new clan for the 470s, but two for the 460s. The decades on either side of the decemviral legislation show a significant rise: seven clans for the 450s and three for the 440s. Then there is a steady decline for the next three decades: two for the 430s, one for the 420s, and zero for the 410s. Then the numbers increase again over the next four decades: four for the 400s (all coming in the year 400), two for the 390s, one for the 380s, and three for the 370s. This last period is not actually a decade because of its shortening in the standard Varronian chronology by several years of fictitious anarchy. Nevertheless, this increase in new clans during the early fourth century is only apparent. Since six military tribunes with consular power were elected for most of these years as opposed to two consuls, the figures need to be converted into percentages for their respective decades for the sake of comparison. They then work out to be $4/49 = 8.16$ percent, $2/52 = 3.85$ percent, $1/60 = 1.67$ percent, and $3/24 = 12.5$ percent. Only the last figure comes close to the average of 20 percent for the period 359–260 B.C., and it seems noteworthy that it is for the period which immediately precedes the restoration of the consulship and the beginning of the power-sharing arrangement between patricians and plebeians. Thus, if there was a period of the early republic in which a group of aristocratic families established a firm grip on the curule magistracies, it would appear to have been the last three decades of the fifth century B.C.

This possibility is further underscored by two other characteristics of the consular *fasti* for these years. The year 423 B.C. is the last year before 366 B.C. in which the consulship is held by someone bearing a name that is known to have been exclusively plebeian in later times: C. Sempronius Atratinus. On the other hand, the 440s and 430s witness for the first time the political emergence of three patrician clans, the last three patrician *gentes* to reach high office during the early republic: a Papirius as consul in 441, a Sergius as consul in 437, and a Folius as consular tribune in 433 B.C. These two phenomena, occurring at roughly the same time, could point to the closing of the patriciate and its assertion of a monopoly on the consulship.

As can be seen from the table in chapter 8 showing the alternation between the consulship and the consular tribunate for the period 444–367 B.C. (see below p. 238–39), these years fall into three phases according to the relative frequency of the two offices. During the first twenty-four years (444–421), there are fifteen consulships and nine colleges of consular tribunes. During the next twelve years (420–409), the two offices are roughly balanced: five consulships and seven colleges of consular tribunes. But during the last thirty-seven years of this period (408–367), there were only two years in which consuls were elected (393 and 392). Consequently, the later ancient belief that the patriciate had dominated the consulship before 366 B.C. would be correct if the patriciate had finally emerged only during the waning years of the fifth century and had at that time asserted and exercised its monopoly over the consulship during the few years for which the Romans elected consuls instead of military tribunes with consular power. Conversely, if the patriciate did not emerge until the close of the fifth century B.C., then the problem of so-called plebeian names in the consular list for the period 509–445 B.C. becomes meaningless, since during that time there would have been no clear distinction between the two orders, and there should have been no major dispute among well-to-do families over issues of eligibility for the office, at least on this basis. The issue, however, would have naturally arisen and would have been a serious matter of debate when, in 367 B.C., the decision was taken to abolish the consular tribunate and to replace it with the consulship and other offices with more differentiated functions and powers. If that is how the struggle of the orders began, it would have been easy for ancient historians, writing at a much later date, to retroject this issue to the beginning of the republic when the consulship was first instituted and to make a false generalization about a patrician monopoly of the office from its inception, whereas actually exclusive patrician control had not been so extensive.

SENATORS, PATRICIANS, AND PRIESTS

Even though tenure of the consulship was crucial from the middle of the fourth century B.C. onwards in defining the Roman nobility, this does not appear to have been the sole criterion for defining the patriciate at the close of the fifth century. Since in later historical times patricians alone continued to fill the offices of interrex, rex sacrorum, and the three major flaminates, some scholars (e.g., Momigliano 1969, 23 ff., and especially Mitchell in Raaflaub 1986, 130–74) have approached the problem of the patriciate focussing on religious authority and expertise, supposing these to have been the preserve of certain elite families due to their hereditary control of priestly offices.[12] Moreover, in addition to the ancient tradition that linked the patriciate with membership in the senate under the kings, there are several other data that point to a clear early nexus involving priesthoods, the senate, the patriciate, and religious authority, indicating that the patriciate was formed out of a group of families who, besides their birth and wealth, distinguished themselves from other Roman aristocrats by their family traditions of special religious knowledge. This interpretation postulates that in early times religion was deeply embedded in Roman society, but as the society was secularized, the close bond between priesthoods and membership in the senate was dissolved and was therefore unknown to the later annalistic tradition, which viewed the early history of Rome's institutions in strictly political terms.

A curious incident described by Livy (27.8.5–10) offers important information connecting priesthoods with the senate. In 209 B.C., the patrician C. Valerius Flaccus assumed the office of flamen of Jupiter (*flamen Dialis*), second in importance in the Roman state religion only to the rex sacrorum. After becoming a flamen, Flaccus asserted that it had been the prerogative of the occupant of this priesthood to be a senator automatically. When the urban praetor challenged Flaccus on this point, the senate took up the issue and decided that, although recent occupants of the office had failed to exercise their privilege in this regard, their behavior did not invalidate Flaccus's right to reassert the ancient practice. Thus, Flaccus was permitted to become a regular member of the senate as the result of holding his priesthood. Given the great importance of his priestly office in the Roman state, the *flamen Dialis* continued to observe many superstitious restrictions (see above p. 138), which to some degree might have been applied in earlier times more generally to other priests. It therefore seems probable that, like these restrictions, *ex officio* membership in the senate had once been the

---

12. I cite here Mitchell's essay in Raaflaub 1986 as opposed to his book of 1990, because the former is a much more concise and coherent exposition of his general approach to the origin and nature of the archaic patriciate, whereas the latter, although occasionally making important amplifications of the earlier essay, is confused and confusing on many issues.

general rule for all or most priests of the state religion.[13] This hypothesis receives additional credibility from the fact that it is useful in explaining three other enigmatic features of the Roman senate: the dichotomy between *patres* and *conscripti, patrum auctoritas,* and the office of interrex.

Livy (2.1.11) and Festus (304L s.v. *qui patres, qui conscripti*) both indicate that the standard formula used to summon the senators to a meeting was "qui patres, qui conscripti estis" = "ye who are fathers, and ye who are enrolled." The distinction between these two bodies became meaningless in later times, and the formula just quoted was shortened to *patres conscripti,* a phrase often used in the ancient literature when foreign ambassadors and Roman magistrates address the senate. In early times, when they were still distinct, *patres* could have referred to those members who were automatically senators by reason of their priesthood, whereas the *conscripti* would have been members who had become senators by some other means, such as enrollment into the body by a magistrate as the result of having held a public office, or simply belonging to a prominent family of long standing.[14] The senatorial body of *patres* explains the origin of the adjective *patricius* = "patrician." Similar adjectives ending in *-icius, -aris,* or *-ius* were commonly used in later times to specify various ranks of senators: *quaestorius, tribunicius, aedilicius, praetorius, consularis, censorius,* meaning that a person's highest office held thus far was the quaestorship, plebeian tribunate, aedileship, praetorship, consulship, or censorship. Thus, *patricius* could have simply meant "one belonging to the *patres* in the senate." The collective term *patres* could have derived from the Roman habit of using the honorific title *pater* in reference to a male divinity (e.g., Liber Pater, Dis Pater, Mars Pater, Janus Pater, and Jupiter): for the same honorific term is likely to have been applied as well to the priestly officials who mediated between the gods and the Roman state. In fact, the spokesman for the priestly college of fetials, who were responsible for conducting the religious and legal solemnities surrounding the declaration of war and the conclusion of peace in early times, was termed the *pater patratus* (Livy 1.24.4–6). Although *patratus* has generally

13. Cornell (1995, 233) erroneously invokes Livy 40.42.8 in support of his claim that the rex sacrorum was forbidden to be a member of the senate. Livy simply says that in order to inaugurate Cornelius Dolabella as the new rex sacrorum in 179 B.C., the pontifex maximus first ordered him to lay down his command as duumvir navalis. The only obvious conclusion to be drawn from this fact is that the priesthood required its incumbent to reside in Rome and not to hold public offices which would require absence from the city. The same prohibition against public service abroad is known to have applied to the flamens of Jupiter and Mars. See Livy *Per.* 19 and 39.45.4.

14. Unconvincing in my view is Cornell's heavy reliance upon Festus 290L s.v. *praeteriti senatores* and his conclusion that "in early times the senate was little more than an *ad hoc* body of advisors with a constantly changing membership, not a permanent corporation of lifelong members" (Cornell 1995, 247–48). This characterization, however, could have applied in some degree to the *conscripti.*

been regarded as the perfect passive participle of the denominative verb *patrare* (= "to accomplish"), Mitchell (Raaflaub 1986, 158) has plausibly interpreted the word as a noun of the fourth declension, analogous to *senatus*. Thus *pater patratus* might have originally meant "father of the fatherhood."

Since even in later historical times sons often succeeded their fathers in holding priestly offices, there would have been in early times a pattern of sons automatically replacing their fathers in the senate as well. Given the problems of infertility, infant mortality, and a short life expectancy in ancient times, strict father-son hereditary succession in the priesthoods and senate must have been often interrupted, but if attempts were made to keep a priesthood within the clan (remember the Luperci Fabiani and the Luperci Quinctiales), entire clans could have used their priestly prerogative as a key element in defining themselves as patrician. The size of the senate during the early republic is unknown, but there were a substantial number of priests forming the Roman state religion; as *ex officio* members, they could have constituted a majority in the senate before the second half of the fourth century B.C. At that time, the increase in the number of magistracies is likely to have led to the secularization of the senate, as the prestige and importance of the priestly body of *patres* were eroded and there was an influx of senators with political and military backgrounds.

According to the later annalistic tradition, in early times all legislative enactments of a Roman assembly (curiate, centuriate, or tribal) were not valid unless they received the concurrent endorsement of the senate. The latter was termed *patrum auctoritas*. Since the word *auctoritas* can have a religious or mystical connotation, the original meaning of the phrase *patrum auctoritas* is likely to have been the sanction given by the *patres* in the senate, who were thought to embody the sum total of religious authority in the state; but as the senate became secularized, and as the distinction between *patres* and *conscripti* was blurred and became meaningless so that the term *patres* began to be used to refer to the senate as a whole, the concept of *patrum auctoritas* was likewise reinterpreted to mean that the senate exercised a general supervisory role over popular legislation (see Friezer 1959, 320–29).

The *patres* in the senate (later interpreted to mean not priests but members of patrician families) were also the ones who chose an interrex from among themselves whenever, as the result of death or abdication, the state was left without chief curule magistrates (consuls, dictator, or military tribunes with consular power). The belief was that in such cases the Roman state (or more likely, its auspices) reverted to the *patres*, who then, as it were, revived the state or curule succession through the office of interrex. There had to be at least two interreges, each holding office for five days, until consular elections were held under the presidency of an interrex, and the newly elected magistrates resumed the pattern of exercising *imperium* and *auspicia* for the Roman state. The reason the first interrex could not hold elections must have been that his tenure of the auspices was felt to be imperfect since they had been assumed *ex nihilo,* whereas his successor had received them in a proper manner from another interrex. Despite the regal character of the title, this office may have never existed during the regal period. It could have been the creation of Roman religious, political, and constitutional theorizing during the fifth century B.C. (Friezer 1959 301–20 and above p. 110). Other than those recorded for the regal period between the reigns of the kings (cf. Livy 1.17 and Dion. Hal. 2.57), the first interregnum of republican date is recorded by Dionysius (8.90.4–5) for the year 482, in which the interreges were A. Sempronius Atratinus and Sp. Larcius Flavus: the former had what is later known only as a plebeian name, and the latter belonged to a family which did not survive beyond the fifth century B.C. If this represents an authentic historical tradition, it could provide further evidence for a late fifth-century date for *la serrata del patriziato.*

THE PLEBEIAN TRIBUNATE

Next to the consulship the most important public office in the Roman state during the fifth century B.C. was that of the tribunes of the plebs (*tribuni plebis*) or plebeian tribunes,[15] but as with many other Roman institutions, we do not begin to have secure evidence about this office until the third century B.C.[16] In later times, the plebeian tribunes were ten in number, and they entered office on December 10, which in the old Roman calendar was the tenth day of the tenth month of the year. This date must have been chosen for the beginning of their official year to promote the unity of all ten tribunes. They were elected by the tribal assembly, in which citizens voted in units according to their geographical tribe. The office was usually held by young aspiring aristocrats around the age of thirty. As indicated by the fact that they were forbidden to be absent from Rome for more than twenty-four hours, their duties were confined to the city and primarily involved conducting legislative and judicial business before the assembled people. The great bulk of laws enacted by the Roman people during the middle and late republic was proposed by plebeian tribunes, usually pursuant to a decree of the senate. Before the creation of permanent criminal courts in the second half of the second century B.C., plebeian tribunes were also

15. For other discussions of the origin of the plebeian tribunate and/or the first secession of the plebs see Meyer 1895; Nestle 1927; Ogilvie 1965, 293–314; Ridley 1968; Mazzarino 1971–72; Urban 1973; Gutberlet 1985, 28–40; Drummond in *CAH* VII.2 1989, 212–27; Mitchell 1990, 131–48 and 179–84; Sohlberg 1991; Eder in *Bilancio Critico* 1993, 97–127; Forsythe 1994, 264–96; and Cornell 1995, 256–65.

16. For detailed treatment of the history and function of this office during the middle and late republic, see Bleicken 1968, 1981.

responsible for prosecuting before the assembled people any curule magistrates accused of misconduct in office. Like the two consuls and other groups of magistrates who shared equal power, a tribune had the right and power to obstruct or veto the action of another tribune (Latin *veto* = "I forbid"). But their power of veto, termed *intercessio* in Latin, also extended to decrees of the senate, as well as to the actions of other magistrates. The surviving evidence, however, suggests that tribunician *intercessio* was employed very sparingly before the politically polarized times of the late republic (see Badian 1972, 697–700). The picture of patricians using compliant plebeian tribunes in early times to exercise their veto to obstruct reformist proposals from their colleagues can be regarded as a late annalistic invention (Oakley 1997, 670). Tribunes also had the authority (termed *ius auxilii*), if they saw fit, to come to the defense of a citizen threatened with prosecution by a tribunician colleague, or with punishment or inequitable military service by a curule magistrate. In later Roman political thought the plebeian tribunes were regarded as public watchdogs and the protectors of citizens' rights.

In order to insure that they could not be intimidated or physically compelled to do things contrary to what they saw fit, the tribunes' office was invested with sacrosanctity. A plebeian tribune was regarded as *sanctus*, meaning that by law he was placed under divine protection so that, if he were physically harmed in any way, the offender would be regarded as accursed (*sacer*) to Jupiter. Someone who harmed a tribune could be killed with impunity by anyone, and his property would be confiscated and dedicated to the cult of Ceres on the Aventine (Livy 3.55.6–7 and Dion. Hal. 6.89). Despite these considerable powers, the plebeian tribunes generally worked closely with the senate and the other magistrates. In times of crisis, however, it was not at all uncommon for one or more of the tribunes to use their tribunician power to champion the cause of Roman citizens in opposing the senate and other elected officials. Indeed, from the time of the Gracchi onwards (133–121 B.C.), plebeian tribunes were frequently at the center of the political controversy, conflict, and even violence that plagued the late republic; and their familiarity with seditious tribunes promoting popular issues in opposition to the senate greatly affected how the later annalists, such as Licinius Macer, Valerius Antias, and Aelius Tubero, portrayed Roman domestic affairs during the early republic.

According to the late annalistic tradition (Livy 2.23–33 and Dion. Hal. 6.22–90), the early Roman state enjoyed internal harmony as long as it was faced with the threat of the restoration of Tarquinius Superbus, but as soon as news reached Rome of Tarquin's death in exile at Cumae, dissension arose between the senate and the people over the issues of debt and military recruitment. This discord began in 495 B.C., in the first consulship of a patrician Claudius, and continued into the following year. When the senate failed to address the question of indebtedness adequately, the people withdrew in a body from the city to the Sacred Mount (*Mons Sacer*) situated three miles away beyond the Anio north of Rome, and there they elected their own officials, two or five in number, whom they called tribunes of the plebs. In addition, they chose two aediles of the plebs (*aediles plebis*), who were to serve as assistants to the tribunes. It was also later believed that on this same occasion the people established tribunician sacrosanctity by taking an oath to punish with death anyone who physically harmed a tribune. Because this ordinance, like some other early Roman laws, pronounced the transgressor to be accursed (*sacer esto*), it was termed a *lex sacrata* (Festus 424L s.v. *sacratas leges*). Because of the threat of war with neighboring people and Rome's dependence upon the plebs for military service, the senate was compelled to agree to the plebeians' demand to be allowed to elect their own officials. The reconciliation between the senate and people was brought about by Agrippa Menenius, and the first plebeian tribunes held office during the year 493 B.C., coinciding with the dedication of the temple of Ceres, Liber, and Libera on the Aventine.

The ancient tradition of the first secession of the plebs, as well as the original nature of the office of plebeian tribune, present the modern scholar with major problems of historical interpretation. As noted above, we do not possess anything approaching a precise knowledge of the early history of this office. Our earliest reliable evidence comes from scattered events of the third century. By that time the plebeian tribunate had been in existence for two or three centuries, and had evolved into the office we know for the middle and late republic. The history of most Roman institutions was marked by both conservatism and change. The Romans of later historical times tended to think that their political and social institutions had been brought into being fully formed by one of the early kings or by a landmark statute of the early republic, and this view affected their historical treatment of institutions. This is perhaps best illustrated by the comitia centuriata, whose organization clearly betrays a long and complex historical development, but later Roman historians attributed its fully developed structure to King Servius Tullius. We are therefore equally justified in suspecting the accuracy of the ancient view of the history of the plebeian tribunate, according to which the office originated fully developed at its outset and remained unchanged for almost three centuries, down to the time when we begin to have fairly secure information about it. Moreover, it is important to realize that the earliest real evidence about this office, in the fragments of the Roman historians of the second and first centuries B.C., dates to the time of the Gracchi (133–121 B.C.), whose controversial and turbulent use of the office ushered in the political violence and polarization of the late republic and gave the plebeian tribunate the reputation of an office "born in and for sedition" (Cic. *De Legibus* 3.19).

When carefully examined, the various elements in the story of the first secession appear to be little more than later inventions designed to explain the origin and nature of the plebeian tribunate. That the dissension arose out of the consuls' attempts to raise an army serves to explain why the plebeian tribunes in later times had the power to obstruct military recruitment. Ungern-Sternberg (Eder 1990 101–2) has shrewdly observed that, although the ancient tradition included the issue of indebtedness in its account of the first secession in order to explain the origin of tribunician *ius auxilii*, the explanation makes no logical sense because tribunician *ius auxilii* could not be used to rescue a debtor from his fate, as made clear by the provisions in the Twelve Tables, (see below p. 217–218). The Mons Sacer seems to have been included in the story in order to explain the origin of the *lex sacrata* that defined tribunician sacrosanctity, but since other *leges sacratae* existed in early times, no such simple etymological explanation is necessary (contra Altheim 1940). Moreover, the famous parable attributed to Agrippa Menenius (Livy 2.32.8–12) has been borrowed from Greek literature (Nestle 1927). In fact, Menenius's involvement in the story probably stems from the fact that the Menenian tribe, one of the original rustic tribes created by Servius Tullius, was located in the area that included the Sacred Mount (Forsythe 1994, 281–82). Even the date of the first secession looks suspicious. It began in 494 B.C. and ended in 493, thus allowing the first plebeian tribunes and aediles to enter office in the same year as the dedication of the temple of Ceres on the Aventine. The coincidence is similar to the one whereby the Capitoline temple of Jupiter Optimus Maximus was dated to the first year of the republic and the first consulship, instead of the third year of the republic as recorded by Dionysius (3.69.2 and 5.35.3) and Tacitus (*Hist.* 3.72). A close connection in the early historical tradition between the dedication of Ceres' temple and the creation of the plebeian tribunate is further suggested by several ancient sources, which say that the first secession was to the Aventine rather than to the Sacred Mount (Forsythe 1994, 280–81). This connection is likely to have stemmed from the fact that in the *lex sacrata* establishing tribunician sacrosanctity Ceres was mentioned as the goddess who was to receive the confiscated property of anyone who broke the law. As the goddess of the earth and the underworld in early Roman religion, however, Ceres was typically included in *leges sacratae* as the divine recipient of the property of the condemned. Furthermore, since Ceres was a goddess primarily concerned with grain and agriculture, her temple must have been placed on the Aventine because foreign trade was conducted in this area, and even in early times that trade could have included the importation of foodstuffs. The plebeian aediles became closely associated with Ceres' temple because one of their primary duties was to oversee practices in the Roman marketplace and to watch over the city's grain supply, but this need not mean that the creation of the plebeian aedileship coincided precisely with the dedication of Ceres' temple.

A likely source for the Roman tradition of the first secession of the plebs is Greek folklore associated with the cult of Demeter in Sicily. The group worshipped at the Aventine temple, Ceres, Libera, and Liber, was patterned after the Greek triad of Demeter, Persephone, and Iacchus (often misconstrued as Bacchus-Dionysus and hence equated with Roman Liber). According to Dionysius (6.17.3), the temple was vowed by the dictator Postumius in 496 B.C. after the Sibylline Books had been consulted for advice concerning a food shortage or a bad harvest. Since Livy has followed a different tradition concerning the battle of Lake Regillus (see 2.21.3–4), he does not mention the consultation of the Sibylline Books at this time, but their advice would account for the Roman importation of the Greek divine triad. Pliny (*NH* 35.154) informs us that the temple of Ceres was decorated with paintings which bore the signatures of Greek artists, Gorgasus and Damophilus; and Cicero (*Pro Balbo* 55) indicates that some of Ceres' sacred rites there were conducted by a priestess of Demeter who was brought in from one of the Greek colonies of southern Italy. Thus it seems likely that Greek lore associated with this cult must have been known to the Romans from an early date. In fact, the plebeian aediles' responsibility for preserving texts of laws in Ceres' temple must have stemmed from a common Greek misinterpretation of Demeter's epithet, "Thesmophoros," as meaning "lawgiver" (Forsythe 1994, 284 with n. 40).

In describing how the people of mainland Greece sought military assistance from Sicily in 480 B.C. to oppose the Persian invasion under King Xerxes, Herodotus (7.153) tells a curious story concerning an ancestor of Gelon, the tyrant of Syracuse who received the ambassadors from the Greek mainland. Gelon's family was from the Greek colony of Gela, and at some time in the distant past a man named Telines had used powerful religious rites of Demeter and Persephone (rites whose nature was unknown to Herodotus) to bring back into the city of Gela a group of political exiles who had taken refuge at a place called Macterium, situated in the hill country near Gela. As a result of his successful reintegration of these political exiles into the community, Telines' descendants were honored with the privilege of a priesthood of Demeter and Persephone. The story looks very similar to that of the first secession, in which the reconciliation was brought about by Menenius Agrippa, and the powerful rites of the Greek goddesses have their Roman counterpart in the *lex sacrata* that created tribunician inviolability. But how or why would the Greek tale of Gelon's ancestry have found its way into the Roman historical tradition?

T. P. Wiseman (1995, 129 ff.) has argued convincingly that many of Rome's early historical traditions were created, propagated, accepted, and reshaped from the middle of the fourth century B.C. onwards through dramatic stage performances, enacted before the Roman people at the time of annual celebrations such as the Liberalia of March 17 and the *Ludi Romani* of early and mid-September. To be sure, myth, ritual, and drama often went hand in hand in the ancient Mediterranean world. Myth was often created to explain ritual, and a myth was frequently acted out as a play at the time of important religious festivals, to honor the gods and to give meaning to the religious celebration. Given the strong Greek associations of the cult of Ceres on the Aventine, it seems likely that the *Ludi Ceriales*, which were celebrated for several days in mid-April to mark the anniversary of the temple's dedication on April 19, regularly included the enactment of myths or stories connected with the worship and cult of Demeter and Perse-phone. Furthermore, since the cult was introduced into Rome at about the time that Gelon became tyrant of Syracuse, one tale associated with the cult from early times could have been the one told by Herodotus as a tribute to Gelon's ancestry, involving civil discord, a secession of part of the citizens, and a reconciliation brought about by one man with the use of purificatory and chthonic rites of Demeter. The tale might have been used to explain the goddess's epithet, "Thesmophoros," interpreted to mean "lawgiver," which would have been appropriate for the tale of Telines ending civil dis-cord in Gela. It is even possible that this story was depicted in a fresco painted by Gorgasus or Damophilus in their decoration of Ceres' Aventine temple. Note that Damophilus's name means "friend of the people."

In any case, the story of Telines and Gela could have been Romanized and reinterpreted by the Romans of the late fourth and third centuries B.C. to explain the origin of the Aventine temple and its close association with the plebeian tribunes and aediles. In fact, according to one ancient com-mentator (Pseudo-Asconius p. 217 Stangl), the *Ludi Plebeii*, celebrated every year with both stage performances and chariot races spread over several days in early and mid-November, were instituted either after the expulsion of the Tarquins to commemorate the establishment of liberty or after the secession of the plebs to commemorate the reconciliation. Since these games were probably not established until the late third century B.C., the explanations are clearly false, but they may indicate that dramas concern-ing the downfall of the monarchy and the secession of the plebs were regu-larly performed at these games and formed an integral part of the celebration's political ideology in later Roman society. It would not have been difficult for the dramatic enactment of an alleged episode in early Roman history to become regarded as a charter myth for the games them-selves. Consequently, the first secession of the plebs should not be accepted as historical.

Once we realize that the origin of the plebeian tribunate should be divorced from the dedication date of the Aventine temple of Ceres, we may reasonably suppose that no secure later ancient tradition existed concerning the date and circumstances surrounding the creation of this office. The annalistic tradition for the events of the fifth century B.C., as seen in the accounts of Livy and Dionysius, contains very few names of plebeian tribunes, and many of the ones recorded (e.g. Icilius and Siccius or Sicinius) are fictitious doublets or even triplets of a single authentic name (Forsythe 1994, 291–94 and below p. 207–208). This shows that, unlike the eponymous consuls, no official list of plebeian tribunes was kept for this early period, or if there ever was such a list, it did not survive into later historical times to be used by ancient historians.

As already mentioned, various aspects of the plebeian tribunate indicate that the office was urban and civilian, whereas the original nature of the consulship seems to have been extra-urban and military. This distinction corresponds precisely to the important concept of *domi militiaeque* (= "at home and abroad") encountered in Roman public law. It therefore appears that these two offices were originally intended to complement one another, and this idea is further supported by the fact that, like the consuls, the plebeian tribunes were at first only two in number, and they had two plebeian aediles to assist them. The later ancient tradition, which has generally been accepted by modern scholars, overlooked these obvious facts, because the creation of the plebeian tribunate was viewed in the context of the struggle of the orders between patricians and plebeians, and was thought to have come into being through revolution. The latter notion (and hence, the modern view of a plebeian state within the state) is likely to have been the product of a later ancient tradition shaped by contemporary political history rather than by the authentic history of the early fifth century B.C.[17] The "revolutionary" explanation for the origin of the plebeian tribunate is quite extraordinary and therefore historically improbable, but it is also unnecessary. A simpler and much less sensational one is possible and seems more likely. The plebeian tribunate was created along with or shortly after the consulship, and the two offices were deliberately designed to complement one another. In the course of time, however, social and political changes in the Roman state led to the plebeian tribunate's being mythologized in terms of the struggle between patricians and plebeians. The emergence of the patriciate during the late fifth and early fourth centuries B.C. had the effect of dividing Roman society into two distinct castes. Non-patrician prominent families were included among the remaining populace, the plebs, henceforth considered to be separate from the patricians. The increase in the number of annually elected plebeian tribunes from two to five and then to ten caused the office to be diminished in prestige relative to the consuls or consular tribunes. As in later historical times, several of the ten annual positions of plebeian tribune must have been filled by members of the less

---

17. Cf. Livy 2.24.1 and 2.44.9 with Cic. *De Re Pub.* 1.31, *Amic.* 41, and *De Legibus* 3.19–20.

prominent families of the Roman aristocracy. This could have caused the office to be avoided by patricians. The latter, instead, defined themselves by their tenure of priesthoods and of curule offices which, unlike the plebeian ones, were more in accord with aristocratic values as offering the potential of military glory to the official and his family.

THE TRIBAL AND OTHER ASSEMBLIES

The second major event in the early history of the plebeian tribunate recorded in the later annalistic tradition (Livy 2.54.3–58.2 and Dion. Hal. 9.37–49) came twenty years after the first secession of the plebs, and involved the creation of a tribal assembly for electing plebeian officials.[18] Livy, however, in his characteristic manner, has not bothered to explain fully the alleged constitutional issues. He so concentrated on individual personalities in order to achieve maximum dramatic effect that his account is confusing and logically incoherent, whereas Dionysius's ponderous verbosity and fondness for detail more accurately reproduce the narrative of the late annalists and help to explicate Livy's heavily edited version. The sequence of events can be briefly summarized as follows. A plebeian tribune of 473 B.C. named Cn. Genucius attempts to prosecute Furius and Manlius, the consuls of the previous year, but on the day appointed for the trial the tribune is found dead in his house. Dionysius (9.38) suggests that Genucius's death was providential, but Livy (2.54.9–10) portrays the tribunes as suspecting the patricians of murder and as being alarmed for their own safety despite their sacrosanctity. After a plebeian named Volero Publilius is nearly brutalized by the consuls' lictors and stirs up the plebs during an abortive military levy, he is elected tribune for 472 and proposes to replace the curiate assembly with a tribal one for electing plebeian officials. Having failed to secure the bill's passage, Publilius is reelected tribune for 471 with a staunch supporter named C. Laetorius. Their tribunate coincides with the second consulship of a patrician Claudius. The two tribunes succeed in carrying their proposal into law despite the fierce opposition of this consul, Ap. Claudius. In addition to the creation of the tribal assembly, according to one ancient version of these events, the year was also significant in marking the increase in the number of plebeian tribunes from two to five.

Like the first secession, serious questions of historicity also surround the ancient tradition concerning these events of 473–471 B.C. The circumstantial details and the names of the tribunes Genucius, Publilius, and Laetorius

---

18. The comitia curiata and comitia centuriata have already been discussed in chapter 4. They are now treated here in conjunction with the tribal assembly. For the subject of the Roman assemblies during republican times, consult Botsford 1909; Taylor 1966; Staveley 1972, 119–216; and Nicolet 1980, 207–316. For a thorough treatment and analysis of the history of the tribes and their role in Roman politics, see Taylor 1960.

are not above suspicion. The only item with the appearance of solid authenticity is the creation of the tribal assembly. Genucius's mysterious death on the eve of his prosecution of the former consuls is obviously patterned after the sudden death of Scipio Aemilianus in 129 B.C., the night before he was scheduled to address the people on the controversial issue of granting citizenship to the Italian allies (Appian *Bell. Civ.* 1.20, and Plutarch *C. Gracchus* 10.4–5). In addition, Volero Publilius's reelection as tribune with Laetorius as his political ally is clearly a late annalistic invention, modeled after the second tribunate of C. Gracchus with M. Fulvius Flaccus in 122 B.C. (Appian *Bell. Civ.* 1.22–24), or possibly Saturninus's reelection as tribune while his political associate Servilius Glaucia was praetor (Appian *Bell. Civ.* 1.28, cf. Sallust *Bell. Iug.* 37.1–2). Consecutive reelection to the plebeian tribunate does not seem to have occurred before 133 B.C., when it was attempted by Ti. Gracchus as a desperate measure to protect himself from his political enemies (Appian *Bell. Civ.* 1.14, and Plutarch *Ti. Gracchus* 16.1), but reelection to the office was not uncommon thereafter. Finally, since the better documented events of the second half of the fourth century have a plebeian tribune Genucius ending a serious sedition by the passage of laws in 342 B.C. (Livy 7.42), followed three years later by the consul and dictator Q. Publilius Philo securing the passage of three other laws believed to have been favorable to the plebs (Livy 8.12.15–16), we may justifiably suspect that these events and personalities of the early fifth and late fourth centuries B.C. have been somehow confused, or used by later ancient historians to supplement their account of the earlier episode with material from the later one. In fact, two of the three laws attributed to Publilius Philo in 339 B.C. involve the power and procedure of the tribal and centuriate assemblies.

Nevertheless, despite some serious doubts about the historicity of these events, the one possible solid fact in the ancient tradition could be the creation of the tribal assembly. Further fruitful analysis of the annalistic tradition is perhaps best offered concerning the consular date rather than the names or actions attributed to plebeian tribunes. The passage of the Publilian Law creating the tribal assembly was regarded as the second major landmark in the early history of the plebeian tribunate, and was supposed to have occurred in the second consulship of a patrician Claudius (471 B.C.). Similarly, the controversy over indebtedness that led to the first secession of the plebs was thought to have begun during the first consulship of a patrician Claudius (495 B.C.), and during this same year the number of the tribes was supposed to have been increased from nineteen to twenty-one by the addition of the Claudia and Clustumina (Livy 2.21.7 and Taylor 1960, 35–37). In addition, both the years 495 and 471 were described as having seen conflict between a consul Claudius and a plebeian named Laetorius (Livy 2.27.6 and 2.56.6–15). The later annalistic accounts of the increase in the number of Roman tribes in 495 and of the creation of a tribal assembly in 471, both during Claudian consulships, appear to contain doublets of a single event. That both were also related to the plebeian tribunate is perhaps due to the latter's association with the tribal assembly. The ancients would have us believe that the tribes were increased to twenty-one in 495, but that a tribal assembly did not come into being until twenty-four years later. This could, of course, be explained by assuming that the tribes were initially used for purposes of census registration and taxation, and were only later employed as voting districts, but the occurrence of these two important events in the first two Claudian consulships is more likely to be a historiographical phenomenon than a historical coincidence. It therefore seems likely that in later times it was known or remembered that a major reform in the tribes and/or the creation of the tribal assembly had occurred during the consulship of a Claudius. The Cassian Treaty with the Latins (Livy 2.33.9) is another example of a key event of the early republic dated by a single consul.

Like the comitia curiata and the comitia centuriata, the tribal assembly organized the votes of individual Roman citizens into units based upon some criterion. In this case, it was the geographical tribe of Roman territory in which the adult Roman male resided. As indicated by Livy 2.21.7, before Rome's conquest of Veii in the early fourth century B.C. the tribes numbered twenty-one, but in 387 B.C. four new tribes were created out of the newly acquired Veientine territory (Livy 6.5.8). Over the course of the next 146 years, the Romans periodically organized additions to Roman territory into ten more new tribes; they always added them in pairs so as to keep their number odd, in order to prevent ties in the tribal assembly's electoral results. Once the tribes reached the total of thirty-five, in 241 B.C., their number was never increased further. In later historical times this assembly elected all the non-curule officials of the Roman state; like the comitia centuriata, it also had the power to enact laws, usually proposed by plebeian tribunes. It even exercised judicial powers for non-capital offenses of a public nature in which the aediles or tribunes acted as the prosecuting officers. Thus during republican times, there existed three different assemblies of the Roman citizen body, of which the comitia curiata was the oldest; but in later times this one had become a vestigial organization, convoked periodically simply to witness adoptions and wills or to ratify the *lex curiata* that empowered consuls and praetors to take the auspices in the field. The other two assemblies, the tribal and centuriate, probably came into being during the early years of the republic and exercised important electoral, legislative, and judicial powers throughout its history. There is, however, a central problem concerning the tribal assembly's composition and terminology. Modern interpretations on this issue have largely centered around the following passage, quoted by Aulus Gellius (15.27.4) from a legal treatise written by Laelius Felix dating to the first half of the second century of our era:

> He who orders not the entire people (*populus*) but some part thereof to be present ought to proclaim not a *comitia* but a *concilium*. Moreover, tribunes neither summon patricians nor have the power to propose anything to them. Thus, measures which are accepted on the proposal of the plebeian tribunes are not properly called laws (*leges*) but plebiscites. Patricians were not bound by these bills until the dictator Q. Hortensius [287 B.C.] carried that law whereby all the Quirites were bound by whatever the plebs had determined.

The distinction between *comitia* and *concilium, populus* and *plebs* made in this passage alone, dating to the middle of the principate, long after the Roman assemblies of the republic had ceased to function, has become the cornerstone of a modern orthodoxy, according to which there must have existed not one, but two different tribal assemblies: a *comitia populi tributa* that comprised both patricians and plebeians, and a *concilium plebis tributum* which included plebeians alone (see Staveley 1955, Develin 1975, and Ridley 1980b). A corollary to this modern thesis is the notion that the plebeians of the early republic formed a state within the state. This interpretation of the tribal assembly, however, though widely accepted, has no support in the extensive writings of Cicero and Livy, who must have been far more knowledgeable in these matters than Laelius Felix of the middle empire. Botsford (1909, 119 ff.) demonstrated long ago that Laelius Felix's distinction between *comitia* and *concilium* simply does not hold up. *Comitia* was a word used by Latin writers to describe formal assemblies (curiate, centuriate, and tribal) convoked into their constituent units to vote on legislative, electoral, or judicial matters. The word was also commonly used to mean "the elections." *Concilium,* on the other hand, was a generic term referring to any kind of public meeting of citizens, including both *comitia* and *contio.* The latter was a meeting summoned by a Roman magistrate in which no voting took place, but some issue of public business, such as a legislative proposal, was openly debated in order to inform the public of the issue before the matter actually came to a vote. It must also be stressed that the supposed technical terms, *comitia populi tributa* and *concilium plebis tributum,* are artificial modern constructions and have no authority in ancient texts. The ancients speak only of a comitia tributa, just as they do of a comitia curiata and a comitia centuriata. In fact, in describing the proposal of the plebeian tribune Volero Publilius to create a tribal assembly for electing plebeian officials, and then the actual use of this assembly in elections for the first time, Livy (2.56.2 and 2.58.1) simply employs the words comitia tributa to designate the body concerned.

Thus, despite general acceptance of the modern orthodoxy, it seems more likely that there existed in republican times a single tribal assembly, which was known as the comitia tributa. It also seems rather dubious that until the passage of the Hortensian Law of 287 B.C. the patricians, who formed the inner group of the Roman aristocracy, were completely exempt from all legislative enactments of the tribal assembly. This later ancient view is likely to be a distortion of a fundamental constitutional principle of the early republic: namely, that all legislative enactments (curiate, centuriate, and tribal) were not valid unless accompanied by a concurrent vote of *patrum auctoritas*. The belief that *populus* represented the entire citizen body, both patricians and plebeians, whereas *plebs* did not encompass the patricians, was a later and erroneous ancient notion. This might have been the view of many patricians and even some plebeians as early as c. 400 B.C., when the patriciate emerged as an exclusive group of families within the aristocracy; and on the basis of this belief, many patricians from the fourth century onwards might have deliberately avoided voting in the tribal assembly. Yet just as the original distinction between the tribunes and the consuls concerned urban vs. extra-urban affairs (*domi* vs. *militiae*), the original distinction between *plebs* and *populus* is likely to have been civilian vs. military, each term referring to the entire citizen body in two different capacities. This hypothesis receives additional support from the fact that the city's sacred boundary, the pomerium, which formed the juristic border between the two spaces designated in the phrase *domi militiaeque*, determined the venues of the tribal and centuriate assemblies. The former always met inside the pomerium, whereas the comitia centuriata was convened outside it, in the Campus Martius.

As suggested by the terms *magister populi* (= master of the army) and the verb *populor* (= "lay waste"), the *populus* referred to the citizens under arms and hence to the comitia centuriata, which elected the consuls for waging war and voted on war and peace. This interpretation is further reinforced by an entry in Festus 224L s.v. *pilumnoe poploe*, in which the latter archaic Latin phrase, meaning "the *populus* armed with javelins [= *pila*]," is cited from the hymn of the Salii and clearly refers to the Romans under arms. *Plebs*, however, referred to the citizen body organized not according to military units but simply on the basis of their residence; and this body, the comitia tributa, elected the officials whose duties were non-military and confined to domestic affairs. A corresponding dichotomy between "the men armed with spears" and "the men not armed with spears" is attested in the religious texts from Iguvium in Umbria.[19] Similarly, just as the military levy of the early Roman state was termed the *legio*, so the enactments of the *populus* formed into the comitia centuriata were called *leges*, whereas those

19. See *Tab. Iguv.* VI.B 62, VII.A 13, 15, 28, and 50, where Umbrian *iouies hostatir, anostatir* = Latin *iuniores hastati et non hastati*.

of the *plebs* organized into the comitia tributa were known as *plebiscita*. Finally, since in later times the tribal assembly was organized simply by tribes and did not have the timocratic structure and voting order of the comitia centuriata, the former would have been more democratic than the latter; but if membership in the tribal assembly was originally contingent upon one's inclusion within the state's military structure as embodied in the centuriate organization, the difference may not have been all that great in early times, before the comitia centuriata came to be differentiated into five classes and included the *proletarii* in a single century.

Since we possess no reliable information concerning the powers and function of the comitia curiata during the regal period, we cannot know how, to what extent, or in what ways the creation of the centuriate and tribal assemblies brought about major constitutional restructuring of the Roman state and redistribution of powers and functions. It seems obvious that laws must have been enacted or customs developed in the course of time to define precisely what each of the three different assemblies could and could not do. Moreover, since in later historical times laws could be enacted by either the tribal or centuriate assembly, there must have been an early law or custom which maintained that each of these bodies was equally sovereign. This conjecture may help to explain one of the three laws attributed to the dictator Q. Publilius Philo of 339 B.C. (Livy 8.12.15), according to which "plebiscites were to be binding upon all the Quirites." When the tribal assembly was first created, it might have been necessary to spell out in a statute that the enactments of this new body (*plebiscita*) had the same validity and binding force as those made by the *populus* in the centuriate assembly (*leges*), and this legislative act could have been carried by a tribune named Publilius, thereby accounting for the Publilian Law which Roman historians dated to 471 B.C. Moreover, if the events of that year were later confused with those of 342–339 as argued above, the earlier tribunician Publilian Law could have been transferred to the much more famous Q. Publilius Philo.[20]

Given the extraordinary influence and power exercised by the Roman aristocracy in early times, we may conclude with confidence from the procedure of the *lex curiata* confirming the authority of the early kings and the consuls that legislative enactments of both the tribal and centuriate assemblies during the early republic likewise required a concurrent vote of *patrum auctoritas* in order to become valid laws. Such a configuration of political power, in which major public decisions were frequently arrived at by agreement between an aristocratic council and a citizen assembly, was typical of Greek city-states during the archaic period. Its presence in early Rome would therefore not be at all surprising, and it would also account for

---

20. For an alternative explanation of this Publilian Law of 339 B.C., together with the similar Hortensian Law of 287 B.C. and one of the three Valerian Horatian Laws of 449 B.C., see below p. 231ff.

the periodic political contention between the senate and the people and their respective representatives, which the later Roman annalists amplified into the struggle of the orders.

It should come as no surprise that both Livy and Dionysius offer explanations for the creation of the tribal assembly in 471 B.C. in terms of the struggle of the orders. Livy (2.56.3) says that the Publilian Law was designed to deprive the patricians of their complete power to choose the plebeian tribunes by suborning the votes of their clients in the comitia curiata. Dionysius (9.41.2–5 and 9.49.5), on the other hand, sees the law as weakening patrician influence by eliminating the need to obtain *patrum auctoritas* before convening the curiate assembly. Livy's explanation makes no sense in the context of the struggle of the orders: since the patricians' clients were presumably plebeians, they would have been included in the tribal assembly too, and could have continued to vote in accordance with their patrons' wishes there. Dionysius's explanation makes more sense, but it may not be anything more than some later annalist's shot in the dark to account for the innovation. Given the archaic nature of the comitia curiata, which is supposed to have been the body that elected plebeian officials before the creation of the tribal assembly, the procedure of the *lex curiata de imperio* could have been taken to show that the comitia curiata's electoral decisions had to be accompanied by *patrum auctoritas*, but such confirmation was not necessary for the decisions of the new comitia tributa. On the other hand, since one of the three laws attributed to the dictator Q. Publilius Philo of 339 B.C. ordained that a vote of *patrum auctoritas* was to precede measures laid before the centuriate assembly (Livy 8.12.15), Dionysius's reason for the establishment of the tribal assembly in 471 B.C. might have been excogitated by some ancient historian on the pattern of this later Publilian Law. As a result, neither Livy's explanation nor Dionysius's may be accepted as satisfactory. Instead, we may conjecture that the comitia curiata was quickly becoming an obsolete organization as Rome developed into a sizable city-state with a rather fluid population. Organizing a new assembly on the simple principle of geographical residence in Roman territory would have been a sensible and rational policy in adjusting a major political institution to fit new demographic conditions.

ROME AND THE LATINS

Down to the Latin War of 340–338 B.C., Rome's foreign affairs were to a significant degree centered upon its relationship with the other communities of Latium.[21] Although the Latins lived in numerous autonomous towns

---

21. For Rome's relations with the Latins in early times, see Alföldi 1965, 10–46, 101–22, and 236–87; Sherwin-White 1973, 3–37; Ampolo in *Crise et Transformation* 1990, 117–33; and Oakley 1997, 332–44. For the archaeological evidence from Lavinium, see Holloway 1994, 128–41, which contains additional bibliography.

such as Rome, Lavinium, Ardea, Aricia, Lanuvium, and Nomentum, they were bound together by a common language and cultural tradition, and from early times this commonality resulted in the creation of interstate cooperation in religious, political, and military affairs. The ethnic unity of the Latins as a whole found clear expression in their participation in communal religious rites conducted every year at Lavinium and on the Alban Mount (Dion. Hal. 1.67 and 4.49). Excavations at Lavinium have uncovered a series of large *u*-shaped altars, which must have been the central focus of Latin religious activities at the site. These thirteen altars range in date from the mid-sixth century to the late third century B.C. We may therefore surmise that a religious league comprising all Latins was already in existence during the second half of the sixth century B.C. Pliny (*NH* 3.68–9) reproduces a long list of peoples who at one time participated in the Latin Festival (*Feriae Latinae*), held every spring in honor of Jupiter Latiaris on the Alban Mount, the modern Monte Cavo, the highest point in Latium. Most of these names are obscure and must have pertained to small communities which no longer existed in later historical times, having been destroyed, abandoned, or absorbed into the larger towns of Latium.

In addition to these shared religious activities, the Latin communities also shared important social, economic, and political rights. These were later codified in Roman law as *commercium, conubium,* and *ius migrandi.* The first of these allowed a Latin of one community to own property in any other Latin town and to conduct commercial transactions without hindrance, as if he were a citizen of the community. *Conubium* was the right of a Latin of one state to enter into a marriage with a Latin from any other state without legal complications. The third of these rights allowed a Latin of one state to take up residence in any other Latin state, automatically becoming a full citizen of the community in which he resided. Although these shared rights were expressive of the social fluidity of archaic society, they were never abolished but were put to new uses by the Romans in later times and formed an important legal institution by which non-Romans were integrated into the Roman social and political system. The three rights were later collectively known as the *ius Latii* and were retained by the Roman state after its dissolution of the Latin League in 338 B.C. From that point onwards, the Romans applied this Latin status to colonies founded throughout Italy, which served as important outposts for the Roman state in strategic areas; and the Latin colonists, termed *socii nominis Latini* ("allies of the Latin name"), formed a class which was intermediate between Roman citizens and other Italian allies. Latin status, however, continued to be used in imperial times as an instrument of acknowledging and promoting Romanization. It formed a halfway stage between foreign and Roman status, and was granted to

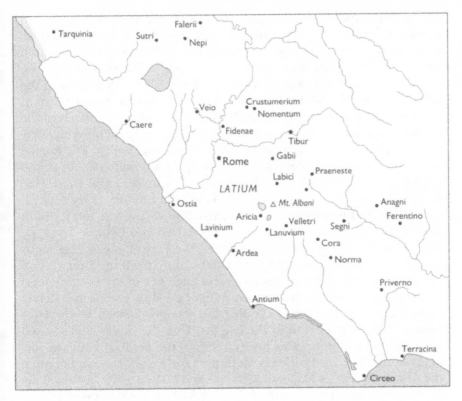

Map 8. Latium.

provincial communities to upgrade them as they became more Romanized. Thus, besides its vital role in Rome's early history, Latin status
enjoyed a long and fruitful history and was a key element in Rome's later
imperial success.

Despite the importance of these shared religious and legal institutions
among the early Latins, the single most significant aspect of Latin communal activity for the history of the fifth century B.C. was military cooperation against common foreign threats. The battle of Aricia fought in 504 B.C.
had pitted the Etruscans under Porsenna and the Romans against the
other Latins aided by the Greeks of Cumae. The latter's victory caused
Porsenna to abandon Rome, and for the next few years there was an uneasy
peace in Latium until, in either 499 (Livy 2.19–20 with 21.3–4) or 496
(Dion. Hal. 6.2 ff.), the Romans and Latins fought a battle at Lake Regillus
near Gabii. According to the Roman tradition, Tarquinius Superbus was
arrayed on the side of the Latins, in hope that a victory would bring his
restoration to royal power in Rome, but when the Romans proved victorious,

he went into exile at the court of Aristodemus in Cumae, where he died in 495 B.C. Consequently, this battle was later viewed as crucial in establishing republican freedom, and it therefore received elaborate treatment in later Roman historical accounts (Forsythe 1994, 258–64). The narrative of the battle itself was patterned in part after a famous event among the western Greeks, the battle of the Sagra River, fought between the Locrians and Crotoneates of southern Italy during the sixth century, in which the heavily outnumbered Locrians inflicted a crushing defeat upon the Crotoneates thanks to the divine assistance of Castor and Pollux. The Roman adaptation was used to explain the vowing of a temple to Castor and Pollux by the Roman dictator Postumius (Livy 2.20.12 and Dion. Hal. 6.13). The temple was dedicated on January 27 in 484 (Livy 2.42.5). Recent excavations have confirmed that the shrine was in fact built during the early fifth century B.C. (see Nielsen and Gronne 1990, 99 and 116). It was a prominent feature of the Forum, measuring 90 by 125 feet. Three columns and their entabulature from the later version of the temple are still standing today and form one of the Forum's most notable landmarks. Given the association of the divine twins with horses and cavalry, the battle of Lake Regillus was proclaimed by the later Romans to have been won by the knights. Thus the victory that secured republican freedom became integrated into the political and civic ideology of the Roman equestrian class, perhaps as early as 304 B.C. when the censors Q. Fabius Maximus Rullianus and P. Decius Mus instituted the Transvectio Equitum (Parade of the Knights), celebrated every July 15 (Livy 9.46.15).

The battle of Lake Regillus was soon followed by a treaty between Rome and the Latins, the *Foedus Cassianum,* which took its name from one of the consuls of 493 B.C. (Livy 2.33.4). With his characteristic lack of interest in such mundane details, Livy does not bother to record the provisions of this agreement but is content merely to note that the treaty was concluded. Dionysius (6.95.2), on the other hand, describes it as having contained the following conditions:

1. They are not to wage war upon one another, nor are they to introduce other parties into the land with the intent to wage war, nor are they to grant safe passage to any such outside parties.
2. In times of war they are to aid one another with all their forces, and there is to be equal sharing of the booty captured in their joint operations.
3. Disputes arising out of contracts made between persons from two communities are to be settled within ten days in the community in which the contract was made.
4. Nothing is to be added to or subtracted from this agreement without the consent of both the Romans and the Latins.

The historicity of these terms in the context of the early fifth century B.C. has been long debated by modern scholars (see Alföldi 1965, 114 with n. 1). Some have objected to the bilateral character of these terms, Rome vs. all the other Latins, as granting Rome too much influence for the early fifth century, although if eastern and southern Latium had already been over-run by the Aequians and Volscians, Roman territory might have constituted half of the area occupied by the Latins, and such a bilateral arrangement could have been appropriate. On the other hand, if the text paraphrased by Dionysius goes back to a document dating to the first years of the republic, it would be as old as the first treaty with Carthage and the inscribed text of the *cippus* of the *lapis niger* from the Comitium, whose language was extremely archaic and would have posed a considerable problem of inter-pretation to later Roman writers, a circumstance which Dionysius fails to mention. According to Cicero (*Pro Balbo* 53), the archaic text of the Cassian Treaty was still to be seen in full public view down to his own day, not far from where the *cippus* of the *lapis niger* stood: "Who does not know that in the consulship of Sp. Cassius and Postumus Cominius a treaty was struck with all the Latins, which, we recall, till recently was inscribed and written out on a bronze column behind the Rostra?" But was the Cassian Treaty of 493 B.C. the only alliance made between Rome and the Latins? Livy (7.12.7) indicates that at least one other treaty was signed with the Latins, in 358 B.C.: "but amid many causes of alarm there was solace in the peace granted to the Latins at their request, and a large body of soldiers was received from them in accordance with the old treaty which they had allowed to lapse for many years." Whether or not we choose to accept Dionysius 6.95.2 as accu-rately reflecting the terms of the Cassian Treaty, the political and military situation in Latium during the early fifth century B.C. would lead us to con-clude that the Romans and other Latins formed themselves into a military alliance against common external threats, and that given the size of Roman territory relative to the other Latin states (see above p. 116), Rome was the main, if not the dominant, member of this coalition.

One question which the provisions listed by Dionysius do not address concerns the supreme command of the league forces. The narratives of both Livy and Dionysius portray the relationship between Rome and the other Latin states during the fifth century B.C. as like Rome's relationship to its Latin colonies during the third and second centuries B.C.: i.e., they rep-resent Rome as the ruling power of Italy, exacting military quotas to serve Roman expansion and able to command obedience from subservient and much weaker Latin communities. In the later annalistic tradition, the Latin forces are combined with those of Rome and are invariably led by Roman consuls or consular tribunes. Rome's unchallenged leadership of the Latin League was even retrojected into the regal period, from the reign of Tullus Hostilius onwards (Alföldi 1965, 101–11). One passage, however, from

Festus (276L s.v. *praetor*), quoting Cincius, the antiquarian of the late republic, hints at a very different situation:

> The Albans controlled affairs until King Tullus. Then after Alba had been destroyed, down to the consulship of P. Decius Mus (340 B.C.) the Latin peoples were accustomed to deliberate at Caput Ferentinae, which is below the Alban Mount, and to administer the command (*imperium*) by common counsel. Consequently, in a year in which by order of the Latin nation the Romans were required to send commanders to the army, several of our countrymen were accustomed to observe the auspices on the Capitol in the direction of the rising sun.

This text makes it clear that before the dissolution of the Latin League command of the combined Latin forces was a matter for common deliberation. On various occasions Rome was asked to provide leadership, but the implication is that other states also sometimes supplied the league army with supreme commanders. This situation certainly must have prevailed during much of the fifth century B.C., when Volscian and Aequian incursions to the south and east made the non-Roman area of Latium the central focus for military operations. Rome must have emerged as the dominant power as these threats to Latium diminished,, but in the fifth century this development still lay in the future.

The Volscians and Aequians posed a major threat to Latium during the fifth century B.C. Rome, however, by reason of its location and the size of its territory was most suitably placed to ride out this storm. Rome's own most serious threat initially came from the Sabines, who dwelled upstream along the Tiber and, like the Volscians and Aequians, attempted to expand downstream toward the coast. By the middle of the fifth century, the Romans had checked the Sabine expansion and were poised to expand their own borders, first at the expense of Fidenae, and then across the Tiber against Veii. The Aequians overran the part of Latium bordering the upper Anio River. Although Tibur and Praeneste were prominent rivals to Rome within the Latin League during the fourth century B.C., they are never mentioned in ancient accounts of the fifth century and therefore might have been taken over by the Aequians during the fifth century (Oakley 1997, 338). It may be significant in this regard that in later times the Latin spoken at Praeneste had its own distinctive characteristics (Coleman 1990). The Volscians occupied the Leppini mountain range and the coastline between Terracina and Antium, which Rome had claimed in the first treaty with Carthage.[22]

The Volscian and Aequian infiltration into Latium was part of a larger demographic phenomenon affecting central and southern Italy during the

22. For fuller treatment of the Volscians, see Coarelli in *Crise et Transformation* 1990, 135–54.

fifth and fourth centuries B.C., in which the Sabellian-speaking tribes of the Apennines migrated down from the mountains and overran and occupied the lowlands. According to the ancient tradition, these major movements of peoples resulted from overpopulation or famine and took the form of a ritual termed *ver sacrum* ("sacred spring"), in which all humans and animals born in the springtime were dedicated to a divinity. The animals were sacrificed; the children were allowed to live, but when they reached mature years, they were driven out of the community and forced to find new land in which to settle.[23] Since an immediate problem of overpopulation could not be solved by this means, seeing that it required fifteen or twenty years for the human offspring to grow to maturity, the sacred spring must have been an institution structured into the society of mountain tribes and periodically employed on a fairly regular basis over generations, in order to forestall overpopulation in agriculturally poor areas which could not support expanding numbers. In addition to converting virtually all of southern Italy into an Oscan-speaking region, these movements threatened and sometimes actually overwhelmed the Greek cities of Bruttium, Lucania, and Campania (see Hdt. 7.170). By the end of the fifth century B.C., the Oscan-speaking element in Campania was substantial and had resulted in the Oscan takeover of Etruscan Capua and of Greek Cumae (Livy 4.37.1–2 and 4.44.12; Diod. 12.31.1 and 12.76.4 with Rutter 1971, Cornell 1974, and Frederiksen 1984, 137–39).

The Volscian and Aequian migrations must have been very disruptive to the society and economy of Latium, especially during the first half of the fifth century, and Rome might have drawn a benefit from these disturbances in the form of Latin immigrants coming to Rome from more seriously threatened communities. Indeed, if we possessed more onomastic information from the other Latin towns, we might discover that such immigration is reflected in the clan names which appear in the early consular *fasti*. Aequian and Volscian infiltration into Latium might also have been responsible for an economic downturn in Rome during the fifth century B.C. J. C. Meyer (1980) has conducted a careful study of Attic black-figure and red-figure pottery imported into Rome and several Etruscan cities during the sixth and fifth centuries B.C., and has tabulated the fluctuations in twenty-five-year segments. During the sixth century, Rome and the other Etruscan cities conform to the same pattern of increased rates of imported pottery, with Rome and the three major coastal cities of southern Etruria (Caere, Tarquinii, and Vulci) reaching their highest rates during the last quarter of the sixth century. During the fifth century, however, these same

---

23. See Dion. Hal. 1.16, Strabo 5.4.12, and Festus 150L s.v. *Mamertini*. The principal modern treatment is Heurgon 1957; cf. Salmon 1967, 35–36 and Dench 1995, 181 ff.

sites imported less Attic figured pottery. Rome exhibits by far the greatest drop-off of any site during the first quarter of the fifth century B.C., followed by Vulci, and then by Caere and Tarquinii to a slighter extent. Inland cities of Etruria (Falerii, Volsinii, and Clusium) continued to increase their rate of imported pottery during the first part of the fifth century, but by 450 B.C. they too were beginning to have declining levels. Meyer has suggested that the particularly sharp decline in Rome's importation of Attic figured pottery during the first part of the fifth century resulted from an abrupt weakening of Roman power in Latium. According to Meyer, the power struggle between Rome and the other Latin states following Porsenna's seizure of Rome might have facilitated Volscian occupation of the coastline from Terracina to Antium, the area once claimed by Rome in the first treaty with Carthage. Veii could also have exploited Rome's difficulties with the other Latins at the same time, by establishing control over the mouth of the Tiber. In any case, as Ampolo has acutely argued (Eder 1990, 484 ff.), since the construction of temples in Rome in later times was always a function of profitable warfare, the virtual cessation of temple construction after 484 B.C. might indicate that for the remainder of the century Rome's wars were not lucrative as they had previously been, during the late sixth and early years of the fifth centuries B.C.

The Roman annalistic tradition described military engagements between the Latins and the Volscians or Aequians for virtually every year of the first half of the fifth century B.C. It seems likely that brief notices of such activity were preserved by the Roman pontiffs in their annual records of the chief events of the Roman state, but the record of this military activity has become so contaminated in later historical accounts, which narrate it in terms of the warfare of the middle and late republic—with frequent set battles, legionary formations, and castrimentation—that little credence can be attached to the detailed descriptions of Livy and Dionysius. Much of the warfare probably consisted of raids and counterraids resulting in the carrying off of captives and booty and skirmishing between the two sides, occasionally punctuated by major campaigns and engagements. In addition to this kind of incessant and indecisive fighting, the Latins attempted to strengthen their overall strategic position by establishing Latin colonies on newly acquired or reclaimed territory adjacent to the enemy. Here again, the annalistic notices of such foundations are likely to be historical, but the particular details surrounding them, such as domestic political debate in Rome over agrarian legislation, cannot be accepted as authentic. The Latin colonies recorded for the early republic, before the dissolution of the Latin League in 338 B.C., are the following:[24]

---

24. Many of these colonies were situated on easily defensible high ground and were fortified with stone walls. For descriptions of their sites and ancient remains, consult Coarelli 1982.

501: Pometia and Cora (Livy 2.16.8)
498: Fidenae (Dion. Hal. 5.60.4)
495: Signia (Livy 2.21.7)
494: Velitrae (Livy 2.31.4 and Dion. Hal. 6.42.3–43.1)
492: Norba (Livy 2.34.6)
467: Antium (Livy 3.1.1–7 and Dion. Hal. 9.59.2)
442: Ardea (Livy 4.11 and Diod. 12.34.5)
418: Labici (Livy 4.47.6–7)
401: Velitrae (Diod. 14.34.7)
395: Vitellia (Livy 5.24.4 and 5.29.4; Suet. *Vitellius* 1.3)
393: Circeii (Diod. 14.102.4)
385: Satricum (Livy 6.16.6)
383: Sutrium (Vell. Pat. 1.14.2) and Nepet (Livy 6.21.4)
382: Setia (Vell. Pat. 1.14.2)

The overall character of these events as the annalistic tradition portrayed them is perhaps best illustrated by the famous exploits of Marcius Coriolanus (Livy 2.33.4–40.11 and Dion. Hal. 6.92–8.62, with Salmon 1930). The tale may have a kernel of historical truth and derive from an authentic tradition concerning the high-water mark of the Volscian irruption into Latium at the beginning of the fifth century. Much of this military success could have been led by a native Volscian commander named Marcius associated with the town of Corioli, hence his surname Coriolanus. In the later Roman historical tradition, however, this apparently native Volscian commander has been transformed into a courageous and capable Roman who, because of his intransigent stance toward the Roman plebs, was driven into exile and led the Volscians to their greatest victories. His surname was explained as resulting from his first act of recorded bravery, before his exile, during the Roman capture of Corioli. Thus, while retaining the basic truth that the Volscians initially enjoyed considerable success against Rome and the Latins, the annalistic tradition preserved Roman national pride by ascribing this success to the fact that the Volscians were led by a Roman. The same pattern of chauvinistic historical revisionism is offered by the case of Tyrtaeus in Greek history. This lyric poet of Sparta, famous for the martial verses he composed during the Second Messenian War of the seventh century B.C., was later transformed by the Athenians into a lame schoolmaster of Athens, brought to Sparta in order to provide the Spartans with the military discipline and leadership needed to subdue their rebellious serfs (Pausanias 4.15.6).

Two other aspects of the Coriolanus story are significant in disclosing how early Roman traditions were generated. Because the two men were near contemporaries, the career of the Athenian Themistocles was mined to add further details to that of Coriolanus (see Cic. *Brutus* 41–43, *ad Att.* 9.10.3, and *Amic.* 42). The former had been the chief architect of Athens's naval policy and thereby of the Greek victory over the Persians in 480 B.C., but not long after Xerxes' invasion of Greece and the Athenian establishment of the Delian League, Themistocles, like Aristeides before and Cimon after him, was officially ostracized by the Athenian people and was therefore obliged to be absent from Athens for a period of ten years. During his exile, however, Themistocles was accused of plotting with the Persians. He fled from Greece before he could be apprehended, and was eventually appointed by the Persian king as lord over several cities of Asia Minor, where he lived out the rest of his life. Thus Themistocles' career represented to the ancients the pattern of reversal of fortune, as well as a signal example of the fickleness and ingratitude of the Athenian democracy. The latter theme was well-suited for the concept of the struggle of the orders, and Coriolanus was accordingly depicted as a Roman aristocrat of fine qualities who was victimized by popular boorishness.

The tale of Coriolanus reaches its patriotic climax when the Roman exile, encamped with the Volscian army near the city of his birth, haughtily rejects peace proposals made to him by Roman officials but yields when confronted by his mother, wife, and two children. Thus, like the stories of Lucretia, Cloelia, and the Sabine women who forced the Romans and Sabines under Romulus and T. Tatius to make peace, the tale of Coriolanus concludes with a patriotic model of behavior for Roman women. This element of the story was probably brought in to explain the origin of the cult of Fortuna Muliebris. According to the ancient tradition (Livy 2.40.11, Dion. Hal. 8.55–56, and Val. Max. 1.8.4), the temple to this divinity was established by the Romans to commemorate the women's success in making Coriolanus withdraw the Volscian army from Roman territory; the temple was supposed to have been built at the place where the women had performed this heroic deed. Fortuna Muliebris is likely to have been a goddess concerned with women and childbirth, and her association with the story of Coriolanus must have stemmed from the fact that the temple's day of dedication was July 6, one day after the Poplifugia of July 5. The latter was an archaic ritual involving the purification of the Romans (probably under arms) and the symbolic routing of their enemies (Forsythe 1994, 322–30). The literal meaning of the ceremony's name, "the routing of armies," must have spawned speculation that these two consecutive days in the official Roman calendar were somehow related, and resulted in the explanation that women had played a key role in turning back the Volscian invasion led by Coriolanus.

SP. CASSIUS, THE FABII, AND THE CREMERA

The nine years 486–478 B.C. contain three important events involving both domestic and foreign affairs of the Roman state: the third consulship of Sp. Cassius, followed by his trial and execution; seven consecutive years in which one of the consuls was a Fabius; and the disastrous Roman defeat at the hands of Veii, at the Cremera River. In 486 B.C. Rome and the Latins were supposed to have formed an alliance with the Hernicans, a people who dwelled in the Trerus River valley (Livy 2.41.1 and Dion. Hal. 8.69.2). Their principal towns were Anagnia, Ferentinum, Aletrium, and Verulae. Since they were situated between the Aequians and the Volscians, such an alliance must have been advantageous to both the Latins and the Hernicans, and we therefore need not doubt the historicity and early date of this alliance; but its assignment specifically to the year 486, the third consulship of Sp. Cassius, might not be authentic. Since Cassius's name was associated with the treaty concluded in his second consulship of 493 between Rome and the Latins, it could have seemed appropriate to later writers to attach the Hernican alliance to his third and final consulship.

Sp. Cassius's third consulship, however, was notorious for his proposed agrarian legislation and his attempt to become tyrant (Livy 2.41 and Dion. Hal. 8.69–80, with Gabba 1964 and Forsythe 1994, 296–301). This was supposed to have been the first time that an agrarian law was proposed by a Roman politician, as well as the first of three attempted seizures of power during the early republic. The other two attempts were ascribed to Sp. Maelius in 440–439 and to M. Manlius Capitolinus in 385–384 B.C. By Cicero's day, these three men had become the canonical demagogues of early Rome, and their actions, interpreted in light of contemporary civil violence, were used to justify the state's strong measures against the Gracchi, Saturninus, Catiline, and others (Mommsen 1871 and Lintott 1970). The extant evidence suggests, however, that the tradition of these demagogues already existed before Gracchan times. The idea of attempted tyranny in fifth-century Rome is historically plausible (Martin in Eder 1990, 49–72). Drews's study of tyranny in archaic Greece demonstrates how an ambitious aristocrat could exploit a local crisis in a developing city-state to make himself its sole ruler (Drews 1972). The alleged seditions of Sp. Cassius and Sp. Maelius were contemporary with the Deinomenid tyranny in Syracuse, Aristodemus's usurpation at Cumae, and the autocracies of Thefarie Velianas at Caere and of Lars Tolumnius at Veii. On the other hand, the historicity of the Roman traditions is not easy to assess, since all three are heavily laden with elements of folklore and etiological appendages. Scholars must carefully examine the ancient material and decide for themselves whether the *aitia* spawned the creation of the tale or were merely later accretions about a hard kernel of historical fact.

Livy and Dionysius seem to follow the same author in describing Sp. Cassius's consulship of 486 and his trial and execution in the following year, and their narratives contain obvious post-Gracchan elements. Like Ti. Gracchus's agrarian bill, Cassius's proposal to divide the public land among the plebs is described as having been opposed by rich and powerful *possessores*

(Plutarch *Ti. Gracchus* 8–10 and Appian *Bell. Civ.* 1.7–12). Cassius's advocacy of the Latins and Hernicans and his colleague's opposition resemble C. Gracchus's proposal to extend Roman citizenship to the Italians and the opposition mounted by the consul C. Fannius (Plutarch *C. Gracchus* 12.1–2 and Appian *Bell. Civ.* 1.23). Cassius's proposal to distribute money to the plebs to purchase Sicilian grain is clearly patterned after C. Gracchus's grain law (Appian *Bell. Civ.* 1.21 and Plutarch *C. Gracchus* 5.2). Both Livy and Dionysius set forth the same version of Cassius's prosecution by two quaestors for *perduellio* and his condemnation by a *iudicium populi*, and they both also retail the same alternative account, according to which he was tried and executed by his own father. Their common source was probably Valerius Antias, who may have been responsible for inventing the story of Cassius's trial by quaestors since one of them was a L. Valerius, and the trial seems to have been patterned after the notorious trial of Rabirius by *duumviri perduellionis* in 63 B.C. (see Cic. *Pro Rabirio Reo Perduellionis*). A post-Sullan source is clearly implied by Dion. Hal. 8.80, which contrasts the senate's refusal to punish Cassius's three sons with Sulla's treatment of the sons of the proscribed. If Antias was the author of the version involving the quaestors, the story of Cassius's execution by his father must have been the earlier prevailing explanation for his death. This account could have been contrived as early as the Hannibalic War as a conservative's monitory antecedent for the episode in which the plebeian tribune, C. Flaminius, proposed his controversial agrarian law and his father unsuccessfully attempted to use paternal authority to prevent its passage (Cic. *De Inventione* 2.52, Val. Max. 5.4.5, Dion. Hal. 2.26.5, cf. Polyb. 2.21.9). Since Sp. Cassius was thought to have been the first Roman politician to propose an agrarian bill, his untimely death was clearly intended to be a warning to any who wished to adopt a similar program.

The one solid artifact at the heart of the ancient tradition concerning Sp. Cassius's thwarted ambitions was an archaic bronze statue dedicated to Ceres, which remained in existence until 158 B.C. when the censors melted it down, along with many other statues (Pliny *NH* 34.30, citing the historian Calpurnius Piso). There were two different interpretations of this statue. One was that it represented Cassius himself, and was testimony to his tyrannical ambitions (Pliny ibid.). The other view, found in Livy and Dionysius, was that it was made from the proceeds of the sale of Cassius's property and was dedicated to the goddess Ceres. It was further maintained that Cassius's house was demolished, and the site lay unoccupied until the temple of Tellus (= the Earth), vowed by the consul P. Sempronius Sophus in 268 B.C., was built on the site (see Florus 1.14.2). It was not uncommon for a temple in Rome to be built on a site previously occupied by a sacred grove or open-air precinct. It is therefore possible that Tellus's shrine was built upon such an area sacred to the same goddess. Moreover, since Tellus and Ceres were closely associated in Roman cult, and since Sp. Cassius had dedicated Ceres' Aventine temple, a member of the Cassian family could have set up a statue to Ceres at this open-air site sacred to Tellus, and this image, associated with both Ceres and the Cassian name, could have formed the kernel of the legend of Sp. Cassius's tyrannical ambitions, his ill-fated demise, the demolition of his house, and the site's consecration to Ceres. The story of this statue would have satisfied the ancients' fondness for the paradoxical reversal of fortune: for Sp. Cassius, who had dedicated Ceres' temple on the Aventine, suffered an ignominious death which led to the consecration of his property to the same goddess.

Finally, the precise location of Tellus's temple is not known, but it was somewhere in the district of the Carinae on the Esquiline (Cic. *ad Q. Fr.* 2.3.7 and 3.1.4, and Dion. Hal. 8.79.3). The two main streets of this area were the Vicus Cuprius (= Good Street) and the intersecting Clivus Orbius. The latter was also known as the Vicus Sceleratus (= Criminal Street), and its name was usually explained with reference to King Servius Tullius's daughter driving her carriage over the body of her murdered father, but the street's proximity to Tellus's temple must have played a key role in the development of the legend about the republic's first alleged instance of criminal political ambitions as well. We may therefore conclude that there is nothing truly worthy of credence in the tradition of Sp. Cassius's execution for harboring unwholesome ambitions.

During each of the seven years 485–479 B.C., one of the two consuls was a Fabius. Such domination of the consulship by a single family is unparalleled in the consular *fasti* of the republic. There are several instances in which two brothers hold the consulship in two consecutive years (e.g., Baebii Tamphili in 182–181 and Popillii Laenates in 173–172 B.C.), and there are only three instances in which members of the same family hold the consulship for three consecutive years (330–328 by the Plautii, 247–245 by the Fabii, and 51–49 B.C. by the Claudii Marcelli). The only other pattern that comes close to the seven consecutive Fabian consulships occurs at the very beginning of the republic, when four of the five years 508–504 B.C. have a Valerius as consul (this excludes the Valerius of 509 as fictitious). The series of seven Fabian consulships becomes even more intriguing when it is noted that this is the first appearance of the Fabii in the *fasti*, that the other consul in three of these years is a member of another clan making its first appearance, and that these three, like the Fabii, are members of clans which later became very prominent patrician families: the Cornelii, Aemilii, and Manlii. It therefore looks as if some kind of major shift in power took place during these years. Modern scholars who accept the historicity of Sp. Cassius's calamitous downfall could interpret the *fasti* of these years as reflecting the political ruin of one aristocratic group and the emergence of another. Unfortunately, as in so many other cases of Roman history before the middle of the fourth century B.C., the surviving ancient sources for this period are rarely above suspicion, and we can do little more than speculate.

Ancient writers were certainly aware of this anomalous series of Fabian consulships, and they were prepared to fill the historical void with the tragic tale of the 306 Fabii who died fighting in defense of Rome at the Cremera River.[25] As in the tale of Coriolanus, parallel events in Greek history were important in the genesis of this tradition. In 480 B.C. at the battle of Thermopylae, perhaps the single most famous battle of Greek history, a force of three hundred Spartans with a few thousand Greek allies was completely annihilated (Hdt. 7.209–31). Another event from Roman history is likely to have encouraged later Roman historians to connect the Fabian consulships of 485–479 B.C. with the heroic story of Thermopylae. Under the year 358 B.C., Livy (7.15.9–11) records that not only was the consul, C. Fabius, defeated in battle by the Etruscans of Tarquinii, but the latter captured 307 Roman soldiers and sacrificed them. The Romans, however, exacted revenge four years later. In 354 B.C. (Livy 7.19.2–3), the Romans defeated the Tarquinienses, and out of the many prisoners taken they sent 358 of the most noble back to Rome and had them beaten and beheaded in the Forum. The number of Fabii who were supposed to have been killed at the Cremera was 306, while only one male was left behind in Rome to continue the family line (Livy 2.49.4 and 2.50.11, and Dion. Hal. 9.22). This makes up a total of 307 Fabii, which is the same as the number of Romans serving under the command of a Fabius who were captured and sacrificed by the Tarquinienses in 358 B.C.

The accounts of Livy (2.50) and Dionysius (9.20–1) of the Cremera disaster of 478 B.C. make it abundantly clear that the fate of the three hundred Spartans at Thermopylae has been the literary model for this Roman tale. In Livy's narrative, the Fabii are both heavily outnumbered and surrounded. After they manage to break through the encircling enemy and take refuge on a nearby hillock, the Veientines succeed in sending forces around to their rear and attack them from higher ground, just as the Persians crossed over the mountain range and attacked the Spartans from behind (Hdt. 7.213–18). In Dionysius's version of the event, the desperation with which the Fabii fought to the death is clearly reminiscent of the ferocity exhibited by the Spartans at Thermopylae (Hdt. 7.223–27). Dionysius's parallel between the Greek and Roman stories is further underlined by the first chapter of his ninth book: for he begins it with the seventy-sixth Olympiad, the year in which Calliades was archon at Athens, and when Xerxes mounted his expedition against Greece; it was at the same time that

25. For other modern treatments of this tale and its possible historicity, see Pais 1906, 168–84; Holleman 1976; and Richard 1988, 1989, and in Eder 1990, 174–99.

the Veientines declared war upon the Romans. Parallelism between the Spartans and the Fabii is further indicated by a variant version of the latter's destruction given by Dionysius in 9.19, according to which they were wiped out when returning in a body to Rome to attend a religious ceremony. This version is clearly patterned after another famous military defeat of the Spartans: the destruction of a Spartan regiment by peltasts under the command of the Athenian Iphicrates in 390 B.C., during the Corinthian War. This disaster occurred when the Spartan unit left the fortifications of Lechaeum at Corinth and began their march back to Amyclae in order to attend the festival of the Hyacinthia (Xenophon *Hellenica* 4.5.11–17). Apparently, some late annalist, not content to leave well enough alone, was eager to display his detailed knowledge of Greek history by substituting the less known Spartan disaster for the more famous one as his model for the Fabian defeat.

Two other factors important for evaluating the historicity of the Cremera disaster are the location of the Fabian tribe and the tradition of the Day of the Cremera, the *dies Cremerensis*. Taylor (1960, 40–41) located three of the original rustic tribes on the Etruscan bank of the Tiber: the Romilia near the mouth, the Galeria farther upstream, and the Fabia even farther upstream, near Veii. Central to this reconstruction was her surmise that the tradition about the Fabian clan at the Cremera suggested the Fabian tribe's location near Veii. The conjecture is doubtless correct, but we need to ask ourselves which was cause and which was effect. Did the location of the Fabian tribe near Veii bring about an actual historical encounter between the Fabii and Veii? Or, as argued above in reference to the tale of Agrippa Menenius and the first secession of the plebs, did the tribe's location and name contribute to the creation of the Cremera legend? If the fight was a real one and not a legend, we might also regard the series of seven consecutive Fabian consulships as resulting, not from some kind of major shift in power, but from the Romans' entrusting military command in an on-going conflict with Veii to persons with important interests in the area of fighting.

In keeping with the early Roman belief in the auspicious or inauspicious nature of the individual days of the calendar, later Roman writers asserted that the Day of the Cremera was inauspicious, but despite unanimity on this point, there was no consistent tradition as to which day of the year the *dies Cremerensis* had been. One view (Livy 6.1.11, Plutarch *Camillus* 19.1, and Tacitus *Hist.* 2.91) maintained that it was the same as the Day of the Allia, *dies Alliensis*, which was in fact well known to have been July 18; one of the epigraphic calendars of early imperial times actually assigns both disasters to this day (Degrassi 1963, 208). Another view, however, was that the *dies Cremerensis* was February 13 and coincided with the day on which Rome was freed from its occupation by the Gauls (Ovid *Fasti* 2.195–96, with Plutarch *Camillus* 30.1 and Degrassi 1963, 265). It is therefore apparent that in later historical times there was no solid information concerning the *dies Cremerensis*, and that in order to fill in this gap in their information, writers borrowed from traditions associated with the Gallic capture of the city. There exist other indications that the events of 390 B.C. have been conflated with those of 478 B.C. as well: the Fabii shouldered the entire burden of the Veientine War, and members of the same family gave the Gauls at Clusium a valid excuse to turn their attack on Rome; the Fabii marched out of Rome through the Porta Carmentalis, and the Gauls ascended the Capitoline at the same spot.[26]

In addition, it should be pointed out that February 13 was the first of the *dies parentales* on which Romans (including the Fabii) were supposed to make offerings to their deceased ancestors, and it preceded the Lupercalia by only two days. As noted, the latter celebration centered around the activities of two groups of Luperci, the Luperci Fabiani and the Luperci Quinctiales. It therefore looks as if the association of the Cremera with February 13 was unhistorical but somehow involved etiological explanations for religious rites engaged in by members of the Fabian clan in mid-February. Consequently, we may conclude that in later times there existed in popular tradition the recollection of a Roman military reversal at the Cremera during the early years of the republic, but apart from this single fact nothing was securely known about it. A legend, however, was developed by having recourse to the battle of Thermopylae, the later capture of Rome by the Gauls, and the Etruscan sacrifice of 307 Roman prisoners of war in 358 B.C. The central role of the Fabii could be historical, but it is also possible that their inclusion in the story was unhistorical and resulted from the Fabian tribe's proximity to Veii, the series of consecutive Fabian consulships in the early *fasti,* and the involvement of a Fabian consul in the affair of 358 B.C.

CLAN WARFARE AND THE *LAPIS SATRICANUS*

The most historically interesting aspect of the Cremera legend has been deliberately withheld up to this point so as to be considered in conjunction with one of the most intriguing recent archaeological discoveries that has a bearing on early Roman history. While excavating on the acropolis of the ancient site of Satricum in October of 1977, archaeologists from the Dutch Institute in Rome discovered an inscribed stone embedded in the foundation of a temple dating to c. 500 B.C. The stone had apparently formed the base of some monument and had been recycled when the temple was built. Since an earlier temple dating to c. 550 had stood on the same site, the

---

26. In chapter 3 of a future collection of essays to be entitled *Concepts of Time in Roman Religion* I intend to treat the ancient traditions surrounding the Day of the Allia and the Day of the Cremera in greater detail.

inscribed stone might have come from a dedication made at that shrine some time before its destruction by fire c. 540–530 B.C. The inscription reads:

ieisteterai Popliosio Valesiosio suodales Mamartei = The companions of Publius Valerius erected to Mars

Shortly after this discovery, a volume was published containing four essays by C.M. Stibbe, G. Colonna, C. De Simone, and H.S. Versnel, which treated the archaeological, epigraphical, linguistic, and historical aspects of this find (see *Lapis Satricanus* 1980 and Holloway 1994, 142–55). A number of possibilities exist concerning the identity of this Publius Valerius: he was a citizen of Satricum; he was the famous P. Valerius Publicola of the early years of the Roman republic; or he was a man from some other community, neither of Rome, nor of Satricum. It should be noted that, according to Livy (6.33.5), when the Romans fought against the Antiates and Latins at Satricum in 377 B.C., one of the two consular tribunes commanding the Roman army was a P. Valerius.

Despite the sensation created by the discovery of an archaic inscription recording the name of Publius Valerius, perhaps an even more interesting question concerns the meaning and significance of *suodales*. In later Roman society, a *sodalitas* was a kind of dining club or brotherhood, usually composed of aristocratic *sodales* and having a religious character in that it was devoted to the worship of a particular divinity (Versnel in *Lapis Satricanus* 1980, 108–12). Since the *suod-* element in *suodales* is cognate with the English word "swear," the term suggests that some kind of oath was taken, binding the members of the group together in a common purpose. Furthermore, the fact that these companions made a dedication to Mars may indicate that one (if not the primary) concern of Publius Valerius and his companions was warlike activity. This interpretation can be reinforced and given greater context by taking note of other possible parallels in the ancient world, such as the war bands led by Homeric heroes, the warlike aristocratic companions of the Macedonian kings during the classical period, and the war bands surrounding Celtic and Germanic chieftains described by Caesar and Tacitus (Caes. *Bell. Gall.* 6.15 and Tacitus *Germania* 13–15, with Versnel in *Lapis Satricanus* 1980, 112 ff. and Bremmer 1982). The lifestyle of all of these was more or less the same: cattle raiding and fighting against hostile neighbors, engaging in hunting and the chase, feasting and drinking together. According to Caesar and Tacitus, the warlords in Celtic and Germanic society were men who, by reason of their demonstrated martial prowess and leadership, attracted to themselves young men eager to win renown through raiding and warfare. The companions were expected to fight beside their leader to the death, and if they abandoned their fellows, they were stigmatized with shame so inexpungible that it often caused the shirker to commit suicide.

The companions honored their leader with gifts, and he in turn was obliged to keep his followers' needs well supplied by bestowing rewards upon them. Booty captured in raids and war fueled these bands of warriors, and a leader was successful only as long as he could maintain this flow of goods among his companions.

Even before the discovery of the Lapis Satricanus, the Fabian defeat at the Cremera was regarded by many scholars as belonging to an early stage in Roman social development, in which the state had not yet completely replaced aristocratic clans and their dependents in organizing major communal activities such as warfare (e.g., Alföldi 1965, 314–15 and Heurgon 1973, 181). The discovery of this inscription, however, has made this view the unchallenged orthodoxy (e.g., Cornell in *CAH* VII.2 1989, 297 and Richard in *Crise et Transformation* 1990, 245–62). Nevertheless, given the unsatisfactory nature of the ancient tradition concerning the Cremera, caution should still be exercised in interpreting the tale as an accurate recollection of early clan warfare. Nonetheless, a few final observations in support of the current view can be made. Livy (2.49.4–5) describes the departure of the 306 Fabii from Rome as attended by a joyful crowd consisting of two parts, the general public and the kinsmen and companions of the Fabii: "sequebatur turba propria alia cognatorum sodaliumque . . . alia publica." Even though these two groups are described as merely seeing the Fabii off, the implication is that under normal circumstances the Fabii would have been attended in such an enterprise by their various followers and dependents. Furthermore, if in fact the Cremera disaster simply involved the Fabii and not the Roman state as a whole, this could account for the fact that there was no later public record concerning the date of the *dies Cremerensis*. On the other hand, the magnitude of the disaster may not have been nearly as serious as the later legend maintains; it could have been exaggerated through identification with the annihilation of the three hundred Spartans at Thermopylae. If so, the later tradition concerning the *dies Cremerensis* was simply an invention borrowed from the Gallic catastrophe of 390 B.C. and the Day of the Allia.

Chapter 7

Rome of the Twelve Tables

Perhaps the single most important and lasting innovation in the Roman state around the middle of the fifth century B.C. was the Law of the Twelve Tables, so-called because this first major codification of law was initially engraved on twelve bronze tablets and was displayed in public. Even though many of this early lawcode's specific provisions eventually became obsolete, it nevertheless continued to be of significance, as it was the precondition for all the subsequent development of Roman law.[1] In Cicero's youth, Roman schoolboys were still being required to memorize its provisions (Cic. *De Legibus* 2.9 and 2.59), and eminent Roman jurists as early as c. 200 B.C. and as late as c. 150 A.D. wrote learned commentaries on this lawcode. In addition, since the Law of the Twelve Tables represented the earliest major Latin text and therefore contained numerous peculiar words and phrases, it received considerable attention from later antiquarians and philologists. As the result of the widespread and sustained ancient interest in this legal text, we are fortunate to possess a very large number of fragments from it (i.e., verbatim quotations or paraphrases). Given the lateness and basic unreliability of the ancient literary sources on Rome during the fifth century, the surviving portions of the Law of the Twelve Tables may provide us

1. For other modern treatments of the subjects covered in this chapter, see Ogilvie 1965, 390–525; Heurgon 1973, 169–73; Scullard 1980, 86–91; and Cornell 1995, 272–92. For other treatments of the decemvirate and the Twelve Tables, see Täubler 1921; Beloch 1926, 236–46; Wieacker in *Origines de la République Romaine* 1967, 293–356; Watson 1975; Gutberlet 1985, 72–98; the essays by Ungern-Sternberg, Eder, and Toher in Raaflaub 1986 (77–104, 262–300, and 301–26 respectively); Wieacker 1988, 287–309; D'Ippolito in Momigliano and Schiavone 1988, 397–413; Humbert in *Crise et Transformation* 1990, 263–87; and Watson 1992. The best critical introduction to and edition of the Law of the Twelve Tables is Crawford 1996, 555–721.

202 ROME OF THE TWELVE TABLES

with our most accurate information about the social and economic conditions prevailing in early Rome.

Since the Law of the Twelve Tables formed an important stage in Rome's internal development, later Roman historians did not fail to portray the political background of this innovation in terms of the struggle of the orders. Codifying the law was first suggested in 462 B.C. by a plebeian tribune, Terentilius Harsa, who proposed the appointment of a commission of five men to accomplish this task. In Livy's narrative (3.9.1–5), the tribune introduces his bill with inflammatory political rhetoric redolent of the late republic, in which the senate and consuls are charged with tyranny, insolence, and a lack of all restraints. The tribune therefore proposes that the appointed commission draft laws concerning consular *imperium* ("legibus de imperio consulari scribendis"), so that the consuls henceforth will be obliged to exercise their power according to what the people have conceded by law, rather than out of their own caprice and licentiousness. Thus we are led to expect that one of the principal issues addressed in the Law of the Twelve Tables would be to define the constitutional powers of the consuls. The extant fragments of the lawcode, however, contain no such provisions. Only a few clauses pertain to constitutional matters. Rather, as we might expect of a lawcode designed for a community's practical use, it is almost entirely concerned with private law (Watson 1992, 14–18). Even if one wished to validate the historicity of Livy's presentation of the original reason for codification by asserting that the provisions defining or circumscribing consular *imperium* have not survived, this argument from silence could be nullified. Given the relative abundance of ancient evidence concerning the nature of *imperium* as well as the ancients' familiarity with the Law of the Twelve Tables, we should expect any such provisions to have been cited in the numerous debates and controversies over governorships and military commands during the late republic and early principate. Moreover, since the ancient accounts state that the commission charged with codifying the law did so with consular authority (*imperio consulari legibus scribundis*), it seems likely that putting the codification in the context of the struggle of the orders was a later annalistic maneuver, accomplished by simply inserting the Latin preposition *de* into the titulature of the legislators, thus converting them from a board *with* consular *imperium* for writing laws into a commission for writing laws *on* consular *imperium* (Ogilvie 1965, 412).

Rome's Law of the Twelve Tables is to be viewed as an important step in state formation (Van Der Vliet in Eder 1990, 249–53). During the archaic and early classical period, Greek city-states rationalized their affairs by establishing annually elected magistrates with defined competences, by organizing a significant portion of their adult male population into a hoplite class for waging war, by instituting coinage and methods of taxation, and by devising lawcodes. Indeed, Hölkeskamp (1992, 95–97) has shown that Greek legislation and written law presuppose a well developed city-state, with differentiated institutions and with established procedures governing their integration and interaction. Rome c. 450 B.C. was engaged in a similar process of institutional rationalization. In fact, the famous lawcode of Gortyn in Crete offers a striking parallel to the Roman codification. Dating to c. 450 B.C., this lawcode is inscribed in twelve columns on the inner face of a circular wall and is similarly concerned exclusively with private law. To say that it was part of a process of rationalization, however, does not imply that the Roman codification occurred without political dissension or in the absence of social or economic discontent. Legislative activity of this sort is by its very nature political and generally spawns political controversy even if none existed before. The actual context is still a far cry, however, from the ancient characterization of the decemviral legislation as an episode in the struggle of the orders. To be sure, the codification of law in some Greek city-states of the archaic period was bound up with severe social and economic conditions which contributed to the rise of tyranny, and the provisions in the Law of the Twelve Tables concerning indebtedness present a very grim picture. Nevertheless, the fact that such harsh conditions were sanctioned by the law indicates that the Roman legislators had no interest in carrying through any major social or economic reforms similar to Solon's famous *seisachtheia* in Athens. Laws ameliorating the conditions of indebtedness were not forthcoming at Rome until the fourth century B.C.

One datum that could possibly point to political tensions at this time concerns a marked increase in the number of new clans reaching the consulship for the first time. As shown in figure 6 (see p. 165), the decade of the 450s witnessed seven new clans attaining curule office for the very first time. In fact, all seven instances occur within the five years 455–451: Romilius 455, Tarpeius and Aternius in 454, Quinctilius and Curiatius in 453, Sestius in 452, and Genucius in 451. Of these, four served on the first board of decemvirs. Yet in the absence of other reliable evidence, this pattern is difficult to interpret.[2] The picture that emerges from the surviving portions of the Twelve Tables is that of a rather traditional agrarian society with marked differences in wealth and status. It must be admitted, however, that a full and accurate picture of early Roman society, economy, and politics is impossible to reconstruct, because legal evidence by itself is usually not the best guide for historical reconstructions, and because we cannot exclude the possibility that some portions of the Twelve Tables were reinterpreted and modernized over time and thus do not accurately represent their original purport. On the other hand, the ancient literary tradition is likewise

2. But see the plausible speculations of Raaflaub in *Bilancio Critico* 1993, 139–42.

rendered suspect by its interpretation of this innovation in the conventional terms of the struggle of the orders. Thus, although we may conclude that the decemviral legislation occurred in a Roman state experiencing political, social, and economic tensions, we cannot in the existing state of our evidence judge with any degree of confidence to what extent, if any, these tensions either brought about or influenced this codification of law.

THE TRIAL OF K. QUINCTIUS

According to both Livy (3.11–13) and Dionysius (10.5–8), in 461 B.C., the year following the promulgation of the Terentilian Rogation, successful senatorial opposition to the passage of this measure was led by the youthful K. Quinctius, the son of Cincinnatus. The young man's actions in the senatorial cause brought about his prosecution on a capital charge by the tribunes before the people. After he was allowed to avoid detainment in bonds by posting surety (*vadimonium*), false testimony secured his unjust condemnation, and he fled into exile. When his sureties had to pay large fines for his absconding, his father was reduced to virtual poverty by repaying these obligations. It was in this condition that legates from the senate found Cincinnatus three years later, when they came to his small farm to inform him that he had been appointed dictator to rescue a Roman army besieged by the Aequians.

The trial of K. Quinctius is most likely fictitious and has probably been historicized from a document that specified the legal procedure of taking *vadimonium* for tribunician prosecutions before the people. Associated with each Roman public office was an official archive containing important information on legal and religious procedures to be followed, procedures which were sometimes conveniently summarized and brought together into a handbook (*commentarius*). A few samples of this kind of material have been preserved by Varro, in 6.86–92 of his *De Lingua Latina*. The antiquarian quotes censorial records in §§ 86–87 for the procedure of the lustrum; consular *commentarii* for the taking of auspices are quoted in §§ 88–89; and in §§ 90–91, he quotes from an old *commentarius* of the quaestor M'. Sergius, the son of Manius, concerning a legal inquiry on a capital charge brought against T. Quinctius Trogus. In the consular document, the name of the consul's attendant is given as C. Calpurnius. The name could be that of an actual person who served as a consular attendant at some time, but it might also have been included in the text merely by way of example, just as Roman jurists used fictitious personal names (corresponding to our John Doe and Richard Roe) to illustrate their legal cases. Varro's quotation from the quaestorian handbook concerning the trial of T. Quinctius Trogus probably derives from an actual prosecution, and the document was preserved and used thereafter as a model. We may surmise that the trial of K. Quinctius was generated from an archival document concerned with *vadimonium*, and that the names of the chief participants, including Kaeso's connection to Cincinnatus, have been added to give this procedure a historical etiology and to lend it verisimilitude, while incorporating it into the structure of the annalistic tradition.

APPIUS HERDONIUS AND QUINCTIUS CINCINNATUS

The annalistic record for the years 464–458 B.C. contains a curious blend of fact and fiction in reference to Roman foreign affairs, which deserves close examination. In 460 B.C., according to Livy (3.15–18) and Dionysius (10.14–16), a band of Sabines numbering either twenty-five hundred or four thousand and led by Ap. Herdonius seized the Capitoline Hill in Rome under cover of night. Dionysius describes the seizure as a military expedition originating upstream from Rome in the Sabine territory, whereas Livy seems to portray this event as an internal insurrection involving exiles and slaves. In any case, given the chauvinistic character of the late annalistic accounts, which showed reluctance to admit that Rome suffered major military reversals, we should accept as historical some kind of Sabine attempt to capture Rome at this time. In order to give the story greater verisimilitude, later writers might have borrowed some of their details for this episode from the sedition in Rome in 100 B.C., in which the plebeian tribune L. Apuleius Saturninus and his followers seized control of the Capitoline but were forced to surrender to the consuls, C. Marius and L. Valerius Flaccus (Appian *Bell. Civ.* 1.32 and Plutarch *Marius* 30). Nevertheless, there is one important detail that is not likely to have been a later fictitious addition to the story. It concerns the vital military support provided to Rome by the Tusculans and their leader L. Mamilius. In acknowledgement of his service to the Roman state in its time of need, Mamilius was rewarded with Roman citizenship (Livy 3.29.6). This grant was recorded by Cato the Elder in his *Origines* (F 25 in Peter 1914), and it is likely to have been remembered by the Mamilian family of Tusculum, who later made their way into the Roman nobility by producing consuls in 265, 262, and 239 B.C., as well as the first plebeian curio maximus (209–174 B.C.).[3]

Whether in 460 L. Mamilius led forces from Tusculum only or whether he was serving as leader of a Latin army, the fact that Rome was indebted to Tusculum for its rescue from the Sabine seizure of the Capitoline prompted later Roman historians to invent for the very next year (459 B.C.) a similar incident in which the Aequians seized control of the Tusculan citadel by

---

3. Each of the thirty archaic curiae was headed by an official called a curio, and the entire curiate organization was headed by the curio maximus. Before the Hannibalic War this latter position had always been occupied by a patrician (Livy 27.8.1–3).

night, and the Romans discharged their obligation to the Tusculans by coming to their aid (see Livy 3.23 and Dion. Hal. 10.20–21). This fabrication conforms to a standard pattern in the later annalists, according to which an actual Roman defeat or major setback is immediately followed by a fictitious Roman victory, which offsets the reversal. Thus, for example, in the year immediately following the destruction of the 306 Fabii at the Cremera, Livy (2.51.4–9) describes how the consuls inflicted a crushing defeat upon the Veientines.

Another annalistic fiction is encountered in the year 458 B.C. and concerns the famous story of Quinctius Cincinnatus, summoned by the senate from his small farm to assume the high office of dictator in order to rescue a Roman army besieged in their camp by the Aequians near Tusculum (Livy 3.26–29 and Dion. Hal. 10.23–25). Three elements are likely to have led to the creation of this patriotic and morally edifying tale: (1) the stories of 460 and 459 B.C., in which Rome and Tusculum rescue one another from enemy occupation of their citadels; (2) Minucius, one of the consuls of 458 B.C., reminded later historians of the famous tale in which M. Minucius Rufus, Q. Fabius Maximus Cunctator's master of the horse during the second year of the Hannibalic War, was rescued from a military defeat by Fabius (see Livy 22.23–30); and (3) the recollection of an actual dictatorship of a Quinctius, involving a brief but brilliant military campaign. This last was the dictatorship of T. Quinctius Cincinnatus in 380 B.C. (Livy 6.28.3–29.10). After defeating Praeneste and its coalition of nine towns, this Cincinnatus returned to Rome, celebrated a triumph, resigned from office on the twentieth day of his dictatorship, and dedicated in the Capitoline temple a gold crown weighing two and one third pounds (Festus 498L s.v. *trientem tertium*). Livy even reproduces the approximate wording of the accompanying dedicatory inscription. The dedication is likely to have survived in the Capitoline temple until the shrine was burned down in 83 B.C., and it must have been the ultimate source of the popular tradition about a dictator named Quinctius Cincinnatus who had somehow rescued the state in a time of crisis and had selflessly resigned from office as soon as he had dealt with the emergency. The influence of the episode from the Hannibalic War upon the tale of Cincinnatus rescuing Minucius in 458 B.C. is clearly seen in the dictator's appointing Q. Fabius Vibulanus as prefect in the city during his absence from Rome and then later placing him in charge of Minucius's liberated camp. Even if such a detail were historical, the names of such minor officials would not have survived from the fifth century B.C. into later historical times. It is obvious that the urban prefect, Fabius, has been added to the story by some Roman historian.

The fame and popularity of the story of Cincinnatus's dictatorship encouraged the later annalists to concoct a similar fiction for the year 464 B.C. (Livy 3.4–5 and Dion. Hal. 9.62–66). As this episode centers upon the

Roman colony of Antium, the presumed hometown of Valerias Antias, this notoriously inventive annalist is most likely the author of this fiction. In this case, when the consul Furius is besieged by the Aequians, T. Quinctius, the consul of the previous year, is empowered as proconsul to raise an army to rescue Furius. Livy (3.4.9) even includes in his narrative the formula of a *senatus consultum ultimum,* by which the senate charged the other consul, Postumius, "to see that the state should suffer no harm" (= "videret ne quid res publica detrimenti caperet"). Both the proconsulship and the s.c.u. are anachronistic. The Roman state did not begin to extend (prorogue) consular commands beyond their one-year term until the beginning of the Second Samnite War in 327/6 B.C., and the first occasion on which a s.c.u. was passed was in 121 B.C., when it was used to empower the consul L. Opimius to take whatever measures he saw fit to suppress C. Gracchus and his supporters (see Cic. *Cat.* 1.2). Valerius Antias's authorship of this fictitious episode is suggested by Livy 3.5.13, where Livy cites Antias for the very first time in his narrative concerning precise figures for battle casualties (cf. Livy 3.8.10). Of the sixty-six fragments surviving from the lost history of Valerius Antias (Peter 1914, 238–75), most come from Livy, and a large number of them concern such matters of invented or exaggerated figures and battles. Antias's inventive hand is probably also to be seen in the L. Valerius whom the proconsul Quinctius appoints as urban prefect.

FACTS AND FICTIONS OF THE PLEBEIAN TRIBUNATE

In 457, five years after Terentilius's proposal, the number of annually elected plebeian tribunes was increased from five to ten. In the following year, 456 B.C. (presumably the first year in which ten plebeian tribunes actually held office), a tribunician law was passed which somehow concerned the status of landholdings on the Aventine. Given the prominence of the temples of Ceres and Diana on this hill, not to mention that the former functioned as the headquarters of the plebeian aediles, the law's central purpose may have been to demarcate the sacred land of these and other less famous shrines from the remaining public and private ground of the hill. This would account for the care with which the bronze stele bearing the text of the law was preserved in the temple of Diana (Dion. Hal. 10.32.4). The later historical tradition, however, viewed this measure as an agrarian law of late republican type, designed to grant land to the urban plebs; and since it was an Icilian Law, the late annalists, eager to embellish their narratives of the struggle of the orders with plebeian tribunes who opposed the senate and consuls, repeatedly recycled this name in different settings, producing the impression that the family of the Icilii was a steadfast champion of the plebeian cause over the course of the fifth century. Consequently, in ancient accounts which followed the dubious tradition that the plebeian tribunes were increased in number from two to five in the first year of their office (after the first secession), an Icilius was inserted among the three additional tribunes there (Dion. Hal. 6.89.1 with 11.28.2). Icilii are likewise encountered during this period as plebeian tribunes in the other two years important to the early history of the plebeian tribunate: 471/0 (Livy 2.58.2 and Diod. 11.68.7) and 449 B.C., (Livy 3.54.11 and 3.63.8–11, and Dion. Hal. 11.50.1).

A similar pattern of the annalists' fictitious recycling of the name of an authentic early plebeian tribune is even more apparent in Dionysius's account of the years 455–454 B.C. (10.36–52), in which the plebeian hero L. Siccius Dentatus figures prominently.[4] Siccius is likely to have been the name of one of the first two plebeian tribunes elected to office. The name is associated with both the first and second secessions in 494 and 449 as well as with the increase in the tribunes' number from two to five in 471.[5] But unlike these three Siccii, who were legendary for their tenure of the plebeian tribunate alone, the hero in this episode of Dionysius is described as having been a distinguished warrior of long standing before becoming embroiled in the politics of these years. The annalistic invention and exaggeration of Siccius's military prowess were probably patterned after and suggested by his name's resemblance to that of Q. Occius, a Roman soldier famous for his brave exploits in Spain during the 140s B.C. Siccius's martial heroism was further enhanced by the bestowal of the surname Dentatus, borrowed from M'. Curius Dentatus, a great hero of the Third Samnite and Pyrrhic Wars, who had been plebeian tribune and thrice consul. Dionysius's immediate source for this episode is likely to have been Valerius Antias. This can be plausibly conjectured from the role of Antium in the narrative as well as from Dionysius's careful enumeration of all the specific military awards that L. Siccius Dentatus had allegedly received over his long and distinguished military career. Such attention to fictitious details involving numbers was characteristic of Valerius Antias (e.g., Plutarch *Romulus* 14.6 and Livy 3.5.12–15).

Dionysius introduces L. Siccius Dentatus into his narrative for the year 455 B.C. by having him come before a meeting of the Roman people to speak in support of the passage of a tribunician agrarian bill. The political

---

4. Briefer parallel accounts of this man's career are Val. Max. 3.2.25, Pliny *NH* 7.101–2, Gell. 2.11, Festus 208L s.v. *obsidionalis corona*, Ammianus 25.3.14 and 27.10.16. For a fuller treatment of the phenomenon of the annalists' fictitious recycling of the few authentic names of plebeian tribunes which survived from the fifth century B.C. into historical times, see Forsythe 1994, 291–94.

5. Ancient sources variously record the names of these personages as either Siccius or Sicinius. For the confusion see Broughton 1951–52, 1:15 n. 1, 19–20 n. 1, and 31 n. 2. For the view that the name Siccius should be preferred to Sicinius, see Forsythe 1994, 292. Cf. Oakley 1997, 441–42.

confrontation, vividly described in terms of the political violence of the late republic (including the anachronism of voting urns), ends when a report comes of an Aequian raid against Tusculum. Despite the fact that he has already served in the army for forty years, Siccius patriotically desists from political bickering, volunteers along with eight hundred other veterans, and joins the consular army. The consuls take the opportunity to rid themselves of this courageous and turbulent fellow by sending him out on a suicide mission against the enemy camp. Contrary to their expectations, however, Siccius succeeds in his mission, returns to Rome, and is elected plebeian tribune for the following year. He employs the powers of his office to prosecute the two consuls of the preceding year and secures a judgment of heavy fines. These trials were doubtless later annalistic fictions suggested by the passage of the consular Aternian Tarpeian Law in this year, a law which somehow regulated legal fines (Dion. Hal. 10.50.2, Cic. *De Re Pub.* 2.60, and Gell. 11.1.2). Siccius's political success and integrity also succeed in subduing senatorial and consular opposition to the Terentilian bill, so that a commission of three men is appointed to travel to Athens and other Greek states, to study their laws in preparation for the codification of Roman law.

THE DECEMVIRAL LEGISLATION

The ancient tradition that this commission traveled to Athens to study the famous lawcode of Solon is obviously fictitious; it was the creation of later historians eager to associate Rome's first major codification of law with the most famous early Greek legislation. Nevertheless, ancient legal commentators sought out parallels between the two lawcodes and judged them to be the result of direct Roman borrowing rather than a case of two unrelated societies devising similar legal provisions independently of one another. The surviving fragments of the Twelve Tables contain three such instances: the property rights of adjoining plots of land (*Digest* 10.1.13), legalization of private associations (*Digest* 47.22.4), and restrictions on mourning at funerals (Cic. *De Legibus* 2.59). Indeed, parallels can even be found between the Twelve Tables and legal provisions of the Old Testament. For example, both legal systems allowed a person to kill a thief or burglar caught in the act at night but not in the daytime (Exodus 22.2–3 and Macrobius *Saturnalia* 1.4.19 with Cic. *Pro Tullio* F 21.50). But this does not mean that the Roman commissioners traveled to Jerusalem to study Mosaic Law.[6] If in fact the Romans had wished to make use of Greek legal models, they would not

---

6. Westbrook (1988) maintains that parallels exist between the Twelve Tables and the legal tradition of the ancient Near East, and he postulates that the Phoenicians mediated transmission from the latter to the former.

have needed to travel to mainland Greece, but could have studied the laws of the Greek states of southern Italy and Sicily. This would be in accord with early Rome's cultural orientation toward the western Greeks rather than the Greek mainland, evident in the Romans' obtaining the Sibylline Books from Cumae and their importation of the cult of Demeter from Magna Graecia or Sicily.[7] According to an alternative tradition (*Digest* 1.2.2.4, Strabo 14.1.25, and Pliny *NH* 34.21), the Greek source behind the decemviral codification was Hermodorus, an Ephesian who happened to be in exile in Italy at the time. Since he was praised by his fellow townsman and contemporary, the philosopher Heraclitus, Hermodorus presumably lived c. 500 B.C. and therefore might not have been alive during the 450s. Thus this tradition, too, might be an unhistorical contrivance of later Roman writers. Nevertheless, unless the verbatim quotation of the Twelve Tables in Gellius 20.1.12 derives from a text whose language had been modernized, the lawcode used the word *poena* to specify a penalty; and since this word came into Latin from Doric Greek, the borrowing could indicate that the Twelve Tables were in some degree affected by the legal tradition of the western Greeks.[8]

Whether or not the Roman embassage to Greek states is historical, the ancient tradition records that after the commissioners returned, the Romans elected ten men with consular power for writing laws. No other magistrates were elected; this board of ten conducted and administered all state affairs as well as carrying out their assigned task of drawing up a coherent body of law for the Roman people. According to the ancient sources, when the Terentilian Rogation was first proposed, it specified that a board of five men should be appointed for writing laws, but by the time the commission was actually impaneled the number of legislators was doubled to ten. This difference was obviously thought to have been related to the increase in the number of annually elected plebeian tribunes from five to ten, which was instituted in the interval between the promulgation of the Terentilian Rogation and the appointment of the decemviral commission.

7. Early Rome's cultural orientation toward the western Greeks as opposed to the Greek mainland or Asia Minor is further suggested by Pliny's statement (*NH* 34.26) that during the Samnite Wars the Romans, ordered by Pythian Apollo to honor with statues the bravest and wisest of the Greeks, set up images of Alcibiades and Pythagoras in the Comitium. The latter was chosen because of his great reputation for wisdom among the western Greeks, and the former was doubtless regarded as the bravest of the Greeks, because he was the architect of the audacious Athenian expedition against Sicily during the Peloponnesian War. But see Wallace in Eder 1990, 289, who is skeptical about this ancient tradition and the explanation of these two statues, and suggests that they were simply brought to Rome as booty from some other Italian community.

8. For Latin *poena* see Walde and Hofmann 1938–54, 2:329–30. For a more detailed examination of the question of possible Greek influence on the Twelve Tables, see Wieacker in *Origines de la République Romaine* 1967, 330–53.

Thus the annalistic tradition viewed the legislators as in part fulfilling the duties and functions of the plebeian tribunate, while at the same time their grant of consular *imperium* made them surrogates for the consuls. This notion of the composite nature of the decemviral board is to be accepted as historical, because legislation was primarily handled by plebeian tribunes throughout the history of the republic (Mitchell 1990, 191–204). Note also that the commission's hybrid character, representing both plebeian tribunate and consulship, suggests that the legislative board was the product of political cooperation, not conflict.

JURISDICTION IN EARLY ROMAN LAW

The all-purpose nature of the decemviral commission raises the question of the origin and early history of the Roman administration of justice. During the middle and late republic, administration of the civil lawcourts lay in the hands of praetors. In 367 B.C., the Romans created the first praetorship, whose incumbent supervised civil litigation in Rome. When this task became too onerous due to the growth in the number of lawsuits, a second praetorship was established in 242. Henceforth, one praetor, termed the *praetor urbanus,* handled cases arising between Roman citizens, whereas the other official, known as the *praetor peregrinus,* was responsible for lawsuits involving foreigners and Roman citizens. The history of Roman jurisdiction before 367 B.C., however, is not so clearly documented or understood. The ancient tradition maintained that Rome's early kings possessed religious, judicial, and military powers, and that when the monarchy was terminated, the king's religious duties were taken over by the rex sacrorum, while his judicial and military powers were assumed by the two annually elected consuls. According to this thesis, the consuls exercised both military and judicial powers from the beginning of the republic until the latter were assigned to the newly created office of praetor in 367. Since World War II, however, the creation and original nature of the consulship have been the subject of much modern scholarly speculation, which has rightly challenged this ancient reconstruction as overly legalistic and historically simplistic (Staveley 1956, 90–112 and 1983, 42–44).

The military origin of the consulship is suggested by two facts: that consuls were elected by the comitia centuriata, which in origin was simply the Roman army acting as an assembly; and that *imperium,* the technical term for the consul's legal authority, was the power to command troops and to issue orders. Thus, the power of jurisdiction is likely to have been a later accretion to *imperium.* During the years 405–367 B.C. the Roman state was, with few exceptions, administered by a board of six military tribunes with consular power. In 366, the boards of tribunes were replaced by five curule magistrates: two consuls, one praetor, and two curule aediles. It seems quite obvious that the six consular tribunes had been performing the duties of these five officials (von Fritz 1950, 37–44 and Stewart 1998, 130). This means that curule jurisdiction can plausibly be conjectured to date at least from the close of the fifth century. In his historical survey of Roman law, the jurist Pomponius (*Digest* 1.2.2.5–6) writes as follows concerning the immediate consequences of the publication of the Law of the Twelve Tables:

> After these laws had been passed, there arose the need of forensic debate, as it is naturally accustomed to happen that their interpretation requires the endorsement of learned men. This debate and body of law, because it came to be composed by learned men without writing, is not designated by any proper name as other parts of the law are known by their names . . . but it is called by the common designation of the civil law. Then at about the same time, from these laws there were composed actions by which people could litigate among themselves. They desired these actions to be fixed and solemn, so that the people might not determine them as they wished; and this part of the law is termed the *legis actiones*, that is, statutory actions. Thus, at almost the same time these three bodies of law came into being: after the Law of the Twelve Tables, the civil law began to flow from them, and from the same source were composed the *legis actiones*. Nevertheless, both the knowledge of interpretation and the actions of all of these lay in the college of pontiffs, from whom someone was appointed each year to preside over the private citizens.

Modern scholars agree that early Roman jurisprudence and the formulation of the *legis actiones* were developed by members of the pontifical college, but Pomponius's final remark goes even further in suggesting that jurisdiction was also originally handled by the pontiffs. Although he is talking about the immediate aftermath of the decemviral legislation, he makes clear his view that before being assigned to curule magistrates, jurisdiction in the Roman state was in the hands of the pontiffs. This makes perfectly good sense. Not only were the pontiffs Rome's early jurisconsults and formulators of the verbal legal procedures (*legis actiones*) needed to initiate a lawsuit, but they were also the officials who possessed expert knowledge of and control over the legal calendar. Each day of the year was characterized as either *fastus* or *nefastus*, the former being a day on which the appropriate Roman official was obliged to be available to preside over legal proceedings, and the latter a day on which legal business could not be transacted. Although it was not the case in later times, this distinction must originally have been sacral in nature and was determined by the pontiffs.[9] Moreover, pontifical involvement in archaic jurisdiction is likewise suggested by a legal custom mentioned by Varro (*Ling. Lat.* 5.180). The antiquarian records that in former days, when litigants were engaged in a lawsuit initiated by the

---

9. For further discussion of the pontiffs' role in the early development of Roman civil law, see Wieacker 1988, 310 ff.

legis actio of *sacramentum,* which required both parties to deposit a sum of money, they made their deposits "at the bridge" (*ad pontem*). Given the original sacral character of this form of litigation (indicated by the term *sacramentum*), the bridge in question must be none other than the Pons Sublicius, Rome's oldest bridge over the Tiber, whose care and maintenance were the responsibility of the pontiffs, and from which their priestly office took its name.

We may therefore postulate that jurisdiction, like all other aspects of early Roman private law, was the responsibility of the pontiffs, and that pontifical jurisdiction was eventually supplanted during the later fifth century B.C. by curule jurisdiction. We may further surmise that the Law of the Twelve Tables played a pivotal role in this process. Once the law was codified in written form, the pontiffs were no longer the exclusive reservoir of such knowledge, but annually elected curule magistrates could be expected to exercise civil jurisdiction competently. If we conceive of the struggle of the orders as consisting in part of resistance to a small number of aristocratic families who laid exclusive claims to privileges and powers on the basis of their hereditary priesthoods and sacerdotal knowledge, the Law of the Twelve Tables can be judged to have been crucial in facilitating the movement of jurisdiction from priestly to magisterial control.

An additional point in favor of this interpretation is the overall secular, nonreligious nature of the Law of the Twelve Tables. This stands in sharp contrast to the motley mixture of public, private, and sacred elements found in earlier known Roman enactments, the so-called *Leges Regiae,* a miscellaneous collection of primitive legal provisions attributed to the early kings (Watson 1972; 1979; and 1992, 19–20 and 87–90). For example, a person convicted of *perduellio* (usually translated as "treason") was hanged from a barren tree. Not only did this punish the perpetrator and prevent his repetition of the foul deed by his execution, but a barren tree was used in order to keep the crime from flourishing in the community. Similarly, a person found guilty of *parricidium* (murder of one's parent or of another close of kin?) was subject to the "punishment of the sack." The criminal was sewn up in a sack together with a snake, a rooster, and a monkey and then cast into the sea, so as not to pollute Roman territory. His animal sack-mates represented the wickedness, brazenness, and perversity of his human character. The Law of the Twelve Tables, on the other hand, contains very few punishments of a sacral nature.

LITIGATION AND ORALITY IN EARLY ROMAN LAW

Litigation in early Rome occurred in two distinct phases. In the first phase, termed *in iure* (= "in the law"), the plaintiff and defendant appeared before a Roman official, while in the second phase, called *apud iudicem* (= "before the judge"), the litigants pleaded their case before a private citizen. In order to initiate a lawsuit successfully, the plaintiff was personally responsible for serving notice upon the defendant; if the latter were sick or enfeebled by age, the plaintiff was required by law to provide him with transportation to court in the form of a wagon. In addition, the plaintiff's claim had to fall within the scope of the law, and the suit had to be framed within the pertinent *legis actio*. The *legis actiones* were a set of legal procedures devised by the pontiffs, and only one particular *legis actio* could be properly used for each kind of case. If the plaintiff employed an incorrect *legis actio* to initiate his suit in the *in iure* phase, he immediately lost the case. Furthermore, each *legis actio* had its own special wording, which had to be correctly uttered in the presence of the Roman official in the *in iure* phase.[10] Assuming that all went well in the first phase, the official would then appoint a private citizen to be the judge of the case. The litigants would arrange to meet with this person, who would hear out both sides and then render judgment. The Roman state therefore involved itself only in the preliminary phase of litigation. Once the official was satisfied that the case lay within the scope of existing law and was couched in the appropriate *legis actio* with its precise wording, the case was handed over to a private individual who served as judge. Thus the *in iure* phase was highly formal, whereas the phase *apud iudicem* was informal. As can be surmised from this brief outline, this judicial system placed a very high premium on personal initiative and knowledge of the law. It is generally supposed that these factors worked to the advantage of wealthier and more powerful citizens and to the detriment of the poor and downtrodden (Kelly 1966, 1–84).

This disposition of early Roman legal procedure to favor the fortunate has been true in varying degrees of legal systems throughout the entire course of human history. One important and distinctive feature of early Roman law, however, was its oral nature. Despite the fact that the law itself was recorded in written form, all early Roman legal procedures were oral and therefore did not require the ability to read or write. Although the insistence upon precise wording, as in the *legis actiones,* could have been an impediment to seeking legal redress, the forms were not so complicated that they could not have been easily mastered by a significant portion of the population. Unfortunately, modern scholars have tended to follow the later ancient historical tradition quite uncritically in believing that down to the curule aedileship of Cn. Flavius in 304 B.C. the pontiffs kept a close guard over Roman legal procedure, so that only those with access to their knowledge

---

10. Detailed information about the *legis actiones,* including their exact wording, is preserved by the jurist Gaius in 4.11–29 of his *Institutes.* They were five in number: solemn deposit (*sacramentum*), demand for a judge or arbiter (*iudicis arbitrive postulatio*), summons (*condictio*), throwing-on of the hand (*manus iniectio*), and taking of a pledge (*pignoris capio*).

could engage in litigation (e.g., Watson 1975, 185–86 and Bauman 1983, 24–28). Such a secretive legal procedure could never have been practicable for a state as large and complex as that of Rome in the fourth century. Moreover, since all legal proceedings *in iure* were conducted in full public view in the Forum or Comitium, they could have been observed by shop-keepers, merchants, artisans, and even peasant farmers who happened to be in town. Thus the notion of a patrician pontifical stranglehold on early Roman litigation makes little sense.

On the contrary, it seems more likely that the later ancient literary tradi-tion both misunderstood the few available facts about early Roman legal history and grossly distorted them by casting them into the stereotypical mold of the struggle of the orders. In early times there could have existed in the Roman community a rich oral legal culture, which many fathers routinely passed on to their sons in order to equip them for adulthood. Two good examples of the formalism and simplicity of early Roman law are *stipulatio* and *mancipatio*. The former was a verbal contract of universal appli-cation. It was legally binding and required only that the two parties involved, standing face to face, verbally express the relevant obligation in the form of a question and answer, both of which had to employ the same main verb in order to signify understanding and agreement. For example, two possible forms of a *stipulatio* could have been the following: (1) "Do you promise to pay . . . ?" "I promise to pay. . . . " (2) "Do you agree to give. . . ?" "I agree to give. . . . " *Mancipatio,* often rendered into English as "con-veyance," was a legal procedure used to transfer ownership of certain kinds of property. Roman law classified all forms of property into two categories: *res mancipi* and *res nec mancipi*. The former comprised land, slaves, beasts of burden, and rustic servitudes (i.e., certain rights-of-way over land). These were the types of property most important for an agrarian society, and it was therefore essential to establish legal title to them beyond doubt. Their owner-ship was transferred by *mancipatio*. All other forms of property were *res nec mancipi*, and their ownership was transferred from one party to another by mere physical delivery (*traditio*). *Mancipatio* was a formal procedure; it required the presence of the two parties concerned, five Roman citizens serving as witnesses, and a person who held the scales symbolic of the purchase and transfer. The exchange of ownership was effected by the recipient's formally stating, "I declare this to be mine by Quiritary title, and be it bought by me with this piece of bronze and bronze scales," whereupon he struck the scales with a bronze coin. Despite their strict formality, both these procedures were simple and oral, and they must have been familiar to and routinely employed by virtually all adult male Roman citizens throughout their lives. Much the same is likely to have been the case with respect to other legal procedures, including the *legis actiones*.

SOCIETY AND ECONOMY

The vagaries of Roman litigation, as well as the social and economic dispar-
ities in Roman society, were mitigated, at least in part, by the institution of
the patron-client relationship, which bound persons of different wealth
and status together in mutual obligations.[11] Dionysius (2.10) describes the
customary rights and duties of this relationship. Patrons were expected to
explain the law to their clients, to defend them in court, to loan them
money, and to pay off their debts; clients were supposed to make contributions to their patrons for their daughters' dowries, for paying off legal fines,
and for offsetting any costs incurred in holding public office. In later historical times these bonds were often hereditary, and aristocratic families
strove to surround themselves with a large *clientela* as emblematic of their
power and influence. A person of intermediate wealth and status might be
a client of someone of higher rank as well as a patron to individuals of lower
status. Thus later Roman society was loosely bound together by a vast interlocking network of such relationships. The institution of patron and client
arose and flourished in early times because of inequalities in Roman society
and because its members derived benefits from these bonds of dependency.

Yet, as might be easily surmised, the institution's function varied according to people's economic resources and personal integrity. Obviously, given
the disparity of power between patron and client, the relationship was readily susceptible to abuse and exploitation. What was supposed to work to the
mutual benefit and protection of both parties could become an oppressive
protection racket. Accordingly, one provision in the Twelve Tables specified
that if a patron wronged his client, he was to be accursed (Serv. *ad Aen.*
6.609). This is the only instance in the Twelve Tables in which this religious
sanction was invoked. Its meaning is not clear. One interpretation is that
the law simply left such abuses up to the gods for punishment (Cornell
1995, 289). The clause more likely means that in order for the patron to be
judged accursed, he first had to be convicted of wrongdoing; then, if found
guilty, the patron was declared to be accursed and could be killed with
impunity by anyone. Even if the patron's wealth and status afforded him
protection from this sanction, he still might have been socially stigmatized
as a dishonest person and could have incurred the legal penalty of *infamia*,
normally imposed upon persons convicted of gross fiduciary misconduct.
Such persons were henceforth forbidden to engage in any legal activity that
involved trust, such as giving testimony, acting as witness for a *mancipatio*, or
serving as a guardian. At any rate, we may properly wonder how effective
the religious sanction was against a delinquent patron. It seems to conform
to what Alan Watson has termed the principle of second best in the law

---

11. For detailed treatment of the history of this shadowy institution, see Brunt 1988,
382–442.

(1992, 48–50). This concept explains the role of oaths in legal procedure during later historical times. In certain well-defined cases in which the presiding magistrate was at a loss to arrive at an informed decision, rather than admit impasse and thereby lower the prestige of the court, Roman law allowed recourse to an oath to the gods as the second-best solution.

In 20.1 of his *Attic Nights*, Aulus Gellius quotes and comments on the provisions in the Twelve Tables concerning indebtedness, which illustrate the harsh conditions awaiting a person unable to pay off his debts in early Rome. The creditor brought the debtor before the Roman official; when it was established that the debtor owed the creditor money and had not paid it, the debtor was adjudged (*iudicatus*) for the amount by the official, and was granted a grace period of thirty days in which to discharge the obligation. If he failed to do so, the creditor again appeared before the official with the debtor, and when it was determined that the debt was still outstanding, the debtor was assigned (*addictus*) by the official to the creditor. At this point the creditor was allowed to lay his hand upon the debtor to lead him away into bondage. The only alternative was for another person willing to take the debtor's place or to pay off the debt on his behalf to intercede by removing the creditor's hand from the debtor and becoming his substitute. This person was termed the *vindex*, which can be translated "claimant" or "protector." The Twelve Tables further specified that only an *adsiduus* could be *vindex* of another *adsiduus*, but anyone who wished could be *vindex* for a *proletarius*. *Adsidui* and *proletarii* therefore represented two basic economic classes in Roman society at this time. The latter apparently took their name from the fact that they were essentially propertyless and were evaluated only in terms of the offspring (*proles*) whom they could beget; whereas *adsidui* were persons who met an unspecified minimum property qualification, perhaps the same minimum which made them eligible for military service. Thus, given the utterly destitute condition of a *proletarius,* another *proletarius* or an *adsiduus* could volunteer to be his *vindex,* but only an *adsiduus* was considered a proper substitute for an indebted *adsiduus.*

In any case, if no *vindex* intervened on behalf of the debtor, the creditor took him away and held him in bonds (not exceeding fifteen pounds in weight) for a maximum of sixty days. During this period the debtor could furnish his own food for his support, but if not, the creditor was obliged by law to feed him no more than one pound of spelt every day. The debtor and creditor might at any time reach some kind of settlement between themselves, but if not, the creditor was required to appear with the debtor in the Comitium in Rome on three successive market days to declare publicly the amount of the outstanding debt. This publicized the debtor's plight to the community at large and provided the opportunity for someone to step forward to pay off the debt. If by the close of the sixty-day period no settlement of any kind had been reached, the creditor could then come before the

Roman official with the debtor for a third time; and when it was determined that the debtor had still not satisfied his creditor, the creditor could surrender the debtor to the official for execution, or he could sell him into slavery on foreign soil across the Tiber (*trans Tiberim peregre*). In the latter case the creditor apparently received the proceeds of the sale as compensation for the unpaid debt. Being sold into slavery across the Tiber among the Etruscans at this period insured that the condemned debtor would lose all the rights of a Roman citizen forever; whereas if he were sold into slavery in a Latin community with which Rome enjoyed rights of *commercium, conubium,* and *ius migrandi,* the person might have been freed from slavery some day and as a freedman of the Latin town could have enjoyed legal privileges shared with Rome, or he could have even reentered Roman society as a citizen by exercising the Latin right of *ius migrandi.* Finally, if there were two or more creditors with outstanding debts against the same man, a third fate might befall the debtor who either could or would not arrange settlements with them. In this eventuality, the Twelve Tables ordained that the creditors "on the third market day shall cut parts (*partis secanto*); and if they cut more or less, it shall be without prejudice."

Some ancient and modern commentators have interpreted this last provision to mean that the creditors were to divide up the debtor's property (see Watson 1975, 123–24 with nn. 38–40), but given the extraordinary harshness of the law, it is more likely that its literal meaning was intended: namely, that the creditors were allowed to cut up the debtor's body in rough proportion to the debts owed them. Like sale across the Tiber, this provision was clearly designed to force the debtor to reach some kind of settlement with his creditors. Even if the debtor was a *proletarius* and had no real assets with which to discharge his debts, early Roman law supplied a remedy in the institution of *nexum,* a form of debt servitude in which the debtor contracted with his creditor to repay the debt by working it off. Persons thus bound were termed *nexi,* and we may surmise that many *iudicati* and *addicti* were reduced to this condition. If interest (not exceeding the Twelve Tables' legal limit of one-twelfth of the principal) had been attached to the loan, economic or agricultural hard times could have been quite ruinous. Similar forms of debt servitude are known to have been current in the ancient Near East and in Greece during the archaic period,[12] and Solon's reform of Athenian society and economy in the early sixth century addressed just such widespread hardship and discontent (Finley 1981, 150–66). The annalistic tradition recorded numerous instances in which indebtedness

12. For the existence of debt servitude in the ancient Near East see Deuteronomy 15 and §110 of *The Lawcode of Hammurabi.* Debt servitude has also been a common institution worldwide up to the present day. For a convenient survey, see Ennew 1981. On indentured service in colonial America, see Van Der Zee 1985.

resulted in social unrest and even political agitation or change during the early republic, and at least some of these reports must be historical. Indeed, the legislative record of the mid-fourth century shows that indebtedness was a major problem at that time (see below p. 261–62), but the later historical tradition about the fifth century contains no such reliable data. Descriptions of fifth-century indebtedness are cast in such conventional terms that they must be viewed with suspicion. As a general rule, given the highly inventive nature of the later annalists in these matters, great caution must be exercised in analyzing all such ancient reports, and each reported instance of social unrest caused by widespread indebtedness should be judged on its own merits and in connection with other related data.

Various provisions of the Twelve Tables are of interest for what they reveal with respect to the concerns and attitudes of early Romans. One clause preserved by Festus (496L s.v. *talionis*) states that "if one person maims another person's limb, and if he does not settle with him, there shall be retaliation." It is noteworthy that here the *lex talionis* is enforced only as a last resort, after the wrongdoer has refused or failed to satisfy the victim. The difference in value placed upon a free person vs. a slave is shown by the monetary penalties for a broken bone: if a free person's bone was broken, the fine was three hundred *asses,* but it was only half that amount for the broken bone of a slave. Similarly, if a free person was caught in the act of committing theft and was not killed, he was beaten and then enslaved to the person whom he had robbed; but if the culprit was a slave, he was hurled to his death from the Tarpeian Rock on the Capitoline Hill (Gell. 11.18.8). The Romans already at this time recognized that children might not be mature enough to form a criminal intent and therefore had to be treated somewhat differently from adults: for if an adult by night secretly cut his neighbor's crops or pastured his animals on them, he was executed by hanging, but if a child under puberty did so, he was beaten according to the official's discretion and was punished with a fine double the value of the damage (Pliny *NH* 18.12).

Two other provisions testify to the early Roman belief in the efficacy of magic and ordain punishment for its use to cause harm. The death penalty was imposed upon one convicted of chanting an evil spell against another, presumably to cause death (Cic. *De Re Pub.* 4.12 with Pliny *NH* 18.17). The Twelve Tables also outlawed the use of magic to charm away the fertility of another person's crops (Serv. *ad Ecl.* 8.99). Although the penalty for this offense has not been recorded, given the lawcode's severity in punishing similar crimes resulting in the destruction of someone's crops, it is likely that if accused and convicted under this law, miscreants lost their lives. It is worth noting that a curule aedile charged someone under this provision of the Twelve Tables as late as 191 B.C., but the accused was acquitted (Pliny *NH* 18.41–43 with Forsythe 1994, 376 ff.).

Several provisions clearly reflect the agricultural orientation of Roman society at this time. If one person's animal got into another person's crops and caused damage, the owner of the delinquent creature could either make recompense for the damage or surrender the beast to the wronged party. According to the *Digest* 43.27.2, a person was allowed to sue his neighbor for the removal of a tree that had been blown by the wind so as to lean over onto the plaintiff's property. Similarly, if the fruit or acorns of one person's tree fell onto the land of another person, the former was permitted to cross into his neighbor's land in order to collect the produce (Pliny *NH* 16.15).

As in other early patriarchal societies, the oldest male ascendent within a Roman household was considered to exercise legal control over its other members and property. Early Roman law, however, subdivided, classified, and institutionalized this overarching authority into three legal concepts. The father of the household (*pater familias*) held his children under paternal authority (*patria potestas*), his wife in his control (*manus* = literally "hand"), and slaves, animals, and all other forms of property in ownership (*dominium*). Slaves could be freed (manumitted) by one of three ways: by registration in the census records as a Roman citizen, by a legal procedure performed in the presence of a Roman magistrate, or by will. The last-named method is mentioned in the surviving portions of the Twelve Tables, and it seems likely that the other two types of manumission already existed at that time as well. Throughout all of Roman history, freed slaves became Roman citizens, were automatically the clients of their former masters or their heirs, and even assumed the *praenomen* and *nomen* of their former owners with their slave name serving as their *cognomen*. Thus a slave named Rufus, when manumitted by his master C. Papirius, became a Roman citizen with the name C. Papirius Rufus. Rome's generous grant of citizenship to freedmen probably stemmed from the fact that in early times slaves were an insignificant portion of the Roman population; since they would have been war captives from neighboring peoples of similar language and culture, freedmen would have been easily integrated into Roman society and could have been regarded as differing little from citizens of Latin states who through *ius migrandi* took up residence in Rome and thereby became Romans. Whatever the origin of this practice, Rome never altered it. From the fourth century B.C. onwards, as Rome's conquest of Italy and the Mediterranean produced a massive influx of slaves, Roman society was constantly receiving into its midst new citizens of foreign origin, through manumission. Such openness contributed to Rome's later success as an imperial power capable of uniting diverse peoples into a workable social system. The demographic significance of this custom was not lost upon the Greeks, including King Philip V of Macedon, who alluded to this Roman phenomenon in a letter written to a Thessalian community in 211 B.C. (*SIG*^{3} 543, cf. Dion. Hal. 4.24).

According to one provision of the Twelve Tables, if a father sold his son three times, the son was freed from paternal authority (Ulpian *Tit.* 10.1). The original significance of this clause must have concerned *nexum* and the intent must have been to place a limit on a father's exploitation of his sons' labor. A father could sell his son to another person. The sale resembled that of a slave, and employed the legal procedure of *mancipatio.* Unlike selling a slave, however, this transfer remained in effect for a stipulated period of time or until an agreed-upon amount of work had been done, at which time the son was "resold" to his father by another *mancipatio.* If the father sold his son two more times, the son was emancipated from paternal authority and became legally independent of his father when he was "resold" to his father for the third time. This interpretation of this provision in the Twelve Tables shows that it complements the provisions on indebtedness, because a father who had one or more healthy grown sons could rely upon them as a valuable resource in discharging debts. The clause may also suggest that in the absence of widespread chattel slavery the early Roman economy might have periodically suffered from labor shortages, which could have been satisfied by fathers' recourse to their sons' labor. If so, a son under paternal authority could have been an important economic asset for a household. However, perhaps already at this time, this clause, was also given a secondary interpretation. It formed the basis of a procedure whereby a father who wished to do so could emancipate his son from his legal authority by selling the son three times to a friend in the presence of a Roman official. Interestingly, later Roman jurists concluded that since the Twelve Tables were silent concerning the selling of daughters, a father could emancipate a daughter from paternal authority by performing a similar ceremony involving a single sale and resale.

Although in later historical times a Roman woman could decide at the time of her marriage whether she wished to come into her husband's legal control or to remain legally independent from him, she had fewer options at the time of the Twelve Tables. In early times there existed three forms of marriage in which the wife entered the *manus* of her husband, and it is likely that they were all mentioned in the Twelve Tables (Watson 1975, 9–19, especially 9–11). The most religiously solemn form of marriage was *confarreatio,* which took its name from the cake of spelt (*far*) shared by the man and woman. The ceremony required the presence of the flamen of Jupiter, the chief pontiff, and ten witnesses. In later historical times, the rex sacrorum and the three major flamens, who had to be members of patrician families, also had to have been married in this way (Gaius *Institutes* 1.112).[13]

---

13. For detailed discussion of the ancient sources and modern views of *confarreatio* and its possible role in the struggle of the orders see Linderski in Raaflaub 1986, 244–61 = Linderski 1995, 542–59. Linderski makes the interesting suggestion that the ceremony was originally an

A second form of early marriage involving *manus* was *coemptio,* in which the procedure of *mancipatio* was used to transfer the woman from her father's paternal authority into her husband's legal control (Forsythe 1996). The third early form of *manus* marriage was termed *usus,* and was simply an adaptation of the Roman legal rule for how one obtained full ownership of property through long-term possession (*usucapio* = "taking by use"). For immovable property, such as land or buildings, ownership required two years of uninterrupted possession, whereas movable things needed only one such year (Gaius *Institutes* 2.42). Thus, in early Roman law, if a woman cohabited with a man for one full year, she was regarded as having entered the man's *manus* by a kind of *usucapio.* Nevertheless, this type of marriage involving *manus* formed the basis of a juristic innovation contained in the Twelve Tables, by which a woman could avoid entering into her husband's legal control. The law specified that if a woman stayed away from her husband for three consecutive nights every year, she would remain legally independent of her husband by interrupting his *usus* (Gaius *Institutes* 1.111 and Gell. 3.2.12). A woman who was in the *manus* of her husband was basically in the same legal position as her children, who were under the husband's paternal authority. Consequently, if the husband died intestate, his children and wife became his heirs and took equal shares of the estate. If a woman did not enter the *manus* of her husband, she remained under the paternal authority of her father until he died, at which time she became legally independent. From the time of the Twelve Tables onwards, women who were not under their father's *patria potestas* or the *manus* of their husbands were still required to have a legal guardian (*tutor*) to assist or oversee their legal transactions. This duty was most often performed by a close male relative, who would have been concerned to protect the family's interests with respect to the woman's dowry. This institution was termed the perpetual guardianship of women (*tutela perpetua mulierum*), and the Vestal virgins were the only females in early Rome exempt from it (Gaius *Institutes* 1.145).

THE SECOND BOARD OF DECEMVIRS

According to the later ancient historical tradition, the Law of the Twelve Tables was codified by two annual boards of decemvirs.[14] The first board drew up the first ten tables of law, performing this and their other duties with the utmost integrity and justice, whereas the second board of legislators,

---

early form of marriage in common use among the Romans, but at some later time the participation of the pontifex maximus and flamen Dialis was added in order to turn the rite into an institution important for the definition of the patriciate.

14. For a somewhat similar skeptical approach to this topic, see the two essays by Ungern-Sternberg in Raaflaub 1986, 78–104 and in Eder 1990, 96–102.

under the leadership of Ap. Claudius, added the last two tables of law and exercised their powers tyrannically. When they refused to leave office at the end of their annual term, a popular uprising, including a second secession, brought about their downfall and the reestablishment of the plebeian tribunate. Simultaneously, senatorial opposition to the ten tyrants was led by Valerius and Horatius, who were elected consuls for 449 B.C. and confirmed the reinstitution of the former political order by the passage of three laws: one that reestablished the right of appeal, another that confirmed tribunician sacrosanctity, and a third which specified that whatever the *plebs* ratified should be binding upon the *populus.*

Virtually every aspect of this ancient historical tradition is suspect. The notion that the legislators had been forcibly removed from power might have initially been suggested to later Roman historians by the names of the consuls of 449 B.C., because the downfall of the monarchy in 509 had resulted in the consulship of P. Valerius Publicola and M. Horatius Pulvillus. In addition, since the annalistic tradition consistently portrayed members of the patrician Claudii as embodying *superbia* (Mommsen 1864, Fiske 1902, and Wiseman 1979a, 57 ff.), the figure of Ap. Claudius was a logical decemviral equivalent of Tarquinius Superbus. Like the overthrow of the Tarquins, the revolt against the second board of legislators was supposed to have been sparked by a wicked assault upon the chastity of a pure and innocent woman. The tale of Lucretia was recycled as the story of Verginia, whose very name reveals the simplicity of the annalists' inventive techniques: for it is merely the Roman name which most closely resembles "virgin" (= *virgo, virginis*). The tale of the evil patrician's cruelty and lust for a beautiful plebeian maiden, which is thwarted only by her murder at the hands of her own father, is rendered more shocking, paradoxical, and sensational when narrated in the context of the prohibition of intermarriage between patricians and plebeians, which the tyrannical board of decemvirs had themselves ordained.

The Roman tale of the decemvirs who became tyrannical and were overthrown is clearly patterned after the well-known story of the Thirty Tyrants of Athens (Xenophon *Hellenica* 2.3.11 ff.). This could have been stimulated in part by the belief that the Romans had used the laws of Solon as a model for the Twelve Tables. Hence, just as the tradition of Rome's transition from monarchy to republic had as its model the fall of the Peisistratid tyranny in Athens, which was soon followed by the establishment of the Cleisthenic democracy, so the famous episode of the Thirty Tyrants served as the mold in which Roman historians cast their accounts of the decemviral legislation. In 404 B.C., after their defeat by Sparta in the Peloponnesian War, the Athenians were forced to abolish the democracy. In its place was appointed a board of thirty who were supposed to draft laws for a new constitution, but instead they arrested, executed, and confiscated the property of suspected political enemies and opponents in order to establish themselves firmly in power. Many other Athenians fled or were driven into exile. After organizing themselves into a military force, the exiles marched into Attica and occupied the stronghold of Phyle, whence they proceeded to the Peiraeus just below Athens itself. Their defeat of the forces sent out against them soon succeeded in forcing the Thirty to abdicate; the democracy was then reinstated. The parallels with the ancient tradition of the decemviral legislation are obvious. After the regular republican offices are suspended, a board of ten is appointed for drawing up new laws, but once the codification is completed the decemvirs become tyrannical and refuse to leave office at the expiration of their annual term; they are forced to resign by a secession, and the sequence concludes with the reestablishment of republican institutions. In addition, the curious topography of this second secession may even be directly patterned after the movements of the Athenian exiles: for in the Roman tradition the plebs first occupied the Mons Sacer, situated three miles from Rome beyond the Anio, but the rebels then returned to the city and joined up with other plebeians in occupying the Aventine Hill.

The ancient tradition, that the first just board of ten men drew up exactly ten tables of law and was followed by a second tyrannical board which added two more tables, is clearly simplistic and therefore *prima facie* appears to be unhistorical. Indeed, the sharp contrast between the two boards of decemvirs conforms to Greek political theory concerning the cycle of constitutions, in which one ideal form of government gives way to its corrupt counterpart, and the latter brings about the establishment of another ideal form. Thus, just as the Roman kingship degenerated into tyranny, which was replaced by the aristocratic republic, so the first board of ten represents aristocratic rule in its ideal form, followed by the corrupt oligarchy of the second board, whose misrule leads to revolution and further political change.[15] Another point against the historicity of the two different boards of legislators is that the codification should not have been so complicated or time-consuming as to have required more than one year and a single decemviral commission. Unfortunately, the neat and tidy arrangement of the surviving portions of the lawcode encountered in most modern editions tends to lend credence to this ancient tradition. Modern editions and translations of the Twelve Tables have generally followed without question the text established by scholars of the nineteenth century (see Crawford 1996, 564–69), in which the ancient material is organized rationally according to specific categories of the law, and the content of each table is confined to a discrete area: e.g., Tables I–II concern legal procedure, Table III indebtedness, Table IV *patria potestas,* Table VIII delicts and related matters, Table IX

---

15. This seems to have been Polybius's interpretation of the decemvirate. See Polyb. 6.11.1. Yet, rather than the result of decemviral oligarchy's being democracy, as the standard theory of the cycle of constitutions would suggest, Polybius regarded the outcome to have been Rome's mixed constitution.

public law, Table X funerary regulations, etc. It is virtually certain, however, that when the lawcode had been completed, a text written on a set of wooden tablets or on a linen scroll was given to an engraver, who then proceeded to inscribe the text upon bronze, and it just so happened that he needed twelve tablets to do the job. Ancient habits of cutting inscriptions would suggest that, even if the lawcode had been neatly organized into specific categories (which is itself an unwarranted assumption), there would have been no attempt on the part of the engraver to insure that the content of each bronze tablet pertained to only one area of the law. Rather, as in the pages of a printed book, the legal text would have been engraved continuously from the bottom of one tablet to the top of the next.

Moreover, the modern organization of the text is based upon very little evidence. Of the 105 provisions that can be reconstituted from ancient quotations or paraphrases of the lawcode, there are only five that provide specific information bearing upon the location of clauses in the text. Three of these refer to the specific number of the tablet, and two other provisions were ascribed to the second board of decemvirs and therefore must have been contained in the last two tablets. Festus (336L s.v. *reus*) cites Table II for a provision concerning an issue of legal procedure; Dionysius (2.27.3) cites Table IV in reference to paternal authority; and Cicero (*De Legibus* 2.64) indicates that Table X contained provisions which placed sumptuary restrictions on funerals. In addition to these three passages, the ancient tradition was unanimous in ascribing the prohibition of intermarriage·between patricians and plebeians to the second decemviral board; and Macrobius (*Saturnalia* 1.13.21) cites both Cassius Hemina and Sempronius Tuditanus for the view that this same second board of legislators had concerned themselves with intercalation. Consequently, given the later ancient view of how the lawcode came into being, these two provisions must have been contained in Tables XI–XII. Thus readers should not be misled by the arrangement of modern editions of the Twelve Tables, but should always keep in mind that the standard organization of the legal material is itself a modern fiction.

THE PROHIBITION OF INTERMARRIAGE

These conclusions are essential in assessing the historicity of the prohibition of intermarriage between patricians and plebeians.[16] Cicero (*De Re Pub.* 2.61–63) cites this clause, which he terms "the most inhumane

16. For a similarly skeptical treatment of the prohibition on intermarriage and the Canuleian Law, as well as explication of the ancient tradition in terms of early restrictions placed upon Roman priests, see Mitchell in Raaflaub 1986, 171–73, which is restated in a somewhat expanded form in Mitchell 1990, 126–29. Unconvincing in my view, however, is Mitchell's explanation for Dionysius's failure to mention the Canuleian Law: namely, that the issue was too technical for his Greek readers. On the contrary, it seems more likely that Dionysius would have welcomed the opportunity to engage in yet another of his long-winded explanations of Roman institutions and practices.

law (*lex inhumanissima*)," as proof of the legislators' cruel and tyrannical nature. Yet, if the analysis in the preceding paragraph be accepted, we should not expect any distinction between the first ten and last two tables of law in their overall character and nature. The ancients, however, did so, and their interpretation of the lawcode's content, especially the last two tables, must have been influenced by the belief that these last provisions had been drafted by evil men. In fact, later historians, hard pressed for solid data upon which to base their narratives, must have studied the last two tables carefully with the purpose of finding something to illustrate the decemvirs' tyranny, and what they came up with was the prohibition of intermarriage between the two orders.

In the Livian narrative (4.1–7), this prohibition was repealed in 445 B.C., a mere five years after its enactment, by the passage of a law promulgated by the plebeian tribune C. Canuleius. The acrimonious debate surrounding this statute is depicted as being bound up with other important political issues: namely, the plebeian demand to have access to the consulship, and the creation of the office of military tribune with consular power. According to Livy, while Canuleius urged the passage of his own bill, the other nine plebeian tribunes proposed a second rogation which allowed the consulship to be held by members of the plebs. Faced with this political onslaught, the senate attempted to quash the latter and more serious proposal by permitting the former to be passed. When tribunician agitation for access to the consulship continued, a political compromise was reached, according to which the consulship would continue to be a patrician preserve, but plebeians would be allowed to hold the office of military tribune with consular power. Cicero (*De Re Pub.* 2.63) briefly alludes to the Canuleian Law in connection with the decemvirs' enactment of the prohibition of intermarriage, but since the text of the *De Re Publica* abruptly ends at this point, we do not know whether Livy and Cicero agreed concerning the larger political context of Canuleius's bill. Dionysius (10.60.5) mentions only in passing that the second board of decemvirs prohibited intermarriage between the two orders, but in his account of the year 445 B.C. (11.53–61) he never mentions Canuleius's measure to remove this ban. This is despite the fact that his description of the political controversy over plebeian access to the consulship is much more detailed than that of Livy.

As a general rule, Dionysius's narrative always includes far more circumstantial details than the parallel passages in Livy. As a result, his narrative frequently elucidates many issues obscured by Livy's rigorous economy of language and preference for portraying emotions and melodrama as opposed to explicating complex political and legal issues logically and coherently. In this instance, both accounts describe the political conflict as pitting one plebeian tribune against the other nine, but Dionysius differs from Livy in that his sole plebeian tribune is a henchman of the senatorial opposition, while the other nine (including Canuleius) urge the passage of a single tribunician measure concerning plebeian access to the consulship. In addition, whereas Livy (4.3–5) has Canuleius deliver a very eloquent speech advocating the repeal of the prohibition on intermarriage, Dionysius (11.57) singles out Canuleius from the other tribunes to have him speak in support of the tribunician proposal concerning the consulship. It is therefore quite evident that Livy and Dionysius used different sources for this year, and that Dionysius's source did not include the Canuleian repeal of the prohibition on intermarriage. Furthermore, given his citation at 4.7.10–12 of Licinius Macer, the Linen Books, and the alleged treaty with Ardea concerning the suffect consuls of 444 B.C., Livy's immediate source for these events would appear to be Licinius Macer; whereas given the agreement between Livy and Dionysius concerning the division between one plebeian tribune and the other nine, as well as the abdication of the first elected consular tribunes, Dionysius's source is likely to have been either Valerius Antias or Aelius Tubero, who followed but adapted the account of Licinius Macer. This same pattern—Macer's account being taken over and adapted by the later two authors—is evident from Livy 4.23.1–3 concerning the names and official titulature of the curule magistrates for the year 434 B.C. Consequently, we can plausibly postulate that the Canuleian repeal of the prohibition on intermarriage was present in the work of Licinius Macer but was absent from that of either Valerius Antias or Aelius Tubero. Unfortunately, the present state of our evidence does not allow us to determine whether or not Dionysius's source for the year 445 B.C. acknowledged the existence of the marriage prohibition, and if so, in what way it was thought to have been repealed.[17] In any case, it is quite obvious that fundamental differences existed in the ancient historical tradition, at least concerning the repeal of the marriage prohibition, and such disagreements may have existed also with respect to the prohibition itself.

The text of the Law of the Twelve Tables must have gone through at least two major stages during republican times. In the first stage, the lawcode was an epigraphic text inscribed on twelve bronze tablets (hence its name), but at some later time which cannot be precisely determined but must remain a matter of speculation, the lawcode became a literary text having the form of a small ancient book (contra Mitchell 1990, 124–26 and 1996, 260–63). In *De Oratore* 1.195, Cicero terms the lawcode "a single booklet (*unus libellus*)" and contrasts its compendious sagacity with whole libraries of Greek

---

17. In this connection it is worth noting that although they accept the historicity of the decemviral prohibition on intermarriage, both Linderski (Raaflaub 1986, 260) and Raaflaub (*Bilancio Critico* 1993, 156) regard the repeal by the Canuleian Law in 445 B.C. as suspect.

philosophy. According to Livy (6.1.10), following the Gallic capture of Rome major public documents such as treaties and the Twelve Tables had to be sought out amid the devastation. This statement can be interpreted in two different ways. Either the inscribed lawcode was recovered basically intact, or it was destroyed by the enemy and therefore had to be reconstructed by those knowledgeable in the law. Yet since several inscribed texts are known to have survived the Gallic occupation of the city, Livy's remark on this matter cannot be given much credence. Rather, it is more reasonable to suppose that the Gallic catastrophe had no appreciable impact upon the Romans' knowledge of the Twelve Tables during the fourth century B.C. On the other hand, since laws inscribed on bronze were often not easy to read but tended to serve a symbolic purpose (Williamson 1987), it is likely that the Twelve Tables became a literary text some time during the fourth century B.C., as the Roman civil law began to be administered by curule magistrates. Since these administrators would have found it more convenient to consult this body of law in book form, the twelve bronze tablets of the lawcode would have become obsolete, and might even have been melted down so that the metal could be recycled.

In any case, the literary text of the Twelve Tables which circulated in later historical times is likely to have been the one published by Sex. Aelius Paetus (consul 198 B.C.) in his *Tripertita*, which stands at the beginning of Roman juristic literature. This treatise took its name from its threefold organization. The first part set forth the text of the Twelve Tables; the second part was a commentary on the lawcode; and the third part explained which of the *legis actiones* were to be used in initiating lawsuits on the basis of the various provisions of this body of law (*Digest* 1.2.2.38). The fact that Cicero and Dionysius could still cite provisions according to their numbered table suggests that this later literary text of the lawcode attempted to maintain the original arrangement of the material as it had been in the epigraphic text. Nevertheless, since about 250 years intervened between the inscribed lawcode and Paetus's *Tripertita*, the later literary text could have been reorganized to some extent, with its contents altered by the interpolation of "updated reinterpretations" of old provisions. This process of modernization is most evident in the actual language and grammar (see Crawford 1996, 571). Even though many of the allegedly verbatim quotations from the Twelve Tables contain archaic grammatical forms, the language is not as peculiar as we might expect from a text dating to the middle of the fifth century B.C. Consequently, the phenomenon of linguistic modernization raises the possibility that a similar process, in the form of reinterpretation and misinterpretation, might have altered the lawcode's content somewhat, especially in the case of provisions legally defunct and hence no longer well understood. This was in fact the case with respect to the provision imposing capital punishment for casting evil spells, which later commentators misconstrued as applying to libel.[18] In this connection it is also worth noting that according to Cicero (*De Legibus* 2.59) the meaning of the word *lessum*, contained in the Twelve Tables, eluded Sex. Aelius Paetus. Furthermore, the lawcode is known to have used words whose meanings had changed somewhat in later times (see *Digest* 50.16.236 concerning the meaning of *venenum*).[19]

The Livian and Ciceronian renderings of the prohibition of intermarriage between patricians and plebeians are quite similar and are clearly not direct quotations from a legal text: Livy 4.4.5, "ne conubium patribus cum plebe esset" = "that there was not to be marriage of *patres* with the plebs." Cicero *De Re Pub.* 2.63, "conubia . . . ne plebei cum patribus essent" = "that there were not to be marriages of the plebs with the *patres*." As discussed in the previous chapter (see above p. 167ff), the combined religious and constitutional significance of *patrum auctoritas*, the principle of *auspicia ad patres redeunt*, and the appellation *qui patres qui conscripti* suggest that the patriciate evolved from and was largely defined by the tenure of hereditary priesthoods; that in early times these priests were *ex officio* members of the senate; and that, like the gods whom they served, they were collectively termed the *patres*. Thus, if the term *patres* was used in a provision of the Twelve Tables, the word should have referred to this group of priestly senators. If their marriage was the subject of the provision, it is likely to have specified that priests had to have been married by *confarreatio*, as continued to be the case for the rex sacrorum and the three major flamens. Moreover, since in later historical times *confarreatio* was preserved in large measure for holders of these religious offices, who were always members of patrician families, we can understand why later ancient historians interpreted a legal provision requiring priests to be married by *confarreatio* as a ban on intermarriage between patricians and plebeians.

As already seen in this chapter concerning the trial of K. Quinctius and the tribunician prosecutions of the consuls of 455 B.C., ancient historians were quite capable of generating fictitious legal proceedings out of authentic statutes or documents. The same clearly applies to Ap. Claudius's verdict concerning Verginia, as well as to the tale of Scaptius and the Roman people judging crookedly in a land dispute between Aricia and

---

18. For the ancient misconception, see Cic. *De Re Pub.* 4.12 = Aug. *Civ. Dei* 2.9, and for a detailed discussion of this matter, see Ronconi 1964.

19. For an archaic Latin legal formula whose meaning has escaped both ancient and modern scholars, see Forsythe 1996.

Ardea (Livy 3.71–72).[20] Thus viewing the prohibition on intermarriage as a later annalistic distortion should not be ruled out, and other considerations can be adduced in support of this notion. Watson (1975, 9–11) has plausibly argued that all three forms of marriage involving *manus* (*coemptio, usus,* and *confarreatio*) were treated in the Twelve Tables. Furthermore, as stated above, ancient evidence indicates that the prohibition on intermarriage and intercalation were treated in the last two tables of the lawcode. If the subject matter of these two tables was pretty much the same, we may cautiously conjecture that these provisions concerned matters of religion. Remember that one provision in the Twelve Tables specified that Vestal virgins were exempt from the perpetual guardianship of women (Gaius *Institutes* 1.145). This clause is of particular interest in the present context, because it demonstrates that the Twelve Tables contained provisions dealing with legal aspects of priestly offices. Thus, neither circumstantial evidence nor the working methods of the annalists are inconsistent with the hypothesis that the alleged prohibition on intermarriage was generated from a legal provision that actually concerned the requirement of priests to be married by *confarreatio.* The sheer improbability of a ban on intermarriage is further suggested by Cicero and Livy, both of whom contrast it with the right of intermarriage between Romans and persons from other Latin communities. The prohibition, therefore, cannot be accepted uncritically as one of the few solid pieces of evidence for the history of the patricio-plebeian dichotomy, as has generally been done in modern scholarship. The ban is probably not historical at all.

THE SECOND SECESSION AND THE VALERIAN HORATIAN LAWS

One final subject pertaining to the decemviral legislation requires comment. This is the historicity of the second secession of the plebs and the three Valerian Horatian Laws of 449 B.C. Given the fact that the second secession is closely bound up with the notion of a second tyrannical board of decemvirs, both of which are patterned after the overthrow of the Thirty Tyrants of Athens, the secession's historicity can hardly be defended. Similarly, since the Valerian Horatian Laws were portrayed as reestablishing the republic following a brief period of oligarchical despotism, we are justified

---

20. Both of these fictitious lawsuits illustrate the Roman legal principle of "the judge who makes the case his own." The Twelve Tables are known to have imposed the death penalty upon a judge or arbiter who was convicted of having accepted money to influence his verdict (Gell. 20.1.7). In Livy's narrative, these two cases serve to offset one another. The case of Verginia is wrongfully decided by a wicked patrician, whereas the land arbitration is foolishly adjudged by the Roman plebs at the urging of Scaptius. The latter case is likewise related to the political strife that breaks out in Ardea as a result of a quarrel patterned after the tale of Verginia, and in the end all is set aright by the prudence and sagacity of the Roman senate.

to view them with extreme skepticism. The law reinstating the right to appeal is nothing more than a repetition of the equally fictitious Valerian Law on appeal dating to the first year of the republic. *Provocatio* was in fact treated in the Twelve Tables (Cic. *De Legibus* 3.11 and 3.44) and therefore did not need to be reinstituted by a special statute. Likewise, if the second secession never took place, there should have been little need for a law reaffirming the sacrosanctity of plebeian tribunes. In fact, the form in which Livy paraphrases this law in 3.55.7 seems to correspond to the constitutional conditions of the third century B.C. and may derive from an actual legal text of that period, because the law encompassed not only plebeian tribunes but also *decemviri,* who must be the *decemviri stlitibus iudicandis,* a board of annually elected minor officials, whose office was created during the third century B.C. (*Digest* 1.2.2.29). Indeed, given the rather simplistic manner in which ancient historians of early Rome constructed their fictions, the mere occurrence of the title *decemviri* in a legal document of the third century could have been responsible for its association with the decemviral legislation of the mid-fifth century B.C.

As already discussed (see above p. 180), according to later Roman antiquarians and jurists (e.g., Gaius *Institutes* 1.3 and Gell. 15.27.4), *populus* comprised both patricians and plebeians, but *plebs* included only the latter. As a result, one major element in the struggle of the orders was supposed to have been the patricians' acceptance that they were also bound by enactments of the plebs. Statutes were consequently believed to have been passed on three different occasions which ordained that whatever the *plebs* had ordered also bound the *populus.* The first of these laws was one of the Valerian Horatian Laws of 449 (Livy 3.55.3). The other two were supposed to have been passed in 339 (Livy 8.12.15) and in 287 B.C. (Pliny *NH* 16.37, Gaius *Institutes* 1.3, and Gell. 15.27.4). Various modern hypotheses have been put forward to explain this ancient tradition.[21] One approach has been to accept all three laws as historical and to suppose that it took repeated passage of the same measure to force the patricians to acknowledge this constitutional principle (Develin 1985, 22). Another approach has been to view all three instances as historical and to suppose that each one concerned some change in legislative procedure; although they were different from one another, the annalistic tradition simply assigned the same effect to all three measures (so Tondo in *Bilancio Critico* 1993, 44–49 and Cornell 1995, 277–78; cf. Scullard 1980, 469–70). A third approach has been to reject the earlier two instances as unhistorical and to accept only the one associated with the third secession in 287 (Drummond in *CAH* VII.2 1989, 223).

21. For further discussion and additional modern bibliography on this subject, see von Fritz 1950, 25–31; Staveley 1955; Ogilvie 1965, 497–98; Maddox 1984; Hölkeskamp 1988b, 292 ff.; and Oakley 1998, 523–25.

Yet the original distinction between *plebs* and *populus* may indicate that none of these laws was ever really necessary. The term *plebs* was always associated with the Roman people organized according to tribes into the civilian tribal assembly, and the enactments of this body were termed *plebei scita*, a phrase clearly analogous and juxtaposed to *senatus consulta*. *Populus*, on the other hand, was the appellation of the same citizen body organized according to military units into the *comitia centuriata*, and its enactments were called *leges*, derived from *legere* (= "to choose"). The connection of *populus* with the military *comitia centuriata* is confirmed by the denominative verb *populari* (= "to lay waste"), and by *magister populi*, meaning "master of the army," a title for the Roman dictator who commanded the infantry forces, in contrast to his subordinate *magister equitum* who led the cavalry (Varro *Ling. Lat.* 5.82 and Festus 216L s.v. *optima lex*). It is plausible to assume that both the tribal and centuriate assemblies were equally sovereign bodies and could pass resolutions, which became binding statutes when accompanied by a vote of *patrum auctoritas*. If so, the only obvious reason for passing a statute like the Valerian Horatian Law would have been to state unequivocally that the enactment of one assembly was no less valid than that of the other. Such clarification might have been desirable in early times, as the centuriate organization slowly evolved from being simply the army in the field to an actual assembly.[22] Nevertheless, this suggestion does not account for the ancient tradition that the same measure was enacted on three different occasions.

Perhaps the most plausible explanation is to understand these three laws as later misinterpretations of a clause found in the Twelve Tables, according to which "whatever the people had ordered last was the law."[23] Modern editions and translations of the Twelve Tables have rightly placed this clause at the very end of the lawcode, because its obvious intent was to indicate that wherever there were differences between the Twelve Tables and earlier law, the provisions of the lawcode were to prevail. Moreover, since this statement embodied an important legal principle, it could have become a constitutional formula used in other statutes that were supplanting existing laws,[24] and this usage could have been repeatedly misinterpreted by later

22. For a more detailed argument along these lines in reference to the supposed Publilian Law of 471 B.C. that created the tribal assembly, see above p. 18off.

23. Note the similarity in wording between the laws of 449 and 339 B.C. and the relevant provision of the Twelve Tables, twice mentioned by Livy: Livy 3.55.3, "ut quod tributim plebes iussisset populum teneret;" Livy 8.12.15, "ut plebi scita omnes Quirites tenerent;" Livy 7.17.12, "ut quodcumque postremum populus iussisset id ius ratumque esset;" and Livy 9.34.6, "id ius esse, quod postremo populus iussisset."

24. A possible analogy might be the Roman practice of placing a standard proviso at the end of a treaty with a foreign state affirming that if both states wished, they could add or subtract anything to the agreement.

ancient historians to fit their overarching thesis of a struggle of the orders (Mitchell 1984, 195–98). Indeed, if this clause was the final provision of the Twelve Tables, as seems likely, its position could have been misconstrued as a final addition made by the consuls Valerius and Horatius. In fact, Diodorus (12.26.1) attributes the drafting of the last two tables of the law-code to these two consuls. As a result, like the other two Valerian Horatian Laws, this one is also to be considered unhistorical.

The notion that the comitia centuriata was originally the only sovereign Roman assembly, and that in early times the plebs in the comitia tributa could not pass enactments binding upon all citizens may have been the product of the political conflict and controversies of the late republic. In 88 B.C. Sulla became the first Roman commander to march on Rome with his army and to capture the city by force. Although this extraordinary act was prompted by his desire to maintain his consular command for the Mithridatic War, he used the occasion to institute some major constitutional reforms designed to weaken the power of plebeian tribunes and to keep them from interfering in the senate's conduct of foreign affairs. Sulla ordained that henceforth only the comitia centuriata was to have the power to enact laws, and he justified this constitutional innovation on the grounds that it represented the ancestral constitution of King Servius Tullius (Appian *Bell. Civ.* 1.59). When he returned to Italy from the Mithridatic War a few years later, Sulla marched on Rome a second time and established himself in control of the state by having himself made dictator. In this capacity, he carried through various constitutional reforms, including severe restrictions on the plebeian tribunate and the reinstatement of his earlier measure about the comitia centuriata. This so-called Sullan constitution was finally dismantled in 70 B.C., but during its twelve-year existence (c. 82–70) it had politically polarized Roman society and had stirred up a tremendous controversy over the proper powers to be exercised by the senate, the people, and the tribunes (see Gruen 1974, 23–28 and Millar 1998, 49–72). There can be little doubt that the parties involved in this struggle (including the plebeian tribune and historian Licinius Macer) made various appeals to Rome's ancestral constitution in order to justify their positions, and these partisan interpretations no doubt had a significant impact on how contemporary historians portrayed the struggle of the orders in the early republic (see Finley 1971).

In conclusion, a critical examination of the ancient historical tradition surrounding the codification of the Twelve Tables leaves very little worthy of credence. Nevertheless, the analysis reveals much about the working methods of the ancient historians and likewise demonstrates that relatively little authentic historical evidence from the mid-fifth century B.C. succeeded in reaching later historical times.

Chapter 8

Evolution and Growth of the Roman State, 444–367 B.C.

THE MILITARY TRIBUNES WITH CONSULAR POWER

Shortly after the codification of the Twelve Tables, the chief executive office of the Roman state was reorganized.[1] Beginning in 444 B.C. and extending down to 367 B.C., the eponymous officials of the Roman state fluctuated between two consuls and a board of military tribunes with consular power (also termed consular tribunes), who were at first three in number but were later increased to four and finally to six.[2] As already discussed in connection with the prohibition of intermarriage between patricians and plebeians (see above p. 226), the accounts of Livy (4.1–7) and Dionysius (11.53–61) are rather different for the alleged political controversy between the senate and people during the year 445 B.C. Although Dionysius fails to treat the passage of the Canuleian Law, which Livy portrays in great detail, the two authors agree in reporting that the decision to create the office of consular tribune resulted from a compromise between the two orders over the issue

---

1. For other modern treatments of the events covered in this chapter, see Ogilvie's commentary on Livy Books IV–V in 1965, 526–752; Heurgon 1973, 173–75 and 180–86; Scullard 1980, 97–108 and 115–19; Cornell in *CAH* VII.2 1989, 298–338; Cornell 1995, 309–22 and 327–40; and Oakley's commentary on Livy Book VI in 1997, 344–733.

2. The consular tribunate has been much discussed by modern scholars, with a variety of opinions expressed as to its nature and the cause(s) of its creation (e.g., political, military, or administrative). See Beloch 1926, 247–64; Cornelius 1940; von Fritz 1950; Staveley 1953; Adcock 1957; Boddington 1959; Sealey 1959; Ogilvie 1965, 539–50; Pinsent 1975, 29–61; Gutberlet 1985, 98 ff.; Ridley 1986; Drummond in *CAH* VII.2 1989, 192–95; Richard 1990; Cornell 1995, 334–39; Walt 1997, 313–18; Oakley 1997, 367–76; and Stewart 1998, 54–94. For the reliability of the *fasti* for these years, see Pinsent 1975 and Drummond 1980. For an explication of Roman thought concerning curule magistrates and the auspices, see Linderski in Eder 1990, 34–48.

of plebeian access to the consulship. In order to avoid the passage of a tribunician bill legalizing plebeian access to the consulship, the senate succeeded in preserving the patrician monopoly of this office by creating the consular tribunate and allowing plebeians to hold this office instead. Consequently, according to the later annalistic tradition found in Livy and Dionysius, the domestic political history of Rome during the period 444–367 B.C. was punctuated by yearly disputes as to whether consuls or consular tribunes should be elected for the next year. After describing in considerable detail how the plebeian tribunes, consuls, and senate clashed over the proposal to open up the consulship to plebeian candidates and how they arrived at their political compromise, Livy (4.7.2) remarks:

> There are those who, without mentioning the proposed law concerning electing consuls from the plebs, say that because the two consuls were not able to handle so many wars at the same time due to a Veientine war being added to the war with the Aequians and Volscians as well as the defection of Ardea, three military tribunes were elected, and they exercised *imperium* and enjoyed the consular insignia.

This statement clearly indicates that there was not unanimity in the ancient historical tradition concerning the reasons why the consular tribunate was established. Some writers interpreted it in terms of the struggle of the orders and the plebeians' quest to attain Rome's highest office, whereas others believed that the office was created merely out of military necessity. Given the rather monotonous and unimaginative way in which some of the later annalists interpreted virtually every step in early Rome's internal development as an aspect of the struggle between patricians and plebeians, we are justified in viewing this ancient approach to the consular tribunate with considerable suspicion. As argued in chapter 7 (see above p. 227), the citations of Licinius Macer, the Linen Books, and the treaty with Ardea in Livy 4.7.10–12, concerning the names of the suffect consuls of 444 B.C., make it likely that Livy's primary source for the first seven chapters of his fourth book was Licinius Macer. Moreover, since Dionysius's parallel account appears to be an adaptation of what we encounter in Livy, Dionysius's principal source is likely to have been an author who followed but adapted Macer's narrative. If so, the author or authors behind Dionysius's narrative would have to be Valerius Antias and/or Aelius Tubero. If this be accepted, both of our extant accounts of these events and their interpretation derive from writers of the closing decades of the republic. The surviving fragments from Licinius Macer indicate that he was fond of finding political motives where none had existed in the earlier historical tradition (e.g., Livy 7.9.3–6, 9.46.3, and 10.9.10–13). In fact, since the two suffect consuls recorded by Licinius Macer for 444 B.C. appear in the next year as the first two elected censors, it seems likely that the suffect consuls are the creation of Macer's erroneous reconstruction or willful interpretation of the Linen Books, which he alone apparently discovered and used.

Since the consular tribunes were initially three in number, the title "tribune" is likely to have derived from the three archaic tribes of the Titienses, Ramnenses, and Luceres, which could still have been used in some form as the basis of military recruitment. This suggests a military purpose behind the office's creation, as well as hinting at a different allocation of Rome's military forces among the state's supreme commanders. In addition, since these officials exercised consular *imperium,* they, like the consuls, must have been elected by the comitia centuriata. Thus the only apparent difference between the consuls and the consular tribunes lay in the title of the office and their number. It therefore appears likely that the reason for this innovation was simply the military needs of the state, as declared by the variant tradition cited by Livy. This surmise gains further credence from two other contemporary innovations: the creation of the office of quaestor in 446 (Tacitus *Ann.* 11.22) and the institution of the censorship in 443 B.C. (Livy 4.8). When taken together, these three innovations constitute a strong indication of a major reorganization in the military structure of the Roman state during the decade of the 440s B.C. The censors were elected in order to conduct a census of the Roman population for the purpose of assessing citizens' property, age, and residence, which in turn determined their voting rights and military and financial obligations to the state. The quaestors were financial officials; in early Rome, when the public and private sectors were both at a rudimentary level of development, their duties are likely to have centered around the disposition of booty, supplies for the army, and other basic needs of the Roman state. We therefore need not doubt that the growth and the changing military and administrative needs of the Roman state were responsible for bringing about the institution of the consular tribunate.

As seen from the information set out below, during the eighteen years 444–427 B.C. there were only five years in which three military tribunes with consular power were elected, whereas consuls were chosen for the other thirteen years. In 426 B.C., the year in which Rome captured and annexed Fidenae, the number of consular tribunes was increased to four for the first time, and during the twenty-one years 426–406 B.C. there were only seven years of consuls but fourteen years in which there were either three or four consular tribunes. Then in 405 B.C., the number of military tribunes was increased to six for the first time; and after that, apart from a few anomalous years in which eight or ten consular tribunes are recorded, the Roman state was headed by six military tribunes for almost every year down to the abolition of the office and the reinstitution of the consulship in 366 B.C. This gradual but rather steady increase in the number of consular tribunes during the late fifth and early fourth centuries B.C. is best explained in terms of a complex combination of Rome's increasing external-military and internal-administrative needs (von Fritz 1950, 37–44). This is clearly evident from the fact that the reorganization of the Roman state in 367/6 B.C. replaced a board of six consular tribunes with five officials with differentiated functions: two consuls for waging Rome's wars, one praetor to oversee lawsuits in the city, and two curule aediles to perform other urban administrative duties such as organizing public spectacles and exercising jurisdiction over the markets in Rome. Given the nature of this transition in 367/6 B.C., we may plausibly surmise that during the period 405–367 B.C., when six consular tribunes were elected almost every year, two, three, and perhaps even four of these officials were occupied with non-military administrative duties confined to the city, but they could be called upon to serve in the field if the need arose. By 367 B.C., however, Rome's position in Latium had become quite secure, so that the urban duties of the consular tribunes could be fully regularized. Consequently, the creation, augmentation, and abolition of the consular tribunate were primarily, if not exclusively, determined by the external-military and internal-administrative needs of the Roman state.

Politics are likely to have been involved in the history of the consular tribunate at two different junctures and in two different ways. First, as argued above in chapter 6 (see p. 166), when the patriciate finally emerged during the last years of the fifth century B.C., the consular tribunate had all but completely replaced the consulship as the chief office of the Roman state (there having been only two consulships in the years 408–367 B.C.); at that time, even though there was no legal ban against non-patricians holding the consulship, the patriciate might have claimed that patricians alone should hold this office. If so, this would explain the overly broad assertion in the later ancient historical tradition that before 366 B.C. the patriciate had exercised a complete monopoly over the consulship since the very beginning of the republic. Moreover, once the number of military tribunes with consular power was increased to six, from 405 B.C. onwards, the relative value of the consulship would have been greatly enhanced in the Roman aristocratic culture, and this increase in the office's prestige could have been responsible for the patricians' assertion of their exclusive right to the office, just as they laid claim to the various religious priesthoods. These considerations would not have been at issue when the consular tribunate was first introduced in 444 B.C. Secondly, when the decision was taken in 367 B.C. to abolish the consular tribunate and to reintroduce the consulship along with three new curule magistracies, a debate would have arisen between the leading members of the two newly emerged orders as to whether and how the consulship would be shared. Nevertheless, this political debate and the eventual agreement to share the consulship equally would have been secondary to the primary decision to restructure the curule magistracies of the Roman state.

The following list of dates illustrates the alternation in time between consuls and military tribunes with consular power, as well as showing the
increase in the number of the latter. The number in parentheses indicates
how many of the magistrates bore names which in later times were exclusively plebeian (see n.6 in chapter 6). Other possibly related events have
been listed below, such as the creation of certain offices or the waging of
particular wars, but it should be remembered that the ancient sources about
Rome's early wars are often unreliable in terms of their precise dating,
nature, and magnitude. Only the most notable wars have been listed here.

457: Increase in the number of plebeian tribunes from five to ten.

451–450: Decemviral codification of the Law of the Twelve Tables.

446: Creation of the office of quaestor (two annually elected).

445: Decision to elect military tribunes with consular power (hereafter
abbreviated mil. trs. c.p.).

444: 3 mil. trs. c.p. (2).

443: 2 consuls (hereafter abbreviated coss.), and the creation of the
censorship.

442–439: 2 coss.

440–439: Food shortage in Rome involving the sedition of Sp. Maelius.

438: 3 mil. trs. c.p. Murder of Roman ambassadors sent to Fidenae to seek
redress.

437–426: Rome's war against Fidenae.

437–435: 2 coss.

434–432: 3 mil. trs. c.p.

431: 2 coss.

430: 2 coss. Eight-year truce signed with the Aequians.

429–427: 2 coss.

426: 4 mil. trs. c.p.

425: 4 mil. trs. c.p. (1). Twenty-year truce granted to Veii, and a truce of
three years made with the Aequians.

424: 4 mil. trs. c.p.

423: 2 coss. (1).

422: 3 mil. trs. c.p. (1).

421: 2 coss. Number of quaestors increased from two to four.

420–419: 4 mil. trs. c.p. (1, in 420).

418: 3 mil. trs. c.p.

417–414: 4 mil. trs. c.p. (1, in 416).

413–409: 2 coss.

408: 3 mil. trs. c.p.

407: 4 mil. trs. c.p.

406: 4 mil. trs. c.p. The ten-year war against Veii begins this year, along
with the introduction of military pay for the first time.

405–396: 6 mil. trs. c.p. (4 in 400, 5 in 399, and 5 in 396). Veii is captured in 396.

403: Enrollment of the Roman cavalry is increased.

395: 6 mil. trs. c.p. Rome makes a treaty with Capena in southern Etruria.

394: 6 mil. trs. c.p. Rome makes a treaty with Falerii in southern Etruria.

393–392: 2 coss.

391–390: 6 mil. trs. c.p.

390: Gallic capture of Rome.

389: 6 or 8 mil. trs. c.p.

388: 6 mil. trs. c.p. (1).

387: 6 or 8 mil. trs. c.p. Creation of four new voting tribes out of the Veientine territory.

386–381: 6 mil. trs. c.p. (1, in 383).

381: Rome extends citizenship to Tusculum.

380: 6, 8, or possibly 9 mil. trs. c.p. Under the leadership of the dictator T. Quinctius, Rome this year defeats Praeneste and its coalition of nine towns.

379: 6 or 8 mil. trs. c.p. (3 or 5).

378–377: 6 mil. trs. c.p.

376–371: Livy records that during these years there were no curule magistrates elected due to civil discord.

370–367: 6 mil. trs. c.p.

366: Reinstitution of the consulship along with one praetor for handling lawsuits and two curule aediles for managing various affairs in the city.

362: Henceforth the Romans elect every year six military tribunes who serve as subordinate officers under the two consuls.

THE SEDITION OF SP. MAELIUS

According to the later historical tradition, the Roman state was disturbed during the years 440–439 B.C. by the attempt of one man to seize tyrannical power.[3] Although they differ in numerous details, Livy (4.12–16) and Dionysius (12.2–3) generally agree that a severe grain shortage led to L. Minucius's appointment as *praefectus annonae* (prefect of the grain supply), but when the equestrian, Sp. Maelius, was discovered to be using his own resources and network of associates to acquire grain in order to gain credit with the people in preparation for seizing absolute power, L. Quinctius

3. For fuller treatments of this complex legend, see Mommsen 1871, 256–71; Pais 1906, 204–23; Ogilvie 1965, 550–57; Lintott 1970, 12–18; Forsythe 1994, 301–10; Wiseman in Linderski 1996, 57–71 = Wiseman 1998, 90–105; and Walt 1997, 319–24.

Cincinnatus was appointed dictator with C. Servilius Ahala as his master of the horse, and the latter killed Maelius when he refused to obey the dictator's summons to answer a charge of attempted tyranny brought against him by Minucius.

As in the earlier tale of Sp. Cassius, the later accounts are so overlaid with etiological and folkloristic elements that it is difficult to ascertain the historicity of this tradition. The story is used to explain at least four things: (1) the existence of the Columna Minucia outside the Porta Trigemina between the Aventine and the Tiber, an area which in later times was dominated by wharves and ship-borne commerce (including grain); (2) the name of the Aequimelium, an area at the foot of the Capitoline Hill where in later times one could purchase lambs and other animals for sacrifice; (3) the origin of the surname Ahala used by the Servilii; and (4) the name of a pool in the Forum, the Lacus Servilius, and the practice of displaying there the severed heads of executed criminals. None of these etiologies can be regarded as historically credible. Furthermore, the presence of the dictator Quinctius Cincinnatus is clearly a variant of the popular Roman tradition of Cincinnatus to the rescue, which we have already encountered in connection with Roman foreign affairs for the year 458 B.C. According to Cicero (*De Senectute* 56), Cincinnatus was summoned from his small farm to be dictator in order to quell the sedition of Sp. Maelius. Thus by the late republic there existed two tales involving the dictator Cincinnatus. In one story he rescued the consul Minucius from a siege of his army's camp by the Aequians, and in the other tale he came to the aid of Minucius, the prefect of the grain supply, to rescue the state from the threat of a tyrant, and the site of the pretender's demolished house became the Aequimelium. It should be noted, however, that in the standard account recorded by Livy and Dionysius the dictator of 439 B.C. does little more than issue a summons to Maelius, whereas the important act of slaying the would-be tyrant is assigned to C. Servilius Ahala. Cincinnatus's inclusion in the story was probably suggested by the fact that one of the consuls of 439 B.C. was a Quinctius; and Servilius, whose deed is supposed to have earned him the name Ahala, was then given the official position of the dictator's master of the horse.

Even though the standard account of this tale contains many obvious post-Gracchan elements, and was used during the late republic to justify harsh measures taken against the Gracchi and Saturninus, Dionysius (12.4) records another version, which he attributes to Cincius Alimentus and Calpurnius Piso. Since Dionysius elsewhere cites Cincius Alimentus together with Fabius Pictor (see 1.79.4 and 2.38.3), his failure to mention Pictor in this passage could indicate that the tale of Sp. Maelius was not to be found in Fabius Pictor. In any case, in this alternative account there is no mention of Quinctius Cincinnatus as dictator. Instead, during a meeting of the senate Servilius volunteers to resolve the crisis by killing Maelius, and he receives the senate's backing to do so. The story therefore resembles that of Mucius Scaevola, who received senatorial approval, according to Livy (2.12.5 and16), to assassinate Porsenna, whose siege of Rome had produced a severe food shortage. The two tales are also similar in that they are both designed to explain the origin of a family's surname: Scaevola = "left-handed," and Ahala = "armpit." In addition, the two stories appear to be historicized folktales involving a one-eyed, one-legged, or one-handed man who frees his people from an oppressor (see Judges 3.12–30), although Scaevola does not become one-handed until he burns off his right hand in the fire, and Ahala's one arm is only temporarily incapacitated by his concealment of his weapon. Nevertheless, it is noteworthy that Dionysius says in his main account (12.2.8) that Maelius ended up with one of his arms cut off.

Despite the etiological and folkloristic aspects of the story, other considerations render it probable that a kernel of historical truth lies at the heart of the sedition of 440–439 B.C. One point in favor of underlying historicity is the fact that, unlike the military crisis of 458 B.C., the event is not simplistically dated to the consulship of a Minucius, which would have been the natural inclination for someone merely interested in providing a plausible historical setting for the tale. Livy and Dionysius record ten grain shortages for the period 496–411 (see Ogilvie 1965, 256–57), and although caution must be used in accepting these reports, it seems highly improbable that they are all fictitious. Several are likely to derive ultimately from pontifical records. F 77 of the *Origines* of Cato the Elder (= Gell. 2.28.6) indicates that grain shortages were recorded on the chief pontiff's whitened board, and the fragment's polemical tone also implies that at least some of Cato's predecessors had incorporated such information into their histories. It therefore seems plausible that Cincius Alimentus dated the story of Sp. Maelius to 440–439 B.C. on the basis of pontifical documentation. Nevertheless, ancient oral tradition and later writers overlaid this bare datum of historical truth with so much folklore and etiology that we are now unable to say anything more than that the Roman state suffered from some crisis at that time, and that it was probably associated with a food shortage, but the severity and precise nature of the emergency cannot be determined.

THE WAR AGAINST FIDENAE

Rome and the Latins continued to be occupied with fighting against the Aequians and Volscians during the second half of the fifth century B.C. Even though it is difficult to assess the significance and historicity of the various campaigns mentioned in Livy, the foundation of the three Latin colonies of Ardea, Labici, and Velitrae in 442, 418, and 401 B.C. respectively suggests steady Roman and Latin success against these two peoples. On the other hand, Livy's account for the year 431 B.C. (4.26–29) deserves to be noted because of a brief passage in Ovid's *Fasti*. According to Livy, the Aequians and Volscians combined their forces in this year for a major campaign against the Latins. Their serious intent was marked by their conducting military recruitment under a *lex sacrata*, according to which the recruits pronounced a dreadful curse upon themselves in the event of defeat (cf. Livy 10.38). This threatening situation prompted the Romans to appoint Postumius Tubertus as dictator, and he succeeded in scoring a major victory over the enemy. The basic historicity of Tubertus's great victory receives support from Ovid's *Fasti* 6.721–24, according to which June 18 was the anniversary of Tubertus's defeat of the Aequians and Volscians. Since this battle is the earliest one for which such an anniversary is recorded, and as it was still noted by Ovid 450 years later, it must have been of considerable significance at the time. In addition, it is worth noting that Ovid's information must derive ultimately from pontifical records.

Rome at this same time took its first step toward expansion by defeating, capturing, and annexing Fidenae to Roman territory. The town lay upstream from Rome on the same bank of the Tiber, opposite the Etruscan city of Veii, Rome's early major rival. According to Dionysius (5.60.4), the Romans had established settlers upon land taken from Fidenae in 498 B.C., and Livy (4.17.1) describes the town as a Roman colony. Before its conquest by Rome, Fidenae was probably already surrounded by two of Rome's rustic tribes: the Clustumina upstream, and the Claudia downstream (Taylor 1960, 34–36).

According to Livy, whose account is our only complete narrative for this war, in 438 B.C. Fidenae defected from Rome and, on the advice of Lars Tolumnius, king of Veii, executed four Roman ambassadors, who had been sent out to investigate. War began the next year in 437. Serving as a mere military tribune (not to be confused with the office of consular tribune) under the dictator Mam. Aemilius, A. Cornelius Cossus avenged the murder of the ambassadors and the violation of international law by killing Lars Tolumnius in single combat. Cossus dedicated the king's captured arms as *spolia opima* to Jupiter Feretrius in his small shrine on the Capitoline. After another year of fighting, in 435 the dictator Q. Servilius brought about the capture of Fidenae by tunneling into its citadel. In 434 Mam. Aemilius was appointed dictator for a second time in response to the threat of concerted Etruscan support of Veii (Livy 4.17–24). After some years of uneasy peace with Etruria, hostilities resumed. In 428, when Cornelius Cossus was consul, Veientine raids upon Roman territory prompted Rome to dispatch a triumviral commission to investigate Fidenate participation. After sending out fetials[4] to demand redress from Veii in 427, Rome declared war. In 426,

---

4. Fetials were priestly ambassadors sent out by the Roman state to make formal demands of redress from a foreign state, and if their demands were not met within thirty days, the Romans then declared war. See Livy 1.24 and 1.32, and Dion. Hal. 2.72 with Watson 1993, 1–9.

after Cossus and three others had been elected military tribunes with consular power, Mam. Aemilius was made dictator for a third time, and he chose Cossus as his master of the horse. During Aemilius's sixteen-day term in office the Fidenates and Veientines were again defeated, and Fidenae was recaptured and finally incorporated into the Roman state (Livy 4.30–34). Thus, according to Livy, the fighting between Rome and Fidenae actually consisted of two different wars, the first one dating to the period 437–435 and the second one occurring only in the year 426, both ending in Fidenae's capture, but separated from one another by an interval of eight years.

Three monuments which survived in Rome into later historical times were associated with the Fidenate War and must have been the only solid data upon which the later historical tradition was based: (1) the statues of the four Roman ambassadors whose deaths at the hands of the Fidenates sparked off the war; (2) the *spolia opima* won by Cossus from Lars Tolumnius; and (3) a gold crown dedicated in the Capitoline temple by the dictator Mam. Aemilius to commemorate his victory over Fidenae. In Livy's narrative the second and third items are linked together (4.20) and date to the first year of the fighting between Rome and Fidenae, thus coming immediately after the murder of the embassy. Yet when the various tales associated with the Fidenate War are carefully examined, it appears likely that later Roman historians, eager to portray the Romans as having exacted swift revenge for the deaths of the ambassadors, transposed events from the close of the war to its very beginning. This phenomenon resembles the fictitious Roman defeat of Veii in the year after the Cremera disaster, as well as the Romans' unhistorical rescue of the Tusculans in 459 B.C. in the year after the Tusculans had aided the Romans against Appius Herdonius. In the case of the Fidenate War, however, real events have been shifted about, duplicated, and reinterpreted to conform to the same chauvinistic pattern of Rome's obtaining immediate satisfaction from an enemy.

To begin with, Lars Tolumnius is likely to have been the actual name of a king of Veii, for at the Portonaccio sanctuary, at which the dedication made by Avile Vipiiennas (= Aulus Vibenna) was found, there were also discovered similar early dedications inscribed with the Etruscan names Velthur Tulumnes and Karcuna Tulumnes (Pallottino 1968, #35, 36, and 38). Statues of the four slain Roman ambassadors were still to be seen at the end of the republic on the Speaker's Platform (Rostra) in the Forum, and their names were still known: C. Fulcinius, Tullus Cloelius, L. Roscius, and Sp. Antius or Nautius (Livy 4.17.2–6, Cic. *Phil.* 9.4–5, and Pliny *NH* 34.23). With respect to the social fluidity of the early Roman aristocracy and the issue of the patriciate and its supposed monopoly of political power in early times, it is significant that only one or two of these men had names which are known to have been patrician (Cloelius and Nautius), whereas the others in later historical times are only known as plebeian. Since the ambassadors must have been senators, these names constitute valuable evidence for the early composition of the senate.

After narrating the death of Lars Tolumnius and Cossus's dedication of the *spolia opima* under the year 437 B.C., Livy (4.20.5) introduces his discussion of the problematic dating of these two events (including Augustus's assertion that they had occurred during Cossus's consulship of 428, for which there was no record of military activity) by stressing that in assigning these events to the first year of the Fidenate war he has "followed all authors before me (omnes ante me auctores secutus)." Although Dionysius's twelfth book survives only in excerpts, one passage (12.5) concerns Cornelius Cossus and suggests that Dionysius's account agreed with Livy's, since he describes Cossus as a subordinate military tribune when he killed Tolumnius and won the *spolia opima*. The imperial writer Frontinus, in his book of military stratagems (2.4.10), describes a stratagem concerning how the Veientines and Fidenates used fire to confuse the Romans when they were attacking Fidenae. The same incident is found in Livy's account of the battle of Fidenae in 426 (4.33.1–2). Yet Frontinus's *Strategemata* 2.8.8–9 apparently concern incidents in this same battle which are not in Livy's account: both the dictator Aemilius and his master of the horse, Cornelius Cossus, order the execution of standard-bearers in order to restore discipline. These latter stories could have been embellishments in other annalistic accounts which Livy chose not to reproduce. Frontinus's text is so terse that the context is unclear, but the executions may have been the Roman commanders' response to the enemy's unexpected use of fire. In Livy the dictator and master of the horse use much less sanguinary means to urge on their men. In any case, Frontinus seems to agree with Livy in not having Cossus kill Tolumnius in the last year of the war.

Diodorus (12.80.1 and 6–8) however, in his characteristic treatment of early Roman affairs, compresses into the single Varronian year 426 B.C. the Fidenate murder of the Roman ambassadors, the Roman declaration of war, the appointment of Aemilius as dictator with Cossus as his master of the horse, and a long indecisive battle with no mention of Tolumnius's death and the *spolia opima*. Despite Livy's emphatic claim that the annalistic tradition was unanimous on the date of Tolumnius's death, he clearly did not bother to read every single ancient account of the Fidenate War written before his day; Livy's statement of unanimity simply indicates that there was complete agreement on this point in the few sources he was routinely using for this period: Licinius Macer, Valerius Antias, and Aelius Tubero (see Livy 4.23.1–3). In his own brief reference to Cossus's winning the *spolia opima*, Valerius Maximus (3.2.4), who often records stories with no Livian parallel, describes Cossus as a master of the horse. This version apparently assigns the episode to 426 rather than 437 B.C. This suggests that Tolumnius's death was variously dated either to the first or to the last year of the Fidenate War. In fact, Tolumnius's death in the last year of the war makes excellent historical sense, for the king's death would have abruptly ended Veientine support of Fidenae, and this in turn would have caused the immediate collapse of Fidenate resistance to Rome and the town's capture or surrender.

What Livy reports about augurs and auspices for the years 437 and 426 B.C. bears out the supposition that Roman historians transferred Tolumnius's death from the last to the first year of the war. After recording the election of Cossus and three others as military tribunes with consular power for 426, Livy writes that Cossus remained in Rome while the other consular tribunes were sent out against Veii. The defeat of Cossus's colleagues resulted in Cossus's appointing a dictator. Since a dictator had always been appointed by a consul and never before by a consular tribune, a special ruling had to be obtained from the augurs to authorize the appointment. After a favorable ruling had been given, Cossus appointed Mam. Aemilius as dictator, who in turn chose Cossus as his master of the horse (Livy 4.31.1–5). When he was dictator for the first time in 437, Mam. Aemilius did not engage the enemy until he had received an affirmative signal from the augurs on the Arx in Rome (Livy 4.18.6). This is a unique instance of the taking of auspices before a battle, besides which, as Ogilvie (1965, 561) points out, the Roman Arx was not visible from the site of the battle. The story of the augural ruling in 426 makes perfectly good sense and has a good chance of being historical, but the taking of the auspices recorded for the year 437 is odd. If the original tradition had been that Cossus killed Tolumnius in 426, after appointing Aemilius dictator and becoming his master of the horse, the augural ruling could have been transformed into that peculiar instance of taking the auspices when Cossus's winning of the *spolia opima* was transferred from 426 to 437 B.C.

This surmise gains further credence from another similarity between the two battle narratives. Before engaging the enemy in 426, the dictator first ordered a legate to occupy a ridge in the enemy's rear. The Romans did not begin the battle until they had received a signal from the legate to indicate that the ridge had been successfully occupied. Then, after the enemy fled into Fidenae pursued by the Romans, the troops of the legate were also ordered against the town and, once inside, they pursued the fleeing host to the Arx of Fidenae (Livy 4.32.9–10, 33.9, and 34.2). Thus in both battles fighting does not begin until the Roman commander receives a signal, and the arx of a city figures in each account as well.

Another likely transposition involves Cossus's official title. Before his appointment as master of the horse, Cossus had been a military tribune with consular power in 426, whereas he is described as a subordinate military tribune in 437 serving under the same man as dictator. It therefore seems likely that Mam. Aemilius's first dictatorship of 437 B.C. is fictitious and the doublet was produced by Roman authors when they transferred the death of Lars Tolumnius and Cossus's winning of the *spolia opima* from the last to the first year of the Fidenate War. Similarly, the same authors removed from 426 and reassigned to 437 B.C. the dictator's dedication of a gold crown to commemorate his victory over Fidenae, but a remnant of the original tradition is detectable in Livy's confused discussion of the role of the Roman *classis* in the fighting of 426 B.C. (4.34.6–7). As explained in chapter 4 (see above p. 113), the term *classis* in early times must have referred to the Roman military levy, but it was misconstrued by later writers to mean "fleet," the misunderstanding prompting them to conjecture that the fighting at Fidenae in 426 somehow involved ships on the Tiber River. It is apparent, however, that the term *classis* was used in the language of the gold crown's dedication. This pattern of transposition, duplication, and alteration explains the peculiar dual character of the Fidenate War in Livy's narrative. It might have been known in later times that the war ended with Fidenae's annexation in 426 B.C., but the precise date of its beginning might not have been known. It could have been assigned to the year 437 B.C. because this was the first year in which a Sergius was consul. The rustic tribe Sergia was located near Fidenae (Taylor 1960, 40), and one surname commonly used among the early Sergii was Fidenas.

THE WAR AGAINST VEII

Following the capture and annexation of Fidenae, Rome's next major step in expanding its borders was the defeat of the Etruscan city of Veii and the acquisition of its territory.[5] This event represents Rome's first really significant conquest and territorial acquisition. Beloch (1926, 620) estimated the size of Roman territory in the fifth century as 822 square kilometers, and that the annexations of Crustumerium, Ficulea, Fidenae, and Veii added 39, 37, 50, and 562 square kilometers respectively to the Roman state. If we take these figures to be approximately correct, it would mean that when Rome acquired Veii's territory in 396 B.C., that alone increased the physical extent of the Roman state by approximately 60 percent. The later Romans' appreciation of the importance of Veii's conquest is seen in the fact that they described the war as having lasted ten years and patterned it after the epic struggle between Troy and the entire Greek host, but, as in so many other cases involving the history of early Rome, they were unable to discover many actual facts about the war (see Ogilvie 1965, 629).

5. The ancient site of Veii and the surrounding area of southern Etruria have been the subject of archaeological field surveys and limited excavations by the British School in Rome. For a summary account of the findings concerning the early cemetery, walls, drainage tunnels (*cuniculi*), and settlement patterns of Veii, see Potter 1979, 61–96, which cites the earlier, more technical archaeological reports.

Figure 7. Terracotta cult statue of Apollo unearthed at Veii.

Yet, it is significant that the three aspects of the war which seem credible are all important religious events, which could have been transmitted to later times by having been recorded in priestly records: the celebration of the first lectisternium in 399 B.C. following consultation of the Sibylline

Books, the consultation of the Delphic oracle, and the *evocatio* of Juno from Veii and her installation in a temple on the Aventine. Cicero (*De Re Pub.* 1.25) indicates that both the *Annales Maximi* and the early poet Q. Ennius in his historical epic poem, the *Annales,* recorded the occurrence of a solar eclipse on June 5 about 350 years after Rome's foundation. The eclipse is generally thought to have been that of June 21, 400 B.C. (see Skutsch 1985, 311–14). Thus, Ennius may have been the first Roman writer to portray the Veientine War in mythic terms by narrating its heroic history in the epic style, including all its attendant divine machinery. He could have used the eclipse to portend Veii's downfall. In addition, an excerpt from Dionysius's lost twelfth book (12.9) cites Calpurnius Piso, a historian of the late second century B.C., for the celebration of the first lectisternium in 399 B.C., described in much the same terms as found in Livy 5.13.4–8. Since Livy's account of the Veientine War seems to have been influenced by the Roman war against Numantia during the 140s and 130s B.C. (see Forsythe 1994, 310–19), the historical tradition that we encounter in Livy's narrative was probably already well established by the close of the second century B.C.

A lectisternium was the Roman adoption of the Greek *theoxenia,* in which the images of gods, dressed in all their finery, were placed on couches before tables laden with viands in order for the gods to participate in the banqueting of public religious festivals. Thus it is entirely plausible that the idea of the lectisternium resulted from consultation of the Sibylline Books at a time of bad harvests and pestilence caused by severe weather conditions. Similarly, Rome's consultation of the oracle of Delphi during the course of the war seems to be borne out by other circumstantial details, and it therefore testifies to Rome's early involvement in the culture of the Mediterranean world. Roman ambassadors in 394 B.C. were said to have brought a gold bowl as a thank offering to Delphic Apollo. In the course of their voyage they were intercepted by Greek pirates from the Lipari Islands, but were released and sent on their way by Timasitheus, whom the Roman senate honored with *hospitium publicum,* a form of honorary Roman citizenship (Livy 5.28.1–4 and Plutarch *Camillus* 8). Diodorus (14.93.5) adds that when the Lipari Islands came under Roman rule 137 years later during the early years of the First Punic War, the Romans granted Timasitheus's descendants immunity from taxes. Appian (*Italica* 8.1) states that the bowl was placed on a bronze pedestal in the Massiliote treasury, and stood there until it was melted down by Onomarchus during the Third Sacred War of the mid-fourth century B.C., but the pedestal remained to be seen. In light of the tradition that the cult statue of Aventine Diana was modeled after the image of Artemis worshipped by the Massiliotes, it is significant that this Roman dedication at Delphi was placed in the Massiliote treasury. Whether the Romans consulted Delphi specifically in reference to the draining of the Alban Lake cannot be ascertained. The Romans did in fact in early times dig a drainage tunnel (= *emissarium*) through the lake's crater in order to control its level, but the date of this project cannot be determined (see Forsythe 1994, 317). In any event, its association with the Veientine War is likely to have produced the tale that the Romans captured the city by tunneling into its citadel; the same stratagem was ascribed to the earlier Roman capture of Fidenae in 435 B.C. (Livy 4.22.4–6 and 5.19–21).

Livy's account in 5.22 of the Romans' transfer of Juno's cult from Veii to Rome is a pious romance which embodies an actual historical event, the formal Roman religious ritual known as *evocatio* (= "summoning forth"), by which the divinity or divinities of a foreign state, soon to be or already conquered, were invited to leave their ancestral abode and come to Rome to receive worship. This procedure, although rarely mentioned in the ancient sources, must have been a common occurrence during the early and middle republic, as Rome conquered one state after another and continued to annex new territory. The ceremony demonstrates that in addition to depriving a conquered state of its political autonomy by incorporation or of its existence by destruction, the Romans also employed religion to remove divine support from the foreign state while simultaneously appropriating it for themselves. Macrobius (*Saturnalia* 3.9.7–8) reproduces the text of the prayer used to evoke the chief tutelary deity of Carthage from that famous Punic city when it was captured and destroyed by the Romans in 146 B.C., 250 years after Rome's destruction of Veii. It reads as follows:

> Whether it be god or goddess in whose protection are the people and state of Carthage, I pray and worship thee, Greatest One, the one who has received the protection of the city and this people, and I seek indulgence from you that you desert the people and state of Carthage, that you abandon their temples, places, sacred areas, and city, that you depart from them, that you cast upon that people and state fear, dread, and forgetfulness, and that having been betrayed, you come to Rome to me and my people, that our places, temples, sacred areas, and city be more acceptable and pleasing to you, and that you be protectors for me, the Roman people, and my soldiers, so that we might know and understand. If you do so, I vow that I will make temples and will perform games for you.

An inference that is probably mistaken has sometimes been drawn from Livy's account of the reaction of the other Etruscan cities to the Fidenate and Veientine Wars. According to Livy (4.23.4–24.1 and 5.1.3–6), following the Roman capture of Fidenae for the first time in 434 B.C., and again in 403 at the beginning of the war between Rome and Veii, a league of twelve Etruscan cities met at Fanum Voltumnae and debated whether they should assist Veii against Rome, and on both occasions the Etruscan cities decided not to intervene. On the strength of these two passages and a few other similar Livian references to Etruscan meetings at Fanum Voltumnae, all dating to the years 434–389 B.C., modern scholars have generally assumed that a league of twelve Etruscan cities existed during the archaic period, and some have even conjectured that similar Etruscan duodecimal leagues were established in Campania and the Po Valley. Luisa Banti (1973, 206–8), however, has cast serious doubt upon these assumptions. If such a league existed, it was probably largely, if not entirely, religious in nature, and the membership must have varied over time. There is no evidence for Etruscan military or political unity against a common enemy, but there is information suggesting that interstate warfare in Etruria was not uncommon. Thus Livy's statements may reflect the existence of communal Etruscan religious celebrations, which later annalists construed in political terms in order to enliven their narratives of Roman foreign affairs with the possible threat of concerted Etruscan military operations against Rome.

Concerning the fate of the Veientine population, Livy (5.22.1) simply remarks that on the day after the city's capture Camillus had the free population sold into slavery. Even if many Veientines had escaped this fate by fleeing the country and taking refuge in neighboring communities before the Roman army closed in on the city, there still must have been a substantial number of people who were sold into slavery. Consequently, this must have been the first major instance of mass enslavement in Roman history. At 5.30.8 Livy indicates that land allotments measuring seven jugera (four and one-half acres) were parceled out of the newly acquired territory, but unfortunately, like his silence concerning the specific number of enslaved Veientines, Livy does not bother to inform us how many Roman citizens benefited from this distribution. Nevertheless, it cannot be doubted that the conquest of Veii constituted a major alteration in Roman society and economy in the increase of both chattel slavery and arable land. Moreover, as discussed above in chapter 4 (p. 106–107), the conquest of Veii resulted in Rome's acquisition of the Veientine stone quarries. Henceforth, for the remainder of the early republic, the Romans all but ceased using their own inferior local Cappellaccio tufa in favor of the better-quality Grotta Oscura tufa from Veii. Blocks of the latter were used to construct the so-called Servian Wall; and even though this project may not have begun until 378 B.C. (see Livy 6.32.1), we may wonder whether any of the stonecutting in the quarries was done by enslaved Veientines.

During the five years following the capture of Veii Rome continued to extend its influence in southern Etruria. Rome's military strength in the area convinced Capena and Falerii to sign alliances with Rome in 395 and 394 B.C. respectively (Livy 5.24 and 26–27). For the years 392 and 391 B.C., Livy (5.31.5 and 32.2–5) reports Roman military activity against Volsinii in central inland Etruria, as well as against the Sappinates. These are an otherwise unknown people, who must have dwelled somewhere in the same general area, and whose name may derive ultimately from pontifical records.

The fighting resulted in the conclusion of a twenty-year truce, but the Gallic attack upon Rome in the following year and the havoc which it wrought ended Roman expansionist designs in southern Etruria for several decades.

THE GALLIC CATASTROPHE AND ITS AFTERMATH

Before Julius Caesar's conquest of Gaul, the Emperor Claudius's annexation of Britain, and the ensuing Romanization of these two areas, the Celts of western Europe were more loosely organized than contemporary Greeks and Romans. The tribe, rather than the city-state, tended to be the basic political unit of Celtic society. The Celts lived in villages and towns in a more dispersed and less tightly structured pattern than the city-states of the Mediterranean area. They tilled the soil, raised livestock, developed their own distinctive arts and crafts, and engaged in trade with Greeks and others for various luxury goods. As mentioned in chapter 6 in reference to the *suodales* of the *Lapis Satricanus* (see above p. 199), the ruling class in Celtic society was a warrior elite, whose members engaged in warfare, cattle raiding, hunting, and feasting (see Rankin 1987, 49–82; James 1993, 52–85; and Polyb. 2.16–34). In addition to warring among themselves, Celtic tribes often preyed upon non-Celtic peoples and areas, especially those that had something the Celts desired, such as land, livestock, or precious metals. In fact, Celtic marauding and overpopulation went hand in hand in enlarging the territorial extent of Celtic settlement and culture. Raids into new areas offered fresh opportunities for Celtic chieftains and their war bands to enrich themselves and to win prestige. At the same time, their plundering incursions often paved the way for more peaceful immigration and settlement; the Po Valley of northern Italy is perhaps the best example of this phenomenon.

Archaeology (Barfield 1971, 149–53) suggests that during the course of the fifth century B.C. Celtic tribes crossed the Alps and occupied virtually all but the northeastern area of the Po Valley. Their settlement of northern Italy is likely to have involved both violent displacement of the native inhabitants and peaceful assimilation. Evidence for violent confrontation between Etruscans and Celts is found on horseshoe-shaped sandstone tombstones from the Etruscan community of Felsina dating to the early fourth century B.C. (see fig. 8). A common scene represented on these funerary monuments shows an Etruscan on horseback attacking a naked Celtic warrior on foot (Holliday 1994, 23–24). By the middle of the fourth century B.C., the Po Valley had become predominantly Celtic in culture and language; it was therefore later termed Cisalpine Gaul by the Romans. Felsina, for example, was eventually occupied by the Celts; when the Romans established a colony at the site in 189 B.C., they named it Bononia (modern Bologna) from the local Celtic tribe of the Boii.

Figure 8. Horseshoe-shaped sandstone funerary stela
from Felsina: top panel depicting a hippocamp and
a serpent, middle panel showing the deceased man
traveling to the underworld in a chariot, and bottom
panel illustrating a combat between an Etruscan on
horseback and a naked Gallic warrior on foot.

   Once Celtic tribes had settled all of the Po Valley that could be easily
occupied either by force of arms or by peaceful infiltration, it was only a
matter of time before Celtic forces crossed the Apennines and raided the
rich cities of Etruria. According to the later Roman tradition, when a large
force of Gauls appeared before the northern Etruscan city of Clusium in
391 B.C., the Etruscans appealed to Rome for assistance, and the meddle-
some interference of three Roman ambassadors from the Fabian clan provoked the Gauls to turn their arms against the Romans (Livy 5.35–36).
Given Rome's military operations as far north as Volsinii in 392 and 391
B.C., Clusium's appeal to Rome, as well as to other states in the region, is certainly plausible, whereas the tale of the Roman ambassadors taking the side
of Clusium in the fighting is a later invention, designed to explain the Gallic
attack upon Rome, the Roman defeat at the Allia, and the enemy's occupation of the city, all as resulting from divine displeasure. Following their victory over the Romans at the Allia, a stream that flowed into the Tiber north
of Rome near Crustumerium, the Gauls occupied Rome itself for several
months and finally withdrew after extracting a ransom in gold. The Gallic
host seems to have dispersed. Some returned home to defend their

territory from invasion by the Veneti (Polyb. 2.18.3), while others continued to wander south and eventually found employment as mercenaries in the army of Dionysius I of Syracuse (Justin 20.5.1–6).

The last fact demonstrates that news of this Gallic rampage through Italy, including the capture of Rome, was broadcast immediately among the western Greeks and was probably first recorded by the contemporary Sicilian historian Philistus. Pliny (*NH* 3.57) and Plutarch (*Camillus* 22.3–4) indicate that the Gallic occupation of Rome was recorded by the Greek historian Theopompus and the philosopher Aristotle during the third quarter of the fourth century B.C. The catastrophe made a deep and lasting impression upon the Romans themselves and left its mark on official practices and the religious calendar. Henceforth, until Rome's conquest of Cisalpine Gaul by the close of the third century B.C., fear of a Gallic attack often prompted the Roman state to take emergency measures by declaring a *tumultus Gallicus,* during which all exemptions from military service were suspended and Roman officials had a free hand in recruiting whatever forces seemed necessary to deal with the crisis. Furthermore, since the disaster had come soon after a censor had died in office and a suffect magistrate had been chosen in his place to complete the lustrum, the Romans thereafter, whenever a censor died, never elected a suffect censor but allowed the censorship to pass without a lustrum's being performed (Livy 5.31.6). Finally, July 18, the day on which the Romans had been defeated by the Gauls, was henceforth marked in the calendar as "the Day of the Allia" (*dies Alliensis*) and was regarded as inauspicious.

As with Porsenna's capture of Rome at the beginning of the republic, the Gallic catastrophe encouraged popular tradition and later Roman historians to make a virtue out of necessity by generating various patriotic and morally edifying tales to illustrate Roman courage and piety in the face of ineluctable adversity: L. Albinius lending assistance to the Vestals in their flight to Caere (Livy 5.40.8–10), the aged Roman senators solemnly devoting themselves to death and then quietly awaiting the arrival of the Gauls (Livy 5.41), and Fabius Dorsuo marching through the midst of the astonished enemy in order to perform religious rites at the clan's customary spot in the city (Livy 5.46.1–3). In addition, the presence of the *dies Alliensis* in the official calendar encouraged later Roman antiquarians to "discover" the origin of other Roman festivals or important events in the circumstances surrounding the Gallic capture of the city (Forsythe 1994, 319–20). Although modern archaeology has thus far not discovered any incontrovertible evidence of Gallic destruction in the area of the city, the Romans of historical times believed that the Gauls had done a rather thorough job of burning and destroying much of the city, and they used this idea to explain why there were so few surviving records prior to the fourth century B.C. (Livy 6.1.1–3 and Plutarch *Numa* 1.2). Similarly, later Romans used the supposed Gallic destruction of Rome and the city's rapid rebuilding to explain the city's disorganized urban layout (Livy 5.55.2–5). On the contrary, as later happened following the Neronian fire of 64 A.D., we might suppose that widespread destruction would have given the Romans an opportunity to impose coherent urban planning upon the city.

The two most famous historical fictions associated with the Gallic occupation of the city concern the exploits of M. Manlius Capitolinus and M. Furius Camillus. According to the ancient tradition, many Romans took refuge on the Capitoline Hill and succeeded in holding out against the Gauls, who occupied and plundered the remainder of the city. By using vague allusions to the Gallic capture of Rome in later poetic accounts, O. Skutsch (1953 and 1985, 405–8) has argued that the Gauls captured the Capitoline as well as the rest of the city, and this notion has been accepted and further developed by Horsfall (Bremmer and Horsfall 1987, 63–75). Even if the tradition that the Romans successfully resisted the Gauls on the Capitoline is false, the later ancient literary evidence scraped together by Skutsch is too vague to prove this point and cannot be viewed as constituting an alternative historical tradition. In any case, Manlius's defense of the Capitoline against the stealthy ascent of the Gauls under the cover of night was designed to explain Manlius's surname, Capitolinus, the epithet Moneta for Juno's cult on the Arx, and other odd Roman customs. Rather than meaning "Warner" and stemming from the warning given by Juno's sacred geese, the divine epithet Moneta is likely to have originally meant "Advisor," "Prompter," or "Reminder" and resulted from the fact that the augurs took the auspices from the Arx in the vicinity of Juno's temple (cf. Ziolkowski 1993).[6] Although the story of the cackling geese and the sleeping dogs may seem probable (see Ogilvie 1965, 734), it is better to regard it as a later invention which served to explain two unrelated customs: why the first public contract to be awarded by the censors was for the feeding of Juno's sacred geese, and why a dog was sacrificed in front of the Capitoline temple (Pliny *NH* 10.51 and 29.57, Plutarch *Camillus* 27, *QR* 52 and 98). The explanation for the primacy of food for the geese in the awarding of censorial contracts is probably no more mysterious than the simple fact that it was one of the oldest public contracts, and simply retained its priority as the business of the Roman state grew. Granting the contract such primacy also agrees with the ancient belief that important matters should always begin with some ceremony or action in acknowledgement of the gods. The sacrifice of the dog on the Capitol was probably a primitive religious ritual whose

6. It is perhaps worth noting that the English words "money" and "monetary" owe their origin to this epithet of Juno, because during the third century B.C. the Romans established their office for making coins near the shrine of Juno Moneta, and the three men responsible for Rome's coinage were popularly known as the *triumviri monetales*.

original meaning had been forgotten by the second century B.C., and for which a historical etiology was concocted. Its primitive Italic origin is suggested by a similar rite known from Iguvium (see *Tab. Iguv.* II.B 15–29).

In the late annalistic tradition Camillus was the dominant figure for this period of early Roman history. Unfortunately, the surviving fragments from the lost historical accounts of Livy's predecessors shed little light on the development of this tradition. The fragments of Claudius Quadrigarius, who probably wrote during the 80s and 70s B.C., suggest that by his day the tradition concerning the Gallic capture of Rome as found in Livy was largely, if not entirely, well established (see Gell. 17.2), but this tells us very little. Livy has clearly arranged his treatment of early Roman history so as to make Camillus's career the chronological centerpiece of his first ten books. Livy's fifth and sixth books form the center of his first decade, and Livy has chosen their beginning and end to coincide with the beginning and end of Camillus's public career. Book V begins with the year 403, the first in which Camillus is recorded to have held public office, and Book VI ends with the year 367, the last year in which he is supposed to have held any magistracy. Livy's fifth book consists roughly of two halves: the war against Veii, and the Gallic capture of the city, both of which are dominated and brought to a successful conclusion by Camillus. In order to dissociate Rome's great hero from the disaster at the Allia and the Gauls' seizure of Rome, the ancient tradition conveniently removed him from the political scene by reporting him driven into exile in the year before the Gallic catastrophe because of a dispute with the foolish and ungrateful Roman people over the issue of the booty taken from Veii (Livy 5.32.7–9). He could then be described as having been formally recalled from exile and appointed dictator in Rome's great hour of need (Livy 5.46.4–11), and in the Livian narrative he is depicted as arriving in Rome at the head of an army just as the ransom of a thousand pounds of gold has been weighed out (Livy 5.48.8–49.5). Thus, like the U.S. cavalry in a melodramatic Hollywood movie, Camillus comes just in time to rescue the Romans from their greatest humiliation by defeating the Gauls on the spot and taking back the ransom.

Livy's account of Camillus's defeat of the Gauls and seizure of the intended ransom could hardly be more chauvinistic and was probably the creation of the annalists of the first century B.C. Other ancient writers give alternative versions of what happened to the ransom. In describing the family lineages of the emperor Tiberius, the imperial biographer Suetonius (*Tib.* 3.2) says that the Livii Drusi derived their surname from a family member who had killed a Gallic chieftain named Drausus in single combat, and the same man recovered the gold with which the Romans had ransomed the city from Gallic territory. Unfortunately, this man is otherwise unattested in ancient literature, but he is likely to have been a propraetor assigned to Cisalpine Gaul during the 230s or 220s B.C. when the Romans were subduing the Celtic tribes of the Po Valley. The Livian family's claim suggests that at the time of this Livius Drusus, the Romans believed that in 390 B.C. the Gauls had successfully made off with the ransom. The Greek geographer Strabo, a contemporary of Livy, records another account of the ransom's fate. According to him (5.2.3, cf. Diod. 14.117.7), the people of Caere defeated the Gauls in the Sabine territory after they had left Rome, and because the Caeretans captured and returned the ransom to the Romans (as well as having given refuge to their priests), the Romans rewarded them with a limited form of Roman citizenship. Indeed, according to Livy (5.50.3), the Caeretans received *hospitium publicum* (= public guest-friendship, honorary Roman citizenship enjoyed by any Caeretan when present in Rome) because they had given refuge to the Roman priests and their sacred objects during the crisis.

Much of the later canonical account of 390 B.C. could have originated in popular oral tradition surrounding the temple of Juno Moneta on the Arx (so also Horsfall in Bremmer and Horsfall 1987, 74). According to Livy (7.28.1–5), this shrine was vowed in 345 B.C. by the dictator L. Furius Camillus, whose master of the horse was Cn. Manlius Capitolinus. The names of these officials are likely to have been preserved in association with the temple in the form of a dedicatory inscription, and later popular tradition might have wrongly construed these names as referring to the great Camillus and the infamous demagogue M. Manlius Capitolinus and linked the two together in patriotic fictions concerning 390 B.C. In support of this surmise is the fact that the consuls of 345 B.C. were M. Fabius Dorsuo and Ser. Sulpicius Camerinus. The only other Fabius Dorsuo recorded in the Roman historical tradition is the man who performed an act of pious heroism in 390 B.C. by leaving the Capitoline and marching through the midst of the astonished Gauls in order to carry out obligatory religious rites. Similarly, the name Sulpicius is linked to 390 B.C. through the consular tribune Q. Sulpicius Longus, who is supposed to have been in command of the Roman forces at the Allia. Thus the names of Camillus, Manlius Capitolinus, and Sulpicius were all associated with the vowing of the temple to Juno Moneta and were also linked in popular tradition with the events of 390 B.C. This linkage might explain why the Capitoline Hill and Juno's geese figure so prominently in the ancient tradition of the Gallic occupation of Rome. It could also account for the creation of the tale concerning Fabius Dorsuo. The consular colleague of Ser. Sulpicius Camerinus of 345 B.C. was converted into the Fabius Dorsuo who marched down from the Capitoline in 390 B.C. to perform ancestral sacrifices.

Whatever the physical destruction which the Gauls inflicted upon Rome and its immediate environs, their marauding activity in central Tyrrhenian Italy caused considerable political disruption in interstate relations. Moreover, bands of warlike Gauls continued to plague the region for the next several decades. Livy's description of Roman foreign affairs in his sixth book reflects the chaotic conditions in Latium following the Gallic catastrophe. His narrative is a complex blend of basic solid facts frequently embellished elaborately with detailed fictitious battle narratives, in which Camillus often figures prominently (see Livy 6.6.6–10.9 and 6.23–26). At 6.4.3 Livy records that Camillus dedicated three gold saucers as war trophies, placing them at the feet of Juno's cult statue in the Capitoline temple where they remained until the shrine was destroyed by fire in 83 B.C. From these monuments later annalists constructed a totally successful lightning campaign conducted by Camillus first against the Volscians, then against the Aequians, and finally against the Etruscans; they dated the campaign to 389 B.C., the year after the Gallic catastrophe, when it was supposed that the Roman state was beset by several major threats at the same time.

Despite the disruption and chaos caused by the Gauls, Rome seems to have restored its power and influence in southern Etruria quickly. Latin colonies were founded at Sutrium and Nepet in 383 (Vell. Pat. 1.14.2 and Livy 6.21.4). For the year 388 B.C., Livy (6.4.8–10) records a Roman incursion into the territory of Tarquinii, where the Romans captured and destroyed the two towns of Cortuosa and Contenebra. Swedish excavations at the modern site of San Giovenale near Tarquinii have revealed a planned town established around 650 B.C. and destroyed at the beginning of the fourth century. Whether or not San Giovenale was the ancient Cortuosa or Contenebra, it is reasonable to explain the destruction of San Giovenale as a consequence of the Roman military campaign mentioned by Livy. This is a striking confirmation of the Livian narrative, whose information on this matter must derive ultimately from pontifical records. During this same period, Rome and the Latins continued to wage war against the Volscians. The fighting centered around the towns of Antium, Satricum, and Velitrae. In 385 B.C. Rome and the Latins founded a colony at Satricum (Livy 6.16.6).[7] In addition to mentioning the appointment of a triumviral commission for founding the colony of Nepet in 383 B.C., Livy (6.21.4) also records that the Romans elected a board of five men to divide the Pomptine land taken from the Volscians into allotments for settlement. In the next year (382), the Latin colony of Setia, located in the same Pomptine district, was founded (Vell. Pat. 1.14.2). Three years later in 379 the same site received additional settlers (Livy 6.30.9). It therefore seems likely that by 380 B.C. the Volscians and Aequians no longer posed a major military threat

7. Under the preceding Varronian year of 386 B.C., Diodorus (15.27.4) says that the Romans sent out a colony to Sardinia, but this seems highly improbable at this time. Given the seemingly limitless ability of Diodorus and his later copyists to mutilate unfamiliar proper names associated with early Roman history, this notice in Diodorus should be regarded as a reference to the Latins colonizing Satricum.

to Rome and the Latins. The events of these years, however, also exhibit disunity among the Latins themselves. Praeneste emerged as a state whose influence in Latium for a time appears to have rivaled that of Rome. In 380 B.C. the dictator T. Quinctius Cincinnatus waged war against Praeneste, broke up a coalition of nine communities, and commemorated his achievements as dictator by placing in the Capitoline temple a gold crown weighing two and one-third pounds and accompanied by an inscription (Livy 6.28–29 with Festus 498L s.v. *trientem tertium*).[8]

Several events mark important steps in the growth and expansion of the Roman state during the two decades following the Gallic catastrophe. In 387 B.C. the newly acquired territory of Veii was organized into four new tribes: the Sabatina, Stellatina, Tromentina, and Arnensis (Livy 6.5.8). This brought the total of Roman voting districts up to twenty-five. In 381 B.C. Tusculum was incorporated into the Roman state by being granted Roman citizenship (Livy 6.26.8 and Dion. Hal. 14.6). This indicates Rome's growing power in Latium relative to other states and presages Rome's absorption of the rest of Latium some forty years later. Although the people of Tusculum were henceforth Roman citizens, the Tusculans still retained their local government and continued to administer their own internal affairs, but as a subsidiary part of the Roman state they no longer had independence in matters of foreign policy. Like other Roman citizens, they were assigned to a Roman territorial tribe (the Papiria, see Livy 8.37.12) and thus enjoyed full political rights in Rome. They were also subject to the same obligations of military service and taxation. During the middle and late republic, an independent community, such as Tusculum, which had been incorporated into the Roman state by being granted Roman citizenship while enjoying internal local autonomy with its traditional institutions, was termed a *municipium*.

Another innovation involving the extension of a limited form of Roman citizenship, which in a modified form proved to be equally important in Roman expansion and incorporation of foreign peoples for the next two hundred years, was the status awarded to Caere.[9] As noted above, the Romans honored the people of the nearby Etruscan city of Caere for their assistance during the Gallic occupation of Rome. Livy describes this honorary status as *hospitium publicum*. The phrase suggests that in matters of private law, any citizen of Caere when present in Rome was treated as if he

8. As noted by Oakley (1997, 608), Livy seems to be mistaken concerning T. Quinctius Cincinnatus's dedication of a statue of Jupiter Imperator, because Cicero (*In Verrem* II.4.129) makes it quite clear that this magnificent statue in the Capitoline temple had been brought to Rome from Macedonia by T. Quinctius Flamininus, the liberator of Greece.

9. For modern discussions of this problematic topic, see Ogilvie 1965, 740; Harris 1971, 45–46; Brunt 1971, 515–18; Sherwin-White 1973, 53–57; Humbert 1978, 405–16; Grieve 1982, 1983; Cornell in *CAH* VII.2 1989, 313–14; and Oakley 1998, 199–202.

were a Roman citizen, but he was exempt from the burdens of Roman taxation and military service and could not vote in the Roman assemblies. He therefore enjoyed a kind of honorary Roman citizenship, and according to Gellius (16.13.7) the Roman censors henceforth kept a special set of records known as the *Tabulae Caerites* in which they recorded the names of people who possessed this limited form of Roman citizenship. By the end of the fourth century B.C. this special status, termed *civitas sine suffragio* (= "citizenship without the vote"), was altered to include the obligations of taxation and military service and was imposed by the Roman state upon various communities, either as a form of punishment for bad behavior or as a halfway stage between foreign status and full Roman citizenship.

A statement in Livy 6.32.1 for the year 378 B.C. suggests that the Romans then began constructing the so-called Servian Wall, made of blocks of Grotta Oscura tufa obtained from quarries near Veii. Parts of the city may have been previously fortified by ditches and earthen embankments, but the Servian Wall provided Rome for the first time with an uninterrupted encircling stone defense work. The decision to build such a structure must have been largely due to the Gallic occupation of the city. Another brief statement in Livy 7.20.9 for the year 353 B.C. indicates that the wall was either still being built twenty-five years later, or it had already been completed and was undergoing repairs. Given the height, breadth, and circuit of this wall, its construction, which involved the quarrying, hauling, and laying of thousands of stone blocks, required an enormous expenditure of labor.[10] When completed, the wall enclosed an area of 608 acres, thus making the city of Rome comparable in size to the great Greek cities of Syracuse and Acragas in Sicily.

THE SEDITION OF M. MANLIUS CAPITOLINUS

According to the later annalistic tradition (Livy 6.11–20), during the two years 385–384 B.C. the Roman state was disturbed by a sedition caused by indebtedness and exploited by the patrician M. Manlius Capitolinus, the same man who had allegedly saved the Capitoline from a night attack by the Gauls in 390 B.C.[11] The sedition ended when Manlius was tried and condemned for treason and was hurled to his death from the Tarpeian Rock on the Capitoline Hill. Thus the man's career was portrayed as representing a paradoxical reversal of fortune, because the place which had witnessed his

10. For more details on the surviving portions of this wall and modern bibliography, see the discussion in chapter 4, p. 107.

11. For other treatments of and commentary on this episode in Livy, see Mommsen 1871, 243–56; Lintott 1970, 22–24; Wiseman 1979b; Valvo 1983; Cornell in *CAH* VII.2 1989, 324–32; Kraus 1994, 146–218; Oakley 1997, 476–93 and 515–68; and Forsythe 1999, 82–86.

greatest service to the state also figured in his calamitous downfall and ignominious execution (Wiseman 1979b). As in the cases of Sp. Cassius and
Sp. Maelius, the sedition of M. Manlius is overlaid with late annalistic inventions, which make it difficult to ascertain what actually happened. For example, as with the earlier two demagogues, part of Manlius's punishment
consisted of having his house leveled, but this detail was probably used to
explain the open area in front of the temple of Juno Moneta on the Arx
(Livy 7.28.5). The site was kept unobstructed by any kind of building not
because of Manlius's fate, however, but because the site was the augurs'
Auguraculum, from which they were accustomed to take the auspices
(Richardson 1992, 45).

Diodorus (15.35.3) places the Manlian sedition in the Varronian year
385 B.C., and in his characteristic manner he describes Manlius's tyrannical
aspirations and death in a single sentence of seventeen words. Plutarch's
account in *Camillus* 36 probably derives from the lost narrative of Dionysius
of Halicarnassus, and is basically a more concise version of the Livian
account. The summary of Dio made by the Byzantine scholar Zonaras
(7.23.10) offers a rather different story. Camillus is appointed dictator to
deal with the crisis, whereas in Livy and Plutarch he is simply elected as one
of the six consular tribunes for 384 B.C. Furthermore, in Zonaras's version
Manlius is arrested with the help of a slave, in a manner reminiscent of the
story of Sp. Maelius and Servilius Ahala. Manlius is then put on trial, condemned, and hurled to his death from the Tarpeian Rock.

Livy's narrative of this episode is the most detailed of the surviving
ancient accounts. It contains obvious fictitious elements derived from the
political violence and rhetoric of the late republic, especially from the
Catilinarian conspiracy of 63 B.C. In 6.18.5–15, Livy attributes to Manlius a
speech in which the demagogue harangues his supporters in his house. He
urges them to stand by him, to take courage in their numbers, and to be res-
olute against their far less numerous enemies. Livy begins this oration with
the evocative words *quo usque tandem,* a clear literary allusion to the initial
phrase of Cicero's famous first Catilinarian oration and to Sallust's imitation and adaptation of the latter in 20.9 of his *Bellum Catilinae.* Just as Sallust
has Catiline speak these words when first addressing the supporters assembled in his house, so Livy has Manlius utter them in an analogous situation.
The obvious literary allusion prompts the reader to associate Manlius with
Sallust's sinister characterization of Catiline. Livy contrasts Manlius's oration in 6.18 with a description of the senatorial opposition's meeting in
6.19. After first recording the opinion of many that the times called for a
Servilius Ahala who would end the internal war by the loss of a single citizen, Livy (6.19.3) adds late republican political verisimilitude to the debate
by his anachronistic reporting of a *senatus consultum ultimum* against Manlius.
The discussion ends with a short speech attributed to the two plebeian

tribunes M. Menenius and Q. Publilius, who propose to prosecute the demagogue before the people on the invidious charge of *regnum* (= "tyranny").
The names of the two tribunes are certainly fictitious and have been taken
over by Livy from one of his sources. The names have been deliberately
chosen to lend further legitimacy to the senate's actions. Menenius recalls
Agrippa Menenius, who was chiefly responsible for reconciling the two
orders at the time of the first secession; and the name Publilius suggests the
two plebeian leaders Volero Publilius and Q. Publilius Philo. The political
significance of Menenius's name is even anticipated in 6.19.1, where Livy
alludes to the meeting in Manlius's house as "the secession of the plebs into
a private home" (*secessione in domum privatam plebis*).

Nevertheless, despite these fictitious accretions from the political climate of the late republic, one single fact seems to demonstrate beyond reasonable doubt that some kind of major disturbance caused by M. Manlius
did in fact take place. Following his execution the Manlian clan agreed
among themselves that henceforth no Manlius would bear the name
Marcus, since the most recent bearer of this *praenomen* had proven to be
inauspicious and even dangerous to the state (Livy 6.20.14). Indeed, the
subsequent history of the patrician Manlii contains no one named
Marcus.[12] Livy's account explains the Manlian sedition as resulting from
widespread indebtedness among the plebs. In 6.14.3–8 he describes how
Manlius won great popular favor by rescuing an indebted centurion from
his creditors. The motif of the honorable centurion victimized by harsh
economic conditions is also found in 2.23, at the very beginning of Livy's
account of the first secession of the plebs. Livy (6.14–15) even employs the
legal terminology of *manus iniectio, vindex, iudicatus,* and *addictus* in connection with Manlius's assistance to others in paying off their debts. Even
though these circumstantial details are likely to be late embellishments,
other data in Livy's narrative for the middle of the fourth century B.C.,
which probably derive ultimately from brief notices in pontifical records,
suggest that indebtedness was in fact a chronic problem during this period.

One of the three Licinian Sextian Laws attributed to the year 367 B.C. by
the later historical tradition concerned a temporary remedy for the allevia-
tion of debt. The law ordained that whatever had been paid thus far in the
repayment of a debt should be subtracted from the principal, and the
remaining sum should be paid off in three annual installments (Livy
6.35.4). In 357 B.C., two plebeian tribunes secured the passage of a law
which fixed the rate of interest at one-twelfth (Livy 7.16.1). This measure
was nothing more than a restatement of a provision in the Twelve Tables

---

12. There may be a single known exception to the ban on this name. If the manuscript's
reading is not corrupt, Livy 42.49.9 states that Marcus was the name of the father of Manlius
Acidinus, a military tribune of 171 B.C.

(Tacitus *Ann.* 6.16). The passage of this law suggests that many creditors had been ignoring the legal restriction on the charging of interest. For the year 352 B.C. Livy (7.21.5–8) records the appointment of *quinqueviri mensarii* for making state loans to help alleviate indebtedness. In 347 B.C. a law further reduced the legal rate of interest by half, and again all outstanding debts were supposed to be paid off in three equal annual payments (Livy 7.27.3–4). For the year 344 B.C. Livy (7.28.9) records that the aediles prosecuted moneylenders before the people. Finally, one of the three Genucian Laws of 342 B.C. was supposed to have been a measure which forbade the charging of interest (Livy 7.42.1). The provision must have been a temporary measure designed to relieve indebtedness. Its historicity gains support from an incident dating to the year 89 B.C., in which enraged creditors attacked and killed the urban praetor when he attempted to enforce this old law in order to ease a financial crisis caused by the circumstances of the Social War (Appian *Bell. Civ.* 1.54).

Widespread indebtedness was not an uncommon problem during classical antiquity, but given the unsatisfactory nature of the ancient sources for Roman affairs during the fourth century B.C., we can only speculate as to the reasons why Roman society seems to have been persistently troubled by indebtedness during the 360s, 350s, and 340s B.C. Disruption caused by warfare between Rome and other Latin states, as well as periodic Gallic incursions, could have been factors, but the problem is likely to have been a complex one, caused by more than one thing. This was a period in which the size of Roman territory was beginning to increase significantly, and successful warfare was no doubt making chattel slavery increasingly common in Roman society. These phenomena could have resulted in major changes in patterns of land exploitation and the utilization of human labor, which might have had adverse consequences for families living on small farms. In any case, in order to accept the historicity of the Manlian sedition, we are obliged to postulate the likelihood that these same factors were already in operation during the 380s B.C., and that they somehow underlay a major political disturbance which ended with the execution of M. Manlius. We may further wonder whether the Roman settlement of Pomptine territory and the foundation of Latin colonies at Sutrium, Nepet, and Setia during the two years immediately after Manlius's alleged execution for stirring up sedition were intended not only to serve strategic goals but also to ease social and economic tensions in the Roman state.

THE LICINIAN SEXTIAN LAWS

The reorganization of Rome's curule offices in 367 B.C. has already been touched upon in chapter 6 in reference to the development of the distinction between patricians and plebeians, in chapter 7 in reference to the history of Roman jurisdiction, and at the beginning of this chapter in reference to the office of military tribune with consular power. It will now be discussed together with the other two alleged Licinian Sextian Laws.[13]

As in the case of other episodes of early Roman domestic affairs, Livy's account in 6.34–42 of this major landmark in Roman political and constitutional history owes much to the political environment of the late republic. The single most obvious fabrication of late republican provenance is the notion that the two plebeian tribunes, C. Licinius Stolo and L. Sextius, were repeatedly reelected and held office for ten consecutive years (376–367 B.C.), and that by use of the tribunician veto they prevented the election of curule magistrates to head the Roman state for five or six consecutive years (376–371 B.C. in Livy's account). As mentioned in chapter 6 in reference to the supposed reelection of the plebeian tribune Volero Publilius (see above p. 178), reelection to the plebeian tribunate for consecutive terms was first introduced into Roman politics by the Gracchi and was attempted by other popular leaders from time to time during the late republic. For example, Sallust (*Bell. Iug.* 37.1–2) records that in 110 B.C. the attempted reelection of two tribunes, L. Annius and P. Licinius Lucullus, forced the elections to be delayed. This action, taken by two tribunes (not one), may have formed the basis of the annalistic fiction concerning Sextius and Licinius, or alternatively, the recently invented story of the latter could have influenced the behavior of the former. In any case, despite the late republican phenomenon of reelection to the plebeian tribunate, it should be kept in mind that no one ever held this office for more than two consecutive years. The idea that two men held this office for an entire decade is utterly fantastic.

Equally incredible is the notion that these two plebeian tribunes used their power of intercession to prevent the election of curule magistrates for six years. Even in the year 52 B.C., the worst period of domestic political violence of the late republic, involving fighting between the gangs of Clodius and Milo, there was only a period of seventy-five days in which there was no curule magistrate to head the Roman state (Asconius 30–36C). The incredible nature of Livy's narrative for this six-year *solitudo magistratuum* is revealed by the fact that he covers this period of time in a single section (6.35.10) as if it were merely a month. In addition, despite Rome's military activities in these years against the Volscians and even some of the Latins, Livy's silence would suggest that Rome's enemies failed to take advantage of the fact that during this period Rome elected no officials for leading armies in the field.

13. For other treatments of and commentary on this complex episode in Livy, see Beloch 1926, 321–32; von Fritz 1950; Pinsent 1975, 62–69; Gutberlet 1985, 127–37; Kraus 1991, 1994, 271–333; and Oakley 1997, 645–724. On the historicity of the legal limit placed on the renting of public land see Toynbee 1965, II: 554–61 and Forsén 1991.

A passage of Aulus Gellius's *Attic Nights* (5.4) shows that these so-called years of anarchy are a late annalistic invention. The passage sets forth a verbatim quotation from the fourth book of the *Latin Annals* of N. Fabius Pictor, who seems to have written his history during the late second century B.C. The quotation concerns the election of the first plebeian consul in 367 B.C. and is not only the earliest but the only information concerning the Licinian Sextian Laws which has survived from the lost historical accounts of Livy's predecessors. The fragment reads:

> Thus, the other consul then for the first time was elected from the plebs in the twenty-second year (*duovicesimo anno*) after the Gauls had captured Rome.

Gellius indicates that the reading *duovicesimo anno* (= "twenty-second year") is incorrect. It should be *duodevicesimo anno* (= "eighteenth year"). The latter reading eliminates altogether the years of anarchy for this period, because in the later Varronian chronology the consular *fasti* recorded nineteen years of curule magistrates for the period 390–367 B.C. Consequently, in this historical account of the younger Fabius Pictor, the eighteenth year after the Gallic capture of the city corresponded to the Varronian year 367 B.C. with no years of anarchy intervening. It has long been recognized that these years of anarchy were probably first invented by later Roman historians as a chronological device designed to reconcile the early Roman list of magistrates with the firmly established chronology of the Greeks. About the only point at which these two independent systems intersected was the Gallic capture of Rome. The four dictator years were a similar late republican invention (see the Appendix). Nevertheless, it seems likely that when or shortly after the years of anarchy were introduced by some Roman historian to make the consular *fasti* line up properly with known events in Greek history, a historical rationale was devised to justify the insertion of these empty years, and this rationale was the alleged political stalemate caused by the two plebeian tribunes Licinius and Sextius. Finally, some modern historians (e.g., Cornell in *CAH* VII.2 1989, 348 and 1995, 400; and Oakley 1997, 650) have considered Diodorus's report of a single year of anarchy for this period (15.61.1 and 75.1) as representing the authentic historical tradition, but this view seems to be based ultimately upon Mommsen's mistaken idea that Diodorus's brief notices concerning events of the early republic derive from the Greek account of Q. Fabius Pictor, whose narrative was free of later annalistic embellishments and inventions. Rather, it is more likely that Diodorus's one-year anarchy simply represents his own characteristically muddled way of handling early Roman history by compressing into a single year a complex episode which in his Roman source spanned more than one year. Note his treatment of the Fidenate War in 12.80, mentioned above in this chapter. It is also significant that in 12.25.2 Diodorus records as one of the Valerian Horatian Laws of 449 B.C. the equal sharing of the consulship between patricians and plebeians. Thus, his account should not be regarded as being anything more than the product of his own confused carelessness.

Having thus established that the period of anarchy and the repeated reelection of Licinius and Sextius are late annalistic inventions not to be given any historical credence, we may now turn to consider the Licinian Sextian Laws themselves. According to Livy (6.35.4–5 and 42.9), Licinius and Sextius proposed and eventually secured the passage of three different bills:

1. That the amounts paid thus far to discharge debts be subtracted from the principal, and that the remaining sums be paid off in equal payments spread over three years.
2. That no one be allowed to possess more than 500 jugera (= 330 acres) of public land.
3. That the elections for consular tribunes be suspended and be replaced by those for consuls, and that one of the consuls be chosen from the plebs.

As discussed above in connection with the sedition of M. Manlius Capitolinus, the first of these measures fits well into the larger context of indebtedness during the middle of the fourth century B.C. Unless it is a duplication of a similar law recorded by Livy for the year 347 B.C. (7.27.3–4), it is likely to be historical. According to an offhand remark made by Cato the Elder in a speech delivered in the senate in 168 B.C., the restriction allowing an individual to rent no more than 500 jugera of public land from the Roman state was a well known fact (Gell. 6.3.40). The same restriction later formed a key element in the agrarian law of Ti. Gracchus of 133 B.C. (Appian *Bell. Civ.* 1.8–9 and Plutarch *Ti. Gracchus* 8–9). Whether it was ordained by law some two hundred years earlier is a matter of speculation. Rome's acquisition of the territory of Veii could have prompted such a measure. Such a restriction might have seemed both reasonable and generous at the time, but if the measure was taken several years after the conquest of Veii, as the ancient tradition records, the imposed restriction could indicate that at least some Romans were already engaged in a form of landgrabbing. If so, the law might serve as the earliest demonstrable indication that members of Rome's upper class were taking their first important step toward the accumulation of sizable landed estates. On balance, the conditions of the early fourth century B.C. may be regarded as consistent with the second Licinian Sextian Law.

Finally, the third measure, reintroducing the consulship with the proviso that one of the consuls be chosen from the plebs, must be historical since the consulship was in fact reinstated, but since for the years 355, 353, 351, 349, 345, and 343 B.C. two patricians were elected as consuls, it is uncertain whether the law of 367 B.C. actually required that one of the two consular positions had to be filled by a plebeian, or whether some other less mandatory arrangement was specified, and the equal sharing of the office was not actually ordained by law until the Genucian Law of 342 B.C. (see Richard 1979, cf. Billows 1989). Alternatively, as described by Livy (7.17.12), the Licinian Sextian Law could in fact have reserved one consular position for a plebeian, but during the years 355–343 B.C. patrician candidates for the consulship might have succeeded in having this enactment overruled at the time of the elections by appealing to popular will and to the provision in the Twelve Tables according to which whatever the people ordered last was the law. The importance of the Genucian Law of 342 B.C. would then be that it specifically outlawed this practice. If so, the election of patrician pairs of consuls between 355 and 343 B.C. would demonstrate clearly that high-ranking plebeians pursuing a public career did not automatically garner the votes of other plebeians, who continued voting in favor of patrician candidates in the centuriate assembly. Whatever the answer to this puzzle might be, we can conclude that the terms of the three Licinian Sextian Laws conform to the larger historical context of the fourth century B.C.

Another question needing serious consideration, however, is whether these three laws were in fact the work of two tribunician legislators who worked closely together as a team, as portrayed in Livy's account. It is certainly possible that although these three measures are historical and belong to the middle of the fourth century B.C., they have been brought together and assigned to Licinius and Sextius by the later Roman tradition in order to portray the events of this period in terms of the struggle of the orders. Similarly, since two plebeian tribunes are associated with these laws, and since two of the laws concern land and debt, whereas the other pertains to the reorganization of the Roman state, one of the legislators might have been responsible for the former, and the other plebeian tribune for the latter, while the two men did not actually work together and might not even have been colleagues but have held their tribunates a few years apart. On the other hand, if we accept as historical their political partnership in proposing and passing these measures, the content and nature of these laws could be taken to indicate the existence of a shrewd political program, which sought to unite and to further the economic interests of the lower strata of Roman society together with the political ambitions and interests of the plebeians of higher station. If so, this would be the first clear instance in Roman history to which the ancient thesis of the struggle of the orders could be said to be applicable. Yet even if this interpretation be accepted, it would reveal a clear dichotomy within the plebeian order: well-to-do plebeians interested in pursuing a public political career along with patricians, and plebeians of lower social and economic standing who had no hope of political advancement but were willing to support plebeian or patrician candidates who promised to watch out for their economic well-being. More-over, since the reorganization of the Roman state in 367 B.C. could not have been carried out without the active participation of leading patricians, the politics of the settlement must have been quite complex, and characteriz-ing it in the simplistic terms of patricians vs. plebeians most likely does not do justice to these events.

Finally, it is reasonable to suppose that this set of reforms, which brought together such divergent political and economic interests, formed a key ingredient in what we may call the plebeian mythology, which in the course of time developed into the tradition of the struggle of the orders. The issues of indebtedness and agrarian reform of the mid-fourth century were later applied uniformly to the much more poorly known events of the fifth century; the notion of a patrician monopoly of the consulship was likewise moved back to the very beginning of the republic; and the origin and early history of the plebeian tribunate, as well as of the plebs itself, was reinterpreted in terms of a struggle between patricians and plebeians.

Chapter 9

Rome's Rise to Dominance, 366–300 B.C.

THE EMERGENCE OF THE ROMAN NOBILITY

The primary purpose behind the reorganization of 367 B.C. was to provide the Roman state with a new set of officials with differentiated functions to replace the board of six military tribunes with consular power.[1] An equally important secondary result of this legislation was the agreement within the Roman aristocracy to share these newly established offices between members of well-to-do plebeian and patrician families.[2] Not only was it agreed to share the two annual consular positions between a patrician and a plebeian, but the curule aedileship was filled in alternate years by two patricians or two plebeians (Livy 7.1.6). There does not seem to have been any kind of regulation concerning the praetorship. Since only one praetor was elected every year, the prestige of this office was greater than that of the consulship, and it was usually held by someone after he had first been consul. If Livy's narrative is to be trusted, the first plebeian to attain this office was Q. Publilius Philo in 337 B.C., the thirtieth year of the office's history (Livy 8.15.9). Another important indication of the power-sharing agreement between

1. For other modern treatments of the events covered in this chapter, see Heurgon 1973, 186–20; Scullard 1980, 108–14 and 119–36; Develin in Raaflaub 1986, 327–52; Cornell in *CAH* VII.2 1989, 333–76; Cornell 1995, 322–26 and 340–57; and the commentary on Livy Books VII–VIII in Oakley 1998.

2. Gelzer 1912 (English translation = Gelzer 1969) remains the single best general survey of the Roman nobility during republican times. Mitchell's essay in Jaher 1975, 27–63 is a briefer and more recent overview of the same subject. Münzer 1920, 8–45 uses prosopography to try to reconstruct the party politics for the period 366–327 B.C. Develin 1979, 1985 and Hölkeskamp 1987 are much more recent treatments of Roman aristocratic politics, and Hölkeskamp's work is more narrowly focused on the period covered in this and the following chapters.

patricians and plebeians is the increase in the number of priests responsible for the Sibylline Books. In 368 B.C. (Livy 6.42.2), their number was increased from two to ten, and the priestly college of *decemviri sacris faciundis* was henceforth composed of five plebeians and five patricians. It seems likely that the religious duties of this priesthood had not suddenly increased so as to require a much larger number of priests. Rather, priesthoods had been monopolized by patrician families, were marks of prestige, and were politically important. Well-to-do plebeians were therefore eager to enjoy this same religious mystique. Thus the expansion of this priesthood and its inclusion of equal numbers of patricians and plebeians is the first clear demonstration of the politicization of Roman priestly offices.

One important consequence of the sharing of the consulship was the forging of political alliances between individual patricians and plebeians. Since one position was to be held by a member of each of the two orders, a characteristic consular election must have had several plebeians running against one another for one slot, while several patrician candidates competed for the other. The consular *fasti* for the period 366–264 B.C. suggest that it was not uncommon for one plebeian and one patrician to pool their political assets in order to secure the election of both. The two candidates thus might have formed a kind of political ticket. The evidence for this phenomenon consists of multiple offices shared by the same two individuals. Although some of these instances could have been coincidences, most are likely to have been the product of deliberate political campaigning. In many instances the patrician and plebeian colleagues might not have been close associates before their first shared consulship, but this joint tenure is likely to have created a strong bond between the two men, who subsequently assisted one another in getting elected to a second consulship:[3] L. Genucius and Q. Servilius Ahala 365 and 362; T. Veturius Calvinus and Sp. Postumius Albinus 334 and 321; Q. Publilius Philo and L. Papirius Cursor 320 and 315; C. Junius Bubulcus Brutus and Q. Aemilius Barbula 317 and 311; P. Decius Mus and Q. Fabius Maximus Rullianus 308, 297, and 295; L. Volumnius Flamma and Ap. Claudius Caecus 307 and 296; Q. Marcius Tremulus and P. Cornelius Arvina 306 and 288; Sp. Carvilius Maximus and L. Papirius Cursor 293 and 272; C. Fabricius Luscinus and Q. Aemilius Papus 282 and 278. There were other instances in which the same two men held both the consulship and censorship together: C. Marcius Rutilus and Cn. Manlius Capitolinus Imperiosus consuls in 357 and censors in 351; P. Decius Mus and Q. Fabius Maximus Rullianus censors in 304; P. Sempronius Sophus and P. Sulpicius Saverrio consuls in 304 and censors in 300;

3. For a much more detailed treatment of the electoral politics for the period covered in this and the next chapters, see Stewart 1998, 151–59. Cf. Hölkeskamp 1987, 74–90.

C. Fabricius Luscinus and Q. Aemilius Papus censors in 275; and Q. Marcius Philippus and L. Aemilius Barbula consuls in 281 and censors in 269. There were also instances in which one person held two consulships with two brothers or members of the same family: C. Sulpicius Peticus with C. Licinius Stolo and C. Licinius Calvus in 364 and 361; C. Marcius Rutilus with Cn. Manlius Capitolinus Imperiosus and T. Manlius Torquatus in 357 and 344; M'. Curius Dentatus with P. Cornelius Rufinus, L. Cornelius Lentulus, and Ser. Cornelius Merenda in 290, 275, and 274.

Another interesting phenomenon in the consular *fasti* for the first twenty-five years after the reorganization of 367 B.C. is the high frequency of iteration. Among the patricians, C. Sulpicius Peticus was consul five times (364, 361, 355, 353, and 351); Q. Servilius Ahala was consul three times (365, 362, and 342); M. Fabius Ambustus was consul three times (360, 356, and 354); M. Valerius Maximus Corvus was consul three times (348, 346, and 343); and double consulships were enjoyed by L. Aemilius Mamercus (366 and 363), Cn. Manlius Capitolinus Imperiosus (359 and 357), M. Valerius Publicola (355 and 353), and T. Manlius Torquatus (347 and 344). Similarly, among the plebeians M. Popillius Laenas was consul four times (359, 356, 350, and 348);[4] C. Marcius Rutilus was consul four times (357, 352, 344, and 342); and double consulships were held by L. Genucius (365 and 362), C. Poetelius (360 and 346), and C. Plautius (358 and 347). In addition to his four consulships, C. Marcius Rutilus was the first plebeian to be dictator and censor (Livy 7.17.6 and 22.7–8). Such iteration might have been a holdover from office-holding patterns and electioneering practices preceding 366 B.C., when it was common for a person to be elected several times to one of the boards of six military tribunes with consular power. Repeated reelection to the two annual consular positions proved to be a different matter, however. It greatly reduced the opportunities of other, less prominent patricians and plebeians to attain the highest office in the state. Consequently, one of the three tribunician Genucian Laws passed in 342 B.C. specified that no one was to hold the same office within a ten-year period (Livy 7.42.2). The consular *fasti* show that this law was obeyed except when the military exigencies of the Samnite and Pyrrhic Wars persuaded the Romans to ignore this measure from time to time in order to have experienced commanders in charge of serious military matters. Nevertheless, during the nine years 340–331 B.C. (333 B.C. is a fictitious dictator year) all nine plebeian consulships were held by nine individuals from nine families which had not yet attained this office since the reorganization

---

4. Livy 7.18.10 indicates that writers disagreed concerning the consuls of 354 B.C. According to some they were M. Fabius Ambustus and T. Quinctius, which would have made this a year in which both consuls were patricians, but according to others the consuls were M. Fabius Ambustus and M. Popillius Laenas. If the latter were true, Laenas held the consulship five times.

of 367 B.C.; and three more new plebeians were consuls in 325, 323, and 322 B.C. Indeed, the success of the Roman political system in incorporating new members into the ruling class is illustrated by L. Fulvius Curvus, the consul of 322 B.C., whose family came from Tusculum (Pliny *NH* 7.136). If the Tusculan Fulvii did not receive Roman citizenship until 381 B.C., when the entire community was absorbed into the Roman state, Tusculum was able to produce its first known consul in Rome in just under sixty years. By the time of the Hannibalic War, the Fulvii were well established as a very prominent and highly successful plebeian family of the Roman nobility.

A third noteworthy pattern in the consular *fasti* for the twenty-five years 366–342 B.C. is a series of six years (355, 353, 351, 349, 345, and 343) in which both consuls were patrician. If a law of 367 B.C. did in fact ordain that the consulship henceforth was to be shared every year by a patrician and a plebeian, these years represent clear violations of the law. Moreover, given the relative frequency with which the Roman electorate after 342 B.C. overlooked the prohibition against one man's holding the same office within a ten-year period, deliberate disregard of the law of 367 B.C. is certainly likely. It could have resulted in large measure from a desire to have proven commanders in charge of Rome's armies at times of expected crises. Noteworthy in this regard is the fact that in the first three of these six years (355, 353, and 351) C. Sulpicius Peticus was one of the two patrician consuls. He had already been consul twice, in 364 and 361, and as dictator in 358 he had inflicted a major defeat upon the Gauls and their Latin allies (Livy 7.12.7–15.8). Another contributing factor might have been the Poetelian Law of 358 B.C., which somehow regulated electioneering practices. Livy (7.15.12–3) simply describes this law as having suppressed the ambition of new men, who were in the habit of attending market days and meeting places *(nundinas et conciliabula)*. The enactment could have intentionally or unintentionally weakened or loosened the law of 367 B.C., and could have been in part responsible for the patrician consulships.

Throughout his seventh book, however, Livy portrays these six years of patrician consuls, as well as some of the other consular elections, in terms of the struggle of the orders, with the patricians striving to regain their monopoly of the consulship, and the plebeians resisting their effort. According to Livy the patrician strategy took one of two courses: allowing the state to revert to an interregnum, so that the elections were presided over by a patrician interrex; or appointing a dictator who could conduct the elections in the patricians' interests. This consistent picture of conflict between patricians and plebeians looks suspicious. Its likely author is Licinius Macer, whose fragments indicate his keen interest in portraying elections in these political terms. For the year 361 B.C., Livy (7.9.1–6) cites Licinius Macer for one explanation of the appointment of a dictator.

According to Macer he was appointed to hold the elections by one consul, C. Licinius Calvus, in order to thwart the perverse ambition of his patrician consular colleague to be reelected, but Livy had found in his older sources that this dictator was appointed to wage war against the Gauls who had encamped on the Via Salaria beyond the Anio. In rejecting Macer's political interpretation of this dictatorship, Livy observes that Macer in this instance was attempting to enhance the glory of his own family (cf. Livy 5.12.9–12, 5.18.1–6, and 5.20.4). Likewise, in his account of 444 B.C., the first year in which there were military tribunes with consular power, Livy (4.7.7–12) cites Licinius Macer for the view that the consular tribunes had to resign from office due to a flaw in their election, so that the state then reverted to an interregnum, and a patrician interrex then presided over the election of patrician consuls in the face of plebeian opposition. In citing Macer for this version of events, Livy notes that these suffect consuls were not to be found in older annals or in the lists of magistrates. Indeed, they were the product of Macer's own imagination, and their election was described as an episode in the struggle of the orders. Thus, we may suspect with justification that Livy's source for the consular elections in Book VII is Licinius Macer, and that the political interpretation consistently placed on these events belongs to this late annalist, whose account should not be given any credence. Another detail which points to Licinius Macer as the source for these consular elections is the fact that in all three passages (7.21.1–4, 22.10, and 25.2) where Livy refers to the law of 367 B.C. concerning the sharing of the consulship, he always calls it the *Lex Licinia,* never the *Lex Sextia* or *Lex Licinia Sextia.*

In the year 342 B.C., a Genucian Law or set of Genucian Laws was passed which further regulated the holding of public office in the Roman state. In order to give this landmark legislation a suitable political context, later Roman historians developed narratives concerning a fictitious sedition.[5] Livy records two very different accounts: one which he follows in his narrative (7.38.5–41.8), and another which he gives as an alternative (7.42.3–6). In the main version, the unrest is peacefully quelled by the dictator M. Valerius Maximus Corvus, whereas in the alternative account the settlement is accomplished by the consuls, without the appointment of a dictator. Although both versions are characterized as secessions, the two incidents are described in very different terms. All the action in the alternative account takes place in or near Rome and seems to involve the civilian population, whereas in Livy's main narrative the sedition involves the army and,

---

5. For other treatments of this alleged affair, see Poma in Eder 1990, 139–57 and Oakley 1998, 361–65. For other discussions of the Genucian Laws, see Hölkeskamp 1987, 102–9 and Oakley 1998, 383–88.

after beginning in Campania, the scene shifts to the Alban Hills and then to the outskirts of Rome.

In Livy's main narrative, a portion of the Roman army is stationed in Campania during the winter of 343/2 B.C. to protect the Campanians from the Samnites. Campanian affluence is responsible for corrupting the Roman soldiers, who then conceive the idea of seizing Capua by force. The corrupting effect of Campanian affluence was a commonplace; Roman historians used it, for example, to explain the demoralization of Hannibal's army, which wintered in Campania in 216/5 B.C. (Livy 23.18.10–16). In addition, the plot to seize control of Capua is clearly patterned after the capture of Messana and Rhegium during the early third century by the Mamertines, who were themselves mercenaries from Campania (Polyb. 1.7, Diod. 21.18, Dion. Hal. 20.4, and Festus 150L s.v. *Mamertini*). The Roman mutineers' summoning of T. Quinctius Claudus from retirement at his Tusculan farm to be the leader of their revolt is clearly a derivative of L. Quinctius Cincinnatus being summoned from the plow in 458 B.C. to rescue a Roman army besieged by the Aequians near Tusculum. A vote of immunity for participation in the secession was supposed to have been carried in the Peteline Grove, the same place where M. Manlius was supposedly condemned by a vote of the people in 384 B.C. (Livy 6.20.11). The latter element might have been responsible for the creation of Livy's alternative account, in which C. Manlius, not T. Quinctius, is forced by the multitude to lead the secession. His name not only recalls M. Manlius Capitolinus, but it is also the name of the Sullan centurion and colonist of Faesulae who spearheaded Catiline's uprising in Etruria in 63 B.C. (Sallust *Bell. Cat.* 27–30 and 32–33). The way in which the consular army and the opposing forces of the secession come together and spontaneously make peace could have been inspired by a similar event in 83 B.C. involving the armies of Sulla and the consul L. Cornelius Scipio (Appian *Bell. Civ.* 1.85 and Plutarch *Sulla* 28.2–3). If these parallels are valid, Livy's alternative account can be dated to the last decades of the republic.

When these later annalistic accretions have been discarded, there remain the provisions of the Genucian Law or Genucian Laws (Livy 7.42.1–2): (1) that it be illegal to charge interest on a loan; (2) that no one should hold the same office again within ten years; (3) that no one should hold two offices in the same year; (4) that it be permitted for both consuls to be plebeian. This curious combination of debt and electoral reforms has prompted Hölkeskamp (1987, 107) to postulate that the politics of 367 and 342 B.C. were similar. Politically ambitious plebeians of the upper class used debt reform to attract the support of other plebeians, and their combined political strength was further employed to pass other measures important for the public careers of politically aspiring plebeians. The first of these four Genucian provisions has already been discussed in the preceding chapter, in connection with indebtedness during the fourth century B.C. and the sedition of M. Manlius Capitolinus (see above p. 262). The other three provisions probably formed a single statute that constituted a kind of early *lex annalis,* designed to place specific regulations on office holding. The reorganization of the Roman government in 367 B.C., the frequency of consular iteration, and the patrician consulships must have formed the immediate background to this legislation. The Romans were now annually electing one praetor, two consuls, two curule aediles, two plebeian aediles, ten plebeian tribunes, four quaestors, and six military tribunes. Some kind of legislation is likely to have been needed to provide a few basic guidelines for how a noble was to pursue a public career; the second and third provisions, outlawing iteration and the holding of two different offices simultaneously, would have served this purpose.

The fourth provision allowing both consuls to be plebeian has long formed a major crux in early Roman history (see Richard 1979 and Billows 1989, 118 ff.), but the recent work by Roberta Stewart on public office in early Rome seems to offer a simple and neat solution to this problem. She has argued that beginning in 367 B.C. and ending in 242 B.C. when the Romans created a second praetorship, the Romans elected the two consuls and one praetor at the same meeting of the centuriate assembly (Stewart 1998, 95 ff.). If Livy is correct in maintaining that in 337 B.C. Q. Publilius Philo was the first plebeian to attain the praetorship, Stewart's hypothesis would require that from 367 to 337 the consular-praetorian elections regularly resulted in the designation of two patricians and one plebeian, except in the six years in which both consuls were patrician. Stewart (1998, 157) has further tentatively suggested that the Genucian Law of 342 B.C. allowed two of these three curule offices to be filled by plebeians, one as consul and one as praetor. This suggestion not only can account for the wording of the Genucian Law, but it also fits with Livy's assertion that plebeians did not have access to the praetorship until 337 B.C. The later historical tradition, written at a time when the consular and praetorian elections were two separate proceedings, apparently misconstrued the Genucian Law as meaning that both consuls could be plebeian, something that was not realized until 170 years later. Since the Romans henceforth consistently elected one patrician and one plebeian to the consulship down to 172 B.C., the Genucian Law must have specified unequivocally that one consular position had to be filled by a plebeian, and by allowing a second plebeian to be chosen at the consular-praetorian elections the law permitted the praetorship to be filled by either a patrician or a plebeian.

In 7.41.4–8 Livy records three other measures passed at this time concerning issues of military service. Their historicity is difficult to assess, but the second provision would fit nicely with the other Genucian Laws on office holding. It specified that no one was to serve as centurion after holding the office of military tribune. Since in later times the centurionate was of lower status than the military tribunate, one purpose behind this provision could have been to define the relative status of these two offices and to require individuals to hold them in ascending order. This would fit with the general character of the Genucian Law as outlined above. Alternatively, this provision also could have been important in drawing a major social distinction between the two offices, for in later historical times military tribunes were usually young men from well-to-do families, and the office was one of the first steps for someone in pursuit of a senatorial career, whereas the centurionate was usually the highest office a commoner could hope to achieve through years of military service. Thus, this provision could have been deliberately or inadvertently responsible for creating the social division between these two offices. Finally, the *Lex Genucia de magistratibus*, as we might call it, was further refined three years later by a Publilian Law of 339 B.C. (Livy 8.12.15–16), which extended the concept of power sharing to the censorship, specifying that henceforth one of the censors should be plebeian.

A second Publilian Law of 339 B.C. can perhaps also be viewed as contributing to the delineation of Rome's newly created curule offices. This second measure specified that *patrum auctoritas* be given before a measure was proposed to the centuriate assembly. *Patrum auctoritas* at this time could refer to the religious authority of the subgroup of priestly *patres* in the senate, or to the senate as a whole. Given the increasingly secularized character of the Roman state, the latter interpretation seems more likely. Unfortunately, Livy's brief statement of this law's content is quite unsatisfactory for explaining its constitutional significance. If Livy is correct in describing this measure as applying only to the comitia centuriata, it would have affected only the comitial activity of curule magistrates. One obvious interpretation of the law would be to view it as having strengthened Roman popular sovereignty to some degree, by obliging the senate to give its endorsement to a legislative proposal beforehand rather than to be in a position to undermine the people's will by withholding their approval after the measure had been passed. Just the opposite, however, can also be extracted from Livy's wording and is probably the more likely interpretation. The law could have been designed to curtail the independence of curule magistrates and the centuriate assembly by requiring that any proposal be first submitted to the senate for debate and approval, before being proposed to the people. If so, contrary to Livy's characterization of it as "most favorable to the plebs and opposed to the nobility," the law would have strengthened the senate's function as the principal deliberative body in the Roman state. This judgment of the law's purpose gains some support from a curious incident recorded by Livy in 7.16.7–8 for the year 357 B.C.: one of the consuls proposed to the army at Sutrium the establishment of a 5 percent tax on manumitted slaves (*vicesima libertatis*). The senate gave the measure its endorsement after the fact, and the plebeian tribunes carried a law which imposed capital punishment upon anyone who henceforth convoked an assembly outside of Rome. Yet this law on the manumission tax had been passed eighteen years before Publilius Philo is supposed to have secured the passage of his law concerning *patrum auctoritas*. On the other hand, Staveley (1955, 29) has astutely observed that the centuriate assembly was responsible for declaring war and making treaties, and that this Publilian law would have guaranteed that such important decisions be made only after the senate had deliberated and offered its advice. In addition, beginning in 366 B.C. the Roman state had three new curule magistrates besides the two consuls: the praetor and the two curule aediles. Since their official duties were confined to the city, they might have been the ones against whom the Publilian Law was targeted. New statutes could have been needed to establish and to define their duties clearly, and a few praetors or curule aediles overly zealous in proposing measures to the centuriate assembly could have been responsible for persuading the senate of the need to interpose itself in this process. If so, the law was designed to integrate the new magistracies, the senate, and the centuriate assembly, but in such a way as to enhance the power and importance of the Roman aristocracy as embodied in the senate.

In light of the foregoing, it is evident that the middle of the fourth century B.C. was the crucial period during which the Roman ruling class developed the general policies and practices that henceforth formed the basis of the Roman aristocracy. The pursuit of a public career was to involve election to office in a generally recognized ascending series of steps. In addition to their legal and constitutional weight, these changes carried with them important social consequences. The Roman nobility hereafter comprised both well-to-do plebeian and patrician families. As figure 6 shows (see above p. 165), the Roman political system was conducive to the upward social mobility of individuals or families of means who had political and military abilities and aspirations. Although the Roman republic was always dominated and controlled by an aristocratic oligarchy, that oligarchy was never a closed group. Entry into the ruling class may not have been easy, but the opportunity was always there for the taking. Elite families from outlying communities newly incorporated into the Roman state could and often did become active participants in the Roman political system, and many of them attained considerable success and made their own contribution to Rome's greatness. Such inclusion served to win over the hearts and minds of erstwhile competitors or enemies and even to appropriate their energy and abilities to the Roman state. It was crucial to the ongoing vitality of the Roman ruling class.

TIBUR, GAULS, GREEKS, AND CARTHAGE

During the middle decades of the fourth century B.C., the Romans waged wars in southern Etruria, Latium, the Volscian coast, and the Auruncan territory and emerged as the dominant power in these areas. Livy records campaigns against the Hernicans for the years 363–360 B.C., and for the year 358 he mentions the creation of two new tribes: the Pomptina and Poblilia (7.15.11), thereby increasing the number of the tribes to twenty-seven. The Pomptina was apparently located in the vicinity of Setia, which had been settled and reinforced a generation earlier in 382 and 379 B.C., on land taken from the Volscians. The location of the Poblilia is not known but has been conjectured to have been either in the same general area as the Pomptina or in the Hernican territory (Taylor 1960, 50–53). During the 350s Rome fought against the combined forces of Tarquinii, Caere, and Falerii, and the fighting ended with the ratifications of a hundred-year truce with Caere in 353 (Livy 7.20.8) and of a forty-year truce with Tarquinii and Falerii in 351 (Livy 7.22.5).

Rome's most difficult fighting during these years was with the Latin town of Tibur and the Gauls. The Tiburtines formed an alliance with the Gauls, apparently with a view to using them to build up their own power in Latium, but six years of fighting against Rome (360–354 B.C.) ended in defeat, and Tibur was forced to concede victory to the Romans. A powerful force of Gauls encamped near Pedum in 358, and was so alarming that several other Latin communities were eager to oppose the invading host by uniting with Rome under the terms of their former alliance (Livy 7.12.7). The Gallic threat to Latium was temporarily ended with their defeat by the Roman dictator C. Sulpicius Peticus, who commemorated his victory by dedicating on the Capitoline a monument made out of the gold torques and armlets captured from the Gauls (Livy 7.15.8). In order to portray this battle appropriately as a great Roman victory, later historians consciously patterned their descriptions after Marius's crushing defeat of the Germanic Teutones and Ambrones at Aquae Sextiae in southern Gaul in 102 B.C. (cf. Livy 7.12.11–15.7 with Plutarch *Marius* 16, 18–21, and Frontinus *Strat.* 2.4.6). For the years 355 and 354 B.C., Livy (7.18.2 and 19.1) reports that the Romans deprived Tibur of Empulum and Sassula. They must have been two small communities under Tiburtine control, and they might have no longer existed by the second century B.C. Their names are recorded nowhere else in all of ancient literature, but their appearance in Livy's narrative can be explained as having derived ultimately from pontifical records which registered the names of captured towns.[6] The Romans' defeat of Tibur and their

---

6. For attempts to locate these two obscure sites see the brief entries on Empulum and Sasulla respectively by Hülsen and Philipp in *Real-Encyclopädie der klassischen Altertumswissenschaft* V2: 2540 and IIA.1:57.

military operations in the vicinity of Privernum prompted the confederation of the Samnite tribes to conclude a treaty with Rome in 354 B.C. (Livy 7.19.4 and Diod. 16.45.8).

In 349 B.C., five years after Tibur's submission to Rome, Latium was confronted with a double threat: a Gallic army on land, and a Greek fleet by sea (Livy 7.25–26). The danger compelled the Roman state to levy as large an army as it could, probably the largest thus far in Roman history. While vigilance in force was maintained along the coast to keep the Greeks from landing, the Gauls were met and defeated in battle in the Pomptine Plain. Once the Gauls were beaten and dispersed, the Greeks had no real hope of carrying out a successful landing, and they therefore sailed off, having accomplished nothing. Since Syracuse had been employing Celtic mercenaries over the previous forty years, there can be little doubt that this campaign against Latium was orchestrated by the western Greeks. Their plan must have been to use the Gauls to defeat or at least to divert the Romans on land and thereby enable the Greeks themselves to disembark their own forces to raid and pillage the coastal districts. Rome's success in dealing with this serious two-pronged offensive was a harbinger of things to come. The next two hundred years in particular demonstrated time and time again that the Roman state never buckled under simultaneous threats from different quarters but always found a way to confront and overcome them.

This Greek expedition against Latium was simply a variation on the Syracusan attack upon Pyrgi and its environs in 384 B.C. This earlier campaign had involved a fleet of sixty triremes and had been designed to provide Dionysius I, the tyrant of Syracuse, with much-needed funds for conducting a war against Carthage. According to Diodorus (15.14), the enterprise had been a great success and had produced fifteen hundred talents of silver from the plundering of the sanctuary at Pyrgi and the sale of captured inhabitants into slavery. By 349 B.C., however, the political situation in central Tyrrhenian Italy had changed. Rome was clearly the dominant power and successfully drove back the marauding Gauls and Greek sea raiders, although the latter might have enjoyed success against other weaker states along the western coast of Italy, about which the ancient sources are silent.

It might have been at this time that the Romans established a small Roman maritime colony at Ostia, at the mouth of the Tiber. Excavations at the site have discovered a stone-wall enclosure made of Grotta Oscura tufa blocks, measuring 627 by 406 feet and covering an area of 5.8 acres. Associated pottery finds suggest a date of construction around the middle of the fourth century B.C. (Meiggs 1960, 20 ff.). The foundation of this guard post could have preceded or could have been in response to the attempted sea raid of the Sicilian Greeks. It is worth noting that although the ancient sources mention a number of colonial foundations for the fourth century B.C., they are silent about this maritime colony. Perhaps the most likely date for the establishment of Ostia is the decade of the 350s, because during the years 359–353 Livy records fighting between Rome and the Etruscan cities of Tarquinii and Caere. Indeed, under the year 356 B.C., Livy (7.17.6–9) records that the Tarquinienses raided the salt works (*salinae*) at the mouth of the Tiber, and in response the Romans appointed C. Marcius Rutilus as dictator, the first plebeian to hold this office. According to Livy, the dictator advanced upon the coast along both banks of the Tiber, took the raiders by surprise, defeated them, captured their camp, and returned to Rome to celebrate a triumph. Marcius's association with the foundation of Ostia would explain why the ancient literary tradition connected the colony with King Ancus Marcius (Livy 1.33.9 and Dion. Hal. 3.44). The 350s or 340s B.C. also might be the chronological context in which we should place an attempted Roman settlement of Corsica mentioned by the Greek philosopher Theophrastus (*Hist. Plant.* 5.8.2). If historical, this expedition must have been dispatched sometime before Theophrastus's death c. 285 B.C., and his wording suggests that it had occurred some time ago.

If we subtract the four fictitious dictator years from the Varronian date of 349 B.C. for the attempted Greek sea raid, we arrive at a probable absolute date of 345 B.C. The correctness of the latter is indicated by Livy 7.28.7–8. Under the Varronian year 344 B.C., in association with the dedication of the temple of Juno Moneta on the Arx he records a double prodigy, which, he says, resembled the portent that had occurred long before at the time of Alba's destruction by Rome: namely, it rained stones, and during the daytime it appeared to be night. The latter is clearly the description of a solar eclipse, and it must refer to a partial eclipse of the sun observable from Rome on September 15 of 340 B.C. In order to expiate the prodigy, the Sibylline Books were consulted, and a formal supplication of the gods extending over several days was decreed and observed, not only by the Roman people according to their tribe, but also by the neighboring peoples under the supervision of a Roman dictator appointed for this very purpose. All this religious information obviously derives from pontifical records. Not only is it historically and historiographically valuable in providing a definite fix on Roman chronology for this period, as well as showing how authentic information could be preserved and passed on in the annalistic tradition, but it is also significant in demonstrating Rome's hegemony over the Latins, who were soon to be directly incorporated into the Roman state: for the neighboring peoples, who according to Livy likewise observed the Roman supplication, must have been the Latins. The religious observance therefore must have taken the form of a special Latin festival (*feriae Latinae*) supervised by a Roman dictator.

In the Varronian year 348 B.C. (= absolute 344), the very next year after the Romans had defended Latium from the Gauls and Greeks, Livy (7.27.2, cf. Diod. 16.69.1) records that Carthaginian ambassadors came to Rome seeking friendship and alliance, and a treaty was concluded with them. This treaty is to be identified with the second treaty between Rome and Carthage recorded by Polybius (3.24), who does not provide a date for the agreement.[7] The treaty was the product of the contemporary state of affairs in Italy and Sicily. In 345 B.C. (= Varronian 349) eastern Sicily and Syracuse in particular were in the midst of a civil war between Hicetas and Dionysius II; the situation was further complicated by the arrival that year of Timoleon from Corinth. His activities over the next several years brought political stability to the Sicilian Greeks and posed a serious threat to Carthaginian influence in the island. The Carthaginians, hoping to keep Timoleon from successfully intervening in this chaotic situation, had met him first at Metapontum and then at Rhegium along his outward voyage to Sicily, but they failed to dissuade or prevent him from arriving in eastern Sicily (Plutarch *Timoleon* 1–2, 7–10, and Diod. 16.66–68). In view of the escalating situation in eastern Sicily, the news of the Roman success against the Greek sea raiders must have prompted Carthage to conclude a treaty with the ruling power of central Tyrrhenian Italy. Carthage's continued interest in Rome is suggested by Livy 7.38.2, which reports under the year 343 B.C. that Carthaginian ambassadors came to Rome with a gold crown weighing twenty-five pounds as a congratulatory gift for the Romans' success that year against the Samnites. The crown was deposited in the *cella* of Jupiter Optimus Maximus in the Capitoline temple. This curious bit of information, involving as it does both diplomacy and religion, may derive ultimately from pontifical records which made note of the event.

The terms of the second treaty between Rome and Carthage recorded by Polybius (3.24) appear to be much more reciprocal than those of the first Polybian treaty. This can probably be taken to reflect Rome's standing as the dominant state in central Tyrrhenian Italy. Nevertheless, as in the first treaty, Rome's sphere of influence is confined to Latium. This detail points to a date prior to Rome's union with Capua in Campania, which was a consequence of the First Samnite War of 343–341 B.C. Thus, the terms of the second treaty are consistent with the political reality of the Roman state in the Varronian year 348, the year in which both Livy and Diodorus mention conclusion of a treaty with Carthage. According to the terms of this second treaty, Roman traders at Carthage or in the Carthaginian sector of Sicily were to enjoy the rights of citizens, and the same applied for Carthaginians present in Rome. The Romans, however, were not to land anywhere else in Libya and were not to visit Sardinia or the Carthaginian area of southern Spain. On the other hand, the Carthaginians were not to harm any of the

---

7. For modern bibliography and further discussion of this treaty, see Scardigli 1991, 89–127.

Latins subject to Rome; and if they captured a Latin community not subject to Rome, they could keep the movable property and captives but were to surrender the place itself to Rome. This last provision concerning the disposition of a captured Latin town appears to be of Roman origin, because a similar arrangement is found in Rome's treaty with the Aetolians during the Hannibalic War (Livy 26.24.11). Besides these provisions, the treaty of 348 B.C. contained reciprocal clauses concerning the wrongful seizure and liberation of persons from either state. This section of the treaty seems to have incorporated the Roman legal procedure of asserting an enslaved person's free status (*vindicatio in libertatem*).

THE SAMNITES AND THE FIRST SAMNITE WAR

During the five-year period 343–338 B.C. Rome fought and won two brief wars: the First Samnite War of 343–341[8] and the Latin War of 340–338. The former resulted in a merger of the Roman and Campanian states, and the latter ended in Rome's absorption of the smaller states of Latium. Rome's use of its victories in these two struggles is very revealing and in many ways formed a blueprint for much of Rome's later success as an imperial power. Even though Rome's earlier conquest of Veii marked the first major step in Roman expansion, the First Samnite and Latin Wars stood at the beginning of a complex series of events which led to Rome's conquest of peninsular Italy in less than eighty years. Rome's principal and most persistent adversary during this period of conquest and expansion was the Samnite confederation.

The Samnites were an Oscan-speaking people who inhabited the Apennine Mountains of central and southern Italy. During the late fourth and early third centuries B.C., when they waged war against the Romans, they were organized into a loose confederation consisting of four distinct tribes: the Caraceni of northern Samnium, the Pentri of the country's central mountains, the Caudini of western and southwestern Samnium bordering on Campania, and the Hirpini of southern Samnium. They occupied a landlocked country, bordered on the east by the Frentani along the Adriatic, on the north by the Marsi in the central Apennines and the Volscians of the

---

8. For detailed treatment of the land of Samnium, its people, and their culture and institutions, see Salmon 1967, 14–186. For a more ethnographic treatment of the ancient peoples of the central Apennines, which complements and updates Salmon, see Dench 1995. For a more summary account see Oakley 1998, 274–84. For detailed treatment of the Samnite hill-forts, which in recent years have been the subject of new investigations, see Oakley 1995 and Faustoferri and Lloyd 1998, which contains additional bibliography. For other treatments of the First Samnite War, see Salmon 1967, 187–207; Frederiksen 1984, 180–85; and Oakley 1998, 284–361.

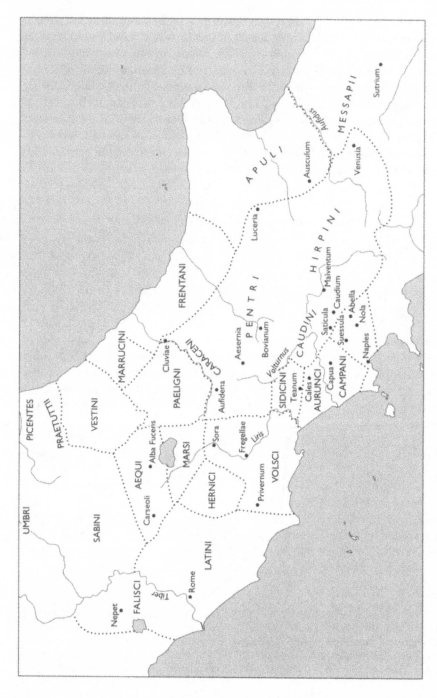

Map 9. The Samnite tribes and neighboring ethnic groups.

Liris River Valley, and to the west and south by the Campanians and Lucanians. Like the Samnites, all these neighboring peoples spoke a Sabellian
dialect and might have actually been related to the Samnites. During the
course of the fifth century B.C. (if not earlier) the lowlands bordering on
Samnium had been gradually occupied by bands of Samnites, who had left
their homeland in part through the ritual of the sacred spring (*ver sacrum*)
in order to rid Samnium of its surplus population. As a result of this migratory activity, by the middle of the fourth century B.C. virtually all of central
and southern Italy, with the exception of the Greek colonies along the coast
and the Messapians of the Sallentine Peninsula, was occupied by Oscan-
speaking peoples, who were descended from simple but hearty mountain
folk.

The Samnites dwelled in a poor land, devoid of major mineral resources
and lacking natural outlets to the sea for maritime commerce. They sustained themselves by a mixed economy of subsistence farming and stock
breeding, chiefly sheep and cattle, but also including pigs and goats (Dench
1995, 111–25). Because of the land's mountainous terrain, the Samnites
practiced transhumance to some extent, keeping their herds in upland
areas during the summer and driving them down into valleys to avoid the
rigors of winter weather. Their towns were few in number and quite small.
Most people lived in simple hamlets or villages, where they had to work
hard to eke out a living. Samnite society was therefore rustic and did not
possess the attributes of high culture. Their political institutions were cor-
respondingly simple. Rather than being organized into city-states like
Greeks, Etruscans, and the Romans, they more closely resembled the Celts
in having the tribal state or folk, termed *touto* in Oscan, as their principal
unit of political organization. Unlike the Celts, however, the Samnite tribes
seem to have possessed a simple form of republican government. The tribe
was headed by an annually elected magistrate who usually bore the title of
meddix tuticus (= Latin *iudex publicus*), and who exercised supreme judicial
and military authority. Epigraphic evidence of the second and early first
centuries B.C. indicates that Oscan-speaking states also had some kind of
senate and assembly. The tribal confederation of the Samnites resembled
the Latin League in being principally a military organization, designed to
pursue the common goals of the four tribes. Policies were probably agreed
upon at occasional meetings of leading men from the different tribes, and
they were implemented by a commander in chief.

Given the poverty of Samnium and the well-established tradition of set-
tling new areas by force of arms, it was inevitable that the Samnites' need
for land would someday bring them into conflict with the expanding and
well-organized state of Rome. The first recorded event in Samnite history is
their conclusion of a treaty with the Romans in 354 B.C. (Livy 7.19.4 and
Diod. 16.45.8). Unfortunately, neither Livy nor Diodorus provides any

specific information about the terms of this agreement, but Salmon (1967, 187–93) has plausibly argued that the two parties agreed to respect one another's territorial interests, and established the Liris River among the Volscians as the obvious boundary between their areas of interest. Yet when the two sides took up arms against one another for the first time in 343 B.C., the cause for their conflict had nothing to do with friction in the Liris River Valley, but stemmed from Samnite attacks upon the Campanians and the Sidicini of Teanum, situated farther south beyond the Volturnus River in northern Campania.

Even though the various details assigned by later ancient writers to the First Samnite War are not above question, the Livian account of how the war came about is instructive in revealing the working methods and chauvinistic ideology of Roman historians. Since Livy chose to begin and end his seventh book with the two major events in Rome's domestic affairs for this period (366 and 342 B.C.), his treatment of the First Samnite War is contained in the last part of Book VII and the first chapter of Book VIII. Nevertheless, at 7.29.1–2 Livy pauses in his narrative to herald the beginning of Rome's long struggle with the Samnites, which he rightly judges as marking a new phase in Roman foreign affairs. He notes that the Samnite Wars led to the Pyrrhic War, and the latter was followed by the great wars with Carthage. Livy and his annalistic predecessors understood that Rome's conquest of Italy had in large measure been determined by the defeat of the Samnites, but their knowledge of the first brief war was probably sketchy. Yet, in order to begin their narratives of this momentous struggle in appropriately monumental terms, they patterned their accounts of the beginning of the First Samnite War after that of the great war fought between Athens and Sparta described by Thucydides, the greatest historian of classical Greece. Like the Samnite Wars, the Peloponnesian War of 431–404 B.C. lasted many years, went through several distinct phases, and ended with the complete defeat of Athens and Sparta's supremacy in the Greek world. Furthermore, using the Thucydidean model of the Peloponnesian War permitted Roman historians to confront important questions of treaty breaking and war guilt.

According to the Livian account Rome was reluctantly drawn into the First Samnite War by circumstances unrelated to the Roman state. When the Samnites attacked the Sidicini of Teanum in northern Campania, the latter sought aid from the nearby stronger state of Capua, the main city of a Campanian federal state. When Capua in turn found itself threatened by the Samnites, the Capuans appealed to Rome for assistance. Although sympathetic to their situation, the Roman senate resisted the Capuan appeal because they did not wish to violate the treaty they had concluded with the Samnites in 354 B.C. This complicated set of relationships and the moral and legal dilemma confronting the Roman senate were adapted from

Thucydides' detailed description of how conflict between Corcyra and Corinth over control of Epidamnus caused the outbreak of the great war between Athens and Sparta (see Thuc. 1.24 ff.). In the Livian narrative, the part of Epidamnus is played by the Sidicini of Teanum, Capua corresponds to Corcyra, Rome has the role of Athens, and the Samnites represent both Corinth and the Peloponnesian alliance headed by Sparta. Just as Rome and the Samnites were bound by a treaty, so were Athens and Sparta. Similarly, both Capua and Corcyra were very powerful but independent states, whose alliance with either side could shift the balance of power in favor of their allies. Consequently, when Corcyrean ambassadors came to Athens and sought an alliance against Corinth, Sparta's most powerful and important ally in the Peloponnesus, the Athenians were understandably divided over the issue, because they thought that a Corcyrean alliance would eventually result in a war with Corinth and perhaps even with Sparta and all its allies. In the end the attractiveness of a Corcyrean alliance won out. Although the Athenians tried not to offend Corinth, they failed, and the ultimate result was a full-scale war between the Athenian Empire and the Peloponnesian League. The speech which Livy attributes to the Campanian ambassadors before the Roman senate in 7.30 resembles in part the speech of the Corcyreans before the Athenian assembly in Thuc. 1.32–36. Yet, unlike Thucydides' careful portrait of Athenian calculations and actions in terms of realpolitik, the Livian narrative stresses the senate's moral rectitude, adherence to legality, and their selfless assumption of the burden of defending the victims of aggression.

The portrait of a Roman senate reluctantly drawn into war to defend another state from the aggression of a more powerful neighbor was common in Roman republican historiography. Virtually all historical accounts were written by the victorious Romans, quite often senators, who were eager to show that Rome always waged just wars (see Polyb. 2.8.3–12). According to this common annalistic thesis, Rome won its empire honestly and with the approval of the gods by defeating one aggressor after another. Needless to say, this ancient thesis of Roman defensive and justified imperialism is to be viewed with grave skepticism.[9] To be sure, much of the fighting during the fifth century B.C. against the Aequians and Volscians was of a defensive nature, but in the end Rome and the Latins prevailed and eventually began to dispossess the enemy of their own territory. The marauding

---

9. The causes of Rome's wars and expansion during the middle and late republic have been much discussed in modern scholarship, but given the inadequate nature of the ancient sources, the same subject in reference to the early republic has not attracted nearly as much attention. Nevertheless, five excellent recent essays on this topic are Rowland 1983; Harris in Eder 1990, 494–510; Hölkeskamp 1993; Oakley in Rich and Shipley 1993, 9–37; and Raaflaub in Wallace and Harris 1996, 273–314.

activity of Gallic armies was rather exceptional. The general rule was warfare involving other well-organized city-states with rational and predictable policies. From the late fifth century onwards Roman expansion through warfare was fairly continuous. Rome did in fact encounter aggressive neighbors, such as the Samnites, but the Romans of the early, middle, and late republic were themselves of an aggressive temperament. In this regard it should be remembered that with few exceptions the Romans conducted their military operations among their enemies, not in Roman territory to drive back an invader.

The Roman aristocracy was pervaded by a military ethos, according to which the greatest honor was won by victory in war, either by individual feats of valor or by commanding successful military operations. This ethos was not only maintained but even fueled by the competitive rivalry which characterized the Roman ruling elite. Similarly, a significant portion of the adult male population of Roman society commonly did several years of military service, and this experience must have been important in educating and habituating much of the Roman leadership and voting public to the idea that warfare was a normal part of life (Harris 1979, 9–53). Many of Rome's Italian allies likewise possessed a well-established military tradition, so that the profitability of successful warfare (slaves and booty) bound the Roman elite, the Roman adult male population, and Rome's allies together into a common interest in waging wars. The Roman state was therefore configured to pursue an aggressive foreign policy marked by calculated risk taking, opportunism, and military intervention. Consequently, during republican times there were few years in which Roman curule magistrates were not leading armies and conducting military operations.[10] Although much the same can be said about many other ancient peoples and states with whom the Romans waged wars, later Roman historians in describing the causes of various wars usually magnified, if not actually fabricated, the culpability of the enemy and suppressed or distorted any wrongdoing on the part of the Romans. In addition, it should be kept in mind that from the time of the Punic Wars onwards, when the ancient sources provide us with a more detailed and clearer picture of the inner workings of the Roman state, the Roman senate is seen to have been well-versed in foreign affairs

---

10. Keith Hopkins (1978, 35) has estimated that during the first part of the second century B.C. more than half of the Roman adult male population saw an average of seven years of military service. For the period 225–23 B.C. he estimates that about 13 percent of the entire Roman adult male population served some time in the army. He regards this level of recruitment as the highest of any complex pre-industrial society, surpassed only by Napoleonic France and Prussia under Frederick the Great—but neither of these latter countries practiced the continual warfare known in the Roman republic. A similar level of military service is likely to have occurred during the period of the Samnite Wars.

and quite capable of manipulating situations or of out-maneuvering enemy states so as to have a just cause for war to buttress an expansionist policy (Badian 1958, 30–31). We are justified in suspecting that the Roman senate possessed such expertise in diplomacy and public relations as early as the second half of the fourth century B.C.

According to Livy 7.31.1–4, when the Roman senate was steadfast in honoring their treaty with the Samnites despite the obvious advantages posed by an alliance with Capua, the Campanian ambassadors circumvented the senators' scruples by formally surrendering themselves and all their possessions into the discretion of the Roman people. By this *deditio* Capua was merged into the Roman state, and the Romans were then morally obligated to defend those who had voluntarily placed themselves under Roman protection. This *deditio* cannot be accepted as historical, but it was designed by later Roman historians to serve two distinct purposes. One was to exonerate the Romans from the charge of having been treaty breakers by explaining how and why the Romans had gone to war with the Samnites in defense of Capua, even though Rome had a standing treaty with the Samnites but no formal agreement with Capua. The second purpose for the *deditio* was bound up with the history of Rome and Capua during the Hannibalic War. Following Hannibal's crushing defeat of the Romans at Cannae in 216 B.C., many of Rome's allies in southern Italy revolted and went over to the Carthaginians. The most serious of these defections was that of the Campanian state headed by Capua. After much fighting and a protracted siege, which employed considerable Roman manpower and resources, Capua was finally forced to surrender to Rome in 211 B.C. Given their implacable resistance to Rome to the very end, the Romans settled for nothing less than unconditional surrender, a formal *deditio;* and Rome's treatment of the surrendered Capuans was very severe (Livy 26.12–16 and 26.33–34). Consequently, later Roman historians applied the *deditio* of 211 B.C. to the beginning of the First Samnite War and used it to explain the war's outbreak and the origin of the alliance between Rome and Capua. In addition to exonerating the Romans from the charge of bad faith in going to war with the Samnites, the device of the *deditio* shifted the war guilt onto the manipulative Campanians. Furthermore, the unhistorical *deditio* of 343 B.C. served to justify the Romans' ruthless exploitation of the real *deditio* of 211 B.C. Since the Roman people had been so gallant in defending the Campanians when they surrendered themselves to the Roman state in 343 B.C., they were obviously well within their rights to punish the Campanians severely for their revolt in 216 and for their unrelenting hostility to the Roman state down to the very day of their surrender.

It is therefore clear that Livy's account of the reluctance of the Roman senate and the behavior of the Campanians cannot be accepted. Nevertheless, his overall explanation for the war, the Samnite attack upon the Sidicini of Teanum and the Campanian appeal to Rome for assistance, may in fact be correct. Teanum commanded an important crossroad for the region and therefore might have been vulnerable to Samnite expansion. According to Livy (8.2.4–5), as soon as Rome and the Samnites suspended hostilities against one another in 341 B.C., the latter immediately proceeded against the Sidicini without fear of Roman intervention. The Romans on their part emerged from this brief conflict greatly strengthened by an alliance with Capua, one of the most important states of central Italy at the time. Campanian society was a hybrid of the more urban culture of the Etruscans of the region and the less-cultivated culture of the Oscan invaders of the fifth century B.C. Although the Oscan-speaking portion of their population could claim kinship with the Samnites, the Campanians must have regarded themselves as having more in common with the growing city-state of Rome than the rough tribesmen of Samnium.

The only other incident in the First Samnite War requiring comment is the episode of the military tribune P. Decius Mus, described by Livy in 7.34–36. Although this man might have performed some feat of bravery at about this time, which then caused him to be the first member of his family elected to the consulship in 340 B.C., the story as it stands in Livy cannot be given any credence. It is clearly a later annalistic fiction cobbled together from two other well-known incidents in Roman history, and it is designed in part to anticipate Decius's self-sacrifice in the first year of the Latin War. The entrapment of the consular army by the Samnites in a deep defile is patterned after the Caudine Forks disaster of 321 B.C. But unlike that historical event, in which the Roman army was forced to surrender to the Samnites, this chauvinistic fiction ends appropriately with an unexpected reversal of circumstances. Not only are the Romans able to extricate themselves from this dangerous situation through the daring and courageous leadership of Decius, but they even succeed in defeating the Samnites and capturing their camp. Decius's brave exploit— volunteering to capture and hold an eminence threatening the enemy while the main force of the Romans slips away unharmed—is closely modeled upon an incident in the First Punic War made famous by Cato the Elder in his *Origines* (Gell. 3.7). In Cato's account, however, the diversionary force under the command of the military tribune was slaughtered to a man except for the leader of the suicide mission. On returning to the site, the Roman army discovered the military tribune badly wounded but still alive amid the Roman dead. But in the fictitious Livian episode all the Romans live happily ever after. Despite the apparent hopelessness of their situation, the force under Decius succeeds in breaking through the encircling Samnites by a daring night sortie and, after reuniting with the main body of Romans, they defeat the Samnites and deprive them of their camp.

THE LATIN WAR AND ITS CONSEQUENCES

Livy's explanation for the Latin War looks like a recycled version of the cause of the First Samnite War. As soon as the Romans and Samnites made peace, the latter proceeded in force against the Sidicini, who in turn surrendered themselves into the power of the other Latin states. When the Latins invaded Samnium, the Samnites asked Rome to intervene to restrain their fellow Latins (Livy 8.2.6ff). Whatever the specific pretexts for this war, it was certainly caused by the growth of Rome's power, which posed a serious threat to the independence of the other Latins. Rome's creation of two new tribes in 358 B.C., and especially its recent alliance with Capua, must have convinced the Latins that they were slowly being encircled by Rome. They therefore took up arms to assert their independence. Given the obvious parallels between this situation and the plight of the Italian allies at the time of the Social War of 90–88 B.C., it is not surprising that later Roman historians used the latter to flesh out their accounts of the Latin War. For example, the Latins' secret plans for war against Rome and the leaking of this information through the Roman aristocracy's network of guest-friends in other states resemble the antecedents to the Social War (cf. Livy 8.3.2–4 with Appian *Bell. Civ.* 1.38 and Plutarch *Cato Minor* 2). Livy (8.8.2) even compares the fighting in the Latin War to a civil war, an apt characterization of the Social War. In fact, the first actual Roman civil war was fought between Sulla and Marius immediately after the Social War.

Livy (8.3.5–12.3) narrates the first year of the Latin War in the greatest detail. Its central theme is the role of the gods in human affairs, culminating in the *devotio* of the consul P. Decius Mus. His act of self-sacrifice to procure victory in battle is an unhistorical doublet of his son's actual *devotio* at the battle of Sentinum in 295 B.C. A fragment of the poet Accius shows that the tradition of these two *devotiones* by father and son went back at least as far as the third quarter of the second century B.C. (Forsythe 1994, 332–33). Livy's narrative for the year 339 B.C. contains a defeat of the Latins in the Fenectane Fields (*Campi Fenectani*), a toponym otherwise unattested. Depending upon how memorable this battle was to posterity, the name of this site could have been preserved by popular tradition, by the tradition of a Roman noble family associated with the victory, or by pontifical records. The year, however, was most notable for the dictatorship of Q. Publilius Philo, who is supposed to have supervised the passage of three laws favorable to the plebeian cause (Livy 8.12.15–16, and see above pp. 178–182, 231–33, and 275–76).[11] Latin resistance was finally broken in 338 B.C., and the terms of the Roman settlement given by Livy in 8.14 can be accepted as historical,

---

11. For other interpretations of these measures, see Hölkeskamp 1987, 109–13 and Oakley 1998, 523–28.

since they remained unchanged down to the Social War of 90–88 B.C.[12] All of the smaller Latin states, such as Lanuvium, Aricia, Pedum, and Nomentum, were directly incorporated into the Roman state, as had happened with Tusculum in 381 B.C. Although these communities became Roman, they were allowed to retain their traditional political institutions and to govern their own local affairs. The two largest Latin states, Tibur and Praeneste, which in the past had rivaled Rome in Latium, had some of their territory taken away, but were left nominally independent as Latin allies, bound to Rome by bilateral treaties which required them to furnish forces to Rome in time of war. Sutrium, Nepet, Ardea, Circeii, Signia, and Setia retained their status as Latin colonies on the confines of the *Ager Romanus*. But Roman territory was further increased by annexing Antium and Velitrae. A small Roman maritime colony was established at Antium to guard the coast. These gains were officially consolidated when the censors of 332 B.C. created two new tribes, the Maecia and the Scaptia (Livy 8.17.11 with Taylor 1960, 53–55), thus increasing the number of Roman tribes to twenty-nine.

The Latin League ceased to exist, because with the exception of Tibur and Praeneste the Latin states had now been absorbed into the Roman state. Rome, however, continued the practice of founding Latin colonies during the course of its conquest of Italy, in order to secure strategic areas.[13] The inhabitants of these colonies collectively formed the new Latium in Roman law. They enjoyed the same legal rights (*commercium, conubium*, and *ius migrandi*) with respect to the Roman state as had the original Latins before the dissolution of the Latin League, but they were individually bound to Rome by bilateral treaties and were subject to Roman military recruitment. These later Latin colonies played a very important role not only in Rome's conquest of Italy but in the Romanization of Italy and hence in Rome's ultimate success in binding the diverse Italian peoples into a single nation. Thus, although the Latin League was abolished, the Romans found a new application of its legal principles.

In addition to preserving the Latin League in an altered form, the Romans likewise continued the communal religious traditions of the Latins by having the consuls conduct the Latin festival every year at the Alban Mount, as well as yearly rites to Vesta and the Penates at Lavinium. The Roman perpetuation and supervision of these venerable Latin cults fostered the growth of the mythical tradition that Rome had been colonized from Alba Longa, which in turn had been founded by Lavinium. Along with the growth of this tradition was another one involving the Trojan ancestry

12. For other treatments of the Roman reorganization of Latium, see Toynbee 1965, I: 129–41; Humbert 1978, 176 ff.; Salmon 1982, 40–56; and Oakley 1998, 538–59.

13. For a detailed treatment of Roman colonization, see Salmon 1969.

of the Latin people. Rome had been described as a Trojan foundation by the Greek mythographer, Hellanicus of Lesbos, as early as the second half of the fifth century B.C. (Dion. Hal. 1.45.4–48.1 and 1.72.2). We do not know when the Romans first began to regard themselves as being of Trojan descent, and when this notion was generally embraced by the Latins, but the process of this myth's genesis probably dates at least as far back as the late fourth century B.C. when the Romans abolished the Latin League and appropriated its religious traditions unto themselves. Central to the Latin association with the Trojans was the hero Aeneas; the later established tradition held that he had landed on the coast of Latium, married the daughter of King Latinus, disappeared from among men while fighting against the Aborigines, and was worshipped by the Latins at Lavinium. Dionysius (1.64.4–5) indicates that Aeneas received worship at Lavinium at an earthen mound thought to be his grave.

Despite doubts expressed by some scholars (e.g., Cornell 1977), archaeological excavations at Lavinium may have discovered this monument, and its history offers an interesting glimpse into the formation of the ancient tradition (Holloway 1994, 135–38). About 110 yards from the row of thirteen altars dating from the middle of the sixth to the late third century B.C., there was a mound measuring fifty-nine feet in diameter, which covered the chamber tomb of some local magnate dating to the middle of the seventh century B.C. At some time robbers tunneled into the tomb and carried off the grave goods of value, but toward the end of the fourth century B.C. the mound was refurbished and a fenced-off porch was built into its side to receive votive offerings. If this burial mound is the monument of the hero Aeneas mentioned by Dionysius, it is worth noting that within less than four hundred years of the burial of the tomb's occupant the local inhabitants apparently had no clear recollection about the grave and were willing to connect it with the Trojan Aeneas.

In addition to incorporating most of Latium into the Roman state, the Romans at this time formed a peculiar bond with the Campanian state headed by Capua, as well as with Fundi, Formiae, Cumae, Suessula, and later (in 332 B.C.) Acerrae (Livy 8.14.10–11 and 8.17.12). The status granted to these communities, which now formed a kind of allied buffer zone to the south of Roman territory, was *civitas sine suffragio* (= citizenship without the vote).[14] This status differed from the honorary *hospitium publicum* given to Caere for its services during the Gallic occupation of Rome (see above p. 258), and in many ways it resembled the legal status which the

---

14. For other discussions of this status, its complex history, and its application to different situations by the Roman state during the late fourth and early third centuries B.C., see Sherwin-White 1973, 38–53; Humbert 1978; and Oakley 1998, 544–59. For the legal relationship between Rome and Capua at this time, see Frederiksen 1984, 187 ff.

Latins had enjoyed with respect to the Roman state before the dissolution of the Latin League. Any state which received this status enjoyed a sharing of civic rights with Rome, whereby the citizens of one state were treated as citizens of the other in matters of private law. In this respect the status resembled both *ius Latii* and *hospitium publicum*. Furthermore, if the citizen of one state took up permanent residence in the other, he would become a full citizen of his new domicile. Besides these legal privileges, the two states were bound to one another by an alliance which obligated each to render assistance to the other in time of war. At the time of the First Samnite and Latin Wars, this peculiar bond, including the alliance requiring mutual military assistance, was probably quite attractive to Capua and the other states which accepted this status from Rome, since other neighboring states posed potential threats. Already by the end of the fourth century B.C., however, when Rome had emerged as the dominant power in all of Italy and was waging military campaigns every year, this form of alliance clearly worked to the advantage of the Romans and to the disadvantage of the other states, from whom the Romans were always demanding and receiving military forces. Thus, this status not only established the sharing of private civic rights between Rome and another community, but it also granted Rome access to the community's manpower, which was a vital factor in Rome's ability to wage war continuously and even on more than one front simultaneously.

THE SECOND SAMNITE WAR

The ten years following the conclusion of the Latin War was a period in which the Romans consolidated their recent substantial acquisitions of new citizens, new territory, and new allies. Beloch (1926, 602) estimated that at the end of the Latin War Roman territory had grown to 5,289 square kilometers, which is about three and a half times his estimate of 1,510 square kilometers for the size of the Roman state in 396 B.C., following the conquest and annexation of Veii. Under the Varronian year 332 B.C., Livy (8.17.10) records that the Romans concluded a treaty with Alexander, the king of Epirus and the uncle of Alexander the Great, who had crossed over into southern Italy at the request of Tarentum in order to defend the Greek cities from the expanding pressure of Oscan-speaking people.[15] The only major military operations conducted by the Romans during these years were directed against the Volscian town of Privernum (Livy 8.20–21). This minor war, however, offers perhaps the first clear picture of Roman standard methods and thoroughness in dealing with resistance. After putting

15. For detailed treatment of this war and an attempted reconstruction of its military history, see Salmon 1967, 214–54.

ROME'S RISE TO DOMINANCE   293

up a valiant effort against Rome for a few years, Privernum was finally captured in 329 B.C., and the principal leader of the resistance, Vitruvius
Vaccus, was apprehended and executed, while the senators of Privernum
were sentenced to live north of the Tiber. Although Livy (8.21.10) says that
the general population of Privernum was given Roman citizenship, it is
likely that they received the status of *civitas sine suffragio,* just like the neighboring Volscian towns of Fundi and Formiae. Besides this modest augmentation, the Romans founded three colonies at this time. In 334 (Livy
8.16.13–14), the Latin colony of Cales was established with twenty-five hundred settlers, on land in northern Campania near Teanum Sidicinum and
the Ager Falernus, one of the richest agricultural districts in Italy. In 329
(Livy 8.21.11), three hundred settlers were sent out to form a Roman
maritime colony at the Volscian coastal site of Anxur, which was renamed
Terracina. It commanded a strategic node along the Volscian coast, a place
where the mountains come down almost to the sea, forming a narrow pass.
In 328 (Livy 8.22.2), a Latin colony was founded at Fregellae on the farther
bank of the Liris River near its junction with the Trerus. It was doubtless
intended to be an outpost to confront the Samnites.

According to Livy (8.22.7–23.12) the Second Samnite War was set in
motion as the result of raids on Roman land in the Falernian district of
Campania by the Greek inhabitants of Palaepolis.[16] This site, whose name
means "Old City" but which probably was originally called Parthenope, had
been colonized by the nearby Greeks of Cumae and formed a dual community with the later colonial community of Neapolis (modern Naples),
whose name means "New City" (Frederiksen 1984, 85–86 and Oakley 1998,
634–36). Despite the Greek colonial origin of Palaepolis and Naples, the
population probably already contained a substantial Oscan-speaking element (see Strabo 5.4.7). This ethnic mixture may explain the people's
alliances with the neighboring Oscan town of Nola and with the Samnites,
as well as their appeal for assistance from Tarentum, the most important
Greek city in Italy at the time (see Livy 8.26–27). Since we have no other
independent sources, we cannot judge how serious were the Palaepolitan
raids on Roman-occupied Campania. Given the working methods of
Roman historians and the behavior of the Roman state in later times in similar situations, we should not exclude the possibility that the reasons for this
conflict were complex, and that Rome bore its share of responsibility for
the escalation of hostilities. It is noteworthy that war broke out soon after
the Romans founded the colony of Fregellae, which might have been intentionally or unintentionally provocative (see Livy 8.23.6). Roman prejudice

---

16. For a detailed treatment of Livy's handling of the Italian expedition of Alexander and
its chronological problem, see Forsythe 1999, 104–6. Cf. Oakley 1998, 405 ff.

against Greeks is clearly evident in Livy's description in 8.25 of how the Greek leaders in Naples opened their gates to the Roman army, while they successfully hoodwinked the Samnite forces in the city and hustled them away. Even if there may be truth in this account, the story is told so as to conform to the Roman stereotype of the Greeks as cunning tricksters. Similarly, when referring to their rejection of Roman demands at 8.22.8, Livy characterizes the Palaepolitans as "a nation more energetic with its tongue than with its deeds." An interesting excerpt from the lost narrative of Dionysius of Halicarnassus (15.5), which is likely to derive from Greek historical accounts (see Frederiksen 1984, 210–12 and Oakley 1998, 640–42), depicts the people of Naples as deeply divided over how to respond to Roman demands. A portion of the aristocracy favored friendship with Rome, whereas the people as a whole were willing to accept military assistance from the Samnites and naval support from Tarentum in a war against Rome.

In any case, when Roman demands were not met, one of the two consuls of 327 B.C., Q. Publilius Philo, led a Roman army against Palaepolis and Naples and the Roman people voted for war. When the Roman siege threatened to drag on beyond the term of Philo's consulship, the Roman people and senate introduced a new practice: the extension of a magistrate's term of office in order to permit him to complete an undertaking. This practice was termed prorogation, and the magistrate who was thus retained in office was termed a proconsul or propraetor, to distinguish him from the newly elected consuls and praetor. Prorogation was an innovation brought about by the exigencies of Roman expansion. It became increasingly more common as commanders waged wars farther and farther from Rome, and as the Roman state found itself fighting on several fronts simultaneously (see Oakley 1998, 658–61). Naples's surrender to Roman arms earned it a favorable treaty, which it enjoyed down to the Social War when the community received Roman citizenship and was integrated into the municipal structure of Roman Italy (Livy 8.26.6 and Cic. *Pro Balbo* 21). While Philo was occupied in besieging Palaepolis and Naples, his consular colleague is supposed to have proceeded into Samnium with an army and ambassadors. When the demands of the latter were allegedly met with a harsh Samnite response, the great war between Rome and the Samnites was about to begin.

The Second Samnite War falls into three distinct phases: (1) 326–321 B.C., characterized by Roman yearly campaigns in or near Samnite territory and finally ending with the disaster at the Caudine Forks; (2) 321–317, known as the Caudine Peace, a period of four years during which the Romans and Samnites did not fight against one another; and (3) 316–304, during which the war was resumed and, after an initial Samnite victory at Lautulae in 315, the Romans eventually prevailed. This war and the Third Samnite War of 298–290 B.C. can be regarded as standing at the twilight of

Roman history. During their childhood and youth Q. Fabius Pictor and L. Cincius Alimentus, who as adults wrote Rome's first two native histories, could have heard stories about these two great wars told by aged Romans who had actually participated in them; at the least, many memories of the wars would still have been current in the form of tales recounted second-hand by Pictor's and Alimentus's parents' generation. In addition, there should have been somewhat more written documentation of these events available to Fabius Pictor and Cincius Alimentus in the form of family and public records. This surmise is suggested by the preservation in Livy's narrative of several toponyms otherwise unattested, which are associated with Roman military campaigns in remote areas of the Apennines: Livy 8.25.4, Rufrium in Samnium captured by the consuls of 326;[17] Livy 8.29.13, Cutina and Cingilia among the Vestini captured by the consul D. Junius Brutus Scaeva in 325;[18] Livy 8.30.4, Imbrinium, the site of a battle fought in Sam-nium by the master of the horse Q. Fabius Maximus Rullianus in 324; Livy 9.41.15, Materina in Umbria captured by Q. Fabius Maximus Rullianus as consul in 308; and Livy 10.3.5, Milionia, Plestina, and Fresilia among the Marsi, captured by the dictator M. Valerius Maximus Corvus in 301. These obscure place-names could derive ultimately from pontifical records, but since the funerary epitaph of L. Cornelius Scipio Barbatus, the consul of 298 B.C., records his capture of equally obscure Samnite sites called Taura-sia and Cisauna (*ILLRP* 309 = *ILS* 1), perhaps more likely sources of this information are family records which proudly enumerated all the moun-tain fortresses captured by members of the family. It is noteworthy in this regard that two of the eight obscure toponyms listed above from Livy are associated with two different military campaigns of Q. Fabius Maximus Rullianus, and that Rome's first native historian, Q. Fabius Pictor, was a collateral kinsman of this man.

Yet despite this evidence for the increasingly improved quality of histori-cal data for this period, we need to keep in mind the parallel remarks of Livy (8.40.3–5) and Cicero (*Brutus* 62) that family records were responsible for contaminating Roman history with exaggerated or fabricated accom-plishments. To these Livian and Ciceronian observations, we may also add that the working methods and patriotic ideology of Roman historians con-tributed their own share of exaggerations and fabrications to the events of this period. This process can perhaps be best illustrated by Livy's account of the year 324 B.C. (8.30–35). His narrative begins with the battle at Imbrinium,

17. Salmon (1967, 27 n. 1) and Oakley (1998, 677) identify this site with Rufrae in northern Campania.

18. Salmon (1967, 220 n. 2) may be correct in conjecturing that these otherwise unknown toponyms are to be identified respectively as Aquae Cutiliae among the Sabines and Cingulum in Picenum.

fought between the Samnites and the Romans under the master of the horse, Q. Fabius Maximus Rullianus, against the orders of the absent dictator, L. Papirius Cursor. Livy says that only one battle was recorded in the oldest writers, and this is the version of events which Livy adopts in his narrative. Since he cites Fabius Pictor for the belief that the master of the horse had burned the spoils taken from the enemy in order to keep the dictator from robbing him of his glory, it is quite clear that Livy's *apud antiquissimos scriptores* (= "in the oldest writers") refers to Pictor. Livy, however, also notes that some writers did not mention this battle at all, and that according to others two battles were fought. Apparently Fabius Pictor knew of this battle and of Imbrinium, a toponym otherwise unattested, from members of the Fabian family. Thus, Livy has preserved for us an incident reported by Fabius Pictor from the Fabian family tradition concerning his kinsman's exploits. Yet it is also worth noting that Pictor's account of this particular episode, involving conflict between the dictator Papirius Cursor and his master of the horse Fabius, might be heavily indebted to the similar conflict between the dictator Q. Fabius Maximus Cunctator and his master of the horse M. Minucius Rufus during the second year of the Hannibalic War, which Pictor witnessed firsthand (see Livy 22.23–30). Some of Pictor's immediate successors failed to mention the engagement altogether, but the later annalists added a second, fictitious battle for the greater glory of Rome and for the enhancement of their narratives. In addition, as is clearly evident from Livy's text (see 8.31–35), they fully exploited the ensuing conflict between Cursor and Rullianus. In fact, Livy himself becomes so caught up in the melodrama of this episode that, although his narrative in 8.30 has depicted a single military engagement at Imbrinium, Livy nevertheless has Rullianus's father, in the course of his passionate defense of his son before the irate dictator, refer to his son's two victories in battle (see 8.33.21). Livy's account of the battle is probably derived in part from Pictor, but later writers are likely to be the source of some elements, such as the report of twenty thousand enemy dead. Livy's elaborate description of the battle's political fallout is most likely based entirely upon later accounts.

An even more blatant annalistic fabrication is to be found in Livy 8.38–39 concerning the year 322 B.C. The version of events which Livy has chosen to follow is clearly designed to glorify the Romans in such a way that the disaster at the Caudine Forks in the following year both is accounted for, as resulting from divine displeasure, and is counterbalanced militarily. According to Livy, since there were reports of an extraordinary military levy being conducted among the Samnites, the Romans entrusted the campaign to a dictator and master of the horse rather than to the two consuls, who carried out their own special recruitment of soldiers. Despite these measures, the dictator encamped so carelessly in Samnite territory that he was forced to withdraw by night. On the next day, when the Roman march was severely hampered by the Samnites, the Romans were compelled to give battle where they were. Because the Romans were fighting on unfavorable ground, and because the Samnites' courage was buoyed up by this fact, the ensuing battle was a total stalemate from the third to the eighth hour of the day. When the Samnite cavalry engaged in a disorderly sacking of the Roman baggage, the master of the horse attacked them with complete success and then turned against the rear of the enemy infantry. The latter panicked, and the Roman foot renewed its effort, which resulted in a total defeat of the Samnites, including the death of their commander. Livy (8.39.10–15) describes the battle's aftermath as follows:

> In the end this battle so shattered Samnite resources that in all their meetings there were grumblings that it was not the least surprising if they were enjoying no success in an impious war undertaken contrary to treaty, because the gods were deservedly more hostile than were men; the war would have to be expiated and atoned for at a great price; and it was only a question whether the punishment of a few would accomplish this with their guilty blood or it would be done by the innocent blood of all. Some were even emboldened now to name the authors of the war. One name especially, that of Brutulus Papius, was heard in the concourse of their clamoring. He was a powerful nobleman and without a doubt was the breaker of the recent truce. The praetors were forced to make a motion concerning him, and they decreed that Brutulus Papius should be surrendered to the Romans, that all the Roman booty and captives should be sent with him to Rome, and that everything which had been requested through fetials according to treaty should be restored in accordance with law and justice. As decreed, fetials were sent to Rome together with Brutulus's lifeless body. He had avoided disgrace and punishment by a voluntary death. It was decided that his property also be surrendered with his body. Yet, none of these things was accepted except the prisoners of war and whatever of the booty was recognized by its owner. The surrender of the other things was made null and void.

Very little, if any at all, of Livy 8.38–39 can be accepted as historical. The lack of any topographical information in Livy's account could be accidental and could simply stem from Livy's own indifference, but it might also indicate that no such information was to be found in Livy's source or sources, because the fabrication did not include such information owing to the authors' preoccupation with other matters. The only reason why the Samnites were able to hold their own in this battle against the Romans is that the latter were fighting on unfavorable ground. Thus this Roman victory serves to mitigate the Samnites' entrapment of Roman forces in a defile near Caudium in the next year. The reported death of the Samnite commander makes their defeat total. The alleged discontent following the battle clearly portrays the Samnites as impious treaty breakers, and their attempted surrender has been fashioned to counterbalance the actual Roman surrender at the Caudine Forks. Attaching the war guilt and its expiation to a single man, Brutulus Papius, not only anticipates but helps to lend credence and legitimacy to the way the Romans are supposed to have extricated themselves from the Caudine Peace by handing over the consul Sp. Postumius Albinus. Moreover, the Romans' partial acceptance of the surrender upholds Roman *dignitas* but also has the effect of shifting some of the divine displeasure onto the Romans, so that the disaster of the following year can be seen as resulting from temporary Roman shortsightedness rather than from Samnite superiority in arms (see Livy 9.1.3–11).

Livy devotes 8.40, the last chapter of the book, to recording a variant to the events of this year and to his complaint about the confused nature of the historical traditions for this period (see above p. 77). According to the variant in this chapter, the military campaign of 322 was conducted by the consuls, and the dictator was chosen merely to conduct affairs in the city in their absence. Besides the fighting in Samnium, the variant included a successful campaign in Apulia led by the consul Q. Fabius Maximus Rullianus. Livy gives the impression that both accounts agreed in the matter of the fighting in Samnium, but this may not have been the case. Failure to record significant differences could simply have resulted from Livy's own reticence and verbal economy. Brutulus Papius is probably an invention patterned after C. Papius Mutilus, a prominent Samnite commander during the Social War and the subsequent period of civil conflict, who, like Brutulus Papius, died by his own hand (Appian *Bell. Civ.* 1.40, 42, 51; Livy *Per.* 89; and Granius Licinianus 36.10). Thus the historical tradition which Livy has chosen to follow in 8.38–39 would appear to date to the last decades of the late republic. This raises the strong possibility that the rejected variant ultimately derived from a much older source which was not replete with the various elements anticipating and counterbalancing the Caudine disaster.

In 321 B.C. a Roman army commanded by both consuls was trapped in a defile called the Caudine Forks near Caudium in western Samnium. The Romans were forced to make peace with the Samnites and probably had to agree to hand over the Latin colony of Fregellae. Livy, however, devotes almost the first half of his ninth book to following annalistic accounts which not only explained away the Caudine Peace but also invented Roman military successes for 320 and 319 B.C. that fully vindicated Roman honor.[19] Thus, just as in the cases of the Cremera disaster, the seizure of the Capitoline by Ap. Herdonius, the Fidenate murder of Roman ambassadors, and the payment of ransom to the Gauls, some later Roman historians felt

19. For more detailed treatment of this portion of Livy's narrative, see Forsythe 1999, 68–73.

obliged to offset the historical Roman reversal at the Caudine Forks with fictitious Roman victories. After describing the Roman army's entrapment at the Caudine Forks in considerable detail in 9.1–7, in 9.8–11 Livy develops elaborate arguments, cast in the form of speeches, to explain how the Romans were legally correct in repudiating the agreement the consuls had entered into. Nevertheless, in 9.5.2–4 Livy makes an important admission. While maintaining that no binding treaty (*foedus*) was made, but the consuls in the field merely bound themselves by a promise (*sponsio*) to have the question of a treaty laid before the Roman people, he indicates that this position was contrary to common belief and to what Claudius Quadrigarius wrote.

The story about repudiation of the Caudine Peace is unhistorical; it was doubtless first formulated in the aftermath of the heated debate over the legitimacy of the humiliating agreement made by the consul C. Hostilius Mancinus with the Celtiberians of northern Spain in 137 B.C.[20] As in the Caudine situation, the Roman senate repudiated the agreement made by Mancinus and expiated the breach of faith by formally handing Mancinus over to the Celtiberians. Livy's citation of Claudius Quadrigarius is particularly interesting. In two other passages (25.39.12 and 35.14.5), Livy cites Quadrigarius in such a way as to suggest that his version of events was taken from the history of C. Acilius. Moreover, a statement in the *Summary* of Livy's fifty-third book suggests that Acilius published his history in 142 B.C., five years before the *foedus Mancinum* and its attendant debate. It is therefore possible that, as in several other matters, Quadrigarius's account of the Caudine Peace was taken from Acilius, who described the Romans as actually having been forced to come to an agreement with the Samnites.

Another historical fragment that has an important bearing upon the historiography of the Caudine Peace, and whose significance has been overlooked by modern scholars, is a quotation from Book XXII of Valerius Antias found in 6.9.12 of Aulus Gellius's *Attic Nights:* "Ti. Gracchus, who had been C. Mancinus's quaestor in Spain, and the others who had guaranteed (*speponderant*) the peace. . . ." All previous commentators on this passage have assigned the fragment's context to the career of Ti. Gracchus during the 130s B.C., despite the fact that the book number clearly argues against this interpretation, for another fragment of Antias (Gell. 6.9.9) cites his forty-fifth book for the trial of Pleminius in 204 B.C. In addition, other fragments from Antias that include book citations clearly indicate that his historical work covered the same period in far more books than did

---

20. Ancient passages which lump these two events together as analogous are Cic. *De Officiis* 3.109; Vell. Pat. 2.1.15; Plutarch *Ti. Gracchus* 7.2; and Appian *Iberica* 83. For the numismatic evidence of the late second century B.C. bearing on these two interrelated events, see Crawford 1973. For the Mancinus affair itself, see Rosenstein 1986.

Livy's. The conclusion is unavoidable. The fragment from Book XXII mentioning Ti. Gracchus actually refers to the Caudine Peace of 321 B.C., and its context must be Antias's allusion to the later Mancinus affair as a parallel, one which in Antias's view lent credence to the earlier repudiation of the agreement at the Caudine Forks. Noteworthy in this regard is Antias's use of the Latin verb *spondere* in the fragment, as well as his reference not only to Ti. Gracchus but to the others who made the pledge. The latter in fact corresponds precisely to Livy's assertion in 9.5.4 that "the consuls, legates, quaestors, and military tribunes made the pledge (*spoponderunt*), and the names of all who pledged (*spoponderunt*) are extant."

Livy's narrative in 9.12–16 is filled with fictitious Roman military successes for the two years immediately following the Caudine Peace. In 320 B.C., the consuls Q. Publilius Philo and L. Papirius Cursor are described as having obtained immediate, full, and appropriate revenge from the enemy. After invading Samnium, near Caudium, Philo and his army inflict a crushing defeat upon the Samnites, who are so terrified that they are pursued into Apulia. When Philo joins up with Cursor at Luceria, the two consuls enjoy similar success in storming the enemy camp. Cursor forces the Samnite garrison inside Luceria to surrender, sends them under the yoke (including the Samnite leader who had been in command at the Caudine Forks) in retaliation for the same ignominy imposed upon the Romans in the previous year, and liberates the Roman hostages given to the Samnites at the Caudine Forks. Then, after describing the Roman recapture of Satricum, Livy digresses on the military greatness of L. Papirius Cursor, which leads into his more important digression in 9.17–19 concerning the hypothetical question, what might have happened if the Romans had encountered Alexander the Great. Although this latter topic may strike the modern reader as silly and out of place, other ancient texts indicate that this was a serious debate involving Greek and Roman honor during the late republic and early empire, and some of Livy's annalistic predecessors had already taken up this issue in the same historical context, the aftermath of the Caudine Peace.[21]

Having filled the first two years of peace following the Caudine disaster with fabrications to vindicate Roman honor, this revised version of Roman history then explained the next two years of peace by saying that the Samnites sought a treaty from the Romans. They had been so thoroughly humbled by the previous two years that they sent ambassadors to Rome in 318 B.C. to beg for a treaty, but they succeeded only in persuading the Romans very grudgingly to grant them a two-year truce (Livy 9.20.1–3). Although we do not actually know whether the Caudine Peace was a

---

21. For a more detailed treatment of this matter, see Forsythe 1999, 114–18.

permanent treaty or a truce for a specified number of years, it seems likely that it was a truce. Since the Romans are said to have granted the Samnites a truce in 318 B.C., we may plausibly conjecture that this element is based upon the fact that the Caudine Peace itself was a truce. If the two parties had concluded a treaty, Roman sources might have attempted to portray the resumption of war in 316 B.C. as a response to Samnite treaty breaking. As demonstrated above in reference to the military activities for the years 324–319 B.C., Roman historical accounts of the Second Samnite War are a complex blend of fact and fiction. Thus, although we cannot hope to reconstruct with confidence a detailed year-by-year account of this war and all its vicissitudes, enough factual material can be extracted from Livy and Diodorus to allow us to discern clearly several major patterns and turning points.

We may plausibly conjecture that the Romans and Samnites did not engage one another in war during the four years 320–317 B.C., but the two peoples are likely to have been active during these years in strengthening their positions internally and with respect to other states through diplomacy and warfare. Livy's report in 9.12.5–8 that the Samnites captured the Roman colony of Fregellae in 320 B.C. may be correct, since the Samnites might have included the cession of Fregellae as a condition of the truce. In any case, hostilities resumed in 316 B.C., but the first major event occurred in the following year. According to Diodorus (19.72.7–8), whose narrative for the later years of the Second Samnite War is somewhat detailed and derives from sources much less chauvinistic than those used by Livy, the Samnites levied an army en masse *en masse* as if to strike a decisive blow, and proceeded against the Romans. The latter responded by appointing Q. Fabius Maximus Rullianus as dictator. Together with Q. Aulius Cerretanus, his master of the horse, Rullianus likewise marched out with a large army and encountered the Samnites at Lautulae near Terracina, where the coastal route (later the Via Appia) between Latium and Campania is narrowest, shut in between the mountains and the sea. The Romans were defeated, and the master of the horse was killed. In 9.23.3–5 Livy follows in his main narrative a version of Lautulae which is far more favorable to the Roman cause, recounting that the battle was indecisive and had to be broken off because of the onset of night. Livy then records a variant account, however, in which the Romans were defeated, and the master of the horse was killed. The aftermath of the battle clearly shows that the Samnites inflicted a major defeat upon the Romans, because the battle was followed by widespread unrest and revolts among Rome's Volscian, Auruncan, and Campanian allies. Strabo (5.3.5) says that the Samnites once plundered Ardea. If this is not to be connected with Pyrrhus's advance upon Latium in 280 B.C. following the battle of Heraclea, the incident could have occurred after Lautulae, and would indicate that the Samnites followed up their victory by marching up along the coast road far into Latium before retreating.

The Romans were fully occupied during 314 B.C. with recapturing places which had gone over to the Samnites after their victory at Lautulae (Livy 9.24–26). The tales which Livy records concerning the retaking of Sora and the Auruncan towns of Ausona, Minturnae, and Vescia appear credible and offer an interesting glimpse into the polarized politics of these small communities caught in the middle of a great war between two powerful peoples. The situation is reminiscent of the civil strife and violence which tore apart Greek city-states during the Peloponnesian War between Athens and Sparta. Unlike the numerous tales of Roman military victories, encountered again and again in Livy and told unrealistically with adolescent chauvinism and bravado, these incidents reflect communities plagued and victimized by their divided loyalties and their attempts to stay on the winning side. After recapturing Sora through the help of a pro-Roman partisan, the Romans rounded up 225 people whom they considered disloyal, brought them back to Rome, and had them publicly beaten and beheaded in the Forum. The retaking of the three Auruncan towns was engineered on the same day by a group of twelve young nobles working in concert with the Romans; when the plot swung into action, it was attended by the large-scale massacres characteristic of bitter internal political dissension.

Both Livy (9.27) and Diodorus (19.76) indicate that the Romans redeemed themselves in 314 B.C. by defeating the Samnites in a major engagement. This victory allowed the Romans to reassert their control throughout northern Campania. As told by Livy in 9.26, the defection of the Campanian federation headed by Capua prompted the Romans to appoint C. Maenius as dictator to conduct investigations into alleged pro-Samnite conspiracies in these communities. Unfortunately, Livy's account of this affair is quite unsatisfactory (see Develin 1985, 145–48). Diodorus indicates that Maenius was actually sent out against Capua with an army, and investigated and settled affairs there only after the city submitted without a fight. Livy, however, makes no mention of an army. Rather, after recording the suicides of the two Capuan leaders Ovius and Novius Calavius to avoid arraignment before the dictator, he says that the investigations then concentrated upon members of the nobility in Rome. Although the unrest and defections after Lautulae might have led to a fair amount of finger-pointing in Rome, Livy's account of these politically motivated investigations seems highly exaggerated and unrealistic. Given his proven track record of fabricating political dissension over the conduct of elections (see above p. 271–72), Licinius Macer is a prime candidate for the invention of the Roman portion of this episode, which looks as if it has been patterned after the trials under the *Lex Varia* of 90 B.C. This law established a special court which tried and convicted several of M. Livius Drusus's adherents for allegedly inciting the Italian allies to revolt, thus bringing on the Social War of 90–88 B.C. It was not until 313 B.C., the year after Maenius's dictatorship, that the Romans brought back under their control the other two chief communities of the Campanian federation, Calatia and Atella (Livy 9.28.6 and Diod. 19.101.3).

Three other incidents mentioned by Livy have the appearance of truth and serve to indicate that the war was fought on both sides with considerable brutality. After Lautulae, the Roman garrison stationed in Luceria was betrayed to the Samnites by the local inhabitants. The Roman soldiers were apparently massacred or enslaved (more probably the former). Luceria was a town in Apulia with which the Romans had become friendly in order to pose a threat to the Samnites in their rear. When the Romans regained control of the town in 314, they exacted revenge by massacring the Lucerians and the Samnite troops in the town, and the site then received twenty-five hundred settlers as a Latin colony (Livy 9.26.1–4). In 311 B.C. (Livy 9.31.1–4), after besieging and starving the Roman garrison of Cluviae into surrender, the Samnites beat and killed the soldiers. On learning of this the Romans marched against the stronghold, took it by force, and massacred all adults in retaliation. In describing Q. Fabius Maximus Rullianus's campaign in Samnium in 307 B.C., Livy (9.42.8) says that after besieging a Samnite army in their camp and forcing them to surrender, the proconsul sold five thousand men into slavery. This is the only remark throughout Livy's entire narrative of the Second Samnite War which mentions enslavement. This particular item could be a later invention designed to magnify Rullianus's glory, but we need not doubt that one result of the war was the selling of large numbers of captured people into slavery.

Also under the year 311 B.C., Livy (9.30.3–4) records two important innovations reflecting the growth in power of the Roman state. The Romans began to elect sixteen military tribunes, as well as two men called *duumviri navales* for fitting out a fleet of ships and keeping it in repair. In the previous year (Livy 9.28.7) the Romans had established a colony on the small island of Pontiae, situated out in the Tyrrhenian Sea west of the mouth of the Liris River. It was intended no doubt to strengthen Rome's lines of communication to Campania. By now there were Roman maritime colonies located on the coast at Ostia, Antium, and Terracina. In addition, since 326 B.C. Naples, an important city with a long maritime tradition, had been Rome's ally. As mentioned above in connection with the foundation of Ostia, the Greek philosopher Theophrastus (died c. 285 B.C.) wrote that the Romans had once sent an expedition of twenty-five ships to Corsica, to explore the possibility of establishing a settlement there (*Hist. Plant.* 5.8.2). Besides these official activities implementing a rudimentary naval policy, Roman maritime privateering is attested in Greek sources for the late fourth century B.C. Under the Athenian archonship of 339/8 B.C., Diodorus (16.82.3) says that Timoleon executed an Etruscan pirate named Postumius, the commander of twelve ships, when he put into the Great Harbor at Syracuse because he considered it to be a friendly port. The man's obviously Latin name suggests a connection with Latium. According to Strabo (5.3.5), both Alexander the Great and Demetrius Poliorcetes complained to the Romans about Antiate piracy, apparently perpetrated in the Aegean or off the western coast of Greece.

The increase in the number of annually elected military tribunes from six in 362 (Livy 7.5.9) to sixteen in 311 B.C. suggests a major change in or restructuring of the Roman army. The six earlier military tribunes had probably been assigned three each to two legions, presumably reflecting a legionary organization based upon the three archaic tribes of the Ramnenses, Titienses, and Luceres. The sixteen military tribunes elected in 311 B.C., however, must have been assigned in groups of four to four legions, indicating a doubling in the size of the normal Roman military annual recruitment. Four legions still formed the usual yearly military levy of the Roman state 150 years later in Polybius's day (Polyb. 6.19–20). This increase in recruitment was made possible by the growth in the Roman state consequent upon the Latin War. In addition to the creation of two new tribes in 332 B.C., another two more were formed by the censors of 318 (Livy 9.20.6 with Taylor 1960, 55–56). They were the Oufentina and Falerna. This brought the number of Roman tribes up to thirty-one. The Oufentina took its name from the river Oufens in the territory of Privernum. Much of its land had been confiscated by the Roman state and had been parceled out to Roman settlers in individual allotments (= viritane assignation) rather than being organized into a colony. The Falerna took its name from the Ager Falernus of northern Campania; this area was likewise a Roman viritane settlement on confiscated land. The two tribes were afforded protection by the Latin colonies at Fregellae and Cales respectively.

It is reasonable to suppose that Roman military organization and methods were modified in various ways as the result of the disaster at the Caudine Forks, the defeat at Lautulae, and the fighting on rugged terrain in central Italy. In fact, Rome might have used the respite of the Caudine Peace to make various adjustments, and the process could have continued after the defeat at Lautulae. To be sure, there was an ancient tradition which maintained that the Romans acquired their manipular organization and weaponry from the Samnites.[22] In 1892, H. von Arnim published a single leaf from a Greek text found in a Vatican collection. It contained a series of four anecdotes from Roman history. Since the text had gone unnoticed

---

22. For more detailed treatments of the problem of the early history and evolution of the Roman army, see Sumner 1970, Rawson 1971b, and Oakley 1998, 451–66. For detailed analysis of the military equipment used by the Romans during republican times, see Connolly 1981, 91–121 and Bishop and Coulston 1993, 48–64.

and unpublished, and since its author is unknown, it has gone by the name of *The Ineditum Vaticanum.* The second of the four anecdotes concerns an encounter between a Roman and a Carthaginian at the Strait of Messina on the eve of the First Punic War (von Arnim 1892, 121–22).[23] The Carthaginian, who is in charge of the Punic garrison in Messana, warns the Romans not to cross the strait to take on Carthage, because unlike the Carthaginians, the Romans have no knowledge of naval warfare. The Roman ambassador or military tribune, probably dispatched to Messana by the consul Ap. Claudius Caudex stationed at Rhegium with his army, is made to reply to the Carthaginian in the following manner. The Romans have always learned things from foreign peoples and have then bested them in the matter. The Romans learned from the Etruscans how to fight with round shields in a hoplite phalanx formation, and they then used this method of warfare to conquer all their neighbors. At a later time they learned from the Samnites how to fight in maniples armed with the *pilum* and *scutum*, and they turned this against the Samnites and defeated them. Although they had no knowledge of siege craft, they learned this art from the Greeks of southern Italy and used their newly acquired expertise to subdue the Greeks. Consequently, the Carthaginians should not force the Romans to take to the sea, because if they do, the Romans will likewise become unsurpassed in naval warfare and will defeat the Carthaginians.

Despite its rhetorical glibness, the passage is likely to be historically valid regarding Rome's adoption of the manipular organization (contra Salmon 1967, 105–7). It differed in two basic respects from the hoplite phalanx previously employed by the Romans. Instead of being armed with a round shield and thrusting spear, the soldier was protected by a *scutum* and used the *pilum* and sword as his offensive weapons. Rather than being round, the *scutum* was broad across the top and tapered slightly toward the bottom edge (Livy 9.40.2 and 8.8.3). The *pilum* was a javelin which Roman soldiers hurled in concert when advancing toward the enemy in order to throw the opposing formation into confusion before closing for hand-to-hand combat. The sword was drawn and used instead of a thrusting spear when contact was made with the enemy. Each Roman legion consisted of sixty centuries, each commanded by a centurion; the centuries were paired together to form thirty maniples. The latter were drawn up in three lines: the *hastati* in front, the *principes* in the middle, and the *triarii* in the rear. But rather than forming a solid phalanx with files and ranks lined up uniformly, the maniples were arranged in what the Romans termed a *quincunx* formation, which had the appearance of a checkerboard. The spaces between

23. The same tale is found in Diod. 23.2, and the basic gist occurs in Salllust *Bell. Cat.* 51.37–38. The precise context of the anecdote is made clear by Diodorus and Zonaras 8.8.

units were filled with lightly armed men who somewhat resembled Greek peltasts. As Livy describes in 8.8, the first line of *hastati* could withdraw into the spaces behind them in order to have the *principes* advance to take on the fighting, and a similar maneuver could be executed to bring the *triarii* forward as the reserve force.

As indicated by the office of the master of the horse, the Roman state had a cavalry force at least as early as the beginning of the republic, but with the emergence of the new patrician-plebeian nobility during the fourth century B.C., horsemanship and equestrian pursuits are likely to have taken on a new aristocratic character. Given the fertility and suitable nature of its terrain, Campania had a well-established tradition of aristocratic cavalry service before this time (Frederiksen 1968), and one consequence of Rome's absorption of Capua and the Campanian League might have been that the Campanian tradition encouraged the development of a similar aristocratic equestrian ideology among the Romans. McDonnell (1997, 206–7) has observed that whereas T. Manlius Torquatus in 361 and M. Valerius Maximus Corvus in 349 B.C. fought their famous duels with Gallic champions on foot, Manlius's son is depicted as having fought his duel in 340 B.C. on horseback. The emergence of a Roman aristocratic ethos involving horse breeding and equestrian education is clearly indicated by the *transvectio equitum* instituted by the censors of 304 B.C. (Livy 9.46.15). This annual ceremony of July 15 was a formal parade of Rome's cavalry forces, and it must have driven into obscurity the archaic military rites of the Poplifugia of July 5, whose focus was the purification of Rome's infantry forces (Forsythe 1994, 325).

Livy reports Roman military campaigns in Etruria and Umbria for the years 311–308 B.C.[24] The previous hostilities he had recorded between Rome and Etruscan states date to the 350s B.C. In 353 Rome granted Caere a truce for one hundred years, and in 351 Rome concluded forty-year truces with Tarquinii and Falerii (Livy 7.20.8 and 22.6). Livy (9.32) says that in 311 all the Etruscan peoples except Arretium combined to attack the Latin colony of Sutrium, Rome's most exposed outpost in southern Etruria, and that the consul C. Junius Bubulcus fought a battle whose outcome was left ambiguous due to the onset of night. Livy's testimony is questionable. First of all, the motif of nightfall ending a battle is also found in the one of his versions of Lautulae that is favorable to Rome. The same motif has probably been employed here to cover up another Roman reversal. Secondly, his claim that all the Etruscan states except Arretium came together to attack Sutrium is clearly exaggerated. Not only does it magnify the threat to Rome, but it places the blame for the resumption of war upon the Etruscans.

---

24. For detailed historical analysis of this Livian material, see Harris 1971, 48–61.

It is noteworthy that the fighting in Etruria coincided with Rome's decision to double its annual military levy. The decision could have been driven by external necessity thrust upon the Roman state, or it could have resulted from the Romans' decision to use the state's manpower resources to embark upon a new military enterprise. Perhaps there is some truth in both these possibilities. Tensions or minor friction between Etruscans and Romans in southern Etruria could have given the Roman nobles, always eager to have new fields of glory in which to operate, the excuse to flex and exercise their muscles. If so, it is very revealing about Roman policy at this time. Rome was a young and vigorous state headed by ambitious and energetic aristocrats, who were eager to utilize the state's growing strength to enhance their own personal prestige and to further Rome's influence and power. Q. Fabius Maximus Rullianus's campaign across the Ciminian Forest into northern Etruria and Umbria in 310 (Livy 9.35–37) and the Etruscan campaign of P. Decius Mus in 308 B.C. (Livy 9.41) were very successful and met with rather little resistance. The states of the region were probably far more fearful of and preoccupied with their Gallic neighbors and were therefore willing to conclude truces or alliances with the Romans, who emerged from the war with Umbrian Camerinum and Ocriculum as new allies. Thus, this brief northern war can be taken to show the opportunistic nature of Roman expansion and imperialism. If this interpretation of the war's causes and motivations is valid, Rome's growing confidence in its strength and abilities appears even more extraordinary when we realize that the Romans were still engaged in a major war with the Samnites. In order to have opened up another front, the Roman senate must have been convinced that they had overcome Lautulae, and that Samnite defeat was now merely a matter of time.

In addition to the reorganization of the Roman army and the increase in its size, two other phenomena demonstrate Rome's rapidly increasing power: colonization and road building. They also further indicate that the Second Samnite War was a period during which the Romans developed institutions which were to become vital for their imperial success. During the forty-seven-year period 338–291, from the end of the Latin War to the close of the Third Samnite War, ancient sources record the foundation of sixteen colonies by the Roman state, thus averaging one every three years.

338: Antium, Roman maritime colony (Livy 8.14.8).
334: Cales with twenty-five hundred settlers (Livy 8.16.13–14).
329: Terracina, Roman maritime colony with three hundred settlers (Livy 8.21.11).
328: Fregellae (Livy 8.22.2).
314: Luceria with twenty-five hundred settlers (Livy 9.26.3–5).
313: Saticula (Vell. Pat. 1.14.4).

313: Suessa Aurunca (Livy 9.28.7).
313: Pontiae (Livy 9.28.7).
312: Interamna with four thousand settlers (Livy 9.28.8).
303: Sora with four thousand settlers (Livy 10.1.1–2).
303: Alba Fucens with six thousand settlers (Livy 10.1.1–2).
298: Carseoli (Livy 10.13.1 and Vell. Pat. 1.14.5).
298: Narnia (Livy 10.10.5).
295: Minturnae, Roman maritime colony (Livy 10.21.7–10 and
    Vell. Pat. 1.14.6).
295: Sinuessa, Roman maritime colony (Livy 10.21.7–10 and
    Vell. Pat. 1.14.6).
291: Venusia (Vell. Pat. 1.14.6).

This flurry of colonial foundations is quite impressive. Although the Roman maritime colonies were small and usually involved only three hundred adult male settlers, the Latin colonies recruited between twenty-five hundred and six thousand adult males. If we assume that many of these settlers were already married and perhaps even had children, these numbers can perhaps be at least doubled. Thus, a considerable number of people, perhaps as many as fifty thousand, were involved in the settlement of these colonies on the frontier of the Roman state. A portion of the settlers would have been Roman citizens from Roman territory, but their number would have been augmented by non-Roman inhabitants of the area, who obtained Latin status by becoming colonists. Consequently, the Latin colonies must have brought together in their populations both Romans and non-Romans. It is also worth noting that after the Genucian Law of 342 B.C., which temporarily suspended the charging of interest in order to relieve indebtedness, there are no other such laws passed. This silence could be the result of the inadequacies of the surviving ancient sources, but it might suggest that even though the primary function of colonization was to serve the strategic military goals of the Roman state, it performed an important secondary social and economic purpose. During the last forty years of the fourth century B.C., the founding of colonies might have helped to alleviate land hunger and indebtedness by offering Roman peasants an opportunity to have a fresh start. The Latin colonies enjoyed local autonomy and governed their own affairs with magistrates, a senate, and an assembly of citizens patterned after the Roman state, but they were liable for Roman military service. In addition to serving as outposts to protect Roman interests against hostile neighbors at the time of their foundation, many of these communities flourished and grew, and as members of Rome's new Latium, collectively termed *socii nominis Latini* (= "allies of the Latin name"), they were a valuable source of manpower for the Roman state in wartime and were also important instruments in the gradual Romanization of Italy.

Another important tool of empire, which the Romans began to employ during this period, and which complemented and reinforced the strategic military goals of colonization, was the construction of roads to facilitate communication between strategically vital areas and to expedite the movement of military forces. It should be pointed out that in order for a state to engage in road construction of this type, the state is likely to be in a position of dominance. Since roads can also be used by one's enemies, the state which builds a road should be confident in its ability to use it and to defend it successfully against hostile forces. Rome's earliest roads were rather crude affairs, probably little more than cleared and widened pathways. If they were paved at all, it was with gravel. Stone pavements were a later luxury.[25] The fundamental object was to clear and level a wide path which could be easily negotiated by foot, hoof, and wheeled vehicles. The roads required the construction of bridges across ravines and streams, and the erection of embankments over marshy ground. In order to reduce labor, the course followed by a Roman road made use of already existing tracks between neighboring communities. Once constructed, the road often encouraged the formation of new settlements or the founding of new colonies along its length.

Rome's first road, the Via Appia, was designed to secure communications between Rome and Capua, but it also was important in connecting Rome to some of the more recently created tribes, such as the Scaptia, Pomptina, Oufentina, and Falerna (MacBain 1980, 362). Construction on it began in 312 B.C. during the censorship of Ap. Claudius Caecus, who supervised the construction, and after whom the road was named (Wiseman 1970, 130–33). The road began at the Porta Capena in the southeastern sector of the so-called Servian Wall, ran south toward the coast, passed through Bovillae and Lanuvium, and then ran through the Pomptine Marshes along the coast. It passed above Circeii, ran through Terracina, turned north to Fundi at the southern end of the Monti Lepini, returned to the coast at Formiae, and crossed the Liris at its mouth, at Minturnae. After reaching Sinuessa on the coast, the road turned inland, passed through Suessa Aurunca on the northern edge of the Ager Falernus and finally came to Capua (Frederiksen 1984, 213–15). Rome's second road, the Via Valeria, was begun in 306 B.C. during the next censorship, now of C. Junius Bubulcus and M. Valerius Maximus Corvus (Livy 9.43.25 with Van Essen 1957 and Wiseman 1970, 139–40). The first segment of this road was the already existing Via Tiburtina between Rome and Tibur. From Tibur

---

25. For the year 296 B.C., Livy (10.23.12) indicates that the curule aediles used a portion of revenues brought in by fines to pave the Via Appia with stone from the Porta Capena to the temple of Mars. Three years later, in 293 B.C., he reports that the curule aediles paved the Via Appia with flint from the temple of Mars to Bovillae (Livy 10.47.4).

the road crossed the Anio, entered the territory of the Aequians, and ran eastward up into the mountains and across the land of the Marsi and Paeligni, two Sabellian tribes who were the northern neighbors of the Samnites. The Latin colonies of Carseoli and Alba Fucens were founded among the Aequians and Marsi along the road's course.[26]

The years 306 and 305 B.C. (Livy 9.42.10–45.18) were the last two years of fighting in the Second Samnite War, and they were an impressive, if not frightful, display of Rome's use of military force. The Roman defeat of a Samnite army and the subsequent capture of Bovianum, the principal town of the Samnite Pentri, forced the Samnites to make peace with Rome in 304 B.C. (with Livy see Diod. 20.90). In the meantime, however, the Romans conducted military campaigns against the Hernicans, some of whom the Romans accused of having aided the Samnites. While the Hernican towns of Ferentinum, Alletrium, and Verulae remained loyal and were given alliances with Rome, Anagnia and the other Hernicans were defeated, were given *civitas sine suffragio,* and were deprived both of local self-government and of normal interstate intercourse with one another. At the same time, the Romans conducted a brutal lightning campaign against the Aequians, who according to Livy had also been aiding the Samnites. Whether this charge was true or false, the Aequians might well have resented the construction of the Via Valeria through their territory, but the application of Roman force settled the situation decisively in Rome's favor. Livy says that thirty-one towns were captured within fifty days, and many of them were demolished or burned. One wonders how many of the inhabitants were taken captive and sold into slavery, and how much of their land was confiscated by the Roman state. Perhaps nothing else better illustrates Rome's extraordinary rise to power in central Italy during the fourth century B.C. than this brief but effective military campaign: the Aequians, it will be remembered, had posed a major problem to the Latins during the fifth century, but by the close of the fourth century Rome was capable of crushing their resistance with relative ease. Like the defeated Hernicans, the Aequians were incorporated into the Roman state, receiving *civitas sine suffragio.*

As a result of the Roman defeat of the Aequians and Samnites, the tribes of the Paeligni, Marrucini, Frentani, and Vestini concluded alliances with Rome. Thus, by 304 B.C. Rome had humbled the Samnites. By constructing the Via Appia and Via Valeria and by founding several colonies it had strengthened its control of the Liris Valley and had forged a secure link with Campania. With the colonies of Luceria, Saticula, Sora, Carseoli, and Alba Fucens (the latter two founded shortly after the war's end), the Romans

---

26. The site of Alba Fucens has been partially excavated by Belgian archaeologists. For a summary report of their findings see Mertens 1981.

had established strong outposts to the south, west, and north of Samnium. Moreover, the new alliances Rome made at the close of the war served to encircle Samnium with peoples friendly to the Romans. Rome had emerged from the First Samnite and Latin Wars as a strong and growing state with flexible political institutions well-adapted for continued growth. The Second Samnite War, especially the reversals at the Caudine Forks and Lautulae, had posed a serious challenge to the Romans. They responded by reorganizing their military structure and by developing other subsidiary practices, such as colonization and road building, which greatly enhanced the military power and capability of the Roman state.

THE PHILINUS TREATY

Under the Varronian year 306 B.C. (= absolute 305) Livy (9.43.26) records that Rome made a treaty with Carthage for the third time. This was none other than the so-called Philinus Treaty mentioned by Polybius (3.26), whose historicity the Greek historian vociferously but wrongly denied (Cary 1919; Scullard in *CAH* VII.2 1989, 531–36; and Scardigli 1991, 129–62; cf. Oakley 1998, 258–62). Philinus was a Greek from the Sicilian city of Acragas. He lived during and after the First Punic War between Rome and Carthage, and he wrote an account of the war, which seems to have been favorable to the Carthaginians (see Polyb. 1.14). Philinus maintained that in crossing over into Sicily in 264 B.C. to eject the Carthaginian garrison from Messana in response to an appeal for assistance from the Mamertines, the Romans had violated a treaty according to which the Carthaginians had pledged not to attack Italy, and the Romans had agreed not to attack Sicily. Despite Polybius's polemic against Philinus and this treaty, there are clear traces of the treaty's existence in the later Roman historical tradition surrounding the question of war guilt with respect to the First Punic War. In order to saddle the Carthaginians with the responsibility of breaking a treaty to begin the war, Roman historians declared that the Carthaginians violated their oaths in 272 B.C. when a Punic fleet appeared off Tarentum while the Romans were besieging it (Livy *Per.* 14 and 21.10.8, and Orosius 4.5). Since the Romans and Carthaginians had agreed to cooperate against Pyrrhus (see Polyb. 3.25), and since Tarentum was the last Greek city holding out against the Romans after Pyrrhus's departure from Italy, the arrival of the Carthaginian fleet near Tarentum becomes understandable in terms of recent events, but it had nothing to do with the outbreak of the First Punic War. Yet in order to counter the Carthaginian charge of treaty breaking, the Romans seized upon this incident to show that it had actually been the Carthaginians who had first violated the treaty. The important point of all this is that none of these charges makes any sense unless we assume that both the Romans and the Carthaginians were basing their accusations of bad faith on the Philinus

Treaty. The Romans seem to have covered up the Philinus Treaty in order to conceal their own misconduct in 264 B.C., while at the same time they used it to cast blame for the same war upon the Carthaginians.

Servius, the late antique commentator on Vergil's *Aeneid,* offers additional support in favor of this treaty's existence and general terms. In commenting on 4.628 of the *Aeneid,* he writes that according to a treaty between the two states "neither were the Romans to approach the shores of the Carthaginians, nor were the Carthaginians to approach the shores of the Romans . . . and Corsica was to be in the middle between the Romans and Carthaginians." These terms are vague, to be sure, but defining Corsica as a kind of no man's land would only make sense if Rome was a power to be reckoned with. Moreover, since the previous treaty of 348 B.C. had included Sardinia and part of Sicily as Carthaginian, the "Punic shores" covered in this treaty poorly paraphrased by Servius must have included these two islands. Under these circumstances, Corsica would have represented the middle ground between Sicily and Sardinia on the one hand and Italy on the other.

The terms of the Philinus Treaty fit well with what we know about the situations in Italy and Sicily in 306–305 B.C. According to Diodorus (20.79), in 306 B.C. the Carthaginians and Syracusans concluded a peace, ending a topsy-turvy war of the previous six years, which had begun with a Carthaginian siege of Syracuse and ended with an abortive Syracusan siege of Carthage. Peace between the two parties was concluded basically on the terms of the status quo ante. Given the ever volatile situation between Greeks and Carthaginians in Sicily, it makes good sense that Carthage would have been interested in entering a simultaneous agreement with the rising power in Italy, to insure that the latter not intervene militarily in the island. In return for Rome's agreement not to interfere in Sicilian affairs, Carthage would have reciprocated by pledging not to meddle in the affairs of Italy. Although Rome had not yet embarked upon a campaign to bring the far south of Italy under control, it had already founded a Latin colony as far south as Luceria, and the imminent defeat of the Samnites clearly established Rome as the greatest power in the peninsula. Thus, the Philinus Treaty, concluded a mere forty years after the previous Carthaginian treaty, testifies to Rome's rapid rise to dominance in Italy during the second half of the fourth century B.C. In the treaty of 348 B.C. Rome was still simply laying claim to Latium, but in the Philinus Treaty Carthage was prepared to recognize Rome as the hegemonic power in the peninsula.

OTHER SIGNIFICANT CHANGES IN THE ROMAN STATE

As might be expected, Roman society underwent significant social, economic, and political changes during the period covered in this chapter. One major change is likely to have been Rome's gradual transformation into a slave-owning society. Incessant and successful warfare over the course of the fourth century must have produced a steady supply of slaves. One clear indication of the growth in chattel slavery in Roman society during this period is a law passed in 357 B.C. which imposed a 5 percent tax (*vicesima libertatis*) on manumitted slaves (Livy 7.16.7–8). It is worth noting that this law was passed by the Roman army at Sutrium, the Latin colony on Rome's Etruscan frontier. It suggests that the army ratified this proposal either before or after a military campaign against non-Latin-speaking people, who must have been prime candidates for the Roman slave market. The other interesting point concerning this law is that the tax was imposed not on the purchase of slaves but on their manumission. If the law was designed to bring in revenue, as seems likely, it indicates that already in Roman society the manumission of slaves (and hence the class of freedmen) was significant enough to be subject to taxation.

Another indication of significant social change along these lines is the passage of the Poetelian Law, which banned or modified debt servitude. There are four ancient accounts of the circumstances surrounding this law: Livy 8.28; Dion. Hal. 16.5; Varro *De Lingua Latina* 7.105; and Valerius Maximus 6.1.9. Cicero's description of this event, in 2.59 of his *De Re Publica*, is unfortunately incomplete. It should come as no surprise that in these accounts the law's passage is related to the struggle of the orders. Livy terms it "another beginning of freedom." Yet the discrepancies among the surviving ancient accounts make it quite clear that by later historical times very little was known about this law apart from its name and the fact of its passage. Consequently, ancient writers concocted what they regarded as the suitable background to the law. The basic outline of the etiological story is that when a handsome young man was forced to become a debt slave, his master beat him for resisting his sexual advances. When the young man ran into the Forum and informed people of his plight, there was such an outcry of indignation that the Poetelian Law was passed. Livy dates the law to the year 326 B.C. when C. Poetelius Libo Visolus was consul, whereas Varro dates it to 313 when the same man was dictator. In fact, it is possible that both these dates are incorrect, and that the law was actually passed in some other year by this man or a kinsman serving as plebeian tribune. If so, later Roman tradition had no clear knowledge of the law's precise date. The texts of Valerius Maximus and Dionysius do not provide a specific year for the law, but they indicate that it was after the Caudine Forks disaster of 321 B.C.

Besides this disagreement over the law's date, there are different versions of the identities of the handsome young man and the lustful creditor. Livy names them as Publilius and Papirius respectively. These two names are clearly fictitious and have been patterned after two of the most illustrious personages of the Second Samnite War: the plebeian Q. Publilius Philo and the patrician L. Papirius Cursor, who were consuls together in 320 and 315 B.C. Valerius Maximus, however, gives their names as T. Veturius and P. Plotius, and he identifies the former as the son of the T. Veturius who was consul in 321 B.C. and was surrendered to the Samnites. Dionysius's account seems to combine elements from these other two versions. The handsome young man is named Publilius and is described as having been a military tribune at the Caudine Forks. Despite these differences in date and nomenclature, the gist of the various accounts involves the same cartoonlike story, which strikingly resembles Livy's tale in 2.23 of the indebted honorable veteran whose mistreatment sparked off the agitation resulting in the first secession of the plebs. The same motif of the honorable indebted soldier is found in Livy 6.14.3–8, in his account of the sedition of M. Manlius Capitolinus. It is therefore obvious that the etiological tale associated with the Poetelian Law must be rejected as unhistorical.

According to Livy (8.28.8–9), the law ordered that "no one should be confined by fetters or by a bond[27] except someone who had deserved punishment (*noxam*) while he was paying the penalty, and that the goods of the debtor, not his body, were to be liable for the debt." Varro, on the other hand, says that "all were released who swore to their good standing (*bonam copiam*), so that they were not *nexi*." These two statements can be taken as complementary and as describing two different aspects of the law. From Livy's paraphrase it appears that the Poetelian Law abolished the provision in the Twelve Tables which allowed a creditor to hold a person judged to be in default of a debt in bonds. The one exception allowed by the Poetelian Law was if the person were guilty of a crime (*noxa*). *Noxa* in Livy's paraphrase of the law could be intended to have a general meaning and could specify anyone guilty of causing damage but not having the means to pay redress according to the law. Alternatively, it could refer to the particular case in Roman law in which a slave or a son under paternal authority stole or caused damage to property, thereby creating a legal obligation for the owner or father to compensate the victim. This could be done either by paying the legal penalty or by surrendering the criminal to the victim, to work off the amount of the penalty. The latter solution was termed noxal surrender and constituted a form of debt servitude. Thus the rationale behind the Poetelian Law seems to have been that since a person guilty of theft or damage to property had already shown that he was not to be trusted, he could with justification be held in bonds while he worked off his legal obligation.

27. I have rendered Livy's *nervo* by the ambiguous "bond." A *nervus* was a device used to confine prisoners or slaves by the neck or feet, and its physical configuration seems to have changed somewhat over time. See Oakley 1997, 501.

Varro's remark hints at something quite different. A person was not forced to work off his debt as a *nexus* if he swore that his property sufficed to cover the debt. As was commonly done in other situations in Roman law, the debtor might have been required by the Poetelian Law to provide someone as a surety to underwrite this assertion. In addition, in order to compel the debtor to swear truthfully, the law could have penalized him by doubling the amount owed if he were caught in a falsehood. There also must have been a legal procedure available to the creditor to foreclose on the debtor's property. There is an implication that if the person's property did not suffice, the debtor could still become a *nexus* who had to work off the amount owed. If this interpretation of the ancient texts is correct, it indicates that the Poetelian Law did not abolish debt servitude, but simply relaxed some of its archaic rigor. Consequently, the Poetelian Law can be explained simply as part of a general progression in the early history of Roman law to ameliorate some of the harsher legal provisions. That debt servitude did continue after the passage of the Poetelian Law is shown by Livy 23.14.3–4. In 216 B.C., following Rome's great losses in manpower in the battle at Cannae, the Romans were hard-pressed to find adequate numbers of recruits. One device employed by the dictator M. Junius Pera was to levy "those who had committed a capital offense, and those who were in chains as judgment debtors." Livy says that six thousand troops were raised from these two categories of convicts. Finally, there is likely to have been a roughly inverse relationship between debt servitude and chattel slavery. During the fifth and early fourth centuries B.C., wealthier land owners might have exploited debt servitude as a means of obtaining dependent labor to work their holdings, but the increasing availability of slaves resulting from Rome's success in war during the fourth century must have provided a more secure and reliable form of subservient human labor. This in turn could have constituted an economic incentive for relaxing the law on debt servitude.

Besides having supervised the construction of Rome's first road, Ap. Claudius Caecus was also responsible for the building of the first aqueduct, the Aqua Appia. This major public work, which provided the city with a steady and reliable water supply, is a rough indication of the increasing size of Rome's urban population and of the city's growing sophistication. At about this same time (or perhaps later, in the early third century B.C.), the Comitium in the Roman Forum was reshaped into a circle measuring about 150 feet in diameter. Coarelli (1985, 11–21) has argued persuasively that this change was inspired by the circular assembly places (*ekklesiasteria*) known from the Greek cities of southern Italy and Sicily. According to the Roman antiquarian tradition, which enjoyed recording such things, the first professional Greek barber who set up shop in Rome did so in the year 300 B.C. (Varro *De Re Rustica* 2.11.10 and Pliny *NH* 7.211). As mentioned above in connection with Rome's military reorganization during the Second Samnite War, the later fourth century is likely to have witnessed the development of an equestrian ethos among the Roman upper class. Since raising horses and training in horsemanship require land, resources, and leisure, the Roman nobility's adoption of an equestrian ethos must have been made possible by their ownership of substantial landed estates, worked to a large degree by slaves.

R.E.A. Palmer (1997, 11–25) has argued persuasively that Polybius's mention of the Treasury of the Aediles as the depository of Rome's treaties with Carthage testifies to the existence of trade between the two states long before the period of the Punic Wars. Since these agreements regulated the commercial status of individuals of one state in reference to the other and its territorial possessions, the curule aediles, who supervised activities in the markets of Rome, were the obvious guardians of these documents and the enforcers of their provisions. Consequently, the Carthaginian treaties of 348 and 306 B.C. can be taken to be the diplomatic manifestations of regular, ongoing commercial activity between the two peoples. Palmer also makes the likely suggestion that Roman purchases of grain from Sicily, reported by the annalistic tradition in times of food shortages during the fifth century B.C., could have involved the Phoenician-controlled sector of the island.

Rome's territorial acquisitions and expansion into the Liris Valley and Campania offered new opportunities to Roman citizens, both rich and poor. Campania not only possessed the richest agricultural land in Italy; it had also long been known for its manufactured goods. Thus, the alliances with the Campanian federation headed by Capua and with the Greek coastal city-state of Naples linked the Romans to areas of industry and trade. One possible indication of Rome's growing importance as a center of manufacture is offered by the famous Ficoroni Cista (Dohrn 1972). This artifact was discovered in a grave at Praeneste in 1738. The two lines of Latin inscribed on its lid (*ILLRP* 1197) say, "Novios Plautios made me at Rome" (= *"Novios Plautios med Romai fecid"*), and "Dindia Macolnia gave [me] to her daughter" (= *"Dindia Macolnia fileai dedit"*). This object is a beautifully decorated, bronze, cylindrical chest, mounted on three claw-like feet and topped with a lid, upon which stand Dionysus and two satyrs (see fig. 9). The flat circular surface of the lid contains three sets of designs: a center circle of floral patterns, a concentric band of four animals, and the outermost concentric band which is filled with numerous human and animal figures. The outer cylindrical body of the chest is engraved with figures of the Argonauts: Jason, Herakles, Orpheus, Lynkeus, the ship Argo itself with some of its crew aboard; but the central scene is Polydeukes tying Amykos to a tree after beating him in a boxing match. The entire cista is almost thirty inches tall, about nineteen inches high minus the lid. The three

Figure 9. Ficoroni Cista from Praeneste.

figures on top of the lid are seven inches high. The cylindrical chest itself is nearly fifteen inches in diameter.

Robert Wallace (Eder 1990, 278–92) has considered this artifact together with the other meager archaeological finds relevant to Rome during the late fourth and early third centuries B.C., and by stressing their scanty and ambiguous nature he has criticized modern scholarly attempts to portray Rome at this time as a major urban center influenced by Greek culture and possessing thriving metalworking and ceramic industries. Although he is correct to caution us against overinterpreting isolated finds, and correct, too, in minimizing the degree to which Roman society as a whole was hellenized during this period, the absence of archaeological data does not necessarily constitute a valid argument from silence. We are certainly justified in supposing that as Rome rose to be the most politically and militarily significant state in Italy, and as a steady stream of war booty enriched its economy, by the close of the fourth century B.C. the city was beginning to attract growing numbers of skilled artisans, of whom Novios Plautios was one.[28]

28. For a brief but thorough treatment of the ancient literary, epigraphic, and archaeological evidence pertaining to Rome's social, economic, and cultural development c. 300 B.C., see Starr 1980.

The curule aedileship of Cn. Flavius in 304 B.C. was marked by important innovations in Roman law, as well as by the fact that he was the son of a freedman. Livy's description (9.46) of Flavius's official activities is very problematic, but when analyzed carefully, this episode reveals much about important changes in Roman society and how they were perceived and distorted by later ancient historians. An examination of the various surviving ancient accounts of Cn. Flavius indicates that there were two different traditions concerning this man's career (Forsythe 1994, 339–47; cf. Bauman 1983, 24–45). One, recorded by Calpurnius Piso Frugi, was that Flavius served as a public scribe until he was elected curule aedile, and that he published the legal calendar and *legis actiones* while holding this office. Ap. Claudius Caecus played no direct role in this version. The other tradition, however, linked Flavius's career to Claudius, whom he allegedly served as scribe and by whom he was enrolled into the senate during the censorship of 312 B.C. According to this tradition, Flavius published the legal calendar and *legis actiones* while still a scribe, after which he was elected to public office. Livy indicates that this latter variant was adopted by Licinius Macer, who was in all likelihood its actual author. That Claudius enrolled the sons of freedmen into the senate is not to be taken seriously. The notion is redolent of the Sullan period, for Sulla the dictator was accused of having enrolled persons of low birth into the senate (Sallust *Bell. Cat.* 37.6 and Dion. Hal. 5.77.5). In addition, falsely ascribing other offices to Flavius before his curule aedileship resembles Macer's manipulation of magistracies in other instances (see above p. 227 and 271). Macer's hand is further evident in the fact that he has Flavius serving as *triumvir nocturnus* before the office was even in existence (see Livy *Per.* 11 and *Digest* 1.2.2.30).

Even though Licinius Macer's direct link between Ap. Claudius Caecus and Cn. Flavius is to be rejected, other considerations suggest an indirect connection between the two men, which most likely formed the basis of Macer's invention. While censor in 312, Claudius was thought to have significantly changed the organization of the voting tribes by not confining the city's inhabitants (including freedmen) to the four urban tribes (Livy 9.46.11, cf. Diod. 20.36.4). Claudius's precise actions and motives have been the subject of much modern scholarly discussion (e.g., Staveley 1959, 413 ff.; Taylor 1960, 132; Bauman 1983, 32 ff.; Cornell in *CAH* VII.2 1989, 395; and Walt 1997, 331–34). Nevertheless, the ancient evidence concerning Claudius's censorship is so plagued with later annalistic sensationalism that we cannot determine how and why Claudius and his colleague actually changed tribal registration. It should be noted, however, that tribal reform of some sort must have been a practical necessity during the late fourth century, in order to accommodate large numbers of new citizens. Besides the creation of four new tribes by the censors of 332 and 318 B.C., the military reforms brought on by the Second Samnite War might have also required changes in censorial registration. In any case, it appears likely that the innovations introduced by the censors of 312 and perhaps their immediate predecessors in 318 and successors in 307 had the effect (intentional or unintentional) of granting greater voting influence to the urban populace, a significant portion of which was now freedmen or of libertine descent. Some peculiar circumstance, such as the absence from the city of numerous freeborn adult males on military service, led to the election of a public scribe and freedman's son as curule aedile. The Roman ruling elite was shocked by this electoral anomaly and took immediate action to prevent its repetition. The censors of 304 limited the voting power of the *ordo libertinus* by registering freedmen only in the four urban tribes. In fact, it seems likely that before 304 Roman freedmen had never been systematically confined to the four urban tribes. Their numbers and voting influence must have been negligible during the fifth century, but Rome's rapid expansion and continuous warfare during the fourth century must have steadily increased their numbers. Flavius's election as curule aedile reflected fundamental social and economic changes in the Roman state, demonstrated the potential political power of the *ordo libertinus,* and convinced the ruling oligarchy that these new forces had to be brought under their control. The censors of 304 B.C. devised the political solution that the ruling elite followed to the end of the republic. Finally, the circumstantial evidence of these events allowed later historians, such as Licinius Macer, to construct a scenario in which an ambitious patrician politician disturbed the tranquillity of the state by orchestrating the publication of the legal calendar, by enrolling the sons of freedmen into the senate, and by advancing one of his own henchmen to public office.

Cn. Flavius's scribal status and his publication of the legal calendar while curule aedile are both historically plausible. By the late republic, the public *scribae* formed a well-organized body of men of equestrian or nearly equestrian status. In fact, C. Cicereius, a *scriba* of Scipio Africanus, was elected praetor for 173 B.C. and enjoyed far more popularity than did Scipio's own son (Val. Max. 3.5.1 and 4.5.3). Thus Flavius's scribal profession should suggest relatively high status in Roman society, where aspiring to public office was not an entirely unrealistic ambition.

Given the fact that the curule aediles exercised jurisdiction over commerce in the city and regularly issued an edict which spelled out Rome's commercial law, it is reasonable to suppose that Cn. Flavius carried out his legal reforms in his capacity as curule aedile. In addition, he could have acquired expertise in Roman law during his service as public scribe. According to the later canonical tradition (e.g., Cic. *Pro Murena* 25), before Flavius's legal innovations the patrician pontiffs had kept the *legis actiones* and the legal calendar secret, but this is a clear instance in which the later Romans exaggerated and distorted supposed major landmarks in their legal history.

As argued in chapter 7 (see above p. 214–15), the later Roman view of early pontifical concealment of the law makes little sense. The notion probably grew out of a misinterpretation of the gradual change from orality to literacy in legal matters. What Flavius did was merely to take the last two logical steps in moving from an oral to a written legal system. The *legis actiones* were published as a supplement to his aedilician edict, and the chief pontiff's temporary monthly notice boards presenting the legal and religious calendar were superseded by erection in the Forum of the entire twelve-month legal calendar, recorded permanently on stone or bronze. It is significant that the antiquated legal habits of the aristocratic pontiffs were abolished by a public scribe, who was doubtless well versed in Roman legal traditions, and by a freedman's son, who was not indoctrinated into the pontiffs' traditional ways but, as an outsider, could see more clearly how the legal needs of the burgeoning populace could best be served.

The Ogulnian Law of 300 B.C. increased the number of pontiffs from four to eight and the number of augurs from four to nine, and ordained that the new priestly positions be filled by plebeians (Livy 10.6.2–9.2).[29] If viewed in the context of patrician pontifical secrecy and control of the legal system, this statute would seem to have been the natural consequence of Cn. Flavius's publication of the *legis actiones* and the legal calendar. But the expansion of curule jurisdiction administered by the praetor's court had long abolished any patrician pontifical monopoly over legal procedure and litigation. Although the pontiffs continued to be extremely important as expert interpreters of the law, both before and after the passage of the Ogulnian Law, Cn. Flavius's actions simply removed any lingering pretense that the patrician college of pontiffs exercised a monopolistic control of the civil law. Like the increase in the number of priests responsible for consulting the Sibylline Books in 368 B.C., this augmentation resulted from the fact that in Roman aristocratic culture these prominent priesthoods were viewed as being akin to public magistracies and as bestowing similar status and prestige. Roman society was becoming increasingly secularized, Roman religion was coming more and more under the influence of Greek culture, and these two trends were seriously eroding the traditional patrician claim

---

29. According to Cicero (*De Re Pub.* 2.26), King Numa Pompilius established five as the number of the pontiffs. Following some earlier scholars, Hölkeskamp (1988a, 58–59) has argued that these five did not include the pontifex maximus, so that the entire pontifical college before the passage of the Ogulnian Law actually comprised six members, thus being equal in number to the augurs. Hölkeskamp (1988a, 61–62) has further suggested that the total of four pontiffs recorded by Livy for the year 300 B.C. represents one pontiff having died and the pontifex maximus not being counted. Thus, according to Hölkeskamp, if we include the pontifex maximus, the Ogulnian Law increased the total number of pontiffs to nine rather than to eight.

to special expert religious knowledge. High-ranking plebeians, who were peers of the most prominent patricians in every other way, were eager to become members of these exclusive religious clubs and thereby to top off their public careers with the added distinction of a priestly office.

If there had been a direct causal relationship between Cn. Flavius's curule aedileship and the Ogulnian Law, we might expect that the latter pertained only to the pontifical college, since the augurs had nothing at all to do with the civil law. In fact, Livy's account may actually indicate that it was the situation surrounding the college of augurs which brought about the promulgation of the Ogulnian Law. At 10.6.7 Livy indicates that when the law was proposed, the augurs numbered four; since they should have been six in number, two from each of the three archaic tribes, he conjectures that two must have recently died. If so, and if the two augurs had happened to die at about the same time so that it was needful to fill two vacancies, the issue of having the two positions filled by one patrician and one plebeian could have arisen naturally. The matter then could have been widened to include the pontifical college as well, and the decision made to incorporate plebeians into these priestly colleges by expanding their numbers. If this reconstruction of events is correct, Cn. Flavius's curule aedileship would not have had any causal link to the Ogulnian Law; connecting the two could be an instance of the logical fallacy, *post hoc ergo propter hoc.*

ROMAN FACTIONAL POLITICS

Before concluding this chapter, a few words deserve to be said concerning modern attempts to analyze Roman aristocratic politics and factions of this period by employing the prosopographical methods which have proven to be so useful in understanding the politics of the much-better-documented middle and late republic. Since the one person about whose political career we are best informed is Ap. Claudius Caecus, much attention has been paid to his public activities and his possible political connections.[30] In addition, Phillips (1972) has written an article devoted to political groupings and individual alliances in general for the period of the Second Samnite War; and Cassola (1962) has written an entire monograph on Roman factional politics for the late fourth and third centuries B.C. These scholars are well

30. See, for example, Fiske 1902, 27–40; Garzetti 1947; Staveley 1959; Nicolet 1961; Cassola 1962, 128 ff.; Ferenczy 1970; and MacBain 1980. Develin (1985, 215–24) is properly skeptical about the value of the ancient literary tradition. See Raaflaub, Richards, and Sammons in Hackens 1992, 35–47 for a judicious survey and assessment of Caecus's public career. For the ancient literary tradition about the arrogance of the patrician Claudii, see Mommsen 1864 and Wiseman 1979a, 57 ff. Cf. Münzer 1920, 8–45 and Develin 1985, 59 ff. for their analysis of Roman politics for much of the fourth century B.C.

aware of the difficulties of reconstructing factional politics in this age due to the unsatisfactory nature of our evidence, and a couple of their conclusions seem sound. For example, it appears likely that there was a Fabian faction centered around Q. Fabius Maximus Rullianus, which included P. Decius Mus; Ap. Claudius Caecus appears to have been a leading figure in another group, perhaps previously headed by Q. Publilius Philo. Yet having reached these general conclusions, there seems to be little else that can be determined with any degree of confidence. Virtually every other argument based upon office-holding patterns or items of information encountered in Livy's narrative is speculative, and in order to build up a larger picture of factional politics, one must erect a structure primarily held together by a whole series of such speculations. It is reasonable to conclude that despite our understandable desire to learn and to know as much about this period as possible, we can only hope to be able to reconstruct an accurate general picture of Roman affairs for this period. Attempting to reconstruct the factional politics for these years probably has as much a chance of succeeding as attempting an accurate and detailed account of the military events of the Second Samnite War. In the latter case, evidence from Livy and Diodorus can be used to extract what might be an accurate general account, but their narratives are so full of fictitious details, which we may not always be able to detect, that we cannot with confidence offer a really detailed reconstruction of events. Furthermore, it seems undeniable that, besides containing fictitious material, the texts of Livy and Diodorus cannot be assumed to have preserved all the significant events of the Second Samnite War. This situation reminds us once more that these events are shadowy. We are able to make out the basic outlines of many objects in this period of Roman history, but we cannot perceive the details.

These same observations are applicable to the study of factional politics. We are in fact fairly well informed about the accomplishments and actions of Ap. Claudius Caecus. Nevertheless, despite this relative wealth of information in the ancient sources, it must be admitted that a full picture of his politics and policies can only be reconstructed by knowing how they fitted into the larger pattern of Roman political life at the time. Besides the scantiness of relevant data, our attempt to make such a reconstruction has been thwarted by the very information preserved in the ancient sources, which have grossly distorted much of Caecus's career by depicting him and his actions in the stereotypical terms of inborn Claudian arrogance. Thus, for example, in his account of the passage of the Ogulnian Law of 300 B.C., Livy (10.6.2–9.2) includes a supposed public debate concerning the proposal, and he has followed his source or sources in making P. Decius Mus the principal supporter and Ap. Claudius Caecus the principal opponent of the measure. It is important to note that in introducing this debate, Livy in 10.7.1 qualifies the view that the debate was primarily between these two men with *ferunt* (= "they say"). In the next section he observes that what they said was more or less the same things spoken years before concerning the Licinian Sextian Laws of 367 B.C. Then in the next section of the same chapter Livy begins the speech he attributes to P. Decius Mus by qualifying it with *rettulisse dicitur* (= "he is said to have related"), and the first six sections of this speech are written in the form of an indirect statement before Livy shifts into direct speech. The use of the qualifiers *ferunt* and *dicitur* can be taken to indicate that Livy himself entertained some doubts as to the historicity of this material in earlier annalistic accounts. In fact, Livy (6.40–1) precedes the passage of the Licinian Sextian Laws of 367 B.C. with a lengthy speech in opposition by another patrician Claudius, and Livy there also qualifies the entire speech with *dicitur.* Obviously, after finding in his annalistic sources the monotonous stereotype of the anti-plebeian patrician Claudii, even Livy felt compelled to put some distance between himself and this material, which he took over from his sources to reproduce in his narrative. Yet, despite Livy's obvious misgivings, modern historians interested in reconstructing the factional politics of this period have routinely used this and other similar material as evidence to support their conjectures about policies and political alliances.

Chapter 10

Rome's Conquest and Unification of Italy, 299–264 B.C.

THE THIRD SAMNITE WAR

The period of peace following the Second Samnite War was brief.[1] Since we are not informed of the exact terms of the settlement of 304 B.C., we have no way of knowing to what extent, if any, the terms of peace created resentment or set up potential areas of conflict and thereby contributed to the outbreak of war six years later in 298 B.C. Livy's explanation of the cause (10.11.11–12.3) casts the blame squarely upon the Samnites, and looks all too suspiciously like his explanation for the beginning of the First Samnite War. When the Samnites approached the neighboring Lucanians for an alliance against Rome, the Lucanians refused. The Samnites then invaded their land and began to lay it waste. The Lucanians sent ambassadors to Rome, to place themselves in the *fides* of the Roman people and to ask them to put an end to the Samnites' violence against their land. The senate received their appeal and sent fetials to the Samnites in the field to demand reparations. Their demands were haughtily refused. The Samnites even went so far as to claim that if the fetials had spoken in Samnium before a public meeting, they would not have been allowed to go away unharmed. Thereupon the senate and people of Rome declared war.

This account portrays the Romans as embarking upon a war in order to defend an innocent people from an aggressive neighbor. The Lucanians treat the Romans as if they are to be counted on to make Italy safe for self-determination. Moreover, the alleged Samnite reply to the Roman fetials further justifies the Roman cause and condemns the Samnites, because the

---

1. For other modern treatments of the events covered in this chapter, see Salmon 1967, 255–92; Harris 1971, 61–84; Heurgon 1973, 209–21; Scullard 1980, 136–53; Cornell, Staveley, and Frank in *CAH* VII.2 1989, 389–485; and Cornell 1995, 357–98.

mere suggestion of harm to fetials is almost as great a sacrilege as if the vio-lence had actually been perpetrated. Such an infraction of international law would have given the Romans a legitimate reason to go to war.

On the other hand, Rome's actions during the brief interval of peace indicate no abating of expansion or in settlement of frontier areas. These ongoing processes suggest that the Roman state was not content to stay within fixed borders. Military campaigns were conducted in Etruria and Umbria to extend Roman influence further in these areas. The Umbrian stronghold of Nequinum was captured and resettled as the Latin colony of Narnia. When both the Romans and Samnites sought an alliance with Picenum, Rome's position in northern Italy was further strengthened by the Picentes' decision to align themselves with Rome. Military operations were also conducted against the Aequians and Marsi, who apparently resented and resisted the Roman construction of the Via Valeria and the colonial foundations of Alba Fucens and Carseoli. Roman settlement in the area of the Liris also continued. In addition to founding the colony of Sora as an outpost against northern Samnium, censors in 299 B.C. created two new tribes: the Aniensis and Teretina, thus bringing the total of Roman tribes up to thirty-three. The Aniensis was located beyond the Anio in the territory of the Aequians, and the Teretina included the coastal area between the mouths of the Liris and the Volturnus (Taylor 1960, 56–59). It is noteworthy that both these new tribes were situated on or near Rome's newly created roads, the Via Valeria and the Via Appia, which apparently facilitated and encouraged Roman settlement. The censorial creation of tribes can serve as a rough gauge for the pace and scale of Roman expan-sion. During the early years of the republic they numbered twenty-one. Their final total was thirty-five, which was not reached until the creation of the last two tribes in 241 B.C., fifty-eight years after the Aniensis and Teretina. During the thirty-three years 332–299 B.C. six new tribes were organized, and during the eighty-eight years 387–299 B.C. twelve tribes were established.

Livy's tenth book contains a detailed account of the first six years of the Third Samnite War (298–293 B.C.), but unfortunately, unlike the Second Samnite War, we do not have the parallel account of Diodorus to compare with Livy; the books of Diodorus's history covering the period from the third century B.C. onwards survive only in excerpts by Byzantine writers. Since the books of Livy's second decade are also lost, our knowledge of the war's last three years (292–290 B.C.) depends upon later epitomes of Livy's history and other similar works by Florus, Eutropius, *De Viris Illustribus,* and Orosius. Indeed, except for Plutarch's *Life of Pyrrhus,* which contains a detailed and valuable account of Pyrrhus's encounter with the Romans, we must rely upon these same works to piece together an account of Roman affairs from the end of the Third Samnite War to the beginning of the

First Punic War.[2] Besides the Byzantine excerpts from the later books of *The Roman Antiquities* of Dionysius of Halicarnassus, there are two other Greek writers of later imperial times whose works are also of some use for this period. Appian, who flourished during the third quarter of the second century of our era, wrote a historical account of Rome's wars organized geographically, but his work too survives only in later Byzantine excerpts. The same applies to the early portions of *The Roman History* of Dio, a Roman senator of the early third century of our era, but in his case the later Byzantine excerpts can be supplemented by Zonaras, a Byzantine historian whose account of Roman history is a summary of Dio.

For the most part, the same historiographical problems inherent in Livy's narrative of the Second Samnite War confront us again in his tenth book concerning the Third Samnite War. There are numerous obscure toponyms not otherwise attested, such as Cimetra in 10.15.6, Murgantia in 10.17.2, Duronia in 10.39.4, and Palumbinum in 10.45.9, which probably derive ultimately from official pontifical records, public monuments, or records kept by Roman noble families. Since the locations of these sites usually cannot be determined, it is very difficult to extract from Livy a detailed, coherent picture of the war's history. The chauvinism of the later annalists has further muddied the obscurity of authentic information with fictitious embellishments. In addition, as in the case of Livy's seventh book (see above/p. 271–72), Livy's tenth book contains several episodes involving political disputes over the conduct of elections, which should be viewed with great caution, and for the source of which Licinius Macer appears likely. The first of these episodes concerns the election, identity, and official activities of the curule aediles of 299 B.C. Livy's account in 10.9.9–13 and 10.11.9 shows that Licinius Macer altered the earlier tradition recorded by L. Calpurnius Piso Frugi, replacing Cn. Domitius Calvinus and Sp. Carvilius Maximus with Q. Fabius Maximus Rullianus and L. Papirius Cursor (doubtless the elder). Besides fabricating the story that Rullianus was first elected consul without being a candidate and was then made curule aedile when he patriotically declined the consulship, Macer invented a grain shortage in order to have Rullianus and Cursor, adversaries of years gone by, cooperate in insuring that the state was not troubled by a food crisis (Forsythe 1994, 347–49). Similarly, Livy's detailed descriptions of the elections for the years 297, 296, and 295, as well as much of the supposed debate over the allocation of consular provinces in 295, are largely, if not entirely, fictitious and derive from the later annalists such as Licinius Macer. Consequently, this material should not be used as factual data by modern historians interested in reconstructing Roman factional politics for this period.

2. For a detailed outline of the events of these years, containing references to the ancient literary sources, see Broughton 1951–52 I: 181–203.

One apparent difference between Livy's descriptions of the Second and Third Samnite Wars pertains to battle statistics. Unlike several battles of the Second Samnite War where enemy casualties are reported as having been twenty or thirty thousand, figures given for enemy dead, enemy captured, and booty realized are drastically scaled down and have the semblance of credibility. Another characteristic of Livy's account of the Third Samnite War is the multiplicity of variant versions. Even though later writers seem to have agreed about where Roman armies campaigned in a given year and what places were captured, they differed over which Roman noble received credit for these successes. This historiographical phenomenon suggests that some historians engaged in considerable rewriting of earlier accounts. For example, for the year 294 B.C. Livy (10.32–37) gives a very detailed description of the military activities of the consuls M. Atilius Regulus and L. Postumius Megellus in Samnium and Etruria. Atilius first conducted war in Samnium with varying success, including an initial defeat at Luceria, followed by a victory and a vow to Jupiter Stator. He then campaigned successfully in Etruria, but was denied a triumph on returning to Rome. His colleague Megellus was delayed from entering the field by sickness, but after dedicating the temple of Victory in Rome, he campaigned in Samnium and celebrated a triumph. Yet at the close of this narrative (10.37.13–14) Livy writes:

> The tradition for this year is hardly in agreement. According to Claudius, Postumius captured several towns in Samnium, but in Apulia he was routed and put to flight, and after being himself wounded he was driven into Luceria with a few of his men; whereas affairs in Etruria were conducted by Atilius, and he celebrated a triumph. Fabius writes that both consuls conducted affairs in Samnium and at Luceria, and that an army was led over into Etruria, but he does not add by which consul. He says that many were killed on both sides at Luceria, and that a temple to Jupiter Stator was vowed during the battle.

Further confusion over the events of this year is created by the *Fasti Triumphales*, which record a triumph over the Samnites and Etruscans by Postumius and over the Volsones and Samnites by Atilius (Degrassi 1947, 72–73).

Livy registers similar major discrepancies from his main narrative for the events of 296, and likewise concerning affairs in Rome before the battle of Sentinum in 295 B.C. After describing (10.17) P. Decius Mus's campaign as proconsul in Samnium during 296, including the capture of several towns and the recording of precise numbers, at the end of the chapter Livy indicates that there were three other versions of these events, in which the same deeds were assigned in various ways to Decius, Q. Fabius Maximus Rullianus, and/or the consuls Ap. Claudius Caecus and L. Volumnius Flamma. Much of Livy 10.24–26 is taken up with a supposed debate over the allocation of the consular provinces at the beginning of 295 B.C., together with a later debate over the disposition of Roman forces and commanders and the strategy to be employed against the coalition of Rome's enemies in northern Italy. Livy indicates that there were other accounts which described even more political contention over these matters than he has chosen to include in his narrative, but he also says that there were versions in which such contention was totally absent, because the consuls P. Decius Mus and Q. Fabius Maximus Rullianus were described as having departed from Rome to assume command in northern Italy without any controversy. Given the nature of the military crisis of this year and of the extraordinary amount of prior planning and preparation which the Romans put into the Sentinum campaign, it should be obvious that these debates are later annalistic fictions, and that the true account was the one in which these quarrels were absent. Nevertheless, Livy has steered what he must have considered to be a moderate middle course through this bewildering welter of different accounts, by accepting some of the wrangling but rejecting the most embellished versions.[3]

Perhaps the most intriguing historiographical conflict is the discrepancy between Livy's narrative of 298 B.C. and the surviving funerary inscription of L. Cornelius Scipio Barbatus. After describing how the Third Samnite War began, Livy (10.12.3–8) says that as consul of 298 Barbatus was assigned Etruria as his province, and after engaging the Etruscans in battle at Volaterrae in the far north of Etruria, he turned to pillaging the land. Barbatus's epitaph, however, cut on his sarcophagus which was placed in the family tomb of the Cornelii Scipiones on the Via Appia, reads as follows (*ILS* 1 = *ILLRP* 309 = Gordon 1983 #5):

> L. Cornelius Scipio Barbatus, born of his father Gnaeus, a brave and wise man, whose handsomeness was most equal to his excellence, who was consul, censor, and aedile among you. He captured Taurasia and Cisauna in Samnium; he subdued all of Lucania; and he took away hostages.

Since the consulship is the only office recorded here in which Barbatus would have conducted military affairs, the natural conclusion is that the three specific deeds listed at the end are to be assigned to his consulship of 298 B.C. It is noteworthy that according to Livy 10.11.13, in making their appeal to the Roman senate for assistance against the Samnites in 298 B.C., the Lucanian ambassadors expressed their willingness to provide hostages to the Romans. Therefore, the logical thing for the Romans to have done would have been to send one of the consuls into Lucania to confront the Samnites and to secure the alliance with Rome by taking hostages. Barbatus's claim to have subdued all of Lucania is perhaps part truth and part Roman

---

3. For a more detailed analysis of this portion of Livy's narrative, see Forsythe 1999, 55–56.

aristocratic exaggeration. Livy indicates (10.18.8) that in 296 B.C. there were disturbances in Lucania arising from the lower social strata, which the proconsul Rullianus suppressed at the invitation of the upper class. This suggests that there existed divisions within Lucanian society over the Roman alliance, and if such a division was present even in 298 B.C., Scipio Barbatus could have campaigned in the area not only to prevent Samnite raids but also to quell any possible resistance to the newly concluded alliance with Rome. Livy's record of Barbatus's campaign in Etruria can be explained in three different ways: (1) it could be an annalistic fiction; (2) as in the case of 294 B.C., Barbatus could have conducted military operations in both Samnium and Etruria; or (3) since Barbatus served under Rullianus in northern Italy in 295 in connection with the Sentinum campaign, he could have conducted military operations in Etruria at some time during the course of that year, and later historians could have transposed his actions then to his consulship three years earlier. In any event, the discrepancy between Livy and the funerary inscription fits with the other cases of variant versions, and it should warn us against depending too heavily upon supposed specific facts contained in Livy's narrative for these years.[4]

The single most significant aspect of the Third Samnite War was the decision on the part of the Samnites to seek allies in order to strengthen their position against Rome. As already noted, the Samnites' attempt to ally themselves with Picenum had backfired. At the close of the previous war Rome had concluded alliances with the Marsi, Paeligni, and Frentani, who bordered Samnium on the north and east; since Rome and Campania were closely bound together by the sharing of civic rights and an alliance, a Roman ally also bordered Samnium on the west. Since Lucania was the one remaining area bordering on Samnium that had not yet joined the side of Rome, it is understandable that in wishing to avoid being completely surrounded by Roman allies, the Samnites first tried to ally themselves with the Lucanians by friendly means, but when this effort failed, they attempted to bring them over to their side by force. In the end, however, their actions in this regard may have played an important part in bringing on the Third Samnite War and in allowing the Romans to get their foot in the door in Lucania.

Despite these diplomatic failures, the Samnites soon found receptive allies on Rome's northern frontier. Roman military campaigns in Etruria and Umbria made these areas logical allies for the Samnites. In addition, although the Etruscans and Umbrians had long feared the Gauls of the

---

4. It should be noted that for the year 298 B.C. the *Fasti Triumphales* (Degrassi 1947, 72–73) record a triumph over the Samnites and Etruscans celebrated by Barbatus's consular colleague, Fulvius Centumalus.

Po Valley, they seem to have decided now that Rome posed the greater threat to their independence, and they even brought the Gauls into this anti-Roman coalition. The first fruit of this diplomacy appeared in 296 B.C., when a Samnite force under the command of Gellius Egnatius joined up with Etruscans in Etruria, but they were defeated by the combined consular armies of Ap. Claudius Caecus and L. Volumnius Flamma (Livy 10.18–19). The news of this coalition of four peoples (Samnites, Etruscans, Umbrians, and Gauls) created great alarm in Rome in 296 B.C., but the military threat did not materialize until the next year. This gave the Romans valuable time to make careful preparations. They conducted a military levy without exemptions, including both *iuniores* and *seniores* and even freedmen (Livy 10.21.1–4). The last were normally not allowed to serve in the legions. Although Q. Fabius Maximus Rullianus and P. Decius Mus had just been consuls in 297, they were reelected for 295 to lead the flower of Rome's forces against this formidable coalition.

The Roman strategy had two complementary parts (Livy 10.27–30). First, they wanted to concentrate as much force as possible against the combined army of the enemy. Both consuls and their armies were chosen for this purpose. Rullianus and Decius probably commanded four Roman legions and an equal complement of allied forces, which must have totaled between thirty and forty thousand infantry. Secondly, the Romans used other troops to distract the various members of the coalition so as to curtail the size of the coalition's principal army, forcing them to disperse their strength to protect themselves against Roman raids. L. Volumnius Flamma had his consular *imperium* prorogued and was kept in command of an army in Samnium. Other troops were held in reserve to protect Rome itself, but as soon as the consuls located the coalition's army and encamped nearby, these forces were sent out into Etruria and Umbria to draw off Etruscan and Umbrian forces. The Roman strategy worked. The Etruscans and Umbrians did not participate in the battle at Sentinum in Umbria, because they were more concerned with protecting their own territory. The two consular armies simply had to contend with the Gauls and Samnites, but this combined enemy army almost proved to be more than a match (Polyb. 2.19.5–6). It seems likely that if they had been faced with all four national contingents, the Romans would have been defeated. In the end the Romans won a hard-fought battle. The consul Decius was killed along with many of his army. The later Roman historical tradition, rightly or wrongly, portrayed his death as a voluntary one. He was supposed to have solemnly devoted himself and the opposing enemy forces to the nether gods in order to assure the Roman victory. His *devotio* was duplicated by later Roman historians, who fabricated a similar death for his father in the first year of the Latin War (Livy 8.9). The battle of Sentinum was clearly one of the great battles of world history. It paved the way for Rome's conquest of Italy over the next thirty years, and Rome's conquest and organization of the ancient Italian peoples into a strong and workable system of alliances was the basis of its eventual overseas expansion and acquisition of an empire.

Another aspect of the battle of Sentinum pertains to Roman religion. T. P. Wiseman (1995, 106–25) has plausibly argued that the myth of the twins Romulus and Remus first came into being during the late fourth century B.C. and that in several important respects it reflects the political, religious, and military circumstances of the period of the Samnite Wars. He explains the oddity of Rome's having two founders as reflecting the division of the consulship between plebeians and patricians. By connecting Remus's name with *remorare* (= "to delay") and the *aves remores* of Roman augury, whose appearance signaled that one should delay the action under consideration, he argues that the Greek eponym Rhomos was changed to Latin Remus because Romulus's twin brother was interpreted as symbolic of the plebeians and their lateness in coming to political prominence. Wiseman also connects the tradition of Remus's murder while leaping over Romulus's Palatine wall as reflecting an important episode in Rome's religious history at the time of Sentinum. According to Zonaras (8.1), the terror in Rome at the news of the formation of the coalition of four peoples was intensified by dire prodigies. The most dreadful was that on three consecutive days the altar of Capitoline Jupiter of its own accord flowed first with blood, then on the next day with honey, and on the third with milk. Besides this, a bronze statue of Victory in the Forum was found separated from its stone base, standing on the ground and facing in the direction of the approaching Gauls. When diviners were consulted about what should be done to expiate these portents, their abominable advice terrified the Romans even more. Wiseman has suggested that this abominable expiation involved human sacrifice. In light of later events in Roman history, the suggestion is a plausible one. Eckstein (1982) has demonstrated that on at least three later occasions the Romans buried male and female Greek and Gallic couples alive in the Forum Boarium to insure against military defeat and the capture of the city. The first of these occasions was in 228 B.C., when the Gauls of the Po Valley were mounting a major expedition across the Apennines against Rome and its allies. The second occasion was in 216 B.C., in the aftermath of Hannibal's defeat of the Romans at Cannae and the ensuing defection of many of Rome's allies. The third occasion was in 114/3 B.C., following the defeat and death of C. Porcius Cato at the hands of the Scordisci in Illyria. In view of the *Dies Alliensis* enshrined in the Roman calendar and the extraordinary measures taken by the Roman state after declaring a *tumultus Gallicus,* we need not doubt that the Romans experienced genuine fear of a Gallic invasion, because it always conjured up frightful memories of military defeat in the field and occupation of their land by a rapacious enemy. Thus it is reasonable to suppose that the rites of human sacrifice of 228 B.C. were simply a repetition or variation of ones performed in 296/5 B.C. preceding the Sentinum campaign.

In further support of Wiseman's interpretation we may note that, despite his very infrequent recording of prodigies throughout his first decade, Livy (10.23.1–2 and 10.31.8) frames his narrative of the Sentinum campaign with brief reports of portents. Unfortunately, he does not bother to go into much detail as to what they were and how they were expiated. He does, however, mention that there were numerous reports of lightning strikes, and that the Sibylline Books were consulted. It is noteworthy that both these things, lightning strikes and consultation of the Sibylline Books, occurred together in 228 B.C., and led to the live burial of the Greek and Gallic couples. Moreover, in addition to suggesting that the Romans committed human sacrifice in connection with the Sentinum campaign, Wiseman has further argued that one version of Remus's murder is to be directly associated with the events of 295 B.C. In later times there were principally two different accounts of Remus's death. In one, he was killed by Romulus when they quarreled about the auspices taken to decide where their city would be founded and after whom it would be named; but in another account Remus was killed when he attempted to overleap Romulus's Palatine wall (Livy 1.6.4–7.2 and Dion. Hal. 1.87). The latter version was usually framed in such a way as to explain the sanctity of the pomerium. Wiseman, however, has plausibly suggested that the original ideology behind this story involved the widespread superstitious notion that the foundation of a major structure could be secured by human sacrifice and by interring the sacrificial remains under or within the structure. Consequently, Remus's death might have initially represented a human sacrifice designed to guarantee the inviolability of Rome's defense works. This ideology, Wiseman argues, is actually detectable in the archaeological remains of the temple of Victory dedicated in 294 B.C., the year after the victory at Sentinum (Livy 10.33.9). Excavations of the temple's site uncovered a grave which seems to have been directly beneath the main altar. Although the grave had been plundered, there remained a cup datable to the fourth century B.C. In addition, this temple was located on the western edge of the Cermalus on the Palatine, and the grave was incorporated into the terracing and defensive wall of the hill. This area of the Palatine was closely associated with Romulus and Remus in the later literary tradition. Thus, these physical remains suggest that human sacrifice might have been used in 295 to secure Roman victory and Rome's protection against enemy assault.[5]

---

5. In this connection it is worth noting that in the course of excavating a portion of the northern slope of the Palatine Hill, Carandini (1997, 505) uncovered, in association with the earliest Palatine wall, a rectangular area marked off by stones and containing four human graves datable to the first quarter of the seventh century B.C.

As might be expected of such a specific issue of early Roman history, Wiseman's thesis connecting the myth of Remus with the events of the late fourth century B.C. and especially of 295 B.C. involves a fair amount of speculation and interpretation of exiguous data. Nevertheless, his reasoning and explanations are certainly within the realm of believability and do not run counter to what we would expect of Roman thinking and behavior. Wiseman seems to be of the opinion that the human remains buried beneath the altar of Victory on the Palatine were those of the person or persons sacrificed in accordance with the advice of the diviners in order to expiate the dire prodigies before Sentinum. Yet if these rites formed the basis of those conducted later in 228 B.C. under similar circumstances, we might instead postulate that the human victims were buried alive—so as to symbolize their possession of Roman territory without actually bringing harm upon the Roman state—as the later victims were. If so, we then should ask whose remains were deposited below the altar of Victory. The most likely candidate for such an honor would have been P. Decius Mus, the plebeian consul who fell in battle at Sentinum. This would actually fit perfectly with Wiseman's overall interpretation of the myth of Remus at this time. If the twins Romulus and Remus were thought to represent the consulship and its sharing by the patricians and plebeians of the Roman nobility, and if Remus was particularly associated with the plebeians, it would have been perfectly logical for the Romans of the day to identify the self-sacrifice of P. Decius Mus by *devotio* at Sentinum with the death of Remus. If Wiseman is correct in his interpretation of the archaeological data of the temple of Victory, we would seem to have a convergence of myth and history at this site. Through the *devotio* and death of Decius, the Romans obtained a victory unparalleled thus far in their history for its magnitude and its implications for Roman security and power. Incorporating Decius's remains into the temple of Victory and the latter into the defensive wall of the Palatine, an area closely associated with Romulus and Remus, integrated all these elements into one.

We should also ask which came first, the myth of Remus's death in association with the Palatine wall, or the *devotio* of Decius and his burial beneath the altar of Victory. It is noteworthy that our earliest secure bit of information concerning the existence of the tale of Romulus and Remus among the Romans comes from the year 296 B.C. Under this year Livy (10.23.12) records that the curule aediles of the year, Cn. and Q. Ogulnius, placed images of the infants Romulus and Remus beneath the statue of the she-wolf at Rumina's Fig Tree near the Lupercal of the Palatine. Livy (10.30.4–7) shows that the battle of Sentinum had attained something approaching mythic status in the accounts of later Roman historians. Its grand scale was already evident in the exaggerated description of Douris of Samos, a Greek historian contemporary with the event, whom Diodorus (21.6) cites for the massive casualties: one hundred thousand enemy slain by the Romans. The omen which allegedly preceded the battle of Sentinum may point to an ideological connection between this victory and Rome's foundation story as well. Before the two armies engaged, a deer with a wolf in pursuit ran into the open space between the two armies. The wolf turned toward the Romans, who opened up a path in their ranks through which it ran and got away safely, whereas the deer turned toward the Gauls, who seized the creature and killed it. The natural timidity of the deer and its death were taken by the Romans to portend that flight and destruction awaited the Gauls, whereas the clean escape of the animal symbolizing the Romans foreshadowed their victory (Livy 10.28.8–9).

The Roman victory at Sentinum shattered the coalition of four nations. These peoples never again combined their forces to oppose Rome. The Samnites, however, mobilized one last enormous effort intended to inflict a decisive defeat upon the Romans. The desperation of the Samnites is evident from their military recruitment under a *lex sacrata*, according to which the soldiers bound themselves by oath not to flee in battle under pain of death (Livy 10.38.3–13 with Salmon 1967, 182–86). In 293 B.C. this army engaged the Romans under the command of the consul L. Papirius Cursor in northern Samnium at Aquilonia, and once again the Romans were victorious. This was the last great battle of the war, and it sealed the Samnites' fate. Cursor followed up the victory by capturing Saepinum, one of the Samnites' main towns. In the next year the Romans captured a stronghold in Apulia, where they immediately established the Latin colony of Venusia. At the same time the consul Q. Fabius Maximus Gurges, the son of Rullianus, suffered a defeat near Caudium in western Samnium, probably due to his rashness or incompetence, but the situation was remedied by Rullianus, serving as his son's advisor. Caudium was eventually taken and with it, Gavius Pontius, the victorious Samnite commander of the Caudine Forks. Gurges was awarded a triumph, in which Pontius was prominently displayed and then executed. In 290 B.C. two consular armies campaigned throughout Samnium to put down any lingering resistance, and the Samnites were forced to accept the terms of alliance imposed upon them by the Romans. After having portions of their land taken from them to become Roman public land, the Samnites became the allies of Rome. Henceforth, they could have no independent foreign policy, were obliged to remain within their borders, and were required to supply troops to Rome whenever asked to do so.

After campaigning in Samnium, M'. Curius Dentatus, one of the consuls of 290 B.C., led his army against the Sabines of the Apennine upland, whose principal towns were Reate, Amiternum, and Nursia. This expedition was probably conducted on the pretext that the Sabines needed to be punished for allowing the Samnites to cross their territory in 295 to unite with the

Etruscans, Umbrians, and Gauls. Dentatus encountered little resistance. Although the Sabines upstream from Rome along the Tiber had posed a threat during the first half of the fifth century B.C., the extant ancient sources fail to mention them for the century and a half preceding Dentatus's conquest of their territory. The Sabines were immediately incorporated into the Roman state by being granted *civitas sine suffragio* (Vell. Pat. 1.14.6 with Brunt 1969), and their land was opened up to settlement by other Romans. On returning to Rome Dentatus boasted of his success, saying that it was uncertain which was the greater: the amount of land or the number of people conquered; if he had not conquered so much land, it would not have sufficed for the number of people taken; and if he had not captured so many people, the amount of land acquired could not have been occupied. The boast is probably to be taken in reference to his campaigns in both Samnium and the Sabine territory. The Greek geographer Strabo (5.3.1) says that according to Fabius Pictor the Romans first realized wealth when they conquered the Sabines. The meaning of this terse statement is unclear. Were the Romans enriched by the booty and slaves resulting directly from Dentatus's military expedition, or did they reap the benefits of the conquest more gradually through settlement and the use of Roman public land for stock raising? Perhaps Strabo's rendition of Pictor's observation is to be taken in both these senses and applied to Samnium as well as to the land of the Sabines. With the conquest and incorporation of the latter area, the Roman state now extended across central Italy from the Tyrrhenian to the Adriatic Sea. It therefore formed a barrier between the Samnites to the south and the Etruscans and Umbrians to the north. This strategic consideration may have been paramount in Dentatus's campaign and the Roman handling of the Sabines. Beloch (1926, 602) estimated that in 290 B.C. Roman territory measured 14,000 square kilometers, which is more than two and a half times his estimated 5,289 square kilometers for the Roman state at the end of the Latin War, just forty-eight years earlier.

One major and immediate consequence of the Third Samnite War was its economic benefit to the Roman state in the form of booty and slaves. This is evident from figures found in Livy's tenth book, which have the appearance of historical veracity. The most striking data are to be found in Livy 10.46, which describes the triumphs of the consuls of 293 B.C. The triumph of L. Papirius Cursor was distinguished by 1,830 pounds of silver taken from Samnite towns, and by 2,533,000 pounds of bronze produced by the sale of captives. His colleague, Sp. Carvilius Maximus, carried in his triumph a mere 380,000 pounds of bronze, but he also rewarded his soldiers with a donative of 102 pounds of bronze each, with twice that amount being paid to centurions and cavalrymen. Moreover, his campaign in Etruria reveals the extortionate methods of the Roman military. Before taking the stronghold of Troilum by force, he allowed the 470 richest persons to go free after paying him a large sum of money. Those less fortunate were apparently killed or taken prisoner and sold into slavery. He granted Falerii a truce for one year on the receipt of one hundred thousand pounds of bronze and that year's pay for his army.

EARLY ROMAN COINAGE

It was probably during the period of the Samnite and Pyrrhic Wars that the Roman state began to have silver coinage issued in its name.[6] Since the land of Italy does not possess deposits of silver or gold, the earliest metallic money commonly used by the native inhabitants of Italy was copper or bronze. The Greek colonies of Sicily and southern Italy, however, adopted the practice of their mother-cities of using silver and gold (acquired through trade) to produce coins which bore the names and heraldic symbols of their communities. In the course of time the non-Greek peoples of Italy did likewise; but in very early times, when payment was made for some transaction among the Romans, scales were used to weigh out unmarked pieces of bronze. This explains why scales were used to symbolize a sale and the transfer of ownership in the legal ceremony of *mancipatio*, long after coinage had rendered the weighing out of bronze unnecessary.

Perhaps as early as the Twelve Tables the Romans may have normally divided a pound of bronze (termed an *as*, plural *asses*) into twelve pieces termed ounces (= Latin *unciae*), because the lawcode seems to have fixed the rate of interest at one twelfth, *unciarium faenus* (Tacitus *Ann.* 6.16). By the late fourth century B.C., the Romans had devised a bronze currency called *aes grave* by modern scholars. This phrase means "heavy bronze," because the coins were whole or fractional divisions of one pound of bronze. The Roman pound originally measured 324 grams and was thus 71.5 percent as heavy as the present-day English pound. Unlike the common contemporaneous Greek practice of making coins by cutting metal bars into cross-sectional pieces and then stamping distinctive patterns into their surfaces using an anvil and incuse rod, these large and heavy bronze coins of the Romans were produced by casting bronze in molds.

The earliest four issues of silver coins of Greek type bearing the name of the Romans had the value of two Greek drachmas, hence their designation "didrachms." Their types were as follows (see fig. 10): (1) helmeted, bearded head of Mars on the obverse and a horse's head on the reverse; (2) laureate head of Apollo on the obverse and prancing horse on the

---

6. For more detailed treatment of this complex and much disputed subject, see Thomsen 1957–61; Crawford 1985, 1–51; and Harl 1996, 21 ff. For the early Roman *aes grave* money, see Haeberlin 1910. For the copper currency bars weighing several pounds, which circulated in early Italy, see Burnett, Craddock, and Meeks in Swaddling 1986, 127–30.

1944.100.2

1969.83.1

1944.100.15

1941.131.6

Figure 10. The Romano-Campanian didrachms. Photographs courtesy of the American
Numismatic Society.

reverse; (3) Hercules on the obverse and the she-wolf and twins on the
reverse; (4) helmeted head of Roma on the obverse and winged Victory
attaching a wreath to a palm branch on the reverse. All four types bear the
legend "Romano," which seems to be an abbreviation of "Romanorum,"
indicating that they were the coins of the Romans.

The chronology of these coins has been the subject of considerable discussion and debate among modern numismatists.[7] Complex arguments
based upon artistic, historical, and numismatic data have been developed
to establish both their relative and their absolute dating. For example,
important chronological evidence is offered by their presence in hoards
with the coins of other states (especially Tarentum), whose chronologies

7. For a survey of modern views up to the mid-1950s, see Thomsen 1957–61, I: 210–47. For
more recent discussions see, for example, Mitchell 1966, 1969; Crawford 1974, I: 35–46; Burnett
1977, 1978, 1980; Crawford 1985, 25–34; Burnett 1989; and Holloway in Hackens 1992, 225–35.

are better understood. When taken together, the data strongly suggest that the four types were not issued simultaneously but in sequence, one after the other in the order listed above. Although modern experts are in agreement concerning this relative chronology, determining their absolute dating has proven to be far more problematic; the situation is complicated further by the desire on the part of some modern scholars to tie this relative chronology in various ways to two events recorded in ancient literary sources. The first one is Rome's alliance with Naples in 326 B.C., and the other is 269 B.C., the year in which the Romans are reported to have begun to use silver for the first time (Pliny *NH* 33.44 and Livy *Per.* 15). Two other bronze coins, one bearing the legend "Romano" and the other its Greek translation "Romaion," have on their reverse a man-headed bull typical of the coinage of Naples during the fourth century B.C. It therefore seems likely that both of these bronze coins were issued by Naples at some time following its alliance with Rome. Naples also might have been the source or one of the sources of the four earliest types of silver didrachms, which have the same Latin legend. Since many modern scholars have supposed that some, if not all, of the four early types of Roman didrachms were produced and issued in Campania, which already had a tradition of making and using silver coins of Greek type, these early Roman coins are often termed Romano-Campanian didrachms.

Scholars, however, differ in assigning precise dates to these specific coin types. For example, Mitchell has argued that these four series of silver coins were issued in an uninterrupted sequence spanning the late fourth and early third centuries B.C. He dates the first type to the late fourth century, the third type to the 290s B.C. (associating the type of the she-wolf and twins with the curule aedileship of the Ogulnii of 296), and the fourth type to c. 272 B.C. when Rome captured Tarentum. He dates to 269 B.C. the beginning of a similar series of three coin types issued at Rome itself and thus bearing the legend "Roma," not "Romano." In more recent years other scholars have interpreted the numismatic data as indicating that the four series were not issued in an unbroken chronological sequence. Crawford assigns the first type to the last decade of the fourth century, the second type to the Pyrrhic War, the third type to 269 B.C., and the fourth type to the eve of the First Punic War. Burnett has proposed a somewhat similar chronology: c. 300 B.C. for the first type, 270 for the second, 264 for the third, and 255 for the fourth.

Whatever the precise chronology, the ancient statement that the Romans first began to use silver in 269 B.C. has been plausibly interpreted to mean simply that the distribution of war booty that year took the form of payments in silver for the first time (Burnett 1977, 116 with Dion. Hal. 20.17). It should be noted that in his historical overview of Roman law preserved in the *Digest* (1.2.2.30), the jurist Pomponius seems to date the creation of the three-man commission for making coins to the earlier part of the third century B.C. These officials in later times bore the cumbersome title, three men for smelting and striking bronze, silver, and gold = *triumviri aere argento auro flando feriundo,* abbreviated in inscriptions as *iiiviri a. a. a. f. f.* Since the Roman mint was located on the Arx, on the Capitoline Hill next to the temple of Juno Moneta, these officials were also termed *triumviri monetales,* and it is from this designation that we derive the word "money."

Although it was not until the Hannibalic War that the Romans developed a fully integrated monetary system of silver and bronze coins (Harl 1996, 29 ff.), the four early series of Romano-Campanian didrachms are significant in several respects. Besides representing Rome's tentative step toward devising coins more manageable than the cumbersome *aes grave,* they demonstrate the importance and closeness of Rome's ties to the communities of Campania from the late fourth century B.C. onwards. In addition, these series testify to Rome's entry into the larger cultural environment of the ancient Mediterranean world. Generally speaking, ancient communities usually adopted the practice of issuing coins in order to facilitate local public finance, which often involved large numbers of payments at a standard rate, such as military pay given to citizen soldiers, mercenaries, or crews of warships, or wages paid to laborers employed in major public works. Rome's earliest silver coinage may therefore be taken as evidence of the growing complexity of Roman state finance. In fact, Crawford postulates that the first isolated series of Romano-Campanian didrachms was minted in Campania during the last decade of the fourth century because of the construction of the Via Appia, which connected Rome to Capua. It is likely that the simultaneous building of the Aqua Appia involved an even greater outlay of public funds; and it should be remembered that the Via Valeria was built during this same decade. Rome at about this same time had doubled the size of its yearly military levy and had begun to keep a small fleet of warships in service, as shown by the creation of the office of *duumviri navales* in 311 B.C. (Livy 9.30.3–4). It is also noteworthy that Rome's second aqueduct, the Anio Vetus, was constructed shortly after the Pyrrhic War, which would coincide with Crawford's and Burnett's dating of the second or third issue of Romano-Campanian didrachms. We may therefore regard Rome's decision to issue silver coins in its name as demonstrating the ongoing hellenization of Roman society, as well as the growing financial complexity or sophistication of the Roman state during the period of the Samnite and Pyrrhic Wars.[8]

8. It should be noted that Holloway has called into question the chronology of Tarentine coinage, upon which the dating of the Roman coins depends to a considerable degree. In lowering the Tarentine numismatic chronology, he has brought all the early Roman didrachms down to the period of the First Punic War, and he regards these issues as stemming from the financial exigencies brought upon the Roman state by the need to build and man large fleets for the very first time.

MILITARY ETHOS AND ARISTOCRATIC FAMILY TRADITION

Various data from literary and nonliterary sources for the period of the Second and Third Samnite Wars present the picture of a Roman aristocracy self-conscious of their power and that of the Roman state, ambitious for and reveling in military glory, and eager to advertise and catalogue their achievements for their contemporaries and posterity.[9] The funerary epitaph of L. Cornelius Scipio Barbatus (consul 298 B.C.) quoted above was inscribed upon a stone sarcophagus in which his body was deposited, and the sarcophagus was placed in an underground burial chamber which received the remains of other eminent Cornelii Scipiones for the next two hundred years. Such a family tomb and its long-term use testify to the existence of a strong sense of family pride, tradition, and continuity. Another inscription, of imperial date (*ILS* 54), purports to list all public offices held by Ap. Claudius Caecus. Many of the tenures mentioned are not attested elsewhere in the surviving ancient sources. The text comes from the Forum of Arretium in Etruria, which imitated the Forum of Augustus in Rome in placing on public display statues and accompanying inscriptions to honor great men of the republic. There is a good possibility that this text derived from the family records kept by the patrician Claudii. If so, the inscription is striking testimony to the way information could be passed down within a family and disseminated to the public. The text reads:

> Appius Claudius Caecus, son of Gaius, censor, twice consul, dictator, thrice interrex, twice praetor, twice curule aedile, quaestor, thrice military tribune. He captured several towns from the Samnites, routed an army of Etruscans and Sabines, prevented peace being made with King Pyrrhus, paved the Via Appia in his censorship, conducted water into the city, and built a temple to Bellona.

Another interesting glimpse into the aristocratic male culture of this period is offered by a fragment of fresco painting on the wall of a chamber tomb found on the Esquiline.[10] Stylistic considerations date the work to the early part of the third century B.C. In four horizontal bands, one above the other, the painting appears to narrate an episode from the Samnite Wars involving negotiations or the surrender of a town. One figure is labeled with the Oscan name M. Fannius, son of Staius, and another figure has the name Q. Fabius. It is therefore possible that the scene concerns an event in the career of Q. Fabius Maximus Rullianus, and thus this might be the tomb

---

9. For this topic see the excellent study of Hölkeskamp 1993, which contains ample additional bibliography.

10. For representations and discussion of the scenes of this painting, see Coarelli in *Roma Medio-Repubblicana* 1973, 200–8, but for a later dating and alternative interpretation identifying both figures as Roman, see La Rocca 1984.

of Rullianus himself. In any case, the painting indicates that, like their contemporary Etruscan counterparts, Roman nobles of this period were often
buried in chamber tombs decorated with paintings which commemorated
their achievements.

The late fourth and early third centuries B.C. witnessed the establishment of temples and similar structures as war memorials commemorating
individual Roman nobles. War trophies had long been a part of Roman aristocratic culture, but from the middle of the fifth to the middle of the fourth
century B.C., these trophies had generally been rather modest and had usually taken the form of dedications placed in already existing temples: the
gold crown offered to Capitoline Jupiter by the dictator Mam. Aemilius in
426 for his capture of Fidenae; the *spolia opima* dedicated in the small shrine
of Jupiter Feretrius on the Capitoline by the master of the horse A. Cornelius
Cossus in 426; three gold saucers dedicated to Juno in the Capitoline
temple by Camillus in 389; a gold crown placed in the Capitoline temple by
the dictator T. Quinctius Cincinnatus in 380; and a mass of gold melted
down from Gallic booty and dedicated on the Capitoline by the dictator
C. Sulpicius Peticus in 358 B.C. The immense profitability of Rome's wars
from the later half of the fourth century B.C. onwards enriched the Roman
state, the soldiers, and their commanders, and enabled the generals to use
a portion of the booty to construct a temple or some similarly impressive
monument to adorn the city and to serve as a lasting memorial to the commander's victory (Hölscher 1978). The earliest such war memorial seems
to have been the *Columna Maenia,* a column set up in the Comitium by
C. Maenius, the consul of 338 B.C., to commemorate his victory over Antium
(Pliny *NH* 7.212 and 34.20). In addition, the Roman custom of using
weapons captured from the enemy to adorn private houses and public
places may have begun during this same period (Rawson in Eder 1990,
161). These traditions were maintained throughout the middle and late
republic, as Roman generals waged countless wars overseas. The result was
that by the time of Augustus, Rome had become a cluttered showcase of
such memorials. Many were swept away in the great Neronian fire of 64 A.D.,
after which the city was gradually rebuilt and became what we now think of
as imperial Rome.

The temples vowed and dedicated by Roman generals during the Second
and Third Samnite Wars clearly reflect Rome's growing confidence and
pride in its military strength. In 296 B.C., during the course of a battle
against the Etruscans and Samnites, Ap. Claudius Caecus vowed a temple to
the war goddess Bellona (Livy 10.19.17). Since Bellona had no place in the
early Roman religious calendar or state religion, she is likely to have been a
creation of the fourth century B.C., and her excogitation can be taken as a
sign of Roman society's preoccupation with warfare. The *-ona* suffix of her
name looks Celtic (cf. Celtic Epona, Dertona, Nemetona, but also Latin

Pomona), making it possible that she was the product of Roman interaction with the Gauls. The temple was built outside the pomerium in the Campus Martius, near the later Circus Flaminius. Throughout the republic it was often the place where the senate convened to receive commanders in the field or foreign ambassadors. In the course of time the shrine was decorated with shields which bore the embossed portraits of famous members of the Claudian family, accompanied by inscriptions that enumerated their public offices and achievements (Pliny *NH* 35.12). Thus, the edifice not only became a well-known public shrine, closely associated with important affairs of state, but also served as a monument that recalled and celebrated the public careers and deeds of the patrician Claudii.

In 311 B.C. the consul C. Junius Bubulcus vowed a temple to Salus. This feminine abstract noun can be translated as "health," "welfare," or "safety." If the vow was made at a critical time in a battle with the Samnites, as Livy's language in 9.31.10–11 suggests, Junius's prayer must have been intended for the welfare or safety of his soldiers in battle. As censor in 306 B.C. Bubulcus let out the public contract for the shrine's construction (Livy 9.43.25), and as dictator in 302 he saw to its dedication (Livy 10.1.9). Valerius Maximus (8.14.6) informs us that the temple was decorated with paintings, and that at least some of them were done and signed by C. Fabius, a kinsman of Rullianus; as a result, the man and his descendants received and proudly used the surname Pictor (= "painter"). It is regrettable that Valerius Maximus does not tell us what these paintings portrayed. Their content could have been cultic or mythological, but the evidence from the nearly contemporary Esquiline tomb makes it quite possible that they somehow depicted and commemorated Bubulcus's public career. The testimony of Valerius Maximus may also indicate that despite the great emphasis placed on martial prowess and accomplishments, members of the Roman aristocracy of this period might have been routinely educated in the liberal arts.

During the battle of Sentinum in 295 B.C. the consul Q. Fabius Maximus Rullianus vowed a temple to Jupiter Victor (Livy 10.29.14). As discussed earlier in this chapter, a temple to Victory was dedicated in the following year by the consul L. Postumius Megellus, who had undertaken to build this temple with fines exacted during his curule aedileship (Livy 10.33.9). Since his first consulship was in 305 B.C., his curule aedileship probably occurred c. 309–307 B.C. The shrine's site, on the Cermalus of the Palatine, may have been chosen to associate Victory with Rome's twin founders, who were believed to be the sons of the war god Mars. Also in 294 B.C. the other consul, M. Atilius Regulus, vowed a temple to Jupiter Stator (Livy 10.36.11 and 37.15–16), whose epithet indicates that he was supposed to make Roman soldiers stand steadfast in battle and not flee. This temple was erected on the Palatine near the Velia. In the later historical tradition, which might have had its beginning at this time, Romulus was thought to have made a vow to the same deity when fighting against T. Tatius and the Sabines in the Roman Forum (Livy 1.13.3–6 and Dion. Hal. 2.50.3). Romulus's connection with Jupiter Stator could have arisen when, in the very next year, the consul L. Papirius Cursor dedicated a shrine to Quirinus, who in later Roman thought was regarded as the deified Romulus (Livy 10.46.7). Quirinus was an enigmatic deity in later times, but he was closely associated with Jupiter and Mars and was generally thought of as a war god (see above p. 137). The other consul of 293 B.C., Sp. Carvilius Maximus, used part of the proceeds of his war booty to erect a temple to Fors Fortuna (Livy 10.46.14).

Perhaps the most interesting war memorial erected during this period was a colossal bronze statue of Jupiter commissioned by the same Carvilius. According to Pliny (*NH* 34.43), this statue stood on the Capitoline Hill and was so huge that it could be seen from the Alban Mount. It was made from the bronze breastplates, helmets, and greaves which Carvilius's army had taken from the Samnites. Thus the size of the monument was designed to represent the magnitude of Carvilius's military victory. Pliny also says that out of the filings of the colossal statue there was made a much smaller one of Carvilius himself, which stood at the feet of the colossal Jupiter. Similarly, Livy (10.46.7–8) indicates that Carvilius's colleague, L. Papirius Cursor, used armor and weapons taken from the Samnites to decorate the temple of Quirinus, but their quantity was so large that he also gave them away to be used to decorate other temples and public places in Latin colonies and allied communities. It seems very likely that the precise figures which Livy records for the amount of bronze and silver carried off in these two men's triumphs (10.46.5 and 13–15) derive ultimately from original inscriptions set up in their temples of Quirinus and Fors Fortuna or engraved on their other military monuments. Livy's brief but detailed catalogue of their booty is identical in nature to triumphal data found in his later books for the years 218–167 B.C. This same information also resembles the content of the famous inscription cut on the stone base of the *columna rostrata* of C. Duilius, which commemorated the latter's victory and triumph over the Carthaginians in the naval battle of Mylae off northeastern Sicily in 260 B.C. (*ILLRP* 319 = Gordon 1983 #48).

The consular *fasti* of the early third century B.C. demonstrate the success of the Roman state in absorbing new elements from outside Rome into its aristocracy. Although the military exigencies of the Third Samnite War produced significant iteration of the consulship during the 290s, the consular *fasti* for the fourteen years 293–280 B.C. contain the names of six clans whose members had never before held the consulship: Sp. Carvilius Maximus (293), M'. Curius Dentatus (290, 275, and 274), Q. Caedicius Noctua (289), L. Caecilius Metellus Denter (284), C. Fabricius Luscinus (282), and Ti. Coruncanius (280). Like the Third Samnite War, the Pyrrhic War produced such consular iteration that no new clans appear in the list of consuls during the decade of the 270s, but there are two new names for the last six years covered in this volume: Q. Ogulnius Gallus (269) and L. Mamilius Vitulus (265). Despite the exiguous nature of our information, enough is known about these eight new clans to indicate that no fewer than five were non-Roman in origin. Two of these families, the Coruncanii and Mamilii, were from Tusculum. Ti. Coruncanius was the first plebeian pontifex maximus (Livy *Per.* 18), but his descendants are not attested among Roman magistrates after the 220s. The Mamilii enjoyed considerable prominence in Roman politics to the end of the third century B.C. In fact, C. Mamilius Atellus was the first plebeian to hold the religious office of curio maximus (Livy 27.8.1–3), but after the Hannibalic War the Mamilii are rarely attested.

Two other families, the Caecilii Metelli and Fabricii, seem to have come from the Latin allied community of Praeneste. The Caecilii Metelli continued to be prominent to the middle of the second century B.C., and from that time onwards they were one of the most illustrious and powerful aristocratic families of the late republic. Inscriptions from a Praenestine cemetery of republican date (*CIL* XIV. 3051–57 and 3128–34) show that the Fabricii and Anicii were members of the local population. C. Fabricius Luscinus was one of the most prominent Roman politicians during the period of the Pyrrhic War (consul in 282 and 278, and censor in 275). Pliny (*NH* 33.17) says that Q. Anicius of Praeneste was the colleague of Cn. Flavius in the curule aedileship of 304 B.C., but no member of his family reached the consulship until 160 B.C. Finally, the name Ogulnius is Etruscan in form; since one of the so-called *Elogia Tarquiniensia* indicates that an early king of Caere was named Orgolnius (Torelli 1975, 39), the Ogulnii attested in Roman public affairs during the third century B.C. might have originated from Caere.

DOMESTIC AND FOREIGN AFFAIRS DURING THE 280s B.C.

A plague broke out in Rome and the surrounding area in 293 B.C., and consultation of the Sibylline Books prompted the Romans to send ambassadors to Epidaurus in Greece in order to import from there the famous cult of Asclepius, the Greek god of healing (Livy 10.47.6–7 and *Per.* 11). About 140 years earlier, the Romans had introduced the worship of Apollo Medicus into the city, after another consultation of the Sibylline Books in order to alleviate a plague (Livy 4.25.3 and 4.29.7). During the Veientine War the Romans had adopted the Greek practice of holding a banquet for the gods and had consulted Apollo's oracle at Delphi but, unlike earlier imported Greek cults, Asclepius's is the first one which is known to have been brought to Rome directly from mainland Greece. This fact is therefore an indication of Rome's growing sphere of international contacts and adoption of things Greek. The ambassadors were sent out in 292 and returned in the same year. The Augustan poet Ovid ends his great mythological poem *The Metamorphoses* (15.622–745, cf. Val. Max. 1.8.2) with a moving account of how the Greek god, in the form of a snake, was transported on shipboard from Epidaurus and placed in his new Roman home on the island in the Tiber River. The Romans slightly modified the Greek form of the god's name to Aesculapius. His temple on the southern end of the Tiber island was dedicated on January 1, 291 B.C. If the Romans at this time already considered January 1 instead of March 1 to be the first day of the year, the day of dedication might have been chosen in order to have the Romans begin each year auspiciously with a day sacred to the tutelary god of health. In the course of time the god's temple became a sacred house of healing involving rites of incubation. People seeking cures prayed and slept in the temple in hope that they would wake up healed, or would be told by the god in a dream what remedy or regimen was needed to heal their ailment. Numerous dedications, some testifying to miraculous cures, have been found in the bed of the Tiber near the island. The Church of St. Bartholomew was later built over this religious site.

According to Zonaras (8.1) the prodigy which preceded the battle of Sentinum—blood, honey, and milk flowing from an altar on the Capitoline on successive days—was interpreted to foretell victory followed by plague and famine. This prediction is likely to have been *post eventum,* and the prodigy itself was probably likewise tailored after the fact to fit what actually happened. We may surmise, then, that the plague of the late 290s B.C. was soon followed by one or more years of bad weather resulting in poor harvests during the early 280s B.C. Major crop failure could account for the secession of the plebs in 287 B.C. As already argued (see above p. 173 and 230), the first and second secessions of the plebs dating to 494 and 449 B.C. are unhistorical, but the tradition of the first secession could have developed early as a Roman adaptation of a Greek tale associated with the cult of Demeter, imported to Rome as the cult of Ceres on the Aventine. The third secession of 287 B.C. should therefore be regarded as the only historical secession of the plebs. It took its form partly from the unhistorical but well-established tradition of the first secession.[11] Unfortunately, since Livy's second decade has not survived, our knowledge of this major event in Roman domestic affairs is very imperfect and rests upon several brief statements or descriptions of the event.

11. For other treatments of this secession of the plebs and of the Hortensian Law, see Maddox 1984 and Hölkeskamp 1988b, especially 292–312.

According to Dio (F 37), widespread indebtedness c. 287 B.C. led to pro-tracted political strife between debtors and creditors. The plebeian tribunes at first proposed that only the principal of loans be paid back, or that debts be repaid in three payments. Although the debtors favored these measures, they were opposed at first by the creditors; when the creditors finally began to compromise, the debtors held out in hope of further concessions. Zonaras (8.1) says this dissension was not resolved until the enemy approached the city. A statement in the *Summary* of Livy's eleventh book says that due to indebtedness there were serious and protracted seditions until the plebs seceded to the Janiculum, a hill on the other side of the Tiber, whence they were brought back by the dictator Q. Hortensius, who did not live out the full term of his office. According to other sources (Pliny *NH* 16.37, Gaius *Institutes* 1.3, Gell. 15.27.4, and *Digest* 1.2.2.8), this dicta-tor secured the passage of a Hortensian Law which ordained that whatever the plebs ordered was to be binding on the entire people.

From this brief outline of the scanty evidence for this event it should be obvious that some features of this secession, especially the nature of the strife and the proposed legislation, bear a striking resemblance to earlier supposed events in the struggle of the orders. These similarities can be explained in either historical or historiographical terms. On the one hand, similar solutions could have been devised for similar problems at different times, and the Romans could have been aware of previous statutes which had handled earlier parallel situations of debt crisis. On the other hand, given the simplistic working methods of later Roman historians, things were often fabricated from misinterpretation or willful invention, or one histori-cal incident was used to form the basis of other unhistorical occurrences of the same thing. The two tribunician proposals to regulate the repayment of debts mentioned by Dio are similar to those ascribed to the plebeian tri-bunes C. Licinius and L. Sextius in 367 B.C. Debt legislation could have been rather conventional, thus making it possible that the laws attributed to both 367 and 287 B.C. are historical; but historiographical duplication of one for the other also cannot be entirely ruled out. Zonaras's statement that a settlement was reached only when a foreign enemy came against the city looks like a stereotypical element of the struggle of the orders as the late annalistic tradition characterized it. In addition, the Hortensian Law is identical to one of the Valerian Horatian Laws of 449 B.C. and to one of the Publilian Laws of 339 B.C. As already argued (see above p. 231–33, cf. p. 181), all three of these measures may be nothing more than a later annalistic mis-understanding of a formulaic statement derived from a provision of the Twelve Tables which was commonly attached to the end of major statutes. The statement simply specified that whatever the people decided last was binding (Livy 7.17.12 and 9.34.6–7). Alternatively, several modern scholars (e.g., Staveley 1955, 20 ff. and Hölkeskamp 1988b, 292–94) have interpreted this measure to mean that henceforth plebiscites ratified by the tribal assembly no longer required a concurrent vote of *patrum auctoritas*.

As a result of these parallels and the brevity of the surviving ancient accounts, not much can be said for certain about this event except that indebtedness at that time is likely to have produced some kind of political conflict. Even if dressed up in the stereotypical motifs of the struggle of the orders and the two earlier unhistorical secessions, this incident preceded the births of Q. Fabius Pictor and L. Cincius Alimentus by only a generation or so. It therefore seems rather unlikely that it is a complete fabrication. Rather, some of its actual elements could have been the basis of the later annalistic interpretation of the other two secessions and of the struggle of the orders in general. Since this secession is said to have withdrawn not to the Aventine or *Mons Sacer* but to the Janiculum, which was otherwise not associated with the plebeian cause or the struggle of the orders, this element could be authentic. This detail suggests that the unrest involved the urban population. Maddox (1983) has plausibly argued that a severe crop failure could have overtaxed Rome's ability to make adequate provisions for its growing urban population. Rome's later republican and imperial history contains several instances in which severe food shortages in the city led to panic and popular demonstrations.

In addition, Macrobius (*Saturnalia* 1.16.30) may offer a more credible interpretation of the Hortensian Law than the other ancient sources give. He cites the early imperial antiquarian Granius Licinianus for the information that according to the Hortensian Law market days (*nundinae*) were to be days of legal business (*dies fasti*). These were days on which the praetor's court was to be open for litigation. Thus, the law seems to have been designed to allow farmers coming into town to transact both their commercial and their legal business on the same day. Given the extraordinary growth in the size of Roman territory in the decades preceding 287, there may have been a substantial number of Roman citizens who did not live within easy traveling distance of a Roman court. Bad harvests during the early 280s B.C. could have produced a sharp rise in indebtedness, and debtors could have been condemned *in absentia* in many lawsuits simply due to the inconvenience of showing up in court on the day appointed for legal judgment. If cases of this sort were sufficiently numerous, political pressure could have been brought to bear upon the plebeian tribunes to intercede on behalf of judgment debtors. According to this interpretation, then, the Hortensian Law responded in part to a need for Rome's legal system to adjust to new conditions produced by rapid expansion of Roman territory during the preceding fifty years.

There are two curious items of prosopography associated with this secession which are worthy of note and speculation. The dictator Q. Hortensius does not appear to be the product of a later annalistic fiction. The Hortensii are not attested in Roman public affairs until the second century B.C., and they were never very prominent. Only two members of the family reached the consulship in republican times (108 and 69 B.C.). Thus, the dictator of 287 B.C. is something of an enigma. Since it was not at all uncommon for a well-to-do family to hold lower public offices for several generations before reaching the consulship, Q. Hortensius could have been one of the ten plebeian tribunes of 288 or 287 B.C. who were attempting to work out a settlement between debtors and creditors, and on the basis of his demonstrated moderation and good faith he could have been appointed dictator to resolve the crisis. Another curious datum is that the consuls of 288 B.C., Q. Marcius Tremulus and P. Cornelius Arvina, had held the same office together in 306 B.C. Although such iteration of the consulship was not uncommon during the preceding Third Samnite War and the following Pyrrhic War, this is the only such iterated consular pair of the 280s. Why would these two men have wanted to hold the consulship for a second time almost twenty years after their first consulship? The meager ancient accounts for this period do not suggest that there was a major military crisis which persuaded the Romans to elect these aged and experienced men to a second consulship in 288 B.C. We therefore may be allowed to speculate that a growing domestic crisis, which did not actually come to a head until early 287 B.C., was responsible for this oddity in the consular *fasti*. Indeed, owing to his accomplishments during his first consulship, Q. Marcius Tremulus may have enjoyed a favorable reputation among the Roman people, which would in turn have made him an ideal candidate to head the state during a time of domestic unrest. According to Pliny (*NH* 34.23), in front of the temple of Castor and Pollux in the Forum there was an equestrian statue of Tremulus, "who had twice defeated the Samnites and by his capture of Anagnia had freed the people from taxation." It seems likely that Pliny's information about Tremulus's deeds reflects the wording of the monument's accompanying inscription.

During the decade of the 280s B.C. the Romans continued to use colonies to consolidate their frontier. The *Summary* of Livy's eleventh book mentions the foundations of Sena Gallica and Hadria. These colonies were on the Adriatic coast and were designed to serve as outposts against the Gauls, as well as to secure the new territorial acquisition resulting from M'. Curius Dentatus's conquest of the Sabines. Sena Gallica was a Roman maritime colony of only three hundred settlers situated in the Ager Gallicus, a strip of land between the Apennines and the Adriatic just south of the Po Valley. It took its name from settlement of this area by the Senonian Gauls, the principal tribe which had descended on Rome in 390 B.C. Hadria was a Latin colony and therefore probably was established with twenty-five hundred or four thousand settlers. It was located about one hundred miles south of Sena Gallica in southern Picenum.

During the years 284–280 B.C. the Romans were engaged in fighting against Etruscans and Gauls in northern Italy.[12] In 284 B.C. a Gallic army crossed the Apennines and laid siege to the northern Etruscan city of Arretium. When engaged in battle by a Roman army under the command of L. Caecilius Metellus Denter, the Gauls inflicted a crushing defeat resulting in the deaths of the general, seven military tribunes, and thirteen thousand Roman soldiers (Orosius 3.22.13–14 and Aug. *Civ. Dei* 3.17). The disaster shows that the Roman fear of a Gallic invasion was well founded. In 283 B.C. another Roman army encountered the combined forces of Etruscans and Gauls at Lake Vadimon just forty miles north of Rome and won an important, decisive victory. Continued fighting went in Rome's favor as well, including the Roman expulsion of the Senonian Gauls from the Ager Gallicus. The Gauls sued for peace and refrained from hostilities against the Romans for the next forty-five years. Meanwhile, Roman consuls campaigned in Etruria in 281 and 280 B.C. and celebrated triumphs over Volsinii and Vulci (see Degrassi 1947, 72–73). Rome's recovery from the defeat at Arretium and its pacification of the Etruscans and Gauls could not have been more timely, because by 280 B.C. Roman involvement in the affairs of Magna Graecia had brought about a war with Pyrrhus, whose victories in 280 and 279 came close to undoing the previous sixty years of Roman expansion.

THE PYRRHIC WAR

With the Pyrrhic War of 280–275 B.C. Rome can be said to have entered the mainstream of ancient Mediterranean history, as well as having emerged from the twilight into the dawn of Roman history.[13] Earlier Greek historians such as Philistus and Theopompus had taken note of the more important events of central Italy during the fourth century B.C. The Pyrrhic War, however, was chronicled by Hieronymus of Cardia and Timaeus of Tauromenium, who lived through it. In addition, King Pyrrhus himself is known to have written personal memoirs. Besides these contemporary Greek historical accounts, there developed a Roman historical tradition of this war which was largely independent of Greek sources. One of the most influential early Roman treatments of this war was the poetic narrative of Q. Ennius in the sixth book of his *Annales*. Ennius's epic recounted the major events of

12. For modern scholarly treatments of the confusing ancient sources on these events, whose details need not be considered here, see Salmon 1935; Corbett 1971; Harris 1971, 79–82; and Morgan 1972.

13. For other modern scholarly treatments of this war, see Wuilleumier 1939, 77–98; Lefkowitz 1959; Salmon 1967, 280–92; Brauer 1986, 121–67; Frank in *CAH* VII.2 1989, 456–85; Raaflaub, Richards, and Samons in Hackens 1992, 13–50; and Lomas 1993, 50–57. Two detailed biographies of Pyrrhus are Lévêque 1957 and Garoufalias 1979.

Roman history in an idealized, heroic manner characteristic of ancient Greek epic poetry, and the Pyrrhic War was not excepted from this kind of treatment (see Skutsch 1985, 328–66). Ennius depicted both Pyrrhus and his Roman counterparts as chivalrous and honorable adversaries (see especially Cic. *De Officiis* 1.38). Since Ennius's *Annales* was a mainstay in educating Roman schoolboys during the late republic, it is not surprising to find this portrait clearly reflected in the Roman historical tradition as a whole (see Gell. 3.8 for a fragment of Claudius Quadrigarius). Although detailed contemporary histories of this war were written and available in later ancient times, they have not survived, and we are unfortunately dependent upon a dozen late epitomes of fuller accounts which now survive only in fragments.[14]

Rome's war with Pyrrhus came into being in a roundabout manner. In 285 or 284 B.C. the people of Thurii appealed to Rome for protection against the attacks of Oscan-speaking Lucanians and Bruttians. Thurii was a Greek colony which had been established in 444/3 B.C. at the former site of Sybaris. Thurii's appeal to the barbarian (i.e., non-Greek) city on the Tiber is a clear indication that Rome had now emerged as the acknowledged hegemonic power of the entire peninsula, and that Roman *fides* could be counted on to provide security against external attacks. Rome accepted Thurii's plea for assistance, and the plebeian tribune, C. Aelius, who carried the proposal to aid the Greek city, was honored by the people of Thurii as their benefactor with the erection of a statue in the Roman Forum (Pliny *NH* 34.32). Exactly what form Roman protection took in 284 or 283 B.C. is not known due to the silence of our meager sources for this period, but in 282 B.C. the consul C. Fabricius led an army against the Lucanians and Bruttians, defeated them in battle, and left a garrison in Thurii (Val. Max. 1.8.6 and Appian *Samnitica* 7.1). Fabricius's military operations on land were apparently backed up by a small fleet of Roman warships. These vessels provoked Tarentum and thus formed the immediate cause of the Pyrrhic War.

According to Appian (*Samnitica* 7.1), by sailing warships in the vicinity of Thurii and Tarentum in 282 B.C., the Romans violated an old treaty with Tarentum, which forbade the Romans to sail beyond the Lacinian Promontory of Croton. This "old treaty" must be the *pax* which according to Livy (8.17.10) the Romans concluded with King Alexander of Epirus during his Italian adventure of the late 330s B.C., when he intervened to protect the Greek cities of the Ionian Gulf from the incursions and expanding pressure

---

14. These accounts are Livy *Per.* 12–14; Dion. Hal. 19.5–20.12; Diod. 21.21, 22.1, 22.6–9, 22.10; Plutarch *Pyrrhus* 13–25; Florus 1.18; Appian *Samnitica* 7–12; Justin 18.1–2, 23.3; Dio Fs 39–40; Eutropius 2.11–14; *Vir. Ill.* 35; Orosius 4.1–2; and Zonaras 8.2–5. There are, of course, numerous other ancient passages which mention or describe aspects of Pyrrhus's career.

of the Lucanians and Bruttians (Cary 1920, 165–70). The treaty was not designed to restrict Roman seaborne commerce, but only to protect the Greeks of southern Italy from Roman naval attack. Rome's extraordinary rise to dominance throughout the Italian peninsula during the following fifty years had rendered this treaty incompatible with Roman interests. Since the agreement had been neither repealed nor updated, however, it was still applicable according to international law in 282 B.C. when the Roman warships sailed along the southern Italian coast at least as far east as Tarentum. Except for Appian, all other Roman historical accounts are silent about this treaty; they portray the Tarentines as acting outrageously when they attacked the Roman warships near their city and sank or captured them. Rome's growing presence in the area, evinced by the Latin colony of Venusia founded in 291 and the installation of a Roman garrison in nearby Thurii, must have been viewed by Tarentum with great concern. Moreover, given the brevity and Roman bias of our surviving sources, we may even conjecture that the Romans were not entirely devoid of ill will toward Tarentum when they sailed their warships near the city in 282 B.C. Indeed, the later Roman historical tradition was careful to thrust the entire blame for the war upon the Tarentines by depicting them as having acted outrageously, impetuously, and even drunkenly when attacking the unsuspecting Roman sailors, but this version of events reveals much more about later Roman patriotic historiography and Roman prejudice against Greeks than about the historical reality of 282 B.C.

The Tarentines followed up their successful attack upon the Roman warships with an assault against Thurii. The town was captured, and the Roman forces present there were dismissed under a truce (Appian *Samnitica* 7.1). When the Romans sent L. Postumius Megellus (thrice consul in 305, 294, and 291) to Tarentum to demand release of all Roman captives and the handing over of the guilty parties, his demands were rebuffed. Later Roman historians embellished their accounts and blackened the reputation of the Tarentines even further by depicting their rejection of Roman demands as delivered in a most insulting and vulgar manner. The Tarentines were described as having jeered at Postumius's Roman toga and his less than flawless Greek diction, and one of them was even supposed to have defecated or urinated on him, thereby dishonoring the international sanctity accorded ambassadors in the most disgusting fashion possible. In the next year (281 B.C.), the Romans sent one of the consuls with an army against Tarentum and its allies. Meanwhile, the Tarentines sent ambassadors across the Adriatic and sought military assistance from King Pyrrhus of Epirus. As a member of the Molossian royal lineage of the Aeacidae, Pyrrhus claimed descent from the great warrior hero of Greek mythology, Achilles; according to Pausanias (1.12.1), when making their plea for intervention and assistance, the Tarentine ambassadors pointed out that the Romans were colonists of the Trojans, thereby suggesting that Pyrrhus was destined to defeat them.

This was not the first but the fourth time that the Tarentines had sought and received military support from across the Adriatic in order to drive back a non-Greek people threatening their city (see Wuilleumier 1939, 77–98; Brauer 1986, 61–86; and Lomas 1993, 39–44). Because Tarentum had been founded in the late eighth century B.C. by the Spartans, the Tarentines first appealed to their mother-city, Sparta, during the 340s B.C.; King Archidamus responded and eventually met his death in Italy while fighting on their behalf (343–338 B.C.). A few years later Alexander, the uncle of Alexander the Great and king of Epirus, also crossed over to defend the Greek cities of southern Italy, and he likewise met his death in battle (Livy 8.24). In 303 B.C. Cleonymus, the brother of the king of Sparta, came to southern Italy and fought briefly in defense of the Greeks against their Italian neighbors before he was distracted by other affairs in the region (Diod. 20.104–5). Thus, Pyrrhus's assistance to Tarentum was in a well-established tradition of transadriatic intervention, but unlike his predecessors, who had been summoned to oppose the incursions and expansion of Lucanians and Bruttians, Pyrrhus was confronting a major and well-organized military power. On the other hand, Pyrrhus was by far the best of the four Epirote and Spartan generals who campaigned in southern Italy on Tarentum's behalf. He had already won a great reputation in mainland Greece as a superior military commander vying for power with the other successors to the remnants of Alexander the Great's vast conquests. Consequently, the Pyrrhic War pitted the best military system Italy had to offer against the military professionalism of the Greek world.

Pyrrhus arrived at Tarentum with an army of twenty-three thousand infantry, two thousand archers, five hundred slingers, three thousand cavalry, and twenty elephants (Plutarch *Pyrrhus* 15.1). The infantry, which formed the core of his army, must have been trained and armed with the Macedonian sarissa devised by King Philip II, which had been the basis of Macedonian military superiority in the eastern Mediterranean and Near East for the previous seventy years. Once Pyrrhus began to receive recruits from among anti-Roman Italian communities, he probably did not arm or train many of them in the Macedonian fashion, but simply allowed them to serve in his army with their traditional weaponry (see Polyb. 18.28.10–11). His own forces brought over from Epirus must always have constituted the central part of his phalanx. Its size, strength, and integrity therefore had to be carefully maintained.

Pyrrhus and the Romans first encountered one another in 280 B.C. at the Siris River near Heraclea in southern Italy. The ensuing battle was a long, drawn-out, hard-fought affair, which finally ended in a Roman defeat involving the Roman cavalry's being thrown into confusion by the strange sight, smell, and enormous bulk of the elephants. Plutarch (*Pyrrhus* 17.4) cites Hieronymus of Cardia for the casualties: seven thousand Roman dead and fewer than four thousand Greek dead, but the latter included many of Pyrrhus's best men. Following Pyrrhus's victory the Lucanians and Samnites, who had thus far been sitting on the fence, defected from the Romans. Pyrrhus then advanced toward Rome through southern and central Italy, perhaps making it as far north as Anagnia (Appian *Samnitica* 10.1) or Praeneste (Florus 1.18.24 and Eutropius 2.12) before returning southward into winter quarters. It might have been on this occasion that the Samnites raided Ardea (Strabo 5.3.5). Pyrrhus's advance upon Latium apparently compelled the Romans to recruit every able-bodied male to mount a defense of Rome itself and other towns in Roman territory, for according to Orosius (4.1.3) the Romans in this year for the first time even resorted to arming the *proletarii* who, because of their poverty and inability to equip themselves, did not ordinarily serve in the Roman army.

Since Pyrrhus expected the Romans to behave like states in the Greek East, willing to conclude a peace agreement following a major defeat, he sent his eloquent diplomat Cineas to Rome to offer terms of settlement. But the history of the Roman state for the past several generations had not conformed to the paradigm by which Pyrrhus was operating. Rome's normal reaction to a major military reversal had been to respond with an even greater effort to overcome the setback. According to the *Ineditum Vaticanum* (von Arnim 1892, 120), which closely resembles Appian *Samnitica* 10.3 on this matter, Pyrrhus proposed that all the Italian Greeks be left free and autonomous, that the Lucanians, Samnites, and Bruttians be allowed to use their own laws and be his allies, and that the Romans merely rule over Latium. Thus, Pyrrhus was applying to Italy the standard propaganda and political ideology long current in the Greek mainland. He was posing as the liberator of Italy, and had hopes that the liberated peoples would become his allies and would acknowledge his hegemony. According to the later Roman historical tradition, when the senate was seriously inclining in favor of these terms, Ap. Claudius Caecus, aged and blind, was led or carried into the senate by his sons, and delivered such a stirring speech full of indignation at the senate's spinelessness that he immediately won them over to his opinion and convinced them to reject the proposed peace terms and to continue fighting on. Wonderful and dramatic as this portrait is, we should seriously question how much support there actually was in the senate in 280 B.C. for accepting Pyrrhus's settlement. We need not doubt that Ap. Claudius Caecus was led into the senate and delivered a rousing speech, but the picture of a Roman senate on the verge of making peace with Pyrrhus on these terms, which would have rolled back all of Rome's gains since the Latin War, is certainly exaggerated.

Cicero (*Brutus* 55 and 61–62) lists Ap. Claudius Caecus among ten other early Romans whom, on the basis of deeds ascribed to them, he conjectures to have been men of considerable eloquence. He indicates that there still existed a text of Caecus's famous speech opposing peace with Pyrrhus, but he raises serious doubts about its authenticity by placing it in the category of aristocratic family funeral orations handed down generation after generation that magnified or even fabricated the accomplishments of the family's ancestors (see above p. 76). Widespread senatorial support for accepting Pyrrhus's terms does not seem to fit well with Roman senatorial leadership since the Second Samnite War. From what we can judge on the basis of their actions, the senate and Roman people do not seem to have been significantly disheartened by the Caudine Forks and Lautulae; they responded to these disasters by reorganizing the military structure, by increasing the level of recruitment, and by aggressively pursuing an expansionist policy which even included the resumption of hostilities with the Etruscans. Nor did Rome back down when confronted with the coalition of Samnites, Etruscans, Umbrians, and Gauls in 295 B.C. The challenge was met head-on and defeated. A few years before Pyrrhus crossed over into Italy the Romans had suffered a crushing defeat at Arretium at the hands of the Gauls, but in the very next year they had mobilized another army and inflicted an equally crushing defeat upon the Gauls and Etruscans at Lake Vadimon, and followed up this success by expelling the Senones from the Ager Gallicus.

Many senators in 280 B.C. might have posed serious questions about Rome's ability to mobilize sufficient manpower to oppose Pyrrhus, especially in view of the losses at Arretium and Heraclea, but the collective will and determination of the Roman senate should not be doubted. The speech of Ap. Claudius Caecus could in fact have been very passionate and eloquent, and by reminding especially the younger senators of what the Romans had overcome and achieved during Caecus's own lifetime, the speech could have dispelled any lingering doubts that the Romans would somehow once again find a way to prevail. In this sense Caecus's speech can be taken as historically significant. Just like its behavior in the aftermath of Cannae, which Polybius so admired, the senate's rejection of Pyrrhus's peace terms following Heraclea well illustrated the true character of this deliberative body. Their resolve was not manufactured for the moment. It was real and was firmly predicated upon the collective resources and adaptability of Roman institutions, and it had been in existence at least since the Second Samnite War. We therefore need not doubt that Cineas was much impressed with the Roman senate, and that he characterized the body as "an assembly of many kings" (Plutarch *Pyrrhus* 19.5).

Following the Roman rejection of his proposed peace settlement, Pyrrhus augmented his own forces with those of his allies and proceeded north from Tarentum into Apulia. The Romans raised two consular armies of four legions with an equal number of allied troops and sent out both consuls, P. Sulpicius Saverrio and P. Decius Mus, to engage the enemy. The two armies met at Ausculum in Apulia (not to be confused with Asculum in Picenum), and they fought two battles on consecutive days (Plutarch *Pyrrhus* 21.5–10, cf. Dion. Hal. 20.1–3). Since they first fought on rough terrain near the wooded banks of a river, the Romans succeeded in holding their own, but on the next day Pyrrhus forced the Romans to engage him again on more level ground, where the frontal assault of the Macedonian-style phalanx and the charge of the elephants overcame the Romans. Pyrrhus's army, however, also suffered substantial losses. Once again, Plutarch cites Hieronymus of Cardia for the casualties: six thousand dead among the Romans, and thirty-five hundred five dead on the side of Pyrrhus, the latter figure coming from Pyrrhus's own *Memoirs*. According to Plutarch, it was at this juncture in his Italian adventure that Pyrrhus remarked that if he won another such battle against the Romans, he would be utterly ruined. According to one later Roman version of these events, the consul P. Decius Mus followed the example of his father and grandfather by submitting himself to ritual *devotio* in an attempt to give victory to the Romans. This instance of self-sacrifice is otherwise not mentioned in the narrative accounts of the Pyrrhic War, and its historicity is to be rejected as a later Roman patriotic fiction.

In the *Summary* of Livy's thirteenth book the battle of Ausculum is immediately followed by the brief statement that "an alliance with the Carthaginians was renewed for the fourth time." Similarly, Justin (18.2.1–3, cf. Val. Max. 3.7.10) places Carthaginian diplomatic overtures to Rome after the battle of Ausculum. A Carthaginian commander named Mago arrived at Ostia with a fleet of 120 warships and offered to assist the Romans against Pyrrhus, but the senate respectfully declined Mago's support. The Carthaginians were obviously concerned that Pyrrhus would prove to be another Timoleon and would cross over into Sicily to aid the Greeks there against themselves, as indeed he actually did in 278 B.C. Carthage was hoping that this situation could be avoided by Pyrrhus's defeat on Italian soil and his withdrawal back across the Adriatic. The Carthaginians were therefore willing to provide aid to the Romans to help them deliver a knock-out blow. It therefore seems likely that this is the context in which we should place the agreement between Rome and Carthage dated by Polybius (3.25.1–5) to the time of the Pyrrhic War.[15] As Polybius reports it, the form of this agreement was conditional. It began "if they make an alliance against Pyrrhus...." This wording might indicate that the agreement was proposed

---

15. For additional discussion, interpretations, and modern bibliography relating to this agreement, see Walbank 1970, 349–51; Mitchell 1971, 644–55; Hoyos 1984; and Scardigli 1991, 163–203.

to the Romans by the Carthaginians, but as stated by Justin and Valerius Maximus (contra Livy's epitomator), it was never ratified by the Romans. The agreement specified how the two parties were to aid one another. They were permitted to support each other in whichever land was attacked (Italy or Sicily). Carthage was to provide the maritime transport, but each side was responsible for paying their own troops.

The first clause of this agreement, which granted explicit permission to both Carthage and Rome to enter Italy and Sicily respectively for the purpose of opposing Pyrrhus, seems to confirm the existence of the so-called Philinus Treaty of 306 B.C. According to that agreement the Romans were not to intervene militarily in Sicily, and the Carthaginians were not to do so in Italy. Despite the statements of Justin and Valerius Maximus that the Roman senate politely declined the Carthaginian offer of assistance against Pyrrhus, a passage in the Byzantine-excerpted text of Diodorus supports the brief remark of Livy's epitomator concerning the actual ratification and implementation of the agreement summarized by Polybius. According to Diodorus 22.7.4, after concluding an alliance with Rome, the Carthaginians took five hundred Roman troops on board their ships, descended upon Rhegium, and destroyed a stockpile of timber intended to be used for ship building for Pyrrhus. A less direct confirmation of the Romano-Punic pact is suggested by Plutarch *Pyrrhus* 24. In 276 B.C., when Pyrrhus was sailing across from Sicily back to Italy to reenter the war with Rome and the other Italian peoples, he was engaged by the Carthaginians in a sea battle in the strait; and even after landing in Italy, he was set upon by an army of ten thousand Mamertines who had crossed over from Sicily to attack him. Since Pyrrhus had proven to be a bane to the Mamertines of northeastern Sicily during his Sicilian campaign, there can be no doubt that at this time the Mamertines were allies of the Carthaginians and therefore are likely to have been covered under the agreement described by Polybius. Thus the statements of Justin and Valerius Maximus should be dismissed as the result of later Roman chauvinism, which depicted the Roman state as neither needing nor wanting any assistance from an equal party in order to conduct its wars, and especially not from the country which later bore the hated Hannibal. Finally, the ratification and implementation of the Polybian agreement would further explain why in 272 B.C. a Carthaginian fleet appeared off the harbor of Tarentum to assist the Romans in their siege of the city, because it was the last holdout from the Pyrrhic War and was still being defended by a garrison left there by Pyrrhus. In later times, of course, the Romans twisted this event into the cause for the First Punic War.

After fighting the Romans to a standstill at Ausculum with no ensuing evidence that Roman resolve was slackening, Pyrrhus was receptive to the invitation of Sicilian Greeks to intervene in the island against the Carthaginians. During his absence from Italy the Romans made considerable progress against his Italian allies. The *Fasti Triumphales* record triumphs by C. Fabricius (consul 278) over the Lucanians, Bruttians, Tarentines, and Samnites; by C. Junius Brutus Bubulcus (consul 277) over the Lucanians and Bruttians; and by Q. Fabius Maximus Gurges (consul 276) over the Samnites, Lucanians, and Bruttians (Degrassi 1947, 72–75). In 275 B.C., when the consul M'. Curius Dentatus was raising troops in Rome for what turned out to be the final battle against Pyrrhus, there was a low turnout for the levy. After Dentatus drew the lot for the Pollia to be the first tribe from which men were to be recruited, and after he received no response to the first name called, he ordered that the person's property be confiscated. When the individual learned of this, he came to the consul's tribunal in the Forum and appealed to the plebeian tribunes for their assistance, but his appeal fell on deaf ears. Dentatus sold not only the man's property but the man himself into slavery (Val. Max. 6.3.4, cf. Livy *Per.* 14). Apparently this single act of severity was enough to overcome the Romans' reluctance to offer themselves for military service. The resistance which Dentatus at first encountered must have stemmed in part from the great demands being placed on Roman manpower at this time. It also could have been due in part to Roman anticipation of another battle involving heavy casualties against Pyrrhus's army and his elephants; but since a plague had broken out in the previous year (Orosius 4.3.1) and was probably responsible for a significant drop in the census figures between 280/79 and 276/5 B.C. (see below p. 363), disease was probably the single most important factor in causing the crisis in military recruitment at this time.

In 275 B.C. one consular army under L. Cornelius Lentulus guarded Lucania, while the other under Dentatus took up a strong position at Malventum in Samnium to await Pyrrhus's advance from Tarentum. In order to keep the two consular armies divided, Pyrrhus detached some of his forces and sent them into Lucania, while he proceeded with the bulk of his army against Dentatus. Pyrrhus decided to position some of his best forces with several elephants in concealment on higher ground to attack the Roman camp while he engaged the Romans in the field, but his plans miscarried. The difficulties of traversing rough terrain in darkness prevented the detachment from reaching their appointed destination. When dawn found them still on the move, the Romans attacked them, and after disposing of this threat, engaged with Pyrrhus's other forces in the open. Both sides scored success in different parts of the field, but the Romans drove back an attack of the elephants upon their camp (Plutarch *Pyrrhus* 25 and Dion. Hal. 20.12). The Romans killed two elephants and captured eight others. Pyrrhus was forced to retreat and soon thereafter abandoned Italy altogether, leaving a strong garrison in Tarentum. Dentatus celebrated his success over Pyrrhus and led elephants in triumph for the first time (Pliny *NH* 8.16). The victory was even commemorated on bronze ingots weighing about five Roman pounds (*aes signatum*) by stamping the figure of an elephant on one side (Crawford 1974, #9). Dentatus used the proceeds of the campaign's booty to finance the construction of Rome's second aqueduct, the Anio Vetus (Frontinus *De Aquis* 1.6). Apparently in recognition of and gratitude for his victory over Pyrrhus, the Romans elected Dentatus consul for a second consecutive year. It was his third consulship (290, 275, and 274).

Rome's defeat of Pyrrhus was a clear declaration to the rest of the ancient Mediterranean world that the Romans had arrived on the world scene of warfare and power politics, and recognition of this fact was no long time in coming. In 273 B.C. King Ptolemy II Philadelphus of Egypt sent ambassadors to Rome to open up friendly diplomatic relations with the victor of Italy (Livy *Per.* 14, Dion. Hal. 20.14, and Val. Max. 4.3.9). The Romans reciprocated by sending their own ambassadors to Egypt: Q. Fabius Maximus Gurges, N. Fabius Pictor, and Q. Ogulnius Gallus. Ogulnius had previous diplomatic experience in the Greek world; in 292 B.C. he had headed the embassage to Epidaurus to retrieve Aesculapius (Val. Max. 1.8.2). He was of Etruscan descent and appears to have been interested in religion. As plebeian tribunes in 300 B.C. he and his brother had sponsored the Ogulnian Law, which had expanded the numbers of pontiffs and augurs and had opened up these priestly colleges to prominent plebeians. While serving together as curule aediles in 296 B.C., the same brothers had placed bronze figures of Romulus and Remus beneath the statue of the she-wolf on the Palatine. This delegation to Egypt, however, must have been headed by Gurges, who had been twice consul, censor, triumphator, and was perhaps the *princeps senatus* at the time of the embassy (Pliny *NH* 7.133). The third member of this group was a Fabian kinsman, who might have been the uncle of the historian Q. Fabius Pictor. The latter was himself destined to perform an important diplomatic mission to Delphic Apollo in the aftermath of Cannae (Livy 22.57.5 and 23.11.1–6).

THE ROMAN ORGANIZATION OF ITALY

The Pyrrhic War finally came to an end in 272 B.C. when Tarentum surrendered to Rome and joined many other Italian states in becoming a Roman ally. The *Fasti Triumphales* and the meager material in the surviving literary sources indicate that during the years 274–264 B.C. Roman armies were active throughout much of Italy in putting down any lingering resistance to Roman power, and victorious Roman commanders continued to vow and construct new temples to celebrate their achievements. There were campaigns in southern Italy as well as in Etruria, Umbria, and Picenum. In 269 B.C. a Samnite hostage named Lollius escaped from Rome and returned to Samnium where he mobilized the last but brief Samnite resistance to Rome

(Dion. Hal. 20.17 and Zonaras 8.7). In 268 B.C. the Sabines had their legal status upgraded from *civitas sine suffragio* to full Roman citizenship (Vell. Pat. 1.14.7). In the same year the consul P. Sempronius Sophus vowed a temple to Tellus (= Earth) when an earthquake occurred during a battle with the Picentes (Florus 1.19). The temple was erected at the putative site of the demolished house of Sp. Cassius, the alleged demagogue of the early fifth century B.C. In the next year (267 B.C.) a temple was vowed to Pales, the obscure Roman deity of flocks, by the consul M. Atilius Regulus when he was campaigning among the Sallentini in the heel of Italy, an area well known for its pastoralism (Florus 1.20). In 265 B.C. the ruling families in the Etruscan city of Volsinii were overthrown by their clients or slaves, and a Roman army laid siege to the place, which was captured in the following year. In accordance with their preference for oligarchical government the Romans suppressed the social revolution, and the Etruscan elite was reestablished in power (Florus 1.21, Val. Max. 9.1 Ext. 2, and Zonaras 8.7). The victorious Roman commander, the consul M. Fulvius Flaccus, returned to Rome, celebrated a triumph, and commemorated his success by building a temple to the Etruscan god Vertumnus, who was probably introduced into Rome at this time from conquered Volsinii through the solemn ritual of *evocatio.* According to Festus (228L s.v. *picta*) the shrine contained a painting showing Flaccus wearing his triumphal garb. In addition, the consul erected a trophy displaying bronze statues captured from Volsinii (Pliny *NH* 34.34). The base of this monument, made of Peperino tufa and inscribed with Flaccus's name, has been found at the ancient sanctuary beneath the Church of Sant' Omobono in the Forum Boarium. Fulvius Flaccus's consular colleague of 264 B.C., Ap. Claudius Caudex, led a Roman army across the strait between Italy and Sicily to assist the Mamertines of Messana against the Carthaginians and Syracusans, thereby initiating the First Punic War. Rome's conquest of Italy was complete, and its long series of overseas wars leading to imperial greatness had just begun.

It might have been during this same period that the Romans extended the course of the Via Appia from Capua through Samnium past the Roman colonies of Beneventum and Venusia to Tarentum and then straight across the heel of Italy to end on the Adriatic coast at Brundisium. Rome's growing involvement in Adriatic maritime traffic is suggested by a curious incident of 266 B.C. When the Greek city of Apollonia on the Illyrian coast sent ambassadors to Rome, two Romans, Q. Fabius and Cn. Apronius, either aediles or men of aedilician rank, became embroiled in a quarrel with the ambassadors and violated international law by striking or beating them. In order to absolve the Roman state from this offense, the senate dispatched fetials, through whom the wrongdoers were formally surrendered to Apollonia, but the latter released the men (Livy *Per.* 15, Val. Max. 6.6.5, Dio F 42, and Zonaras 8.7). Unfortunately, the ancient sources do not bother to tell us what business had brought the Apolloniate ambassadors to Rome in the first place.

As had happened during the Second and Third Samnite Wars, colonies were established throughout Italy to secure Roman control of various areas (see Vell. Pat. 1.14.7–8). In 273 B.C. the Latin colonies of Cosa and Paestum were founded on the Etruscan coast and at the Greek coastal site of Posidonia in Lucania respectively.[16] Five years later in 268 B.C., two more Latin colonies were founded: Beneventum and Ariminum. The former was at the site of Malventum in Samnium, and the colony was given the more auspicious name of Beneventum. Ariminum was established on the Adriatic coast at the northern edge of the Ager Gallicus to control the coastal route leading into the Po Valley. In 264 B.C. Firmum was founded in Picenum, and in the next year Aesernia was established in northern Samnium. Toward the close of the First Punic War the Romans founded two more important Latin colonies: Brundisium on the Adriatic in the heel of Italy in 244, and Spoletium in Umbria in 241 B.C. In addition to these Latin colonies, the Romans might have founded two Roman maritime colonies during this same period. In 264 B.C. Castrum Novum was established on the Etruscan coast near Tarquinii (Vell. Pat. 1.14.8, contra Livy *Per.* 11), and it might have been at about the same time that the Roman colony of Pyrgi was founded over the Etruscan site, where excavations indicate violent destruction during the first part of the third century B.C. (Colonna 1966, 21). Thus, if we include the two colonies of Sena Gallica and Hadria established during the 280s (Livy *Per.* 11), the Roman state founded ten colonies during the twenty-seven years 289–263 B.C.

The conquests and territorial expansion of the Roman state during the eighty years 343–264 B.C. had enormous consequences for Rome, for its citizenry, and for the other peoples of Italy. The city of Rome itself must have experienced substantial growth in population, and this in turn would have created a more complex urban environment. By the close of the period covered in this volume Rome was serviced by two aqueducts: the Aqua Appia and the Anio Vetus. War booty had begun to have its effect in adorning the city with temples and other victory monuments. A mint was established in Rome, probably during the early third century B.C., and the newly created board of *triumviri monetales* began to oversee the production of Roman coinage. Because Rome was the center of a powerful and rapidly growing state, into which large quantities of booty were flowing, it is reasonable to suppose that the city was a magnet for skilled artisans and merchants. A type of black-glazed plate, decorated by impressed small stamps (hence its name, *Atelier des Petites Estampilles*) and dating to the early third century B.C.,

16. The ancient site of Cosa has been extensively excavated. For a detailed treatment of this town's history, see Brown 1980.

is common in the vicinity of Rome and was probably a local product. Its distribution along the Tyrrhenian coast of Italy, southern France, Spain, Corsica, and the Carthaginian-controlled areas of western Sicily and North Africa testifies to Roman commercial links throughout much of the western Mediterranean (see Morel 1969). Similarly, Roman citizens' involvement in seaborne commerce as far afield as the eastern Aegean is indicated by a bilingual inscription (Latin and Greek) found at Lindos on Rhodes and dating to the first half of the third century B.C. It records a dedication to Athena Lindia by L. Folius, the son of Maraeus (*ILLRP* 245).

State revenues must also have been enhanced by the renting out of public land, the amount of which quickly grew as the Romans confiscated tracts of land from conquered peoples. The growth and complexity of Roman state finances was probably the reason for an increase in the number of annually elected quaestors in 267 B.C., probably from four to six (Livy *Per.* 15). Increased complexity in Roman urban life is further suggested by the creation of three other boards of minor officials (*Digest* 1.2.2.29–31 and Livy *Per.* 11): *quinqueviri uls cis Tiberim* (= "five men for the nearer and farther sides of the Tiber"), *decemviri stlitibus iudicandis* ("ten men for judging lawsuits"), and *tresviri capitales* or *triumviri nocturni* (= "three men for capital matters" or "three men for the night watch"). Even though the precise duties of these officials are not well attested, their titles alone bespeak an urban environment requiring administration, policing and law enforcement, and the handling of increased litigation. The *quinqueviri* were each assigned one of five administrative districts of the city, four on the left bank of the Tiber and one on the right (Livy 39.14.10). Before these officials were instituted, their urban administrative duties might have been discharged by the ten plebeian tribunes, two assigned to each of these five regions. The dual title of the *tresviri capitales / nocturni* suggests that they were responsible for crime prevention by using night patrols, as well as for supervising the executions of those convicted of capital offenses. It therefore seems likely that in order to perform these duties, they had at their command a body of public slaves and other freeborn or libertine attendants. They must have worked closely with the *quinqueviri uls cis Tiberim* (see Livy 39.14.10).

Despite the paucity of reliable data for this period, there are clear indications that Roman society was absorbing aspects of Greek culture. Three prominent plebeian politicians adopted Greek surnames: Q. Publilius Philo (consul 339, 327, 320, and 315), P. Sempronius Sophus (consul 304), and Q. Marcius Philippus (consul 281). As already noted, the scenes painted in the temple of Salus by C. Fabius Pictor raise interesting questions concerning the education members of the Roman upper class received during the late fourth century B.C. The introduction of the cult of Aesculapius from Epidaurus in Greece is a striking illustration of the growing hellenization of

Roman religion. S. Weinstock (1957, 211–18) has plausibly suggested that the establishment of cults to Victory and Jupiter Victor during the Third Samnite War reflects religious influence from the contemporary Hellenistic world. According to Cicero (*Disp. Tusc.* 4.4) Ap. Claudius Caecus wrote a Pythagorean poem which contained the maxim that each man is the fashioner of his own fortune. Pythagorean philosophy had become well established in the Greek cities of southern Italy and Sicily during the fifth century B.C. and continued to be significant long thereafter. It was probably during the period of the Samnite Wars that some learned Greek of southern Italy concocted the idea that Rome's second king, Numa Pompilius, had been a pupil of Pythagoras, and that this fact accounted for many peculiarities of Roman religious practices. The notion of Numa's Pythagorean learning was apparently still current in 181 B.C. when some people in Rome (perhaps members of the recently persecuted Bacchanalian cult) tried to pass off a collection of religious writings as those of Numa and Pythagoras (Livy 40.29.3–14 and Pliny *NH* 13.84–87). Roman historians, however, realized early on that Numa's discipleship under Pythagoras was a chronological impossibility (Livy 1.18.2–3, Dion. Hal. 2.59, and Cic. *De Re Pub.* 2.28–29). The prestige enjoyed by Pythagoras in Rome during the Samnite Wars is further suggested by Pliny *NH* 34.26. According to this passage, the Romans erected statues of Pythagoras and Alcibiades in the Comitium during one of the Samnite Wars, because they were commanded by Apollo to honor the wisest and the bravest of the Greeks. In addition to having written a Pythagorean poem, Ap. Claudius Caecus wrote a legal treatise or pamphlet entitled *De Usurpationibus* (*Digest* 1.2.2.36), but apart from the title nothing is known about this work. Pomponius, a jurist of the second century of our era, records Caecus's authorship of this work, but indicates that the book was no longer in existence in his day. It had probably not been preserved beyond the second century B.C.

Rome's conquest of Italy must have wrought tremendous social and economic changes throughout the entire peninsula. Roman arms opened up new areas into which Roman citizens could migrate and settle. Arable land often must have been plentiful. Rome's numerous colonial foundations and the creation of new tribes testify to large-scale emigration from Latium and the incorporation of native foreigners into the Roman state. At the same time, the wars of conquest were certainly very deleterious to many non-Roman populations, what with the ravaging of the land, the enslavement or killing of tens of thousands of human beings, seizure of movable property as war booty, and the confiscation of portions of conquered territory as Roman public land. Emigration from Latium to Latin colonies and into new areas of Roman territory must have been counterbalanced by a substantial increase in the slave population of Latium and the growth of sizable estates. Public land is also likely to have formed a new realm of economic opportunity from which enterprising individuals could profit by stock raising or other activities. For example, Dionysius of Halicarnassus (20.15) says that the Romans deprived the Bruttians of half the Sila Forest, which contained magnificent stands of trees suitable for ship building and the manufacture of pitch of the best quality. Thus, despite the limited amount of precise data for the early third century B.C., we may nevertheless plausibly conjecture that social and economic conditions in Italy at this time were dynamic and fluid, as the Romans and other Italian peoples accommodated themselves to new realities brought on by Roman conquest.

By 264 B.C. peninsular Italy was firmly under Roman military control. Its population consisted of three different categories of people. First of all, there were the Roman citizens. They occupied the actual territory of the Roman state, which stretched across central Italy from the Tyrrhenian to the Adriatic, extended southward in a strip down along the Volscian coast to the Bay of Naples, and included northern Campania. According to Roman census figures, which seem to be credible from the early third century B.C. onwards, the adult male Roman population at this time numbered more than a quarter of a million.[17] Secondly, there were the states allied to Rome. In geography and population they formed the largest of the three categories. They were the various Etruscan, Umbrian, Picene, Sabellian, Messapic, and Greek communities of northern and southern Italy, who still exercised local autonomy over their own affairs but were bound to Rome by individual bilateral treaties. Generally speaking, these states were governed by republican constitutions of various configurations, and political power was largely in the hands of local landed elites, who had the same basic social, economic, and political interests and outlook as the Roman aristocracy. The third category of people in Roman Italy were the Latin colonies scattered throughout the peninsula. Since their inhabitants enjoyed Latin status and had Rome as their mother-city, they were closely bound to the Roman state by law, language, culture, and sentiment. Though numerically the smallest of the three categories, their numbers were deployed geographically to best safeguard Roman interests in the lands of the allied communities.

Rome held the commanding central position of this legal structure, which integrated all these peoples into a single military organization. Both the Italian allies and the Latin colonies were bound directly to Rome by individual treaties which spelled out their rights and obligations. As long as domestic tranquillity was maintained, Rome was content to allow the allied

17. For 293/2 B.C.: 262,321 (Livy 10.47.2); for 289/8 B.C.: 272,000 (Livy *Per.* 11); for 280/79 B.C.: 287,222 (Livy *Per.* 13); for 276/5 B.C.: 271,224 (Livy *Per.* 14); and for 265/4 B.C.: 292,234 (Eutropius 2.18). For a detailed discussion of what these figures represent, see Brunt 1971, 15–25.

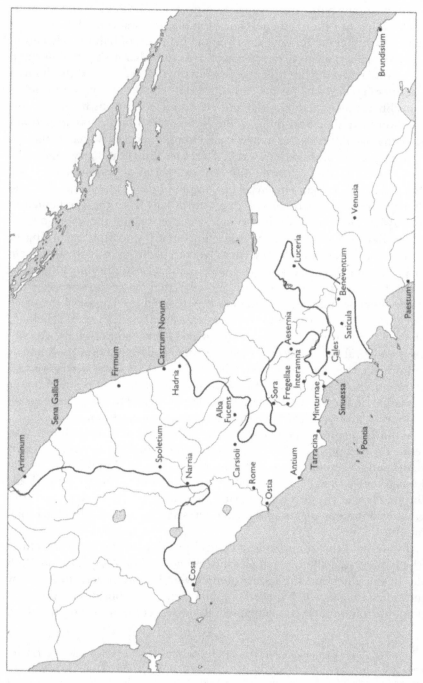

Map 10. Roman territory and colonization c. 250 B.C.

TABLE 2. Total Manpower for the Regions of Italy 225 B.C.

Infantry	Cavalry	Category
41,600	2,400	Romans in consular armies
60,000	4,000	Allies in consular armies
20,000	1,500	Romans guarding Rome
30,000	2,000	Allies guarding Rome
8,400	800	Forces in Sicily and Tarentum
50,000	4,000	Sabines and Etruscans
20,000	0	Umbrians and Sarsinates
80,000	5,000	Latin colonists
70,000	7,000	Samnites
50,000	16,000	Iapygians and Messapians
30,000	3,000	Lucanians
20,000	4,000	Marsi, Marrucini, Frentani, Vestini
250,000	23,000	Romans and Campanians

and Latin communities to govern their own affairs without interference, but all major issues of foreign affairs were determined by the Roman people and senate. Unlike the Greek world, where leagues and federations of states commonly employed representative bodies, the Roman organization of Italy had no such multilateral institutions; it was merely the large and dominant Roman state linked to all the other Italian peoples by a complex network of alliances. Most important for Rome's future as an imperial power in the Mediterranean was the access which these treaties gave Rome to the manpower resources of peninsular Italy.

An overall picture of the impressive scale of the Roman military organization of Italy at this time can be obtained from Polybius 2.24, which lists the military manpower available to the Roman state in 225 B.C. at the time of the last major Gallic invasion across the Apennines (see table 2).[18] Besides cataloguing the various forces deployed against the Gauls, Polybius gives the total manpower for the different regions of Italy. Since the historian Fabius Pictor is known to have participated in this military campaign (Orosius 4.13.5), Polybius must have taken these specific figures from his historical account, which in turn was based upon accurate contemporary official records. The numbers given below can be taken to correspond

18. For a detailed discussion of these figures, see Brunt 1971, 44–60 and Baronowski 1993.

rather closely to what they were in 264 B.C. They add up to a total of 730,000 infantry and 72,700 cavalry.[19]

Besides these resources of manpower, the Roman military organization was undergirded by the economic resources of Italy. We are given a glimpse of this Roman military iceberg in Livy's description (28.45.14–20) of the material support which many of Rome's allies gave in 206 B.C. for the construction and outfitting of the fleet needed by the expeditionary force commanded by Scipio Africanus for the invasion of North Africa:

> The peoples of Etruria, each according to their ability, first promised to assist the consul. Caere promised grain and supplies of every kind for the naval allies. Populonia promised iron, Tarquinii sail-cloth, and Volaterrae ship timber and grain. The people of Arretium said that they would furnish thirty thousand shields and an equal number of helmets, as well as javelins, spears, and pikes (fifty thousand of each), axes, shovels, sickles, basins, and mills as many as forty ships would require, one hundred twenty thousand measures of wheat, and travel money for the officers and oarsmen. Perusia, Clusium, and Rusellae promised a large quantity of grain and fir timber for building the ships, which they took from public forests. The peoples of Umbria and the entire Sabine territory, including Nursia, Reate, and Amiternum, promised soldiers. Many Marsic, Paelignian, and Marrucinian volunteers gave in their names for service in the fleet. Although they had an equal alliance with the Romans, the people of Camerinum sent an armed cohort of six hundred men.

SOME FINAL ASSESSMENTS

Like those of other significant communities of central Tyrrhenian Italy, the site of Rome experienced a major physical urban transformation and organization into a city-state during the seventh and sixth centuries B.C. Although Latium was not as blessed with natural resources as much of Etruria and Campania, Rome's location at an important spot on the Tiber insured that its social and economic development during the archaic period generally matched that of the most advanced communities in Etruria. Thus, by the beginning of the fifth century B.C. Rome was the largest and single most powerful state in Latium. This granted Rome a leading position in the Latin League. The community had evolved politically to the point of having replaced kingship with the republican institutions of

---

19. It is noteworthy that this total of slightly over eight hundred thousand men capable of bearing arms during Fabius Pictor's lifetime is exactly ten times the figure which he attributed to the very first census conducted by King Servius Tullius (Livy 1.44.2). It therefore seems likely that Pictor estimated that from the first census down to his own day the manpower available to the Roman state had increased tenfold.

the consulship and the plebeian tribunate for conducting military and domestic affairs respectively. Rome's geographical position protected it from the worst effects of Volscian and Aequian infiltration and raiding. By the end of the fifth century, the Latins had obtained the upper hand against these invading highlanders, and Rome itself had begun to expand its territory by conquest, first by capturing Fidenae, and then by defeating and incorporating Veii. The Gauls' victory at the Allia and their occupation of Rome marked only a temporary setback and caused disruption in Latium for a generation or so.

In the meantime the Roman state had also undergone considerable internal change. In addition to the codification of law embodied in the Twelve Tables, new institutions, such as the censorship and the consular tribunate, were created to cope with the growing external-military and internal-administrative needs of the state. Although during the later part of the fifth century an inner group of aristocrats succeeded in defining themselves as patrician by reason of their birth, wealth, and presumed special relationship with the divine, their attempt to monopolize the consulship was relatively short-lived and was abandoned about two decades after the Gallic catastrophe. Taken together, the political settlements of 367 and 338 B.C. launched the Roman state on a course of spectacular conquests of all the various peoples of peninsular Italy. These two settlements laid down regular procedures by which new members were to be integrated into the Roman ruling elite, and by which foreign communities were to be integrated into the Roman citizen body and alliance system.

In addition, during the second half of the fourth century B.C. the Romans developed institutions and practices characteristic of the middle and late republic and fundamental for their conquest of the Mediterranean. Political power was distributed among the magistrates, the senate, and the assembly of citizens so as to form the mixed constitution which Polybius praised so highly in his sixth book. During the Samnite Wars, the Romans further refined their military institutions and developed colonization and road building as instruments to consolidate the gains achieved by warfare. Simultaneously, Roman expansion began to have important social and economic effects: increased opportunities for members of the Roman lower class to improve their economic condition, the significant rise in chattel slavery and of a freedman element in the Roman civic body, the beginnings of the accumulation of considerable wealth by members of the Roman upper class, and Rome's growth and increased complexity as an urban entity.

At the conclusion of the Latin War in 338 B.C. not only were the Latins granted Roman citizenship, but even many Volscians and Oscan-speaking Campanians were made *cives sine suffragio*. Latin status was given to Romans and non-Romans who became members of Rome's Latin colonies. Even though Rome's wars resulted in the enslavement of thousands, manumission seems to have been quite common from early times, and all freed slaves became Roman citizens. The consular *fasti* for the period of the Samnite and Pyrrhic Wars display a pattern of steady social mobility into the Roman aristocracy. Thus, even though Roman society was very hierarchical and not at all democratic, it was far more open than the city-states of Greece. As a result, Rome succeeded in uniting the very diverse peoples of Italy into a single confederation, whereas the states of mainland Greece, although bound together by a common language and culture, never overcame the exclusionary nature of their institutions to form a lasting union. Greek unity was achieved only when imposed by the superior force of a foreign power such as Macedon or Rome. It is also noteworthy that when the Roman state failed to address the grievances and aspirations of its Italian allies over the course of the second century B.C., the ultimate result was the explosion of the Social War of 90–88 B.C., in which the non-Roman inhabitants of central and southern Italy took up arms against Rome. This brief but bloody war was only ended when Rome agreed to extend its citizenship to all the inhabitants of Italy south of the Po. By the time of Julius Caesar's assassination two generations later in 44 B.C. Italy had become Romanized, and the same process (albeit at a much slower pace) was already under way in the overseas provinces.

Throughout its entire history Roman society and politics were always dominated by an aristocratic oligarchy. Although the term oligarchy has always had a pejorative connotation in political parlance, and although classical Athens is generally given high marks for its democracy with equitable sharing of political power within its citizen body, the historical record demonstrates that the latter proved to be incapable of building a lasting imperial system, and guarded its citizenship so jealously that Athenian society was always relatively closed. Roman society, on the other hand, although dominated by an oligarchy with political power distributed in a hierarchical fashion, was far more receptive of foreigners; and this social and political receptivity was chiefly responsible for Rome's lasting success as an imperial power. Like many other peoples throughout history, the Romans were quite successful in war, but conquest alone does not explain Rome's success in forging its conquests into an empire which endured for several centuries.

Early Roman Chronology

From the year 300 B.C. onwards the Roman list of consuls is secure, and Roman dates are absolute, but this is not the case for the period preceding 300 B.C. The reason for this needs to be understood in order to appreciate fully the historical and historiographical difficulties surrounding some of the more important problems of early Roman history.

The dates used throughout this book for Roman affairs before 300 B.C. are those of a chronological system worked out by the Roman antiquarian Atticus, who published it in his *Liber Annalis* (Book of Chronology) in 47 B.C. This chronology was accepted by Varro (hence the modern term Varronian chronology) and was consequently employed thereafter by the Roman state as the official system for determining an absolute date from the supposed foundation of Rome (*ab urbe condita*). Thus, this scheme was used in the famous Augustan inscriptions listing Rome's chief magistrates from the beginning of the republic and the celebration of triumphs from the reign of Romulus, the *Fasti Capitolini* and the *Fasti Triumphales*. Because of its widespread use and acceptance during imperial times, it has been generally adopted by modern scholars for the sake of convenience.

The Varronian chronology dates the foundation of Rome to the year 753 B.C., the first year of the republic to 509, the Gallic capture of the city to 390, and the first plebeian consulship to 366 B.C. It also includes an anarchy for the five-year period 375–371 (i.e., years in which allegedly no consuls or consular tribunes were elected), as well as four dictator years for 333, 324, 309, and 301 B.C. The latter were years for which there were no consuls recorded, but instead a dictator and a master of the horse were supposed to have been in office for the entire year. Drummond (1978a) has cogently argued that the dictator years were first invented by Atticus partly in response to Julius Caesar's tenure of the dictatorship beyond a six-month term during the 40s B.C., but they were also probably used by Atticus to make minor adjustments to Roman chronology of the late fourth century so as to synchronize Roman affairs with events in Greek history. Furthermore, a fragment of N. Fabius Pictor, who wrote a history of Rome in Latin toward the end of the second century B.C., indicates that this work did not contain any years of anarchy, suggesting that these five years were a later annalistic invention (see above p. 264).

Greek historical accounts, independent of the Roman tradition, suggest that the Gauls captured Rome in the year 387/6 B.C. (see Polyb. 1.6.1 with Justin 20.5.1–6). Thus, if we remove both the dictator years and the years of anarchy from the Varronian chronology, the Roman date for the Gallic capture of the city is lowered to 381, about five years too late. Consequently, modern scholars have generally supposed that the consular *fasti* for the fourth century were slightly defective in that they somehow omitted five years of eponymous magistrates, that Roman writers at some point realized this, and that they adopted at least two different chronological devices (years of anarchy or dictator years) in order to remedy the gap. The simplest means would have been the insertion of five years of anarchy, containing neither eponymous magistrates nor major events to be recorded. Atticus apparently devised the four dictator years at least in part as an alternative chronological solution, but since his chronology included both the years of anarchy and the dictator years, his reconstruction had the effect of raising early Roman chronology by as much as four more years. As a result, the Attican/Varronian chronology, used by the ancients from the Augustan age onwards and by modern scholars, cannot be regarded as an absolute chronological system before the year 300 B.C.

It should also be understood that our two major ancient accounts of early Roman history, Livy's first decade and Dionysius's *Roman Antiquities,* do not employ the Varronian system, although annotated modern editions of their works generally equate their consular years with it. Livy, for example, differs from the Varronian scheme in having six instead of five years of anarchy, and his narrative does not include the four dictator years. The dictators and masters of the horse for these four years are included as normal republican dictators during the consulships of the years preceding the dictator years of the Varronian system. Nevertheless, since the Roman annalistic tradition recorded events by the years of the eponymous magistrates, it matters little that Livy and Dionysius did not use the Varronian chronology, because ancient accounts tended to be in general agreement in assigning a specific event to its consular year, regardless of how that year in a particular author's chronological scheme is now to be translated into our own B.C. dating system.

WORKS CITED

For additional bibliographical references the reader should consult Salmon 1967, 405–16; Heurgon 1973, 261–312; Richard 1978, 601–26; Raaflaub 1986, 379–433; Hölkeskamp 1987, 259–76; *CAH* IV. 1988, 864–82; *CAH* VII.2 1989, 673–771; Eder 1990, 562–86; Cornell 1995, 472–91; Dench 1995, 227–45; Smith 1996, 256–81; Oakley 1997, 735–67; and Oakley 1998, 782–820. With minor variations (e.g., *TAPA* for *TAPhA*) the abbreviations used below for the titles of scholarly journals are those of *L'Année Philologique* and *The Oxford Classical Dictionary*.

Adcock, F.E. 1957. "Consular Tribunes and their Successors." *JRS* 47: 9–14.

Afzelius, A. 1942. *Die römische Eroberung Italiens (340–264 v. Chr.)*. Copenhagen.

Akten des Kolloquiums zum Thema die Göttin von Pyrgi: Archäologische, Linguistische und Religionsgeschichtliche Aspekte (Tübingen, 16–7 Januar 1979). 1981. Instituto di Studi Etruschi ed Italici. Florence.

Alföldi, A. 1965. *Early Rome and the Latins*. Ann Arbor.

Altheim, F. 1940. *Lex Sacrata: Die Anfänge der plebeischen Organization*. Albae Vigiliae 1. Amsterdam.

Ammerman, A.J. 1990. "On the Origins of the Forum Romanum." *AJA* 94: 627–45.

———. 1996. "The Comitium in Rome from the Beginning." *AJA* 100: 121–36.

Ampolo, C. 1970. "L'Artemide di Marsiglia e la Diana dell' Aventino." *PdP* 25: 200–10.

———. 1975. "Gli Aquilii del V. Secolo a.C. e il Problema di Fasti Consolari più antichi nell'Anno 487 a.C." *PdP* 30: 410–16.

———. 1976–77. "Demarato: Osservazioni sulla Mobilità Sociale Arcaica." *DdA* 9–10: 333–45.

———. 1980. "Le Condizioni materiali della Produzione: Agricoltura e Paesaggio agrario." *DdA* n.s. 2: 15–46.

Ancillotti, A., and R. Cerri. 1996. *Le Tavole di Gubbio e la Civiltà degli Umbri*. Perugia.

Anzidei, A.P., et al. 1985. *Roma e il Lazio dall'Età della Pietra alla Formazione della Città*. Rome.

Astin, A.E. 1978. *Cato the Censor.* Oxford.

———. 1982. "The Censorship of the Roman Republic: Frequency and Regularity." *Historia* 31: 174–87.

Aubet, M.E. 1993. *The Phoenicians and the West: Politics, Colonies, and Trade.* Cambridge.

Badian, E. 1958. *Foreign Clientelae 264–70 B.C.* Oxford.

———. 1966. "The Early Historians." In *Latin Historians.* Edited by T.A. Dorey. London.

———. 1972. "Tiberius Gracchus and the Beginning of the Roman Revolution." *ANRW* I. 1: 668–731.

———. 1990. "The Consuls, 179–49 B.C." *Chiron* 20: 371–413.

Baier, T. 1997. *Werk und Wirkung Varros im Spiegel seiner Zeitgenossen.* Hermes Einzelschriften 73. Stuttgart.

Baldi, P. 1999. *The Foundations of Latin.* Berlin and New York.

Banti, L. 1973. *Etruscan Cities and Their Culture.* Translated by E. Bizzarri. Berkeley.

Barfield, L. 1971. *Northern Italy Before Rome.* London and New York.

Baronowski, D.W. 1993. "Roman Military Forces in 225 B.C. (Polybius 2.23–4)." *Historia* 42: 181–202.

Bauman, R.A. 1983. *Lawyers in Roman Republican Politics: Study of the Roman Jurists in their Political Setting, 316–82 B.C.* Munich.

Beard, M. 1980. "The Sexual Status of Vestal Virgins." *JRS* 70: 12–27.

———. 1985. "Writing and Ritual: A Study in Diversity and Expansion in the Arval *Acta.*" *PBSR* 53: 114–62.

———, and J.A. North. 1990. *Pagan Priests: Religion and Power in the Ancient World.* Ithaca.

———, J.A. North, and S. Price. 1998. *Religions of Rome.* Vol. 1 *A History.* Cambridge.

Beloch, K.J. 1926. *Römische Geschichte bis zum Beginn der punischen Kriege.* Leipzig.

Bernardi, A. 1945–46. "Patrizi e Plebei nella Costituzione della primitiva Repubblica Romana." *Rendiconti dell' Istituto Lombardo, Classe di Lettere, Scienze morali e storiche* 79: 1–14.

Best, J., and F. Woudhuizen. 1989. *Lost Languages of the Mediterranean.* Leiden.

Bickermann, E.J. 1947. "Apocryphal Correspondence of Pyrrhus." *CP* 42: 137–46.

———. 1952. "*Origines Gentium.*" *CP* 47: 65–81.

———. 1969. "Some Reflections on Early Roman History." *RFIC* 97: 393–408.

Bietti Sestieri, A.M. 1992. *The Iron Age Community of Osteria Dell' Osa: A Study of Socio-Political Development in Central Tyrrhenian Italy.* Cambridge.

Bilancio Critico. 1993. *Accademia Nazionale dei Lincei, Atti dei Convegni Lincei 100, Convegno sul Tema: Bilancio critico su Roma arcaica fra Monarchia e Repubblica, In Memoria di Ferdinando Castagnoli (Roma 3–4 Giugnio 1991).* Rome.

Billows, R. 1989. "Legal Fiction and Political Reform at Rome in the Early Second Century B.C." *Phoenix* 43: 112–33.

Bishop, M.C., and J.C.N. Coulston. 1993. *Roman Military Equipment from the Punic Wars to the Fall of Rome.* London.

Blakeway, A. 1935. "Demaratus: A Study in Some Aspects of the Earliest Hellenization of Latium and Etruria." *JRS* 25: 129–49.

Bleicken, J. 1968. *Das Volkstribunat der klassischen Republik: Studien zu seiner Entwicklung zwischen 287 und 133 v. Chr.* Zetemata 13, 2nd ed. Munich.

————. 1981. "Das römische Volkstribunat: Versuch einer Analyse seiner politischen Funktion in republikanischer Zeit." *Chiron* 11: 87–108.

Blench, R., and M. Spriggs eds. 1997. *Archaeology and Language: Theoretical and Methodological Orientations.* London and New York.

Bloch, R. 1961. *The Etruscans.* London.

————. 1963. *The Origins of Rome.* London.

Boardman, J. 1980. *The Greeks Overseas: Their Early Colonies and Trade.* New York.

Boddington, A. 1959. "The Original Nature of the Consular Tribunate." *Historia* 8: 356–64.

Bömer, F. 1957–58. *P. Ovidius Naso: Die Fasten.* 2 vols. Heidelberg.

Bonfante, G. and L. 1983. *The Etruscan Language.* New York.

Bonfante, L. 1970a. "Roman Triumphs and Etruscan Kings: The Latin Word *Triumphus.*" In *Studies in Honor of J. Alexander Kerns.* Edited by R. C. Lugton and M. G. Saltzer. Mouton.

————. 1970b. "Roman Triumphs and Etruscan Kings: The Changing Face of the Triumph." *JRS* 60: 49–66.

————. 1978. "Historical Art: Etruscan and Early Roman." *AJAH* 3: 136–61.

————. 1981. "Etruscan Couples and Their Aristocratic Society." In *Reflections of Women in Antiquity.* Edited by H. P. Foley. New York.

————, ed. 1986. *Etruscan Life and Afterlife: A Handbook of Etruscan Studies.* Detroit.

Bonnet, C. 1983. *Le Dieu Melqart en Phénicie et dans le Bassin Méditerranée: Culte national et officiel.* Leuven.

————. 1988. *Melqart: Cultes et Mythes de l'Héraclè tyrien en Méditerranée.* Leuven.

Botsford, G. W. 1909. *The Roman Assemblies from Their Origin to the End of the Republic.* New York.

Bowman, A. K., and G. Woolf, eds. 1994. *Literacy and Power in the Ancient World.* Cambridge.

Bradford, J. 1950. "The Apulia Expedition, An Interim Report." *Antiquity* 24: 84–95.

————. 1957. *Ancient Landscapes.* London.

Brauer, G. C., Jr. 1986. *Taras: Its History and Coinage.* New Rochelle NY.

Bremer, F. P. 1896. *Iurisprudentiae Antehadrianae Quae Supersunt.* Leipzig.

Bremmer, J. N. 1982. "The *Suodales* of Poplios Valesios." *ZPE* 47: 133–47.

————, and N. M. Horsfall. 1987. *Roman Myth and Mythography.* Bulletin of the Institute of Classical Studies Supplement 52. London.

Brendel, O. J. 1995. *Etruscan Art.* New Haven.

Bridenthal, R. 1972. "Was There a Roman Homer? Niebuhr's Thesis and its Critics." *History and Theory* 11: 193–213.

Broughton, T. R. S. 1951–52. *The Magistrates of the Roman Republic.* 2 vols. Cleveland OH.

————. 1986. *The Magistrates of the Roman Republic.* Vol. 3, *Supplement.* Atlanta.

Brown, F. E. 1974–75. "La Protostoria della Regia." *Atti della Pontificia Accademia Romana di Archeologia (Serie III) Rendiconti* 47: 15–36.

————. 1976. "Of Huts and Houses." In *In Memoriam Otto J. Brendel: Essays in Archaeology and the Humanities.* Edited by L. Bonfante and H. von Heintze. Mainz.

————. 1980. *Cosa: The Making of a Roman Town.* Ann Arbor.

Brown, T. S. 1958. *Timaeus of Tauromenium.* Berkeley.

Brunt, P. A. 1969. "The Enfranchisement of the Sabines." In *Hommages à Marcel Renard.* Vol. 2. Collection Latomus 102. Edited by J. Bibauw. Brussels.

————. 1971. *Italian Manpower 225 B.C. to A.D. 14*. Oxford.

————. 1980. "On Historical Fragments and Epitomes." *CQ* n.s. 30: 477–94.

————. 1988. *The Fall of the Roman Republic and Related Essays*. Oxford.

Bucher, G.S. 1995. "The *Annales Maximi* in the Light of Roman Methods of Keeping Records." *AJAH* 12: 2–61.

Buck, C.D. 1904. *A Grammar of Oscan and Umbrian*. Reprinted with additions. Darmstadt, 1928.

Buranelli, F., ed. 1987. *La Tomba François di Vulci*. Rome.

Burckhardt, L. 1990. "The Political Elite of the Roman Republic: Comments on Recent Discussion of the Concepts of *Nobilitas* and *Novitas*." *Historia* 39: 77–99.

Burkert, W. 1992. *The Orientalizing Revolution: Near Eastern Influence on Greek Culture in the Early Archaic Period*. Cambridge MA.

Burnett, A.M. 1977. "The Coinages of Rome and Magna Graecia in the Late Fourth and Third Centuries B.C.," *Schweizerische Numismatische Rundschau* 56: 92–121.

————. 1978. "The First Roman Silver Coins." *Numismatica e Antichità Classiche* 7: 121–42.

————. 1980. "The Second Issue of Roman Didrachms." *Numismatica e Antichità Classiche* 9: 169–74.

————. 1986. "The Iconography of Roman Coin Types in the Third Century B.C." *Numismatic Chronicle*, 8th ser., 6: 67–75.

————. 1989. "The Beginnings of Roman Coinage." *Annali dell' Istituto Italiano di Numismatica* 36: 33–65.

Cambridge Ancient History, III.3: The Expansion of the Greek World Eighth to Seventh Centuries B.C. 1982. 2nd ed. Cambridge.

Cambridge Ancient History, IV.: Persia, Greece, and the Western Mediterranean c.525–479 B.C. 1988. 2nd ed. Cambridge.

Cambridge Ancient History, VII.2: The Rise of Rome to 220 B.C. 1989. 2nd ed. Cambridge.

Campanile, E., ed. 1988. *Alle Origini di Roma*. Pisa.

Carandini, A. 1990. "Palatino, Campagne di Scavo delle Pendici settentrionale (1985–1988)." *Bollettino di Archeologia* 1–2: 159–65.

————. 1997. *La Nascità di Roma: Dei, Lari, Eroi e Uomini all'Alba di una Cività*. Biblioteca di Cultura Storica 219. Torino.

Cary, M. 1919. "A Forgotten Treaty Between Rome and Carthage." *JRS* 9: 67–77.

————. 1920. "Rome's Early Treaties with Tarentum and Rhodes." *Journal of Philology* 35: 165–72.

Cassola, F. 1962. *I Gruppi Politici Romani nel III Secolo a.C.* Trieste.

————. 1982. "Diodoro e la Storia romana arcaica." *ANRW* II. 13.1: 724–73.

Chassignet, M. 1986. *Caton: Les Origines (Fragments)*. Paris.

————. 1996. *L'Annalistique Romaine, Tome 1: Les Annales des Pontifes et l'Annalistique Ancienne (Fragments)*. Paris.

Civiltà del Lazio Primitivo. 1976. Exhibition Catalogue. Rome.

Classen, C.J. 1963. "Zur Herkunft der Sage von Romulus und Remus." *Historia* 12: 447–57.

Coarelli, F. 1982. *Lazio, Guide Archeologiche Laterza*. Bari.

————. 1983. *Il Foro Romano I: periodo arcaico*. Rome.

————. 1985. *Il Foro Romano II: periodo repubblicano e augusteo*. Rome.

————. 1988. *Il Foro Boario dalle Origini alla Fine della Repubblica*. Rome.

Coleman, R. 1990. "Dialectal Variation in Republican Latin, with Special Reference to Praenestine." *PCPS* n.s. 36: 1–25.

Coli, U. 1958. *Il Diritto pubblico degli Umbri e le Tavole Eugubine*. Milan.

Colonna, G. 1966. "The Sanctuary at Pyrgi in Etruria." *Archaeology* 19: 11–23.

Connolly, P. 1981. *Greece and Rome at War*. London.

Corbett, J.H. 1971. "Rome and the Gauls." *Historia* 20: 656–64.

Cornelius, F. 1940. *Untersuchungen zur frühen römischen Geschichte*. Munich.

Cornell, T.J. 1974. "Notes on Sources for Campanian History in the Fifth Century B.C." *MH* 31: 193–208.

———. 1975. "Aeneas and the Twins." *PCPS* n.s. 21: 1–32.

———. 1976. "Etruscan Historiography." *Annali della Scuola Normale Superiore di Pisa*, 3rd ser., 6.1: 411–39.

———. 1977. "Aeneas' Arrival in Italy." *LCM* 2: 77–83.

———. 1978. "*Principes* of Tarquinia." *JRS* 68: 167–73.

———. 1980. "Rome and Latium Vetus 1974–79." *Archaeological Reports* 26: 71–89.

———. 1986. "Rome and Latium Vetus 1980–85." *Archaeological Reports* 32: 123–33.

———. 1991. "The Tyranny of the Evidence: A Discussion of the Possible Uses of Literacy in Etruria and Latium in the Archaic Age." In *Literacy in the Roman World*, Journal of Roman Archaeology Supplement 3. Edited by M. Beard et al. Ann Arbor.

———. 1995. *The Beginnings of Rome: Italy and Rome from the Bronze Age to the Punic Wars (c. 1000–264 B.C.)*. London.

Corpus Speculorum Etruscorum. 1981–95.

Crake, J.E.A. 1940. "The Annals of the Pontifex Maximus." *CP* 35: 375–86.

Crawford, M.H. 1973. "Foedus and Sponsio." *PBSR* 41: 1–7.

———. 1974. *Roman Republican Coinage*. 2 vols. Cambridge.

———. 1985. *Coinage and Money under the Roman Republic: Italy and the Mediterranean Economy*. London.

———, et al. 1996. *Roman Statutes*. 2 vols. Bulletin of the Institute of Classical Studies Supplement 64. London.

Crise et Transformation des Sociétés archaiques de l'Italie antique au Ve Siècle av. J.-C. 1990. Collection de l'École Française de Rome 137. Rome.

Cristofani, M. 1967. "Ricerche sulle Pitture della Tomba François di Vulci: I Fregi decorativi." *DdA* 1: 186–219.

———. 1972. "Sull'Origine e la Diffusione dell' Alfabeto Etrusco." *ANRW* I. 2: 466–89.

Cross, F.M. 1972. "An Interpretation of the Nora Stone." *Bulletin of the American Schools of Oriental Research* 208: 13–19.

D'Agostino, B. 1977. *Tombe Principesche dell' Orientalizzante antico da Pontecagnano*. Monumenti Antichi 49. Rome.

Degrassi, A. 1947. *Inscriptiones Italiae, XIII. 1, Fasti Consulares et Triumphales*. Rome.

———. 1963. *Inscriptiones Italiae, XIII. 2, Fasti Anni Numani et Iuliani*. Rome.

De Grummond, N.T., ed. 1982. *A Guide to Etruscan Mirrors*. Tallahassee.

Dench, E. 1995. *From Barbarians to New Men: Greek, Roman, and Modern Perceptions of Peoples from the Central Apennines*. Oxford.

Dennis, G. 1985. *The Cities and Cemeteries of Etruria, Abridged With New Material*. Edited by P. Hemphill. Princeton.

Densmore Curtis, C. 1919. "The Bernardini Tomb." *MAAR* 3: 9–90.

——. 1925. "The Barberini Tomb." *MAAR* 5: 9–52.

De Puma, R.D., and J. P. Small, eds. 1994. *Murlo and the Etruscans: Art and Society in Ancient Etruria*. Madison WI.

De Sanctis, G. 1956–69. *Storia dei Romani*. 2nd ed. 4 vols. Florence.

Develin, R. 1975. "*Comitia Tributa Plebis*." *Athenaeum* n.s. 53: 302–37.

——. 1977. "*Lex Curiata* and the Competence of Magistrates." *Mnemosyne*, 4th ser., 30: 49–65.

——. 1979. *Patterns in Office-Holding 366–49 B.C.* Collection Latomus 161. Brussels.

——. 1985. *The Practice of Politics at Rome 366–167 B.C.* Collection Latomus 188. Brussels.

Devoto, G. 1974. *Le Tavole di Gubbio*. Florence.

——. 1978. *The Languages of Italy*. Translated by V. Louise Katainen. Chicago.

Dohrn, T. 1972. *Die ficoronische Ciste*. Berlin.

Dorey, T.A., ed. 1971. *Livy*. London and Toronto.

Drachmann, A.B. 1912. *Diodors römische Annalen bis 302 a. Chr., samt dem Ineditum Vaticanum*. Bonn.

Drews, R.C. 1972. "The First Tyrants in Greece." *Historia* 21: 129–44.

——. 1981. "The Coming of the City to Central Italy." *AJAH* 6: 133–65.

——. 1988a, "Pontiffs, Prodigies, and the Disappearance of the *Annales Maximi*." *CP* 83: 289–99.

——. 1988b. *The Coming of the Greeks: Indo-European Conquests in the Aegean and the Near East*. Princeton.

——. 1992. "Herodotus 1.94, the Drought ca.1200 B.C., and the Origin of the Etruscans." *Historia* 41: 14–39.

——. 1993. *The End of the Bronze Age: Changes in Warfare and the Catastrophe ca.1200 B.C.* Princeton.

Drummond, A. 1978a. "The Dictator Years." *Historia* 27: 550–72.

——. 1978b. "Some Observations on the Order of Consuls' Names." *Athenaeum* n.s. 56: 80–108.

——. 1980. "Consular Tribunes in Livy and Diodorus." *Athenaeum* n.s. 58: 57–72.

Dumézil, G. 1966. *Archaic Roman Religion*. 2 vols. Translated by Philip Krapp. Chicago.

——. 1979. *Marriages Indo-Européens à Rome*. Paris.

——. 1980. *Camillus: A Study of Indo-European Religion as Roman History*. Translated by A. Aronowicz and J. Bryson. Berkeley.

Dunbabin, T.J. 1948. *The Western Greeks: The History of Sicily and South Italy from the Foundation of the Greek Colonies to 480 B.C.* Oxford.

Dunkle, J.R. 1967. "The Greek Tyrant and Roman Political Invective of the Late Republic." *TAPA* 98: 151–71.

——. 1971. "The Rhetorical Tyrant in Roman Historiography: Sallust, Livy, and Tacitus." *CW* 65: 12–20.

Eckstein, A.M. 1982. "Human Sacrifice and Fear of Military Disaster in Republican Rome." *AJAH* 7: 69–95.

Eder, W., ed. 1990. *Staat und Staatlichkeit in der frühen römischen Republik*. Stuttgart.

Elliott, J. 1995. "The Etruscan Wolfman in Myth and Ritual." *Etruscan Studies* 2: 17–33.

Enea nel Lazio: Archeologia e Mito. 1981. Exhibition Catalogue. Rome.

Ennew, J. 1981. *Debt Bondage, A Survey.* Anti-Slavery Society Human Rights Series, Report #4. London.

Evans, E. C. 1939. *The Cults of the Sabine Territory.* Papers and Monographs of the American Academy in Rome 11. New York.

Faustoferri, A., and J. Lloyd. 1998. "Monte Pallano: A Samnite Fortified Centre, and its Hinterland." *JRA* 11: 5–22.

Ferenczy, E. 1970. "The Career of Appius Claudius Caecus after the Censorship." *Acta Antiqua Academiae Scientiarum Hungaricae* 18: 71–103.

Finley, M. I. 1971. *The Ancestral Constitution, An Inaugural Lecture.* London.

———. 1981. *Economy and Society in Ancient Greece.* London.

Fiske, G. C. 1902. "The Politics of the Patrician Claudii." *HSCP* 13: 1–59.

Fitzmyer, J. A. 1966. "The Phoenician Inscription from Pyrgi." *Journal of the American Oriental Society* 86: 285–97.

Flower, H. I. 1995. "*Fabulae Praetextae* in Context: When Were Plays on Contemporary Subjects Performed in Republican Rome?" *CQ* n.s. 45: 170–90.

———. 1996. *Ancestor Masks and Aristocratic Power in Roman Culture.* Oxford.

Foresti, L. A. 1979. "Zur Zeremonie der Nagelschlagung in Rom und in Etrurien." *AJAH* 4: 144–56.

Forsén, B. 1991. *Lex Licinia Sextia de modo Agrorum: Fiction or Reality?* Helsinki.

Forsythe, G. 1990. "Some Notes on the History of Cassius Hemina." *Phoenix* 44: 326–44.

———. 1994. *The Historian L. Calpurnius Piso Frugi and the Roman Annalistic Tradition.* Lanham MD.

———. 1996. "*Ubi Tu Gaius, Ego Gaia:* New Light on an Old Roman Legal Saw." *Historia* 45: 240–41.

———. 1999. *Livy and Early Rome: A Study in Historical Method and Judgment.* Historia Einzelschriften 132. Stuttgart.

———. 2000. "The Roman Historians of the Second Century B.C." In *The Roman Middle Republic: Politics, Religion, and Historiography c.400–133 B.C.* Acta Instituti Romani Finlandiae, vol. 23. Edited by C. Bruun. Rome.

Fowler, W. W. 1899. *The Roman Festivals of the Period of the Republic, An Introduction to the Study of the Religion of the Romans.* Oxford.

———. 1911. *The Religious Experience of the Roman People.* Oxford.

———. 1912. "Mundus Patet 24th August, 5th October, 8th November." *JRS* 2: 25–33.

Fox, M. 1996. *Roman Historical Myths: The Regal Period in Augustan Literature.* Oxford.

Fraccaro, P. 1957. "The History of Rome in the Regal Period." *JRS* 47: 59–65.

Frank, T. 1924. *Roman Buildings of the Republic: An Attempt to Date Them from their Materials.* Papers and Monographs of the American Academy in Rome 3. Rome.

———, ed. 1933. *An Economic Survey of Ancient Rome.* Vol. 1, *Rome and Italy of the Republic.* Baltimore.

Frazer, J. G. 1929. *Publii Ovidii Nasonis Fastorum Libri Sex, The Fasti of Ovid.* 5 vols. Edited with translation and commentary. London.

Frederiksen, M. W. 1968. "Campanian Cavalry: A Question of Origins." *DdA* 2: 3–31.

————. 1984. *Campania*. London.

Frier, B.W. 1979. *Libri Annales Pontificum Maximorum, The Origins of the Annalistic Tradition*. Papers and Monographs of the American Academy in Rome 27. Rome.

Friezer, E. 1959. "*Interregnum* and *Patrum Auctoritas*." *Mnemosyne*, 4th ser., 12: 301–29.

Gabba, E. 1964. "Studi su Dionigi d'Alicarnasso III: La Proposta di Legge agraria di Spurio Cassio." *Athenaeum* n.s. 42: 29–41.

————. 1991. *Dionysius and the History of Archaic Rome*. Berkeley.

Galinsky, G.K. 1969. *Aeneas, Sicily, and Rome*. Princeton.

Garoufalias, P. 1979. *Pyrrhus, King of Epirus*. London.

Garzetti, A. 1947. "Appio Claudio Cieco nella storia politica del suo tempo." *Athenaeum* n.s. 25: 175–224.

Gelzer, M. 1912. *Die Nobilität der römischen Republik*. Leipzig.

————. 1969. *The Roman Nobility*. Translated by R. Seager. London.

Gentili, B. 1975. "Storiografia Greca e storiografia Romana arcaica ." In *Atti del Convegno: Gli Storiografi Latini Tramandati in Frammenti*. Studi Urbinati di Storia, Filosofiia, e Letteratura 49. Urbino.

Gierow, P.G. 1964–66. *The Iron Age Culture of Latium*. 2 vols. Lund.

Ginge, B. 1993. "Votive Deposits in Italy: New Perspectives on Old Finds." *JRA* 6: 285–88.

Giovannini, A. 1985. "*Auctoritas Patrum*." *MH* 42: 28–36.

Gjerstad, E. 1953–73. *Early Rome*. 6 vols. Lund.

Goody, J.R. 1986. *The Logic of Writing and the Organization of Society*. Cambridge.

Gordon, A.E. 1975. "Notes on the Duenos Vase Inscription in Berlin." *CSCA* 8: 53–72.

————. 1983. *Illustrated Introduction to Latin Epigraphy*. Berkeley.

Grandazzi, A. 1991. *La Fondation de Rome*. Paris.

————. 1997. *The Foundation of Rome: Myth and History*. Translated by J.M. Todd. Ithaca.

Grande Roma dei Tarquini. 1990. Exhibition Catalogue. Rome.

Grieve, L.J. 1982. "The Etymology of *Municeps*." *Latomus* 41: 771–72.

————. 1983. "*Tabulae Caeritum*." In *Studies in Latin Literature and Roman History*. Collection Latomus 180. Edited by C. Deroux III. Brussels.

Gruen, E.S. 1974. *The Last Generation of the Roman Republic*. Berkeley.

————. 1992. *Culture and National Identity in Republican Rome*. Ithaca.

Gutberlet, D. 1985. *Die erste Dekade des Livius als Quelle zur gracchischen und sullanischen Zeit*. Beiträge zur Altertumswissenschaft 4. Hildesheim.

Hackens, T., ed. 1992. *The Age of Pyrrhus: Archaeology, History and Culture in Early Hellenistic Greece and Italy*. Archaeologia Transatlantica XI. Louvain.

Hadzsits, G.D. 1936. "The *Vera Historia* of the Palatine *Ficus Ruminalis*." *CP* 31: 305–19.

Haeberlin, E.J. 1910. *Aes Grave: Das Schwergeld Roms*. 2 vols. Frankfurt.

Hall, J.F., ed. 1997. *Etruscan Italy: Etruscan Influences on the Civilizations of Italy from Antiquity to the Modern Era*. Provo UT.

Hallett, J.P. 1970. "Over Troubled Waters: The Meaning of the Title *Pontifex*." *TAPA* 101: 219–28.

Harden, D.B. 1963. *The Phoenicians*. London.

Harding, A. E., and H. Hughes-Brock. 1974. "Amber in the Mycenaean World." *BSA* 69: 144–72.

———. 1984. *The Mycenaeans and Europe.* London.

Harl, K. W. 1996. *Coinage in the Roman Economy, 300 B.C. to A.D. 700.* Baltimore.

Harmon, D. P. 1978a. "The Public Festivals of Rome." *ANRW* II. 16.2: 1440–68.

———. 1978b. "The Family Festivals of Rome." *ANRW* II. 16.2: 1592–1603.

Harris, W. V. 1971. *Rome in Etruria and Umbria.* Oxford.

———. 1979. *War and Imperialism in Republican Rome.* Oxford.

———. 1989. *Ancient Literacy.* Cambridge MA.

Havelock, E. A. 1982. *The Literate Revolution in Greece and its Cultural Consequences.* Princeton.

Healey, J. F. 1990. *The Early Alphabet.* Reading the Past, Vol.6. Berkeley.

Hencken, H. 1968. *Tarquinia and Etruscan Origins.* London.

Henzen, G. 1874. *Fratres Arvales: Acta Fratrum Arvalium Quae Supersunt.* Berlin.

Herm, G. 1975. *The Phoenicians: The Purple Empire of the Ancient World.* Translated by C. Hillier. London.

Heurgon, J. 1942. *Recherches sur l'Histoire, la Religion, et la Civilisation de Capoue préromaine.* Paris.

———. 1957. *Trois Études sur le Ver Sacrum.* Collection Latomus 26. Brussels.

———. 1964. *Daily Life of the Etruscans.* Translated by J. Kirkup. New York.

———. 1966. "The Inscriptions of Pyrgi." *JRS* 56: 1–15.

———. 1973. *The Rise of Rome to 264 B.C.* Translated by P. J. Cuff. Berkeley.

Hobsbawm, E., and T. Ranger , eds. 1983. *The Invention of Tradition.* Cambridge.

Hölkeskamp, K. J. 1987. *Die Entstehung der Nobilität: Studien zur sozialen und politischen Geschichte der römischen Republik im 4. Jhdt. v. Chr.* Wiesbaden.

———. 1988a. "Das *Plebiscitum Ogulnium de Sacerdotibus:* Überlegungen zu Authentizität und Interpretation der livianischen Überlieferung im Jahre 300 v. Chr." *RM* 131: 51–67.

———. 1988b. "Die Entstehung der Nobilität und der Funktionswandel des Volkstribunats: die historische Bedeutung der *Lex Hortensia de plebiscitis.*" *Archiv für Kulturgeschichte* 70: 271–312.

———. 1992. "Written Law in Archaic Greece." *PCPS* n.s. 38: 87–117.

———. 1993. "Conquest, Competition, and Consensus: Roman Expansion in Italy and the Rise of the *Nobilitas.*" *Historia* 42: 12–39.

Holland, L. A. 1961. *Janus and the Bridge.* Papers and Monographs of the American Academy in Rome 21. Rome.

Holleman, A. W. J. 1976. "Myth and Historiography: The Tale of the 306 Fabii." *Numen* 23: 210–18.

Holliday, P. J. 1994. "Celtomachia: The Representation of Battles with Gauls on Etruscan Funerary Urns." *Etruscan Studies* 1: 23–45.

Holloway, R. R. 1981. *Italy and the Aegean 3000–700 B.C.* Louvain.

———. 1994. *The Archaeology of Early Rome and Latium.* London.

Hölscher, T. 1978. "Die Anfänge römischer Repräsentazionskunst." *MDAI* 85: 315–57.

Hopkins, K. 1978. *Conquerors and Slaves: Sociological Studies in Roman History.* Vol. 1. Cambridge.

———. 1983. *Death and Renewal: Sociological Studies in Roman History.* Vol. 2. Cambridge.

Horsfall, N.M. 1979. "Some Problems in the Aeneas Legend." *CQ* n.s. 29: 371–90.

Howard, A.A. 1906. "Valerius Antias and Livy." *HSCP* 17: 161–82.

Hoyos, B.D. 1984. "The Roman-Punic Pact of 279 B.C.: Its Problems and Purpose." *Historia* 33: 402–39.

Humbert, M. 1978. *Municipium et Civitas sine Suffragio.* Collection de l'École Française de Rome 36. Rome.

Jacoby, F. 1950. *Die Fragmente der griechischen Historiker.* Vol. III.B. Leiden.

———. 1958: *Die Fragmente der griechischen Historiker.* Vol. III.C. Leiden.

Jaher, F.C., ed. 1975. *The Rich, The Well Born, and the Powerful: Elites and Upper Classes in History.* Secaucus NJ.

James, S. 1993. *The World of the Celts.* London.

Jehasse, J. and L. 1973. *La Nécropole préromaine d'Aléria (1960–1968) avec une Étude des Grafites par Jacques Heurgon.* Paris.

Kelly, J.M. 1966. *Roman Litigation.* Oxford.

Kenyon, F.G. 1951. *Books and Readers in Ancient Greece and Rome.* 2nd ed. Oxford.

Kierdorf, W. 1980. "Catos *Origines* und die Anfänge der römischen Geschichtsschreibung." *Chiron* 10: 205–24.

Klein, J.J. 1972. "A Greek Metal-Working Quarter: Eighth-Century Excavations on Ischia." *Expedition* 14: 34–39.

Klotz, A. 1937. "Diodors römische Annalen." *RM* 86: 206–23.

Kraus, C.S. 1991. "Initium Turbandi Omnia A Femina Ortum Est: Fabia Minor and the Election of 367 B.C." *Phoenix* 45: 314–25.

———. 1994. *Livy: Ab Urbe Condita, Book VI.* Cambridge.

Lapis Satricanus. 1980. Archeologiche Studien van het Nederlands Instituut te Rome, Scripta Minora V. The Hague.

La Rocca, E. 1977. "Note sulle Importazioni Greche in Territorio Laziale nell' VIII Secolo a.C." *PdP* 32: 375–97.

———. 1984. "Fabio o Fannio: L'Affresco medio-repubblicano del'Esquilino come riflesso dell' Arte 'rappresentativa' e come Espressione di Mobilità sociale." *DdA*, 2nd ser., 3a: 31–53.

Last, H. 1945. "The Servian Reforms." *JRS* 35: 30–48.

Latte, K. 1960. *Römische Religionsgeschichte.* Munich.

Lefkowitz, M.R. 1959. "Pyrrhus' Negotiations with the Romans from 280 to 278 B.C." *HSCP* 64: 147–76.

Lévèque, P. 1957. *Pyrrhos.* Paris.

Levi, M.A. 1983. "Roma arcaica e il connubio fra plebei e patrizi." *PdP* 38: 241–59.

Lincoln, B. 1991. *Death, War, and Sacrifice: Studies in Ideology and Practice.* Chicago.

Linderski, J. 1986. "The Augural Law." *ANRW* II. 16.3: 2146–2312.

———. 1995. *Roman Questions: Selected Papers 1958–1993.* Heidelberger althistorische Beiträge und epigraphische Studien 20. Stuttgart.

———, ed. 1996. *Imperium Sine Fine: T. Robert S. Broughton and the Roman Republic.* Historia Einzelschriften 105. Stuttgart.

Lintott, A.W. 1970. "The Tradition of Violence in the Annals of the Early Roman Republic." *Historia* 19: 12–29.

Lomas, K. 1993. *Rome and the Western Greeks 350 B.C.–A.D. 200: Conquest and Acculturation in Southern Italy.* London and New York.

Lübtow, U. von. 1952. "Die *Lex curiata de Imperio.*" *ZSS rom. Abt.* 69: 154–71.

Luce, T. J. 1965. "The Dating of Livy's First Decade." *TAPA* 96: 209–40.

———. 1977. *Livy, The Composition of His History.* Princeton.

MacBain, B. 1980. "Appius Claudius Caecus and the Via Appia." *CQ* n.s. 30: 356–72.

MacKendrick, P. 1983. *The Mute Stones Speak: The Story of Archaeology in Italy.* 2nd ed. New York.

Maddin, R., T.S. Wheeler, and J.D. Muhly. 1977. "Tin in the Ancient Near East: Old Questions and New Finds." *Expedition* 19: 35–47.

Maddox, G. 1983. "The Economic Causes of the *Lex Hortensia.*" *Latomus* 42: 277–86.

———. 1984. "The Binding Plebiscite." In *Sodalitas: Scritti in onore di Antonio Guarino.* Vol. 1. Edited by V. Giuffre. Naples.

Magdelain, A. 1964a. "Note sur la Loi curiate et les Auspices des Magistrats." *Revue historique de Droit français et étranger* 42: 198–203.

———. 1964b. "*Auspicia ad Patres Redeunt.*" In *Hommages à Jean Bayet.* Collection Latomus 70. Edited by M. Renard and R. Schilling. Brussels.

Manganaro, G. 1974. "Una biblioteca stoica nel ginnasio di Tauromenion e il *P. Oxy.* 1241." *PdP* 29: 389–409.

Mazzarino, S. 1945. *Dalla Monarchia allo Stato Repubblicano: Ricerche di Storia Romana Arcaica.* Catania.

———. 1971–72. "Sul Tribunato della Plebe nella Storiografia Romana." *Helikon* 11–12: 99–119.

McDonnell, M. 1997. "Review of T. J. Cornell, *The Beginnings of Rome. . . .*" *CP* 92: 202–7.

Meiggs, R. 1960. *Roman Ostia.* Oxford.

———, and D. Lewis. 1975. *A Selection of Greek Historical Inscriptions to the End of the Fifth Century B.C.* Oxford.

Merrill, E.T. 1924. "The Roman Calendar and the Regifugium." *CP* 19: 20–39.

Mertens, J. 1981. *Alba Fucens.* Brussels.

Messerschmidt, F., and A. von Gerkan. 1930. *Nekropolen von Vulci. JDAI* 12. Berlin.

Meyer, E. 1895. "Der Ursprung des Tribunats und die Gemeinde der vier *Tribus.*" *Hermes* 30: 1–24.

Meyer, J.C. 1980. "Roman History in the Light of the Import of Attic Vases to Rome and South Etruria in the 6th and 5th Centuries B.C." *Analecta Romana Instituti Danici* 9: 47–68.

———. 1983. *Pre-Republican Rome: An Analysis of the Cultural and Chronological Relations 1000–500 B.C.* Analecta Romana Instituti Danici Supplementum XI. Odense.

Michels, A.K. 1949. "The Calendar of Numa and the Pre-Julian Calendar." *TAPA* 80: 320–46.

———. 1953. "The Topography and Interpretation of the Lupercalia." *TAPA* 84: 35–59.

———. 1967. *The Calendar of the Roman Republic.* Princeton.

Millar, F. 1998. *The Crowd in Rome in the Late Republic.* Ann Arbor.

Mitchell, R.E. 1966. "A New Chronology for the Romano-Campanian Coins." *Numismatic Chronicle,* 7th ser., 6: 65–70.

———. 1969. "The Fourth Century Origin of the Roman Didrachms." *Museum Notes* 15: 41–71.

————. 1971. "Roman-Carthaginian Treaties 306 and 279/8 B.C." *Historia* 20: 633–55.

————. 1984. "Historical Development in Livy." In *Classical Texts and Their Traditions, Studies in Honor of C. R. Trahman*. Edited by D. F. Bright and E. S. Ramage. Chico CA.

————. 1990. *Patricians and Plebeians, The Origin of the Roman State*. Ithaca.

————. 1996. "*Ager Publicus*, Public Property and Private Wealth during the Roman Republic." In *Privatization in the Ancient Near East and Classical World*. Edited by M. Hudson and B. A. Levine. Cambridge MA.

Momigliano, A. 1957. "Perizonius, Niebuhr, and the Character of Early Roman Tradition." *JRS* 47: 104–14.

————. 1958. "Some Observations on the *Origo Gentis Romanae*." *JRS* 48: 56–73.

————. 1969. "The Origins of the Roman Republic." In *Interpretation: Theory and Practice*. Edited by C. S. Singleton. Baltimore.

————. 1977. "Athens in the Third Century B.C. and the Discovery of Rome in the Histories of Timaeus of Tauromenium." In *Essays in Ancient and Modern Historiography*. Middletown CT.

————, and A. Schiavone, eds. 1988. *Storia di Roma*. Vol. 1, *Roma in Italia*. Torino.

Mommsen, Th. 1864. "Die patricischen Claudier." In *Römische Forschungen*. Vol. 2. Berlin.

————. 1871. "Sp. Cassius, M. Manlius, Sp. Maelius, die drei Demagogen des 3 und 4 Jahrhunderts der römischen Republik." *Hermes* 5: 228–80.

————. 1879. "Fabius und Diodor." In *Römische Forschungen*. Vol. 1. Berlin.

Morel, J. P. 1969. "Études de céramique campanienne: L'Atelier des petites estampilles." *MEFR* 81: 59–117.

Morgan, M. G. 1972. "The Defeat of L. Metellus Denter at Arretium." *CQ* n.s. 22: 309–25.

Morris, I. 1992. *Death-Ritual and Social Structure in Classical Antiquity*. Cambridge.

Moscati, S. 1968. *The World of the Phoenicians*. Translated by A. Hamilton. New York.

————, ed. 1988. *The Phoenicians*. Translated by P. Barras et al. New York.

Müller, V. 1943. "The Shrine of Janus Geminus in Rome." *AJA* 47: 437–40.

Münzer, F. 1905. "Atticus als Geschichtsschreiber." *Hermes* 40: 50–100.

————. 1920. *Römische Adelsparteien und Adelsfamilien*. Stuttgart.

Nagy, B. 1992. "The *Argei* Puzzle." *AJAH* 10: 1–27.

Nash, E. 1968. *Pictorial Dictionary of Ancient Rome*. 2nd ed. 2 vols. New York.

Nestle, W. 1927. "Die Fabel des Menenius Agrippa." *Klio* 21: 350–60.

Nicholls, J. J. 1967. "The Content of the *Lex Curiata*." *AJP* 88: 257–78.

Nicolet, C. 1961. "Appius et le double Forum de Capoue." *Latomus* 20: 683–720.

————. 1980. *The World of the Citizen in Republican Rome*. Translated by P. S. Falla. Berkeley.

Nielsen, I., and C. Gronne. 1990. "The Forum Paving and the Temple of Castor and Pollux, and Fragments of Architectural Terracottas from the First Temple of Castor and Pollux on the Forum Romanum." *Analecta Romana Instituti Danici* 19: 89–117.

Nougayrol, J. 1955. "Les Rapports des Haruspicines étrusque et assyro-babylonienne, et le Foie d'argile de Falerii Veteres (Villa Giulia 3786)." *CRAIBL* 509–19.

Oakley, S. P. 1995. *The Hill-Forts of the Samnites*. British School at Rome Archaeological Monograph 10. London.

———. 1997. *A Commentary on Livy Books VI-X*. Vol. 1, *Introduction and Book VI*. Oxford.

———. 1998. *A Commentary on Livy Books VI-X*. Vol. 2, *Books VII-VIII*. Oxford.

Ogilvie, R.M. 1965. *A Commentary on Livy Books 1-5*. Reprinted with additions and corrections 1970. Oxford.

———. 1976. *Early Rome and the Etruscans*. Glasgow.

Olshausen, E. 1978. "Über die römischen Ackerbrüder: Geschichte eines Kultes." *ANRW* II. 16.1: 820–32.

Origines de la République Romaine: Entretiens sur l'Antiquité Classique. 1967. Fondation Hardt 13. Vandoeuvres-Geneva.

Pais, E. 1906. *Ancient Legends of Roman History*. London.

Pallottino, M., et al. 1964. "Scavi nel Santuario Etrusco di Pyrgi." *Archeologia Classica* 16: 49–117.

———. 1968. *Testimonia Linguae Etruscae*. 2 vols. Florence.

———. 1969. "L'Ermeneutica Etrusca." *Studi Etruschi*, 2nd ser. 37: 79–92.

———. 1975. *The Etruscans*. Translated by J. Cremona with a new introduction by D. Ridgway. Bloomington IN.

———. 1991. *A History of Earliest Italy*. Ann Arbor.

Palmer, L.R. 1954. *The Latin Language*. London.

Palmer, R.E.A. 1969. *The King and the Comitium*. Historia Einzelschriften 11. Wiesbaden.

———. 1970. *The Archaic Community of the Romans*. Cambridge.

———. 1974. *Roman Religion and Roman Empire*. Philadelphia.

———. 1990a. "A New Fragment of Livy Throws Light on the Roman Postumii and Latin Gabii." *Athenaeum* n.s. 78: 5–18.

———. 1990b. "Cults of Hercules, Apollo Caelispex and Fortuna in and around the Roman Cattle Market." *JRA* 3: 234–44.

———. 1997. *Rome and Carthage at Peace*. Historia Einzelschriften 113. Stuttgart.

Parke, H.W. 1988. *Sibyls and Sibylline Prophecy in Classical Antiquity*. London and New York.

Pascal, C.B. 1981. "October Horse." *HSCP* 85: 261–91.

Pasoli, A. 1950. *Acta Fratrum Arvalium*. Bologna.

Pearson, L. 1987. *The Greek Historians of the West: Timaeus and his Predecessors*. Atlanta.

Perl, G. 1957. *Kritische Untersuchungen zu Diodors römischer Jahrzählung*. Berlin.

Perlwitz, O. 1992. *T. Pomponius Atticus: Untersuchungen zur Person eines einflussreichen Ritters in der ausgehenden römischen Republik*. Stuttgart.

Peter, H. 1914. *Historicorum Romanorum Reliquiae*. 2nd ed. Vol. 2. Leipzig.

Peterson, R.M. 1919. *The Cults of Campania*. Papers and Monographs of the American Academy in Rome 1. Rome.

Phillips, E.J. 1972. "Roman Politics During the Second Samnite War." *Athenaeum* n.s. 50: 337–56.

Phillips, J.E. 1982. "Current Research in Livy's First Decade 1959–1979." *ANRW* II. 30.2: 998–1057.

Pichlmayr, Fr. 1970. *Sexti Aurelii Victoris Liber De Caesaribus*. Leipzig.

Piganiol, A. 1962. "Les Origines d'Hercule." In *Hommages à Albert Grenier*. Collection Latomus 58. Edited by M. Renard. Brussels.

Pinsent, J. 1975. *Military Tribunes and Plebeian Consuls: The Fasti from 444 V. to 342 V.* Historia Einzelschriften 3. Wiesbaden.

Pinza, G. 1905. *Monumenti Primitivi di Roma e del Lazio antico.* Monumenti Antichi 15. Rome.

Platner, S.B., and T. Ashby. 1929. *A Topographical Dictionary of Ancient Rome.* London.

Poccetti, P. 1979. *Nuovi Documenti Italici à Complemento del Manuale di E. Vetter.* Pisa.

Posner, E. 1972. *Archives in the Ancient World.* Cambridge MA.

Potter, T.W. 1979. *The Changing Landscape of South Etruria.* London.

Poultney, J.W. 1959. *The Bronze Tables of Iguvium.* Baltimore.

Powell, B.B. 1991. *Homer and the Origin of the Greek Alphabet.* Cambridge.

Pritchard, J.B., ed. 1969. *Ancient Near Eastern Texts Relating to the Old Testament.* Princeton.

Pritchett, W.K. 1975. *Dionysius of Halicarnassus, On Thucydides.* Berkeley.

Prosdocimi, A.L., ed. 1978. *Lingue e Dialetti dell' Italia Antica.* Popoli e Civiltà dell' Italia Antica 6. Rome.

Purcell, N. 1989. "Rediscovering the Roman Forum." *JRA* 2: 156–66.

Raaflaub, K.A., ed. 1986. *Social Struggles in Archaic Rome, New Perspectives on the Conflict of the Orders.* Berkeley.

Radke, G. 1979. *Die Götter Altitaliens.* Münster.

Rankin, H.D. 1987. *Celts and the Classical World.* London and Portland OR.

Ranouil, P.C. 1975. *Recherches sur le Patriciat: 509–366 av. J.-C.* Paris.

Rathje, A. 1983. "A Banquet Service from the Latin City of Ficana." *Analecta Romana Instituti Danici* 12: 7–29.

———. 1990. "The Adoption of the Homeric Banquet in Central Italy in the Orientalizing Period." In *Sympotica: A Symposium on the Symposion.* Edited by O. Murray. Oxford.

Rawson, E. 1971a. "Prodigy Lists and the Use of the *Annales Maximi*." *CQ* n.s. 21: 158–69.

———. 1971b. "The Literary Sources for the Pre-Marian Army." *PBSR* 39: 13–31.

———. 1976. "The First Latin Annalists." *Latomus* 35: 689–717.

Rebuffat, M.R. 1966. "Les Phéniciens à Rome." *MEFR* 78: 7–48.

Redman, C.L. 1978. *The Rise of Civilization from Early Farmers to Urban Society in the Ancient Near East.* San Francisco.

Renfrew, C. 1987. *Archaeology and Language: The Puzzle of Indo-European Origins.* Cambridge.

Rich, J.W., and G. Shipley, eds. 1993. *War and Society in the Roman World.* London and New York.

Richard, J.C. 1978. *Les Origines de la Plèbe Romaine: Essai sur la Formation du Dualisme patricio-plébéien.* Paris.

———. 1979. "Sur le plebiscite *ut liceret consules ambos plebeios creari* (Tite-Live VII.42.2)." *Historia* 28: 65–75.

———. 1988. "Historiographie et histoire: L'Expédition des Fabii à la Crémère." *Latomus* 47: 526–53.

———. 1989. "L'Affaire du Crémère: Recherches sur l'évolution et le sens de la tradition." *Latomus* 48: 312–25.

———. 1990. "Réflexions sur le Tribunat consulaire." *MEFR* 102: 767–99.

Richardson, L., Jr. 1992. *A New Topographical Dictionary of Ancient Rome.* Baltimore.

Ridgway, D. 1973–74. "Archaeology in Central Italy and Etruria 1968–1973." *Archaeological Reports* 20: 42–59.

————, and F. R. S. Ridgway, eds. 1979. *Italy Before the Romans: The Iron Age, Oriental- izing and Etruscan Periods.* London and New York.

————. 1992. *The First Western Greeks.* Cambridge.

Ridley, R. T. 1968. "Notes on the Establishment of the Tribunate of the Plebs." *Latomus* 27: 535–54.

————. 1975. "The Enigma of Servius Tullius." *Klio* 57: 147–77.

————. 1979. "The Origin of the Roman Dictatorship: An Overlooked Opinion." *RM* 122: 303–9.

————. 1980a. "*Fastenkritik*: A Stocktaking." *Athenaeum* n.s. 58: 264–98.

————. 1980b. "Livy and the *Concilium Plebis*." *Klio* 62: 337–54.

————. 1983. "*Falsi Triumphi, Plures Consulatus*." *Latomus* 42: 372–82.

————. 1986. "The 'Consular Tribunate': The Testimony of Livy." *Klio* 68: 444–65.

Roberts, D. 1993. "The Iceman." *National Geographic* 183.6: 36–67.

Roma Medio-Repubblicana: Aspetti Culturali di Roma e del Lazio nei Secoli IV e III a.C. 1973. Exhibition Catalogue. Rome.

Ronconi, A. 1964. "*Malum Carmen* e *Malus Poeta*." In *Synteleia Vincenzo Arangio-Ruiz*, vol. 2. Edited by J. Napoli. Naples.

Rose, H. J. 1924. *The Roman Questions of Plutarch.* Oxford.

————. 1933. "The Cult of Volkanus at Rome." *JRS* 23: 46–63.

————. 1934. "Two Roman Rites." *CQ* 28: 156–58.

————. 1944. "Manes Exite Paterni." *University of California Publications in Classical Philology* 12: 89–93.

Rosenstein, N. 1986. "*Imperatores Victi:* The Case of C. Hostilius Mancinus." *CA* 5: 230–52.

Rosenzweig, I. 1937. *Ritual and Cults in Pre-Roman Iguvium.* London.

Rowland, R. J., Jr. 1983. "Rome's Earliest Imperialism." *Latomus* 42: 749–62.

Ruoff-Väänänen, E. 1972. "The Roman Public *Prodigia* and the *Ager Romanus*." *Arctos* n.s. 7: 139–62.

Rüpke, J. 1993. "Livius, Priesternamen, und die *Annales Maximi*." *Klio* 75: 155–79.

————. 1995. *Kalender und Öffentlichkeit: die Geschichte der Repräsentation und religiösen Qualifikation von Zeit in Rom.* Berlin.

Rutter, N. K. 1971. "The Campanian Chronology in the Fifth Century B.C." *CQ* n.s. 21: 55–61.

Ryberg, I. S. 1940. *An Archaeological Record of Rome from the Seventh to the Second Century B.C.* Philadelphia.

Sachs, A. 1948. "A Classification of Babylonian Astronomical Tablets of the Seleucid Period." *JCS* 2: 271–90.

Sacks, K. S. 1983. "Historiography in the Rhetorical Works of Dionysius of Halicar- nassus." *Athenaeum* n.s. 61: 65–87.

Säflund, G. 1930. *Le Mura di Roma Repubblicana.* Lund.

Salmon, E. T. 1930. "Historical Elements in the Story of Coriolanus." *CQ* 24: 96–101.

————. 1935. "Rome's Battles with Etruscans and Gauls in 284–282 B.C." *CP* 35:23–31.

————. 1967. *Samnium and the Samnites.* Cambridge.

————. 1969. *Roman Colonization Under the Republic.* London.

————. 1982. *The Making of Roman Italy.* London.

Santini, C. 1995. *I Frammenti di L. Cassio Emina: Introduzione, Testo, Traduzione e Commento.* Testi e Studi di Cultura Classica 13. Pisa.

Scardigli, B. 1991. *I Trattati Romano-Cartaginesi*. Pisa.

Scheid, J. 1990. *Romulus et ses Frères: Le Collège des Frères arvales, Modèle du Culte public dans la Rome des Empereurs*. Paris.

Scholz, U.W. 1989. "Zu L. Cassius Hemina." *Hermes* 117: 167–81.

Schuller, W., ed. 1993. *Livius: Aspekte seines Werkes*. Xenia: Konstanzer althistorische Vorträge und Forschungen 31. Constance.

Scullard, H.H. 1967. *The Etruscan Cities and Rome*. London.

———. 1980. *A History of the Roman World from 753 to 146 B.C.* 4th ed. London.

———. 1981. *Festivals and Ceremonies of the Roman Republic*. Ithaca.

Sealey, R. 1959. "Consular Tribunes Once More." *Latomus* 18: 521–30.

Shackleton Bailey, D.R. 1986. "*Nobiles* and *Novi* Reconsidered." *AJP* 107: 255–60.

Sherwin-White, A.N. 1973. *The Roman Citizenship*. 2nd ed. Oxford.

Skutsch, O. 1953. "The Fall of the Capitol." *JRS* 43: 77–78.

———. 1985. *The Annals of Quintus Ennius*. Oxford.

Slagter, M. 1993. Transitio Ad Plebem: The Exchange of Patrician for Plebeian Status. Ph.D. diss., Bryn Mawr College.

Smith, C.J. 1996. *Early Rome and Latium: Economy and Society C. 1000 to 500 B.C.* Oxford.

Sohlberg, D. 1991. "Militärtribunen und verwandte Probleme der frühen römischen Republik." *Historia* 40: 257–74.

Solin, H. 1983. "Varia Onomastica V." *ZPE* 51: 180–82.

Sommella Mura, A. 1981. "Il Gruppo di Eracle ed Atena." *PdP* 36: 59–64.

Spindler, K. 1994. *The Man in the Ice*. New York.

Spivey, N.J., and S. Stoddart. 1990. *Etruscan Italy: An Archaeological History*. London.

Stadter, P.A. 1972. "The Structure of Livy's History." *Historia* 21: 287–307.

Starr, C.G. 1980. *The Beginnings of Imperial Rome: Rome in the Mid-Republic*. Ann Arbor.

Staveley, E.S. 1953. "The Significance of the Consular Tribunate." *JRS* 43: 30–46.

———. 1954–55. "The Conduct of Elections during an *Interregnum*." *Historia* 3: 193–211.

———. 1955. "Tribal Legislation before the *Lex Hortensia*." *Athenaeum* n.s. 33: 3–31.

———. 1956. "The Constitution of the Roman Republic 1940–1954." *Historia* 5: 74–119.

———. 1959. "The Political Aims of Appius Claudius Caecus." *Historia* 8: 410–33.

———. 1972. *Greek and Roman Voting and Elections*. London and Ithaca.

———. 1983. "The Nature and Aims of the Patriciate." *Historia* 32: 24–57.

Steinby, E.M., ed. 1993–96. *Lexicon Topographicum Urbis Romae*. 3 vols. Rome.

Steingräber, S. 1985. *Etruscan Painting: Catalogue Raisonné of Etruscan Wall Paintings*. New York.

Stevenson, R.B.K. 1947. "The Neolithic Cultures of South-East Italy." *Proceedings of the Prehistoric Society* 13: 85–100.

Stewart, R. 1998. *Public Office in Early Rome: Ritual Procedure and Political Practice*. Ann Arbor.

Sumner, G.V. 1970. "The Legion and the Centuriate Organization." *JRS* 60: 67–78.

Swaddling, J., ed. 1986. *Italian Iron Age Artifacts in the British Museum*. Oxford.

Täubler, E. 1921. *Untersuchungen zur Geschichte des Dezemvirats und der zwölf Tafeln*. Berlin.

Taylor, L.R. 1923. *Local Cults in Etruria*. Papers and Monographs of the American Academy in Rome 2. Rome.

————. 1960. *The Voting Districts of the Roman Republic.* Papers and Monographs of the American Academy in Rome 20. Rome.

————. 1966. *Roman Voting Assemblies from the Hannibalic War to the Dictatorship of Caesar.* Ann Arbor.

Taylour, W. 1958. *Mycenaean Pottery in Italy.* Cambridge.

Thomas, R. 1992. *Literacy and Orality in Ancient Greece.* Cambridge.

Thompson, J.W. 1942. *A History of Historical Writing.* Vol. 1. New York.

Thomsen, R. 1957–61. *Early Roman Coinage: A Study of the Chronology.* 3 vols. Copenhagen.

————. 1980. *King Servius Tullius: A Historical Synthesis.* Copenhagen.

Timpe, D. 1972. "Fabius Pictor und die Anfänge der römischen Historiographie." *ANRW* I. 2: 928–69.

Torelli, M. 1971. "Il Santuario di Hera a Gravisca." *PdP* 26: 44–67.

————. 1975. *Elogia Tarquiniensia.* Florence.

————. 1976. "Greek Artisans in Etruria: A Problem Concerning the Relationship Between Two Cultures." *Archaeological News* 5: 134–38.

————. 1977. "Il Santuario Greco di Gravisca." *PdP* 32: 398–458.

Toynbee, A.J. 1965. *Hannibal's Legacy: The Hannibalic War's Effects upon Roman Life.* 2 vols. Oxford.

Trieber, C. 1888. "Die Romulussage." *RM* 43: 569–82.

————. 1894. "Zur Kritik bei Eusebios." *Hermes* 29: 124–42.

Trump, D.H. 1966. *Central and Southern Italy Before Rome.* London and New York.

————. 1980. *The Prehistory of the Mediterranean.* New Haven.

Tykot, R.H., and T.K. Andrews, eds. 1992. *Sardinia in the Mediterranean: A Footprint in the Sea, Studies in Sardinian Archaeology Presented to Miriam S. Balmuth.* Sheffield.

Ungern-Sternberg, J. von, and H. Reinau, eds. 1988. *Vergangenheit in mündlicher Überlieferung.* Stuttgart.

Urban, R. 1973. "Zur Entstehung des Volkstribunats." *Historia* 22: 761–64.

Vagnetti, L. 1970. "I Micenei in Italia." *PdP* 25: 359–80.

————, ed. 1982. *XXII Convegno di Studi Sulla Magna Graecia, Magna Graecia e Mondo Miceneo: Nuovi Documenti.* Taranto.

Valvo, A. 1983. *La Sedizione di Manlio Capitolino in Tito Livio.* Memorie dell' Istituto Lombardo, Accademia di Scienze e Lettere XXXVIII.1. Milan.

Van Berchem, D. 1959–60. "Hercule Melqart à l'Ara Maxima." *Atti della Pontificia Accademia Romana di Archeologia (Serie III) Rendiconti* 32: 61–68.

————. 1967. "Sanctuaires d'Hercule Melqart: Contributions à l'étude de l'expansion phénicienne en Méditerranée." *Syria* 44: 73–109 and 307–38.

Van Der Meer, L.B. 1982. *"Ludi Scenici et Gladiatorum Munus:* A Terracotta *Arula* in Florence." *Bulletin Antieke Beschaving* 57: 87–99.

————. 1987. *The Bronze Liver of Piacenza: Analysis of a Polytheistic Structure.* Amsterdam.

Van Der Zee, J. 1985. *Bound Over: Indentured Servitude and American Conscience.* New York.

Van Essen, C.C. 1957. "The Via Valeria from Tivoli to Collarnele." *PBSR* 25: 22–38.

Vanggaard, J.H. 1988. *The Flamen: A Study in the History and Sociology of Roman Religion.* Copenhagen.

Verbrugghe, G.P. 1979. "Three Notes on Fabius Pictor and His History." In *Miscellanea di Studi classici in Onore di Eugenio Manni.* Vol. 6. Rome.

———. 1982. "L. Cincius Alimentus—His Place in Roman Historiography." *Philologus* 126: 316–23.

Versnel, H.S. 1970. *Triumphus: An Inquiry into the Origin, Development, and Meaning of the Roman Triumph.* Leiden.

Vetter, E. 1953. *Handbuch der italischen Dialekte.* Vol. 1. Heidelberg.

Vine, B. 1993. *Studies in Archaic Latin Inscriptions.* Innsbruck.

———. 1999. "A Note on the *Duenos* Inscription." UCLA Indo-European Studies. Edited by V.V. Ivanov and B. Vine,Vol. 1. Los Angeles.

von Arnim, H. 1892. *"Ineditum Vaticanum."* *Hermes* 27: 118–30.

von Fritz, K. 1950. "The Reorganization of the Roman Government in 366 B.C. and the So-called Licinio-Sextian Laws." *Historia* 1: 3–44.

Walbank, F.W. 1970. *A Historical Commentary on Polybius.* Vol. 1, *Commentary on Books I-VI.* Oxford.

Walde, A., and J.B. Hofmann. 1938–54. *Lateinisches etymologisches Wörterbuch.* 3rd ed., 2 vols. Heidelberg.

Wallace, R.E. 1998. "Recent Research on Sabellian Inscriptions." *Indo-European Studies Bulletin of the Friends and Alumni of Indo-European Studies (University of California Los Angeles)* 8.1: 1–9.

Wallace, R.W., and E.M. Harris, eds. 1996. *Transitions to Empire, Essays in Greco-Roman History, 360–146 B.C., in Honor of E. Badian.* Norman OK.

Walsh, P.G. 1963. *Livy, His Historical Aims and Methods.* Cambridge.

———. 1974. *Livy.* Greece and Rome, New Surveys in the Classics 8. Oxford.

Walt, S. 1997. *Der Historiker C. Licinius Macer: Einleitung, Fragmente, Kommentar.* Stuttgart and Leipzig.

Watson, A. 1972. "Roman Private Law and the *Leges Regiae*." *JRS* 62: 100–5.

———. 1975. *Rome of the Twelve Tables.* Princeton.

———. 1979. "The Death of Horatia." *CQ* n.s. 29: 436–47.

———. 1992. *The State, Law and Religion: Pagan Rome.* Athens GA.

———. 1993. *International Law in Archaic Rome: War and Religion.* Baltimore.

Weinstock, S. 1946. "Martianus Capella and the Cosmic System of the Etruscans." *JRS* 36: 101–29.

———. 1957. *"Victor* and *Invictus."* *HTR* 50: 211–47.

Westbrook, R. 1988. "The Nature and Origins of the Twelve Tables." *ZSS rom. Abt.* 105: 74–121.

Whatmough, J. 1937. *The Foundations of Roman Italy.* London.

Wieacker, F. 1988. *Römische Rechtsgeschichte: Quellenkunde, Rechtsbildung, Jurisprudenz und Rechtsliteratur.* Vol. 1, *Einleitung, Quellenkunde, Frühzeit und Republik.* Handbuch der Altertumswissenschaft. Munich.

Williamson, C. 1987. "Monuments of Bronze: Roman Legal Documents on Bronze." *CA* 6: 160–83.

Winter, J.G. 1910. "The Myth of Hercules at Rome." *University of Michigan Studies, Humanistic Series* 4: 171–273.

Wiseman, T.P. 1970. "Roman Republican Road Building." *PBSR* 38: 122–52.

———. 1979a. *Clio's Cosmetics, Three Studies in Greco-Roman Literature.* Leicester.

WORKS CITED 389

———. 1979b. "Topography and Rhetoric: The Trial of Manlius." *Historia* 28: 32–50.

———. 1983. "The Credibility of the Early Annalists." *LCM* 8: 20–22.

———. 1994. *Historiography and Imagination: Eight Essays on Roman Culture.* Exeter Studies in History 33. Exeter.

———. 1995. *Remus: A Roman Myth.* Cambridge.

———. 1996. "What Do We Know About Early Rome?" *JRA* 9: 310–15.

———. 1998. *Roman Drama and Roman History.* Exeter.

Wissowa, G. 1912. *Religion und Kultus der Römer.* 2nd ed. Munich.

Woodhead, A.G. 1962. *The Greeks in the West.* London.

Woudhuizen, F.C. 1992. *Linguistica Tyrrhenica: A Compendium of Recent Results in Etruscan Linguistics.* Amsterdam.

Wuilleumier, P. 1939. *Tarente des origines à la conquete romaine.* Paris.

Zancani Montuoro, P. 1977. "Tre Notabili Enotrii dell' VIII Sec. a.C." *Atti e Memorie della Società Magna Grecia* n.s. 15–17: 9–82.

Ziolkowski, A. 1993. "Between Geese and the Auguraculum: The Origin of the Cult of Juno on the Arx." *CP* 88: 206–19.

Zorzetti, N. 1990. "The *Carmina Convivalia*." In *Sympotica: A Symposium on the Symposion.* Edited by O. Murray. Oxford.

INDEX

Compositor: International Typesetting & Composition
Text: 10/12 Baskerville
Display: Baskerville
Printer and binder: Maple-Vail Manufacturing Group

CPSIA information can be obtained
at www.ICGtesting.com
Printed in the USA
JSHW021437011119
2211JS00001B/40